Music and Dance in California and the West

RICHARD DRAKE SAUNDERS, Editor

BUREAU OF MUSICAL RESEARCH, INC.

WILLIAM J. PERLMAN, Director

HOLLYWOOD — 1948   Published by DRAKE-WILLIAM

TABLE OF CONTENTS

OPERA

DANCE

TEACHING

LIBRARIES

FILMS

RADIO

ACTIVITIES

FOREWORD

This volume is a more ambitious project than the earlier editions published in 1933 and 1940, respectively. The territory it covers is considerably more extensive, its content of much wider scope, and its compilation and printing was infinitely more expensive.

Inclusion of articles, biographies, and musical activities was determined on the merit of material and on the importance of individuals. It is possible that a few personalities and germane items have been omitted. But such omissions are entirely due to a lackadaisical attitude on the part of those who were requested to furnish the desired information.

With the cessation of hostilities, the renaissance of music began. Concerts, operas and symphonies never have been so fully attended. Never before have music schools had such large enrollments, and private teachers such long waiting lists. Primarily, our aim was to reflect this renaissance, to present a comprehensive survey of the musical growth and development in all communities, large and small, in California and the West, and to make this volume a reference work worthwhile.

It is our endeavor to represent this progress in cycles of seven years. Our first edition was published in 1933, the second in 1940, but the present edition, scheduled for 1947, was delayed owing to a shortage of satisfactory paper.

It is with a genuine feeling of satisfaction that we affix an approximate "finis" to our task. But before doing this we wish to acknowledge gratefully our indebtedness to Belle Forbes Cutter, Victor Young, Mark Warnow, Ray Heindorf, Arnold Schoenberg, Boris Sirpo, Paul Pierre McNeely, and all the other members of our Honorary Editorial Board for the articles they have contributed and for their moral and financial support without which this volume could hardly have been brought to a successful conclusion.

William J. Perlman, Director
Bureau of Musical Research, Inc.

Hollywood, California
January 1, 1948

PREFACE

A book such as this is the product of many minds. The editor's function is to see that the thoughts of its contributors are expressed without too much violence to the simpler rules of grammar, and to collate material of interest to all readers.

Care has been taken to select those articles which make points of individual value. At least, they reflect the attitudes and opinions of a cross-section of Western musicians and dancers. Some of the authors are well known, others less so: the criterion has been the article's import, not the prominence of its author.

Neither musicians nor dancers make any pretensions at being writers. Most of them frankly stated that they would rather write a sonata or a ballet, which they felt better qualified to compose. What they have written, therefore, is in the effort to convey thoughts that could not be expressed in the medium of music.

Whatever these articles may lack in literary nuances, they have the qualities of sincerity and candor. They have been written to share an experience, to plead a cause, to clarify a situation. The editor has endeavored to tamper with the originals as little as possible.

An editor, like the director of a film, receives the lion's share of the credit. His name is in the largest type, and in the most prominent place. Yet whatever his ability, the finished product also represents the combined skill and abilities of his co-workers.

It is perhaps only fitting that a volume dealing with music should have been produced under the most harmonious and concordant conditions. In all the meetings of the staff and of the board of directors, a remarkable spirit of amity and good fellowship has made the production of this work a most pleasurable task. The only differences of opinion were really minor dissonances which resolved easily into unison.

So it is with pride and affection that I thank those who have done so much to make this book a reality. Our invaluable secretary, Jo Louise Palumbo, has handled the difficult routine with diplomatic finesse, in addition to reading proofs, writing tactful letters, and maintaining a sense of humor.

The most tricky matters of typography were smoothed away readily by the skill of Fredric Reid. Claire Robson has handled deftly the involved details of book-keeping, to say nothing of pacifying the various rapacious bureaus of city, state and federal government who obviously think all business is conducted only for their fulsome benefit. The title page design is the artistic work of Lorraine A. Perlman. And the members of our honorary editorial board have given generously of their time and experience.

And last, but only in the theatrical sense of "top billing," is my comrade, as well as coadjutor and friend, William J. Perlman.

—Richard Drake Saunders

Is It Fair?

By ARNOLD SCHOENBERG

IT has become a habit of late to qualify esthetic and artistic subjects in terms borrowed from the jargon of politics. Thus mildly progressive works of art, literature or even music might be classified as "revolutionary" or "left wing," when they only evolve artistic possibilities. On the other hand, old-fashioned products are called "reactionary," without any clarification of what its antonym might mean in contrast.

No wonder, then, that there are people who call the method of composing with twelve tones "bolshevik." They pretend that in a "set of twelve tones," upon which such compositions are founded, since there is no tonic nor dominant, every tone is considered independent, and consequently exerts equal functions.

This is wrong in every respect; yet it is curious to note that even the exact contrary has been contended.

The German composer, Paul von Klenau, during Hitler's times, composed a whole opera in twelve tone style. After a successful performance, he published an essay in which he "demonstrated" that this method was a true image of national-socialist principles!

This, of course, also is politics—though of the opposite color.

As a matter of fact, the structural independence of the single tone is rather limited in a set of twelve tones, because every tone is bound unchangeably to a definite place.

For example, observe the following set:

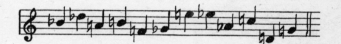

In a "fascist" interpretation, the basic set accordingly would represent the leader, the Duce, the Fuehrer, on whom all depends, who distributes power and function to every tone, who also is the originator of all the three mirror forms, and who is responsible for all the subsequent transpositions of the basic set and its derivatives—to function as sub-Fuehrer in minor affairs.

Whether this concept is an advantage or a handicap to the composer or to the listener, certainly it has nothing in common with "Liberty, Equality and Fraternity," neither with the bolshevik, fascist nor any other totalitarian brand.

Most important: is it an evaluation?

Subjective and Objective

By IGOR STRAVINSKY
as told to Sol Babitz

TO SAY the essential and say it quickly is necessary because the attention span of today's audience is limited.* This means to strip the music of unnecessary instruments (for essential sound) and unnecessary notes (for essential form).**

The over-orchestrated and over-emotionalized music of the nineteenth century has caused the new composer to react in the direction of cleanness and simplicity which may be deceptive because of the rhythmic and musical complexity contained.

Since musical criticism is not yet fully recovered from the old standards of pomp and heroics, the deliberate renunciation of these ingredients by a composer makes these critics uneasy, striking as it does at the roots of their understanding. In order to maintain their equilibrium they invite the new ideas into their hall of fame and call it "cold objectivity" little realizing that their own "warm subjectivity" is now alas, only warmed over.

As if the new approach and unfamiliar sounding music were not sufficiently embarrassing, there is the additional dilemma of technical mastery in the fields of orchestration, counterpoint, etc. Much simpler than accommodating to this newness is to wash one's hands of the whole problem and round out the myth of "cold objectivity" by calling it the natural partner of technical facility. [Stravinsky often speaks of his "feeling for the right thing"; strange language for a "cold objectivist" who has nevertheless always taken such pains to balance the subjective and objective elements in his creative method. S.B.]

The story of the blind men and the elephant illustrates many aspects of the objectivity theory both from the auditor's and composer's point of view. The blind man who touched the trunk of the elephant was objectively correct when he said the animal was like a snake. Equally correct was the blind man who likened the elephant to a wall when he touched its side. Each was objectively correct in terms of his own immediate comprehension; but he could have been more correct had he investigated further.

Our understanding of new music is quite similar and it is for this reason that serious listeners, aware of this "blindness" demand a second and third hearing of music which sounds truly new.

There is a qualitative difference in the "blindness" of the composer in the presence of an, as yet, uncomposed piece of music. The composer who is creating the new animal also is feeling his way into the unknown. But this blindness, which is called "inspiration" is a most subjective state, in which the artist seeks within himself—in the excitement of the conflicting ideas which live in his mind.

The result of this search is an expression which must be put on paper . . . . objectively. The creative artist must not permit the necessary subjectivity of his gropings to penetrate into the finished work. When this is successfully accomplished, the auditor of the new work receives the impression of something new, yet something permanent and vaguely familiar.

The mere fact of the individual's existence is a guarantee of subjectivity; the creative problem is to *objectivise* the subjectivity. A consistent problem of balance in the process of writing is the relationship between harmonic and contrapuntal factors. Here the problem, which is identical with that which confronted Palestrina, lies in maintaining the continuity and integrity of each voice as it moves horizontally on the staff but not at the expense of the vertical harmonic sound.

All attempts to bypass this problem have met with failure. There is an artificial objectivity which maintains that if the notes are "worked out" according to rules the sound will take care of itself.*

* * * * * *

* Alfred Frankenstein "Stravinsky in Beverly Hills" MODERN MUSIC (1942)
**"As one reads the score (of Stravinsky's Symphony in C) the form unfolds before the eye as clearly as that of a classic work. The page as a whole reveals a visual difference indicative of the new sounds contained. The manuscript is very white, perhaps whiter than any of Stravinsky's other scores—an unforgivable sin in the eyes of the pedants who have been held spellbound by the increasing blackness of symphonic scores during the last one hundred years. There is none of the conventional doubling, no outward attempt at tonal balance. One may detect elegance but never affectation." MUSICAL QUARTERLY (January, 1941). Sol Babitz in Stravinsky's *Symphony in C* (1940) observes: Upon re-reading this excerpt Stravinsky said, "Wait till you hear the finale of my *Orpheus* (1947); it is as dry as the Arizona climate."

(*Continued on page* 152)

Form Makes the Symphony

By GEORGE ANTHEIL

I have been asked to write four or five pages of double spaced typewriting on the subject of "Modern Symphonic Form". It is a nice assignment because, curiously enough, I have spent the last six years of my life almost exclusively in the study of this subject as it applies to modern composition; and I relish the idea of attempting, at least, to boil it all down to its most important basic elements.

In the final analysis, the quintessence of symphonic form of any period is expressed best and most fully in its symphonies. The chamber string quartet or sonata, or at the other swing of the pendulum the solo concerto, are both slightly too possessed and limited by outside factors to be the best examples. Let us, therefore, consider the modern symphony.

I believe, first of all, that the symphony of all times and periods is a spiritual as well as an abstract musical canvas, and that any "symphony" written to present purely abstract musical values is a misnomer. In other words, I believe that every symphony ever written could be subtitled "The Life Of Man" as seen by the composer of that particular period while writing that particular symphony. It is like a great novel which shows some complete large section of life, and has some deep spiritual moving comment upon it. This makes me reject many modern symphonies which, although they may be admirably constructed, or filled to the brim with exciting musical ideas, sounds, or constructions, yet miss in the fundamental reason for being of the "grand symphony".

I could mention a number of recent symphonies by several of the greatest of modern composers which, in my estimation, utterly miss the point of the symphony per se; yet this short article is no place for such criticism. I will only say here that I can never consider that the so-called "abstract beauty" of a harp and bassoon chord can in itself be considered an excuse for the creation of music—which, finally, must come from that nebulous thing we call "man's soul." Or his conscience, if you are a modern thinker.

A symphony is the greatest expression of music as we know it today.

Secondly, I believe that the symphony is also the most sophisticated expression of music as we know it today, or yesterday, or a hundred years ago or more. There is, frankly, no such thing as "musical primitivism" in the symphonic form. It is a highly complex organization, and insists upon being constructed with the highest degree of musicianship and musical resource. Therefore, when some modern composers (here to be unnamed) label three or four movements of a suite a "symphony", without any of the basic elements of true symphonic form being therein present, it is to laugh. Yet one could be surprised at the number of American "symphonies" yearly performed over the great radio chains which are no more basically "symphonies" than Paddy's pig. They are series of musical contraptions lengthened out into approximately the length of a symphony; they glue themselves together by a vague arrangement of "cyclic form" (whatever that is, but this is what their composers tell us) but have practically no development except that by sequence or primitive contrapunctual device. Perhaps the two most important elements of symphony construction are emphatic statement of material capable of development, and the highest sophisticated development of same, each in its various proper places, with a maximum of contrast. These two elements most young American symphonies do not possess; yet Mozart, Beethoven, Brahms, even Mahler and Bruckner possessed them to the highest degree.

Great music will not be written until these two elements once more become apparent in the pages of written music.

Thirdly, the modern symphony and the future symphony may not merely be a filling of new sophisticated wine into old sophisticated bottles, if one will forgive the mixed metaphor. A modern symphony may well pass my first test (that it must be a great complete spiritual bird's eye view of some part of the modern composer's conscience) and even my second (or that it must be highly sophisticated in its construction, bearing out the main elements of

(Continued on page 136)

The California Plan

By PAUL A. PISK

PRIVATE music teaching is a necessary complement to music education in public schools. Whereas the study of music appreciation, singing and musical group activities like chorus, school orchestra and band are duly emphasized in our grade and high schools, it is obvious that the American school system cannot devote enough time to teaching applied music, especially piano, voice production and string or woodwind instruments. Therefore the studio teachers assume an important role in the musical training of our youth. In the general recent upswing of musical interest and of musical knowledge as a cultural factor, adults in increasing numbers also desire technical music training. They want not only to listen to music but to take an active part in it by acquiring facility of playing. So they turn to the private music teacher for instruction.

As music teaching in U.S.A. is a free profession and there is no compulsion to belong to any official organization, nor the necessity for securing any credential, it often happened, especially in the first decades of our century, that the standards of private music teaching did not quite live up to its educational responsibility. The California Music Teachers Assn. was organized around 1910 not only as a society for protection of professional interests but as an educational body. It declared as one of its main purposes the raising of the artistic and pedagogic level of its members. Farsighted leaders in this association felt the necessity for a definite program to achieve that goal. The president of the California Music Teachers Association in 1940, Mrs. Winifred Lucia Fisher, herself a nationally known singer, voice teacher and choir director, conducted a careful survey of the requirements for music degrees in the institutions of higher learning in the U. S. and in Europe. Aided by a committee of outstanding music educators, she worked out a system of self-education for teachers. It was named the "California Plan" and has been unanimously adopted by the Association. Today, only a few years since its inauguration, more than a third of the general membership have either completed the degree work or are active in the studies required by the Plan.

The inaugurators of this Plan have divided the field of study into five groups: music theory (ear training, sight singing, harmony) music literature (music history, forms), music education (educational psychology, psychology of music, teaching methods, the so-called "normal" courses) and applied music (performance and presentation of students. Teachers who already have acquired theoretical and historical background in music through studies in accredited colleges, conservatories or universities or who have been active in the concert field are given credit for these subjects after proper evaluation and may be exempt from taking examinations in the first two groups. Every candidate for the California Plan, however, has to meet the requirements in the educational and practical fields.

The California Music Teachers Assn. is an entirely private and voluntary organization. Therefore, its plan of certification lacks official approval. The future goal, however, will be intensive cooperation with the State Board of Education so that California Plan certificates and degrees will be acknowledged by the State similarly to teacher's credentials.

At present, the Plan offers three degrees for its candidates. The Colleague's degree is somewhat similar to a Bachelor degree of a college. The Child Specialist degree emphasizes the pedagogic and psychological aspects of music for those who concentrate on the teaching of children. After having received either of these degrees the candidates may go on in their studies for a Fellow's degree the requirements of which are patterned after a college master's degree. More detailed study of theory, counterpoint, even an original thesis are necessary for its completion. The Fellow must show outstanding professional ability either in performing, teaching or musical scholarship.

The difference between this scheme of self-educa-
(*Continued on page* 139)

14

The Distaff Side

By ELINOR REMICK WARREN

THE place of women in the field of music has long been a disputed issue. It is not the intention here to trace the careers of the many women who have succeeded in their chosen professions, but rather to discuss the opportunities and the practical aspects for women in a life of music.

It is true that there still remains a lingering prejudice against women taking their place on an equal basis with men. Paradoxically, it is not only the men who engender this prejudice, but as often it is a lack of comprehension on the part of the aspiring young woman to analyze herself and her temperament in relation to the demands and responsibilities of the professional life she would assume.

Among singers, women have long achieved fame and success alongside men. It is in the instrumental and especially in the composition fields that women have been slower to achieve equal acceptance.

The question is argued as to whether women lack sufficient innate endowment of talent or whether, all things being equal, they have the same opportunities to develop their talents along professional lines. Certainly the recent war has dispelled much of the feeling against women's activities in music (as well as in many other lines) as is testified by the many women in symphony and studio orchestras who continue to maintain their place there.

There are still a few die-hards who are reluctant to accept the thought of this professional equality. There are those whose highest compliment to a woman's creative works or instrumental performance is by declaring it has the excellence of a man's. There is the case of the prominent musical publisher who insisted upon using only the initials of a certain woman composer's given name, because her compositions were "good enough to have been written by a man." But the old prejudices are surely breaking down. Women shall have their spot in the sun, if they themselves are willing to grasp their opportunities and responsibilities.

It is an interesting observation that most teachers of children state that in the aggregate the girl pupils show more aptitude, interest and diligence than the boys. There are the boys of exceptional talent, but for group classification the little girls are invariably in the lead. Why is it then, as the years progress, so many of the formerly promising girl students abandon their serious studies and the relatively small number of boys who have "stuck it out" go on to the fore?

The fundamental hurdles are biological and psychological. It is not a lack of talent, not a lack of physical strength, nor a lack of wisdom and steadfastness of purpose. Most women, even if endowed with all these attributes, are unwilling to devote themselves completely to a career if it means a life apart from marriage, children, and a home. In a few happy exceptions, a satisfactory blending of the professional and home life have been achieved; but only under unusual circumstances of complete understanding and co-operation. In such a case the family life becomes, instead of a distracting, difficult problem, an enriching experience.

One great concert artist, a woman of international success, says she solved the problem which faces most normal women by resolutely avoiding marriage with its inevitable responsibilities, and substituting romance. She might be in love anew every day, but nothing would keep her from her rehearsals and concert tours.

To most other women this is an unacceptable substitution for a happy home life, the achievement of which necessitates the family receiving first consideration. This means that one's achievements in music, if maintained professionally, must be scaled to a longer period of accomplishment, but with continued steadfastness of purpose. Even then, it is possible only when a woman's family, especially her husband, contributes actively to her career by real helpfulness in aiding her to arrange for sufficient time and mental freedom to maintain a continuing flow of effort each day.

This problem, of course, is the same for women in any career, except that it is magnified many times over in an art which necessitates an early beginning plus uninterrupted application through the years.

(*Continued on page* 136)

15

Where Is Latin-American Music Going?

By ELISABETH WALDO

BECAUSE of the richness of its heritage, fascinating possibilities of future development, and growing public interest in the United States and abroad, the music of our neighboring countries of Latin America is destined to a significant place.

Although it is an accepted fact that twenty per cent of popular music played through the media of screen, records and juke boxes is of Latin American character, an inquiring audience wants to hear what lies beyond the Rhumba and Samba.

The great painters of Latin America, with their individualistic works, have been the first serious artists to gain recognition for their countries because they have dared to assert their own flavor and atmosphere rather than depend upon Europe.

The principal contributing elements of Latin American music are the Indians, the Spanish (with Moorish overtones) and the Negro, of African origin. The romance of the "gaucho" riding the *pampas* (plains) of Argentina, the Andean "llama" drivers with their inseparable little plaintive flutes known as "quena", the beating of exotic jungle drums of various forms and tones, tunes from Coastal plains and high mountain ranges, a variety of folk songs and dance forms as plentiful as in any part of the world, all as colorful as their nations are different, provide a background of warm and colorful folk culture for the composer of to-day who is throwing off the shackles of "pseudo-classicism" to develop his native individualism.

When we consider the great strides made in the last fifty years by such composers as Heitor Villa-Lobos and Camargo Guarnieri of Brasil, Carlos Chavez and Manuel Ponce of Mexico, Andre Sas of Peru, Guillermo Uribe-Holguin of Colombia, to mention but a few, it is evident that this evolutionary development of transplanting the richness of native folk material into sophisticated music forms is well under way.

Although the colonial life was condusive to the development of the folk songs, new vistas developing through the media of radio, screen and symphony orchestra, contribute to the development of native talent and education.

The radio networks which can now be heard in jungle interiors as well as in metropolitan areas, are being patterned after our own. Mexico and Argentina lead the film output, and Cuba, Brasil, Chile, Venezuela, Peru, and Colombia have growing industries. With the possibility of available materials now at hand, sizeable domestic industries may be developed. For those Spanish and Portuguese countries who do not find sufficient satisfaction in American pictures dubbed into their native tongues, this would be a tremendous advancement as well as another medium to preserve records of historical development.

In the realm of musical education, Brasil possesses excellent conservatories and music schools. Cali, Colombia has one of the most modern conservatories in South America. Beautiful opera houses such as the Bellas Artes of Mexico, the Teatro Colon, of Buenos Aires, and Manaus Brasil, are significant of a large and appreciative opera public.

Although Italiante traditions dominated opera before 1910, South America has to its credit the presentation of many native operas. One of the best known, *Malazarte*, by Oscar Lorenzo Fernandez, sequences of which have been incorporated into the Ballet Russe repertory, has as well, choreography by Brasil's most famous painter, Candido Portinari.

No article on Latin American music would be complete without mentioning the "big three" of popular melodies. Cuba's Ernesto Lecuona, Mexico's Augustin Lara, and Brasil's Ary Barroso, have created an art of composing for the International market with such song hits as *Siboney, You Belong To My Heart,* and *Brazil.*

In present-day Europe the percentage of Latin-American music performances, classical and popular, exceeds that from the United States and the demand is on the increase.

Musicologists are only today authenticating some of the musical findings of the Aztec, Maya and Inca Empires, restrained for many centuries when music went underground at the time of the Conquest. So the twenty Republics of Latin America today with their ancient cultures, picturesque Cathedrals reminiscent of old-world Spain, and the dynamic life of the new world, and musical young America, may indeed possess the same joy as their ancestors in finding a "place in the sun."

The Past Once Was New

By ERNST KRENEK

MUSICIANS of all kinds and music lovers in general do not think very highly of the value of music history. Professional interpreters do not see why they should occupy themselves with historical problems, for the music which they are called upon to perform mainly originated in the nineteenth century. The tradition of that music seems lively enough that no special studies are necessary in order to comprehend its meaning. The average music lover has much the same attitude, for he hardly ever hears any music earlier than Bach. The contemporary composer, finally, is either identified with that tradition, too, or if he is progressive, he frequently thinks that he ought to keep himself as free as possible from influences of the past.

Thus music history is left to specialists interested in that field for reasons of their own. The average musician comes into contact with it only in the history courses of conservatories and colleges, which he takes because they are "required". It is the task of the teacher of such courses to convince his charges that knowledge of history is not only necessary to get the requirements "out of the way", but to attain full and respectable musicianship.

History is of vital interest only if it is related to the present. The mere information that Francesco Landini wrote the only three-part canon in the fourteenth century is of possible interest to the collector of such items. A musician will be interested in it only when he understands why and in what respects that canon is remarkable as a work of art.

There are two ways in which history may be put into a relationship to the present. During the nineteenth century, which was dominated by the idea of evolution and progress, earlier phases of music were looked upon as preparatory to the proud consummation of the present, as imperfect attempts toward creating those values which were supposed to be the ultimate purpose of the whole evolutionary process. Seen from such an angle, the subject matter of history indeed is not particularly engaging, for if we actually have reached the peak of perfection, why should we bother with the tentative results of our less fortunate and relatively unenlightened ancestors?

During the last thirty years our attitude has somewhat changed. Two devastating world wars and their disturbing consequences taught us rudely but effectively that the pride of our fathers and grandfathers was less than justified. We can not any longer cherish the illusion that we have reached anything near perfection. Thus we have also learned to look upon history with greater humility, willing to acknowledge our ancestors' accomplishments on their own merits.

If they have not done exactly what we do and like, we do not any longer think that this is due to their having been primitive, or simple-minded, or restricted in their mental capacities by obsolete prejudices. If they expressed themselves in ways which are not our ways, we do not blame their ignorance, but try to understand that they had different intentions at least as honorable as our own, and therefore developed different methods of expression and reached different results, no more or less perfect than ours.

If this point of view guides our historical studies, history becomes a very attractive field and gains much vital importance. Let us take, for instance, the early attempts at polyphonic writing in the twelfth and thirteenth centuries. It is easy to see that a motet by Petrus de Cruce, or an organum by Perotin, is less comprehensive in scope and elaboration than a symphony by Beethoven. But seen in their own frames of reference and related to what those early composers had to work with, their compositions are of eminent interest, as they show no less a degree of inventiveness and expressive intensity than the works of later masters. If we stop looking at Plain Chant as the primitive effort of dim-witted barbarians who did "not yet" know how to use harmony, we can admire in those amazingly fine and delicately wrought melodic lines perfect specimens of the craft of composition, the basic principles of which have remained the same for more than a thousand years.

In substituting for an unfair and supercilious attitude toward the past one of insight and respect, we have to avoid the opposite mistake of idolizing history

(*Continued on page* 136)

17

With and Without Honor

By WILLIAM GRANT STILL

TEN years ago, we made notes for an article on the composers of serious American music—prophets with and without honor in their own country. On looking over these notes today, we have found that there has been very little change in the basic situation. For composers who may be considered established (if such a situation is possible in their own lifetimes) the only change is that there are a few more performances for a few more composers. For newcomers, the obstacles are such that many of them may prefer to take the easy way: money through popular music. For the unfortunate fact is that serious American music is still in the position of having to sell itself to the American public.

It may well be said that the problems that confront the serious American composer today are the same that have confronted composers in all times, but it is also true that there are slight variations in these problems, in conformance with the times and the setting.

In the past, it was difficult to get hearings for new American works. Today, a composer who has something worthwhile to offer may come to any one of several open-minded and versatile conductors and be assured that he will be given consideration and, very possibly, a performance. This is due to the pioneer work done by such men as Howard Hanson, and (to name but a single instance of a conductor of foreign birth who has made it his policy to play American works) Leopold Stokowski.

But what about repeated hearings for an American work that has won favor on its initial performance? Dr. Hanson has tried to give good works repeated hearings in Rochester, and some others have indicated their willingness to do the same thing. But this is all too seldom the case. Our native works are too often simply classed as novelties, played once if at all, then forgotten.

There are still almost no opportunities for the adequate production of American operas. There are, on the contrary, people who persist in efforts to discredit them, possibly in an effort to propagandize and thus preserve traditional works that are staged and restaged, year after year. And the recording companies, long a sore spot with the majority of serious American composers, still persist in their refusal to record works of any but the favored few, thus leaving a great volume of serious American music unrecorded and therefore unavailable to the masses of people, and removing from many composers a valuable source of revenue. As for the individual concert artists now touring the country, only a few give enough attention to works produced by their countrymen.

Yet those conductors and recitalists who do perform American works have said that these are received with intelligent interest and with genuine enthusiasm by their audiences, especially when these audiences are composed of people, young or old, who have questing minds and spirits. Such people not only love the classics which they have known all their lives, but are willing to explore and appreciate the new.

There is always an economic aspect to musical problems. In the old days, composers had royal patronage, or were subsidized by publishing houses. The modern substitute for this is an organization such as ASCAP, fellowships from various foundations, or commissions, which are infrequent at best. In the past, publishers were wary of printing native compositions (excepting popular songs, which stood a chance of making a great deal of money from a small outlay) but nowadays practically all of the standard publishers are giving consideration to native composers. Not all of the works of all of our composers are printed, it's true, but surely more today than in years gone by.

As audiences have come to appreciate the American music they hear, so have many of the critics. They too have become accustomed to this new mode of expression, still in the formative stages, and often they come forth with intelligent opinions which the composer may weigh and from which he may learn. There still lingers a tendency to judge the new works by the standards of the old, or by the tastes of the reviewer, and as a result the composer often wavers, wondering whether his course, or that of the critic, is the right one. The wise composer is apt to follow his own inner convictions and come out the winner in the end.

The average young composer has a weighty problem, in that he may wonder which of many musical styles he will employ. Should he follow the classic tradition that he learns in the conservatory (as many people will expect, their view being that nothing we can produce can equal the European product), or should he adopt an ultra-modern style? Should he write in an idiom related to jazz, since that is one that finds favor with so many of our young people, who will be the musical audiences of tomorrow? If he is sincere and a true artist, he will turn to that style which best expresses what he wishes to say in music and, in doing so, he undoubtedly will develop involuntarily a personal idiom which no one else can or will duplicate.

In a sense, this latter problem is allied to another, which has been present in the lives of many composers after the Romantic period. Should the composer simply try to express *himself* in music, or should he try to write music with national characteristics? If he wishes to follow the latter course, how can he define our national music, since it is still in the formative period? After all, no single type of music can be termed the *only* American music, for no music could represent the entire nation unless it is a composite of all our racial, nationalistic and regional groups. Our representative music should be as much of a "melting pot" as is the country as a whole. This last problem, as with the choice of style or idiom, can be solved by the individual composer. No stranger has the right to influence him in this decision.

Yet it is unfortunate that so many strangers, even other composers, will attempt to influence their colleagues. We find today cliques of composers, even as there were ten or twenty years ago, so assured of their own superiority that they are positive that all others are misguided. These musicians have a tendency to be over-critical in print, perhaps from selfishness or jealousy, and perhaps simply because another composer adopts a style different from theirs. They lose no opportunity to communicate their scorn to anyone who will listen.

This is a foolish procedure, for one can scarcely expect everyone to write in the same style, and who would want this to happen? It would remove all variety, color and initiative from our music and make it an imitation of the things the European experimentalists were doing years ago. There is a danger in the lack of ability to appreciate a piece of music, even if it is written by someone else, purely on its own merits. Thus these particular composers have created for themselves a peculiar problem. In their campaign to advertise their own works as the only ones, and themselves as the "Messiahs" of American music, they have attempted to suppress, by one means or another, all music which does not agree with their own ideas. Such a proceeding does more to discredit than to advance American music on the whole.

Fortunately, an equal number of American composers have been astute enough to recognize and to fight this narrow procedure. These latter are not as able politicians as the former, but they are working steadily and their efforts are constructive.

Perhaps one of the problems that is most evident today is the need for a creator to withdraw from the rush and bustle of modern life in order to become quiet and to allow inspiration to flow freely. With so much going on all around, so much nervousness and so many business details to care for, it is necessary not to forget that the most valuable inspirations are those which come from a Divine source. These must be translated into understandable musical terms despite the vicissitudes of our contemporary world.

The American composer is not without honor. One could go on and on, citing instances of increasing attention to his works. One could also balance all such statements with facts of continued inattention. Certainly, America is gradually becoming aware of its own culture. There are those of us who would like to see this awareness grow faster and more steadily than it has done up to the present time. We feel that it would be a boon to America as well as to the individual American artists, and that it would be a means of helping America to take her place as a leader among nations.

No nation can be respected if it does not respect itself, and surely cultural values and the people who create a body of living culture in any nation are worthy of that nation's interest.

Little Town's Big Music

By JOHN J. GROSS

THE conductor lowered his baton and the 1100 enthusiastic auditors burst into wild applause. This was the realization of a dream come true. For the citizens of the small mid-Columbia town of Hood River, Oregon, this was the moment toward which their musically-minded, progressive citizenry had worked. An audience of 1100 represented better than one in eight of those resident in the whole prosperous apple-growing Hood River Valley.

The time was 1943, at the completion of the first winter music festival of the Hood River Music Assn. organized the preceding spring, and the guiding genius of the musical enterprise, which had won the enthusiastic plaudits of the capacity audience, was a vital Finnish conductor, teacher, and composer, Boris Sirpo.

Friend of the world-renowned Jan Sibelius, student at the St. Petersburg Conservatory from 1907 to 1911, later under Sevcik, Jacobsen, Kulenkampff, Schrecker, and others in Berlin, Prague, and Vienna, Sirpo had brought his great gifts to America following the Russo-Finnish war of 1939 in which his home had been destroyed along with the musical monuments to his career in his native Finland.

"Mr. Sirpo," declared his friend Sibelius, "has a very rare and natural gift for discovering unusually talented violinists and teaching them in an individual manner." And that gift was fully disclosed in the concert which ended on that December night in 1943. Presented semi-annually since that time, the Hood River Music Festival, under the direction of Boris Sirpo, has justified the faith of that small group of local citizens and amateur musicians, who believed that a cultural tradition of community could become a real and vital enterprise in the Valley.

From a mere handful of youths who wished to make music, the effort has grown to recognized eminence, not only in the Valley, but throughout the State and the entire nation. In 1944-45-46 the festival attracted widely-known and respected visiting artists, and boosted its lists of sustaining members to several hundred.

The Junior Symphony Orchestra, which began with a personnel of ten at its first rehearsal, has since been expanded into a symphony of more than 60, with a chorus of comparable size.

Young American artists have been recruited for guest appearances with the Hood River group. Young men and women from the community have gone forth after studying, fired with a passion for music and an unswerving faith in and loyalty to their friend and leader which has developed in them a degree of muscianship they would otherwise never have known.

The story of Hood River's good fortune and Boris Sirpo's American dream began at the same moment: that fateful day in 1939 when air-borne destruction laid in ruins all that Boris Sirpo had built through the years that he devoted to enriching the musical life of Finland. But the preparation for the enterprise belongs to the years which this talented artist had devoted to the development of community music in his own Finland. Born in 1893, Boris Sirpo interrupted his studies in the musical capitals of Europe to return to his home town of Viipuri in 1914. His city should also become a great musical center, not only for Finland, but for all Europe as well. Such was the ambition which he undertook to realize. In 1918 he founded the Viipuri Conservatory, the focus of musical activity in Karelia, which he continued to head until his coming to America. In 1920 he created the Viipuri String Quartet and a little later, the Viipuri Chamber Orchestra, which was acclaimed widely on a succession of continental tours with the late Bronislaw Huberman as soloist. In 1928 Sirpo became conductor of the Viipuri Symphony Orchestra which, under his direction, was recognized as among the finest of Scandinavian musical organizations. In addition he conducted performances of opera and, in 1932, the great National Singing Festivals.

In 1939, following the great success of the Viipuri Music and Art Festivals in Helsinki, which he directed, Mr. Sirpo was appointed conductor of the recently formed "Symphony Chorus" of Viipuri. It was at this stage of his career, one of Finland's most successful and highly esteemed musical leaders, the friend and intimate of the musically great of Europe, that he was faced with the necessity of starting anew, of creating a place for himself in another land. All that he had spent half a lifetime in building lay in ruins about him when Boris Sirpo came to America. With him was his wife and and his foster son Haimo Haitto, his student at the Viipuri Conservatory, who, though still a child, had won the international competition of the British Council of Music which proclaimed him the most talented young violinist of Europe. Youthful star of the European film, "The Little Fiddler," and soloist of many European concert stages.

Arrived in America, the Sirpos toured the nation under the auspices of Finnish Relief and the Red Cross. Young Haitto appeared as a guest soloist with the Philadelphia Orchestra, following which the Sirpos spent some time in Hollywood where the youth appeared in a picture and Boris Sirpo arranged musical scores.

Such work, however, could not long prove congenial for a musician of his temperament. He dreamed once more of fostering community music, of developing a musical tradition such as he had seen grow through the years in Viipuri. Sibelius recognized, as did his other friends and intimates, that Sirpo's genius lay mostly in his great gifts as a teacher. His own considerable abilities as a composer had always been subordinated to the imperative necessity of pouring all his energies into the training of yet another talented young musician. And the youth, if he truly loved music, always caught fire with the inspired direction he received.

Accordingly, the Sirpos came to Portland, where they purchased a home and opened a studio. The wooded hills of the Oregon Coast and the green Willamette Valley fields were not unlike their native Finland, and here perhaps there would be the opportunity to continue the work that had been so abruptly broken off in the ruins of Viipuri.

Like other world-famed musicians who had found their way to America, like Ernst Bloch who came to make his home on the Oregon coast, like Darius Milhaud at Mills College in California, like Hindemith and Honegger, Boris Sirpo found the new land congenial, and he began to feel a growing affection for his adopted country. But affection must be demonstrated. Teaching alone was not enough. He knew that he must find another and more characteristic manner of expressing his love for and gratitude to America. He wished once more to create an orchestra, to shape a great musical organization for the region, which might be a continuing source of community pride and pleasure.

Thus it was that the dream of the exiled Finnish conductor coincided with the desire of a musically-minded community. Hood River, Oregon, approximately 65 miles east of Portland on the Columbia River, wanted the kind of music the children of the community were receiving through the instruction of Boris Sirpo.

The Hood River Music Assn. was organized and Sirpo was invited to form a symphony orchestra. The idea spread. The list of sponsors soon grew from the original handful to well over a hundred. Contributions from the very beginning of the enterprise averaged approximately sixty cents for every citizen in the community, an evidence of enthusiastic popular support which led Hilmar Grondahl, music editor of the Portland *Oregonian*, to write admiringly, "Just figure what Portland could do toward symphony and chorus with an average contribution like that!"

As rehearsals progressed, the symphony orchestra with a nucleus of junior members began to attract the increasing interest and attention of their parents. It was not enough to sponsor good community music; parents decided they too wanted to participate, and so a choir was organized. From the length and breadth of the valley, children and adults came faithfully throughout the spring and winter months to attend weekly rehearsals, devoting themselves to the making of music with a zeal of which only inspired amateurs are capable.

Since that first concert in 1943, the Hood River Music Assn. has presented two music festivals annually, one in summer, one in winter. In 1944 Heimo Haitto, who had enlisted in the American army after finishing high school in Portland, appeared with the orchestra as guest soloist. In 1945 the Association presented Marie Rogndahl, brilliant young coloratura soprano, with orchestra and chorus. But perhaps Hood River was proudest of its own youthful artist, little Susan Eby, who appeared with the orchestra in the 1946 festival playing a violin concertino by Pleyel. Two years before she had begun receiving instruction on the instrument. Now at the age of seven she was playing brilliantly in her first concert, as well as demonstrating convincingly the significance of the Hood River success story.

Observers agree that there is something contagious about Hood River's growing passion for good music. Youth and age meet in music on equal terms. It is, all agree, a great equalizer. And parents find that they can hardly be less enthusiastic than their children, or children than their parents. Often whole families participate in orchestra or choir, and children who are little more than toddlers anticipate the time when they may take an instrument into their own hands. A sense of the importance of the enterprise in which the community is engaged seems to have been communicated to all the participants. They are serious about music, and their music is serious. A program may feature Bach and Beethoven or Hindemith and Honegger, but whether classic or modern it must be good music. "No woogie-boogie" as Sirpo says. There is no question concerning the serious interest of the children who grow up knowing good music, and who, when they are ready for college, have been following Sirpo for advanced instruction to Lewis and Clark College in Portland where he is professor of violin and orchestral music and conductor of the college symphony orchestra.

The year 1946 marked yet another milestone for orchestral music in the Northwest, and another personal triumph for Boris Sirpo with the formation of the Portland Chamber Orchestra, an ensemble of fifty strings drawn from the ranks of musicians prominent in the musical life of the city and the State. Playing without compensation for the joy of the music, the ensemble held weekly rehearsals from October until its first concert in May, which was hailed by critics and public as the musical event of the year.

But Sirpo was not through. Perhaps he had paid part of the debt. There was now a music association in Hood River which brought music to all the people. There was the beginning of a musical tradition in the mid-Columbia valley which promised to widen and deepen. There was a Chamber Orchestra in Portland which would continue the work begun in Viipuri. But, he says, "We can do wonderful things in the future. We can build tradition. We can bring festivals to all the people. We can give all a part in their country's musical culture." And behind his words there is an idea, a big idea, an ambitious idea, so ambitious that the telling of it causes him to stammer helplessly and express his enthusiasm with gestures and grimaces as his inadequate command of English fails him and he begins anew with any one or a combination of the seven other languages he speaks.

In 1948, Sirpo believes, the Hood River Music Festival can count itself grown-up. The community is ready, the musicians are ready for a festival ex-ceeding all others in scope, in planning, in imagination. A single concert was good, but why not a week? A boldly ambitious festival with symphony, opera, oratorio! A day for children alone, with internationally famed guest artists! And so Hood River is planning, working, preparing. Eagerly, they have met and accepted the challenge given them to surpass all their previous achievements in successfully presenting four full days of music in August of 1948. And perhaps in the challenge lies the memory of the great Viipuri Music and Art Festivals of 1939 which Boris Sirpo directed, and the desire to make a further payment on the debt of gratitude which he feels he owes to his adopted homeland.

There are always the skeptics, of course, but they have found themselves members of an ever-dwindling minority as the 3,500 citizens of the little town have rubbed their eyes from season to season in the presence of the succession of musical miracles that have been performed. For the coming festival Hood River is preparing to play host to from 5,000 to 8,000 visitors. Elaborate plans have been made to entertain the guests. Committees on housing, entertainment, and transportation are quietly going ahead with the necessary preparations, for these people realize that the 1948 music festival is Hood River's great opportunity. They understand that such a festival gives the community and its youth an unparalleled personal relationship with the outstanding personalities of the musical world. They are coming to realize that a common unity may be forged in their adherence to the spirit of the music which they create and help to foster. And they see the possibility of winning for their community a nation-wide reputation as a leading musical center of America. The attainment of such objectives will require the concentrated efforts and unflagging interest of all the people, but residents of Hood River have become zealots in the cause.

On the first evening of the coming festival the musicians of the Alma Trio will appear in concert, followed on the second evening by the Portland Chamber Orchestra which will feature as soloist a renowned, though yet unnamed, artist. On the third day, Saturday, the children of the valley will present another of their remarkable performances with choir, orchestra, and soloists. Saturday evening's concert promises a treat to musicians and music lovers, for Arthur Honegger's powerful and gravely stirring *Le Roi David* will have its second performance in

(*Continued on page* 137)

Scherzo

By MAURICE ZAM

HUMOR is a rare and priceless gift. Without it life is a painful *canto fermo*. It lubricates the emotions—gives tone to the mind—releases tension and illuminates with startling clarity many a hidden truth. It is a health giving vitamin which helps preserve one's equilibrium in the face of life's realities. Humor is the flower of the intellect. No wonder it has been called the cousin of philosophy!

In art only a genius can give it the earmarks of immortality, for the vulgar and the commonplace are always ready to poisin its spirit. A musical "slip on the banana peel" may tickle the ear, but would have no artistic value. Humor in the hands of the true artist will not be a fabrication of shallow puns, nor a degrading parody of an artistic creation —the caricature that tries to turn the sublime into the ridiculous. Rather will he seek in humor the drama of humanity.

Humor in music has had a slow evolution for obvious reasons. Music and religion have been inseparable companions during the greater part of man's history. Only when music, divorced from its religious roots, developed independently, could it be fertilized by the spirit of humor. The Gregorian Chant is a perfect expression of the demands of Church music. For it excludes any suggestion of elemental passion and forbids the intrusion of a personal nature. As these elements are indispensable to humor, the early Christian Fathers rightly considered that humor does indeed detract from the sanctification and edification of the congregation.

This moral attitude associated humor with the Devil, and those who indulged in such wickedness were looked upon as treading the road to perdition. This may explain our guilt complex whenever laughter disturbs our conscience. As a consequence, musical chastity and humor were enemies, and composers for the Church were prevented from exhibiting any undignified harmonic or melodic inflections. On the other hand, it is interesting to note how in literature, churchmen such as Rabelais, Sterne and Swift easily cast aside their professional solemnity for comedy.

It was, therefore, only in the music of the people that humor could flourish. The innate sense of folk humor was reflected in popular dance music, street songs and folk songs, which have inspired and refreshed composers of every period. Consciously or subconsciously, the spontaneity of folk music became the spiritual basis of secular music. The madrigal of the 16th century, which flourished in England and Italy, gave humor a decided impetus. Weaned from the Church, it had complete freedom to experiment with tonal effects. Especially in merry England did the madrigal achieve a high state of comedy which eventually flowered into the Gilbert and Sullivan operettas.

On the other hand, early Italian opera with its artificial revival of Greek drama, crystallized into an antique spectacle, thus contributing little to the growth of humor. As an antidote, the opera buffa, or comic opera of the 18th Century, abandoned the mythological plots of Greece and chose subjects from every day life. The comic opera revealed the superb possibilities of humor and gave birth to a series of glorious masterpieces, such as Pergolesi's *La Serva Padrona*, Mozart's *Marriage of Figaro*, Cimarosa's *Matrimonio segreto*, Rossini's *Barber of Seville*, Smetana's *Bartered Bride*, Wagner's *Die Meistersinger*, Verdi's *Falstaff*, Strauss' *Rosenkavalier* and Hindemith's *Neues vom Tage*.

The desire for "comedy relief" is demonstrated in the term "scherzo" used by Monteverdi and other composers of the 17th century. However, the scherzo never quite became a joke. Haydn was more successful in the elusive domain of humor, for there is in Haydn's music, when he wants to be jolly, unsophisticated comedy and the healthy aroma of peasant soil. Some of his minuets, when brought to life by a sympathetic interpreter, are pure scherzo in feeling.

Mozart, as a man of the theatre, had a more lucid and penetrating insight into the psychology of musical humor. Who can forget his inimitable characterizations of Leporello and Papageno! Whether in tragedies or comedies, Mozart gave humor its appropriate expressiveness. It is a mistake however, to believe that this lightness had its origin in his happy

(Continued on page 130)

From the Pueblos to the Movies

By WILLIAM J. PERLMAN

THE present-day position of Los Angeles as a world music center has been attained in a comparatively short time. It was not until after the advent of sound in motion pictures that famous singers, musicians, composers and conductors flocked to Southern California to make music for world-wide audiences through the medium of the "talkies."

The city's earlier history is made up of localized musical eras, comprizing successively the folk music of the Indians, the Spaniards, the Mexicans and the quasi-folk music of the American pioneers. The European type of concert hall music was first introduced in the late seventies.

Music played a vital and intimate part in the everyday life of the Southern California Indians. Its extent and variety are surprising in view of the primitive nature of those "Stone Age" people. Song and dance were the Indians' chief mode of expression. Their myths of creation, telling of a Sky God and an Earth Goddess, founders of all life, were chanted in rhythmic, melodic tunes. They had songs with instrumental accompaniment for rain-making, mourning, hunting, and other occasions. Different tribes had their own versions of the Creation Myth. Some families had songs describing local landmarks, the verses serving as "title guarantees" to prove the right to a particular parcel of land.

This native music was characterized by the use of many unorthodox scales. Their primitive instruments fluctuated in pitch and vocal intonation, and the scale successions they achieved cannot be duplicated by the twelve fixed keys of the piano. Their rhythmic patterns were more complex than those of many other American tribes and were at times curiously suggestive of syncopation. Each song was a series of phrases, or measure repetitions, often with melodic ornaments and variations of rhythm that suggest the plaintive and colorful quality of Oriental music.

Instruments used by Southern Califonia natives included flutes blown with the mouth or nose, rattles made of shells or dried skins filled with pebbles, crude drums, wooden clappers and musical bows which the Indians played so expertly that they are said to have been able to "talk" and make love with them.

A curious custom was the singing of traditional "war songs" against neighboring tribes or families. The "foes" had usually long since become good friends, but the songs had been handed down from father to son and each successive generation felt duty bound to sing them periodically, angrily stamping the ground as if trampling on the graves of their enemies. One of these harmless feud songs has been translated as follows:

"Bury him now, plant him now:
And then they buried him, and then they planted him:
PEHUETEMATEWILWISH" (the enemy's name).

When the Indians were Christianized by the Franciscan Missionaries in the late eighteenth century, they were taught to play the guitar and mandolin and to intone in Latin for church ceremonials. Gradually they were induced to forsake their tribal ceremonies and primitive folk music. However, these rituals persisted in isolated places until recent time. Old Indians who remembered the songs have been persuaded to sing many of them for phonograph recordings which are preserved at the Southwest Museum in Los Angeles.

Spanish and Mexican folk songs were the music of Los Angeles for some seventy years after the founding of the city in 1781. Of the lazy, carefree pueblo, Charles F. Lummis, author and devoted collector of Southwestern folklore, wrote: "There was no paying $5 to be seen chattering in satin while some Diva sang her highest. There was no grand opera and no fool songs. There were songs of the soil, and songs of poets and of troubadors, in this far, lone, beautiful, happy land; and songs that came over from Mother Spain and up from Stepmother Mexico. But everybody sang; and a great many made their own songs, or verses to other songs . . . They felt music, and arrived at it."

There were romantic and amorous, melancholy and jocular songs, all with the charm, rhythm and richness of melody characteristic of Spanish music. The guitar was the favorite instrument. Almost everyone played it. The young bloods of the pueblo were so addicted to the old Spanish custom of serenading their sweethearts that the city fathers, in 1838, passed the following ordinance: "All individuals serenading promiscuously around the streets of the city at night, without first having obtained permission of the mayor, will be fined $1.50 for the first offense, $3 for the second, and for the third punished according to law."

The songs of the dons lived on for a time under American rule. Then as the new generations took more and more to Yankee ways and Yankee music, the traditional melodies were gradually forgotten. A few may perhaps still be heard in the vicinity of the Plaza, but most of them exist today only in phonograph records made by Lummis, who recorded more than 450 songs sung for him by the last survivors of the old era.

During the fifties and sixties much of the town's music was provided by Army and civilian brass bands, with occasional visits by light opera companies from Mexico and traveling minstrel shows from the East. But Los Angeles also heard its share of gambling house "orchestras" with Mexican-Indian players, who, according to Horace Bell, chronicler of that boisterous epoch, "sent forth most discordant sound, by no means in harmony with the eternal jingle of gold." At the same time, Los Angeles began singing songs brought in by the pioneers, many of which remain popular today—lusty forty-niner songs like *The New Eldorado*, brought down from the northern mining camps—nostalgic lyrics like *Home, Sweet Home*—facetious ditties of the *Clementine* type—and, somewhat later, rollicking cowboy songs.

With the influx of American residents during the seventies Los Angeles gradually shed the buckskin habiliments of the frontier town. Band concerts were given more regularly, pianos in private homes were no longer a novelty, and cultural groups were formed for the presentation of amateur entertainments such as the "Unitarian Thursdays," which included piano solos and song recitals. However, it was not until the boom days of the middle eighties, when thousands of fortune seekers rushed to the city, that Los Angeles took its place as an American community and started to assimilate the culture of the Eastern United States.

Since then, the development of local musical consciousness and institutions have kept pace with, or even surpassed, the city's unusually rapid growth. Folk music was supplanted by concert hall music. Theatres and opera houses were built; road shows

came in increasing numbers, and the world's famous artists included Southern California in their itineraries.

The first serious effort toward the appreciation of the classics began more than a half century ago with the inauguration of a series of chamber music concerts given privately by an instrumental group consisting of the talented members of the Heine family, and with the formation of the Hadyn Quartet by Harley Hamilton, a newcomer to Los Angeles. At that time, in 1883, there was in Los Angeles another excellent chamber music ensemble of strings, flutes, brass, and piano—the nucleus of which was the Berth family. This organization played nightly, first at the old Vienna Buffet, later at the Palace, corner of Broadway and First Street.

In 1893, four members of the newly-formed Woman's Symphony Orchestra, Edna Foy, Channeil Ferris, Dora James, and Madge Rogers, organized the Lute Quartet and gave concerts during the latter part of 1893 and the year following.

Shortly after the turn of the century, Alice Coleman and Blanche Rogers, two talented young pianists, took the initiative in promoting chamber music in Los Angeles. In 1905, Miss Coleman (now Alice Coleman Batchelder), transferred her musical activities to Pasadena where she had taken residence, and ever since has been that city's most outstanding sponsor of chamber music. She is the founder and director of Pasadena's famous Coleman concerts.

Miss Rogers (later Blanche Rogers Lott) was a member of the Jennison Trio, one of the first prominent chamber groups to follow the establishment of the Los Angeles Symphony Orchestra. She has also been actively connected with other groups, including the Rogers-Krauss-Opid Trio, the L'Ensemble Moderne and the Los Angeles Chamber Music Society, of which she was the founder.

Another young woman who played a worthy role in the chamber music history of Los Angeles was the pianist, May MacDonald Hope, now Mrs. John Coryell of Sacramento. She sponsored and maintained several musical trios whose personnel included such artists as Calmon Luboviski, Sylvain Noack, and Ilya Bronson.

In 1918, Albert C. Bilicke, a Los Angeles music patron, brought from Vienna Adolph Tandler, Rudolph Kopp, and Axel Simonsen—all musicians of prominence. With Ralph Wylie, they formed the Brahms Quartet. Later, Oskar Seiling, a Joachim pupil who had come to Los Angeles in 1906, replaced Mr. Wylie. In 1912, the group was joined by Homer

(*Continued on page* 126)

Mirthful Melody

By RAYMOND FRANKLIN SHRY-OCK

LIGHT opera, musical comedy and operetta, should be due for a renaissance in this country. It is optimistic indeed to hope that Vienna can experience a resurgence of those melodious successes which, to our delight, invaded our land during the first two decades of this century. War and its aftermath may suffer, even in invaded lands, composition of serious symphonic works. A lone individual with requisite skill may, in his cold and gloomy abode, derive inspiration of a like nature from the historic events pressing inexorably against his sensitive nature.

Light opera, however, brilliant and bubbling with mirth as it must be, requires a felicitous combination of circumstances, surrounded by a happy atmosphere to flower or even for the seed to be planted: a fascinating "book" or libretto, charming lyrics, catchy and appropriate melodies to set the populace awhistling. To conceive of two or three gathered together in a reasonably cheerful mood to collaborate for this happy issue is too much to expect in a war-riven land. With minds on the bread line and bodies all too reactive to deficiencies in calories the proper setting just isn't there; and where is the enthusiastic impresario, the generous "angel" also necessary to the scene?

True, we have been in the wars; but our homes and conditions are intact, our artistic life untouched; the draft, too, has been lenient in assignments to our talented musicians, hardly curtailing time and opportunity for creative endeavor. Then why all these revivals of past hits in the field of light opera and musical comedy? Gilbert and Sullivan have been repeated so often that their shades must be crying, "enough, enough!" Herbert, Friml, Lehar, Romberg and like talented tunesters have held the post for decades and deservedly so, but it is now time to hope for a series of new successes by young composers and librettists. These need not be perennials continuing from generation to generation. There were a number of operettas from the 'nineties on for some twenty years which were hits and made money in their time which this generation has never heard of.

It is well worth the try, and a fascinating pursuit it would be.

There are talented and erudite American composers busily writing serious music: symphonies, tone poems, choral works and novelties. These will hardly be diverted from this class of composition. It is to a different crop of talent we must look for the delight in treading airier realms.

The requirements are not too light though the subject is. First, there must be the gift of melody. This generally comes through a musical background: musical or musically inclined parents; the experience of hearing light and serious music from childhood which stores the subconscious with a synthesis, a sea, of rhythm, melody and harmony readily drawn up to the conscious at will, separated, combined or "mixed" by good taste for the particular requirement at hand. It is understood that the love of good music of all styles will have induced the prospective composer to continue this storing by voluntarily attending performances of various kinds: symphonic, choral, grand and light opera, recitals, even to night spots, for all will be grist to his mill; attending not alone for emotional reaction but to analyze what makes the compositions tick. A study of standard harmony from a good teacher to dress his melodies most attractively. (He might be warned to refrain from headaches possible through study of speculative textbooks in which theorists strive to explain extremes of Schoenberg, Stravinsky, Tcherepnin and company. This will only serve to separate him from the public he aims to please.) A working knowledge of standard counterpoint to make the most of his choruses and, if he writes his own orchestrations, to manage the instruments well. A careful analysis of a Mendelssohn symphony and an early Beethoven and, say, the former's Elijah, together with a few successful grand and light operas.

Then, with plenty of resultful practice, considering, too, that he has a working knowledge of the piano, he is ready to look for his librettist. This should not be too difficult with many clever writers available

(*Continued on page* 137)

Stranger In His Own Land

By MORRIS RUGER

IF our country is to come of age, artistically as well as scientifically, the same sympathetic and financial encouragement which is offered to the promising young scientist, must be available for the talented young American composer. As it stands today, a composer must possess a fair degree of social and political talent and be willing to spend considerable time in their cultivation if he wishes to have his works performed in any significant manner.

This situation is all the more distressing considering the amount of money spent on serious music each year in this country and the high degree of perfection maintained in its performance. American artists of competence and distinction are to be found in all branches of music, but new American music seldom is heard, neither on the programs of solo artists or by the many fine orchestras which are functioning in almost every section of our country. The part played by the large recording companies and the radio networks is even less significant.

These facts have been pointed out many times before, but so far little improvement has taken place. There have been some attempts to explain the apparent lack of good American symphonic music by categorically stating that Americans do not have talent for musical compositions. This idea is utter nonsense, as anyone with experience in a conservatory or university music department is well aware.

What is not generally known however, are the many difficulties of a non-musical nature that stand between a composer's ideas and the public performance of his works. It might be well to examine a few of the more serious of these difficulties with a view to paving the way for their eventual solution.

The first problem is one of education. Most people know of the many years of technical training required to become a doctor or an electrical engineer, but are often quite unaware of the exacting nature of the preparation and training of a competent composer.

In general, his education must develop along three separate fields more or less simultaneously. He should become a good performer, preferably a pianist with a working knowledge of at least one other instrument. The problem of securing a fine teacher is of course a difficult one which requires the investment of a considerable sum of money.

Training in the theoretical aspects of music including harmony, counterpoint, orchestration, composition, is even more difficult to acquire. It used to be necessary to go to Europe for this training, but that is no longer the case. However, there are still very few schools where this all important part of his education may be pursued in a satisfactory manner. This again requires the investment of a considerable sum of money.

The third part of his education is possibly the most troublesome to acquire. Since no one in his right mind expects to make money from the composition of serious music, if he wishes to teach in a college, or the public schools, he must be prepared to get an A.B. or a master's degree. This is a four to six year undertaking with very little of that time devoted to the study of music.

Let us assume our young composer has managed to surmount these many and varied obstacles—that he has learned the craft of musical composition and that he has achieved at least a minimum of economic security. The question now remains as to when he will find time to compose. Making a reasonable living is usually considered to be a full time job. Since making a living and composing music are more or less mutually exclusive terms, he is forced to do his composing at odd hours as best he can. Too many people still believe in what might be called the "stork legend" in reference to the birth of a new musical composition. The composer is pictured retiring to a garret and there amid moonlight and pink clouds, his long sensitive fingers gliding lightly over the piano keyboard, he delivers himself of a masterpiece. He then returns slightly pale, but happy, to present it to an eagerly awaiting world.

This picture, however dear to the public's heart, is far removed from the facts as they actually exist. The composition of music is usually a long and ofttimes gruelling process, requiring tremendous concentration and great physical as well as emotional stamina. Undoubtedly, there would be a lot more

(Continued on page 138)

Consider the Children

By FRANK HUBBELL

THE mind of a child is like a blank phonograph record, sensitive and receptive to each passing impression, and retaining those impressions permanently. Today's children are tomorrow's adults, and the educational efforts of one decade become the cultural habits of the next. Therefore it is every musician's obligation to help the new generation to develop and attain a discriminating appreciation of good music.

There are far too many adults who, through no fault of their own, might bluntly be termed musical morons simply because, as children, they received little or no opportunity to partake of the pleasure that comes from hearing and understanding fine music. Such people are truly unfortunate, their lives needlessly incomplete. Had they in childhood been exposed to good music, its enjoyment would have grown with them as they themselves matured.

Some of the world's greatest composers have recognized the necessity of writing music especially for children. Not tinkly, popularized banalities, but sincere and valid music of genuine integrity—music whose appeal is so thoroughly universal that it delights the adult as well as the child, and thus fulfills a dual purpose.

Among the brooding despondencies and melodic magnificences of Tchaikovsky, for instance, you come, surprisingly, upon the sparkling fairy-tale vignettes of the *Nutcracker Suite*, so gay, so obviously airy and youthful, that merely to listen carries you back to a time when you yourself were young. That master French impressionist, Debussy, was another whose genius frequently turned toward compositions for children. Ravel explored similar paths to the child mind with his *Mother Goose* suite. Humperdinck's score for a legendary *Hansel and Gretel* contains moments of sheer childlike beauty, and in a more modern idiom, Prokofiev has blended youthful charm with subtle whimsy in his *Peter and the Wolf*, as well as in the less-celebrated *Summer Day* suite.

There are others, too. But not enough.
Not nearly enough!
Why?

Can it be that most of our contemporary composers are so lost in the race for quick fame and quicker fortune, so preoccupied by daily drudgery, that they have become blind to the urgent need for creating a solid, substantial musical idiom for children?

Not to mince words, are musicians less intelligent than baseball magnates, for example? Organized baseball goes to great lengths in a foresighted effort to interest youngsters in the game: sandlot teams are sponsored, sixteen-millimeter movies are produced and exhibited—in fact, everything possible is done to create future "fans." Commercial considerations aside, why shouldn't musicians make just as sincere and determined an effort to reach the child mind and teach it to enjoy the better things in music?

True, many of our better orchestras are trending in this direction with their special concerts for school children; this is a splendid thing. But it answers only half the problem. In a concert, the music is performed. But first that music must be written. And there is not enough of it. Composers should devote more time and effort to creating good music in the youthful vein. It could be, and should be, a completely unselfish project, undertaken for the sheer joy of accomplishment and the satisfaction of engaging in a needed task.

As a composer and arranger, my own interest in the realm of children's music was first crystallized some years ago when I was given the opportunity to write the score, including ballet numbers, for an operetta called *Mother Nature's Children*, produced in 1937. This assignment brought one lesson into sharp focus: my researches taught me the enduring value of simplicity. That is the major ingredient in successful music for children. All the finer compositions in the field are simple, direct—and therefore charming.

Simplicity need not be cheapness, however. Good taste is the cornerstone upon which the structure must be built, and good taste is never sleazy nor shoddy. By establishing these sound principles of musical good taste in the mind of the child, you plant a seed which will take root and grow and flower throughout that child's entire life, blossoming into years of ability to appreciate the best things which music can offer.

And make no mistake about it, music plays an important and vital role in all our lives, more so than in any previous era. Whether we are professional musicians or non-professional listeners who depend mainly upon radio, movies and phonograph records for our musical enjoyment, almost all of us are placed in intimate contact with music in one form or another, many hours a day. It is for us to teach our children musical discernment; to encourage them to separate the wheat from the chaff. And it is the composer's obligation to make sure that there shall always be plenty of wheat in the form of good music—and not an oversupply of corn!

In recent months it has afforded me much satisfaction to put these theories to the acid test of practice. Through a series of fortunate circumstances I was engaged as composer-conductor for a concern currently specializing in phonograph record albums for children. The company has developed a new idea combining phonograph records and comic books, attractively packaged in colorful sets.

Unlike most of those on the magazine stands, eschewing blood-and-thunder melodrama and bang-bang adventure, these publications emphasized charming fantasy in their picture-stories. And every word, every action shown in the drawings, came to life upon the accompanying phonograph records. There were sound effects, too; but, most important, there was music.

My task was to compose, arrange and conduct the musical backgrounds, interludes and tunes. This music would not be mere subordinate material, and I was not asked to hack out mechanical "bridges" between action sequences, as in the average radio show. Instead, my compositions were to be an integral part of each story—and the stories were so written that they depended upon the music for completeness and unity.

Here, then, was a problem demanding sincere thought. The first story was called *Lonesome Octopus,* an under-water fantasy in which a humanized octopus organizes an orchestra made up of his fellow-creatures of the sea. He does this as a favor for a friend—a nice little sugar-coated moral touch which subtly teaches the child the value of generosity and unselfishness. But the organizing of the Octopus Orchestra, and treatment of the music it subsequent-

ly performs, represented a challenge worthy of any composer's ingenuity, especially since the entire thing had to be performed in less than six minutes of narration and playing time, divided into the two "sides" of the record.

I had to decide what instrumentation would fit the story. I then had to develop a theme which could first be played as a solo melody, unaccompanied. Next, one by one, the other instruments had to be introduced in a way which would display each instrument's characteristics, as well as its proper place in building orchestral ensemble. Brief counterpoints had to be composed for the various instruments, all so interwoven that they would blend contrapuntally in a united whole when once the entire orchestra began playing.

It had to be done clearly and simply, with no hint of complexity. Morever, I had to keep in mind that there would be a sequel—called *Grumpy Shark*—which would pick up where *Lonesome Octopus* left off, adding still more instruments and telling a new musical-picture story similar to the first, but yet fresh and definitely different in plot and treatment.

Above all, I had to remember that while my music must appeal to the child and illustrate certain fundamentals of orchestration, the tune itself must be sufficiently lilting to catch the ear of the adult as well.

It was an assignment requiring experimentation, careful planning, and close collaboration between composer and script-writer. The music may not be classical in the highbrow sense of the word, but it delights the children who hear it. And that, after all, was my purpose in writing it.

I feel that television ultimately will play even a larger role in the development of musical good taste in children than radio itself has played. For television, like motion pictures, will bring visual educaton to the world, specifically to the younger generation, provided it is properly channeled and wisely used. Let the child see a composer at work; let him actually watch the process of setting down the notes in their proper position. Let him see each instrument taking its rightful place in the eventual ensemble, and let him behold the entire orchestra playing, as he hears it play.

Televised programs of that nature actually should be just as enticing to adults as to youngsters—for after all, the adult is but a grown-up kid. If "the child is father to the man", music well can be godfather to both!

If the Shoe Fits

By RICHARD DRAKE SAUNDERS

MOST musicians and dancers continually complain that not enough people are appreciative of their Art (with a capital A), especially as distinguished from the art (with a small a) of their immediate competitors. Impresarios sing the same refrain, to the effect that not enough patrons of serious music can be lured into concert halls. And statistics inform us that while some twenty-five per cent of the public is interested, more or less, in worth-while music, less than five per cent actively patronize musical and choreographic attractions.

The reason, quite frankly, is that most musicians and dancers are so completely self-centered that they repel others, instead of attracting. If they would benefit their own lot, it is high time that they matured emotionally and intellectually. They ask universal appreciation; let them ask themselves what they are doing, and what they can do to deserve it.

First of all, musicians—and I will include dancers in this category hereafter, for the sake of brevity—take a perverted pride in declaring that they have no aptitude for business. This is stupid, in the present era. It is a holdover from an age when the musician fawned upon some noble patron to ask for alms. By disassociating himself with "vulgar" business, he placed himself in the same class as his noble patron, even though as a poor relation. It was a disgustingly servile attitude then; it is even more so today.

Whether the musician likes it or not, nowadays he is in business; furthermore, he is in business for himself. He never will be successful if he merely licks the boots of wealthy patrons, whining for a handout. He may get a certain measure of charity, but he never will get respect in that way. He must realize the value of what he has to offer, and expect remuneration for his services in the same manner as a doctor, lawyer or other professional man. That remuneration should be based upon the time involved, considering his experience and the investment he has had to make in securing his training in his profession.

The professional who has a manager is protected in his engagements; the instrumentalist who performs as a member of the union is protected similarly, as is the concert and radio artist in comparable organizations. But the artist who has no manager is still fair game for the "music" clubs who want free programs. And the music teacher seldom knows the value of his services.

The impresarios who complain about lack of patronage have only themselves to blame. They—one and all—never have even tried to sell the one thing that could ensure them full houses; the music itself. Instead they have been content to be rubber stamps for the concert managers, and devote their whole attention to selling personalities. The result is unique emphasis on the individual and none at all on what he may be playing, singing or dancing. Unless the personality is adequately glamorized, the house will be empty.

This practice has led to the ridiculous extreme of continual bookings for artists long since passe, while competent talent is given the cold shoulder. When a "name" artist has been built up by a management, by hook or crook, they continue to sell him as long as that name has drawing power, without regard to his ability. His voice may be reduced to an octave without resonance, or his violin tone to a thin and febrile squeak; his pianism may have lost its efficiency and accuracy, or his legs may wobble uncertainly: what do the managements care if they can sell him.

The impresarios will accept such has-beens unquestionably because an established name requires less "selling effort" than a new one. Always it is the name they sell; never the program, or the music itself. On the contrary, they will discourage the artist from offering new works in the fear of offending some patrons with their roots in the last century, without considering that a few novelties might make a few new patrons.

Neither will the local impressarios lend a hand to aid local talent. "It is too hard!" they wail; "no one will come to the concert." Few, indeed, are the impresarios willing to take the time and trouble to stir a bit of local pride and push a resident artist, not with just one concert, but with enough engagements to establish him. After he wins fame they will be quick enough to claim credit for any small help or bit of advice, invariably seen through a high-power magnifying glass.

Musicians are far from being the best patrons of their colleagues' concerts (and there we must except dancers, who are commendably good patrons of dance events). When they do go (on passes, if it is humanly possible to get them), they rarely attend any event outside of their own specialty. A reasonable modicum of pianists will attend piano concerts, singers will attend voice events, and so on. But it is rare indeed for the singer to purchase tickets for a violinist, for a dancer to patronize the orchestra, in fact, for any musician to attend an event outside of his immediate and specialized field.

Whenever they go, the musicians eagerly await the intermission when they may parade in the foyer for the express purpose of belittling the performance to everyone within hearing distance. "Of course he has a good tone," they may admit, "but his technic is deplorable." Or it may be: "A brilliant technic, if you like, but it cannot make amends for his lack of interpretation." Good points are conceded grudgingly, while there always is the inevitable "but, of course—"

This customary procedure does the cause of music no good. The layman, who cannot help overhearing these tirades, naturally wonders if there is an honest standard of performance at all. Or it merely may fortify his opinion that all musicians are crazy, anyway.

Musicians are not good company in social groups because they are so completely immersed in their own branch of art that they seldom are able to converse intelligently on any other subject. It is shop talk or silence with them. They wonder audibly why they are invited only to make music, yet it is quite literally the only thing they can do to contribute to a social gathering.

It is quite time that musical folk took a look at themselves in the mirror of public opinion instead of the mirror of their own self-esteem. They would find that a few simple alterations of habits and methods would rebound to their advantage.

Just for a beginning, they might stop bemoaning their unhappy lot. A musician lives in the shadow of great beauty, and he should realize this fact fully, not merely partially. It is the fascination of music itself which really binds a musician to his task, and makes amends for whatever other shortcomings there may be.

Contemplating his business dealings, let the musician look to other professions or skills for a model. The physicians, who pride themselves as belonging to a self-styled "noble profession," never hesitate to send their bills, nor to turn the unpaid ones over to a collection agency. The saying that "the laborer is worthy of his hire" is a very old one.

During compilation of this volume, I talked with a number of teachers who declared they were busy every moment from early morning to late at night, yet complained in the next breath that they barely were making a living. Advised to raise their fees, they recoiled in fright lest they might lose pupils. Yet simple mathematics would prove that if they lost half their pupils by doubling their fees, they would have half their time for rest and relaxation, if nothing else. Services, like commodities, should rest on the law of supply and demand.

The professional who has no manager should be aware of his own value in the competitive market, and set his fees accordingly, raising them as opportunity permits, in the same manner that a manager would act for his client. A demand for his services will bring him to the attention of a good manager sooner than anything else.

Local impresarios should realize that they are a part of the community, and not endeavor to "milk" it for the benefit of outside managements. They should make an honest effort to stimulate civic pride, also, to "sell" their communities on music itself. They should try to benefit resident artists who have the ability to become concert attractions.

Musicians should make more effort to patronize concerts, particularly those of resident artists, who deserve the utmost aid from their colleagues. They should make a point, too, of hearing forms of music apart from their own specialties, where they might even discover valuable pointers to apply to their individual work.

Indiscriminate carping criticism in public places hampers the cause of music in general. Here, again, musicians might observe the practice of the doctors, who never publicly criticize another physician, no matter how incompetent or inefficient they might know him or her to be.

Above all, musicians and dancers should realize that they are one with the life about them, not a group chastely set apart. Let them interest themselves in all the other factors of existence today which will make them better company, better citizens, and—in the long run—better artists.

What Price Culture?

By MARLIN SKILES

FOR the past quarter century the American public has inherited a wealth far and above any monetary value. It is a wealth that in past history was reserved for that minority fortunate enough to acquire it by means, title or long, serious study. It is one of the greatest of art forms: Music.

After centuries of slow, tedious development the dam has burst and Mr. Public, with the aid of many ingenious inventions, finds himself in an avalanche of creative and interpretative endeavor. It is his for the asking. The vast stockpile of good music now is open to rich and poor alike, to take as wished with a bare minimum of effort to acquire it and the most ideal circumstances in which to enjoy it. All for the turn of a switch, the drop of a tone arm on a record or the payment of a small fee at a theatre box office. Pretty cheap for an education in music appreciation, don't you think?

Mr. Public, realizing the golden opportunity, buys himself stacks of records, listens to symphony programs and discovers that even motion pictures are presenting threads of good music along with the visual entertainment. He has learned to pronounce correctly "viola" and "'cello" and has become aware that the English horn actually is not a horn at all and is not necessarily associated with the British nation. He has advanced quickly, true to his American tradition.

As it is fashionable to discuss music intelligently, this may be accomplished by the simple means of reading columns and books by critics who "must know their business." Of course this takes a little time but it is not necessary to read everything. Just memorize the more important points and there you have it.

He now goes to his symphony concerts, applauds vigorously after each number and concedes that classical music is pretty damn good regardless of who wrote it. The music of that popular young foreign composer must be sheer genius because of his reams of publicity, especially as his name is difficult to pronounce. He has been told, and accordingly believes that the best motion picture scores are the ones he is not conscious of while viewing the picture.

He knows that Debussy is good, because someone is always playing his music, but give him the *1812 Overture*—there's music with guts, good and loud. He never misses tuning in on the Sunday Symphony but suddenly remembers that the lawn needs watering or that the most soothing way to take a nap is to be accompanied by music. He will put a stack of records on his automatic machine and spend a delightful evening arguing politics with his guests—accompanied by music.

This doesn't stop with Mr. Listener. It continues and in fact increases along the line to the people who make it possible for Mr. Public to become educated. They who pay the bills, who sign the checks, who buy talent in wholesale lots much as they would a carload of oranges. They presume to dictate which music, what kind of music and how this music should be played. It is an undeniable fact that it is suicide to perform a modern composition on a commercial radio program unless it is played by a Heifetz. In some strange way this modern music becomes digestible when played by Heifetz but not when played by Joseph Jones, violinist, over station HOWL, Keokuk. Mr. Radio Producer finds a formula which attracts interest (usually the first one presented) and that formula is repeated as long as the people continue to buy soap or until the advertiser decides to play with billboards instead of radio.

And then there is Mr. Motion Picture Producer. He clamors wildly for the services of any Academy Award winner and pays him fabulous amounts, knowing all the while that the music award usually rides along with the best picture of the year. He will pay a symphony composer handsomely for a score and struggle along despite the composer's lack of technical knowledge of the film craft, smiling all the while as the budget soars higher and higher.

Fortunately the motion picture composers, individually and collectively, are progressive and have elevated their form of art to a very high plane, the majority having achieved a comparative skill as craftsmen. A really *bad* motion picture score is practically unknown, so it seems a bit ridiculous then

(*Continued on page* 140)

32

Off With His Head!

By MILDRED NORTON

OF all his colleagues in the critical field, only the music critic has reason to be smug. Come inflation, depression or the end of the world, he can be sure of a steady job throughout eternity.

Painting, poetry and the dance may have their place in heaven, but if so, our classic literature on the subject fails to mention them. On the other hand, look at the publicity job that has been done on the state of music behind the Pearly Footlights. Gabriel, we are given to understand, cuts loose every now and then with some hot licks on the trumpet, celestial harps twang persistently, and anywhere you turn you're almost sure to bump into cherubim in a cappella choir formation.

Such activities, badly organized though they obviously are, could add up to quite a busy musical season, and while there are two schools of thought as to whether any critic could possibly get within yodeling distance of St. Peter, it is a reasonably safe bet that his experience in browbeating ushers here below would eventually get him seated somewhere near the eighth row center of the celestial aisle.

Since it would seem, therefore, that the music critic is not easily to be shaken loose from his toehold on either this or the following world, the next best thing might be to try to improve his species sufficiently to make him a tolerable member of the human family. As things now stand, the critic goes the performer one better, in that he not only lives for his art, but frequently manages to live despite it. This last sometimes entails great agility on his part, the discretion to dart suddenly behind a protecting pillar in concert halls and the avoidance of dark alleys for several days after some critical blast of his has incited to mayhem a temperamental tenor or fiddler.

As a matter of cold record, however, the popular impression of the music critic as a kind of Looking Glass figure, shouting "Off with his head!" like the Red Queen, has become outmoded in an age when anyone can draw his own conclusions about a piece of music or its performance simply by turning his radio dial. From now on the critic is going to have to offer something in merchandise beyond the arbitrary dictum of his opinion, and he is going to have to present his case in terms that have valid relationship to the needs and experience of the common man.

To do this, he will quite possibly come to concern himself less with the pedantries of his craft than with his power to expand the capacity of his readers for enjoying, understanding and judging music on their own account. To sharpen the public's ear, to arouse its interest in good music well performed, and to incite its indignation when it is offered the banal or the mediocre—these should be among the critic's prime functions in an age tyrannized by the commercial fallacy that only the vulgar, the trite and the easily grasped are properly the cultural portion of the masses.

Rightly to exercise this office, the well-equipped critic needs a keen perception of musical values, and the imaginative resources to communicate an aesthetic experience vividly, in words that will neither intimidate, affront nor bore his readers. Such a combination of musical taste and literary talent, plus the equally essential attribute of personal integrity, has been rare in the annals of musical journalism, but that it has been achieved more than once is confirmed by the writings of such men as Philip Hale, James Huneker and Lawrence Gilman, to mention but a few of the superior critical minds produced in America alone.

The critic of the future, even more perhaps than those of the past, will need to possess spiritual and intellectual horizons extending well beyond the microcosmos of his own subject, if he is to relate it in true proportion to its own time and to the dynamic curve of history. The critic who takes time out from his perusal of Tovey and Grove to orient himself as a world citizen is going to approach his critical chores much better fortified against provincialism and pedantry alike.

With all this must go a great feeling of responsibility toward not only the material he is discussing but toward the effects for good or ill his viewpoint may have on the public's reaction. While it is highly doubtful that the critic's opinion exerts any small fraction of the influence he likes to think it does, the

(Continued on page 139)

Music Heals

By ESTELLE HOLMELUND

THIS CHILD is as good as dead. He never will be able to sit up. It is only a matter of a short time before he will go blind. His heart is so weak that he cannot live more than a year or so anyway. Frankly, it is a waste of time and money to do anything for him."

This was the verdict of the doctors of a prominent West Coast hospital after week-long examinations of three-year-old Jimmy, eight years ago.

Jimmy was born a victim of cerebral palsy, a disease that so far had been a stepchild of medical science. At least, the thirty-odd physicians who were consulted admitted their inability to cope with the case. I finally had to face the fact that if Jimmy was to be saved it would be up to me both to find the way and to do the work.

Today our boy is eleven years old and an exceptionally attractive youngster, intelligent, active and always cheerful. He has not yet gained complete physical control and coordination but he can walk without braces, use his hands for many delicate tasks and is an outstanding cub scout.

Music became one of the most important factors in his life when he was still very young and his music appreciation has gradually developed to a marked degree. He is particularly fond of symphonic music and finds in it expression for his own thoughts and feelings as well as fascinating pictures of both real and imaginary things and events, his own life and struggles and the goal for which he is fighting.

My first great problem was to make him move his arms and legs. The idea struck me that it might be possible to use music for this purpose. So with the help of radio and victrola I set to work to make the baby conscious of rhythm and movement of arms and legs in step with it. Changes in tempos and rhythms required corresponding changes in the execution of the exercises and soon our work started to take the form of games. This gave our antics a meaning to him—it was fun, and we began to look forward to our sessions of home-made gymnastics with anticipa-

tion of a good time. I started to use costumes to fit the songs and melodies and added a new feature to our games—we could let the lift of the rhythms carry us to strange foreign lands. A globe of the world and pictures from the National Geographic made these musical flights more real.

Little by little, arms and legs gathered strength so that Jimmy could move them a trifle and support his weight and begin to crawl. He could do this only as long as he received the stimulation and timing of rythmical music, singing or counting. He moved both arms together and the legs the same way. Counting to slow two-four or four-four music I drilled him in a rhythm that he soon could follow listening to the music alone, without my continuous counting and verbal urging.

Walking was the next step. I started by tieing Jimmy to the back of a heavy chair in an upright position. Then I played some lively melodies for him, waltzes and folk dance music. The idea was to stimulate his desire for physical action and to animate this ambition so vigorously that he would forget his feeling of inability through the only stimulant strong enough to lift him out of himself—music.

Several weeks of this work with the chair as a support resulted in a kind of awkward dance which was still far from coordinated movement, but it was a physical expression of what the music created in his mind, and this was important.

The next step was to teach him the motion of walking, to move one foot at a time. For this purpose I placed him in a padded Taylor Tot and continued my routine of counting to music. I soon discovered that my counting of two-four time confused him until it struck me that my previous counting of one-two still was understood by Jimmy to mean the same as it did when I drilled him in crawling—to move both legs together on "one" and both arms together on "two." From then on I counted only "three" and "four" and he soon got the hang of following the rhythm with one foot at a time.

Military marches always had a very strong effect

on Jimmy. As soon as he was old enough I made it a habit to dress him in little army or navy uniforms when I played such warlike music for him. I had pictures of soldiers and sailors standing at attention and parading across a large mirror. Costumes and visual objects as usual helped to create the right atmosphere, but it was the martial music that lifted him out of himself and made him forget that it was supposed to be impossible for him to straighten his body into a military posture and lift his feet high for marching. Another result of the military music feature was that Jimmy got a drum of his own that he loved to beat with his hands until he could work out a rhythm by himself or accompanying my piano or the victrola.

I neglected no opportunity to develop his sense of rhythm as soon as I began to realize how important it was. Wherever we went we played games with it. I counted time to the movement of people's feet passing by and to the motions of horses walking, trotting and cantering in a riding arena. Counting to the rider's "posting" was excellent practice in combined rhythms.

Jimmy had been well drilled in the sense and understanding of the rhythm of horseback riding before he got into the saddle himself. When this great moment came he was for some time unable to keep his balance unaided, so I walked beside the pony to steady him, humming a little melody or counting in step with the slow, regular motions of the pony. Very gradually he began to get an actual feel of the rhythm of the pony's motions and the thumping of its feet against the ground accompanying the faint creaking of leather became music, a melody that he knew how to follow. Balance then came easily and after thirty-five riding lessons he could ride his pony without outside help. He was, however, able to balance himself only as long as the horse was in motion. When the pony came to a gentle stop, Jimmy would fall off. Without the stimulant of rhythm, Jimmy's body ceased to obey.

The steady, regular motions of the pony seemed to take the place and perform the duties of the many missing connections in his system between brain and limbs and make the necessary exercise possible that would give his muscles the strength on which all physical control depends. After three months of pony riding he was able for the first time to sit upright without support on a stool.

Pony riding also provided a form of massage that resulted in loosening and stretching of muscles in permanent spasms that were threatening to pull his legs tightly together and even across each other.

We continued to build on our experiences in the pony ring, using the little hummed tunes and counting with which we followed the motions of the pony, in connection with other physical exercises, always with the same response.

Ever since Jimmy began to understand musical instruments he has wanted a violin more than anything else. For obvious reasons I kept postponing the disappointment it would be for him to get one and compromised on piano lessons instead. He went into this new enterprise wholeheartedly. Music and rhythm was in his blood by this time and his desire to produce his own melodies was strong enough to create mental awareness of each separate finger and enforce control of it.

On his seventh Christmas the violin finally appeared. He took like a man his disappointment over his lack of reach and the stubborn refusal of his hands and fingers to work and even open. Instead of giving up in despair he set out to overcome, privately and quietly, the obstacles that stood between him and mastery of his violin. He would sit for hours pulling at the fingers of his left hand and pressing the fingers open by flattening his hands against the table top. There were days when I was asked to take the violin out ten or twelve times so that he could measure his arm and try his hands to see how much they had improved. He is not yet able to handle the instrument, though ukuleles, mouth organs, recorders, a real snare drum and the piano are providing some consolation. But he has accepted the challenge and he is going to play that violin some day.

Jimmy had three pickaninny dolls that he was so fond of that they had to be put to bed with him every night. One day I had an idea that resulted in the construction of a puppet show with a regular stage, curtain, footlights and all other accessories including strings for simple manipulation of the performing pickaninnies. Without music Jimmy would "freeze" on the strings, but if I played on the piano an appropriate melody for the dolls to dance by, Jimmy came to life and manipulated his strings with perfect efficiency. Obviously, music was doing to Jimmy what gas does to an automobile.

During his early childhood Jimmy, of course, had little opportunity to get acquainted with the world outside his own room. Telling stories and showing pictures will always do something to bring the wonders of far-away places into your home. So will movies, carefully selected. But in Jimmy's case it took music to give imagination wings. Music would not only bring the world into Jimmy's room, it would take him out to any place he wanted to go and take in whatever was going on there. So, when the day's excursion was decided on, Jimmy's transportation was provided in the form of cowboy music, a martial march, some sacred music, a symphony under the stars.

For Jimmy the daily grind consisted, among other things, of reading, writing, typing, modeling in clay, finger painting, drawing with crayon and chalk. Due to his condition most of these things were extremely hard work for him and I reached a point where I begin to despair. Again music came to my rescue. Records played softly on the victrola produced a marked improvement in energy and concentration. The steadily flowing rhythm forming the background of the music had a surprisingly stimulating effect on his thinking, motions and emotions. It gave him the strength to carry on with tasks that ordinarily were too much for him.

One of Jimmy's many defects used to be a chin that rested normally on his collar bone. His head was the the same time thrown back and slightly sideways with the result that his mouth was hanging wide open. Besides being very unattractive, this purely physical defect invariably seemed to convince even supposedly intelligent people that Jimmy was half-witted or worse. The fact that he was unable to speak did not improve the impression he made. The stimulation of music must be given credit before all other means attempted for the fact that today he can articulate with sufficient conscious control to make it possible for me to understand him.

Counting and keeping time with our hands to very slow four-four time, using the down-beat and the timing of the rest of the measure, established the basic rhythm for pronouncing the vowels. Later on, when we started to work on whole sentences, we used the four beats in the measure for the pronunciation of four syllables. This gradually developed into longer sentences following a steady rhythm in order to make each syllable distinct and separate. We are now using various forms of music with different tempos and varying rhythms in order to improve articulation and vocal expression.

For the general purpose of preparing him for a period of work I have learned to choose and use music to establish the right atmosphere and subse-

quent favorably attuned condition of Jimmy's nervous system and mood. In order to establish the quietly detached condition of mind desirable for religious training I would play an *Ave Maria* or a *Largo*. Relaxation and rest were invited by slow, swaying lullabies. The gliding motions of arms and hands when writing were inspired by waltzes. If faster movements were called for I switched to the lively tunes of folk dances. When I needed all he had of mental alertness and highstrung concentration I got results with Sousa's marches. . . . When he needed an outlet for pent-up emotions and time off for a little primitive exuberance, ballet music was called for. Symphonic music has always had great power over him and I have been able to use it to control and guide his emotions and moods and consequently also his thoughts and the molding of his mind.

Music therapy in hospitals remains as yet in the experimental stage. This, however, does not detract from the many outstanding achievements which have been accomplished by music therapists who have been working with mentally sick patients, but rather means that no set approach has been devised through which an operator can be assured the mentally sick patient might be reached.

Different approaches on the part of the therapists are needed. Operators who are improvisors, who can catch the mood of the patient and then carry the patient along to reach the mood desired by the therapist, can do much to provide relief and satisfaction to the patient.

The music therapist must be prepared for the unexpected rather than the normal reaction, when presenting a program of music therapy. The operator must contact the patient at the patient's level, bearing in mind that a good song for a particular patient cannot be determined beforehand. The operator must select and play music especially suited to the patients of each ward. Play or sing softly and low, rather than high and loud. Careful tabulation of the patients' reaction to the program then should be made.

Preliminary steps now are being made to conduct the music therapy program on a strictly prescriptive basis. The local Music Work Shop consists of a five-fold program for the Veteran's Administration hospital, Naval and Civilian hospitals. 1. Entertainment, 2. Teaching of instruments, 3. Music appreciation and patients' participation, 4. Organists and choirs or church, and 5. Music therapy.

The Inside Story

By ERNEST KANITZ

QUITE often we hear the radio announcer say, "And now Mr. X will give you the inside story behind the news." Most people seem to take for granted that there always is a story behind the news. Whether this radio custom does or does not make sense, is not for musicians to decide. We should be more concerned, however, when we hear a similar question raised in connection with a musical composition. "What is the story behind the piece"? This is what many persons are likely to ask when presented with a musical performance, particularly of a new piece whose "inside story" they have not yet been told.

Usually the program notes or the radio announcer inform the listener as to the piece he is about to hear. They tell historical facts regarding the composer, his life and his background, as well as the themes and structure of the work, all of which is a highly commendable procedure; but very often they also give out one of the above mentioned "stories." This, in my opinion, is bad in all cases where music is played which has not been clearly linked with extramusical ideas by the composer himself.

We have sacred music whose purpose and story everybody knows, or learns, through the words which are being sung. The same is true of secular vocal music. There is, on the other hand, secular instrumental music of two different types. One is music accompanying dance or dramatic action—from the village fiddler's dance tunes to the modern ballet, from incidental music for Baroque court plays, to the intricacies of the Wagnerian music drama. Adding to these the more recent branch of motion picture music, we realize that in all three cases, dance, operatic, and film music, the story unfolds while the music is being played.

The other type is music written for no other purpose than for entertainment through music. We have become used to calling it symphonic, if written for orchestra, chamber music, if written for small groups. This type of music has no "inside story"; at least the composer, in most cases, keeps silent about it, if there is one, and both the commentator and the public should honor his silence and not ask indiscreet questions. We call such music *absolute* when comparing it with pieces of another, relatively young, kind of music which is purposely descriptive in character; here the composer announces the action he wants to describe with his music through an explanatory story, through a poem, sometimes through the title only. Such music we call program music.

The descriptive type, having occurred only sporadically in the pre-classical and classical eras, enjoyed a tremendous development in the second half of the 19th century, up to the time of World War I. It seems to be on the decline again, since 1918, as far as the number of pieces composed in the last twenty years is concerned. Orchestra leaders all over the world, however, still seem to be quite fond of the type, and a great number of music commentators, authors and music teachers overemphasize the programmatic side of music by giving mostly unjustified interpretation to the pieces of contrary character. Thus they extend the influence of a rather unimportant style long beyond the time when it should begin, and actually has begun, to become obsolete.

A piece of program music will only live in repertory, for a period longer than just the first few years after its first performance, if it contains inspired music in well balanced form and therefore can be enjoyed as pure music also by listeners who do not realize that a program, or story, exists at all. To name a few examples, Beethoven's *Pastoral Symphony* and Strauss' *Eulenspiegel* will still be played often when *Wellington or the Battle of Victoria* and *Heldenleben* will hardly get more than a few performances here and there.

Even in music for the stage, the movies or the dance, it is this absolute, the purely musical, which keeps it alive, often long beyond the time when the interest for the drama or action it had been written to accompany has long vanished. The sheer musical qualities are the ones that count most, and in absolute music it is not the composer's intention to impress his listeners by anything else but melody, harmony, form and instrumental color. Through these four elements the mood and spirit in which the piece was written can be expressed perfectly and will easily be carried to the listener's mind. No more is necessary.

None of the other arts can be as detached from matter and material thoughts as music. The arts of

(Continued on page 131)

Where Now?

By THEODORE KOLLINE

WHAT may be the future of contemporary music? We speak of modern music as dating from Bach, and contemporary music as that composed since the turn of the century. In the last category the leading composers still living are Richard Strauss, aged 83; Sibelius, 81; Vaughn Williams, 75; Arnold Schoenberg, 73; Ernest Bloch, 67; Stravinsky and Villa-Lobos (interesting contrast), both 66.

The first-named threatens to outlive his musical immortality. The others have ceased to enrich our musical literature with any new or important developments, with the exception of Villa-Lobos. Our younger creative men like Shostakovich, Prokofiev, William Walton, Hindemith and Roy Harris, should be at their creative peak now and continue their output for a least two more decades. Will they? And in what direction?

Modernity becomes more and more synonomous with atonality. Biologically the ear soon becomes accustomed to the wildest violations and the cruelest torture. The tyranny of the fourth has replaced the tyranny of the third, and the passion for "originality" at any cost, has become the dangerous obsession of the younger generation. Vaughn Williams once explained to an orchestral player, "It *looks* wrong, and it *sounds* wrong but it's *right!*" The writer repeatedly warns his composition students against that easy originality which defies logic, sanity or form, paths which when regarded may provide a nucleus for distinctive individuality.

While it is no longer necessary to nurture the budding creative hopeful entirely upon Haydn, Mozart, Chopin and Brahms, it is equally dangerous to sustain him exclusively upon a diet of Schoenberg, Stravinsky, Milhaud or Ives. Incidentally, the Schoenberg "Twelve-tone theory" was first promulgated by the Viennese composer Joseph Mathias Hauer but with totally different results.

Never before in musical history has there been such an eager acceptance of contemporary music with its atonal nihilism, its formlessness, its shrieking defiance. And why? Because it faithfully reflects the chaos and confusion of the world we live in. Its only harmonic feature is that it is in harmony with our age. However, the creative spirit must beware of trends which may before long become cults. Music no more than any other art can afford to lose sight of its dual role and purpose, which is not merely to reflect exoteric functional living but also to reflect upon it, to comment thereon from within, to express the eternally fixed human and spiritual values, with an individual voice.

Within the past twenty-five years the tremendous speeding up of life by means of the radio, the motion picture and the airplane has made possible a hundred years of development. The implications cannot be overlooked. Composition students may now be reared upon Bach and safely leap to Liszt, Musorgsky, Debussy, Ravel, and Stravinsky without harm, because the structural and expressive elements of the classics and romantics are all safely deposited therein. The old experiments of a George Antheil and an Edgar Varese have irrevocably ended, for a new impetus comes with every generation. The commercial snare of the motion-picture with its inevitable "background music" has fantastically replaced the ubiquitous stuffy salon music of years ago. But what can be expected of a center which glorifies the successful moron and repudiates the unsuccessful genius?

We have witnessed a passing age spend itself, extravagantly, intensely, and furiously. The pioneer work has been done, and it is the fate of the pioneer to leave the harvest to successors. Free and unfettered ultra-chromaticism has inevitably lead us to the brink of the perilous abyss of atonality. Where now? One thing is certain. Who have never known the self-discipline of solid craftsmanship, can never know the meaning of real freedom. Most of the younger composers today are bereft of an esthetic faith and there is a serious need for a new esthetic. A new Renaissance of culture may be a furtive dream but it is nonetheless a spiritual necessity.

Since the future of civilization may be within the province of the Americas and the Russias, we may do well to ponder the prophetic elements discernable in Shostakovich, Prokofiev and Villa-Lobos. The

(*Continued on page* 138)

Keep Your Tools Sharp

By MARY CARR MOORE

THEATRICAL subjects are apt to be taken lightly, in the minds of many. Music composition (as with poetry) is often mistakenly considered to be a "gift" bestowed upon the few by the Muses, and emanating from the desire to create original work, rather than from an understanding of the process.

Often one is at a loss to convince the inexperienced composer (without discouraging him completely) of the necessity for a thorough understanding of the mysteries of notation. How entirely out of place, for instance, is an E flat sprinkled into a thoroughly respectable B major chord!

There is such a grave necessity for a complete understanding of the many modes and scale patterns, of modulation and chromatic alteration, that without the guidance of thorough musical understanding, the young composer is entirely discouraged by the time his errors are ironed out.

The science of notation, from the time of Terpander and his first addition to the Greek tetrachord (650 B.C.), through the marvellous deductions of Pythagoras (500 B.C.) and the gradual development and expansion through the centuries to the present, is well worth the interest and attention of any serious music student.

So often, in giving advice to an ardent young composer (young in experience, perhaps—at any age) it is difficult to explain the awkwardness of certain phrases, which *sound* exactly as the composer desires —but would be completely confusing to the performer—accustomed to certain patterns of notation. In other words, "two, too and to" sound alike, but have a different meaning; on the contrary, "through, though and trough," look much alike yet have different sounds.

In the early phases of harmony, the student becomes accustomed to the proper use of scale passages, intervals and triads; he finds it of illuminating interest to discover the connecting links between the different keys; as, for instance, the three major triads, in every major key, and the two major triads in the relative and tonic minor keys. Gradually, to his interest, he realizes that the tonic triad of any major key may become in turn, the dominant triad of a key a fifth below, or the subdominant triad of a major key, a fifth above. The inter-relationship of keys, within the range of several sharps, or several flats, is surprising; and the many modulatory effects obtained, by the addition of one or more accidentals, as well as the return to the original key, is almost inexhaustible.

The diminished triad, on the vii° of any minor key, and its diminished 7th, may be written (with only four notes) in five different manners; supplying on the three semi-tones (G-sharp; A natural, and A-sharp) the fifteen keys of the minor scales: (a-minor, with signature of its relative major, C) and the seven sharp keys, as well as the seven flat keys. In each key, of course, one or more notes are subjected to an enharmonic change. It is easy to realize what a difference it would make to substitute, say, a B-flat, for an A-sharp; although the piano tone is exactly the same.

In more modern harmony, the use of the whole-tone scale (six notes) is bristling with difficulties, which are never quite the same. One has to consider the implications—in other words, "Let not your right hand know what your left hand doeth"—as is the case in Debussy's *Jardins sous la pluie,* where the descending phrase of the right hand reaches A-flat, simultaneously with the left hand ascending phrase as it touches G-sharp. The notation calls for this sequence, but the sound is of a perfect octave. The diatonic, chromatic, whole-tone, and pentatonic modes, in each case, bring about, an entirely different mood.

After the mastery of harmony (group-writing) with its stately architecture, its modulations, suspensions and organ-points, one is initiated into the mysteries of counterpoint, dealing with two or more combinations of melodic phrases. In turn these lead to the marvellous combinations of canon and fugue, in which forms John Sebastian Bach left us such riches. Following on to the texture of the complete orchestral instrument—I wonder if anything of human creation can be more akin to the marvels of "the stars in their orbits?"

Sometimes when I am told by an inexperienced

(*Continued on page* 127)

Music Flows With the Tide

By DEZSO DELMAR

EVERY period in musical history has a distinct mood, an idiom typical of its time.

What then are the shaping forces of those particular moods? There must be several, since artistic appeal is of a complex nature, and depends upon the emotional responses of the listeners.

These emotional reactions cannot be constant. They change with the dynamic flow of social events, yet the composers who have tried to interpret the changes in new and original musical idioms seldom have received plaudits from their contemporaries. Only gradually and painstakingly, through the effort of a persistent minority, has each new musical idiom finally been understood and appreciated.

The reason for the lukewarm attitude of the public toward any innovation, in any artistic endeavor, is deeply rooted in the current of life which stirs the emotional and psychological responses. If a new composition is to achieve any degree of success, it must necessarily fathom the emotional life of the public at a particular time. Unless a composition meets this requirement it is doomed to failure. Throughout history, new musical idioms survived only when the emotional needs of the masses were satisfied by them.

Bach and Handel's compositions during the reformation era appealed to religious instincts. With their mental gaze riveted on the radiant glory of the Creator, Bach and Handel sang His greatness and stressed the smallness of man. Man's place in the universe was the song that flowed in an unending stream from their harmony, melody and rhythm. From the harmonic aspect, their idioms abound in a lavish variety of discords, emphasizing that only the faithful will be saved.

The idioms employed by Haydn, Mozart, and young Beethoven were radically different from their predecessors. All art, and music particularly, then was sponsored by an esoteric aristocracy, and the composers of that age were obliged to give expression to the frivolities of their sponsors if they were to live. The music they wrote reflected the grace, charm and lightheartedness of the so-called elite. Serious thought had to be subordinated to form, and discords which infrequently crept into their compositions were well-groomed and well-mannered.

There is, however, a remakable transition in the musical ideas of Beethoven between his earlier and later works. This transition chronologically coincides with the social and political changes. Feudalism tottered under the hammering blows of a new ideology which championed the masses. The common man assumed importance.

Beethoven turned apostle and crusader of this revolutionary movement. His imagination was fired by the struggle in which the common man was locked with the forces obstructing his freedom. His music grew beyond the conventional in an elementary plebeian sense. The graceful minuet yielded to the scherzo, and he even had the temerity to introduce folklore as a motif, as in the *Scherzo* of the *Pastoral Symphony*. In the *Seventh Symphony*, Beethoven rejoiced with the humble on earth to celebrate their release from bondage. In the choral finale of the *Ninth*, he envisioned man rejoicing in the thought of fraternity and equality.

While Beethoven's prestige and popularity continued to rise in proportion to the mounting importance of the masses, concurrently other tendencies asserted themselves. The social and political upheavals at the close of the 19th Century augmented the freedom of the individual, and Beethoven gave expression to the revolutionary movement in his compositions. He glorified the yearning, suffering, and aspirations of the masses alternately in moods of ecstacy and despondency. And thus was born the romantic movement, stressing the individual and national life streams, exemplified in the compositions of Chopin, Schumann, Liszt, Grieg and Tchaikovsky.

At the turn of the Twentieth Century, with the advent of radio and sound, the music-consuming public grew by leaps and bounds. The modern composer is linked with the masses, and if he is to gain recognition, he must fathom their heartbeats.

In a single generation, the hopes of man were blasted by two bloody cataclysms. A disillusioned world is now seeking stability, and the task of the composer is to give expression to its aspirations. If the masses will be able to identify their own emo-

(*Continued on page* 130)

Unbalanced Symphony

By RUTH HAROLDSON

THE middle of the 20th Century finds us reaching high points of scientific research and artistic attainments by both men and women. In the field of music, however, one phase remains almost exclusively the privilege of men—the actual playing of great symphonic literature, while women's major participation and contribution is delegated to those countless committees which support the symphony.

This article does no more than mention a concern. It is not necessary to "plead" the cause of "women in symphony" because many hundreds of women have proved themselves in orchestras in limited numbers whenever opportunity has been granted.

During the war years women were admitted to symphony orchestras in a ratio of one to seven. This year finds fewer women employed in major orchestras, with managers indicating that the ratio will soon be 1 to 20. One of the war years—1943—found five women each in Cincinnati, St. Louis, and Philadelphia; 4 in Cleveland and Detroit; Chicago had 6; San Francisco, 8; Baltimore, 11; Los Angeles, 12; Indianapolis, 13; Kansas City and Washington, 16 each; New Orleans, 17; Seattle, 21; and Houston, 26. Boston, Minneapolis and New York followed the tradition of 100 per cent male membership. Of thousands of local women players, 10 women were employed this summer in the Hollywood Bowl Orchestra and 10 this winter in the Los Angeles Philharmonic. However, several women are employed in radio and motion picture studio symphonies, several have gone to second rate orchestras elsewhere in the country, and many have entered the field of chamber music.

In a cross-country survey, managers give no definite reason for the current return to a 95 per cent male symphony except that, while their own particular conductors "have no prejudice against women, naturally they will employ men instead if there is a choice." Because it is a fact that conductors do differentiate between men and women to the ratio of 1 to 25, "women in symphony" remains a controversial issue. If women instrumentalists have not convinced mid-20th century male conductors of their musical value and personal stamina—and they have

had open-door opportunity during the recent war years to do so—the field just might return to one almost exclusively devoted to men.

However, a few superlatively skilled women may always merit "drafting" in several major symphonies. Those women who have over-ridden the remaining obstacles and prejudices must of necessity be outstanding instrumentalists, many of them holding first chair positions. A few of these are the first flute in Hollywood Bowl, first bass in Kansas City, first horn in Chicago, first trombone in St. Louis and Kansas City, first oboe at Warner's for 11 years, and first bassoon in Portland.

In spite of the discouraging professional outlooks and predictions, educational institutions are enrolling more and more women in instrumental and conducting courses. Public school orchestras have been a splendid proving ground for interested talents where boys and girls share half and half in personnel. The cream of high school orchestras become the college music majors and conservatory students and continue to get the best training possible.

These students, along with hordes of American business men, housewives, and highly gifted amateurs with symphony playing as an avocation, flock into many volunteer orchestras several evenings each week to study and play the best of symphonic literature. Again, the personnel is half men and half women. In Los Angeles County alone, there are over 30 active volunteer symphonies. From these training-ground groups men and women alike go to major symphonies to continue in their chosen fields.

Heretofore the place of women in professional symphony has usually been on women's committees that secure the inevitable "patronage" for symphonic organizations. This is one of women's greatest contributions to symphony, because time has not altered the fact, as has been true in all history, great music still is subservient to sponsors, patrons and donors.

Present day philosophers and educators believe that the difference between men and women is biological only and not a psychological and temperamental problem. Perhaps this biological difference is why
(*Continued on page* 142)

The Movement West

By ROWLAND W. DUNHAM

THERE was a time when important activities were concentrated on the eastern sea coast—Boston, New York and Philadelphia. Nearly all famous musical personages were Europeans who lived in lands then rather far removed.

After the First World War many of these foreign celebrities found a haven as well as a far more comfortable living within the United States. Then came another conflagration far more devastating than the first. Not only did Jews find a desperate need for protection from Hitler and Musolini but Gentiles as well began to emigrate for perfectly obvious reasons, in large numbers. Nor was this confined to performing artists. Composers and musicologists arrived in significant numbers. Today there remain relatively few musicians of eminence who maintain residence in European countries.

With the increase of opportunity west of the musical hub of New York, the movement west has assumed proportions which must be of major importance to the building of a country-wide musical picture. Several reasons may be cited for this diffusion of musical talent.

California with its need for composers and first-rate performers in the movies and a salubrious climate to which natives refer in such glowing terms, has attracted many important persons. Symphony orchestras of increasingly high calibre require the services of players not easily discovered in their respective localities. There is little need to point to the avid public interest and support in these ventures. The city with a good orchestra becomes at once a musical high-spot. Operatic adventures, either amateur or professional, add impetus to the movement.

Conservatories and music departments in the universities and colleges of the West have demonstrated increasingly higher standards. Not only do most of them have faculties of real worth, often partly imported from eastern cities where they have established a fine reputation, but the students they are turning out offer a distinct challenge to the students to be found anywhere.

Fortunately talent is not insular. Musicality and application of natural endowments appear in about the same proportion in Arizona as in New Jersey. Under skilled guidance of competent teachers young

That Useful Microtone

By DAVID ZEIKEL

THEORETICAL works accompany their timorous approach to the microtone with profuse apologies and utter disparagement. Warning signals are lifted high in order to discourage their investigation and use. Atonal music is held up as a shining example, and in recent years the Schillinger method of tonal expansion and contraction has come into favor.

What the theorists fail to realize, however, is that the present-day dance orchestra has become the exclusive exponent of this much discussed, but too little used, tonal subdivision. True, the terms indicated to the performer for their use are rather loosely employed by the arranger. Even the musically uninitiated must be cognizant of the fact that the lip-smear or lip-slur is an impossibility when a bowed instrument is considered. However, this is a minor matter, and one that can easily be corrected. In my *Introduction to Quarter-Tone Playing* I use only two additional symbols; the *minus*; which *lowers* the note a quarter-tone and the *plus*; which *raises* the note a quarter-tone.

I hold to the unshakable belief that if the contemporary composer of serious music will occasionally listen to his popular prototype, he will make use of this *common* practice, with even greater accuracy than has been heretofore given the microtone. And he will add another valuable technical device to his repertory.

---

artists are now developing all over this country. Some of these young people find it possible to do advanced study in eastern centers. Many complete formal work in their home environment. Others disappear from the musical scene, especially the girls who find a satisfactory husband. Apparently the days of European study is largely over. Nearly all the great teachers are already in our midst .

This movement west corresponds to a similar trend in other fields. Domination by eastern powers has already passed its day of docile acceptance. In music the land west of the Mississippi is sure to be the scene of independent activity in performance and creative art that will bring about the realization of a truly musical America.

New Times, New Rules

By THOMAS P. CANDELL

THERE is no such animal as "Modern Music." No one ever has made a truer statement than Paul Hindemath who said "in no other field of artistic activity has a period of over-development of materials and of their application been followed by such confusion as reigns in this one."

It is also true that in the last century new discoveries have been made in the tonal domain but these new discoveries have apparently gone unnoticed by many of our American music departments today, for they are merely teaching what has been handed down to them for the past one hundred and fifty years.

The rules of the Masters still prevail as strongly as ever with no deviation; of course it never occurs to music instructors that if Bach were with us today the rules would be slightly different. It is unfortunate that the art of music must suffer until our "great educators" decide that music could possibly have advanced a little.

I do not wish to infer that we should throw away entirely the teachings, knowledge, or rules of Richter or Prout, but I do affirm that in present day music some improvements have been made upon those teachings and rules.

As a result of musical instruction today, students are able to write smooth chord progressions, talk at great lengths about the Masters, and explain the various species of counterpoint. But that won't buy them a cup of coffee or pay their rents.

We have just come through another great war. I don't think we would have fared so well had we used the weapons that George Washington was accustomed to, and yet many of our weapons were basically the same—only greatly improved. Why, then, don't we improve on our weapons in music. Why must we work with the same traditional tools.

Doctors, lawyers, draftsmen, and other professional men depend on research for improvement in their respective fields. In music we depend upon analysis. In order to halt the confusion which reigns in our field we must arm ourselves with pages from the music of today— find out what is going on and

(*Continued on page* 141)

Distinctly Different

By LEO ARNAUD

FEW laymen understand the difference between arranging and orchestrating a musical composition. In fact, most of them have the impression that orchestration is a much more difficult task and requires more originality than arranging. This is entirely erroneous. To arrange means to translate the thoughts and emotions of a composer through the means of voices and instruments. Orchestration simply involves the combining of instruments of different timbres so as to obtain contrast and color.

The foregoing definitions somewhat overlap. In order to draw a line of demarcation between them the American Society of Music Arrangers has made certain distinction.

The task of the orchestrator is to distribute the parts of a musical composition to the various instruments of the orchestra, to transpose them in their respective clefs in the score or partitur. But a composition turned over to the orchestrator must be complete in form. It must have melody, harmony, structure— bass, contrapuntal lines, figurations and obbligati.

The task of the arranger is quite different and more complicated. The piece of music placed in his hands is usually incomplete in form. It is generally a simple melody, partially harmonized. It requires creative ability on the part of the arranger to develop length and embellish the theme or original melody so as to give it substantial and tonal qualities. Primarily, the arranger must have at his finger tips the knowledge of counterpoint.

If a piece of music already has been arranged for orchestra and is merely to be transcribed for voices, without any further creative contribution, such work comes under the heading of orchestration.

An ungifted arranger easily can mar the beauty of an original manuscript score. Many a fine composition has lost its original quality owing to the arranger's lack of inspiration. On the other hand, many a mediocre composition owes its popularity to clever treatment and many a tune that was doomed to an "early death" was saved by the imaginative work of a talented arranger.

The distinction between arranging and orchestrating had to be made because the Musicians' Union, having no jurisdiction over creative work, has fixed a rate of compensation for orchestrators only, not for ar-

(*Continued on page* 140)

The Turbulent Twins

By JULIUS GOLD

KNUD JEPPESEN in *The Style of Palestrina and the Dissonance* suggests that consonance and dissonance are subjects among several others awaiting solution. But like the powerful donkey's tail, Jeppesen is behindhand in his information on this important problem. The solution of it was advanced several years before he was born. But he and his confreres, along with the physicists, have speculated incessantly on the nature of consonance and dissonance without seeming to realize the tragic absurdity of subjecting music to physical as opposed to metaphysical analysis. One may well speak of the metaphysics of music in the sense that it is beyond the scope of physics, for music is not a physical phenomenon.

It was the illustrious theoretician Bernhard Ziehn who brought to bear the light of a penetrating mind on this disconcerting question, and now for the first time it is possible to understand the true meaning of the terms under consideration. The facts were given by Ziehn more than sixty years ago in his monumental *Harmonie- und Modulationslehre*, and again in his *Manual of Harmony* published in 1907. Like all of Ziehn's didactic writing, the exposition of the subject is characterized by pithiness and brevity. As I shall not attempt to improve upon it, it is given here in its entirety:

> The terms *consonance* and *dissonance* have nothing in common with the idea of *euphony* and *cacophony*. These terms are only generic names of chords and intervals.
> Consonances are the major and the minor triad, and those intervals which occur in these triads, that is: large and small Third, large and small Sixth, and perfect Fifth, Fourth and Octave. All other chords and all other intervals are dissonances.

Thus it may be seen that consonance as opposed to dissonance is merely a logical, not an acoustical phenomenon.

Ziehn was the first to give the study of harmony a genuinely scientific validity, and that without resort to physical experimentation. In the words of Ferruccio Busoni, he did not attempt to measure feeling in mathematical symbols, nor did he draw boundaries by old standards. And Winthrop Sargeant interpreted

To Practice Or Not To Practice

By VERA BARSTOW

THERE has been a long established belief among musicians that it is necessary to practice slavishly in order to attain technical mastery of their instruments. Lately, however, the more progressive thinkers have arrived at the conclusion that well-directed, thoughtful efforts bring quicker results.

Kreisler speaks for the latter group in a recent magazine article and uses as an example the way one fires a pistol. One sets the trigger, takes aim and then fires. So with the fingers, the mind directs the finger, it aims and then falls. I agree entirely Kreisler's idea of procedure and constantly tell my pupils that five minutes of careful, well-directed practice is worth more than three hours of the other kind.

The difficulty in stressing care rather than the amount of time spent is that many pupils jump to the conclusion that very little practice is ever required. It is important that the student does not acquire this standpoint. He must realize that even to think about the varied technical problems requires application, and to acquire skill even after knowing how to direct the fingers or bow does take practice.

Understanding of the problems and how to master them, alone will not attain the desired results any more than practice for its own sake. But the one who thinks first and directs his efforts will indeed master his instrument sooner than the one who practices arbitrarily a given number of hours.

———— ⟶ ◆◀ ————

article "Bernhard Ziehn: Precursor" which appeared in the April 1933 issue of *The Musical Quarterly*: Ziehn's position with perfect understanding in his

> Ziehn was stunchly opposed to the tendency which manifested itself among practically all the leading theorists of his time, and which had received enormous impetus from the researches of Helmholtz: to base, or to attempt to base, the theory of harmonic structure upon the physical phenomena of resonance. While Ziehn's procedure was scientific in an inclusive sense of the term, the data from which he drew his conclusions—the data which he marshals with such astounding scholarship in his various writings—were drawn, not from what he considered to be the totally irrelevant domain of natural science, but from the literature of music itself. "Not the laws of physics, but the masterpieces of music are the standard of judgment for the science of music."

The Well Tempered Musician

By SAMUEL BALL

WHEN we speak of a "well schooled musician" we mean to offer the highest phrase for one who presumably has met and conquered every academic problem. Yet it would be still higher praise to speak of a "well balanced musician," for in proper balance lies the keynote to artistic as well as scholastic success.

A novice may be well schooled, even exceptionally well schooled, yet fail to give us artistic satisfaction from the concert stage merely because he lacks the balancing factor of experience. The teacher may be well schooled, yet have but a small class because he is overly pedantic, lacking the balance of a genial or friendly personal rapport with his pupils.

In my own instrument, the piano, this factor is particularly important because its very mechanism tends to augment or emphasize faults. Either you strike the right note or the wrong one; there is no happy medium. Similarly, the performer is either in a state of balance or of imbalance; there are no degrees of the former.

It is obvious that the ideal concert is one wherein the technical and interpretative functions are on a par; any disparity is both noticeable and disturbing. Where one is considerably better or worse than the other, the auditor will be more distressed than if both are sub-standard, provided they still remain even.

But the technical and interpretative functions each comprise a multiplicity of factors, which in themselves should be equivalent at the various stages of the individual's progress in music. No one, or no group should outweight the others.

This is, of course, an ideal state which is realized by few performers, even the greatest, before the public today. There is no need to cite names; everyone knows pianists of amazing digital dexterity whose concerts leave one cold, or others with wondrous tonal quality handicapped by poor control; singers who know every role and lied, yet have lost their voices, or vocalists who hold a tonal thrill yet forget their lines.

These artists might have succeeded despite a state of imbalance in the beginning. More likely their faculties were relatively even during the time they were rising to fame and the inequalities were accentuated later by emphasis and preference for a particular phase. But their present discrepancies cause many a headache to the teacher who must explain to his students that they must not do some of the things they hear done on the concert platform.

It is obvious that the pupil must be made to realize from the outset of his studies that technique is a means to an end, and never entirely an end in itself even in the presentation of etudes whose primary object is to show technique. In such cases, that very brilliance is and should be modified by whatever understanding, comprehension and emotional attitude the performer is capable of bringing to it.

At the other end of the scale is the over-emotional performer who makes his presentation "schmalzy" despite technical competence. This situation is well illustrated on the radio at nearly every hour of the day and night in the so-called "popular" music. But what is less clearly understood is the differentiation between the emotional states of approach to Tchaikovsky, Beethoven, Chopin or Debussy. The performer's attitude must be fixed mentally before he starts to play or sing that particular work.

The concept of balance between emotional and technical states, therefore, cannot be set at equal parts of each. Their proportions must be relative with respect to every individual work, and may be modified as well by the circumstances under which that work is presented, or even its position on the program with respect to other works.

As the technical and emotional factors are subject to considerable division within themselves, these likewise are relative in their functions according to the individual work and its particular presentation. The extent to which these vary are demonstrated by the different editions of masterworks wherein editorial opinions sometimes become actual distortions.

When we enter a room which is properly proportioned and in which the color scheme is blended skillfully so as to be pleasing to the eye—a room which is balanced in its decor, we say that the room is "in good taste." Similarly we speak of music as being in good taste when it is properly balanced, yet we

(Continued on page 141)

The Sibelius I Knew

By ILMARI RONKA

I saw Jean Sibelius for the first time as he descended the steps in his home at Jarvenpaa, Finland. Tall and large-framed, his baldness gave him a marble-like appearance, but he wore a welcoming smile such as his pictures invariably belie, and extended his large hand in a warm clasp that made me feel at home immediately.

He asked about American orchestras, even mentioning the Hollywood Bowl, and I gave him what information I could at the time, 1936. A picture of the Cincinnati Symphony, of which I was then a member, pleased him greatly, as well as a note from its conductor, Eugene Goossens. "I can hear this orchestra when I look at the picture," he observed. His own experience of the United States dated from 1917, when he conducted several programs of his own works.

Even then I was amazed at the master's vitality, yet I have heard that to this day he still walks without any noticeable slump in posture and that his step is still sure. He found his age difficult to remember, himself. "I forget it often," he declared, "and then I become provoked when I find I am unable to walk as briskly as I would like to."

In his younger years he was an enthusiastic nimrod, and would leave his home before dawn on hunting trips with friends. He always has enjoyed long hikes, and even to this day often walks through the virgin woods of his estate, containing many species of pine and white birch overlooking a beautiful small lake, stopping to observe the wild flowers, trees and birds, and to admire the sunsets as he always has done.

He takes little account of weather. It has been said that some years ago he left his house during a rainstorm. Mme. Sibelius, noting his absence, began a search and finally discovered him standing in the rain not far from the home. She begged him to come in the house, but he merely reprimanded her for interrupting his thoughts and asked her not to do so again.

His reflexes were comparable to those of a much younger man. Once he had just seated himself in his favorite chair and had lighted his cigar when it slipped from his fingers and dropped to the rug. Before I could stand in an effort to retrieve it for him, he had picked it up. An inveterate smoker, he lights one cigar after another. "I am a slave to my cigars," he admits, "but I love them!"

"I always compose," he declared. "In sixty years I do not remember many times when my thoughts have not been of composition." When not writing, he often turns to books. He is an ardent reader of history of all nations, and enjoys reading memoirs as well. Often he is at his radio, where he turns on the instrument at full volume in order to hear "all the voices."

Once when the late Kyosti Vehanen and I were lunching with the Sibelius' in 1938, the subject of airplanes arose and Vehanen asked the master if he had "ever been up?" "Indeed," was the smiling response, "I've been up in the ether very often!"

A renowned gourmand, Sibelius became fond of the food of many lands during the travels of his earlier years. Though he seldom has left his Jarvenpaa home during the last twenty years, his favorite dishes often are available to him. These include oysters, duck, and many varieties of wild game.

Sibelius' wardrobe is extensive, for he is sartorially exacting as well as fond of variety. In the summer months he seems to prefer white, lightweight suits. But it might be mentioned that his loose, oversized collars are almost a legend.

The Sibelius estate is called Ainola, after Mme. Sibelius, whose first name is Aino. There have grown up five daughters, celebrated for their beauty, in the large house, unpretentious as its master's music, but furnished in the best Finnish taste.

One of the immortals of music, Sibelius loves life with its diversity, perpetualness and mystery. He loves his home and family, his country and all mankind. For his music is not merely nationalistic. It belongs to the ages.

Once when discussing the heavenly bodies with a group of friends, Sibelius said, "there may or may not be life in other planets. But one thing is certain: there is music there—as there is everywhere!"

A New Field Opens

By ANTHONY GALLA-RINI

ONLY recently have the concert possibilities of the accordion begun to be realized by a few progressive musicians and a small group of forward looking accordionists. Yet there exists a large and only partially explored field which has been surprisingly neglected by performers, composers and impresarios. A large and eager public awaits the training of more and better performers and the development of a more comprehensive and individual literature.

Too many accordionists are merely players on the instrument and nothing more. They can play a melodic line and support it with simple harmonic treatment, but they are far from realizing the potentialities of the instrument. It is as if most pianists had not progressed beyond the third grade of piano study.

Still more unfortunately most of the really competent accordion players devote their talents more or less exclusively to popular music, and secure applause by apparent brilliance that makes few real technical demands.

At the root of this situation is the limited repertory of music available to the student, no matter how high his aspirations. Only lately, through the efforts of a small group* is a printed literature of serious music beginning to take shape.

The classic masters wrote nothing for accordion, which is not surprising since the instrument was only invented in 1829 by Damian in Vienna. Ebeneezer Prout, writing of it in Grove's Dictionary, calls it "a small pair of hand-bellows, to one side of which is affixed a key-board, containing, according to the size of the instrument, from five to fifty keys." He observes later: "It will be seen that the capabilities of the instrument are extremely limited, as it can only be played in one key, and even in that imperfectly; it is, in fact, but little more than a toy."

During the last century that "toy" has grown into an instrument of very different caliber, whose limitations have been expanded until they certainly are no less than those of the piano.† For example, the accordion today has five sets of reeds (12 reeds to each set) for the left hand, amounting to 60, and four sets (41 to each set) for the right hand, 164 in all, making a total of 224 available to both hands.

The right hand of the performer must be trained in all the designs of fingering that occur to a pianist or an organist. While the thumb of the left hand is not used, the remaining four fingers must be trained equally; although the left keyboard consists of buttons instead of keys, the manner of phrasing and style of fingerings are the same as those in the right hand.

All dynamics are effected by the bellows, which must be mastered and treated in much the same manner as the bow in the hands of a violinist. Reversing the bellows properly, sometimes required in the midst of a phrase or during a held note, demands virtually the same technique, and the accordionist must learn to judge instinctively the air capacity (thought of in terms of tone capacity) that remains in the bellows when extended at various lengths. Moreover the accordion requires proper employment of couplers in the same manner as the organ.

The accordion has its own problems, such as the fact that execution on the left hand keyboard is "blind," since it is not visible to the performer. But its technique, on the whole, is neither more nor less difficult than the piano, violin or organ, if it is to be mastered properly.

The important point is that the accordion is an instrument of extended range with a wide variety of colors available in its tonal palette, capable of executing music of orchestral opulence. It can and does stand alone as a concert instrument, requiring no accompaniment by piano or other instruments. It can appear as solo instrument with a symphony orchestra, or it can accompany a voice, violin or other instrument of more limited harmonic capacity.

Most needed at this time is a more extended repertory for the instrument, not of transcriptions or arrangements, which may safely be left to the skilled

(Continued on page 135)

---

*Led by Galla-Rini, who has contributed more original compositions and arrangements than any other in the field.—Ed.

†The inventions and improvements by Galla-Rini himself have been responsible in a large measure for the advancement of the instrument during the past fifteen years.—Ed.

Guitars and Soft Music

By RAY MEANY

ALOHA! With the soft and dreamy strains of *Aloha Malihini*, we invite you to drift and dream with us across the blue waters of the Pacific to Hawaii.

According to notes found in the hands of dependable authorities, one or two Spanish ships were wrecked on the coast of Hawaii back in the 16th Century. Their sailors were believed to be the first white men to set foot on Aloha Land. The ukulele and steel guitar, thought by most people to be native Hawaiian instruments, were imported to the Islands by them, and other Spanish and Portuguese settlers or visitors.

As to the steel guitar, there are many contradictory stories among which the following is as authentic as any other:

While stretched lazily on the beach, someone (a beachcomber, no doubt), got the idea of trying to pluck out a tune on the guitar while sliding the back of a knife on the strings; soon the weird tones were picked out and then assorted into an easy hula, which is usually a short two- to four-line verse. At the time, the guitar was used in the Islands in what the natives term the slack key and picked finger style.

On my last trip to the Islands, I came in contact with ancient Kamainas (old timers) who demonstrated the old style of guitar picking. The first man or one of the very first to experiment seriously on this idea of playing with the steel was Joseph Kekuku who developed a method all his own, then came to the mainland, where he made a hit with his individual and fascinating interpretations.

Many of the younger generation are under the false impression that the guitar is more or less a novelty or a new instrument. Nothing could be farther from the truth. The guitar is really one of the oldest instruments in the world: some of our professors of ancient history even claim that the guitar was in existence before the flood.

Some give the credit to Jubal as being the first man to originate a guitar. Even Noah was said to be a performer. In Egypt, where he settled after the flood, there is evidence of the guitar being a popular instrument. The lute of ancient times and the old guitar differ only in shape and perhaps in the type of strings used, as well as special tunings used during various periods. In ancient Greek works, we find mention of the cithara, which is the predecessor of today's modern guitar.

Like most other instruments, the guitar has gone through many changes which still are in process. One has only to stop, look and listen to the modern electric guitar to realize this continuous change, and marvel at the ingenuity of the modern guitar manufacturer and the large strides made in the past few years in the guitar world.

If we are to believe that eminent guitarist, Andres Segovia, the guitar was introduced into Greece shortly after the Trojan era, about 1000 B.C. and used mostly by the rhapsodists of that period. One of the most talked about in ancient times was Terpander, who became a celebrated guitarist, teacher and composer. Even Socrates learned to play the guitar in his last years of existence, proving the old saying that a person is never too old to learn an art. Franz Schubert was fairly well versed in the guitar and many of his famous compositions were composed with its aid. According to some historians, he was too poor to own a piano.

You have only to listen to a few of the best popular orchestras on the air to pick out the unmistakable rhythm of the standard guitar keeping rhythm for the lead instruments in the band, or the sweet strains of the steel guitar in its melodic slides, glissandos, tremolos or modulations to realize that the guitar stands out in potentiality and beauty of tone quality. Yes, the guitar is as standard as the piano or any other instrument. Its future is secure. However, for the benefit of those who wish to establish themselves in the guitar world, I would make plain that this instrument is not a novelty to toy with. It requires study, practice and concentration. Some seem to think that a few easy lessons will make anyone an accomplished guitarist, but it takes years of study and long practice periods to reach the goal.

Tune To the Times

By LOUIS KAUFMAN

THERE is a wonderful anecdote about Johannes Brahms and the young Gustav Mahler, which deserves to be true, even if it never actually transpired. The story goes that as the old and young masters were walking in Vienna's famed Prater, Brahms remarked to Mahler that the age of great music and its composers seemed to be drawing to an end and that they seemed to be at the closing period of a noble art. At that moment the two men had reached a bridge crossing a swiftly flowing stream, and young Mahler replied, "Look, Master, there goes the last wave."

Perhaps ours is the only time that reveres the arts of the past so greatly and appreciates the accomplishments of former masters of music, painting, sculpture, architecture and literature so highly that as a rule whatever is accomplished in the contemporary arts is regarded condescendingly. A notable exception seems to be the acceptance of modern literature, which commands a wide and appreciative audience.

Collectively speaking, concert audiences are very intelligent. The younger generation, especially, is beginning to wonder why it is necessary to hear only the outstanding masters of the Nineteenth Century at each and every concert. People like variety in food, literature and art. Why shouldn't they enjoy it in music? This might even apply to the performance of the less familiar works of classic and Romantic composers.

I do not think that a concert hall is to be mistaken for a schoolroom and that programs should be presented as a Reader's Digest version of the history of music, in chronological order. Planning programs according to the date of the composer's birth can find one in the late Nineteenth Century by 10 p.m. after an early Eighteenth Century beginning. Unfortunately, this process does not often permit audiences to hear the efforts of composers of the Twentieth Century. The relentless hands of the clock should not be the greatest factor in determining the arrangement of the music comprising concert programs.

A violinist who lives in an age of rocket planes, atomic power, and radar should certainly not leave his audience dreamily in a musical world of only the romantic past.

Musicians should keep up with the times they live in. One way for performers to accomplish this is to play the works that present-day composers are writing in North, Central and South America, in England, Russia, France, Italy, Czechoslovakia, Hungary or wherever music worthy of performance is being created.

It is the duty of the violinist, as well as the conductor of a symphony orchestra, to present this new music, which is as important for our day as any of the composers of the past were for theirs.

However, programs must be as well-balanced as a good meal. All roast beef can be as monotonous and unsatisfying as all pastry. The old and new works are mutually enhanced by a fresh and unexpected juxtaposition. If any artist played only new works he would omit the wonderful heritage of our musical past and do a great disservice to the audience, as well as the young composers. To understand our own age, we must have a firm knowledge and respect for the past.

Just as a good museum should exhibit the arts of all epochs and countries, including our own, the violinist should play today's music to give audiences an opportunity to make their own evaluations and to give them greater pleasure in the widening of their musical experiences.

In speaking of music that should represent our time, I refer to the works that are well-written from a viewpoint of craftsmanship and inspiration and are sincere expressions of the composer's moods, aspirations and hopes.

My own experience has been that audiences are, as a mass, nearly always right in their reactions. If the music or a performer is repudiated in the larger centers, that same music and musician will not be likely to be well-received in the smaller communities. The reverse of this situation is also true. People know when they are being bored and will forgive almost everything except that. For this reason, too, audience response is one of the best cues to good program planning. One of the results of a well-balanced program is that audiences will accept and enjoy the new music. Eventually they will even demand it.

(Continued on page 152)

Not So Hot

By WILLIAM van den BURG

MANY articles have been written on jazz, from one extreme to the other. Radio programs and the motion pictures have often given it a great build-up as to its musical value, often going so far as to belittle the great masters. Primarily dance music, jazz is a great money maker. It has been cheaply exploited and sold to the public at a wrong evaluation concerning its place and value.

Sometimes fine or even well-known musicians have helped this false build-up, often for selfish reasons. No doubt many jazz enthusiasts are sincere, but jazz has become popular less for its actual musical value than for other reasons.

As dance music it serves a social and even a psychological function. It helps to reduce the inhibitions and self-consciousness between boy and girl. Its practical orchestration enhances its popularity. Never in history could one get a dance orchestra that could make more noise with so few musicians. Thus permitting people to talk more without covering the orchestra.

The instruments used are the easiest to learn; excluding the piano, they require far less training than the violin or 'cello.

Another factor is that modern dances can be faked easily. One needs but a few lessons at most. Many persons just shuffle along, more walking than dancing, putting in a dash of rhythm according to their limited ideas. So in reality it is the dance which has become popular, rather than its music.

The influence of jazz music on the greater forms of music has been very little. Great music is like life itself; it speaks to the mind as well as to the heart. One might call it a subconscious philosophy. The spirit, philosophy and even the morals of the time in which the (great) composer was born always will be felt strongly in his writing.

The nature of each composer differentiates his self expression besides the influence of the time in which he lives. That is why we have all kinds of music; religious, romantic, impressionistic, realistic, patriotic, sentimental, sensual, cynical, or intellectual. Great music is a mixture of all these. It stands alone and has always a certain message to give. Besides being entertainment, one has to listen intelligently to receive the full value of its content.

Great music is a happy marriage between the heart and the mind. Jazz is purely entertainment music; it goes in one ear and out the other, leaving practicall no intellectual impression.

Jazz in its purest form, the way I have heard it performed by negroes in a theatre in Philadelphia, is like folk music all over the world; a primitive form of self-expression which shows real talent, sincerity and vitality. In this form it is like gypsy music and never will change. Because its strong rhythm is so easy to dance, it was adapted readily using mainly the ryhthm, orchestration, phrasing and some obvious effects in color but losing actually its main value as a spontaneous, primitive art. Like gypsy music it will never have a great influence on the other forms of music, because it is not cultivated. It is like a wild flower or plant.

In an age where money making seems the most important thing, we are sacrificing a great deal of our precious radio time for an abundance of superficial entertainment, which may in the long run have a deteriorating effect in lowering our spiritual and intellectual powers.

Many of our composers and musicians are wasting much of their precious musical gifts by devoting all their talents to the field of entertainment music. They are using the modern self-service, taking harmonies and melodies from the classics. This exploitation has been used for a great build-up for popular music, making a "mountain out of a mole-hill." by often calling it "modernizing the classics". Dance music has become part of the machine age; it is factory made.

Jazz and its derivatives, such as swing, should be evaluated for what they are, not berated for what they are not. Great music will not miss a theme temporarily borrowed, whereas the song hits of today will be buried tomorrow. Nor can craftsmanship ever take the place of genius.

Tradition Is Tangible

By GASTONE USIGLI

OF particular interest to those who occupy themselves with the mechanics of opera making are the many changes, alterations, cuts and transpositions that are effected in several operas of our standard repertory, namely those Nineteenth Century operas in which the *melos* is entrusted chiefly to the voice or voices.

Whereas symphonic works customarily are performed as their printed scores indicate, and all dynamic and agogic nuances are (or should be) well within the boundaries that the most imaginative interpretation permits, the performance of these operas does not represent, in many instances, a faithful rendition of the original intentions of the composer.

If these operas are followed with the printed (original) score in hand, or faithfully fixed in mind, sometimes startling changes may be perceived. Doubtless every sensitive musician has concerned himself at one time or another with the question of which of these are fully justifiable and which are objectionable.

Many years ago it was my privilege to serve as assistant to Lorenzo Mascheroni, who had conducted many of Verdi's operas under the master's "friendly supervision," including the first performance of *Falstaff*. I am indebted to him for having in many respects satisfied the interest I felt even then in this matter.

Of the many conventional changes that had been adopted in Verdi's operas, some had been sanctioned by the composer, obviously those that were prompted by: (a) (in arias) the characteristics and the individual limitations of the human voice, thus permitting a more effective projection of the voice and a smoother unfolding of the vocal line, and (b) by the requirements of the dramatic action in a recitative or in an *arioso* episode.

These conventional changes actually constitute a sequence of nuances, to be applied deftly and subtly, that greatly enhance the musical discourse. At their best, they form what is called the *operatic tradition*. The term and its meaning indeed is much invoked and much abused; also, conversely, much ignored by those who choose to conduct the human voice with relentless rigidity.

Practically every detail and nuance of this sound and intelligent tradition can be sensed by an experienced and imaginative conductor, because true to the norms of good musicianship. Through a skillful analysis of the vocal *melos*, in relation to the dramatic situation, the conductor can judge the proper amount of increasing or decreasing, lingering or pausing. In many instances these depend upon the nature of the *melos*, the meaning of the words, and the vocal tessitura.

Both musical and dramatic considerations often should militate against repeating the second section of an aria or of a concerted episode, when these amount to mere reiteration, as well as against the strange practice prevailing in modern times of opening cuts in sections long since discarded because of their obvious musical weakness. There is no more reason to include such episodes than to perform in most cases the long repeats of older symphonies; in both cases, the considerations of form that originally had prompted those devices have ceased to exist.

Another important aspect is that of substituted notes in the course of an aria or a cadenza. In some instances these have radically altered the original vocal line, often to the extent of deforming it because of arbitrary patterns adopted by the performers.

A logical solution would be for the best version of all these traditional changes (best because sanctioned by the practice of great performers, vocalists and conductors) to be incorporated in a revised edition of the printed scores.

This would aid materially in correcting a condition in which operatic tradition now often is invoked both pro and con, to a degree that verges upon the preposterous.

Opera With a Suitcase

By ERICH WEILER

OPERA in English is beset with so many problems that its realization in America seems well nigh impossible. Many attempts have been made to find it a permanent home, much has been written and said on this subject, but little of constructive or lasting value has been accomplished.

A few operas with English librettos and with claim to permanence have been written. One of them has a definite right to immortality: *Porgy and Bess*, by Gershwin. Deems-Taylor's *King's Henchman* and *Peter Ibbetsen* have merit and deserve revivals. Menotti's *Amelia Goes to the Ball* and *The Old Maid and the Thief* possess humor and great theatrical virtues, as do his last Broadway success-operas *The Telephone*, double-billed with the exciting *The Medium*, all one-act operas.

It has been said by some that opera in English will come into being when a genius comes along and writes them for us. But the problem is not as simple as that. The need for a large repertory of well-translated operas has also been advocated; but the creation of such a repertory is one of the doubtful solutions, and a very difficult problem in itself.

Even if the complete repertory of the Metropolitan and San Francisco Opera Companies were suddenly and miraculously produced and presented in good, singable English versions, well staged under fine direction, with our best American singers, (of which there are already a great many) it would still be more than doubtful if opera in English would thereby become more popular than it is already. It might be meritorious and worthwhile to work towards such a goal, but we might also even ruin what has been accomplished so far.

For a lack of appreciation of opera in English has been shown every time it has been tried on a large scale. Our public, through a long period of time, has been conditioned to hear opera in a foreign tongue. Of many attempts I need only mention the Savage Opera Company which toured this country some years ago and failed. In spite of the Sadler Wells Opera House in London, with its long record of opera sung in English, it cannot be said that a native operatic art has been created successfully in England.

In this connection it is interesting to note that even with Mozart's highly successful operas *The Abduction from the Seraglio* and the *Magic Flute* as pathbreakers, it took many decades before German opera became popular in Germany.

Italian opera companies and Italian impresarios have for over two hundred years been the pioneers of opera in every country of the world, and their hold on operatic life cannot be broken so easily, especially not here where conditions for native opera are still in an unfavorable and embryonic stage.

Before coming to a solution, or at least to a clear exposition of the problems involved, we must understand and admit that opera, the "art of the sung drama" can only be *fully* appreciated when the words are understood by the listeners. There is no doubt possible: opera should be sung in English. Why it is not appreciated, why at present it cannot be successfully presented, is another story.

Why should we listen to opera in English? It is a paradox that in none of the traditional lands of opera, in Germany, in Italy and in France, opera can be presented in a foreign tongue. In Germany operas are sung in German; all French and Italian operas are given in translations, some of which may be infinitely worse than the original. In France it is the same: Wagner and the Italian operas are given in French. And in Italy the audience would consider it a sacrilege to listen to opera in anything else but Italian.

The highbrow's contention that translations are always bad is based on snobbery. Many of the earlier Italian operas have texts which are very bad Italian, and translation might actually improve them. The Wagner texts are in proverbially clumsy German. Paradoxically, the same outraged listener will listen to Schubert's lieder with the greatest delight, and be ignorant of the fact that some of Schubert's best songs are set to very inferior poetry.

For the intelligent listener of opera it is important to understand every phrase of the operatic text. He knows that the success and the thrill of the music lies in the closeness with which words and music are welded by the genius of the composer.

The story of the opera is not as important as this

knowledge of the words. No reading of libretto and studying of the synopsis will give the listener to *Goetterdaemmerung*, or *Louise* or *Pelleas* or *Boris Godunov* a full understanding and appreciation. Even *Rigoletto* or the *Barber of Seville* (be they ever so enjoyable without knowledge of the words) are infinitely more enjoyable if the words, phrases and situations are thoroughly understood.

It is often said that even Italians do not understand the words the singers are singing. This, of course, is not true. In Italy, at least in the better opera houses, the singer's success depends on his ability to make the audience understand the words. The better the singer, the clearer his enunciation, the better his making the meaning clear behind the music, by fine acting and fine phrasing.

It may, at times, be difficult to understand coloratura singers in their high registers, or the individuals in ensembles of many voices. But these places are relatively unimportant and can be looked up and studied later. By far the greater part of the opera is usually well understood by the audiences in any European opera house.

The paradox of our opera appreciation is deepened by the fact that here light opera, radio or night club audiences, or people listening to crooners, will never stand for the mumbling of words, for unintelligibility. In fact, the audiences which are supposed to represent the less cultured part of our public detest listening to words which are not understood. Theirs, to some extent at least, is a truer appreciation of song and singing.

Opera audiences are different. They come to listen in a vague, confused and dreamy mental state. They have been conditioned: they take opera as something for the elite, something esoteric, something requiring study of libretto and synopsis, of languages, of Grove's Dictionary, and what not. It never becomes clear to them why this should be so. They glory in this false approach and invent theories to prove it desirable. In a frenzy of artistic snobbery many such opera-habitués hide behind the thesis that operas are spoiled by translations, and they defend the status quo from being disturbed.

They pity the Europeans who have to hear operas in "vile translations" who are compelled to understand the phrases as they are sung from the stage. It is incomprehensible to them that opera ought to be comprehensible from first to last note. They become uncomfortable when chance phrases are understood. To them it seems silly that La Traviata should ask, while singing, for a "glass of water" from the maid, or that Pinkerton should offer the consul a "glass of whiskey" accompanied by the orchestra.

Their enjoyment increases in the ratio of incomprehensibility. They get their pleasure from the "glorious voices," the scenery, the costumes, the guessing game with the synopsis, the discussions of the artists after the performance, the antics of the exhibitionist conductor, the orchestra, and the social amenitites. But they neglect to enjoy the greatest thrill opera has to offer: the emotions aroused by the impact of great musical moments expressed by the composers through *voices, written to important words,* interpreted by the singers and the orchestra.

There are more paradoxes to illuminate. Wagner, through all his life, fought for the "music drama," and for the importance of the "word" and the understandability of his works. He often preferred the singer whose words were understood to the singer with the better voice. He practically abolished the ensemble singing and the chorus (after *Lohengrin*) hoping to compel the audience to listen to the singer's "speeches" just as in the drama. Here Wagner's operas are given in German, in uncut versions, to crowded houses, without the audience understanding one word. Surely a testimonial to the power of great music, but certainly no compliment to the discernment and intelligence of the auditors.

No composer tried harder to bring music and text in closer relationship. His themes change with every word, all the musical changes only gaining meaning as underlining the actions and words of the characters of the stage.

The same, of course, holds true for such operas as *Pelleas, Louise, Electra* or *Salome,* and in varying degrees for every opera ever written. But the opera snob is not vanquished by these arguments. He wants operas presented in their original tongue, like manuscripts, under glass, in a museum.

There are other super-esthetic opera fans who consider opera an obsolete and hybrid art form, who pride themselves on never having made the attempt to understand sung words. They hold it to be an unnecessary part of appreciation. They will, however, rave about a lieder-recital where opera is given in homeopathic doses. They do not realize that their appreciation of misunderstood musical snatches is definitely below the public's appreciation of Bing Crosby and Frank Sinatra.

The worst enemies of musical art are not the untrained, unsophisticated lovers of popular music: they can often be found among the aesthetic, the intellectual snobs, and the habitués of the concert halls.

There is one more objection often heard in connection with opera in English. It is the old, old fallacy that English is not a singable language. To use a paraphrase: This is the last refuge of a musical scoundrel. Purcell, Handel, (*Messiah, etc.*) Haydn, (*Seasons, Creation*) Weber, (*Oberon*) Sullivan, and many other composers have written glorious music to singable English texts, and no one in his right mind can disregard the many fine English songs which have endeared themselves to audiences for generations, not to mention the many modern songs which are in every good singer's repertory.

Needless to say, the same purist will never object to the nasal qualities of French, or the guttural sounds coming from German throats during singing.

I maintain that if the Bible or Homer can be translated and enjoyed in many languages, the same can be done for any opera, even *Rigoletto*. If the translation is good, and it it is sung by good singers, the audience will enjoy it.

This brings me back to the "conditioning" of American audiences *NOT to listen* to words during an opera performance; but it also illuminates the enormous power and greatness of operatic art. that so many people have learned to love opera, even without full understanding and proper appreciation.

Nothing has so immediate an effect and appeal as a well trained, beautiful human voice—even when the words are not understood. I repeat: this thrill is immensely heightened once the listener has learned to grasp the meaning behind the sung phrases, and their relationship with the music, created by a master. The various interpretations by different artists multiply the pleasures of the listener. One change in a cast can sometimes make a new and greater work out of an old and apparently shopworn opera. That is why old, good operas can be repeated again *and* again.

How false is the approach of the "purist" can be shown by a recent performance of *Fidelio* in English which had been presented a few years previous in German. The text of *Fidelio* is an antiquated, badly written lyric drama, forged into greatness by Beethoven, and emphasis on the liberty theme. The musical numbers alternate with spoken dialogue. When it was given in English, the intelligentsia was disappointed and praised the German version as the better one. But for him who understood German, the first version was even more unbearable than the English one.

The stodgy, silly, sentimental, antiquated lines were ranted intolerably (with an assortment of various foreign accents) in the most amateurish fashion. As to the English version, no one realized that a little revision of the spoken text, and emphasis on good acting and delivery could have made the English version infinitely superior.

A performance of Puccini's *Girl of the Golden West* in English was disliked by the highbrows for similar reasons. The few lines of the "Give-me-a-glass-of-whiskey" variety caused titters in the audience. The subject of the opera gave additional discomfort. The "locale" was too close to home. To watch miners of the Bret Harte age sing a drama (by Belasco) in Pucciniesque accents was too unusual, and roused the "conditioned" audience out of its accustomed dream state.

In this the audience was not much different from another, a Venetian audience, in the year 1853, which condemned Verdi's opera *La Traviata*, at first hearing. That great Verdi opus was a complete failure, not so much because of the stout soprano who looked too healthy for a consumptive, but mainly because the opera was presented in what was for that day everyday dress, the costume of the day, and an everyday drama.

In the *Girl of the Golden West* the miners seemed ludicrous to the unintelligent audience, singing ensembles and arias; but the audience forgot completely that if the miners had sung in Italian, it would have seemed even sillier to them. It was a Western audience.

It took *La Traviata* about twenty years to become popular, and not until it was performed in the then antiquated 1860 costumes. The first audiences had been conditioned to see operas in old costumes only. Maybe the *Girl of the Golden West* will gain in popularity when the costumes and the locale will be more remote.

This brings us to the problem of librettos for young American composers. It is always something of a mystery to me when prospective creators of the "first American opera" make a frantic search for an "American" text with an "American" subject. They contradict the whole history of opera. *Aida*, the *Barber of Seville, La Boheme,* or *Butterfly* are not Italian subjects, nor do they show Italian life. *Carmen* is not a French girl; neither are *Faust* or *Mignon* French. *Don Giovanni* and *Electra* are not German. Even the characters stalking around in Wagner's dramas are very un-German, to say the least. What is important in a libretto is first of all: Is it good? The next questions might be: Is it operatic? Is it good theatre? Is it human? Does it have universal interest? Are the characters real?

The composer might ask himself the questions: Do I know how to write for the human voice? Have I an understanding of the operatic forms? Have I a sense of the theatre? Am I practical?

The last question embraces all the others. I do not exclude Wagner or Strauss from this criterion. Both, in spite of their modernity, were men of the theatre. And Wagner, before branching off into the more radical music drama, had written the *Flying Dutchman, Tannhaeuser* and *Lohengrin*.

I know of a highly gifted composer who is at present doing fine work for one of the major studios. When he was young, enthusiastic and ambitious, he composed an opera in English. For a libretto he chose a story of a very mystical play, which, like the *Woman Without a Shadow* (by Strauss) needed a very elaborate and complicated synopsis, a blueprint, and much preparatory study to understand the characters represented. The plot was so intricate that a lecturer would have been needed to explain to the audience what really happened and what was meant by it.

For his singers he used the untried, unpractical and difficult technic of Schoenbergian *Sprechgesang* instead of the pleasant and tried advantages of bel canto singing. An enormous scenic apparatus was needed to put the opera on the stage, and to add to his innovations, he used a super-Straussian orchestration with every conceivable instrument demanded.

He then offered his monumental score to the two or three opera houses in this country. A simple computation showed that their budget would have to be strained to national proportions in order to give a first performance. His score was returned with thanks and many compliments, and my friend was greatly surprised that no one wanted to produce the work on which he had worked so long and with so much love.

This illustrates one very important side of the "Opera in English" problem. It also has bearing on the "Opera in Translation" problem. It is the disregard of the practical side which has held up a reform in our operatic life. Before opera here can be what opera once was in other countries, we must put emphasis on the practical and realistic sides of the problem.

My contention is that it is not enough to translate operas, give good performances and then imagine that therewith opera in English has been created and that from then on audiences will come flocking.

All opera is in a state of transition. The motion pictures and the radio have dealt heavy blows to this expensive art form. We are on the threshold of television, and further changes in the theatrical field are in store for us. While people will always love to sing, and will always love to hear singing, hardly

any new operas are being written. The European field has dried up, a process hastened by two world wars, but which already had begun long before 1914.

New problems beset the endangered art of opera on every side. The abovementioned new entertainment fields are already experimenting with new forms in which music and singing play integral parts.

We must also understand that opera once upon a time was entertainment, just as the motion picture is today. People went to opera often, and expected new operas every year. Verdi, in his early years, had to sign contracts with managers, who also hired the librettists. And he, as well as his numerous now forgotten rivals, had to turn out their works to order, just as the movies are brought out today. Nearly all the great opera composers learned their trade under such conditions, driven to perfect their art because of the public hunger for new operas, for the entertainment form of that era.

To have works of genius, many works must be produced by many composers and librettists. There must be a great public demand, there must be audiences. Before Verdi wrote *Rigoletto*, not yet his greatest work, he wrote many other operas. So did Rossini, Donizetti, Bellini, Auber, Boieldieu and many other composers of the day. Only few works remain of the many operas written, just as only few motion pictures will be worth showing a hundred years from now. The important fact remains: many works must be written for many audiences in order that great works are produced.

Under the impact of Wagnerian theories opera is not supposed to "entertain", it is supposed to raise the listener to mystic heights of musical exaltation. An American composer or librettist would feel ashamed to aim for less when writing an opera. He forgets that there are only two kinds of opera: good or bad. Only two kinds of music: good or bad. Only two kinds of libretto: good or bad.

When Shakespeare wrote his plays he wrote them for a public and did his very utmost to hold the attention of his audiences by all the powers at his command. The plays *did* entertain, and as Shakespeare's art grew, they became plays for all time, *without his specially aiming for the praise of posterity*. We might as well admit: some of the greatest art was produced this way, and many of the finest works were *written to order*.

It never hurt a great master to write music to order. Bach, Handel, Haydn, Verdi, Mozart, and most of our classic (and some modern) composers wrote works on demand, and for a demand. Mozart, Verdi, Bizet and Puccini never forgot what they owed the audience, without ever lowering their own ideals. What much of our young composers are doing is not creative and is not living art. If opera is to be kept alive, it cannot be done by artificial means, by museum art, even though a much larger public has begun to show interest in opera.

The mainstay of opera today is the star system and the social display connected with opera. The genuine opera-lover alone can never support and keep alive the few large opera companies we have. These companies serve a good purpose; but they will not last forever, unless new and healthier operatic activities spring up in every American city and nourish the roots from which good opera must come. Many smaller and less pretentious opera groups must be formed to cultivate and create opera sung in English.

Their first aim must be to seek new audiences. This can only be done by a new repertory, by new works and new translations. There must be different types of presentation.

The American public has never taken too kindly to the recitatives in opera, to the stodgy conventions and to the luxury aspects of "Grand Opera." *Porgy and Bess* became a commercial success only after some spoken dialogues were introduced into the work which made it more acceptable to the general public. The success of *Carmen Jones* is also an example which throws light on this peculiarly American desire to "understand" opera.

Europe, for generations, has had an intermediate type of opera which educated the public for the more pretentious "Grand Opera" and appealed to a part of opera lovers who stayed away from the more expensive type of opera. There was the "Spiel-Oper" and "Singspiel" in Germany, and there was the "Vaudeville" and "Opera Comique" in France. (None of these types should be confused with "Operetta" or "Light Opera") America has seldom had opera of the above mentioned varieties, as we have tried to skip immediately into the more elaborate type of Grand Opera.

I believe that the envisioned little opera groups should cultivate the "Opera Comique" (opera with spoken dialogue) at first. They must follow a narrow and difficult road. Much experimentation and preparatory groundwork must be done.

A real native art of opera can only be created if we retrace our steps, if we abandon the top-heavy, expensive apparatus that is the rule in the established opera houses. We must try to travel with lighter baggage. In this connection I must again mention Menotti whose operas were successful because of their small casts and small scenic requirements.

And this should be the first guiding principle of any small opera group: keeping the budget to the smallest dimensions by limiting the repertory to the small cast and the small orchestra operas. Special arrangements, or performances with two, or even one piano can be of artistic caliber if carefully arranged, rehearsed and prepared.

The second principle should be the new repertory, largely chosen from the comic field, with special emphasis on entertainment value. Works should be of the type of *Cosi Fan Tutte* and *Abduction from the Seraglio* (Mozart) all with spoken dialogue, and works by Donizetti, Gretry, Boieldieu, Lortzing, Auber, and others should form the nucleus of such a repertory.

Limitation to the comic field need not vulgarize the presentations, nor should inferior music be utilized for the new repertory.

San Francisco's Comedy-Opera Guild, under the leadership of the author, has produced something like ninety performances in about ten years. *Bruschino the Grouch* (Rossini) *Secret Marriage* (Cimarosa) *Village Singers* (Fioravanti) *Rendez-Vous, Bourgeois* (Isouard) *Good Night, Mr. Pantalon* (Grisar) *Orpheus in Hades* (Offenbach) *Impresario* (Mozart), were among the most successful of its presentations.

Spoken dialogue should be used extensively in these productions. Teamwork, fine singing, good ensemble and natural acting would compensate for the lack of chorus and the decor of the big companies.

Most important would have to be understandability and an entertaining repertory. Translations would have to be home-made, if exchange with other groups could not be arranged. Dialogues would have to be written with great care, and the dialogue would have to sparkle with good and lively humor. No tasteless changes would be necessary in the making of new versions of old operas.

Groups should seek sponsor help to commission American librettists and composers to write for them in a simpler medium, for small groups and small orchestra. There is no harm in going back to older models, to simpler themes, to a less hectic period in the development of opera. Neither is there any harm in making sensible revisions of good old operas which are no longer played.

Music remains beautiful when it is well made and well presented, but theatrical conventions, plots and dialogues tend to become stodgy and unperform-

(*Continued on page* 137)

All Voices Can Sing

By LILLIAN EVANTI

ALTHOUGH few Negro artists have had an opportunity to appear in Grand Opera, the ice has been broken and it is safe to prophesy that many others will be heard in the not too distant future.

It has fallen to my own happy lot to have the distinction of being the first Negro soprano to win acclaim in the major European opera houses of France and Italy. I made my debut in Nice in the role of Lakme and sang later in Monte Carlo, Mentone, Toulon, Montpelier, Nimes and Paris. In Italy I made my debut as Rosina in *The Barber of Seville*, and sang in Milano, Turino, Palermo, Lucca, Reggio Emilio. I have had the pleasure of utilizing a repertoire of twenty-four operas in five languages.

In the United States I sang the title role in *Lucia de Lammermoor* with the Philadelphia Orchestra in Robin Hood Dell, after being chosen by Conductor Alexander Smallens in a competitive audition.

Baritone Todd Duncan has sung with success in the City Opera of New York, numbering among his roles those of Escamillo in *Carmen*, Tonio in *Pagliacci*, Scarpia in *Tosca*, Athenael in *Thais*.

Camilla Williams, a young Negro soprano, has interpreted *Madame Butterfly* in the City Center Opera. Ellabelle Davis got her chance to sing in opera in the Palacio de Belles Artes, Mexico City, and La Julia Rae sang *Aida* with the Chicago Civic Opera Company.

Salmaggi has given three Negro sopranos the opportunity to interpret *Aida*: Catarina Jaboroe, Edith Sewell, Minta Cato. He also engaged the late Jules Bledsoe to sing Amonasro. Tenor Paul Smith sang *Othello* in Carnegie Hall and Florence Cole Talbot sang several performances of *Aida* in Italy.

After singing the role of Violetta in *La Traviata* in French and Italian, I finally had the opportunity of interpreting it in English with the National Negro Opera Company in performances given in Pittsburgh, Chicago, Washington and New York. Although I was the only professional in the cast, the calibre of my colleagues won emphatic plaudits from the reviewers. Tenor Joseph Lipscomb was formerly an elevator boy in one of Pittsburgh's department stores. Baritone Charles Coleman was a teacher at Greensboro, N. C. College. Other capable young artists who interpreted leading roles during the five performances were Horace Wilson and William Franklin, baritones, and Oscar Griffin, tenor.

Production of *Carmen Jones* brought forth Muriel Rahn, Muriel Smith, Carlotta Franzel and Napoleon Reed. Others who may be expected to appear in the operatic roles in the near future include Charlotte Murray, Etta Morton and Anne Brown.

Among the organizations who have given performances with Negro singers are Howard University, Negro Musicians Association (Detroit) and Jefferson High School, (Los Angeles.) Doubtless there are many others that have not come to my personal attention.

At the present time the greatest handicap to Negro artists in opera applies equally to their white colleagues. That is the deplorable lack of opera houses in this country. As early as 1935 a bill was presented to Congress by the late William Sirovich of New York, providing for the establishment of a Portfolio of Science, Art and Literature, and though it was favored by hundreds of prominent artists, nothing yet has come of it.

The Negro has natural ability in dramatics and in vocal music, a fact that long has been recognized. Such operas as William Grant Still's *Blue Steel* and Clarence Cameron White's *Ouanga* still await production; so do many others by other American composers. I am confident that when opera becomes better recognized as an integral part of the musical development of this country, Negro artists and composers will share in this operatic advancement.

The Opening Way

By ISABEL MORSE JONES

MAN is supposed to change every seven years. Glancing back to the 1940 edition of *Music and Dance in California*, we find opera in the West outwardly the same; broadened perhaps, but seemingly very little deeper in its hold upon people. But there have been subtle changes and these indicate a trend.

Andres de Segurola then voiced his belief in the necessity of producing opera in English. He also wrote of the need for better looking, slimmer opera singers, and more opera houses in which our young people could appear. In conclusion he spoke for nationalization of opera.

Vladimir Rosing, now developing an opera company from a flourishing school, wrote seven years ago that opera caused controversy because it was economically unsound and artistically far behind the time and the taste of its audience. He placed the blame on the musical public and the musical snobs who go to opera and pay high prices to see dramatic stupidity. He begged for dramatic criticism as well as musical, derided opera as nothing but a poor relation to films.

These critical evaluations have since increased in number. This paeon of voices has reached business and government, and we are beginning to support leadership dedicated to something nearer the ideal.

The West is basically Latin in its culture. Opera being essentially a European and dominantly Latin art-form, it is quite natural that San Francisco, with its Italian, French, and smaller Spanish groups, has taken the lead in opera-giving here. Since the memorable earthshaking of 1906, the Metropolitan Opera of New York has not ventured to dispute the title. Chicago has sent its opera company out, but for the last twenty-five years San Francisco has proudly bestowed our grandest opera.

Under the direction of Gaetano Merola, Northern and Southern California welcomes the San Francisco Opera Co. with large audiences. Plans are made for longer tours and closer affiliations among the western cities. The productions admittedly are not surpassed in cast, in superlative choral work, in a symphony orchestra with an operatic heart, and stage sets that are not only traditional but fresh.

Other operas are heard in Seattle, Portland, San Francisco, and Los Angeles, either organized on the spot for a few performances, or included in the annual tours of the San Carlo and occasional appearances of the National Opera, directed by Giorgio D' Andria.

But the future lies with the growth of workshop opera. At Stanford University, there is Jan Popper's opera group. In Riverside, Marcella Craft and Isabella Hutchings have developed the Riverside Opera. In Pasadena, Richard Lert is reviving the opera group which he and George Houston developed to a high point of success cut off by Houston's untimely death.

In Los Angeles there is the promising American Opera Co., an outgrowth of the American Opera Laboratory which has made a point of opera in English and intends to produce light as well as grand opera. Singers are trained by General Director Hugh Edwards and artistic director Rosing. During the winter of 1946-47, the Laboratory gave performances of standard operas with several casts for each, under the musical direction of Curtis Stearns. The Philharmonic Auditorium, which is destined to become a people's theater when the more expensive importations are moved to the contemplated new opera house, was used for three notable presentations in the early Fall of 1947, preceding the impressive jubilee season of the San Franciscans.

This is a strong effort in the direction of community opera. Jerome Hines, a young Southern Californian who has reached the "Met", led with the part of Mephistopheles in *Faust*. He has steadily climbed from audition to audition, his operatic experience including roles with the San Francisco, Central City, Colorado, and New Orleans companies.

Other California singers such as Nadine Connor, Nan Merriman, Florence Quarteraro, Felix Knight, and even Lawrence Tibbett, have had to struggle for experience in New York. Among the few giving young singers opportunity here are the opera reading clubs, Hollywood and Euterpe, with large audiences gathering once each month to listen to dramatized, costumed singing of major works.

Adolph Heller, an opera club director, with Henry Reese staging, brought the Pacific Coast its first hearing of Benjamin Britten's *The Rape of Lucretia* in the Ebell Theater in 1947. Sergei Radamsky and a dedicated band of devotees have organized another group. Their initial event was *Boris Godunov*, and this, too, was conducted by Heller. In this opera the cooperation of film-actor Richard Hale as Boris added much to the success. This coalition between film and music theater is always fruitful.

The Summer seasons of opera have been confined to Hollywood Bowl's occasional and expensive performances, and Summer opera at Stern Grove, San Francisco, conducted by Kurt Adler who trains the brilliant chorus of the San Francisco Company.

In Southern California there is Hugo Strelitzer, a chorusmaster of special attainment. His workshop opera at City College in Los Angeles had a sudden rise only to be cast down by War II. Back at the expanded college, Strelitzer is building anew. Another opera class is trying its wings at a local conservatory, directed by Gastone Usigli.

With the University of California at Berkeley awakening the opera public with the work of its faculty member, Roger Sessions, *The Trial of Lucullus*, last Spring, the signs of today point to renewed interest in Western composers. George Antheil, Louis Gruenberg, Erich Korngold, Richard Hageman, and Italo Montemezzi, who live here, have several operas waiting performance. Probably there are composers not so well known who are harboring masterpieces. Where in the world are there creative resources of music and the theater to equal those in the Southwest?

Cosi fan Tutte was produced at Leland Stanford University by Popper, polished off by two performances in "The City," and then taken to Hollywood for a three weeks' run. It had to be reduced to chamber opera with only six principals and no chorus, but the essential beauty of Mozart was heightened. Such traveling groups are welcome additions to Western opera fare.

Radio opera is important to Westerners. Thousands listen to the broadcast on Saturday from New York and on the Sunday evening hour sponsored by Standard. The Metropolitan Opera is aided by Western financial support. The New Yorkers are acknowledging their debt in 1948 by a tour which includes the West.

Opera broadcasts emanating from San Francisco are directed by Gaetano Merola, California's foremost man of opera. He is deeply concerned over the lack of opportunity for young talent. In his opinion the reason that "singers of this generation cannot begin to compare with those of the past" is that "life moved at a vastly slower tempo." It is true five to ten years of study and singing of small parts was a usual preparation for opera a few years ago. That foundation was lasting. Today we have a different story.

With only two major resident houses—the Metropolitan and San Franciscan, and the Chicago Opera House used for occasional opera, the country is badly lacking in opportunity. The San Francisco season is too short for any but the best publicized singers to be presented in major roles, and the Metropolitan is too dependent on box-office, also. The public pays to hear favorite stars, not to hear operas. This is also true of the guarantors.

Training and experience are not to be had in Western cities except in the small and meagerly supported groups mentioned above. So singers with European background will continue to get the coveted roles in American opera unless this condition is improved by citizen and government-supported local companies in every sizable city.

The young singer of today is not to be blamed if he turns to the quick success of radio or films. He cannot waste his youth in a desert of waiting while he pays out all he can earn in individual lessons in a studio with never a chance to sing .

California could lead in establishing new music theaters. There should be seasons of four or five months with an opera a week and the principal roles given to the well-known singer or two who happen to be on concert tour in the vicinity. Each city's orchestra could be used and the chorus recruited by the civic music organizations. Native composers should have their chance to be heard. This is the way it has been done in Italy, mother of opera, and there is no better way.

The Cycle of Modern Dance

By ELEANOR KING

THE term modern dance presupposes two things: awareness of the present and a free manner of expressing that awareness, in contradistinction to the classical dance, which is concerned with the attitudes of the past and their formal and arbitrary expression.

Its origin goes back about forty-five years ago to a rebellious young girl in San Francisco who made a prophecy: "She is coming—the dancer of the future; the free spirit who will inhabit the body of new woman—the highest intelligence in the freest body—and she will belong not to one nation but to all humanity."

Isadora Duncan's revolutionary concept of dance as expression of the soul of the dancer was the impetus, the seed from which modern dance stems. Its philosophy is based on democratic as opposed to aristocratic principles; it applies the test of psychological truth to its motivations (let us remember truth does not always wear a pretty face) and its technique acknowledges a debt to Newtonian science, to Darwinian studies of emotion and to the physical extensions of the range of movement contribute to its great leaders, Doris Humphrey, Martha Graham, Hanya Holm and Charles Weidman, who have considerably changed the depth and contour of dance since Isadora's advent.

It is difficult for us today to appreciate how narrowly confined were the physical and mental horizons of our mothers and grandmothers until Isadora appeared, discarded the weighty garments of Victorianism, and dared to dance naturally, simply and greatly, as she lived, the emotions which she felt. Isadora has been called "the greatest woman genius since Sappho", and her conception of dance as Chorus, the soul of Tragedy, lifted the dance as an art to supreme expression of the spirit of man, stimulated countless artists, philosophers and poets, and left a legacy which takes on stature with the years. Though there is not yet a monument to her name in San Francisco, there is a living and growing testament to her vision in the movements of young dancers all over the country.

The history of modern dance is a history of reactions. Isadora began in revolt against the decadent ballet of her time, to dance romantically, subjectively the emotions which she felt. She used the best accompaniment available at the beginning of this century, and danced to the music of Gluck, Wagner, Mozart, and Schubert. This unfortunate shackling to the chains of previously composed music proved the most serious downfall for her followers: after Isadora, there was a dreadful era of imitation instead of realization—the cheesecloth era of interpretative dancing. Artificial sentimentalism, the quality Isadora abhorred in the ballet, was rampant, and it flourished until the late twenties.

If Isadora was the great mother of modern dance, Ruth St. Denis may be called her godmother. Appearing about the same time as Isadora, mistress of pageantry and incense, rather than of choreography, Miss Ruth and Ted Shawn, who pioneered in the still much-needed field of dancing for men, together made "Denishawn", their school in Los Angeles, important as the source of the second generation of rebels. Part priestess, part performer, Ruth brought exotic elements of Asiatic religious cults into American concert halls. Her aim was, and continues to be, to establish dance as a religious ritual. In her own words: "The meaning and purpose of art is to communicate the hidden perfection of God—to reveal the full chord of human personality."

In the latter part of the twenties three young Denishawn dancers rebelled from the Denishawn ideals. They were Martha Graham, singly, and Doris Humphrey and Charles Weidman together. They were tired of dancing as Javanese, Burmese, Singalese, Indians and every nation under the sun except their own. They said "Our lives must have meaning and expression, too. We must set out to discover for ourselves what it is." The original Humphrey-Weidman manifesto was "to find the outer form for the inner need". Miss Graham answered the question: "What is form?" with "Form is the memory of physical content." And "where do form and content meet?" with "Form and content meet in action."

"Significant form" became the new banner cry.

Concentrating on movement, eschewing all the appurtenances of the commercialized theatre, they explored movement per se, just as the painters and composers before them had explored light and color and sound as entities in themselves. To establish movement as an art in itself, independent of literary plots, or dubious weddings to program music, there were dances without any music at all (as Miss Humphrey's "Water Study" and "Drama of Motion"), with simple percussion or woodwinds, or more importantly, with the music written after the dances were composed. Costumes were functional, settings minimal. This was great pioneering in a period of obsequious borrowing of European culture. Actually it has required another fifteen years and a second world war for American artists really to awaken to their own resources. Modern architecture and modern dance were, and are, from this period on, considered the most vital forms in America.

After a decade of this insurgent movement—(we seem to have a new generation of dancers every ten years, the time it takes to make an artist)—there was a new rebellion in the ranks of the Expressionists. The younger dancers, Anna Sokolow, Jane Dudley, Sophie Maslow, William Bales, José Limon, Sybil Shearer and myself among others, began to chafe under the rigors of abstraction. Some of us said "Abstraction is not enough—or rather it can go too far in abstracting meaning." And so elements of the formerly tabu theatre began to creep in.

Outcries for bread, for justice, not only were danced but were spoken. The warmth of the speaking voice was added, and if the dancers' own voices were thin and breathy, still the ice of abstraction was loosened, and a strong return to the concept of dance as theatre took hold, which is where we are today, completing the cycle: dance revolting from theatre (Isadora) into concert form (Graham-Humphrey-Weidman-Holm) and back to theatre again (second and third generations both).

Contributing factors in the development of modern dance must be mentioned. One was the five-year Bennington plan, where the techniques of leading dance artists were taught each summer to dancers and teachers from all over the country. This helped to break down the tendency of special cultisms and to establish principles of modern dance in education which are now being applied in most of the colleges and universities throughout the country. The other was the pioneer work of John Martin, one voice crying in the wilderness, who with his column in the New York Times helped to prepare an enlightened public response to the dance forms of our own time.

At the end of the five-year Bennington plan the curriculum included not only the techniques of the major modern artists but also—counterrevolt: ballet! Are we right back where Isadora began, nearly half a century ago? Let us see.

Ballet and modern dance now exist side by side and retroactively influence each other. The fields of technique are wide open. Every dancer is free to make use of them all, to adapt the ones she needs for her own ends. Danilova recommends modern dance for ballet dancers; Graham uses a ballet barre. The dancer's technical resources are, therefore, unlimited. The only ceiling is in the extent of imagination, depth of wisdom and amount of taste each individual dancer can bring to her art.

With these enormous technical gains since Isadora's day there comes also the enormous responsibility of keeping technique in its rightful place, as a means toward and not the end of expression. The present tendency toward the prevalence of walky-talky dancers preoccupied with properties and extraneous materials that have nothing to do with movement can be carried right into the camp of the enemy —where the means become more important than the ends.

We ask of a modern dancer: "What is she dancing about?" And we find that the content of her dances dictates the form of the movement. That there should exist confusion in the public mind about modern dance is to be expected, since not only is it a microcosm of the turbulent age we live in but also its forms are so individual and varied. And this is the point of departure in comparing the 400-year-old-classical system against the 40-year-old modern dance.

Modern dance, then, has no arbitrary code of movement. The laws of force and gravity dictate its kinetics, its range includes every degree of tension from vibrating, shaking, swinging, thrusting, pushing, pulling to complete flexion of every part of the body, with the main focus upon the expressive **center of** the torso. In range of dynamics, use of space and experimentation with time factors, modern dance is infinitely more varied and free than the classic form.

Classical dance is based on five (only) positions of the feet and arms, one position of the spine—rigid vertically—and about fifty techniques for the legs alone. (I count the fundamental exercises listed in Agrippina Vagonova's *Fundamentals of the Classic Dance*—(Kamin Dance Pub., N. Y.). Its movement is mainly peripheral, aerial, and its most brilliant achievement in turning velocity. Its vocabulary is precise, static, and arbitrary. Originally designed for and performed by Renaissance kings and their courts in elegant and corsetted costumes with voluminous headdresses, the inheritance of this encrusted formality has often stifled the soul of expression in ballet and left an anachronistic exhibition of meaningless movement 400 or, at best, 100 years behind the times (the cultural lag being what it is).

In classical dance the frontal position in the three-dimensional frame is the norm. In modern dance, the back of the dancer, lying, sitting, kneeling, standing, leaping can be just as eloquent as the front view, and is often more refreshing. Modern dance can be equally at home in the round as in the three-dimensional frame, and it importantly uses the fourth dimension. I consider a movement good if it is good from all sides as well as from the front, just as sculpture is. How often one stands in the wings and sees unfortunate angles of the body from that view which are not apparent to the spectators. When the body's action is correctly aligned, there will not be this jar or line, of weight in the wrong place.

Modern dance is taught in a democratic manner. Principles of movement are given to the student and individually applied. Each has to work out her own salvation, her own use and command of these laws. It is her responsibility to develop them in her way, whereas in classical dance, nothing is left to the student's imagination or wits—everything is codified, unalterably fixed and learned by rote. The result of course is a highly trained machine with the mentality left out.

As a young student I had the revealing experience of dancing in the League of Composers' production *Sacre du Printemps* under Leonide Massine's direction. I was astounded that no word of meaning or interpretation was ever given to the company. The sequences were learned as so many links in an unrelated chain, whereas in Miss Humphrey's group, where I was a student, thorough mental climates were built up before each major work was put into action. Books, related works of art and discussions were part of the conceptual background. It was always a fascinating experience to see the individual dancer's growth, response and contribution to this preparation.

Of course it must be admitted that modern dancers exist who do not follow this pattern, who, perhaps, under the pressure of time, or inertia, have chosen the short-cut, the easiest way, of dictating the movement with the meaning left out; or what is even worse, stringing sequences of unrelated techniques

together, adding a title and presenting it as a dance. But since that obviously isn't a dance and is soon forgotten, it need not concern us here.

The human body has changed very little since the Greek Chorus arose several thousand years ago, as Antony Tudor once pointed out in a Seattle lecture. It still expresses the ideas and emotions of men and women in that most concrete reflection of life which is action. It is the mirror and unconscious reflection of the attitudes of our culture. And our culture, extraverted as it is, is movement-possessed. From Calder's mobiles, or Mickey Mouse to supersonic flight, we have symbols about us of this compulsion for movement. Even sculpture must move, when movies hypnotize the world and men annihilate space.

The modern dancer is concerned with truth and meaning of experience; the classical dancer is concerned with physical exploitation of technical skill. Noverre in 1760, Fokine in 1904, and Agnes De Mille, Tudor and Jerome Robbins (to come down to our own day) are the exceptions to the latter category, in that they have employed movement with psychological truth as the motive factor in their choreography. Yet the octopus of academic ballet undermines the gains made by these few truly modern choreographers. In comparison to their worth, Tudor's works are seldom performed on the road, and both De Mille and Robbins are now choreographing on Broadway.

The balance of the programs which are dazzlingly held up before coast-to-coast audiences year after year continue on a nursery or, at most, adolescent level of intelligence. This acceptance of the past which keeps the ballet producing its incredible round of mechanical dolls, sleeping beauty fairy-tales, bewitched or phthisic heroines from the 19th Century, explains the reaction of timid souls to modern dance who are disturbed by the unaccustomed movements, and who fail to look deeply enough to grasp the meaning behind the movement.

The magnificent creative power of the best works of modern dance during the past two decades* should be preserved in some form (and moving pictures, good as they are, are only a two-dimensional answer) such as a repertory system if we are going to have a basis for continuity of the great tradition of modern dance. We need a basis for that continuity. And we need to keep the pattern clear. Is it time for another revolt?

* **Graham's** *Primitive Mysteries, Letter to the World* etc. Humphrey's *New Dance, Inquest, Shakers* etc. Weidman's *Atavisms, A House Divided* etc.

Opera On Its Toes

By LUCIEN PRIDEAUX

THE primary purpose of a ballet in opera is threefold: (a) as a diversion from a (customarily) tragic story, (b) to help continue or emphasize the theme of the story, and (c) to add color or to give a national character to the work.

Although these aims have been recognized by the composer at the time the work was created, in performance the ballet too often is relegated to an obscure position either because the impresario does not realize its importance or because the choreographer is incapable of coping with his material.

An opera ballet is not written in detail, like the music, nor does it rely on tradition like the staging. It begins and ends with its individual choreographer, who sometimes is not aware of his special responsibilities.

To choreograph a ballet the subject of the opera first must be considered. If the piece is of a fantastic nature, the job is quite simple; the scope is unlimited so the mind may run riot. But if the opera is historic or national in character, as so many are, then weeks of research in libraries or museums are required. All details, such as costumes from head-dresses to shoes, must be noted. The religion, manners and customs of the people must be taken into account, for they influence the style to be employed.

Mode of dress or costume will dictate the steps and manner of movement. In the period when women wore corseted dresses and long trains, the steps were stiff and stately. When men wore very tight trousers, their bows were (necessarily) slight bends mostly done with head and chest. In early Greek and Roman times, especially in the bacchanals so popular in opera, the body was given free play of expression.

The choreographer must have a sixth sense, supported by musical training. The mere fact that the music is written in 3/4, 4/4 or 6/8 time is not enough; he must delve deeply into the important factors of phrasing, mood and expression.

This limitation is all too often apparent in broken-counted music, where the choreographer is palpably at sea and takes the easiest way out. If the music is wild, the dancers run about waving their arms and jumping like banshees. In soft, quiet music, the company lies on the floor while the prima ballerina strikes artistic attitudes.

The choreographer must refrain from putting his own favorite steps into every ballet, for repeating his own dances is an inexcusable mistake. The music itself must suggest all steps as well as characters to him. In good taste he cannot use a Russian style to interpret an Italian theme, nor a modern technic to a Tchaikovsky melody.

Nor must the ballet be overly involved; it should be so constructed that it tells its own story with few or no program notes. A definite sense of color must be brought to it by the really successful choreographer, who also should be a competent costume and scenic designer.

An ideal operatic corps de ballet should have at least half as many men as women in its personnel. Since there is much "line" work in opera, the dancers should be as evenly matched as possible, each girl preferably 5 feet, 5 inches tall, weighing about 120 pounds, each boy 5 feet, 9 or 10 inches tall, weighing about 150 pounds. It may be noted that when a girl raises on toe she adds considerably to her height, and should not tower over her partner.

The ballet can be compared with the piano keyboard, the boys carrying the heavier work and giving the needed support comparable to the bass, while the girls do the more fanciful or quicker work of the treble. At no time, except in burlesque or comedy, should the boys' work become effeminate nor the girls' work masculine. Each must serve their separate duty to complement the other.

In opera today there is most use for the interpretative style of dancing, such as in *Tannhaeuser*, *Thais*, or *Orpheus*, seconded by character dancing as in *The Bartered Bride, Carmen,* or *Il Trovatore*, while the classic ballet as in *La Gioconda* or *Hamlet* is least used.

The premier danseur and premiere danseuse must have dynamic personalities, outstanding showmanship, and sound technique, for their appearances on the stage are of short duration, usually only five or six minutes in a whole performance and sometimes only a couple of performances a week. They must

(Continued on page 126)

Let the Music Dance

By PAUL SCHOOP

PAUL DUKAS, who drew heavily on pantomimic ideas for his incomparable *Sorcerer's Apprentice*, once remarked to me, "music should express both the lowest and the highest attributes of human behavior." In this sense, we have innumerable emotional levels upon which the composer may operate, ranging from abstract music, such as liturgic chorals, through the symphonic forms, and into the more descriptive and program music.

Some composers achieve only the technical understanding necessary for many of these forms; some will explore emotional depth as well. Among the latter, who will of necessity develop a deep understanding of human nature, and of the heights and depths of human behavior, one may express himself in one of the most exciting of musical fields: the pantomime, or the modern theatre of ballet or dance, more recently called simply "ballet".

Music for the ballet has been written in many different ways. The manner adopted in a particular case will depend upon the dancer, choreographer or group for which the composer writes, and also the manner in which his own background and intentions influence his choice of style. That is to say, a symphonic composer is not likely to write for a caricaturist dancer, and a man whose work has been the composition of music for cartoons of such things as dancing kittens would be unhappy within the framework of a passacaglia or sarabande for an abstract dancer.

Broadly, there are two standard procedures in creating a ballet. Either the composer "tailors" the music to fit a particular dancer or group, or the dancer uses an already finished composition. There are, of course, minor variations in both of these methods.

If a composer has a good understanding of rhythm and phrasing—if he has a good "dance sense"—he will be able to turn out compositions without any collaboration from a dancer which may, nevertheless, be easily adapted to performance by any choreographer or dancer. If the composer lacks this feeling for dance forms, the dancer will have an arduous time creating a choreographic expression of the music.

Unfortunately, many composers who have written for ballet have not taken it very seriously—far less seriously, say, than their symphonies. This is probably one of the main reasons why there is so little good ballet music, and why famous choreographers have told me that they seize eagerly upon any piece of suitable music outside the ballet field, as a means of expressing their ideas. This method has led to a number of excellent productions, but it is rare that such music is ideal from a choreographic and technical point of view.

One major reason for this shortcoming, in my opinion, is the lack of a really adequate, coordinated notation for music and dance. There is not the easy correlation between bars of music and dance steps that there is between musical phrases and words when the composer is writing for the human voice. A comprehensive notation, intelligible alike to composer and choreographer, would eliminate the fairly common occurrence in which an entire ballet could be danced to a completely different musical composition with trifling alteration, and would result in a far more firmly integrated pattern of musical and choreographic rhythms.

Many great composers (Beethoven, Schubert, Gluck, to name but a few) have written ballet music, but for some psychological reason, difficult to understand, it is rarely performed. A striking exception is Tchaikovsky, whose ballet music is widely employed. Unlike many great composers, he possessed a deep love and understanding of the ballet, and even Diaghilev, who sought only the finest and most distinctive things, eagerly adapted the music of Tchaikovsky.

The greatest danger which ballet faces is that tradition—vitally necessary to the ballet—can easily deteriorate into stale routine, choking progress and endangering its life. From time to time there must appear on the horizon strong personalities (such as Diaghilev) who can retain the best elements of tradition, yet infuse new life by attracting new composers and new choreographers to an intimate collaboration which can result in outstanding productions and true progress.

(Continued on page 140)

Flamenco and Castanets

By INESITA

A WORD must be said to defend a beautiful treasure that has continued to exist strongly in the face of many national crises—the Dance Art of Spain.

Too often I have heard persons remark that they did not understand Spanish dancing. Perhaps the reason for this is that there really isn't enough of it. There have not been really sufficient fine Spanish dance artists in the United States to acquaint the public fully with this bewitching form of expression.

There is so much to enjoy in all the variety of Spanish dancing that one must study each style alone and compare one with the other to realize the inspiration for all of them.

In Spain, the art to receive its highest development was dancing. It was put above every other type of characteristic or national dancing and revered by all who understood. Of all the dance forms, the Spanish dance, I believe, gives the most opportunity for range of motion. There is no part of life that a dancer, using this art as an expression, cannot mirror to an audience. It is the perfect medium for a dancer, as it not only employs a supple body and strict rhythm, but demands an expressive face, as well as coordination of every muscle to the tip of each finger. For the dancer practically must play his or her accompaniment with the various percussion instruments used in these dances, such as the castanets, finger cymbals, and panderas. The "taconeo", or heelwork, is another added accomplishment difficult to achieve and combine with the rest of the movements.

A typical Spanish dancer, in the imagination of many, is a smiling "Senorita" with flouncing petticoats, a comb perched high in her hair, chattering her castanets and accomplishing nothing more than violent motion, coupled with just plain noise. There is a great deal more to it than that.

Spanish dancing is divided into two outstanding types—the classic and the flamenco. The flamenco or gypsy type is actually what supplies the red corpuscles to the whole of Spanish dance art. This group contains the dances usually recognized by a very flexible body, sharp heel work or "taconeo", graceful arm movements, and quickly changing tempos expressing every move and caprice.

As a rule these particular dances are done without the use of castanets and are more often accompanied by finger snapping known as "pitos". Bulerias, farrucas, and alegrias, to mention only a few, are members of this group.

The classic types or purely Iberian dances, such as the Sevillanas, Malaguenas and Jotas, have more dignity and majesty than the flamencos, but do possess their own personality and brilliance. There is, of course, endless variety to these dances, and only after seeing all of them can one fully appreciate this subtle and intriguing art.

Often it is said that when one knows the basic forms of the Spanish dance, a visit to the bullring to see the "Corridas" helps to make the student understand the feeling for which he strives. There is definitely a line drawn between what is innately Spanish and what is fakery and false.

There in the "plaza de toros" one can watch the "torero" with his strict and studied movements in his duel with the bull. After one has mastered the technic of the dance, one can find in the bullfighter's performance the answer to Spanish dancing. It is an arrogance coupled with a sweetness, together with the tenseness of a tiger that make up the attitude or the "bravado" of the Spanish dancer. Aside from the other dramatic qualities of the spectacle, the tiger-like performance of the "torero" is akin to that atmosphere that belongs to Spain's art alone.

In performing the various phases of this art, the dancer runs the gamut of emotions and moods. I think it is comparable to a violin concerto—the upper part of the body, the arms, facial expressions and hands, could be likened to the violin in its solo; and the lower part of the body, the hips, legs and feet, to the orchestra carrying the rhythms and accompaniment for the whole.

Spanish dancing is not always as violent and passionate as many people think. The flamenco or gypsy dancing of Spain is the most passionate of all the Iberian forms, yet it still has the great reserve and dignity which identifies every real Spanish

(Continued on page 143)

Choreographic Beginnings

By SERGE LESLIE

IN the preface to her book, *Theorie de la Danse,* Mme. Bertha Bernay, eminent danseuse of the Paris Opera, observed that in her extensive research for excellent treatises on this art she found only two works which she considered of aid and utility to students, modestly failing to mention her own contribution. The works she cited were the *Blasis-Lemaitre* manual, and the *Letters of Noverre.*

Authors of the 19th century regarded two late 16th Century books, one by Fabrito Caroso and the other by Thoinot Arbeau, among the most important works of all time.

Authors, scholars and dancers of the 20th Century have been searching feverishly for earlier works of equal or greater importance in order to push back the horizon farther into the past. There are several manuscripts and books so seldom quoted or listed in catalogues of bibliographies as to be considered in the light of "discoveries." However, to my mind, these works fall short of the standard set by Caroso and Arbeau.

The 15th Century yielded a few valuable contributions; first the *Basses Danses* translated by Ernest Clossen in the first quarter of this century, contemporaneous with the manuscript of Jean Ambroise of Pesaro held in the Bibliotheque of France under the year of 1416. The work on *Basses Danses,* sometimes called the Golden Book because the lines of the music and the letters representing the choreographic steps were written or ruled in gold and silver on a black background. In spite of the excellence of this work, the technical precisions are few, but the system of using a letter under or above a note of music to denote a step, does anticipate Thoinot Arbeau by almost a century and a half. The steps described in Capital Letters are as follows: R. *reverence;* S. *pas simple;* D. *pas double;* B. *branle;* r. *demarche.* One or two other steps are named but not described.

The works of Antonius de Arena fall in much the same category. There are several editions of his published in 1536, 1670 and 1758.

For absolute clarity we must turn to the work of Thoinot Arbeau (Jean Tabourot), first published in 1588. This book was partially translated into German by Czerwinski, reprinted in French, carefully annotated by Mme. Laura Fonta, in 1888, and painstakingly translated into English in its entirety by Cyril W. Beaumont, in 1925. The title of this work is *Orchesography.* Here positions and stances such as *marque pied* and *marque talon, pieds pari and pieds larghiz* are described and drawn. Also, the number of steps named and described, in addition to those named in the manuscript of *Basses Danses,* now include the *grue,* the *ruade,* the *ru de vache, entretaille,* and *les cinq pas de la gaillarde,* or the five steps of the dance called the *Gaillarde.* This information is most helpful. These steps are clearly described. Students and ballet masters engaged in reconstruction of late Renaissance Dances have drawn heavily on this work. Michel Fokine used very nearly the actual dances in his *Diane of Poitiers* for Ida Rubinstein, and also for his ballet *Don Juan* produced in London.

However, it is unlikely that the dance at that period was limited to such relatively few steps. Arbeau, in the beginning of his dialogue with Capriol, quotes Athenaeus, Scaliger and Lucien who claim the dance to comprise hops, sways, jumps, bendings, changes, limpings, slidings and a thousand and one other transitory movements. In the main Tabourot was unable, any more than the Greek authors had been, to define these phases or qualities of movement within the limitations of an actual step and thus give it a concrete form susceptible to reproduction. It remained for Fabrito Caroso to attempt this vast task.

Caroso's book, *Il Ballarino,* was first published by Francesco Ziletti of Venice in 1581. It contains within its covers twenty-two full page engravings of Giacomo Franco, a large section of rules on dancing describing steps and movements, and a great many airs for the lute with couplets to be sung and others to be danced.

While a number of authors admired *Il Ballarino* as a work of art, they ignored it as a technical treatise of value, and centered most of their attention on Arbeau's *Orchesography.* They observe, with some justification, that the work is obscure and very difficult to decipher. After a great many years study of this work, I am more inclined to think Caroso wrote these rules or explanations of steps for people who had either studied with him or in similar schools, and thus was more of an *aide memoire*."

To my way of thinking, if it were not for *Il Ballarino*, we would have no true understanding of how large and wide a base the dance rested upon in the last half of the 16th Century. For instance, Caroso described several kinds of *balzetti*, (*bouncing steps*), *zoppetti*, (*hopping steps*), and *trabuchetti*, (*leaping or throwing steps*), that later sometimes were called *chetti* or *chetty* or *jete*, by Feuillet in 1700. Among the fifty-odd rules, some explaining several varieties of the same *pas* or step, were explanations for practically every general classification of Feuillet's *Orchesography* which appeared a full century or more later. Without making this an entirely technical treatise, one must mention the fact that Caroso has many varieties of *coupes, chassees, fleurets*, and *changements, brises, cabrioles, entrechats, pirouettes* and *tours en l'air*. In addition to *les cinq pas de la gaillarde* which he uses in combination with Thoinot Arbeau, he has other short combinations of steps. His numerous *seguiti* are really short combinations of three steps each. His *groppo and groponetta* are five and sometimes six steps in one phrase or combination. *Gruppo* or *Grupett* in musical terminology of the 18th Century may indicate a certain kind of trill. It could be easily ascertained whether 16th Century musical dictionaries such as *Tinctoris* have used this term as early as Caroso. However, in the manner of tempo or comparison there could be no analogy between the musical *gropetto* and the choreographic one, except that they both represent a grouping or clustering of values.

I have in the past transcribed after considerable effort some six of Caroso's dances to the musical accompaniment he provides. They are perfectly feasible, and possible to perform. He has not written the name of the step above the music as Arbeau but has given the musical duration of each movement, whether a *minima, semi-minima, grave* or *perfetto*. Again let me repeat if it were not for the *Il Ballarino* of Fabrito Caroso, we would arrive at the period of Octave Feuillet amazed at the progress of the dance in the 17th Century.

The work of Cesare Negri published later, in 1602 and 1604, is hardly clearer than that of Caroso and will, by its obscurities, frighten away all but the hardiest specialists. But the engravings, more numerous than those of Caroso, explain a great many things. His notes in the preface and first chapters

also provide a great deal of knowledge of the status of dance academies in Venice, Florence and Milano. He mentions artists and ballet masters engaged for the French Court and the subsidies they receive.

Perhaps the most famous contribution of the 16th Century is Beaujoyeux's *Ballet Comique de la Reine*, published in libretti or book form in 1582. The engraving of the nobleman's harangue before Henry the Third and the Queen-Mother has been widely published. Another work of this type that appeared in 1681 is "*Le Triomphe de l'Amour.*"

The title of this Opera-Ballet is *Ulysse all' Isola di Circe*. It was produced in Brussels in 1650 for Philippe the Third, then Regent of Spain. The exact number of engravings has not, to my knowledge, been listed in any bibliography. Possibly the National Galleries at Brussels has a complete copy. It is a very rare document with invaluable information for the dancer. The machines and decoration are by Sr. Battista Angelini, the music by Signor Giuseppe Zamponi. In the composite plate facing page twenty-three, there are several illustrations of dances which are excellent. The Primo Ballo, *Minatori Introdotti da Guinone* (The Introduction of the Minators by the Gnomes), and the Secondo Ballo, *Messicani Sotto Scorta da Zefiro* (The Mexicans Forming Escort for Zephyr) are animated and well within the style of Jacques Callot for the grotesque, zest and humor.

The third entry *Floridani Introdotti da Flora* to me is a revelation. The dancers are in light tunics and maillot, heelless slippers and executing a great number of steps and attitudes nearer to the Carlo Blasis conception of purity of line, although the positions have not yet reached their final determined position, yet a strong step forward. Some of the ballet are in arabesque, a demi-arabesque; first arabesque, more in harmony with those of Blasis than the example we have in Lambranzi's, *New and Curious School of the Theatre*. There are arabesques with one arm bent and the hand on the hip. The whole conception of the design places the drawing and the posture well out of the eccentric and well within the range of demi-character if not classic in conception. There are numerous attitudes, as fully developed in openness and vigor as the ones Blasis claims originated with the statue of Jan de Bologne, also attitudes with one hand on the hip as well as those employing opposition of the arm and knee drawn up.

We should be very thankful for these brief flashes of richness in attitude and movement. I am inclined to think authors and ballet masters of these periods were not overly eager to thoroughly analyze and

(*Continued on page* 134)

Every Detail Counts

By SERGE OUKRAINSKY

SPEAKING of choreography, I believe I can best illustrate its meaning by an incident that happened during one of my classes in pantomime. I asked one of my students, a young lady, to show me how she would sit in a chair on a stage. She sat down most gracefully. But I told her that there were many different ways of sitting down, depending upon the place, the time, and the occasion. Before sitting, she should have inquired about the epoch, whether it was in the time of Cleopatra or Semiramis, Marie Antoinette or Queen Victoria.

Any girl could portray a modern sophisticated woman sitting in a drawing room with her legs crossed, smoking a cigarette. However, this same behavior on the part of a woman seventy-five years ago would have been deemed vulgar and unladylike, unfit in polite society. Once we are acquainted with the character and the epoch, the way to sit would depend upon the lady's mood at a particular moment —whether she was gay or sad, frivolous or serious, tired or sprightly. By taking all these factors into consideration one would know how to sit properly.

Our own generation has seen the decline of the ballet, its renaissance and its decadence. In the old choreography of Petipa the story was used only as a pretext for adagios and variations (well enough composed), compiled without rhyme or reason to some old-fashioned stage action invariably ending in a glorified ineptness with the ballerina standing on toe, dressed in the ubiquitous tutu, regardless of the period.

The renaissance of the ballet, started by the genial Michel Fokine and followed up by Diaghilev, Pavlova and my own company, and at present by Anthony Tudor, primarily concerns itself with choreographic composition that will make the ballet a live picture, interpreting the music, and using the dance only as a medium of expression, just as singing is used in opera to advance the story and emphasize its period. In other words, an artistic cooperation between the librettist, costumer, scenic artist, composer and choreographer.

Who of modern composers would, for instance, write an opera in the idiom of Donizetti after Wagner, Stravinsky and Richard Strauss? None would be so foolhardy. And yet in the ballet, many choreographers are doing just that by introducing a musical potpourri, reducing it to dance school exhibitions and gymnastic exercises, disregarding artistic quality for the effect of cheap circus stunts, and retrograding to the pre-Diaghilev period.

Recently I saw a ballet wherein dancers supposedly representing Queens wore no skirts and had greater resemblance to burlesque queens than to those of royalty. That is the reason why the present-day ballet is in a state of decadence. Many can still remember the superb Diaghilev presentation of *Till Eugenspigel*, staged by Nijinsky, with scenery and costumes designed by Robert Edmond Jones.

There is quite a difference in technique between the artist dancer and the good student dancer. I had the pleasure of seeing Nijinsky in *Les Sylphides*. At the rise of the curtain he held the ballerina in his arms. She stood on one foot, a dreamy far-away expression on her face. The other members of the ensemble, draped, lay on the floor, feet turned up, knee hugging knee, in a pose you could see in Grecian statues and find in the paintings of Bellini and Carpaccio.

This same pose at a dance school would be incorrect inasmuch as it requires a fourth position. But the pose was just right for the character Nijinsky portrayed, and gave further evidence of his artistic knowledge of Plastique. Later I saw *Les Sylphides* again but the dancer had no knowledge of Plastique. He simply stood in the banal, conventionally correct fourth position. It was no longer the romantic *Sylphides* of Nijinsky, but a studio rehearsal of a conventional ballet. The dancer in the studio needs technique on the stage plus Plastique—a rare gift.

The composer of an opera or a symphony must have a thorough knowledge of harmony and composition if his work is to stand on its own feet. Naturally, with a good orchestra and a great conductor his work will sound even better. The choreographer's

(Continued on page 134)

Set the Standards High

By MELITA KRIEG

THERE is a thorn in the flesh of all competent teachers of music: the old saying that anyone who fails as an artist can always turn to teaching and earn an easy living. This has obtained credit and force in some circles because the unsuspecting student has not been acquainted with the standards he should require of his teacher.

The time has come when those who bring a lifetime of effort, research, and experience to this lofty profession must raise the banner of excellence even higher, and keep it afloat in the breeze of understanding. Acknowledgment of the good that can come from association with a successful artist is granted, but we must be mindful of the difference between enriching a student's background and teaching him the rules of music. A teacher who can offer both is doubly blessed, while the student benefits in direct proportion.

Good teaching makes the same demands for perfection in performance on the teacher that it does on the student, and the alert student will do well to seek the teacher who performs well, understands why he does what he does, and is able to give the student a working knowledge of how he too can reach the same perfection. The influence of this sort of standard, expected by the student, offered by the teacher, is far-reaching and effective. It annihilates the canard that our country is too new to offer thorough music education for the serious student.

This same new country which some would cheat of its rightful place in the world of music has fostered a profession which in a surprisingly short time has become one of the richest in the land. The student who seeks a career as a professional musician sets his goal in a field full of opportunity and rich in promise. Since millions of dollars are to be made in this lucrative business, millions of dollars likewise are spent learning this important way of making a living. And here is the thorn.

Into every good teacher's experience there comes a student or succession of students who after many years of haphazard but costly training present themselves with very little to show for their time and money; more often, and which is worse, much that is bad. To be successfully trained a student must study with a highly trained and successful teacher who is thoroughly familiar with the subject and who is able to teach it.

Little can be said about the teacher who works by no set standard of rules except to say: "Beware!" Beware of the one who has studied for a number of years, played a little, enough to impress his neighbors, even to the extent that they are willing to entrust their youngsters to his care for the *first lessons*. The unsuspecting parents have not understood how terribly important it is that those first glimpses into the wonderful world of tone should be given by one imbued with the proper perspective of this intensely fascinating and inspiring subject.

And again, beware of the very talented person who has studied hard, performs extremely well but has never taken the time, nor even has been conscious of the necessity, to broaden his horizon beyond himself and his own ambitions. He is short in patience, nervous, high strung, irritable, lacking the insight into another's mental complexities. The student of such a one is generally shy, fearful, rarely composed, and seldom confident in his own right.

Good teaching is a highly specialized profession. It requires much from one who expects to be paid well. It exacts a lifetime of work. In return it fits the competent teacher with a thorough and complete training in his special instrument as well as in the complementary subjects and makes of him an able performer. He has thrilled to the feeling of playing, of mastery over his instrument and himself. Finally it endows him with an ability to search the temperaments of his individual students with a warmth of feeling and depth of understanding so necessary in developing the sensitive and complex nature most often presented.

Sooner or later the truth of the matter catches up with both teacher and student, and the old saying is discredited by that reliably honest one which which says, "By their *works* ye shall know them."

Schools Signpost the Road

By ESTELLE CARPENTER

FROM the earliest ages, people have expressed their elemental emotions through the arts, especially through song, dance and instruments. Strains of martial music make the heart beat faster, the feet step quicker, the spirit grow lighter. The power of rhythm affects one and all. Dance rhythms bring a motor-exhilaration and an immediate response.

The child should have personal experience with dance rhythms and forms to completely understand music intellectually and emotionally. Upon these musical experiences, the child's musical, emotional and aesthetic nature are founded.

Emphasis is given to vocal and instrumental work in the various stages of the school life in most of our educational systems. The play period, with its free and suggested rhythms, motivates the love of music in early childhood. From these experiences is evolved the ear-training, rhythm, sight-seeing, part-singing, theory, development of the correct child voice, music appreciation, and choral singing.

During the adolescent age, the high school period, individual ability, skill and taste should be discovered, encouraged and developed. It is here that music in education is a most important factor for guidance and preparation as a life's vocation or a pleasant diversion.

Thousands of pupils in our high schools, junior colleges, universities and conservatories elect courses in various music subjects such as choral, voice culture, glee club, a cappella choir, part singing, band, individual and class instruction in voice, instruments, theory, harmony and composition. And since the courses of study are preparatory to definite ends in professional or liberal education, the purpose of the work in these institutions is large vocational.

Many of our soloists, composers, conductors, symphony artists have received their first early training in our schools. The school roster includes such illustrious names as Mario Chamlee, Myrtle Claire Donnelly, Nathan Firestone, Radiana Pazmor, Henry Hadley, Charles Kullman, Jan Peerce, Raoul Jobin, Frederick Jagel, Thelma Votipka, Rise Stevens, Grace Moore, Josephine Tuminia, Katherine Meisle, Margaret Harshaw, Florence Quartararo, Clara Mae Turner, Percy Askam, Richard Bonelli, Lawrence

Tibbett, Robert Weede, Francesco Valentino and Leonard Warren.

Various States provide splendid junior colleges, where expanded music courses are given for advanced study, preparatory to the elective courses of the universities, music colleges and conservatories. In California there are 46 junior colleges giving music courses. To those who are preparing to teach, definite courses are given in public school music.

Music appreciation in education was given prominence when, as chairman of music week for the San Francisco public schools, I inaugurated in 1921 the "Music Memory Contests" in all schools, with 40,000 children participating and preparing for the tests over a period of some months. Shortly after this I secured, through the Board of Education, authorization to purchase 100 phonographs and 3,000 selected records. These were distributed from a central office of the School Department and thus a regular course of music appreciation was introduced in San Francisco. This course was later much amplified when the Standard Hour was born. On my suggestion, the Parent-Teachers Clubs and the Board of Education provided radio sets for each of the schools, to listen to the great music of the masters not only in San Francisco but throughout California and the West.

One of the great values of music in education is its power to stir into action patriotic fervor and loyalty to country. This is so clearly indicated through the singing of patriotic and folk songs, which vitally grip the young. These songs have lived for many years—they have survived by reason of the truth they express. At no time in our nation's history has the need for patriotism been so great to re-affirm our faith to our Union, our home, cities and towns.

The emotions may be intensified and uplifted by the continuous use of music that will have the correct effect upon the impulses. This power of music in song is so forceful because it reaches "the innermost center of us all, whence truth abides in fullness" and arouses the essence of the man or child. It quickens the mainspring of action.

When a child is possessed of this power of pure

song it is a precious gift. The method of vitalizing the child through song is happily strengthening the right emotions which lead to right action, at the same time affecting the quality of the voice.

As the inner spirit is developed through song, so it is strengthened by the effects of listening to the great masters' works as produced by symphony orchestras of note. So the first Young Peoples Symphony Concerts were presented in San Francisco in 1922 fulfilling a long-cherished dream of mine . . . that of thousands of children listening to a great symphony under a master's hand. These concerts were given in the San Francisco Civic Auditorium under Alfred Hertz, with an average attendance of 9,000 children paying 25c each.

The success of these series later resulted in the Board of Education continuing the concerts free of charge, for a number of years. Later, the Young Peoples Concerts were given by a committee of music-minded sponsors in downtown theaters. Subsequently, the San Francisco Musical Association presented the Young Peoples Symphony Concerts through a committee of interested music-loving citizens under the direction of the late Ernest Schelling. These concerts have been continued up to the present time under Rudolph Ganz. That the concert series through the years have represented a most important part of our planned music in education is attested to their continued success. Attendance is always complete and the keen attention and evident enjoyment of the young listeners is a joy to behold!

All over the country, cities and communities are instituting these Young Peoples Symphony Concerts and in some places they are given in conjunction with the various school systems, with their music departments using community orchestras of counties and cities.

During recent years there has been a growth in symphony orchestra music throughout the country. This has been the result and reward for the intensive effort on the part of educational forces and music-lovers. The great symphony concerts all over the country have been aided materially by the Young Peoples Concerts. Many places support municipal bands and orchestras, notably in San Francisco, where citizens are taxed a small amount for these musical organizations. The interest of the general public in all forms of the better music such as presentations of individual soloists, in concerts, chamber music and grand opera are traceable to the earnest and efficient efforts of music educators throughout the country.

In the schools, music in education has brought about the finished musical performances at patriotic exercises, graduating and closing exercises, open house days, principals' meetings, parent-teachers meetings and fathers' nights. School plays, pageants and festivals, interspersed with musical selections are given in auditoriums and school yards. Recitals, operettas, light operas and musical selections given for education week, public school week, music week, dedications of new schools all motivate individual and group music instruction, as well as dramatic feeling and expression. Thus, through interest in these musical school affairs, the parents are brought into the school circle and the home and school become a unit with parents, pupils and teachers all interested partakers in each project.

One of the most effective mediums for the advancement of music in education is the activity of the recreation departments in cities and towns. Their musical activities include glee clubs, classes in folk dancing, junior symphony orchestras and community singing. An excellent example of this work is found in the San Francisco recreation department, where children are instructed in the glee clubs and folk dancing under general supervisors. A junior symphony orchestra under a well-known symphony conductor is the pride of the students and parents alike for their excellent work on such occasions as the Christmas fetes in the San Francisco Opera House.

Thus, in San Francisco we meet the challenge to inculcate in the American youth an understanding of the faith of our fathers. In song and music in great assemblages they proclaim the faith in our democratic freedom. A concrete example in devotion to patriotic duties has been manifested in the observance of Armistice Day, where 6,000 pupils from all the public, private and parochial schools voluntarily attended at the Civic Auditorium and sang patriotic songs from 1927 to 1941 in honor of those who had made the Supreme Sacrifice for their country. This was paralleled by the great Lincoln Day celebration at which 5,000 to 8,000 upper grade pupils participated.

Through music the human relationship, with its respect for others, its friendships, its home activities and its civic responsibiltes has become more potent . . . through these experiences, music in education will extend through the adult life in community service and good citizenship.

Music will bring to all the people a new state of mind, for music renews the spirit of youth, and is the leaven which transforms the every day routine into an ecstacy of life.

The Attitude Counts

By JANE STANLEY

THE American ideal for music study is perfectly expressed by David Patterson in his definition: "Music is still an art in the making. Not a science gone to seed, nor a set of museum pieces, but creative expression and growth; not just adornment and display, but an ideal in fine skill; not just passive pleasure for listeners, but participation and ennobling experience; not just a mark of social distinction, but a socializer and homemaker; not just a public event, but a companion in solitude; not just a business or career, but a way of happiness."

The student's motivation expressed to the teacher usually is simply that of appreciation and the general proficiency to play the "not too long" and well-loved standard pieces. Comparatively few aspire to professionalism. But the desire to "understand music" is universal, and where finances permit most children are given that opportunity. Parents of a hopeful artist take a "look-see" with a "few" lessons. The result of this trial depends on many things beside just so-called talent.

Attitude becomes the important thing, the attitude of nearly everyone concerned: self, family, relatives, neighbors and neighbors' children. The family may be impatient about hearing constant practice—the neighbors sentimental about it all, or understanding, or super-critical, or musically ignorant. Their children may resent the student's practice schedule as interfering in play with them, or compare their teacher's possibly less exacting assignments. Relatives are compared—cousins with cousins, an older child with one younger who may have studied longer and therefore plays better, a gifted student with one less brilliant but just as much in earnest. None of these things need be taken too seriously, but unless the student is sympathetically considered in these emotional experiences a sense of inferiority develops, resulting in complete discouragement and a cessation of study.

Young children are usually curious and obedient to study; older people have more determination; but adolescents are a problem! They resent studying music because of its persistent routine and practice. "I thought music would be all just fun!" Outside-school activities are multiplying and are likely to be so much more fun because they are done with others instead of in solitude. Discipline of any sort, from themselves or anyone else, is off. They are beginning to be put on their own and are enjoying that freedom. The physical is predominant, the emotions not yet needing direction or expression. Yet this is the best time to fix the fundamental essentials of reading, technic and routine. Firmness in discipline should not be slackened even though it is difficult for the teacher as well as the parent.

To stop at this time is to lose most that has been gained, with the danger that much time may elapse before the urge to concentrate again appears. If insistence is needed it should be used. No one would be so fantastic as to allow a child to discontinue school because of rebellion against routine. Yet these are the reasons often used in determining the fate of music lessons. Incidentally, because of the intensity of modern competition, of which the child of this age is more than conscious, the adolescent may be very reluctant to be a beginner. For the one who has already started, routine builds solidity and prepares for the emotional development which often happens suddenly and forcefully.

The music teacher, after all, takes part in a limited amount of the entire process. The alloted weekly time for music lessons at best is less than half the time given to any one subject in school, and this one is much more highly complicated. The subject most nearly related in difficulty is learning another language. What child could achieve fluency in a foreign tongue after only two or three years study with bi-weekly lessons of an hour each? Why, then, expect the child to become proficient at the piano, spectacular in public performance, or understanding of the subject after such superficial study? Public schools allow much more time for ordinary subjects.

The teaching of appreciation and some definite instruction in performance of solo voice or instrument in the public schools is constantly increasing, and we all pay tribute to that growth. We frankly ask why not start the child there to see if any musical talent is evinced and try to measure the child's ability? The answer is obvious. One cannot judge

(Continued on page 128)

Triad Out of Tune

By LENNARD ANDERSON

THREE individuals are concerned when a music lesson is given: teacher, pupil and parent. If each of the three would faithfully discharge his or her duties towards the other they would indeed form a harmonious triad.

Each must live up to certain obligations in order to reach their goal. The teacher should, of course, maintain a high standard by continued study. He should endeavor to make the most of the natural gifts possessed by his students, and should not lose patience with those who do not manifest natural talent. It is the teacher's duty to educate the non-musical as well as those with genuine talent.

Every new pupil should be approached by the teacher in an attitude that will replace fear and unrest with trust, confidence and regard. Instead of devoting the entire lesson period to the correction of wrong notes, some time could be spent profitably to the correction of the student's mental attitude. Harsh criticism only tends to incapacitate and unnerve the pupil.

The era of the long-haired foreign pedagog striding back and forth, fuming and raging over a pupil's errors happily is almost a thing of the past— I lost my hair long ago. It has been found possible to know something about music and yet retain one's mental balance. There is no reason why a fine teacher with a comprehensive knowledge of music should not maintain the same mental balance accredited to representative men in other professions.

If the teacher is to attain any degree of success, he must primarily make it as pleasant as possible for those willing to travel the road to musical perfection. First and foremost, he must take into consideration the psychological bent of his pupils.

In no study other than music would the parent venture to dictate to the teacher what or what not to do in developing a child's talents. By interfering in the methods of procedure and teaching, parents often are more troublesome than the students. One of the most difficult problems that confronts the teacher is to please both student and parent at the same time. Of course, one cannot entirely disregard parental desires. Good will is a requisite of entrusting children to the hands of a particular teacher.

However, parents can render invaluable assistance

(*Continued on page* 133)

No Par For the Course

By MARSHALL B. CHASHOUDIAN

THE present day student of the violin has many advantages over his counterpart of twenty-five years ago. It was almost a necessity in those days to go to Europe in quest of good teaching. In Boston, New York, Philadelphia and Chicago there were a few teachers of note, but to count the cost, a European training was much less expensive and more inspiring.

Teaching staffs in our American universities, private and endowed schools now surpass those of Europe and the great number of very young students who show outstanding talent and facility proves how that quality of teaching has progressed. Yet apart from these and a small number of competent private teachers, the field is loaded with so-called pedagogues who have few qualifications for their chosen profession.

Such teachers guide students to a nebulous end which either discourages them or launches them on a long period of breaking down first impressions and building up again from a sound foundation. This experience has a bad effect. The student becomes skeptical and in many cases falls victim to a psychosis, a neurotic tendency which manifests itself in the habit of running from one teacher to another in hopes of finding the cure for his particular failings.

On the other hand, real talent can protude in spite of poor teaching. Heifetz would be a great violinist no matter who taught him.

We have proved in this country that our athletes and sports participants are second to none in the world. In the first instance, our educational system encourages play, demonstrating that health of mind and body is built upon these outlets. Secondly, choice of supervisors and coaches in various branches of athletic competition is given careful and serious consideration. The coach for any High School football team is a man who has qualified at some time or another as a player of distinction and trained in the subtlety of imparting his knowledge.

Thousands play golf, most of them instructed by professionals who themselves have for many years played in recognized competition, and mastered the game's grip-stance-knees-hips-head-eyes-wrist-arms-swing and concentration ramifications. They

(*Continued on page* 142)

Free For the Asking

By GLADYS CALDWELL

THE year 1948 marks the seventieth anniversary of the Los Angeles Public Library, and also the appointment of its fourteenth City Librarian, Harold Louis Hamill. Music, however, was not considered legitimate library material until 1889 when Tessa Kelso, city librarian, defied tradition to the extent of buying music scores for circulation. By 1914 the Arts were felt to be of sufficient importance to warrant the establishment of a separate department, and since that date a steady development in its resources has brought the Art and Music Department to first place in non-fiction circulation of the Central Library. Many factors contributed to this accomplishment: chief among them is the year by year purchase of books and music selected with the aim of maintaining an even balance between materials of current interest, and scholarly works of permanent value.

Many gifts have enriched the collection. In 1922 William Andrews Clark, Jr. presented the Library with a benefit concert given by the Philharmonic Orchestra. It was a community affair in the happiest sense of the word. Sponsored by the Music Teachers' Assn., a committee was formed consisting of Mmes. Emma M. Bartlett, A. B. Cooke, G. W. Mabee and M. H. Pehr and Miss Vera Blythe. Olga Steeb gave her services as soloist. The result was $1,140 to spend for books and scores.

Through the efforts of the Parent-Teachers Assn. the valuable music library of the pianist and pedagog, Jaroslav de Zielinski, was acquired. Besides several thousand scores it contained authoritative works in English, French, German and Polish on the history and technique of music and the lives of composers.

No account of the Department's development would be complete without mention of the regal gifts of Mrs. Elizabeth Sprague Coolidge. Beginning in 1927 chamber music concerts were given for a period of thirteen years in the Lecture Room of the Library, either as her personal gift, or under the auspices of the Coolidge Foundation of the Library of Congress. Such world famous groups as the Aguilar Lute Quartet of Madrid and the Pro Arte, London, Brosa, Roth and Gordon String Quartets performed the various programs. So popular were they, that long before the concerts began every seat was filled, and many unable to get in listened quietly in the Children's Court.

The next step forward in the growth of the music collection was in 1934, when again the Library was the recipient of a magnificent gift from Mr. William Andrews Clark, Jr. By the terms of his will, the entire collection of orchestral scores, which he had built up for the Philharmonic Orchestra, was donated to the Los Angeles Public Library "for enjoyment and use by the general public". The collection comprises 752 full orchestrations; practically the entire repertory of classics, as well as many lesser known compositions. They are in constant demand and are proving a powerful aid to cultural development in the smaller communities of Southern California. So grateful for their use is one orchestra of a neighboring town, that at the end of its season each year, the Library receives a check for the purchase of an additional score.

In the past decade librarians have become increasingly conscious of the need for visual and auditory aids to supplement the printed page of books and scores. Lecturers are depending more and more on films and slides as illustrations of their talks, students of foreign languages and literature study from records, and the music student wants to hear interpretations other than his own of the world's great music.

Fortunately the Los Angeles Public Library was the recipient in 1930 of a gift of $10,000 from Mrs. Alice M. Bluett, as a memorial to her husband. By the terms of the bequest it was to be used for the benefit of the blind. Since government agencies deliver books to the homes of the blind, it was decided to spend the interest of this money for recorded music which could be enjoyed by all. During the depression years of the 1930's noonday concerts of recorded music were given daily, the programs arranged by staff members and presented by W.P.A. workers. With the end of such government projects in 1942 the concerts continued through volunteer help, for the past four years under the able direction of Mr. Brown Shoenheit. These regular Tuesday evening concerts of

(Continued on page 138)

The Library Lends a Hand

By JESSICA FREDRICKS

THAT public libraries should include music departments, is still a novel idea to many people. As the collection of music and the work of the department in the San Francisco Public Library presents a good example of such procedure, its story may not be considered too personalized to be given here.

Starting in 1917 with some 3000 volumes of music and 500 books about music, it has by now more than doubled its collection of music and gathered together ten times as many books about music. This in addition to hundreds of pictures, 12,000 pieces of sheet music and a working collection of choral music where any single title may run into a dozen or a hundred copies.

The question naturally arises as to the use and value of such a department and its appreciation by the music loving and book loving people of the community. The best answer is to imagine that section of San Franciscans without a music department. While in general, libraries have not been glamorized to the public, nor sufficiently heralded, this collection and the activities growing out of it, would be sorely missed, of that we are certain.

In a public library the scope of the collection must be particularly wide. Not the scholars and research workers, the students and teachers, and not the general reading public have to be considered individually but all of them, as members of a tax paying American community, must be able to satisfy their needs in the library they help to support.

Hence we have all the standard classics in each category, hundreds of volumes of piano music, the great heritage of song, sacred and secular, violin music "the whole world plays" and similarly through the fields of music for flute, clarinet, horn and other instruments.

The entire history of opera can be studied through the vocal scores on the library shelves. Another outstanding collection is that of chamber music, where in addition to the standard works in the conventional combinations, can be found scores of items. All of these may be withdrawn for home use, in generous quantities at a time.

Backing all this music, providing information for the students and enjoyment for the amateur, are the books on music history, biography, essays, theory, appreciation, studies. Books on how to read and how to play and how to listen. Popular books they are, too. Over the course of the last thirty years we can see a great change in the study habits and musical outlook of our reading public. Books on counterpoint, orchestration, histories that are not written down to a supposed level of taste, biographies that are realistic, these are popular books.

"The other side of music in the air" might be the title of the miniature score section. They are the special joy of the hundreds of listeners one can visualize in homes and studios, who follow with the library score as the orchestras play the music they love. Like the chamber music this is also a field we like to keep growing, because of its appeal to youth.

In the field of scholarship, the public library can hardly hope to compete with collections in the big colleges or with our own Library of Congress. But we purchase the fine and definite sets of the masters: Gluck, Bach, Handel, Beethoven, Mozart, Brahms and others. And we make a serious attempt to have adequate material for musicologists and their students.

Reference work is very important and a vast amount of research is required to keep it going. Magazines are clipped for pictures and biographies of personalities currently dear to the public, obituaries are gathered to keep the encyclopedias up to date and material is preserved dealing with the newest composer in the field or the oldest one, almost but not quite forgotten. Once a library gains something of a reputation in the reference field there ensues much interesting correspondence and many live contacts.

Out of all this have grown many special services to the public. There is, for instance, an exchange list whereby amateurs can find other players to complete a chamber music group, or a student may locate a practice studio or get second hand books. Dozens of such requests are listed. A survey of the city's own musical activities is very useful to have on hand for reference regarding the orchestras, big and little,

(Continued on page 132)

Music By the Yard

By WILLIAM LAVA

HOW ON EARTH do you manage to get so many new themes in such a short time, week after week" This little poser is practically the very first question thrust at me, in any discussion of my work as a composer of music for the films. Doubtless the average non-writing musician, or the layman interested in music generally, finds it hard to understand just how a film composer can keep grinding out music, day after day, week unto week, year by year, without running out of material.

Well . . . all I can say is, it's not easy. However, in routining one's self to a lifetime of writing music at the drop of a hat, so to speak, it behooves the composer to acquire, adopt, assimilate or otherwise endow himself with the facility for grasping thematic material from the thin air. It would be silly for me to protest that a certain amount of natural talent or adaptability to this specialized type of music writing is not required—quite the contrary; without this precedent aptitude, even if only to a small degree, the novice will find the going quite tough indeed. There have been many times when, during the process of attempting to irritate the musical oyster I have found a strange delight in uprooting what few hairs remain on my (now) rapidly glowing scalp.

According to some composers, the use of themes for characters or as basic story motifs, is a backward approach to the project, and stamps the user as a man lacking in originality, or the vitality to knock out a cracker-jack of a music score for a potent drama. The "rebels" class themselves as "the modern group" of composers of film music, and of course throw all the others into a category which they describe by using the one pungent word, "hack." The present theory of this new school of thought on filmusic is that no thematic material be used that contains a potent strain or melody; rather that the music be abstract in its content, and of a mood nature and meandering in its development. The idea behind this reasoning is the argument which so many of these writers advance, that to be truly effective, filmusic must not be noticed by the audience in the theatre, must not be so powerful melodically as to draw attention from the drama unto itself.

Now as far as this belief ever becoming popular with the film producers, I do not hestitate to state my conviction that such will not come to pass either soon, or in the far distant future. There may be one or two producers who will allow themselves to be influenced by this theory in their acceptance of the music to be used in their pictures, but I am sure that it will only be the result of their confusion rather than their enlightenment.

As a matter of fact, I have even seen this confusion evident amongst these composers themselves. In one instance, in a newspaper article describing his feelings on the same subject, one gentleman claimed that film composers should not succumb to the theory that filmusic is effective only when it is not noticed by the audience, while in all of his film scores and in his private utterances amongst colleagues he operates on the theory that the abstract form is the least likely to distract from the film drama, and that the use of melody is a practice to be left to the old guard. In another instance, an ardent advocate of the abstract form is breaking all his own rules by turning out some very wonderful film scores containing any number of delightful and effective melodies. In this case, failing to practice what he preaches has proved to be to his definite benefit and advantage, and I heartily recommend that he continue philandering in this manner.

I am firmly convinced that a good melody is a far better demonstration of a composer's natural ability than the most involved contrapuntal arrangements or conglomerate harmonic constructions. If a theme is established for a certain individual in the film drama, certainly there is a basis for its use throughout the film as a character reference, and the same theme utilized in the various moods that are created by the unraveling plot is a most effective skein to assist in our following the progress of that plot.

Let's get back, now, to our subject of accumulating these sometimes controversial themes, and examine the various methods of approach employed by some of the men now engaged in that branch of artistic hysteria. If we step down low enough to reach basic essentials, we'll find that there is very little difference in the manner that each composer sets himself to work—they may apply themselves in any one of a hundred or more idiosyncratic spasms, but the basic element is still there—regardless of his approach he still must bridge the gap between pencil and blank score page, and the fill is supplied by the muse in one way only, veritably from the dark recesses of his cranium, by the simple expedient of tapping the fertile reserve of material held in storage there.

If you are a nervous character, and if you have a tendency to exhibit this nervousness in a manifestation of strange mannerisms, while engaged in the pursuit of love's labor, there is every reason in your favor for assuming that you would make a very fine filmusic composer. In granting this conclusion, it must be remembered that you must know a little something or other about music—in our business nobody ever forgives you for working at something about which you know nothing, no matter how successful you may be at it.

Few days go by wherein someone fails to make a remark about the weird and bizarre manner in which I set myself to work. Needless to add, that in so remarking, they are overlooking the prerequisites mentioned in the two preceding paragraphs. But no matter what people may think about my "unusual" methods of operation, somehow I manage to get the work done, and in the time allotted to me, regardless of how narrow the confines of that allotment. When I decided on the title for this article, it seemed to me the only true description of what the average composer for films has to contend with. Literally the job calls for a turnout of music by the "yard" so to speak, although the actual measurement is the foot length. (So many feet of film per second of time.)

Now, let me answer that question in the very opening paragraph of this symposium—you can't do it without having the ability to do it before you even know you've got the ability. You can't do it if you can't think quickly in an emergency. You can't do it if you can't sit down and read a script, or see a brand new film drama, and feel the mood of the new opus immediately on viewing, and at the same time translate that mood in terms of music. You can't do it if you can't understand the idiosyncrasies of a producer or director who tries to tell you what he likes as a musical background for his picture. You can't do it if you can't think of music in terms of linear measurement, and as a plastic substance, subject to remolding at all times. You can't do it if

you can only think of music as something for the concert hall and as a sacred entity thereof. And at last but certainly not least, believe me when I say that you can't do it if you haven't got a strong constitution and a strong mind.

I may have overlooked one or two other details in this listing, but if you can fill the bill on the above mentioned, the missing qualifications probably would be taken care of automatically. In line with the statements made regarding time allotments, I might add that unless you are prepared to meet the occasions wherein music must be written by you almost as quickly as it could be played, you are not going to be very happy in the field. If this is an exaggeration of the true situation, I feel certain that there are enough composers in Hollywood who would gladly endorse the exaggeration as a solemn truth, if only for the purpose of lashing back at the people who insist on making it necessary for the composer to do his work on each picture in such an unfairly short length of time, while all other technical points are accomplished without the bugaboo of a deadline.

When a composer sets himself to creating a new work for the concert hall, his thematic material is usually the result of an inspiration that might have popped up at some previous time, and which he has at hand ready to be arranged in the particular form that he wants this particular piece to be played. However, in writing for the films, his thematic material must evolve from the topic or mood presented in the picture, and the style of presentation of the music depends also on the pace set in the picture. I will not attempt to describe the many possible variations of this relationship, but the basic idea set forth covers every possible situation, except in the case of musical features.

In a musical movie, one that contains songs by some well-known popular songwriter, the background musical score almost without exception, contains thematic material using these same songs either wholly or in part, and the treatment is obviously guided by the mood and pace of the scene in each instance.

It's not easy to set forth in a few paragraphs all the things that arise in the scoring of a motion picture, and I must admit that not all of it would make interesting reading. However, I do hope that in giving this little insight on the manufacture of motion picture music, I haven't belittled the profession, or made it look unglamorous and ordinary. Actually it is a very exciting, interesting and diversifying kind of work, and I am very happy to be right

(Continued on page 128)

Time Tells the Tale

By NATHANIEL FINSTON

IN the summer of 1928, Paramount Pictures, like all the other companies, went into sound; recordings were made in the Victor Studios at Camden, New Jersey. Later, in November, the music and sound departments in Paramount Pictures' studios, in Hollywood, began the first music department for any picture studio on the West Coast. It was my good fortune to be then an executive and the musical head of this major film company, and to convert and install the music requirements, at the transitional point, from silent to sound pictures.

Everyone knows how pictures sounded, and what the music consisted of in those days—rather lowly and fairly insignificant. But no longer do you hear the horrible sizzling sounds from the screen; no longer the limited and rather immature music and renditions. Musical instruments are now recorded and reproduced with great fidelity; in fact, were you in the next room, you could hardly tell whether it was a recording or the actual rendition by the performer in person.

However, we have not reached the ultimate by far, although great progress has been made by the combined efforts of research and technical groups in music and sound. While sound recording has made important advances, too often we are still hampered with "reproduction" in theatres and other public places because of their acoustical or mechanical shortcomings.

The art of music, or music as an art in pictures, has not advanced that rapidly, nor as far—although progress has been made. Take for instance, play, operetta, opera, or even the drama: over and over again one wishes to hear excerpts of this music. It is tuneful in many instances, and reaches classical and academic heights. *L'Arlesienne* music is constantly played in concert form even though set incidentally to a drama. The Rogers and Hammerstein, Irving Berlin, Victor Herbert, Sigmund Romberg and Rudolph Friml operettas, to say nothing of Johann Strauss, all have haunting and lilting music that can be performed as separate and solo numbers. Wagner, Puccini, and Verdi excerpts can all be played in three- or four-minute selections but who asks for "The Ride" or "Sunrise Music" from a given picture epic; or "Dance of the Hours," "Ballet Music,"

"Magic Fire", or the "Entrance Music" from any recent pictures?

The time must come (and I hope very soon) when picture music is of sufficient importance and musical value that it will be requested, heard and respected at critical performances by major musical organizations. The music as present, for the most part, is only the "picture frame to the picture". There was such a time in grand opera, ballet and incidental music to dramatic plays, when the music was undistinguished, uninteresting, and rather inferior. Contributions by great composers changed that, but music in pictures is not yet of sufficient stature to be given the same importance and prominence.

This must and will also come, of course. It may be that composers, given a freer hand, or subjects better integrated to music, will help to hasten this advance. There abounds smart orchestration and experienced musical craftsmanship which undoubtedly result in good and interesting overall musical jobs in pictures that still cannot rate the musical importance (to the story) that Wagner, Puccini, Bizet, Verdi, Tchaikovsky, Johann Strauss, Herbert, Coward, and a host of others, have rated for their music to dialogue, action, ballet, costumes and scenery.

Yet we have made great progress in less than twenty years, and there is reason to be optimistic that "music in pictures" will merit a very important concert rating and value as extant in operettas, dramas and ballets.

It should be said, however, that too often the inspired musician is hampered in many ways and by many people around picture production; in other words, the last word musically or "power of decision" rests too often with a "power executive". If uncompromising story material will not be sympathetically librettoed to give music a chance, if spacing in dialogue will not permit music to be heard, if boxoffice, or commercial whim, is the only barometer—and if the apostle of such judgments is a high-placed executive "protecting" these problems against the "highbrow" musicians—then the advancement of important picture music will continue to be delayed. But, in other ages, the developments of arts, crafts and science took time—so today, it will again, to develop sound and music in pictures.

The Growing Art

By MIKLOS ROZSA

WITH the advent of sound in motion pictures, a new form of expression has been developed in the field of dramatic music. The new form not only has posed new artistic problems, but it has brought about vital social and economic changes in the life of a Twentieth Century composer. The present-day composer, unlike his precursor of the Eighteenth and Nineteenth Centuries, no longer need depend upon the bounty of a patron. Many of our foremost contemporary composers already, or eventually will write music for the movies.

The cinema is a synthetic art, a combination of drama, acting, and music, closely allied to the Wagnerian ideal of *Gesamtkunstwerk*. The only difference is that music on the screen plays but a subordinate part to the unfolding of the story.

In the early days of silent movies it became apparent that an element of sound would have to be introduced if this new form of entertainment were to survive. Thousands on the screen strutted about and moved their lips, yet no footsteps or words were audible, and the hushed silence in the theater was disturbed only by the monotonous drone of the projection machine. The introduction of sound was imperative, and music was its logical medium.

The first musical accompaniment was by means of phonograph records, and the music played had no relationship whatsoever to the story unfolded. Later, as the movies grew in length, the phonograph was replaced by piano or organ, though these, like the phonograph, made no effort to correlate music with action. Music merely served to create an agreeable atmosphere to please the spectators, or followed the tempo of movement on the screen.

As pictures increased in length, and theaters in size, cinema music underwent a corresponding change. Gradually more and more instruments were added to the piano, until toward the end of the "silent" era every first-class movie theater housed a complete symphony orchestra, conducted by a competent musician.

With a symphonic orchestra installed in the pit of a theater, the musical accompaniment to the picture was no longer a willy-nilly concoction of unrelated tunes, but selected and well-sustained melodies, suited to the action, mood, rhythm of the story on the screen. Thus the music accentuated the rhythm with pleasant sounds, resulting into the hitherto novel effect of synchronization.

The new musical accompaniments put the symphony conductors in the movies on their mettle. They had to delve into classical literature to find melodies suitable for the scenes of different moods. In order to alleviate this burden, a new printed literature appeared that supplied the conductors with a combination of musical arrangements to any and all cinema stories—farce, comedy, drama, tragedy.

But the quality of the music so dispensed was meretricious. The most commonplace melodic traditions of the Nineteenth Century were used. Hackneyed and dramatic titles, such as *Agitato* and *Appassionato* were constantly repeated. Later, as the screen stories grew emotionally more intense, the ready-made music literature supplied accompaniment for all screen eventualities, for fights, battle scenes, love scenes, thunder, storms, quarrels, funerals, weddings—the whole gamut of human emotions and elemental disruptions. It formed a large and varied repertory but none of it could stand the acid test of time and all now is happily forgotten.

Invention of electrical sound amplification brought about a revolution in cinema music. The new invention pushed the symphony orchestra out of the theater and replaced it with the sound track which enabled the recording of whole musical scores on records. An added advantage of this device was that it afforded the same musical accompaniment to small theaters that could not afford the luxury of a symphony orchestra.

The first sound pictures, apart from their technical innovations, brought no marked improvement to the musical accompaniment as rendered by the symphony orchestra. They were just picturized operettas and theater accompaniment by canned music. For a while, pictures even lost their aesthetic integrity of the silent era. Song "hits" predominated, and stories and action were subordinated to those songs. Film composers degenerated into song writers. Real-

(*Continued on page* 133)

Drastic Decade

By RUDY DeSAXE

TWENTY years is not a long time in our passing parade, yet we well may wonder at the many developments brought about in the motion picture industry in two short decades. The technique of writing music for the films has undergone very definite changes.

Most of us still remember the large orchestras employed by various theatres, when silent pictures had to have a background of music in order to enhance the action on the screen. A musical score, as we understand it today, was then nonexistant. Unless special numbers or songs had been composed particularly for a picture, very little original material ever was written.

Most of that music was compiled from classical, semi-classical, operatic, popular and various other sources, the selection and compiling being left to the discretion of the conductor.

Yet, from this haphazard manner of compiling a musical background—crudely timed to the action on the screen—eventually sprang our elaborate, streamlined motion picture score of today, expressly composed for a particular picture, and recorded right into the film.

Through years of trial and experimentation, music finally has become one of the most necessary items in film production. No picture is made today without a musical background of some sort.

Composing music alone costs the motion picture industry over one million dollars each year, and this figure does not include cost for conducting, orchestrations, arrangements and performing orchestras. The yearly expenditure of such enormous amounts of money can mean only that the industry considers music a very important factor in making pictures.

A film score is not written with the intent of standing out or predominating. Being an integral part of the picture and created to fit the mood and the action, it is not meant to interfere or clash with the development of the story or distract the audience from interest in the plot. The public must remain only half-conscious of the music in the background, but should we take away that music entirely, something definitely will be missing.

Music thus becomes as important to a film as the excellent designing of a set, proper lighting of scenes, good editing or clever recording. But in many respects it is more important than these, for it deals with moods and the portrayal of human emotions. The ability to communicate such emotions to the listener through the medium of music and connect them with visual action on the screen, is unquestionably an artistic achievement.

While film music has its limitations, it does not have to be relegated entirely to background scoring. It can be a work of art. Some of our picture scores are excellent. They stand on their own merits and easily can be compared in quality with some of the best symphonic works. Many in fact have been performed by major symphony orchestras.

In this country we have been perhaps a bit slow in giving that same recognition to the values of film music. While the motion picture industry is willing to spend five times as much money on a score as the British do, yet it does not bother to capitalize upon it. The general attitude, still prevailing among many Hollywood producers, is that of dismissing or minimizing the importance of a good musical score. From their viewpoint, music is something of a "necessary evil," required only to enhance the action on the screen.

It is needless to point out how wrong this attitude is, for no artistic endeavor can be classified as a "necessary evil." That the general public does not share this viewpoint is manifest by the many thousands of letters received every year by the various studio music departments, here in Hollywood. All such letters show a definite interest in picture music, a desire for better acquaintance with the composer's work and a strong wish that more film music could be made available to the public through commercial recordings.

Music in the films, in this ever-changing world, is as modern an expression as motion pictures themselves. We cannot stop progress. Such music is bound to grow in importance as a part of our national heritage, just as much as pictures have become a part of our daily life.

The time has passed when a film score was some-

(Continued on page 132)

Select For Yourself

By CONSTANTIN BAKALEINIKOFF

SUPPOSE *you* had a million dollars invested in a brand new film. Suppose, too, that you could select virtually any composer to underscore, or write the background music for it. Whom would you select?

You would have a wonderful roster from whom to choose. In Hollywood and vicinity, within easy reach of the telephone at your elbow, is the greatest array of composer talent the world ever has known, an array that requires many pages in the biographical portion of this volume.

At your call, for an adequate fee, are men whose names are on the lips of every musical family, whose works have been played in every concert hall and by every leading symphony orchestra. They are men who not only know every intricacy of modern composition and instrumentation, but have contributed to the advancement of these phases of music.

Similarly at your call are men who have underscored many films, whose chief claim to distinction lies in the craftsmanship they have acquired over years of practice. All of them have written scores, at one time or another, that have won high commendation because of their suitability to the individual films.

All these composers, whether classified as ornaments of the concert hall or merely as appendages to the silver screen, have one thing in common: they have written mediocre works as well as good works. Only the mediocre items by the concert composers lie quietly collecting dust in cupboards, while those of the film writers have gone, willy-nilly, into the pictures for which they were written, where they contrived to serve a purpose, even if an undistinguished one.

The mediocrities of the concert composers, it must be considered, are works composed at leisure, with ample time and scope for frequent consultation with the Muse and solution of technical problems. While those of the film composers are works produced under the utmost pressure, many of them written within a few days and often in hours customarily used for sleep.

You have, moreover, the space of two weeks—fourteen days, including Sundays—for the music to be written and orchestrated and the instrumental parts copied out. It was long considered remarkable that Rossini could compose essentially the same amount of music in two weeks, but that is the average time allotted to a Hollywood composer. Occasionally a producer generously grants three weeks, but more often he will insist that ten days is adequate.

Perhaps you may decide that Mr. Blank, who has just created a furore with his new symphony (for percussion, piccolo, viola d'amore, heckelphone, basset-horn, tenor horn, theremin, alto clarinet and four zithers), is just the composer you want. You have heard his opus in the Philharmonic Auditorium, and consider that it has exactly the proper touch of novelty.

Unfortunately the program notes aver that Mr. Blank required seven years to create his masterpiece, counting from the time the great idea germinated to the final stroke for the fourth zither. How much could he do in two weeks?

You know that you will be perfectly safe in selecting Mr. Nemo, who has written many scores in two weeks or less, with and without sound effects. But Mr. Nemo's record, while indubitably efficient, is far from inspiring, being a monotonous vista of class B films. In fact, the only review of his work you recall having seen was a film critic's statement that "the music was by Nemo."

Mr. Nemo has the advantage of being under contract to the studio, so that his services are available at a minimum of expense. Whereas Mr. Blank, despite his years of starving for art's sake (according to the program notes) certainly would not descend to besmirch his artistic reputation by scoring any film for less than a very large fee, cash in advance.

The only thing of which you are sure is that each composer will adhere to the musical idiom he has already established, with the qualification that Mr. Nemo will be reasonably elastic while Mr. Blank will be inexorably inflexible.

There are a few other complications. The producer would like you to use Mr. Ecks (who has scored pictures for him before), one of your best friends has phoned to impress you with the abilities of Mr. Wye (who probably owes him money), and one of the

(*Continued on page* 143)

The Mood Comes First

By RUDOLPH KOPP

SOME great composers would have been quite incapable of writing satisfactory film scores. Debussy, for instance, was a stylist. He was concerned with the development of his own individuality as a composer, and would not have been easily adapted to a screen composer. Wagner, on the other hand, could have done magnificently had the medium of motion pictures been at hand. For he was peculiarly gifted in writing music to a mood or a scene.

In general, music for the screen involves the same basic principles as music for an opera. That is to say, it must support the story, giving it aid when necessary and full cooperation always, but never obscuring it. A screen score is not and cannot be written primarily for the concert hall, nor aimed at securing an Academy Award.

The musical score is intended to decorate and assist the dramatic action of the picture. A sympathetic screen score can do much to make the picture a success. The opposite is equally true, meaning that a score which is written for its own effect alone will obtrude upon the dramatic story to the consequent loss of both factors.

The young composer, whose ambition is to write a film score, should first look very carefully at his own music. He should analyze it as objectively as possible, and form his conclusions without prejudice. First, he must have a sound musical education. He must have a complete mastery of his medium and he must be able to write with ease and fluency at all times, and under the most trying conditions. For screen scores must be turned out in a limited time without regard to whether or not the composer has a headache or happens to feel out of sorts at the moment. The film studio is no place for a composer who thinks first of his temperament.

One of the most difficult problems for any screen composer is to know when a scene should have music and when it should not. Few pictures require continuous underscoring. It is a problem that can be solved partly by experience and partly by intuition. It always requires a judicious blend of both.

A motion picture score does not require the same texture as a work for concert hall. Thick scores sound heavy and moody in recording, and the objective of sonority cannot be reached by such means. Certainly, a motion picture score is not merely harmonization of a melodic line, but counterpoint must be used skillfully.

Perhaps this is one reason why excerpts from motion picture scores are only occasionally useful in the concert hall. A lofty attitude adopted by some critics often gives the public the wrong impression of such selections. Screen excerpts at a concert must be judged for what they are and no more. They are intended as screen media.

Another factor a young composer should take into account is that the effort to be "different" at all costs is out of place when writing for the silver screen. A producer who has from a half-million to a million dollars invested in a picture will not look favorably upon a composer who wishes to experiment in sound patterns for unusual effects. In some instances, the producer may appear too conservative, yet considering the circumstances, he cannot be blamed for caution on the musical side.

One successful work does not make a composer fitted for film scoring. Before the studio music department head will take a chance of engaging a composer, the latter must be able to show a number of works. Certainly, the composer must demonstrate his facility, for he will be asked to turn out a score in from two to six weeks. He must know his orchestra thoroughly, and be able to indicate to his orchestrators what he desires in the way of instrumentation. He must know choral writing, for a chorus is often an important feature in a score. One of the most important factors is that of modulation, which must be easy and deft at all times.

A screen composer must always be on his guard against plagiarism. I do not think that any composer on or off the screen would knowingly utilize another's work, but there always exists a danger in some portion being reminiscent of some item of standard fare, or even a novelty the composer may have heard and quite unconsciously reproduced. The composer, therefore, must have a thorough familiarity with both old and new works, in order to be able to avoid such similarity. The film composer must possess originality in its fullest sense.

Where Seldom Is Heard an Encouraging Word

By ALBERT SENDREY

I WENT through futile motion No. 17 again last week. The boys and girls who are pursuing music (or whom music is pursuing) at L. A. City College had me in to ta.k to them about composing and arranging for motion pictures and radio. Their favorite subject was inevitably brought up: how does one go into writing for radio or pictures on a paying basis?

The musical tribe at L.A. City College is the same eager, practical, intelligent cross-section of citizenry you find all over America. With the one exception that the major network shows emanate from New York and Hollywood, and 99% of all motion pictures from Hollywood (comprising Burbank, Culver City, and West Los Angeles). Which gives the local kids something young music students in Des Moines and Dallas don't have: access, if in their dreams only, to the source of America's entertainment. And so they want a road map to a job.

Caught in this trap, I always try gentle dissuasion. I point out that the ratio of those studying music to those who will get a studio job is discouraging, and suggest they turn to other outlets for their talents. Actually, to get a job in a motion picture studio writing music anyone has to be not only lucky, but to stay on the job he has to be a minor genius. He must have the same command over the carpentry of writing music as a great juggler has over his plates, clubs, and balls—harmony and counterpoint must long have ceased to present the slightest problems, the range of the instruments making up the symphonic palette must be as familiar to him as the driver's seat of an old and faithful automobile which he has driven for ten years or more. He must know the volume weight of each register of each instrument against all groups and possible combinations of groups of other instruments, to achieve balance in his writing and clarity in his intentions.

The valuable boys are those who know their way around this maze of technical preliminaries, who have made a study of microphone writing by hearing their own mistakes before anyone else does, and never repeating them. They all are expert composers, even if their job consists of arranging and orchestrating only, and they all are expert arrangers and orchestrators even if they never write a single score page again in their lives. No matter how successful they may be, they must continue to keep abreast, and even be ahead of the contemporary trends of music styles, for their own work can be heard by fifty million people, and copied by fifty thousand, though in parrot fashion. This means that their own ideas will soon reach them again from behind, as a sort of public domain, and force them to invent new ways of writing in order to keep up with themselves.

This answers the most frequently put question: "Is a thorough musical education REALLY necessary to get into radio or pictures?" Well, brother, it sure helps.

Imagine having to compose ten minutes of music in a day, creating it, as you go along, in the orchestral coloring which expresses the picture or radio show for which you are writing, and yet allowing possible dialogue to be heard clearly. This means the ability to judge, again in weight, the density of the musical texture. Imagine having to turn out, from someone else's sketch, forty score pages a day, each page containing every woodwind, brass, percussion and string part, with a few harps and celeste thrown in, and doing this with an incomplete knowledge, due to insufficient preliminary studies! Ask a machinist to make you a threaded bolt, but give him no lathe and screw threading machine, but only a file and some hexagonal bar stock.

I tell the kids that no one really bore any permanent scars from several years of hard study at a good music school. This does not convince them. Most of them seem to wonder whether they've been wise to go to school. They feel they could have found an arranging job with some small band and picked up all the knowledge as they went along. Then, in a year or so, they'd knock at the studio gates and say: "Here we are, we're expert arrangers and orchestrators now, how about a job at $300 a week?" Poor sad sacks.

(Continued on page 143)

Conducting On Cue

By IRVIN TALBOT

THE conducting and interpreting of musical film scores is a much more exacting and difficult art than is generally understood.

It is not only necessary for the conductor to catch his cues, but also to give a musicianly reading and try to help balance the orchestra during recording; last, but not least, is the desire to please the composer who, in many instances, forgets that cues must also be caught. There are times when one cannot linger upon beautiful chords and pet modulations.

Some composers conduct their own scores. Others, either afraid that they might be carried away with the sound of their own music and disregard the picture, or might not feel at home with the baton technic required in picture conducting, prefer to concentrate on balance, cueing of scenes and freedom to offer suggestions. In this case they prefer a conductor specialist in synchronization to assume the conducting and mechanical details.

Hollywood has many very fine composers and orchestrators. I am one of the fortunate ones to have the pleasure of conducting their scores, "breaking down" pictures into musical sequences and following through with the mechanical details, I have often been asked how one approaches the matter from its inception.

The picture, after it is assembled to what is called a "cutting print", is run in advance of the regular cueing, for the general musical director and composer. This is done to give them an idea about the picture, and very often a meeting is held afterwards to discuss the approach, thematic material, etc. After the picture is ready to be turned over to the music department, it is first sent to the laboratory and a "dupe" print is made for our personal use. A regular cueing is then called, and the general musical director, composer, sound department, sound and music cutters, producers, often the director and story editor as well, run the picture and stop between each reel and discuss where music will start and stop.

In some studios the general musical director has the cues in advance and will run the picture with the composer assigned and discuss all musical matters with him.

The reels are then turned over to the chief music cutter, to "break down" each musical sequence, viz: to give us the timing *all* action, dialogue, etc., down to the one-tenth of a second. This is typed and copies are given to the composer who, if he wishes, can then check cue sheet against picture, and review scenes as many times as necessary.

Most composers compose in three or four line sketches which they turn over to their orchestrators (who in many instances also see the picture before commencing to work) with suggestions as to color, whether large or small orchestra, and where action requires the sound to be full and richly instrumented or transparent where the dialogue is consecutive. In some instances composers do all their composing in orchestral form, and sketches are made afterwards from the scores.

Most conductors rehearse from the scores and conduct the actual recordings from sketches which have all the cues and timings, thereby eliminating turning of pages, as the "mikes" are everywhere and pick up the least sound of rustling paper.

The composer creates his music according to the cue sheet stopwatch timings, so the conductor starts his stop watch on the starting cue, and conducts the music, shaping it to the action; keeping in mind the fact that he must be at such and such a bar at the prescribed timing, in order to catch entrance of characters, changes of mood or action.

The first recording is usually done on playback wax so that everyone concerned can hear the orchestral balance, then the wax is played back with the dialogue to check whether the orchestration interferes with the dialogue.

If that is O.K., the next recording will be a "take", which is recorded on film, but at the same time a wax playback is also recorded, in case of a request for a playback.

In the transformation period; that is, when studios first started recording musical accompaniments on records, a "take" lasted about ten minutes, no intercutting was possible, Now all sequences are recorded

(*Continued on page* 142)

Scissors Save the Score

By ROY WEBB

ONE might think that the problems of writing music for films would be very simple, and that any man versed in the technical knowledge of musical form would be able to fill successfully the position of film composer.

This is far from being the case. In the first place, it usually is necessary for the composer to subserve his music to the requirements of the picture and enhance its moods. In doing this many interesting incidents have taken place.

One practice is to put temporary music in the picture when it is sent for preview. This is done by selecting suitable music previously recorded and putting it roughly in the film. Then when the picture comes to its final cut the composer is called in to write the permanent score, to be recorded and mixed in with the picture.

But often the producer has grown so used to the preview music that the composer is met with such comments as "Don't like the new music nearly so well," "You haven't got the right mood!" or "I think I'll keep the old music." In such cases the composer should supervise the selecting of temporary music so that the picture is treated to his liking. Then his final job will parallel the first one and in the end everybody will be happy.

Last-minute cuts and changes are always in order, and when the problem of cutting fifteen or twenty seconds out of the middle of a recorded composition comes up, the solution is not always easy. I have seen a clever music cutter take the middle out of a long chord with a snip of the scissors and a patch of cement! It is hard to describe many similar problems which arise, but I wish to express my personal thanks to my friends the music cutters, who have done wonders in keeping my own work smooth and still musical.

An important part of a film composer's technique is in selecting the starts and stops of the various pieces of music. In order to do this well the picture should be run several times, so that the composer may become very familiar with the flow of the picture as well as the dramatic values which need to be strengthened or embellished. Many times the act of stopping the music after a terrific build-up has the tendency to point up the following scene and intensify its importance.

In addition to this, conversation must be protected. When music is played under dialogue or comment, great care must be exercised in writing music that is powerful enough to give value to the scene, yet smooth enough not to interfere with intelligibility.

One very difficult job for the average composer is the necessity of adapting himself to write in many different moods according to the requirements of the picture. Naturally, every composer has his own style, and if he writes in the style of Sibelius or Puccini it might be difficult for him to change into a Gershwin. In the initial years of scoring pictures every composer was expected to be able to write all different types of music, but slowly things are changing so he is "cast" for each picture the same as an actor. This is a great step forward.

A very fine composer (whom I will not name for obvious reasons) once wrote a score for a picture which would have been very successful if played on the concert stage, but when played with the picture it didn't seem to fit. The producer appreciated the quality of the music but saw that something drastic had to be done. With the help of a music cutter he went to work on the film. Imagine the composer's surprise at the first run of the picture when he found music written for reel two in reel seven, and the music for reel ten in reel one, as well as other revisions to place the music in more effective spots. Had the composer been a motion-picture technician as well as musician this would not have happened.

Another important thought to be retained in film composing is the suitable mixing of music and sound effects. For example, I had a whole reel in which a waterfall was seen in the background. To be effective, the music had to be treated so that the sound of the waterfall belonged to the composition. The usual water effect, harp arpeggios and woodwind figurations, was left out and very deep tones of brass and woodwinds were used instead. It was especially effective because the picture was a dramatic one and the sombre feeling was heightened. Many other scenes such as storms, battles, or street scenes, have

(Continued on page 144)

The Speeding Hour

By BERNARD KATZ

AS a youngster nothing gave me more pleasure than attending an afternoon performance in a silent movie theatre when the organ or pit orchestra was not present. As the plot unfolded I could inwardly hear a large orchestra playing music which I felt was more appropriate than the hackneyed music used during that era. Perhaps this interest has been one of the reasons why I enjoy my work as a composer-conductor despite the difficulties it presents.

Few radio listeners realize the many responsibilities imposed upon the musical director during a broadcast. His music and timing should be so perfect that it attracts no undue attention. Even musicians employed in radio have little conception as to what actually goes on behind the scenes. This is quite logical because the musician, reporting for orchestra rehearsal, finds upon his stand a legible part from the pen of a skilled copyist, carefully extracted from an orchestral score which previously has been timed to the split second.

The necessity of speed in the preparation of a radio score is a perpetual problem. I often have had to compose and orchestrate twenty-five to twenty-seven minutes of continuous underscoring within a day and a half. A film studio would have allowed at least three weeks for this amount of music. This element of speed has prevented many composers from entering radio as few nervous systems can attune themselves to composing with one eye on the clock. More discouraging is the fact that after the final dress rehearsal, retiming the script may necessitate cutting a great deal of music. I have often worked through the night composing and orchestrating a montage or background only to find at orchestra rehearsal that the entire sequence has been cut from the script. Cutting music to fit a script can create more problems than the actual labor required in composition.

Over a period of time my library has grown to the point where it embodies every type of music bridge and background necessary to cue any radio production. This accumulation of music is used only when a music bridge has been added to the script before air time or when it has been necessary to substitute a new script. The composer-conductor of today should strive for a completely new and original score for each program. However, an original score should not exclude the use of a published melody if such a composition can aid the continuity of a script.

It is important for the radio composer continually to bear in mind the necessity of writing simply and effectively at all times. This is especially necessary when one has a small orchestra. I have occasionally complicated scores by the use of too much counterpoint and too many difficult passages; this may have been interesting from the musician's viewpoint but required more rehearsal time than was at my disposal. It takes confidence to write simply and adhere to the script.

Once while scoring an important dramatic production, I realized that one of my backgrounds did not fit the script. Having at my disposal a large orchestra, I utilized too many instruments at one time, thereby cluttering up a section of underscoring which was more effective by the use of a simple melodic line played as a 'cello solo with an occasional tympani beat to denote the passing of time. On the dramatic program *This Is My Best* an unusual treatment of music was required in the production of *The Storm*. As a narrator described the movement and influence of an imaginary storm from its origin in one part of the earth to its final disappearance in a far remote section, music played a predominant part in the interpretation of changing moods and augmenting sound. For this type of broadcast an orchestra of symphonic proportions is necessary. Programs of this nature have done much to arouse interest in radio underscoring.

Authenticity in composition as to period and style necessitates many hours spent in historical and musical research. However, there are times when native music is not commonly recognized and it is preferable to "fake" a style in order to conform to the layman's conception. I was required to background a script which called for a considerable amount of Balinesian music. Upon completion of the score I had the feeling that my efforts had been in vain, therefore I engaged a small orchestra of Balinesians to replace my orchestra at the required intervals in the script. The results were far from satisfactory as it seemed that no one in the production end of the program was sufficiently versed in Balinesian music to fully appreciate or identify it in its true form. In reverting to my original score, I was amazed to find that it was exactly what the program required. I had composed according to my own conception of Balinesian music, thereby matching a mood with the everyday radio listener.

This same situation has arisen in the scoring of music based around the Elizabethan period. It was necessary to compose in a style which expressed the American listeners' conception as to how music was written and played during that era. Often it proves necessary to be authentically correct as to the use of instruments such as the bagpipes, concertina, banjo, etc. At other times it is more effective to simulate the color of these instruments by the use of odd combinations in the orchestra.

It is quite impossible to enumerate the various styles and types of bridges and montages used in radio underscoring as every script must be treated individually. I have always found it quite easy to compose music for a well written script, be it of the heavy dramatic type, or one of clever light comedy. The uninspired script, however, demands music of a neutral nature which is difficult to compose. One often hears musical scores on the air which are far superior to the quality of the script; this factor is objectionable because the score, in this case, is over-emphasizing the lack of good continuity.

Despite the fact that many radio stories based upon tension, mystery, and the supernatural require the use of ultra-modern harmony and unconventional orchestral color, I always endeavor to keep my bridges and backgrounds interesting by the use of melodies which are intended to develop musically along with the plot. Experience has proven also that the members of the orchestra are inclined to perform with more musical taste when required to play a score with refined melodies and interesting harmonic structure. Nevertheless, there are times when radio music must be treated as an adjunctive to the sound effects, such as the rumbling of the ocean, the splashing of a waterfall, the roaring of a locomotive, etc. Occasionally in modern radio production it is advantageous to replace sound effects entirely with music, thereby building up the listeners' imagination with musical sounds instead of actual ones.

Many excellent results are achieved in radio background scoring by assigning the work of composing and orchestrating to more than one individual. However, because of the great amount of time lost by conflicting ideas, I prefer doing my own composing and orchestrating.

Before attempting actual composition on a new script, I make it a practice to study every detail of the story, carefully marking places where the music must act as a background and where it is required to be out in the open, thereby acting as a bridge or interlude. My next procedure is to discuss with the author and program director all situations which will musically aid the program. Their well intended suggestions, if carefully translated into music, can save the composer endless hours of groping in the dark for ideas.

The next step, particularly in a heavy dramatic program, is to compose a theme which will musically designate the mood of the entire story. The quality of this theme can do much to enhance the general development of the plot. If the story allows, I try to introduce a portion of this theme in each bridge, giving the music an opportunity to unfold along with the plot. Secondary themes are also helpful in depicting certain moods or describing characters in the story. After these themes have been composed, I develop them into an overture, which is customarily referred to in radio as "show music". This overture is most effective when it does not exceed a playing time of eighteen seconds, and for a fast moving light comedy script, twelve seconds is sufficient. It is extremely difficult for the symphonic composer, who does not have the time element to cope with, to realize that a radio bridge which runs two to four seconds over its normal timing, can destroy the dramatic pace of a well timed radio production. This feeling for correct timing seems to be natural with most radio composers, although many errors are made before it is fully mastered.

After my overture and music bridges are completed, I endeavor to lay out plans for the composition of all music which will be used for background purposes. At this point the timing element must be carefully worked out, because one must take into consideration the approximate pace to be used by the various actors reading their lines. In this type of music I find it necessary to write flexibly, that is having an extra bar or two ready in the event that the pacing should be slower, or having in mind certain practical cuts which can be made instantly should the pace speed up, as is often the case once the program is on the air.

Upon completion of all composition, it is desirable to get together with the cast for a reading rehearsal. At this rehearsal I play all of the score on the piano, giving the producer an opportunity to time his script. This is also valuable from the composer's standpoint,

(*Continued on page* 145)

New Sounds On the Air

By MARK WARNOW

SOMEONE once said that there are only three things you can do on the radio: say words, make sounds and play music. Forgetting sounds for the moment, we can bow briefly to a few Corwins and Toscaninis, then retire sadly in the realization that radio, in presenting words and music, has been far more concerned with quantity than quality.

In a sense, this has been an inevitable development. There was, first of all, the wild mushrooming of radio, and with it an almost frenzied need to fill the air. Radio was a toy; people played with it; almost any program was a pleasant novelty.

Time brought commercialization and the subsequent rise of the advertising agencies and sponsors to positions of dominance. They are the ones who changed radio programming from an end in itself to a means, the means by which they could sell a product. This meant devising a show that would appeal to most people, thereby selling the most product.

With more and more sponsors competing for this same group of listeners, production has fallen into tried and true cliches rather than experimentation or high quality material. And those listeners of discrimination, to whom radio is no longer merely a toy but an instrument of culture, find radio listening worth little or no time.

If it is words you want, there are not enough Corwins or Shirers or Theatre Guilds. And if it is music you want, there are not enough Toscaninis or Heifetzes, Kerns or Ellingtons.

This, then, is the general situation confronting the American listener. And it is not a happy one. The Metropolitan is the only steady broadcaster of opera, and that but a couple of hours each week during the season. Of the symphonies, the NBC and New York Philharmonic are the year in and year out groups. Others such as the Boston, Cleveland and Chicago symphonies appear less consistently. Chamber music? None. Light Opera? None. Musical comedy? None. Jazz? Eddie Condon for half hour a week.

Probably the only classification in which the supply meets the demand is popular dance music, with orchestras of usually dubious merit broadcasting from hotels, dance halls, and disc-jockey turn-tables for unceasing hours, days and nights.

It is no secret that more people like popular dance music than any other kind of music. It is, actually, our present day folk music and serves as such. But the fact that more people prefer it does not mean that all people do. Nor does it mean that this group of "more people" cares only for this type of music.

The fact is that many listeners take the music they get because they can't get anything better. And many potential listeners don't even turn on their sets because they can't get what they want.

Normally this would be a problem, a problem demanding an answer. But in these highly abnormal times, an answer has already started on its way.

I'm speaking of FM (frequency modulation) broadcasting. Operating on different wave length channels, FM makes room in the air for innumerably more stations. On the economic side, it is said that the physical operation of FM stations will cost far less than regular broadcasting. And, finally, there is a fidelity of reproduction with FM that should warm the ears of music lovers who have never quite grown reconciled to static and surface noise.

It is my firm belief that the emergence on the American radio scene of hundreds, maybe thousands, of these new FM broadcasting stations will have an inestimable effect on the music situation in this country.

What I am looking forward to is, in a word, specialization. By operating more cheaply than the current type of station, FM stations will be able, or perhaps forced to aim their programs not at the large majority of potential listeners, but rather to segments of the population. In this way they will answer more specific needs and achieve a quality of presentation heretofore unrealized.

If an analogy be needed, take the magazine field. Although "Life" magazine may from time to time feature a spread on modern housing, "Architectural Forum" or "California Arts and Architecture" are among the sources to which modern housing enthusiasts will turn. The fact that the "Atlantic Month-

(*Continued on page* 129)

Mozart vs. Mayhem

By MEREDITH WILLSON

WE gotta new thing around our office
Every day we say to each other "A successful radio program must be absorbing"
and you know what we do that for?
We do that to remind ourselves that the "whodunits" no matter how bad have a suspense quality that proves to be very absorbing to the great majority of radio listeners and whether you like it or not
once you get in on the beginning of one of those things you pretty near gotta stay with it at least till you find out who done it
That's just plain ordinary human-nature curiosity
Now unless you are an all-out music lover or professional composer or something
this element which makes for big Hoopers—this quality of being absorbing to the point where you "just *gotta listen*"—is missing from the musical programs
On the face of it it's pretty ridiculous for Toscanini to have just about the lowest Hooper rating you can get when the worst two-by-four most badly transcribed murder mystery that would be refused by any self-respecting pulp magazine
can knock out a seven to twelve rating with no trouble at all and those electric-organ bridges! Bro-*ther!!*
How do you fix this?
Well
the way to start trying to begin to think of some way to fix it is for everybody in the radio business (who would like to improve the status of musical programs) to walk around muttering to each other "A successful radio program must be absorbing"
We haven't got all the answers as yet but at least the wheels are going around like for instance:
(1) The networks could see to it that their musical programs be more ingeniously built and what is equally important that
(2) the complete daily and nightly schedules of programs as they relate one to the other be plotted with some intelligence and that
(3) no expense be spared to "propagandize" such carefully thought-out presentations
Sunday I heard the New York Philharmonic play the seldom heard *Alpine Symphony* of Richard Strauss

I remembered to listen not because it had been built up for me by way of spot announcements or newspaper plugs but only because I saw it tucked away in an obscure radio column and I had not heard it since I played one of the flute parts in that same New York Philharmonic twenty years ago
You know something
the general public—"the great unwashed" as Harrison Holloway used to say—is just now—thanks to the modernism that has come and gone and thanks to the melody renaissance that has been sweeping over us—this great public is just now in the frame of mind to become completely absorbed in a work like that great *Alpine Symphony* of Mr. Strauss and some real honest provocative advertising of this event would have done a great deal towards proving that musical programs can also be *really* absorbing
On this same Sunday and following this thrilling hour of wonderful music there occurred another very fine hour presentation of George Kaufman's *George Washington Slept Here*.
This theatre of the air was on another network but what's the difference
A little *Miracle of Thirty-Fourth Street* backscratching is maybe what we need in the radio business
At any rate I can see a vast potential audience slithering up and down the dials hunting for the Sunday afternoon transcribed adventure of *Joe Jerk-Face, Boy Goon*
or *Bertha Bloodhound, Girl Revolving-Door*
while a combination of the world's most absorbing music followed by the finest possible contrast: a George Kaufman comedy
was probably averaging a two and a half or three rating
Can't you just see the ads they coulda dreamed up—the same kind that pulled the Philco program up from a desperate seven or eight to the present sixteen or more
But no
One of the world's memorable performances of a symphony the public could understand took to the air with no fanfare at all

(*Continued on page* 145)

Ethereal Substance

By JACK MEAKIN

COMPOSITION of music for radio presents basically the same exact problem as composing music for any dramatic art form. The composer who sets himselm the task of writing an opera, an operetta, a dramatic song, a descriptive tone poem, a Broadway play, a scene for a motion picture, or the background for a radio script has one primary purpose—to describe in music the mood and movement of the particular story and situation involved. Composition of radio music differs only in the particular technique of the medium itself.

In radio, orchestras generally are smaller than in in any other field of dramatic music for two reasons: (1) budget limitations of the sponsor and (2) because larger orchestras are not absolutely necessary. The tricks of reproduction wrought by electronics and radio engineers have made it possible to produce for the ear of the listener the sound of a large orchestra with a comparatively small group of musicians.

For example: a group of four violins placed strategically around a microphone can sound like a much larger group over the air. By adding, in unison with the four violins, the singing tones of a Hammond organ in the upper register, the effect is surprisingly like a large and complete violin section. Many of our leading dramatic radio productions such as *Suspense, The Whistler, Mr. District Attorney* and *Screen Guild* use orchestras of from seven to fifteen pieces.

Even the largest dramatic orchestras on radio do not equal in size those used for concert, opera or motion pictures. Thus a radio composer learns to think in miniature, so to speak. He learns to score in terms of various combinations of individual instruments rather than the large sections of the familiar symphony orchestra. He learns, too, that when a radio script calls for music back of the dialogue the music must be scored lightly and orchestrated thinly, otherwise the dialogue will not be heard.

Radio, the newest medium of entertainment, appeals to only one of our six senses, the ear. Because of this, radio has brought about the development of its own particular type of musical expression, the so-called music "bridge". In all other forms of entertainment the composer has the advantage of a scenic background to help him depict his musical mood. The audience at the opera, or at a musical play or at a movie can *see* the action as well as hear the dialogue and music. The audience can also see the setting in which the action takes place. In radio the audience can only *hear* the action. [The music (along with narration) must provide the setting in which the action takes place. Therefore, radio music must be extremely descriptive.]

Music must substitute for the curtain rising and falling at the beginning and end of every act. The musical "bridge" must take the place of a scene change on the stage or a dissolve on the movie screen. It must completely describe the mood at the end of one scene and just as completely transport the listener to the mood at the beginning of the next.

This brings us to another problem for the composer—the time element in radio. Practically all radio programs being no longer than a half-hour in length (except for a few rare cases) it is necessary for the musical bridges, curtains and transitions to say as much musically as possible in the shortest length of time. For example, in the case of scene changes as described above, the composer must first establish the closing mood of one scene and then make the complete transition to the beginning mood of the next scene all in the space of approximately ten seconds. Thus musical development for radio is entirely different than the normal thematic development as applied to other types of composition.

To sum up: the composition of music for radio differs from composition in other entertainment fields in four basic concepts: (1) radio orchestras are smaller and differ slightly in instrumentation. (2) background scores for the radio orchestra are necessarily lighter and thinner. (3) radio music must take the place of scenic backgrounds. (4) The radio composer must say musically as much as possible in the shortest possible time.

The Commercial Scarecrow

By ROBERT VAN EPS

W E WHO have chosen the creative arts for our means of sustenance by working in radio or moving pictures have learned to observe the word "commercial" as a treacherous term. And this is quite natural, since our conditioning arises from the fact that sponsor, producer, director or instrumentalist is quite in the habit of using the word indiscriminately to describe all types of music from symphony to jazz.

Consequently, many arrangers are so very obsessed with the "commercial scarecrow" that they become self-bullied into writing a poorly sorted variety of gaudy-sounding frills so that their contributions at rehearsal prove to be unworthy of any effort from the orchestra, not to mention the resultant waste of music paper. However, if they comprehend the imaginary fears of our "scarecrow", they will form the habit, as part of their work, of immediately ejecting the word "commercial" from their minds while creating, but not without the necessary consideration due for the type of show and the particular orchestra involved. When the latter procedure is practiced, the result is usually good because it is sincere., and so the producer or director will then often say: "Didn't I tell you? or, "Now that's commercial." Whereas, what they are trying to say is that it is a musicianly but *sincere* interpretation of whatever it is meant to be and nothing more nor anything less.

The term "commercial" in art is a misnomer and the word sincere could well be substituted. Is it not a strange coincidence that all of the many successful talents in music right down to our hill-billies have found their success because their sincere efforts brought about a true sympathetic appeal within their audiences? Is it not, then, this certain quality of sincerity that causes the listener to recognize and to appreciate? I think it is and I believe that a sincere musical effort crowned with the necessary amount of talent will sell itself. But one must have faith in being sincere for the audience is quick to recognize this quality and just as quick to recognize a carbon copy or fake.

The radio and motion pictures are the greatest known means of mass contact. In view of this, then we must be aware that they are capable of selling anything: good, bad or indifferent. For example, it is the opinion of some advertising firms that even though a housewife may turn on a soap opera at low volume, not to listen particularly, but more to keep her company during her chores, much of it—advertising and all—will penetrate via her subconscious mind. One would immediately deduce that they would be apt to sell more soap if their programs were entering human consumption via the conscious mind.

It should be remembered that our vast listening audiences are composed of many varying tastes. Also, let us not forget that it is simply a fact, despite the stubborn dreams of some sponsors, that we cannot capture all this vast mass of listeners with one broad sweep, more particularly in one short half hour of time. Motion pictures have a greater advantage over radio shows because the running time of a movie is long enough to display many more varieties of taste.

Audience taste, of necessity, *must* be divided into groups because the average listener is not endowed with tastes broad enough in scope to extend from the humor of Spike Jones to the serious concerts of a Philharmonic orchestra. If the die-hard sponsors would realize this, they would benefit by taking the task of deciding upon which type of audience they wish to capture and then hire persons whom by their very own natures are best fitted to do the job *sincerely* instead of expecting them to copy any number of styles at random. Of course, to be endowed with the aptitude for imitation is, indeed, a definite asset, but this should only be resorted to when the script makes it absolutely necessary. Every one of us learns much, either consciously or subconsciously, by apeing but this should be confined to private research and should not be forcibly stuffed into the public air waves or movie houses in the present massive proportions. If all the present energy used to copy this or that successful program could be diverted into an honest effort to delve into newer flavors, the musical standard would immediately rise. (This could also apply to script writers).

How much more the sponsor would gain could
(Continued on page 147)

Heard But Not Seen

By EDWARD TRUMAN

MUSIC as a fine art and as a profession has advanced by tremendous strides since its general use in broadcasting and motion pictures. These two universal mediums of distribution have spread music—and American music in particular—over the face of the globe and made it available and acceptable to millions of people.

Some may say this applies only to so-called "popular" music. Not so. Not only has public taste been lifted to a plane where it appreciates the role of the orchestrator, the scorer and the arranger of melodies in the popular field but also this advance of musical taste is carried over into a greater appreciation of the classics and the works of contemporary serious writers.

As money and what money will buy has become the American standard (even in music), satisfactory salaries for individual professional performers have become the criteria to judge whether or not it "pays" to be a skilled artist. Radio and films, more than any other parts of the music industry today, have opened new fields where superior performing skill counts in terms of the almighty dollar.

So, if only for this single reason,—good wages—excellent renditions of all types of music are the order of the day on the air and on the screen. The important thing is that a great body of excellent musical talent has been built up in the radio and picture industries. With that reservoir always available to give a superior performance, we can expect the fine art of music to emerge.

What composer, for instance, does not enjoy hearing his music played by the best musicians? What conductor can fail to appreciate the saving in rehearsal time and effort when an experienced orchestra is at his disposal? Such orchestras, serving exclusively the radio and movie industries, are permanently installed at the three program centers (Chicago, New York and Los Angeles) of the four radio networks and at the major film studios.

Frank Black, director of music for NBC, recently commented that a program he was conducting was able to originate at these centers without difference in quality of performance, but that elsewhere he required longer rehearsals, lacking an orchestra with concert experience.

Once a screen credit which read "and the MGM Symphony Orchestra" actually referred to a motley crew of pickup musicians culled from symphony, radio, concert or bar-room.

Since 1946, after negoiations with their union, film musicians were formed into permanent orchestras at principal studios and for the first time, movie credits like the one above really became true.

We have seen the background music or the "underscore" emerge from the Mickey Mouse stage into an integral part of the drama. Many moviegoers now pay admissions to hear the music alone. Even some below average films have been saved by serious music, such as *Suicide Squadron* which introduced *Warsaw Concerto*.

Max Steiner, now at Warner Brothers, is perhaps responsible for compositions becoming an integral part of movies. His *Symphonie Moderne* started a cycle that included *Humoresque, Laura, For Whom The Bell Tolls, Duel In The Sun,* and many more.

Not all the best work in music has been done by the writers for feature pictures. The brunt of the battle to get good music into movies was borne by the documentary films made by the U. S. government before World War II. *The Plow That Broke the Plains* is a good example, with *The River* a close second.

The British put their best composers to work on wartime documentaries, scores from which are being played from time to time now as concert pieces, though the films themselves were never booked here. Illustrative of this work is Wiliam Walton's *Spitfire Fugue.*

The British have displayed great originality here, a deftness for copying techniques there, until Hollywood is sorely put to it to hold its slight lead in music for the films. The exchange of writing talent which is beginning now is a healthy sign that points to more and better music in the films of both countries.

In radio we have seen amateurs banned at Interlochen and, on the other hand, complete acceptance of music by the great symphony orchestras of the na-

(*Continued on page* 144)

Every Trick Is Needed

By JOHN ROY WEBER

MUSIC arrangements specifically for radio use may be divided roughly into three major categories: (1) feature arrangements, which are musical compositions in the tradition of master works; (2) vocal accompaniments and background music designed for a specific use in contrast with the standard vocal arrangements intended to serve all purposes, as produced by song publishers since the days of vaudeville, and (3) transition and cue (background) music for dramatic shows, in contrast with the old stage or silent motion picture prepared scores.

The former consists of musical inventions and combinations of harmonic progressions, whether utilizing a motive, phrase or material complementary to a given lead theme, and is creative arranging as practiced by any composer. Any set of variations, whether by Bach, Beethoven, Brahms or a contemporary studio arranger, falls into this category. For instance, Paganini wrote a series of variations for violin on an original theme. Brahms later wrote variations for piano on the same theme, and Rachmaninoff still later used the same theme as the basis of a work for piano and orchestra. The pattern is applied to symphonic work by Dvorak in his *"New World" Symphony*, regardless of whether the themes utilized were Negro folk themes, as often has been claimed, or whether they were original Czech folk themes, as the composer stated.

This type of arranging is much used in radio work, a form that may be classified as abstract music because of its organic musical growth. It includes feature numbers such as a song wherein the subject is "exposed" as thematic material.

In a song featured by a vocalist, the arrangement becomes background and accompaniment, with intervals of abstract composition. Such an arrangement always is written as a complement to the vocal lead, with synchronizing mood, expression and points of climax. This is virtually independent from the vocal lead, which may be inaudible to the musicians when the singer is using a separate microphone. In that case, the conductor often follows the score while using earphones connected directly with the broadcast board to guide him in keeping with the singer while controlling the orchestra as to volume and balance.

Producing fine music as atmosphere and interweaving the original thematic and rhythmic material of an arrangement depends entirely upon the ingenuity and talent of the arranger. A music "setting" preparatory to the entrance of the soloist or the exposition of the lead theme often may be a work of near genius, and may give the feeling and emotion of a tone poem, continuing as a background and never overshadowing the main lead. Some very beautiful music has been produced in this manner in connection with some mediocre songs.

As a background for dramatic shows, radio music follows the pattern and cueing devices of the old silent-picture music, though modern and better written arrangements replace the stilted forms of "hurry," "mood pensive," "plaintive," "dramatic suspense," and their like.

Orchestrations for such shows require special combinations of instruments, according to the type of show, ranging from suspense effects to reference themes suggesting individual characters. For instance, suspense might be obtained through the use of muted brass, bass clarinet and horn; the character of Mortimer in the *Charlie McCarthy* show is suggested by his arrival to a clumsy lilt by a bassoon.

Concert items of the standard repertory sometimes require special arrangements to suit a specific ensemble. In this case both arranger and sound engineer endeavor to reproduce the original effect as closely as possible. Where program music has been written with an ear for microphone technique, arranger, engineer and conductor generally collaborate in placement of "mikes" for balance and volume.

Dance, jazz or popular music usually is arranged "solid", meaning that the full brass blows loudly and it is up to the sound engineer to mix or balance the result. The same term is often applied to the string section, though properly speaking, solidity can be obtained only with a sufficient number of players, rather than with a few performers playing loudly.

Technically incorrect runs or other passages can crucify that prima donna of the orchestra, the violin, or hamper performance in all instruments. The ar-

(Continued on page 147)

(Continued on page 147)

Must Music Be Edited?

By HELENA LEWYN

THOSE of us who humbly seek the faithful interpretation of what the great composers sought to present, maintain that with few exceptions what is commonly known as "editing" would better have been left undone. It actually can be deterrent to the cause of music making. The more humble we are, the less we are inclined to alter the intentions of the composer as expressed at the outset upon the printed page. And so we ask, does not the printed text express the inner meaning of the master's message sufficiently without so-called editing?

Toscanini has said "the professional faithfully follows the score, the amateur does not". He is undoubtedly a purist, in that he reads without the added "expression marks" of an editor the hidden meaning between the lines of the music staff. In like fashion we who realize that the force and beauty of interpretation can only be attained by conscientious attention to the musical content of every measure, resent revision and edition of great works which contain a thousand and one marks which the composer has intentionally omitted.

Need we be told that because the musical line ascends, we must make a cresendo or vice versa. Or that when two notes of equal value are slurred, whether the second one is higher or not, that we should play the first one (nearly always) slightly stressed? Isn't it in the music? How could one do otherwise? These are the very simplest and most obvious dynamic means of expression, yet we see music pages literally cluttered with such marks until "the forest cannot be seen because of the trees!" What an inspiration it is to find the text of, for instance, the Beethoven *Sonatas* as printed by Breitkopf and Haertel with nothing added. It is like a walk in the Spring in wide open spaces!

It is quite evident that mercenary aims are the inspiration for publishing houses to print different editions of precious and what should be priceless creations of the masters as they put *their* inspirations down in the form of notes, dots and dashes for posterity to use; these firms thereby enlarge their catalogs by engaging an editor to revise the already satisfactory text of a composer.

The works of Brahms had been published by Simrock during the composer's life and were edited by him with his usual meticulous care, according to his biographers. At the time the Brahms copyrights expired, Sauer was doing some editorial work for the firm of Peters. So Sauer was engaged immediately to edit the complete works of Brahms, even though Sauer was not known as an exponent of or an authority on Brahms, and seldom had included the master's music on his programs. Fortunately he did nothing to detract from their beauty, lending his name rather than using his pen.

It is in the realm of phrasing, dynamics and pedaling that the most flagrant misuse of the editorial function occurs. Since many composers have not indicated fingering, suggestions along those lines may be acceptable and justifiable. Music written during the early classical era by Rameau, Couperin, the Bachs, Scarlatti, Handel and others was composed for clavichord or organ. Therefore the continuation of sound as that retained by the use of our modern pedal was unthought. The first pedal was invented in 1760, ten years before Beethoven's birth, and had to be pressed by the knee. It intrigued the young Mozart, but he regarded it skeptically and warned against its use! Yet we find "edited" works by these same masters indicating overuse of the pedal, thereby definitely changing the character of the compositions.

The first real pianoforte music was published in London in 1773; three *Sonatas* by Muzio Clementi, Opus 2, written especially for the technical and instrumental treatment to which the newly introduced pianoforte was responsive. And it was only in 1795 that the piano replaced the clavichord or harpsichord previously used by composers who were most times performers of their own works. During the Nineteenth Century development of the modern pianoforte made great progress and the pedal of today was in existence during the third era of Beethoven's life; consequently during the lives of Schubert, Schumann, Chopin, Brahms and Liszt.

The modern piano is stronger built and has much more sonority, permitting more pedal to be used. It could be argued that because the sound of the earlier instruments was thinner composers would have indicated more pedal had they known the capabilities of today's instrument. That is perhaps the reason the "editor" indicates much pedal. But overuse is not the answer, for pedaling can change the phrase and alter the dynamics as much as any other factor, proving irksome to the serious performer or student.

Music has a grammar; clauses, phrases, sentences and paragraphs. Its punctuation includes periods, commas, as well as exclamation points, as purposeful as in any spoken language. The observance of phrasing is as important as taking a breath in speaking or singing. Phrases of great length would be awkward even though the hands do not have to breathe. A phrase is usually of the duration of one breath, yet editors offend in that particular realm, altering the musical thought by too long or too short cutting of the phrase line already indicated by the master.

We know that Bach, Haydn, Beethoven, Mozart, Schubert, Schumann, Mendelssohn, Brahms and Liszt meticulously examined their proofs. In the case of Bach there is a divergence of opinion as to what is absolutely authoritative. It was because every time he rewrote any work, he tried to do it even better than the last time and since few of his works were printed during his lifetime, alterations were made on the manuscripts by his pupils and sons as well as by himself. He lived during an era of improvisation and most of his works were written for immediate use, or not written down at all. Incidentally it is interesting to note that at the end of a great number of his works he wrote, *Soli Deo Gloria, (To God alone the Glory)*!

The Bach Gesellschaft now has printed the Master's works in their most authoritative autograph. Bach thought in terms of legato and seldom wrote a staccato mark. He wrote his two and three part *Inventions* with the particular purpose of developing a cantilene style of playing and an independence of the fingers of each hand, playing two and three voices against each other. Yet we find countless editions of Bach with staccato marks in profusion!

Unfortunately it cannot be said that Chopin examined the printer's proofs with the greatest care. We have had to depend on pupils and friends who had in their possession the master's works at the time of his death for authenticity as to details. Nevertheless we have enough material to judge what may have

been intended and what not, and to resent many of the editions that have been advanced. Because there is little authority, editors all the more should stop trying to further their versions of Chopin's works. We prefer to do the reading between the lines ourselves without their assistance!

The ideal reprint of a work would be in giving the original work with all comments either in the form of foot-notes or in a color such as red, thereby eliminating confusion with the original text. At least the publishers should state at the beginning of each work that all inking by the editor will be in brackets.

The works of Debussy, Ravel and contemporaries in most instances have been protected by copyright laws to date. In all probability the works of a composer printed during his lifetime will be authentic.

The full orchestra score used by the Conductor is the authentic reference for the solo part of a concerto whether for piano, voice or other instrument.

It must not be assumed that because a work is printed in a foreign country that it is authentic, nor that an edition published in this country lacks authenticity. The onus or credit, as the case may be, rests with the individual editor.

To cite specific instances, certain editions by Hughes and Joseffy cannot be recommended because of the many alterations in phrasing, dynamics and pedaling. Epstein's edition of the Mozart *Sonatas* are full of dynamics contrary to the composer's custom, and bristle with sforzandi, with staccati indicated where Mozart actually wrote slurs. Similarly, changes in phrasing, notation and tempi can be observed in the same *Sonatas* edited by Klee, Koehler and Ruthardt, sundry editions of Scarlatti *Sonatas*, Bach's *Well Tempered Clavichord* and other standard works.

Recently G. Schirmer has isused the *Goldberg Variations* by Bach in their original form with the annotations of the editor on another staff, a highly commendable move in the right direction and something for which the music world should be grateful. The firm also has published five Mozart *Concerti* in an authentic edition. Kalmus has published some Bach works well edited (if a few extraneous staccato marks are disregarded) by Bischoff, and authentic editions of Beethoven's *Sonatas* and *Concerti*, Mozart's *Sonatas*, Chopin and other works. The International Edition deserves mention as well.

In the long run, it is certain that the good editions, which conform best to the composer's intentions, will triumph through recommendation and use by careful teachers. May there soon be more of them!

Repetition Spells Success

By DOROTHY ZIMMERMAN

ANY well-learned performance may be called a habit. Since we learn an act or form a habit by doing the act over and over again, repetition is a most necessary procedure when learning or mastering a skill.

Learning amounts to a change or modification of behavior through modified structure, especially brain structure. Each muscle has its motor nerves coming out of the brain or spinal cord; the motor nerves carry stimuli out from the center whereas the sensory nerves conduct or carry stimuli into the center. Through repetition and learning "patterns" are formed, so that the same groups of neurones are used time after time, whenever the same familiar skilled act is performed. It is well known that the end-brushes and dendrites in a much used synapse grow and make better connections after exercise or atrophy through disuse. Therefore repetition and review are always expedient when learning or mastering a skill.

Piano instruction is no exception. Continual repetition is an absolute necessity. This creates no problem today—a day of attractive material attractively presented. It is not difficult to find teaching material which is educational yet interesting and recreational. Nevertheless many teachers do not make use of repetition, which is a necessary tool when building a strong musical foundation.

When teaching beginners, some instructors find it satisfactory to use one of the many modern day teaching courses. Most of the courses familiar to all consists of three, four or five books. These books are carefully and progressively graded, and the scope of material is most comprehensive. Nevertheless, I find them inadequate, for they do not make allowances for repetition. Any one course is narrow and confining; however, any one may be highly satisfactory when used, simultaneously, with four, five or six of the others.

To be more explicit: in books for beginners, each new item or problem has a page all by itself. At the most, two pages are devoted to the study of each new note or item. Do two pages allow for repetition? Do the opportunities for repetition, which they

offer, help pupils to work independently of their teachers and parents? Do they stress self-activity? No. Yet a child learns by doing, not by telling.

It is true that a pupil learns by observation or by demonstration. Still, the learning process does not stop there. He also learns through insight. The latter way is just as necessary and important as the former. The ideal way is a grand mixture of the two. In other words, use a page or two from one book for demonstration purposes. Then be sure that the pupil has four or five additional books where the same item or problem is presented in a similar way for his home practice. These extra books make allowances, not only for repetition without monotony, but also for learning through self-activity and insight. Repetition and new material give fresh insight into the problem.

In addition, the repetition afforded by these extra books increases the pupil's interest and confidence. Each book has a different appearance in size and color, in light, dark, large or small print, in illustrations and in stories. With the teacher's help the pupil is able to master the problems in one book. Whereupon he is assigned exercises in the other books involving the same problem in changed surroundings. If he understood the explanation in the first book, he is likely to carry over this knowledge to the second, third and fourth book. All of this adds up to increased self confidence and independent study work.

This repetition makes it possible for the beginner to have longer practice periods. In this way he forms practice habits which he can use to advantage in later years. (Many advanced pupils forget that it is necessary, time and time again, to repeat over and over, the difficult passages in a long composition. They believe that they are practicing when they play a piece from beginning to end.) With beginners, many additional books simplify this problem of adequate practice time.

Repetition produces good sight readers. It helps pupils to do two or more things at once, all of them being part of one performance, which is called over-

(*Continued on page* 139)

All Means To an End

By C. PURVES-SMITH

SO MANY contradictory books upon the subject of pianoforte technic have been published that the reader may well ask "What is a truly rational approach to the subject?" Even today, at least one school, headed by a world-famous pianist, advocates what appears to be a rigid position of the hands, metacarpals depressed, with lifting of the fingers to achieve a hammer-like action. At the opposite extreme are many weight enthusiasts, some of whom go so far as to suggest that there may be no conscious finger articulation, but that all playing should consist in transferance of arm weight, the digits merely acting as a series of supports.

Among these varied opinions there are, happily, some which recognize the important fact that all of these so-called "schools" have trained their share of acceptable pianists and that, though some of these have not scaled the topmost peak in execution, their circumscribed approach is effective if applied only to suitable literature.

In setting out to build a pianoforte technic, it is evident that neither the teacher nor the student can afford to confine his aims to a pedantic adherence to any dogma. Instead, he should determine to master every technical device employed by the greatest pianists so as to be ready to employ that most practical for every passage.

When we examine the equipment of a Rachmaninoff or a Horowitz, we generally find it impossible to catalogue them under such headings as "weight school" or "finger school". Technic, with these artists, is all-inclusive, being applied as dictated by the aesthetic requirements of the composition. Withall, a free and relaxed muscular basis is maintained throughout, which enables the maximum of attention to be directed toward interpretation and which conserves energy for those occasions when rigidity may be required to produce special effects.

When asked about hand position, Sergei Rachmaninoff repeatedly said that the correct fundamental position found the fingers naturally curved as when the hand hangs loosely at the side. Since this is the position in which the muscles are relaxed, it is that from which special hand-shapes may be most readilly assumed.

It is universally accepted that posture must be erect and that distance from the keyboard must be such that the arms are not hampered in crossing in front of the body. On the question of height, there is some divergence, but it seems obvious that the bench should, at first, be so high that the maximum of tone will result from the minimum of effort. Under the elementary laws of mechanics, this is when the elbow is level with the keyboard, as the upper arm hangs loose. Variation from this normal bench height may later be considerable, but should depend upon the personal experience of the pianist rather than upon arbitrary adherence to any particular preference on the part of the teacher.

Finding that they are able, thereby, to secure more musical and facile results from the very beginning, many expert teachers advocate weight playing exclusively for the commencement stages. The generally superior quality of the playing of early students from these studios indicates that this is a wise choice. The strongest case for such a commencement is that the student forms the habit of resting, where possible, during performance and will later fall back upon weight technics whenever these provide the required musical results. There is the further consideration that a well-mastered weight technic, including the ability to increase from forearm to full-arm weight, becomes the most satisfactory basis for full-toned legato passage playing as well as for the playing of slow chord groups. Properly controlled weight must be coordinated with absolute lateral and rotary freedom, so that the arm mass may be centered above the playing finger. The student must transfer weight not only through finger articulation but also through forearm rotation, and must learn to adjust the arm and hand to secure the best position for playing black or white keys. On occasion, the wrist must be able to assume a fairly high position in order to establish a direct line of action between the arm and the fingertip.

The teacher who first concerns himself with the development of a weight technic is on the safe road. He is building a good foundation upon which more complex technics may later grow without danger that

(Continued on page 127)

The Initial Adventure

By LILLIAN STEUBER

THE performer, as a communicator of musical ideas between composer and listener, has the responsibility of making those ideas clear and understandable. Above all, he must project to the hearer the spirit and emotion animating the music. This obviously demands sensitivity, perception and imagination which will establish the difference between a literal reading and one which, penetrating into the essence of a work, brings forth a vital musical experience.

In either case certain basic study is requisite and the initial approach to a new work is of the utmost importance, particularly when it is to become a permanent part of one's repertory. Having a vast musical world to explore, it is necessary that time spent in learning new works be well utilized by close observation and a sound plan for study.

The form of the work and its harmonic structure can be studied advantageously away from the instrument and any rhythmic problems can be solved prior to the first reading at the keyboard. It is of great value to "hear" the work mentally before becoming concerned with the actual playing.

When the first reading takes place it is imperative that many things be observed simultaneously. Having been steeped already in the key, the harmonic plan, being aware of chromaticism or modulations, it is assumed that flaws in the reading of notes would occur infrequently. Incorrect notes, however, are not always easily discerned unless the reading is coupled with particularly keen listening in order to be sure that the notes seen on the printed page are actually being reproduced.

More frequent oversights appear to be in the exact duration of notes and rests. This has a vital bearing upon the musical structure since the loss of sustained inner or bass notes will create a thin, inadequate, musically unintelligible sound. Doubtful note values will create a rhythmically unstable effect and the awareness of these values is insufficient without the actual forming of muscular habits—the holding and releasing of notes. This must be done in the beginning when the new set of mental, aural and muscular habits connected with that particular work begin to be formed. At that time the fingering suited to the phrasing as well as the consciousness of dynamic and touch indications will need to be established.

The closest observation and concentration are essential. Since a new groove, so to speak, is being made in the mind, a relatively slow tempo would seem to be inevitable. It is my conviction that the elements of the work should be integrated from the start, not gradually superimposed, and this crystal-clear impression has much to do with security in memorizing.

When the fingers are capable of producing the desired touch and variety of tone, pianists have the good fortune to have at their disposal an agent for bringing to the work greater warmth, subtle coloring and new tonal beauties. This is, of course, the pedal, which can enrich or mar the performance with equal ease. Its misuse makes it evident that inexperienced or uncritical performers seldom utilize the precious opportunity of listening to and evaluating their own playing. The mechanism of playing would appear to have the curious effect of closing their ears.

One of the great needs is for instuction in practicing. Many earnest and ambitious students waste an incredible amount of time because their objectives are not clear or because they have not developed resourcefulness in handling the various problems. To my mind, the function of a teacher is to bring to the student an awareness of how to cope with these needs, to explore with him the works of significant composers and to build self-reliance.

Obedience is not the goal, rather must the student realize which are the vital things to be sought in the work and how their communication is to be achieved. It is essential that the student be well guided in the choice of editions, whenever possible using the Urtext and seeking, through his own study, direct contact with the composer. Any drastic departure from the text or distortion of the evident musical ideas would fall into the category of eccentricity which has little in common with the distinction and nobility of enduring music.

The need is great for gaining a comprehensive view of musical literature. Pianists, having a wide field from which to choose, are in danger of overlooking

(Continued on page 129)

The Eternal Foundation

By TEALA BELLINI

IT is rather an amazing fact that Johann Sebastian Bach, who laid the foundation of our modern concept of music, still remains the necessary basis for study in the education of every musical aspirant.

Bach utilized and pointed out virtually every phase of music in use today, including syncopation, dissonance and the most advanced treatment of harmony and counterpoint. Proper presentation of his music taxes the most advanced technic, demanding the utmost from the performer as firmly as the most formidable works of Schoenberg, Prokofiev or Szymanowski.

Every instructor of piano will concede the necessity of teaching Bach to each and every pupil, and it may be assumed that virtually every teacher does so. But the all-important manner in which they approach this teaching is one that is too little discussed.

Certainly Bach never should be taught as an exercise, which is the way too many teach it. Granted that a properly assigned Bach selection may achieve the same purpose as an exercise on certain occasions, great care must be taken to avoid such a connotation in the mind of the pupil.

Nearly every pupil regards exercises as merely so much dry, uninspired work, and if Bach is identified in such a manner, the pupil eventually will have only that much more of a handicap to overcome.

First of all, the teacher himself should love Bach. All well grounded, progressive teachers do so as a matter of course, yet many of them are inclined to take Bach for granted, and to assume that the student somehow will appreciate the Bachian values at first sight. Others, doubtless including those whose appreciation of Bach had been stultified in their own student days, do not realize what they themselves are missing, and consequently offer little or nothing to the pupil in this important phase of education, whatever their qualifications in other directions.

Such teachers owe it to themselves to take a refresher course, or to delve deeply into the subject. They will find it of material advantage, not only to themselves but to their students as well.

There is a regrettable tendency today to regard Bach in the same category as Cicero and Caesar, to feel that the language in which he has expressed himself is a "dead" language, merely because it is old. Yet the language of Bach has no parallel with Latin, since it remains today as fresh, vital and comprehensible as the day it was written.

Personally, I never have had a student who did not develop a love for Bach, a fact that can be attributed largely to my own affectionate care in presenting the music to the pupil, as well as the pupil to the music.

First of all, the student should be made to feel that he has attained a real milestone in his progress by being allowed the privilege of studying Bach. It should be an event in the student's lifetime, a much desired, greatly desirable and therefore earnestly sought-after goal.

The student must appreciate what he is doing at all times. He must comprehend construction, voice leading patterns, and the ascent and descent of scale line. He must grasp the fact that he is working upon a perfect model which, sooner or later, he will recreate for others in as perfect a manner as he is capable.

Many instructors ignore the obvious fact that Bach must be played with an entirely different touch than the music of any other composer. Its delivery must be so in order to attain the crystal purity of tone that is a requisite of its interpretation.

Pedals should be used sparingly and often not at all, except in the case of chorales or organ works transcribed or arranged for piano, which require pedaling to carry organ points and special effects. For the pedals of our modern instruments did not exist in Bach's day.

Furthermore, Bach should be practiced with varied rhythms (personally I use eight different ones) to achieve the utmost in flexibility. It should be practiced too, with what I term a "brushing staccato" to bring forth absolute equality of tone.

For Bach, like Shakespeare, never will die. He stands, a towering figure, among the immortals. And we who practice the art of music are the exponents of his living, vital force.

Background To Foreground

By TILLI DIETERLE

THE role of the accompanist is perhaps as demanding, if not more so, as that of the soloist, while burdened with the additional challenge of following the unpredictable tempo changes and subtle tone-color shadings characteristic of every solo artist.

In the field of accompanying, there are two classifications of actual working assignments:

First, there is the role of staff accompanist. A pianist in this position is automatically expected to know every composition ever published, and must be able to transpose it into a dozen different keys. He must also sight-read original manuscripts and special arrangements to the satisfaction of the performer, as well as to the hearers.

Second, there is the less strenuous position of a regularly hired accompanist. In this situation, rehearsals are scheduled at given intervals, enabling both soloist and accompanist to work out the finer details that otherwise are neglected due to the lack of time.

Needless to say, the staff musician is under a greater nervous strain, but he in turn also shares in an endless number of comical situations. The radio networks, film studios, and theatrical companies are always in need of a good-natured, versatile pianist who can toss off anything from Verdi's operas to *Pistol Packin' Mamma*.

In my own experiences in accompanying, I have found manuscripts worn from years of use, showing evidences of spilled liquids in many spots, also musical scores cursed with the invariable missing pages. When sections of a composition or an arrangement are gone, the remarks are usually:

"Fake it—there's nothing to it—just sixteen measures of straight rhythm in C, then a fast arpeggio into E flat,—and—be sure to follow me when I get to the new theme—you see, I do it a little differently from other people's versions—" and so on.

It's these little incidents that place a staff job in the ulcer-provoking category.

One often hears of the staff pianist put in the position of an arranger. When a new melody is being written, often the song writer wants a quick sketch of his little "masterpiece" worked out as a band number. So our, poor overworked, imposed-upon pianist sits down and writes parts for trumpet, trombone, tenor and alto sax, clarinet, piano, guitar, bass, drums, and possibly a group of fiddle parts for good measure. All he can do is philosophize and call it part of a day's work.

Another angle to the business of accompanying is the amount of responsibility assumed, particularly when playing through auditions. The performer making the audition has perhaps a film contract or a Broadway part at stake. A sincere musician can't help but feel the "do-or-die" pressure which exists under these circumstances. The would-be star is having his big chance; a mistake in the accompaniment might completely spoil his possibilities. Therefore, each audition must be regarded as a separate assignment in itself, requiring special attention for various details. In an afternoon of general auditions, as many as twenty-five to thirty people may be heard, each taking about ten minutes of actual playing time. In 1946, eleven hundred people were heard just in regular weekly auditions held at the West Coast office of Rogers and Hammerstein the Second, Broadway show producers.

As for the regularly contracted accompanist, the duties and problems are somewhat different. Here, a perfect unity of artistic balance may be achieved through the painstaking efforts put forth by both soloist and accompanist, on a daily or semi-weekly rehearsal schedule. As any concert artist knows, hours, weeks and months of hard concentrated practice must take place before one dares to step out before a critical audience, not mentioning critical reviewers.

The accompanist must be the perfect assistant, musically, to the artist. He must not detract from the soloist by flaunting audience-attracting mannerisms, or, figuratively speaking, "upstaging" the other party. There is also the matter of "covering up" in case of an error, such as a forgotten passage. This may happen even to a veteran of hundreds of concerts; the accompanist must be prepared for an accident of this nature throughout the entire presentation.

(Continued on page 144)

Let Them Shine

By CONSTANCE JEANETTE SHIRLEY

COMPETITION is so keen today that our younger aspirants to the concert field must have a prodigious piano technic. They must be able to play with the prestissimos and fortissimos of a Horowitz before the public will clamor to hear them and a concert career is assured.

Exciting technical display will always call forth bravos; it stirs the audience. But we forget that the speed and strength which the exceptional pianist possesses are the very things that enable him to create an artistic performance providing he does not sacrifice poetry, beauty of interpretation, clarity, and feeling for artistic dramatic effects. Let the public clamor for technical fireworks: the sharper the pencil, the finer the line; the keener the tool, the more beauty achieved.

Too often, however, the striving for power and speed results in a harsh tone quality and a loss of clarity; the former being due primarily to the fact that teachers and pianists are so concerned with the display of power in the attack that the release is completely ignored. Yet the release is of equal importance.

In fact, the work "attack" with its implications is perhaps the root of the trouble. Approach conveys a truer meaning and eliminates the thought of wild grabbing and hard, uncontrolled hitting. Unfortunately we have seen and heard plenty of both even from so-called artists.

Speed without clarity and beauty of tone is a total loss. Yet to sacrifice the romantic beauty, grace, and buoyancy of a Chopin *Waltz*, for instance, for a faulty display of speed would seem to be the aim of many radio and concert performers.

Consider for a moment the remunerative struggle. The limited outlet for performers in the pianistic field precludes the assurance of a livelihood. Even outstanding pianists must resort to teaching despite having spent considerable money and many years in study.

There is a place for but one or two pianists in any small orchestra group throughout the country. Compare this with the openings for string players and singers in radio, motion pictures, orchestras, choirs, and light or grand opera.

(*Continued on page* 147)

Pianists In Retrospect

By SYLVAN BREYN

"Music, when soft voices die,
Vibrates in the memory."
. . . Shelley

WHENEVER I think of luminaries in the world of pianistic art, there come to mind memories of those great men, Busoni, Godowsky and DePachmann. They possessed the power of penetrating to the depth of the soul and conveying the noblest ideas of beauty. They displayed more than the mere mechanical phase of piano playing, imparting the perfection of their art by revelation of beauty in the re-creation of the works they performed.

Each possessed the greatest individuality and distinctive conception. Their playing was based on complete knowledge of aesthetic values, aided by interest and study of musical history, philosophy, poetry and literature. They did not neglect particular traits; they did not generalize; they did not conglomerate the composers into a mass. They produced natural distinction between each master's works. They were able to distinguish between simplicity and magnificence, between melancholy and mirth, thereby rendering to art the emotions of the beautiful and sublime.

My first experience in hearing Ferruccio Busoni was a memorable one. As a mere youngster, I followed his career by avidly reading all the reports and notices of his playing which appeared in musical magazines. I had dreamed of the day when I would hear this pianistic giant.

His stage entrance remains indelible in my memory. Here was a large-looming musical personality, a magnificent figure, who seemed to fill the atmosphere by his presence. From the moment he began to play, I was carried away by his magic spell. He seemed to develop Olympian proportions with the performance of each work and when at last he arrived at a Liszt group, his playing was monumental. There was none of the flashy vulgarity that many pianists attach to the works of Liszt and which a large share of the public delights in expecting. His Liszt emerged as music of striking sonority and complex colorings, unequalled in the annals of piano playing. It was not Busoni the pianist, displaying his phenomenal technique, but Busoni the composer,

(*Continued on page* 146)

That Terrible Child

By ARIEL RUBSTEIN

A YOUNG PIANIST embarking on a pianistic career devotes a great deal of time to developing its technic, studying a repertory, and trying to perfect his playing so he will have a definite and solid background before he is ready to appear before an audience, and earn a place for himself on the concert stage. In practicing Bach and Czerny, in working on scales and arpeggios, in memorizing the pieces, he is so absorbed with so many immediate factors of the purely mechanical hurdles, that one primary element so necessary for a good artist, has been completely overlooked and forgotten. This element is the knowledge and analysis of the instrument itself.

A good general, before planning a campaign in battle, makes a searching study of the strong and weak points of his adversary. After thoroughly determining what they are, he prepares his campaign accordingly. An instrument to a young pianist is also an unknown enemy to be conquered, muzzled and subdued to the point of slavery, where it will obey its new master unquestionably without hesitation at the slightest command of the master's fingertips.

Among all the musical instruments, a piano is in quality of tone, in warmth, expression, the most negative of instruments. Where a singer or a brass player can produce a uniform tone for the length of his breathing ability, where a violinist or any other string player can draw a tone for the length of his bow, a pianist can only strike a key and helplessly see the tone disappear. On all other instruments where tone is produced that tone can be increased from pianissimo to fortissimo. If a pianist will employ the sustaining pedal he will get the impression that his tone is somehow lengthened, but he will lose the purity of the original tone because the vibration of undampened strings will add the sonority of the whole keyboard.

On the other side of the ledger, no other concert instrument has the range of the piano. In the lower register it can play notes lower than contra-bassoon and in the upper register it will play above the piccolo and flageoleted violin. The ability of the pianist to strike at the same time as many notes as his fingers are capable of reaching, has enabled composers to

(Continued on page 149)

The Printed Page Lives

By MAY MacDONALD HOPE CORYELL

THE opinion has been expressed by some critics that the piano is solely an instrument of percussion and brilliant technic, and not capable of expressing the personality of the artist. This opinion is erroneous. The piano of today is a great and wonderful instrument, capable of expressing various moods and emotions, one which enables the artist not only to produce beautiful tonal color and wonderful orchestral effects, but also to express his own personality and interpretations.

A great deal of discussion and various means and methods have been advanced to break down the percussive idea and prove that a singing tone can be produced on the piano. Piano technic should mean not only brilliant mechanical perfection and speed, but also tone and interpretation.

Looking back over a period of time, my thoughts and gratitude return to Teresa Carreno, a protegee of Anton Rubinstein. I had the rare privilege of studying a number of years with her. Time has proved her ideas of tone and relaxation to have been far in advance of her period. The demands Carreno made of her pupils are the very qualities to which pianists of today aspire in order to acquire perfection.

I always have been taught that a simple and natural approach to the piano is best—as free from mannerisms and unnecessary movements of the hands, arms, head or body as possible.

Some years ago, weight and pressure in the touch were still spoken of by many pianists as eccentric and not quite understandable. The highly arched hand, with fingers lifted, high and rigid arm, was still considered the only method of playing. Carreno's simple instructions that the hands should be rounded and the fingers rest lightly but firmly on the keys were almost revolutionary, particularly when the added instruction, "with controlled relaxation," was given.

Mr. Charles E. Cook has remarked in his book *Playing the Piano for Pleasure* that the two great artists of the piano who attained the highest degree of relaxation in their playing were Teresa Carreno and Leopold Godowsky. I heartily agree with him. Dur-

(Continued on page 148)

Music Also Serves

By CLAUDE A. WARD

WITH few exceptions, most services of worship include music in some form. Some very conservative groups continue to ban the use of any instrument, such as the pipe organ or the piano, contending these are "secular" and therefore inappropriate in the house of God. However, most religious groups have accepted music as fulfilling a definite place. In the liturgical churches, the scripture readings, prayers, responses, and other portions often are chanted by clergy and choir. With this acceptance man unites the spirit of religious fervor with the emotional expression of an aesthetic art. At this point his God becomes very real to him as he utilizes the blending of tones and overtones with inspired text to convey more successfully to the Almighty the thoughts and desires of his own heart.

Probably the most important function of sacred music in the service of worship is inspiration. As the worshipper enters the church at the stated time for service, he symbolically approaches the throne of his God for one or all of three reasons, adoration, praise, petition. That he may adequately prepare himself for this experience almost every church has secured a pipe organ, which blends its varied qualities into the interpretation of great compositions in the *Prelude*. The more faithful and devout respect its intent by utilizing this period in preparation for the portions of the service which will follow.

Whatever may be the form of the opening of the service, after the entrance of the choir and the clergy, there will come the singing of a hymn by the congregation and choir. Here is one of the few opportunities for the individual to participate in the expression of adoration, praise and petition. It is also one of the points at which many of our churches utterly fail. This because their musical program has never included instruction in the field of religious education which would prepare young people for active participation in the "adult" services of worship. So-called "Sunday School Hymnals", "Songs for Little Children", and other materials of like nature have left boys and girls thoroughly unfamiliar with the immortal hymns included in the average church hymnal. Hence, much of our congregational singing has deteriorated to something

resembling a race between the choir and congregation to determine which will reach the "Amen" first.

A positive note should be sounded, however, to commend the several movements in America which are making valiant attempts to correct this error. Their yeoman efforts and their courage and conviction will eventually bear fruits in great congregations of singing worshippers. Commendation should also be expressed to the publishers of hymnals for the all too long delayed practice of placing the words of the stanzas between the lines of music, rather than at various other places on the page. Finally, congregational hymn singing as a great religious opportunity must be more seriously approached by the church leaders, for only through inspired congregational singing will religion become something which is vital to each individual who worships in the house of God.

At some point in the service of worship there will be a musical presentation by a specialized group—choir or quartet. Under no circumstances should such a selection of sacred music be regarded as entertainment. Rather, there should exist a definite element of inspiration pointing, if possible, to the context of the sermon which probably will follow. Whether or not the latter is possible, this "anthem" should, through a text of inspirational message, and music of worthy liturgical form, bring the worshipper another step closer to the throne of God and the spiritual sustenance which he will receive.

This places upon the person or persons responsible for selecting the anthems a very grave responsibility. Personal likes and dislikes must of necessity be subservient to the final intent of the service and the place which this particular anthem will take in that service of worship. Also every choir or quartet should fully realize a definite responsibility to the individual in the pew, conducting themselves with the same dignity and reverence as befits the members of the clergy.

Other elements such as solos, responses, calls to worship, or choral benedictions, will vary with the many types of service which are used. In the solo, the term "sacred music' is employed as loosely as

(*Continued on page* 149)

An Organist Looks Over His Shoulder

By CLARENCE MADER

IN this day of superlatives it is interesting for the organist to reflect that he plays upon the most complex musical instrument the world has ever known. Not only is it the largest, most expensive, mechanically the most complicated and tonally the most diverse, but also the most imaginative and most baffling. How to construct an organ, compose for it, and perform upon it, are questions with so many answers that musicians in general stay away in droves and cloak themselves in apathy and distrust. Fortunately recent trends in organ design and organ playing are bringing to a focus the critical appraisal of discriminating musicians, and are inspiring some of our best composers to write for the organ.

The organ is the only musical instrument that never will know completion. It is the least standardized, and has the greatest flexibility of design. Its size is regulated by purse and purpose; its quality by tonal engineer and craftsman. Tailor-made from the ground up, every organ, honestly built, is an artistic creation which has no counterpart anywhere. While the piano and violin have remained practically unchanged for years, the organ has ever been in a state of flux. It follows current musical practices, and in the past thirty years has obliged by dipping to the all-time low of the dreadful cinema organ, and rising again to the present clarified classic ensemble which gives bold outline to the music of a Hindemith or Piston. The story of the steps leading to the development of the modern organ is one of the most fascinating in the musicologist's notebook.

Even if a complete account of the earliest organ may never be available, enough light came in 1885 when a clay model of the *hydraulus* was found at Carthage, that we have a rather unbroken record from 300 B.C. We know that the organ existed in several forms in the pre-Christian era, and that it was of Oriental extraction. We know that in the first century there was an organ with ten rows of pipes called a *Magrephah* which was used in the elaborate Temple services at Jerusalem. But our most positive knowledge came from that little clay model made in the second century.

It showed the *hydraulus* to be an instrument standing about 10 feet high and 4½ feet wide, containing 57 pipes, arranged three to each of its 19 "keys". Air pressure was provided by the action of side pumps through a valve to the wind chest, and so into a compressor standing in water held in a central container. The scale included a number of chromatic notes, a feature later lost for many centuries. This organ had already been in active use for about four centuries when the model was made, as records credit the invention to an Egyptian named Ctesibius (300 B.C.).

There are many references to organs in early writings but accompanying drawings never have been found. However, an obelisk erected in Constantinople by Theodosius in 390 shows an organ of 8 pipes, and Claudian, the poet, in the same year mentions an organ of "brazen tubes".

We are in the habit of thinking of the organ as a symbol of religious music but there is no record of its having been used in Christian Churches until the first half of the fifth century. Actually the early Christians would have none of it as the *hydraulus* was strictly a secular instrument, used for court ceremonies and the gladiatorial arena. Not until 450 was the organ reported as the hand-maid to religion. The Spanish city of Grado, at that time, had a church organ about 2 feet long, 6 inches broad, and furnished with 15 playing slides and 30 pipes.

By the year 700, England had acquired a taste for organs and her artificers were already ornamenting the front pipes with gilding. In 757, Pepin, the father of Charlemagne, requested the emperor of Byzantium to send an organ to France. The gift was not long in arriving and proved to be a "wind organ with pipes of lead". Germany's first organ, patterned after the Byzantine model in France, came in 812. The year 980 saw the completion of an organ at Winchester with more than 400 pipes, the giant among organs up to that time.

Information given by Theophilus proves that in the eleventh century something was known of "voicing", the art by which the quality of pipe tone could be regulated. But the chief problem of the organ builders was still the matter of a steady wind supply and a system of controls for admitting the wind into the pipes.

Bellows, singly, in pairs, or multiple pairs were pumped by hand, or by the weight of a man standing with his feet on two bellows, raising the one as he lowered the other. At the time of the Winchester organ the method of controlling the wind supply to the pipes was by a slide, which alternately covered or exposed the underside of the holes leading into the pipes. That method was a great advance over the earlier one where, in order to have a single pipe sound, it was necessary to cover the other pipes with the hands.

The Cathedral of Magdeburg claims the distinction of having the first keyboard. It came in the days when Guido's system of notation was still new. There were 16 notes, but what they were is not known. (It should be remembered that most organs up to this time were diatonic instruments with a possible B flat key added, and that the pitch was predominately treble. Not until the fourteenth century were the four additional chromatic notes added).

An organ erected in Halberstadt Cathedral in 1361 seems to be the first with more than one keyboard. The keys of this instrument were only 4 inches from center to center and had a fall of 1¼ inches. Such refinement must have been greeted with enthusiasm by organists everywhere as earlier keyboards sometimes had a keyfall of a foot! This century also saw the common acceptance of two small organs called the Positive and Portative. The former eventually became attached to and an important division of the main organ. The latter was small enough to be carried about in processions and taken to merry outings in the country.

At the beginning of the fifteenth century the great church organ had become the most important instrument for the performance of polyphonic music, and most notable churches in Europe had one and often two. Buying an organ in those days required a requisition for materials and labor something like the following which was found among the records of Ely Cathedral:

    20 stones of lead
    4 white horses' hides for 4 pairs of bellows
    Ashen hoops for the bellows
    10 pairs of hinges
    The carpenter, 8 days making the bellows
    12 springs
    1 pound of glue
    1 pound of tin
    6 calf skins
    12 sheep skins
    2 pounds of quicksilver
    Wire, nails, cloth, hoops and staples
    Fetching the organ-builder, and his board, 12 weeks

It was in this century that one of the glories of the organ was developed—namely, the pedal organ. The first pedal board (1429) is ascribed to Valbecke, a Fleming. Alert German and French builders took up the new practice at once, out-distancing Italy by a full hundred years. (England didn't get around to it until 1772). Progress through the fifteenth century was so rapid that long before 1600 most continental organs had two or three manuals and an independent pedal organ, though early pedal divisions seldom had a compass of more than an octave, and but few chromatic notes.

The good work of the organ builders came at a fortuitous moment, for the great instrumental genius of Merulo, Gabrieli and Frescobaldi was about to be unleashed. When Merulo played it is said that the church doors had to be closed to prevent people from crushing each other in their eagerness for admission. Frescobaldi, organist at St. Peter's in Rome, played for audiences of 30,000, according to Baini. This flood of interest in the new instrumental style had its immediate effect on organ building and the industry flourished as never before.

In passing to the next era we must note the date 1527, the year the first American organ was made. It was built in the Mexico City School of Fray Pedro, from which came a stream of little organs and Indians trained to play them.

The organ of Bach's day was a nearly perfected instrument. The only noteworthy improvements to follow were mechanical. The first was the Barker pneumatic lever in 1832, a device that greatly lightened the labor of playing. Previously, the touch in large organs was enough to paralyze a strong-armed organist. The second forward step was unveiled at the Paris Exhibition of 1867 when the first organ harnessing electricity to operate its action was displayed. Subsequent development led to power driven blowers, giving a steadier wind supply, and to a faster, lighter action, making possible organs of mammoth size and consoles detached from the organ proper at any desired distance.

Modern controls at the console have made the resources of the instrument more flexible, but have so multiplied the extraneous movements of hands and feet that console management is now an art in itself. Organists sometimes envy their brethren of a century ago when it was proper and fashionable to employ one or two assistants to pull the stops, allowing the organist the comparative peace of mind of a pianist, for instance, who can give full attention to putting down the keys that make the music.

Inspired Instruments

By MADALYN PHILLIPS

INSTRUMENTAL music in the church can be traced back to the time when the sky formed a roof above the worshippers and a tree or a mountain offered a suitable place for religious devotion. It is recorded in the Bible that about 4000 B. C. Jubal invented instruments which were in use after the flood. He is spoken of as being "father of all such as handle the harp and the organ." In ancient times music was used entirely in religious services. Even the savages, in their own way, were devout and used rhythm, by beating upon the ground with sticks, in connection with symbolic dances for their expressions of religious fervor.

One office of music in the ancient occult ceremonies of the Egyptians and Hindus was that of suggesting definite ideas through associated symbolism. Music was a sacred art in Egypt, guarded jealously by the priest, whose ceremonies and funeral rites were displays of instrumental performances. Naturally, the music of ancient times expressed the primitive thought of each country.

The Hebrews seem to have been the first to express more of the "divine" service. It was pronounced by some as "sentimental", but regardless of this criticism, it was more devout and consecrated. To them, each tune and each instrument had its own individual meaning, never were used on other occasions. These Hebrew instruments are mentioned throughout the Bible. It is also noticed that in The Book, accompaniments by instruments are recorded in the references pertaining to expressions of gratitude, praise, humility, and exultation. The instruments had their ethos or moral character and great care was used in selecting the right one to express the desired emotion.

In India and China the drum was and is a characteristic religious instrument. It is not used merely to mark accent or to express a climax, but has a definite symbolic meaning. All Chinese ritual instruments have symbolic names. Astronomy governs their pitch. A metal bell is struck before each strophe of the *Hymn to Confucius* and is answered by a stone-chime. Chinese ritual music is sung in the key of C major with the fourth sharped. At the end of each verse a large drum is struck three times and is an-

swered by two other drums. At the end the "tiger-box" is beaten. Other instruments are used, each tone of which has a detached meaning to the Chinese and each is identified with either some special god, a color, a planet, an official or other entity.

In Rome the organ was at first considered a scientific toy or experiment, especially by the monks, and was barred from the church. The method of playing (described elsewhere in this volume) was another reason for antagonism. Who could possibly experience spiritual "uplift" when a gymnastic "organist", by pounding one key alone, would set off as many as ten diapasons—tuned in fifths and octaves? They neither knew nor cared when this would happen. To some people it was terrifying; to others it was amusing, but it was not considered conducive to the purpose of the church. Gradually the many improvements in organ building and the development and selection of real musicians to play made the "king of instruments" most important in the western churches, although the organ still is seldom used in the Eastern Empire.

For a long time instrumental music disappeared from the temples and the early synagogues. It was condemned by Clement of Alexandria, Saint Chryoston and Saint Ambrose. This was due, according to some, to the sensuous effect upon the emotions, which it seemed to excite as well as the association of instruments with superstitious pagan rites. According to them, a Christian maiden should not know what a lyre or a flute was or the reason for its use. At this time these instruments were used in performances on the stage in sensuous scenes and thus became identified. Even today, would not some of our instruments be considered "out of place" in church services?

In the church of today there remains much symbolism which would seem fully justified providing the sincere religious spirit be upheld and demonstrated. The Bible constantly reminds one that without the spirit, symbolism and rituals become "as sounding brass and a tinkling cymbal." Therefore, is it not just as necessary for the instrumental part of any church service to be of the proper spirit in order to signify all that the service typifies?

It has been said that the organ is a most mechanical instrument. If so, the fault must be with the musician at the console. Is the mechanism of an organ any more mechanical than any other instrument? Some will answer this question by referring to the "touch" used in playing, claiming this is not noticeable on the organ. Others are just as sure that individual "touch" is definitely recognizable in organists as in other instrumentalists. The writer is of the opinion that the spiritual content of the music as well as the spiritual understanding of the musician is the determining factor.

The necessity for spiritual enlightenment and devotion on the part of composers and organists is important and essential. Palestrina reached a higher spiritual plane in his music although there were several devout church men in the field of music during his time. Willaert was the originator of antiphonal organ work in the church. During the Seventeenth Century German culture was based upon the old choir chorus, hymn tunes and organ music. Then a more varied and characteristic expression could not be kept out of the church—the Passion Music and cantata of the Eighteenth Century with its accompaniment. However, Schuetz, in the Seventeenth Century, had employed the organ bass as an accompaniment to all the parts of his *Seven Words* except that which represented Christ, when string instruments were used.

Johann Sebastian Bach's purpose in life was to enrich the musical treasury of the church. His high ideals and motives, coupled with his great genius, enabled him to reach a height in sacred and secular music that no one has ever surpassed. He was a devout and consecrated Christian who never thought of his art other than as part of the church. To him there was no separation. Although he created no new styles in music, yet his work was superior and his devotion to the Lutheran Church was as great as Palestrina's devotion to the Catholic Church. It is noteworthy that his organ works are played in both Catholic and Protestant Churches in Europe and America—and their use is increasing.

In the Protestant Church, the organ solo had grown into an established feature of the service, while in the Catholic Church it had less intrinsic value—more of an embellishment. Up until this time organ playing in Germany had reached the point of being more an extemporization upon choral themes. Improvisation on original or borrowed themes was an unwritten law of the German Church and it became

quite an art. The organ expressed the dignity, gravity and moral earnestness which prevailed.

When the organists of today attain the great spirituality of thought and the deep moral responsibility which was so characteristic of Bach, it is certain that they will give to their audiences the great message found in his work. Then, no longer is it heard that Bach sounds like "technical exercises." How can one give that which Bach put into his music without at least a glimpse and a little understanding of his great depth and profoundly religious nature? After Bach there was a period when organ playing degenerated and the composers were not able and did not care to perpetuate the old traditions. The whole trend of the musical world was toward secular music. In the Nineteenth Century, both in compositions and in performance, church music associations and societies were established in Germany to protect the music and to keep it on a more efficient basis.

Handel, a naturalized English subject, gave many miscellaneous compositions to the libraries of music in churches. But in England the organ did not occupy an important position. It was merely a support to the voices and was not used in the service as a solo instrument. Long after Handel's time few organs in England had complete pedal boards or manuals and many had none at all. The orchestra figured prominently in places of worship during the Restoration Period. But church music in England has never been more satisfactory than it is today because of the deep rooted religious reverence and culture of the people.

In the United States, as in other countries, Synagogues and Catholic Churches require traditional music. However, in some of the Synagogues, the organist is permitted to select his instrumental solos. In the orthodox service of the Synagogue there is no instrumental music whatever.

To those who believe that instrumental music is unimportant or unnecessary in church services, let it be said that many persons receive a message in music that they do not find elsewhere, and it is so important that if it is less than a standard of musical excellence, it can ruin an otherwise ideal service.

In the churches of today, organists are gradually admitting that the electronic organ definitely has its place, yet it never can be considered in the same category as the pipe organ. Organists also are viewing, with growing interest, the library of new and modern music publications. The music committees

(*Continued on page* 141)

Oratorio Carries On

By MAURICE GOLDMAN

ONE of the most social of all arts, and the most universally beloved, music appeals to large groups of people and gives large opportunities for cooperation. Oratorio being one of the larger forms of musical composition, is enjoyed largely because of this basic fact. A large body of singers joined in sympathetic and emotional expression, almost invariably performing music of a deeply religious nature, appeals deeply to human interest. Hence the reason for a striking growth in popularity of the oratorio in both Europe and America during the past century.

The oratorio draws its style, form and ideals from both church music and opera. It is related to the cantata and has especially significant differences with the operatic form.

In the main seats of the early classic music drama, Florence and Rome, the term "opera" had no specific meaning in the century of its appearance. In the early Seventeenth Century it usually signified a narrative lyric poem set to music in the monodic style. The various stages or episodes were connected by a recitative called *testo* (text). This later became the narrator or the *Evangelist* as witnessed in the Passions of Bach. The term *cantata* appeared early in the century and was used loosely in many aspects of music before assuming its present form. Similarly the term *oratorio* after a few years of uncertainty, became in 1640 the form which we attach to it today.

Simply stated, oratorio differs fundamentally from opera in that it does not use stage settings and dramatic action. Oratorio puts the listener in a mood for imaginative contemplation. Oratorios have been staged occasionally, but this does not basically alter the original conception. Nevertheless in a dramatic version of Mendelssohn's *Elijah*, staging the aria *Is Not His Word Like A Fire* would have a tremendous effect on the audience. This form of sacred opera flourished during the Sixteenth and Seventeenth Centuries and later evolved into the true oratorio form which featured the chorus as the "action" part of the performance, with occasional dramatic interruptions by the narrator or other solo parts.

Among those who contributed to the development of sacred opera and oratorio were Filippo Neri, Cava-lieri, Barberini, Mazzochi and Carissimi, whose accomplishments in the field of Latin oratorio are especally significant. When the great Handel was hard pressed for time he very conveniently "lifted" 'whole scenes from the works of Carissimi. One of the finest samples of extraordinary and deeply reflective church music is Carissimi's *Jeptha* and it seems regrettable that so few of his works are published today. Most distinguished composer among those who preceded Bach and Alessandro Scarlatti (1659-1725). He was one of a versatile family who wrote distinctive music in all forms of opera, cantata or oratorio. One of his most famous works is *The Martyrdom of Saint Theodosi*. A prolific early German writer was Heinrich Schuetz (1585-1672), sometimes called the father of German music. Through his familiarity with the Italian style, he laid the groundwork of the modern German oratorio, in his *Resurrection, Seven Last Words* and the four *Passions*. Bach's tremendously important contributions to church music are well known.

Handel, the greatest of oratorio writers, wrote some forty operas, none heard today though his oratorios are still sung over and over again. During his time he had no rival. His first oratorio was *Esther*, written in 1720, produced in 1733. Then in rapid succession came the most magnificent series of choral works ever to be penned by one man. They were *Saul, Israel in Egypt, Messiah, Samson, Hercules, Belshazzar, Judas Maccabeus, Judas, Solomon, Suzanna, Theodora, Jeptha*, and *Triumph of Time and Truth*. During this period the oratorio developed from the simple form of Carissimi to the massive structure of Handel's later works. "Papa" Haydn later followed with two outstanding contributions, *The Creation* and *The Seasons*.

In the early nineteenth century, little was contributed to oratorio until Spohr wrote *The Last Judgment*, considered his mastepiece. Following Haydn's *Creation* the most thoroughly satisfying oratorios to be written were those of Felix Mendelssohn, who fostered a general revival of choral writing and singing. At the age of twenty he revived Bach's *St. Matthew's Passion* and before his brief span ended he

(*Continued on page* 150)

Singing For Fun

By NORMAN SORENG WRIGHT

EVER since man discovered that two or more voices singing different tones at the same time could be pleasant to listen to, and fun to participate in, there have been choral organizations. From earliest times these groups of singers have not lacked audiences of appreciative listeners. This is not surprising when we stop to consider that in all of music only the singing voice is direct. In every other musical art there is an instrument between the performer and the listener. The hand of a child playing a single note on the organ will sound no different than the same note played by Marcel Dupre. An amateur playing a single chord on the piano will not sound very different from Artur Schnabel playing the same chord. However, a single tone sung by one voice will never sound the same as the tone of another. With the instrumentalists the difference lies in the development of their technique. No one not vitally interested can enjoy the early attempts of a string player to make music, but often the song of a child will cause one to listen with pleasure. The completely untrained voice may be beautiful.

Even today, when our ears are so accustomed to sound from every side as a part of our daily lives: juke boxes blaring through open doors; radios sounding from the houses we pass and from the cars that pass us; motor horns that play tunes and even organ music broadcast from church steeples, I have seen the effect of the direct singing voice on a chattering crowd. We were revisiting the San Luis Rey Mission in the company of a particularly talkative group of young people. When we came into the inner court we could hear chanting. Everyone immediately quieted. It was apparent to me as a musician that we were hearing a rehearsal, yet such was the power of the appeal of the singing voice that even the noisest ones stood transfixed to listen.

One of the rare experiences of my early musical life was listening to a group of Egyptian fishermen sing as they pulled in their nets. The leader, a burly fellow with a strong and pleasant baritone voice, improvised verses of variable length and melodic context, and his companions joined lustily in a chorus which was ever the same. I listened, entranced, for hours. Though I could not share in the added pleasure of understanding the words, the whole meaning was clear to me through the music. Humor, pathos, grotesqueries were all apparent, and hugely enjoyed by the not inconsiderable number of onlookers.

It was a well-known fact during my student years in Paris that the choral singing of some of the amateur groups far surpassed the singing of the professional choristers at the Opera and the Opera Comique. Undoubtedly the level of performance was more consistent by the professional groups. They never sang as badly as the amateurs sometimes did, but by the same yardstick they never reached the heights of inspired performance that we occasionally heard in the churches, or at schools. I remember very well hearing two performances of Franck's *Beatitudes* within a few weeks time. The first was done by an all professional orchestra and chorus in one of the concert halls in Paris. The other was a performance by the Schola Cantorum with student orchestra and student chorus. The orchestra was much better in the first performance, but the chorus in the second so far surpassed the first that the performance as a whole was better. Yet I have no doubt that the individual voices in the professional group were better and that the task of teaching them their parts was infinitely easier. Perhaps some of the professional chorus singers are like the chorister at the Paris Opera who came to his director and asked to be excused from the matinee because he had the opportunity of earning more money by singing for a wedding. The director excused him, but was very startled on the day of the matinee to see the young man in the chorus apparently lending himself wholeheartedly to the performance. At the intermission he approached the singer and asked him how he happened to be there. The singer replied, in a whisper, pointing to his throat, that he couldn't sing at the wedding because he had a severe case of laryngitis and couldn't utter a sound.

In no other branch of music is the untrained performer an asset to an organization. This goes back to my original premise that the human voice does not have to be trained to be beautiful. The only requirements for a singer in an amateur chorus are

(*Continued on page* 151)

Together We Sing

By VAN A. CHRISTY

TEACHING instruments in class has been an accepted procedure for a considerable time. While teaching voice in classes has lagged behind the instrumental, it is no longer a questionable experiment but a proven success, especially in the beginning stages of vocal study. That class voice training is here to stay is attested by the fact that over a dozen text books, some of them in wide usage, have been published on the subject.

Voice classwork first became prevalent in teacher training colleges as a substitute for private voice work where students could not afford the cost of private lessons or where sufficient well trained teachers were not available. In spite of many classes being taught by private voice teachers untrained in the specialized techniques of class voice teaching, the project, on the whole, has proven a surprising success. The practice has now spread and is common, not only in the colleges and conservatories, but in the more progressive high schools and even in some junior high schools. California lags behind middle western states in offering voice class work as a standard elective in the high school but the subject is rapidly expanding into more schools and has the strong endorsement of most music educators.

Many college music departments offer class voice in the first and second year and a number also in the third and fourth years of the curriculum. The common practice in high schools where class voice is offered is to limit the work to one year. It is frequently a prerequisite to membership, or accompanying membership in an a cappella choir or a glee club. It is a universal comment that the quality of choral work in the school vocal ensembles improves rapidly where voice class work has been properly installed. It is true that the major objective of the teacher in such voice classes often has been to train skilled ensemble singers. Nevertheless, many students also are taught to do excellent solo work.

There has been a recognized need and an ever growing demand in the high schools for the development of a choral training program on a par with that in the instrumental field. It is a well known fact that high school pupils in the past two decades have benefited greatly from a tremendously expanded program of class work in the instrumental field. The practical limit of instrumental technical development has been fairly well achieved in some of the most progressive schools, but not so for the vocal development.

Under prevailing conditions, the quality of work done in the vocal ensembles in many schools has reached a practical limit that can be extended only by developing better individual singing ability, better technic and more maturity of tone than exists in untrained voices. Teachers in high schools cannot possibly find the time nor the energy to do this by private teaching. Neither is the taxpayer willing to provide funds for the expensive procedure of furnishing additional teachers for private music lessons in the public schools. The majority of students cannot afford or be persuaded to take private vocal lessons from local teachers. The only practical answer is voice class work.

Boys and girls genuinely interested in chorus or glee work usually desire to learn to sing well as soloists if they can do so through a classroom technic that does not immediately single out their individual shortcomings for public attention. Where choral ensemble work is well established, voice class work finds a fertile field and will always prove popular if properly taught. It should be regularly scheduled like any other class activity and receive commensurate credit. The most effective work is done in schools where the subject is scheduled as a "solid", meeting five periods weekly.

A year of voice class work is sometimes required as a prerequisite to later membership in select choral groups. In schools where this plan is not yet feasible, two periods of voice class lessons per week in connection with chorus or glee club has proven possible, e.g., chorus or glee club is scheduled on Monday, Wednesday and Friday and voice class work on Tuesday and Thursday. Choral directors using this plan are almost unanimous in praising the results as significantly raising the standards of choral ensemble work as well as giving students a fundamental background and needed experience for solo singing.

The following plan for a vocal curriculum is recommended to colleges as both practically and musically satisfactory in achieving high educational and performance standards:

1st Year—Class voice only, three times weekly (For those of little or no previous training in solo singing).
2nd Year—Two class lessons and one private lesson weekly.
3rd Year—Two private lessons and one class lesson weekly.
4th Year—Two private lessons weekly.

Such a plan of vocal study needs, of course, to be implemented by a regular schedule of student recitals. Voice classes should grow progressively smaller so that more time can be given to the advanced individual student. A class of six to eight advanced students is considered maximum for best results.

Many authorities believe that it is unnecessary to spend much time with the individual student in the initial stages of development and that classes of fifteen to twenty-five can be handled efficiently in the fundamental work of the first year. They contend and have ably demonstrated that it is an inefficient use of time to attempt to classify voices and give much attention to individual problems until the second or third semester; that the fundamentals of proper posture, breath support, relaxation, vowel production, attack, legato and proper practice habits, which can be taught as easily and rapidly to large groups as to an individual in the first year, will automatically eliminate most of the difficulties of the individual student; and that the voice then, and only then, can be safely classified.

Vocal material used is in a medium range. When a song or an exercise goes either too low or too high for easy production for some individuals, they are instructed to desist in singing. When two-part songs are used, the student is instructed to sing the part which is easier for them at the time.

The instructor is expected to explain and amplify information given in the text, to present suitable examples when needed, and to assign exercises and songs to individuals either from the text used or from some outside source. It is well to emphasize that class voice, as it is best taught, incorporates gradually an increasing attention to the individual. In small advanced classes this amounts to considerable time being allocated weekly to each student. Some individual singing of phrases or short sections of a song should be done the latter part of the first semester and some of the more able students should be urged to volunteer to sing an entire song of easy grade.

An introduction to individual singing is best achieved through selecting one row to sing alone, then three or four students, and eventually only two. In fact, small ensemble work of duets, trios, quartets, etc., should be encouraged and their work incorporated as an integral part of the class activities. While most of early class voice work should be devoted to singing exercises and easy unison songs in a limited range, the singing of part songs should begin at an early date. Most text books designed for class voice are weak in that they do not include enough good duets of an easy grade.

Students in more advanced solo singing classes should not only obtain verbal and written criticism by the instructor but also from the members of the class. Such criticism should always be constructive and follow observations regarding good features of the performance observed. Written class comments regarding specific factors outlined by the instructor usually have been found more effective than verbal. Power of critical discrimination develops most rapidly through this phase of class work.

Some of the major advantages of the voice class plan are:

1. Cost to the pupil is low. In most schools no special tuition is charged.
2. Use of a text prepared by an authority and an organized procedure for studying voice better guarantees a logical and thorough supervised study and practice of the fundamentals involved. It is much easier for a teacher to carefully plan and organize class work and keep exact progress in mind than it is to organize and remember the progress of many heterogeneous individual voice pupils.
3. Reduction or elimination of self-consciousness, timidity and fear, first through ensemble singing with others and then through frequent solo singing before a class. The class furnishes a practical laboratory for performance experience. In an alert class, students may learn as much or more from one another as they do from many teachers.
4. Gaining assurance, poise, good posture and stage deportment much more easily and quickly than is possible through private voice study alone.
5. Frequent opportunity to hear others sing with similar faults or similar virtues. This procedure—
   a. Develops power of diagnosis and analysis of vocal difficulties and makes the student not only a better singer but a better critic and a better teacher of voice if he ever wishes to teach.
   b. Promotes a more rapid development of the powers of discrimination in relation to judging good singing.
   c. Gives a better chance to evaluate both one's vocal assets and vocal difficulties by comparison with other voices. It is well to remember that students learn as much or more from hearing the difficulties of others corrected as they do from observing the best of singing techniques.
   d. Gives a wider acquaintance with song literature and a broader knowledge of types and classification of voices.
   e. Stimulates many students, who otherwise would never do so, to continue advanced study with private teachers.

Ten of the most vital class voice objectives are:

1. To promote greater joy in singing and desire for progress.
2. To establish habitually correct habits of articulation.
3. To correct speech defects and improve the quality, ease and carrying power of both the speaking and singing voice.
4. To teach intelligent ensemble as well as artistic solo singing.
5. To train the ear and the aesthetic taste of the pupil.
6. To habituate correct posture and breath control.
7. To guide and establish correct and habitual practice methods.

(Continued on page 148)

A Song For Everyone

By JOHN ELLIS

IT HAS BEEN SAID that music is a universal language and the amateur chorus participant certainly has found truth in that statement. Moreover he has discovered a means to become better adjusted, socially; he has found a more adequate channel for the expression of his emotions, and an effective way of energizing and stabilizing his morale. Many have found that active membership in a group singing together for the love of music has proven to be, in this day of speed and struggle, an excellent "safety valve". Through the resource of singing, the nervous strain of living is diminished and the spirit lifted to a much higher level.

The desire for choral music as a recreational activity is increasing steadily. Music groups interested primarily in song have sprung up throughout the country and now one may see, upon perusing the various national musical periodicals, choral programs presented by organizations from Southern California to upper Maine.

In the past, colleges and churches have been the main sphere of choral activity, but now, for the great number of persons unable to attend the universities, and to accommodate those interested in secular as well as sacred music, singing organizations are being included as civic enterprises. Financial support for these endeavors may be obtained through internal revenue, while groups not sponsored by a city or town usually operate by the membership or public subscription method.

Since group singing is growing in popularity, most major radio programs employ some type of vocal effects, other than the principal vocalists. The influence of glee club arrangements has made a desirable impression upon the vocal-minded public. Both domestic and foreign recordings of choral groups have increased in sale, and the recorded repertory eventually will equal, in all probability, the orchestral library available.

Many a well prepared and sensitive musician has hesitated to enter the field of training a group of amateur singers, especially church choirs, where often the only music required is a sort of "religious vaudeville". This deplorable situation is being remedied, in the Southland, by the efforts of the Choral Conduc-tors Guild of Southern California, whose primary aim is improvement of music in the churches.

To mold a group of trained vocalists to present good music is a simple task in comparison to the training of an amateur group. The only way to achieve this latter goal is the self-discipline of endless patience. Not only must the director have a thorough knowledge of harmonic structure, of the special technique of choral conducting, of the relative importance of time and tempo, but he must be a psychologist as well.

His also is the big problem of educating his personnel in the understanding of good music, as well as training them in the correct use of the vocal apparatus. It is up to him to explain correct breathing and good tone, and to provide a clear understanding of interpretation. Most important of all, the director must realize that to hold the interest of his group, each rehearsal must be a finished performance on his part. But the results of patience and thorough preparation can be satisfying to the director, the chorus and to the audience.

Undoubtedly the bane of every choral director's existence is the teaching of the various voice parts by rote. This problem can be overcome partially by establishing separate part rehearsals handled by section leaders, or by instituting a fifteen minute pre-rehearsal period of solfeggio and sight-singing study. The use of one or the other of these methods will eliminate much of the tedious and uninteresting portion of a rehearsal.

At times the choice of music presents an issue. The musical taste of the public as well as the choristers will depend upon the quantity and quality of the music to which they have been exposed; however, it is easier to educate the chorus than the audience. Likewise, the type of music presented must vary in different localities. The radio has changed this situation to a degree, but when choruses have good music presented to them for performance preparation, various opinions may arise. This presents a challenge to the director, and it is up to him to give his chorus proper understanding and appreciation.

This writer recently proved this assertion. Within

(Continued on page 131)

Stresses Stop the Song

By BELLE FORBES CUTTER

WITH what opulent delight have concert and opera goers in the past listened to the voices in the era now referred to as the "Golden Age of Bel Canto". I recall conversations with musical friends who were privileged to have heard some of the glorious voices of that day. One, I recall, had heard Patti. Many had known of the singing of Melba, Scotti, the De Reszkes, Eames, Bonci, Sembrich, Nordica, Maurel, Plancon, Scalci and Calve, to name a few of the great ones, and remembered well the operas in which every member of the cast had been a finished singer. In fact, there was never an opera given in those days in which one was compelled to listen to any *bad* singing. It was consistently excellent.

The number of fine singers today is deplorably low. What has happened? Our country is teeming with talented young men and women possessing lovely, natural voices. Where we once had hundreds of singing teachers we now have thousands. Schools are turning out graduates by the tens of thousands. These graduates are better musicians, which is something to be grateful for, but *what* of the voices? Whenever a rare voice is discovered and added to the roster of the Met its beauty lasts but two or three years. Are they given roles for which they are not vocally ready? Are young voices pushed beyond their capacity? Or have we teachers become so commercial that we urge icarian flights on the beginner only to watch his subsequent fall into the sea of ruined voices.

After all is said and done, it is the teacher to whom we must look for the sound foundation that is to carry the student to a successful career. It is the teacher whose ear must be attuned to beauty; whose ideals must stand against the variable winds of radio and motion picture styles; whose knowledge and understanding must combat "cow tones" and "straight" tones and the tremulous wobble of the over-heated popular singer. Beauty should no more be out-moded than truth or honesty or mercy, and "bel canto" should be the sum and substance of the singing teacher's profession. Unless the teacher is a true lover of "beautiful singing" and has the know-

ledge of how it can be achieved, a futile struggle begins for the student.

Far too often, the unwary beginner is ushered into a studio to discover that there all thoughts of comfort and pleasureable singing are to be put aside. He must now bring the voice "up and out" of the throat and force it into the nose, or the top of the head, or work it through the Eustachian tubes or jam it against the cheek bones. He is told that the jaw must be held rigid, the diaphragm locked and never used, that he must sing louder and harder, that respiration must be tempestuous and that he must feel as though he were carrying heavy weights. I have been amazed through the years to watch the would-be singer hopelessly mesmerized by illogical notions and floundering statements which should not only have been queried, but flatly contradicted.

If these teachers of so-called "beautiful singing" begin by telling the new student to "meow" like a cat or growl and snarl like beasts of the forests, the young singer should beware, lest in the end, his feline or adanoidic tones may be too abhorrent for even his own family to endure.

Nothing succeeds unless based upon principle, and the underlying principle of singing is most tangible of the loveliness, comfort and control gained by its application. The illustrious Old Masters of singing were well aware of this. Physiologically, they had measured the possibilities and limitations of the human throat. They recognized the need for normalcy and its resultant ease, and they demanded "bel canto" of every student and were satisfied with nothing else.

What hypnotic charm has a teacher to bind a pupil to a method which is the direct antithesis of what is being used by the successful artist? How can they possibly believe that tension, brute force, a smarting throat and ungainly contortions of the body could ever bring harmony and radiance to a voice? When you watch the agonized eyes and mouth, the facial grimaces, the heaving chest, the swelling throat muscles, the color of the amateur's face changing from pink to purple, you wonder at anyone choosing a profession which seems to demand such suffering. Why spend time and money for such tortuous "half-

(*Continued on page* 148)

Why Not Say It?

By RAY CRITTENDEN

THE progressive voice teacher does not look askance at any measure which will aid him to correctly diagnose vocal difficulties. The mystery is why there persists (with a small minority, it must be admitted) an antiquated pedagogy based solely on empirical ideas with an equally out-moded terminology used to convey its meaning.

An expression heard frequently in voice studios is that the student is producing a "throaty tone." This is to convey the idea that there is tensing of the constrictors. Why not say just that; for fundamentally, all tones, good or bad, are produced in the larynx (throat) and amplified in the pharyngeal throat space immediately above the larynx. The oral, post-nasal and naso-pharyngeal spaces still higher in the skull are modifiers and not *producers* of resonance. These are facts which have been proven in the scientific laboratories as conclusively as the accepted fact that H_2O is water. Why then do we continue to use expressions as "throaty tone," "singing in the mask," "placing the voice" in some arbitrary spot, etc.

To be sure, the successful teacher uses imagery and empirical terms constantly in his work, and he is justified so long as their use does not conflict with physiological facts. The trouble is that many of us do not go deep enough to uncover the common underlying principles. Vocal methods can be reconcilable with science. When they conflict, the differences and disagreements frequently are in the type of imagery used and can be located not in the factual physiological processes but in the delusive realm of the purely empirical approach. Why not use imagery that conforms to physiological law?

Voices are impaired many times by the insistance of a teacher that the pupil carry a "heavier load" of dynamics in his tonality than is consistent with the muscular development and coordination the pupil possesses at the time. Science demonstrates that the vocal chords adjust themselves to various tensions, lengths and weights in accordance with other physiological laws. If the tension of a violin string is quadrupled, the pitch is raised an octave; shorten the length one-half, and it will be raised another octave; reduce the weight one-half, and the pitch is raised another octave. Obviously, the greatest danger to the vocal chords is in overloading the tensing mechanism, or literally carrying too heavy an adjustment, particularly in the upper range of the voice. Science cautions us, "thus far, but no farther." The laboratories are helping us to recognize sounds whose decibel content is too high for safety. Conversely, we are able to demand the full "potential" of the pupil without danger of vocal impairment.

There are two sets of muscles, the crico-thyroids and the arytenoids, controlling the length, weight and tension of the vocal cords. The first group (crico-thyroid) is the heavier and functions to produce tones of loud intensity or low pitch. Muscles of the arytenoid group are predominately in action when tones of high pitch or soft intensity are being sung. It has been found through X-ray and phonetic devices that both groups are active and coordinated in great singing. Aside from the aesthetic, this implies that the voice is one of exceptional quality, dynamics and range. A remarkable feature revealed by scientific research is that the action of these two groups of muscles can be separated one from the other, thereby permitting (through specific exercises) a strengthening of each group. This, in the opinion of the writer, is one of the most significant and exceedingly valuable contributions science has made to the voice teaching profession.

Science is in accord with the popular studio expression, "Sing with an 'open throat'", for it has been proven conclusively that the back throat or pharyngeal space is the principal resonator of the human voice. Its ability to adjust its size, large or small, to the frequency of tone being produced conforms to the laws of physics. But tones thus produced often create a sensation of vibration in the head cavities above, which gives rise to the erroneous notion that the sound is being resonated in those spaces; or even worse, that it is actually produced there.

These sensations are described in amazing and astonishing variations of imagery. One teacher tells the student to "open the mouth as wide as possible, because the larger the mouth opening the larger the resonance and volume of tone." Another, "practice the most closed oo until the voice is 'placed up'." The use of imagery i.e. "head resonance," "getting the tone in the mask," "forward" or "against the teeth" is an attempt, physiologically, to relax the velum in order to open the passage into the head. It thus weakens the fixity of the upper fulcrum from which the pillars and other swallowing muscles operate, permitting the weaker downward pulling muscles to enlarge the throat.

Thus there is the curious anomaly of the nose and head passages adding almost nothing in the way of resonance, and yet being of great importance in securing indirectly a proper setting of the throat resonators. And from this paradox come most of the misunderstandings not alone between voice teachers and scientists, but among voice teachers themselves.

One of the most interesting contributions science has made has been through the medium of X-ray moving pictures secured by Dr. G. Oscar Russell in the phonetic department of Ohio State University. These pictures show the value of the proper taking in of breath to loosen interfering muscles and relax the jaw. Also this proper "in-take" is shown to prepare the laryngeal pharynx as a resonator for the tone which should follow almost simultaneously this inspiration of breath. Even the slightest hesitation between this intake of breath and the starting of tone results in a partial collapse of the walls of the throat. This ensuing flabby condition is the antithesis of all that is required of a resonator. A "stroke of the glottis" will invariably be heard if the tone starts with a vowel. This, as a matter of fact, is an infallible way to ascertain if faulty tone production is caused by this collapse.

In the light of this factual information, instructions by certain voice teachers to deliberately "pause" between breath and tone is positively pernicious; for the attempt to resonate tone in such an ill-prepared resonator creates inflammation in the mucous lining of the throat and is a positive cause of vocal fatigue. With continued intensive singing, a chronic soreness many times develops.

Practically all voice teachers of standing are in agreement that the student should learn to sing with a large open throat throughout the entire pitch range. It is relatively simple to establish this condition in phonating vowels, but the addition of consonants with the complexity of middle and tip tongue activity creates a problem of coordination much more difficult to solve. Most vocal-research scientists are in agreement that the vowel has its inception in the larynx, through adjustments in the ventricle, and that it is completed in the laryngeal-oral pharynx. So it is

evident that excessive shaping of the lips for singing vowels should be avoided. The front mouth is the area for consonant utterance rather than vowel formations. The only consonants which originate in the back mouth area are "ng," "k," "q," and "r,"

Also the open throat has a powerful semi-reflex to overcome in the swallowing group of muscles, which in many singers are in a state of partial contraction ready to act in the process of swallowing. This tension is dangerous to good voice quality. The measurement of this and many other muscular and nerve tensions, i.e. shoulders, arms, powerful back muscles, etc., can now be ascertained with remarkable accuracy by the use of instruments recently developed in the laboratory for Clinical Physiology of Chicago with the assistance of the Bell Research Laboratories.

With the use of these facilities, as the instruments become more available for studio purposes, a simple check-up requiring but a few moments could be made periodically to measure progress in attempting to secure ideal muscular tonicity. These instruments can detect hidden tensions in other vital nerve centers, particularly, those involved in reflexes from powerful structural muscles which often play havoc with correct posture.

Many teachers are reluctant to accept the real facts concerning vibrato, even though phonetic laboratories in our finest graduate schools inform us that "vibrato is present in all great singing whether we hear it or not, or whether the singer is conscious of it or not." In the near future, measurements will be standardized and made available on phonograph records with norms to increase the capacity for hearing not only the presence of vibrato but differences in vibratos. Without the aid of science, we would still be in the dark and at the mercy of fickle opinion regarding our conceptions of the nature of the vibrato.

The terms "high" and "low" as they are used to indicate changes in pitch are not factual terms, for there is literally no perpendicular change of level for so-called "high tones" and "low tones." A higher cavity is not used to resonate a tone of high pitch than for one of low pitch, rather, the changes that take place are in the size and shape of the back-throat resonators, synchronized with the pitch mechanism adjustments of the vocal cords. From a psychological standpoint therefore, it is questionable whether or not the usual studio parlance in this regard does not present "mental hazards" for the student to hurdle.

It is also questionable whether a teacher should definitely classify a student's voice (tenor, soprano,

(Continued on page 145)

Is the World Sick Vocally?

By RENNAY SHRY-OCK

WE ARE living in an era unsurpassed for its extensive desire by multitudes to express themselves through song. With these far-reaching desires have come attendant dangers for both student and teacher. This current mania for singing indulged by countless aspirants regardless of native talent, has placed an unprecedented responsibility directly in the lap of the vocal teacher.

Fomented by radio, screen and stage, with standards of performance for the most part that decry and abuse the legitimate to the extreme, the gullible novice in the field of singing has a sickly heritage to start with. Flamboyancy, the keynote of most entertainment fare thrust upon the ears of our young people today, is an insult to average intelligence. I said, "our young people," but being gifted naturally with a faculty for imitation, young and old alike ultimately and unwittingly fall before the persistent onslaught of blaring radio programs and juke boxes. No wonder a perverted sense of what constitutes *correct* singing is the result.

I can hear someone say, "Granted, but you are dealing expressly with the commonplace; the vaudeville or night-club type of vocalist. Now, for example, in concert and opera—." And, bristling with indignation, we are launched upon another argument over what upon rather frequent occasions one is forced to listen to politely and try to accept, (if fair judgment permits) as the "highest example" of vocal art in the field of opera, or (with tongue in cheek) both light and grand opera productions. Concert is the only possible happy exception to these hectic and deplorable practices, and even here, due to a scarcity of truly capable artists, we are fed all too lean a diet.

At best it appears we are a sick world vocally. I believe these terse calculations can be safely based upon obvious true and authoritative values as evidenced and recorded in most of the performances of fifty to seventy-five years ago as compared with those of today. With few exceptions, the average singer of the present day, frequently one who has spent years in study under so-called reputable instructors, is entirely devoid of true understanding in the basic principles which constitute a correct vocal premise. Student and teacher in many cases will argue to

the contrary, but a shoddy performance is proof positive. Certainly any good vocal teacher will bear me out when I insist that faulty intonation, diffused vocal color, strident tones and slovenly enunciation (to say nothing of the "sag" that has crept into musical interpretations of all descriptions) can hardly be accepted as vocal standards of the highest calibre. Yet these ailments are prevalent in most singers today to the eternal aggravation of the intelligent listener and ofttimes to the humiliation and discomfort of the performer himself.

This presents a pretty dour picture, one may say, sounding like the prating of the pessimist. But, perhaps we can find a remedy for an obviously decadent singing public. Anyone eager enough can weigh the good against the bad and through an unbiased, intelligent survey reveal a multitude of symptoms which challenge the vocal teacher for clarification. For upon the heads of "voice specialists," vocal coaches, voice technicians, voice builders, et cetera, rests the responsibility. Heaven knows, the capable and enlightened teachers can ill afford to slacken their vigilance for an instant. Something should be done to arouse a more general knowledge of the true Art of Singing, that our children and children's children may be able to evaluate correctly and perform with higher standards, ceasing to tolerate the mediocre and slipshod in vocal practice. We have been too reticent in this matter by putting up with this condition so long.

How is this to be done? Truly a frightening question when flung in the teeth of voice teachers and coaches whose number is legion and of whom, judging by the current results, about 90% are a vastly overrated and confused throng. Their efforts, to a startling degree, have earned the unmitigated contempt and utter disillusionment of countless trusting souls who have placed their talents in the hands of these unwise and unlearned tutors. This frank statement is stimulated by twenty-five years of personal observation and experience by the writer as teacher of singing during which time students and performers of all ages, talents, degrees of development, frustrated and otherwise have come for consultation and vocal help. More times than not they have brought with them vocal "diseases" of varied description which are to a great degree the result of former poor training, placing the arduous and lengthy task of reestablishment of the original or latent natural voice upon both teacher and student, a feat that takes untold patience and time to accomplish even in the most diligent.

We who teach this most misunderstood of all subjects are fully aware, by token of the intangible and elusive nature of the human voice, that frequently both teacher and student, no matter how sincere, are subjected to failure in their results due to the lack of sound knowledge regarding the true functions of a balanced vocal equipment; a sheer case of "the blind leading the blind." Herein lies the danger; a most prevalent "disease", and thus vocal practices of untold variety spring up, instituted as "methods", some of exceedingly weird origin. A few of these run rampant for the sole purpose of commercialization while others make a feeble attempt toward honest development despite a pathetic lack of ability.

There has been no effective attempt made to curb or discourage these practices by authoritative control and proven methods as should be the action in most of the great music centers. Yet, ultimately such control should be put in effect with fair and equitable premises established for correct training provided by actual demonstration before an unbiased, impersonal examination board drafted from the tried and eminently successful specialists in the Art of Singing. We should be thankful there are still a few of these authorities left in this country. This plan could be very far reaching in its scope and would strike at the seat of the trouble.

Foremost is the sadly neglected and deplorably deficient vocal training as taught in the average public school and college. The widespread picture that this presents is one of poor posture, poorer breathing, diffused, off-key singing, wrong classification of voices, forcing of frail young singers, and last but certainly not least, the regrettable injury to the sense of hearing—a most important adjunct in the Art of Singing. Irreparable damage is sometimes incurred. Teachers of public school music who handle young voices should be equipped with real vocal understanding through specialized training and then examined for proper credentials before assuming responsibility.

This public school vocal picture is more serious than most persons realize, for many young promising talents have been handicapped and abused in the schoolroom by unthinking, poorly-trained instructors.

So much stems from these beginnings that true exponents who bear the name of specialists in the field should rise up at once and do something about it! In fine, dropping all prejudices or differences (that we as a class are noted for) which will cause undue argument over technicalities, let us come out of our smug corners and be concerned only with the basic truths about singing that will help this vocally sick world to redeem itself.

Briefly, what are these truths? They are the basic natural principles that govern good vocal expression in anyone, namely: A supple, relaxed body with correct posture—the perfect, pure vowel (tone) expressed with meticulous care in its individual physical forms—the loose, low, relaxed open throat in every operation—the ever keen sense of hearing—an energized, automatic breathing form, elastic and poised—flawless enunciation with specific consonant (sound) forms—and imagination. These can form the structure for that subtle balance in performance so necessary in all art, and known as the perfect voice. Coupled with the latter must be the emotional and artistic interpretation which makes for real artistry.

There is a perfect voice (vocal color or timbre) latent or active, inherent in all voices—young or old—lyric or dramatic—male or female, which has its personal, unique color (quality) as individual as the human face. In its perfection (balanced use) it possesses the following attributes: clear, vital brilliance—pure vowel color—perfect intonation—full range—easy, free facility—and power without pressure. Acquisition of these characteristics in any voice, great or small, brings it back to its natural "habitat" or intention, (that center of spontaneous control) where expression is the essence of freedom and beauty.

Vocal teachers should strive to acquire that certain unique sensitivity and particular perception that will permit them to recognize without a shadow of a doubt the true *native* beauty and capacity of each individual voice. Without this ability to perceive the true potential voice in a student, no matter how obscure it may seem upon first contact, there is every reason to expect partial or total failure in the training of that voice to any heights of accomplishment, unless, as has happened, the singer is found to be a "natural" and sings well in spite of his training. Even here such a one may upon occasion find himself upon a dangerous precipice if too lacking in technical understanding.

This *perfect voice* can only be expressed as the epitome of pure tonal color, a master pattern,

(*Continued on page* 151)

How Does It Sound?

By ALEXANDRE CHERRIER

IN searching for a voice teacher, a student's first question often is: "What method does he teach, Italian, French, or German?" The question is as ridiculous as the answer in most cases. Name and country have little to do with methods. National methods do not exist any more, as teachers of the same country have their own individual ideas and opinions; but tradition holds us fast if we do not break its shackles. There can be only one way to sing correctly, and that is, "The Natural Way". Fundamental laws are the same: it is the comparative ability of the teacher to explain them and his capacity to realize the possibilities of each individual voice, which leads to success.

When a voice student enters the studio he has but a faintest notion of how good tones sound, even in his own voice. He may have excellent taste, may have heard much good singing, and possess a natural voice of real musical quality, yet have no means by which to judge the sound of his own voice.

Such pupils lack a standard. They are apt to be hurt and offended when they cannot hear how their own voices sound, assuming that they are being accused of lack of musical perception. This point must be handled carefully, for it is vital to successful work that friendly relations be established between pupil and teacher.

Pure tones depend upon perfect vocal adjustment, and not once in a hundred times does a pupil come to the teacher with a freedom in tone emission which has enabled him to develop a perfectly pure tone. His ear has become so accustomed to the quality of tone which he has always heard from his own voice, that he considers that quality not only desirable, but distinctly and peculiarly his own—something like the color of his eyes and not to be changed. Nearly always something is objectionable in his manner of voice production which interferes with his ability to produce the best tones his vocal apparatus is capable, so that the tone to which his ear has become thoroughly adjusted must be changed.

A student must have something to go on, some tone picture in his mind to guide him, since it is necessary to form a mental picture of a definite tone before a sound can be uttered. The teacher must explain that pure tone is the result of perfect elasticity in the tone-producing apparatus, relaxing the breathing and throat muscles, so that the muscular system may be in normal condition for action.

The pupil may be sensitive to good tone when he hears it from others, but this fact may blind him to the correct tone for his own voice. The tones he has most admired in others will have been those full resonant, mellow tones which come from the completely poised and matured artist, the result of years of study which have brought mastery. The pupil desires at once to give out his voice with the same fullness and volume, which is simply physically impossible. The volume and quality which he rightly admired in the finished artist has been achieved only through long years of work in the right manner.

The ideal of novices is nearly always volume, power, and resonance. Beauty of tone quality is really another way of saying freedom of tone production, and unless this condition is established in the first place, with the understanding on the part of the pupil as to why it is necessary, there is no chance for the development of the volume, power, and range which are essential to success.

The pupil comprehends the means of producing the desired tone more readily through the sensations of ease and freedom in production than through the effect the quality of the tone produces on his ear. With sensations of ease and freedom, he can be brought to understand the definiteness of physical sensation. Then gradually his ear becomes adjusted to the sound, and he learns to recognize that certain sensations in the production of tone always produce a certain quality of tone. Not until these facts have become perfectly clear to his mind, has he any true idea of the tone quality which belongs to his own voice.

Anybody who can speak in a normal tone proves that he possesses a voice which could be used for singing. Whether or not he will sing depends on that faculty of the brain which is sensitive to musical impression, and which is commonly called "an ear for music".

It is not, however, the physical ear, but the faculty of the brain which counts. That the pupil is able to speak exites no surprise, for it is one of the commonplaces of life. He modulates his voice to express many emotions without causing comment, for everybody else can do the same, but the idea that his singing voice is fundamentally the same, moved through the same means, governed by the same natural laws in the same manner, is at first a most astonishing thought.

When you can make the pupil grasp the elemental fact that his singing voice was put into him by nature for the express purpose of being used for singing, and that he will learn how to do it by practical experiment, in the same way that he learned to swim and skate, then there is an understandable basis on which to work. Young singers, and a good many old enough to know better, have the notion somewhere in the back of their heads that singing is a gift, that they have it, and the teacher in some mysterious way "brings it out" while they take their ease as he does the work.

If at the very beginning, pupils learn to adjust themselves to definite laws by nature, instead of seeking some secret way, they will comprehend that they are dealing with natural laws and bodily functions. They would not delude themselves with pleasing, but totally unreal fancies.

Singing being a natural function, it must conform to law. The only way of telling this is through the result. If you are learning a new movement in skating and fall down, it is painfully evident to you that you did not do it in the proper way, since we understand enough about gravitation to know that if you offend the law you are punished immediately, no matter what you may have intended.

Yet in singing, pupils keep on, time after time, trying a way that will not work, not understanding that they must be proceeding on an incorrect theory. If their idea is correct, that is what nature intended, and the result will be good; if not, nature is not at fault; they simply are doing the wrong thing. They do not understand that they must conform to natural law, which always works in a perfectly definite manner, but have the idea that singing is artificially acquired muscular control, and if they persevere, sometime they will get it. Understanding that singing is the result of a natural function does not make people singers, but it does give the clue to the truth. If intelligently followed, it will save students from a number of the common pitfalls into which so many tumble.

An unruly tongue often is cited for difficulties where, if the truth were better understood, the blame does not rest on the tongue at all. In many cases it is easy to be seen that the tongue is drawn back and all "bunched up" so that the passage through the back of the mouth, which should be open to admit the free outflow of the tone, is almost closed. This makes the tone thick and muddy in quality, renders distinct enunciation impossible, and presents a problem which must be solved if the singer is ever to gain proper control of his voice.

The back of the tongue forms the front of the throat, so if there be any improper tension in the throat, the tongue will be stiffened and unable to perform its functions in enunciation, and will interfere with the free emission of the tone. But the tongue is not causing the trouble, it is merely a visible signpost indicating that trouble exists down below. The vital functions, the interaction of the breath and throat which actually produce the tone, are hidden away from sight, while some of the bad results that come necessarily from improper breath action are plainly visible. Some singers adopt all sorts of expedients to get the tongue forward out of the way, holding the back down with a spoon, or even in some cases taking hold of the tip of the tongue with the fingers and drawing it forward by main strength. But nothing is done to correct the real difficulty. When the tongue acts in this manner it is simply a sign of improper tension in the throat.

Why do so many singers enunciate so indistinctly that it is often impossible to tell what language they are using? Usually, because they are not thinking of what the words mean, but have their minds fixed on making what they feel to be a good tone. Of course, if they do not make a good tone nobody will care to listen to them, but unless they use their skill to give expression to the meanings of both poetry and music, they will find that few are interested in what they do.

Young singers get so bound up in the consideration of the technical side of their work that they forget that technic is but the means to an end; the expression of beauty is the true purpose of singing. The distinct enunciation of the words is one of the ways in which this beauty is given to the hearers, and unless it is there, the singer will be uninteresting. Put your mind on making the words mean something, then they will begin to come out clearly. If they don't, you will be conscious of the fact, and you will then learn to make them expressive.

Many singers labor under the delusion that keeping time renders music mechanical and detracts from its expressive power. This merely shows that they are immature and do not understand the laws

(*Continued on page* 149)

The Vocal Flight

By BELL T. RITCHIE

PADEREWSKI, in addressing Sembrich when a young woman, told her she had three pairs of wings with which to fly to fame: as a pianist, as a violinist, and as a singer. When she realized she had a voice, she chose the last as her greatest treasure and with it passed to supreme success.

Not only is the human voice a most thrilling instrument, but it is unique in its power of the spoken word wherewith to utter thoughts common to the soul of the listener, and give to him the highest emotional beauty of the human soul. The door is open for the singer through the medium of his voice to lift his audience by means of words into realms of imagination quite beyond material experience.

At the outset the student should appreciate his unique position and power, to say nothing of the joy that personally will be his. It can live only in being given to others. The first tone he makes must be through a desire to give to one listener the beauty he feels from within. This leads to the foundation of tone—the breath which controls his life or soul.

Thinking of giving beauty makes the breath flow instead of being held. One should never think of holding a tone, rather think of letting the breath flow through one in tone. This makes effortless singing. If we keep our mind on loveliness, the emotions are quickened and the throat tends to remain open, causing a depth of tone to well up from below.

When we first began to sing, we must realize that the breath is like a person, highly sensitive. It has been accustomed always to speech but not to tone. Sustained tones frighten it at the outset. If we begin with the medium voice, which is used in speech, taking no more breath than needed for speech, the breath will flow naturally, the muscles of the neck, tongue and throat will all relax as in speaking. In a quality half singing, half speaking, the whole set-up will respond readily.

Our greatest fault is taking too much breath. In speech we never think of it, and so are constantly supplied, but when singing, we are prone to fill up with breath which cannot expend itself in the medium voice; hence we have strangulation, gasping for more breath when we really have too much. Begin the opening phrase of a song with no more care than when speaking. Yet there must be control of the abdominal muscle, which, linked with the side ribs and those of the breast, control the lungs. In this place there is tension, for the whole burden of song, be it light or intense, is given over to this muscle.

Many untrained singers subconsciously believe the voice is controlled in the mouth, hence the constriction that follows. Whereas, if we simply open our mouths, think, "Thank God I can sing" and just let it flow, amazing ease will come. We can enjoy the flow in the realm of beauty when the throat is open naturally; the marvelous mechanism of head and throat cavities will serve us, and beauty itself is here. Should one have difficulty in breathing naturally, by sitting down, and throwing the body over the knees, the huge muscles of the pelvis region will at once show where control of the breath lies.

The organs of speech are the tip of the tongue, the middle of the lips, and the teeth. In singing it seems to me that it is fundamental to have correct enunciation. Certain consonants are said with the tongue, others with the lips. One must feel the words on the lips; as Plunket Greene says, "literally taste them." Again, Walford Davies says one must feel them "dancing on the lips." The function of the jaw is simply to bring the lips, tongue or teeth together; it has no control of the tongue itself.

Confining enunciation to the organs of speech, this control of lips, tongue, and teeth engages the deep abdominal muscle connected to the diaphram. Long phrases may be carried on with no thought of breath by simply staying on the words. One discovers marvelous breath supply by just thinking of the words. Sing as if you were carrying on a conversation, telling something interesting to someone. Always see the end of your phrase, hear it and you will have supply. Keeping your mind on the end will bring all the breath required; gradually longer tones will appear as a natural matter.

Another most important factor in singing—one at the basis of its power—is *rhythm*. Rhythm is the onward urge like the tread of passing soldiers on parade. The final consonant of any word is linked with the first syllable of the following word; like the

(*Continued on page* 141)

A Cobblestone Road

By SERGEI RADAMSKY

DURING some thirty years, while actively engaged in opera and concert singing here and abroad, I have heard many disparaging remarks about the lack of muscianship and one-track-mindedness of singers. The criticism was that their only concern was voice, voice and again voice.

Singers of today are a great deal more versatile, especially American singers. John Charles Thomas has sung in light opera, vaudeville, Italian and French opera, on the concert stage and on the radio. Lawrence Tibbett, besides the opera and the concert stage also appeared as star on the screen, and is vitally dynamic and a socially-minded personality. Many singers are more than mere vocalists.

It seems paradoxical that in this country where specialization has reached so high a level, singers really are the least specialized. The majority of American concert and operatic singers are conversant with French, Italian, Spanish and German. Many of them have even learned to sing in Russian, Swedish, Polish, Yiddish and Hebrew, and perform in grand opera, light opera, oratorio, radio and the films.

Concert programs often consist of arias from operas, operettas and oratorios, including art songs and folk songs of European and Latin American countries in their original tongues, placed before auditors who understand only English. The American concert singer also translates and recites the poetry or substance of the song or aria, and often tells charming little anecdotes, at times very boring.

Singers of the past decades had a less difficult task. Their repertoire mainly consisted of Italian arias, with a smattering of French, and an encore in "pidgin" English. Wilner, Hynemann, Julia Culp, Elena Gerhardt specialized in German lieder almost exclusively. Caruso occasionally would break into folk songs. But for all they added to his fame, he might better have confined himself to *Ridi Pagliacco*.

As previously stated, the American singers are more versatile. Geraldine Farrar sang in excellent German, Italian and French. Marian Anderson sings her complete repertory in the original tongues. Jan Peerce is equally at ease in seven different languages and in as many styles. Edward Johnson and Reinhold Werrenrath were equally versatile. So is Richard Crooks. Richard Hale, a superb actor and narrator, renders all his songs in their original languages. There are at least one hundred lesser known singers who can please an audience with their interpretations in various languages.

With the overpublicized, fabulous salaries of film, radio, and operatic stars, and the recently enacted G.I. Bill of Rights, tens of thousands of men and women are studying to become singers. No doubt many of them are qualified, but few are aware of the difficult road that lies ahead. And those of the teaching profession are to some extent responsible for the carefree attitude manifested by young students towards their future career.

How many teachers tell these young people the truth about their lack of qualifications, Their excuse is that if they don't teach them somebody else will, or that no one can tell who will or will not make the grade. Hard work, money, connections, good looks, may pave the road to success. No doubt, they can. But there are certain indispensable requirements, such as vocal material, youth, musical aptitude, good health, desire to study, ability to sacrifice and above all, a knowledge of the hazards to be encountered on the road to a successful career. Many gifted students never arrive because they focus their attention only on the glamorous side of the profession. The newspapers seldom relate the accounts of young people who have given the best years of their lives and their last dollar, and ended in bitter disappointment.

During my years in Milano I came across many Americans who spent many years and many dollars and never learned to sing. Their lives were sad and, in some cases, tragic. Of the several hundred American students in Milano between 1923-1925, only Frederick Jagel has reached the top, and several have managed to earn a livelihood. Of the rest, the women got married, some of the men went into business and the majority of the unsuccessful ones became vocal teachers.

(*Continued on page* 135)

Why Sing?

By MADGE de WITT

SO you want to learn to sing! Of course you do, or you wouldn't be consulting me about your voice problems. But there's something else I must know about you before we get to work—something even more important than your overwhelming desire to be a singer. It's simply this:

Why do you want to sing? Let's examine your motives. What are your aims? Are they fame, wealth, position? If these are your aims, then I feel sorry for you. Go get yourself a good job and make singing your hobby. We can't build a sturdy house on such a shaky foundation.

But if you love songs—if you love music—and if you want to become a singer because of your great love for music and for singing, then I'm interested in you. You have possibilities. You are on the road to greatness, even though you may not be aware of it.

Examine your motives. If they are selfish—"how much will my singing bring to me?"—then you're licked before you start. But if they are unselfish—"what will my singing do for others?"—then you're ready to roll up your sleeves and get started.

You will find that singers are "developed"; they are not "born". Voices are "evolved"; they unfold; but in order for them to unfold, the mental soil must be well-cultivated.

Yes, your mental attitude and your intellect are the main prerequisites for successful singing. How could you possibly ever get the mechanics of good singing if you can't direct your thought correctly towards achieving them? If you can't do it mentally, how could you ever hope to do it physically? The teacher must understand this technic and be able to direct the student accordingly.

If you can first create a mental picture of these fundamentals, you'll go ahead faster than the student who works entirely from the mechanical viewpoint. Even if he should achieve mechanical perfection, his voice may have no "soul"—and a voice without a heart and soul will never be truly successful. If your mental concept of singing is perfect, your mechanical production of the tone will be perfect.

You must have a dogged desire to master each step along the way, no matter how tedious the ground-work may be. You must be willing to master scales before trying an aria from your favorite opera. Your intellect must be pliable and adaptable; you must be willing to understand and to reason out the fundamental principles of voice culture.

Of course, there must be some degree of natural talent. But talent is not sufficient unto itself; a combination of sincerity, intellect, work, and talent is the formula for success.

Having arrived at the correct mental state, the first step is voice training—the head above the jaw. The placing of sound in the nasal passages gives a brilliance and positive quality to the voice. If you can visualize the head as a sounding box with the various bone structures as tuning forks, you can understand how the pressure of air or breath, coming from a free and open throat upon these tuning forks, produces a tone. Throat tones lack resonance and have a rough, grating sound.

Breathing is the foundation of voice culture. Proper breathing necessitates the expansion of the pelvic muscles and the depression of the diaphragm, which in turn, causes an expansion of the abdominal muscles over the solar-plexus. This method of breathing develops capacity and reserve. It creates the control and power which enables you to keep the breath "inside" and likewise sing from the "inside." (The rise and fall of the chest does not indicate proper breathing; as a matter of fact, it usually indicates improper breathing.)

Enunciation, languages, and expression are important factors; they, too, are necessary to round out a singer—but they are studied after the voice itself has become strong and perfected.

Pathos and depth of emotion are most important. You must sing from your soul and heart in order to penetrate the soul and heart of your listeners. Warmth and personality or the lack of warmth and personality are as obvious in a voice as in an individual.

Suppose you found a piece of unpolished jade. It might be fairly pretty in its natural state. But when you take this jade to a stone-cutter and have it

(Continued on page 152)

Why Not Sing?

By ALTA TURK

WHAT person is there alive who has not felt sometime an urge to express himself in song? And why is it that the average man leaves that urge unsatisfied, and depends upon a few whom he considers "chosen people" to sing the songs that would give him so much pleasure and satisfaction to sing himself, when it is possible for everyone with the desire and average intelligence to sing and to sing well?

If the average man knew just how simple and easy it is to sing, more people would be enjoying that activity. Soon the average person would be singing better than the artists of the day, and the artists would be singing still better because more would be expected of them as the audience would have a greater appreciation and understanding of singing. Auditors naturally would demand more and it would be a challenge to each artist to raise the standard. As it is, many artists now think they have to "sing down" to their audience.

Singing is the amplification of the correct speaking voice, in other words—glorified speech.

The principle underlying singing is so simple that it is profound, and like all simple truth is overlooked. The value of it may be lost to most people, yet that principle belongs to all.

Singing is a natural emotional outlet, activity, or means of self-expression, as much as talking, walking, dancing, swimming, laughing or crying, and serves the same purpose as any of the arts. The only difference is the method of release.

Singing ranks high among the arts because it combines all the fundamental principles of the others, plus the use of the spoken word, which is our highest form of culture, and the most valuable means of contact in our social order.

The standard of singing today is the lowest among the arts. Why? Because to understand the voice thoroughly, one must equally understand human nature in general and himself in particular. There is a secret fear in the hearts of most of us that if we become too intimate with ourselves, we may find we are not all we would like to be.

When a balance of the mental, emotional, and physical energies is reached, with the aid of the reasoning power, we have coordination, and the re-

(Continued on page 151)

Vocal Millionaires

By GENNARO M. CURCI

OF major importance to teachers and students is a clear understanding of the difference between resonance and noise. The first and most important problem for a singer should be to acquire in his voice the greatest amount of resonance. Resonance must be the only source of power and with it comes beauty.

All instruments, string, wind or percussion, have their "cassa di risonanza" (resonance chamber) without which rich and agreeable tones cannot be produced.

The human voice, like all other instruments, has its own "resonance chamber," which consists of the intricate formation of pharynx, frontal sinus and nasal cavities. If the tones produced by the vocal cords do not pass through the "resonance chamber", the result is poor and of an unpleasant quality, merely noise. No matter how strong those tones may be, they still will remain noise.

The richness of this sounding board can be either a natural gift or one acquired through methodical study. Without discussing the artistry or musical intelligence of any great singers, I will only mention the very few who, in my opinion, by nature possessed the gift of an exceptional "resonance chamber".

Among the women of the last three decades who possessed or still possess naturally resonant voices are Melba, Burzio, Galli-Curci, Bori, Raisa, Destinn, Muzio, Rethberg, Agostinelli, Ponselle, Stignani, Besanzoni, Milanov, Flagstad, Pons, Traubel and Sayao. Some of these queens of the opera produced beautiful and powerful tones with little pressure of their breath, because their "resonance chambers" were so sensitive and responded quickly without forcing their voices.

For this reason such dramatic sopranos as Raisa, Burzio, Rethberg, Destinn, Muzio, Agostinelli and Ponselle could deliver beautiful legato (that is the "bel canto") and also rapid passages with the fluidity of a coloratura. The same lovely "bel canto" can be heard today from the voices of Flagstad, Milanov and Traubel. And for the same reason we have heard Melba, Bori and Galli-Curci (three lyric coloraturas) give power and dramatic color in such operas as *Boheme*, *Butterfly*, *Mignon* and Puccini's *Manon*, yet without forcing their voices. Today we still have

(Continued on page 150)

Poise Means Freedom

By HARRIET HOLT

POISE or the lack of poise, as understood by critics, is that attribute which seems to cover all the undefinable good or bad points in a performance. When we leave the realms of technic and musicianship we may well be in the realm of poise. Webster tells us that poise is "balance" or "to make steady or stable." The artist must have physical, mental, and emotional poise. They are interdependent and each is useless without the other.

Physical poise is the first phase noticeable to the listener. The relaxed body, proceeding with simplicity and surety, induces self-confidence and at once the audience also relaxes, to enjoy the performance. The artist's posture, and manner of walk and stance, should be vital and enthusiastic, but unhurried. His attitude before each number should express these same qualities. Thus he prepares himself and his listeners, through this moment of vitalized relaxation, to more thoroughly enjoy the emotional content of each succeeding number. Actually, physical poise is the outward manifestation of mental poise, but the mechanical technic of body movement can be learned through study and application of correct eurythmics.

Mental poise is all-important. Without it there can be no physical or emotional balance. Voice and body complement and reflect thought. As the artist thinks and feels, so is his voice. The stable, well balanced mind is alert and easily aware of situations and circumstances and can cope with them. Sensitive mental perception is necessary to understand subtle values whether they be audience reaction, artistic capabilities or emotional and musical content of the composition.

With mental relaxation and clarity, one is free to feel and then produce. Seconds of stillness serve to let the artist sense his own confidence and assurance, enabling him to express through inspiration along with his technical knowledge. The artist should never dwell on past mistakes, but rather take them as lessons. He should not mentally pull away from any difficult posture or expression, for this denotes uncertainty. His mental poise must open the door to imagination and inspiration. He must trust his thought. Mentally and emotionally the voice must be commanded with authority and given generously in

(Continued on page 151)

Simplicity In Song

By NICHOLAS E. BARABE

IF one is taught to sing easily and without effort, one of the basic points in teaching, and also to achieve naturalness when performing, so that nothing can detract from the song, it will be found that simplicity and spontaneity go hand in hand. Since voice is the most difficult of the musical arts because of the intangibility of its instrument, teachers should and must reduce all factors to their simplest form. To clutter an already complicated situation with mystery and more intangibility is not only ridiculous but dishonest.

As the son of a dental surgeon, I had opportunity to study more of the physiological aspects of voice production than the average student. Space does not permit here a full explanation of the complete physical action in every detail. But much can be given simply and without unnecessary complications by the teacher.

Though all teachers know, or should know, that physiological procedure is dependent always on mental facility, they sometimes, through lack of interest or for some other reason, allow a pupil to sing without the slightest evidence of constructive thought. If the preponderance of voice students were morons, one could perceive the significance of such phrases as "throw your voice into the corner," or "when you sing your low tones, imagine you are singing into a bucket," or perhaps an even more priceless bit of instruction would be: "When you wish to sing a high tone, take a deep breath, drop the jaw, lower the head to achieve the illusion of singing over something, then throw the tone upward and forward." But thank goodness, moronic pupils are definitely in the minority.

Long periods spent by students in the various studios throughout the world, listening to abstract phrases and vocal abracadabra could well be eliminated. A simple explanation of the physiological and mental processes concerned in working out a vocal problem, accompanied by correct vocalizes, would save untold time and money for the aspiring singer. Too often there is a certain amount of hush-hush, and "this was handed down to me and is not generally known" at each lesson. If such is the case, the pupil, to borrow from our ancient friend Omar Khayyam, "comes out by that same door wherein he went."

(Continued on page 150)

Sing and Like It!

By BRIAN SULLIVAN

SO you want to sing? Take each rung of the ladder slowly and carefully, if you would reach the top. I know that I am far from the top of that ladder, but I believe that each of us has experiences that strengthen us and make the next step easier to scale. I know, too, that the moment I consider I have acquired sufficient musical knowledge, and begin coasting on that premise, I will be heading for a fall.

Keep your singing career ever new, ever fresh: never allow it to become a routine matter. Make every performance seem as though it were the first, rather than the last.

Make every word count in your own or foreign languages, and learn other languages to speak as well as to sing. Auditors, I have learned, love to have each word literally bounce on their eardrums. They love to feel they are with the performer from start to finish. Never swallow your words, or lose them in an effort to prove what a terrific voice you have.

Never limit yourself as to the amount of studying you will do—can a musician ever know too much about music?

Naturally a singer must have that certain quality in his voice that will carry him through many successful years, but first and foremost, one must *love* to sing. I know the fact that I sincerely love to sing has helped me, and is helping me towards my goal.

Acting is essential. Why shouldn't our movements, our mannerisms on the stage be as natural and as well balanced as our musical tones? By all means study acting under the guidance of a skillful coach, and learn to make your acting and singing works of art by harmoniously combining them.

And then there's that big little word "patience." If one note, one phrase seems difficult to reach, don't leave it until you have conquered it. Be the master of your score!

Take every singing engagement that you personally feel will give you more experience. Church singing teaches true musicianship and the quiet dignity a singer needs. Oratorio makes a singer control himself emotionally. But by all means, do not type yourself; be proficient in all phases of singing.

Watch your appearance! Audiences are very clothes-conscious. They notice our poise, our hair, our weight—everything.

The Arduous Road

By MEBANE BEASLEY

THE aspirant to a singing career should bear in mind a few vital, pertinent points.

He will need a strong, healthy body, governed by an alert mind, for the road to success is not easy, nor is it paved with roses. It requires stamina, determination and the ability to withstand physical as well as mental hardships.

He must retain a conscientious love for singing, for only that we love do we do well.

He must possess correct body control and singing position, deep breathing and breath application, understanding of the soft palate and how and why it functions, control of largnyx, proper vowel and consonant formation, and the right muscular development and coordination.

He must be equipped with sight singing, languages, properly selected and prepared repertory, and stage technic. He must have a pleasing personality and an attractive personal appearance. And he must be under the right management and have the right publicity promotion.

The aspirant who is unwilling to spend at least five years in mastering the above points should seek another vocation. For singers who are unprepared only cheapen the profession, while facing inevitable discouragement themselves.

In the very exercise of their profession, teachers dedicate their lives to preparing young people who want to be singers. They should be very careful in the selection of pupils, not to waste or misdirect talent. Each pupil is an individual study in himself. Some of the most talented are the hardest to teach, and in such cases love and patience is necessary. But the ultimate reward is a successful artist.

Don't be a slave to your work. Read, play, relax at some kind of sport, such as golf or tennis. Keep physically fit, for all singers are expected to possess an unlimited amount of energy.

Be sure to have confidence in yourself. If you let discouragement creep into your consciousness, you can say good-bye to a vocal career.

Sing, sing, sing—and enjoy every note!

Pueblos To The Movies

Grunn, one of the Southland's outstanding pianists and, under the name of Brahms Quintet, continued to concertize for seven years.

Another chamber music group, one which had an important bearing on the musical future of the city, was the Saint-Saens Quintet, organized about 1910. Its first violinist was Edwin H. Clark and its 'cellist the philanthropist William A. Clark, Jr., who sponsored the group, the concerts being given to invited audiences. The particular significance about this quintet was that, through it, Clark became so interested in music and its mission that he founded the present Los Angeles Philharmonic Orchestra, in 1919, and financed it to the extent of three million dollars.

Besides Clark, founder and sponsor of the Philharmonic Orchestra, credit is due two other men for its ultimate success, Lynden Ellsworth Behymer and Walter Henry Rothwell. Behymer had taken an active interest in the musical life of the city since 1886. He assisted in the formation of the first Los Angeles Symphony Orchestra, and was its business manager for eighteen years. And it was he, too, who brought Adelina Patti, Sarah Bernhardt, Enrico Caruso, and other world renowned stage and operatic personalities to Los Angeles.

Rothwell lifted the Philharmonic Orchestra to a high standard. He practically built the orchestra, combining skill, perseverance, and patience to bring out the best in his musicians. The Philharmonic Orchestra was his creation.

Upon Rothwell's death, in 1927, the baton was entrusted to the hands of Georg Schneevoight. Artur Rodzinski, assistant conductor of the Philadelphia Symphony Orchestra, succeeded Scheevoight in 1929. When Rodzinski assumed the conductorship of the Cleveland Symphony Orchestra, in 1934, he was followed on the podium by Otto Klemperer who, owing to serious illness, was forced to withdraw in 1939 and the conductorship divided between Bruno Walter, Albert Coates and Leopold Stokowski.

Perhaps no other single event has done more for the advancement of music in Los Angeles than the acquisition of the Hollywood Bowl, a natural amphitheatre in the Hollywood Hills. Since then, the "Symphonies Under The Stars", presented each summer for eight weeks, has attracted world-wide attention.

The genesis of the Hollywood Bowl dates back to 1916, when a performance of Julius Caesar was staged under that heavenly cyclorama. Other dramatic productions followed. But when the idea of open-air concerts was first suggested, a number of impresarios and musicians pooh-poohed it. However, despite difficulties and discouragements, the group sponsoring the idea incorporated, in 1920, under the name of The Community Park and Art Association, and F. W. Blanchard was chosen president. The other officers and directors included F. E. Keenan, Mrs. Mary Rankin Clarke, Mrs. Artie Mason Carter, E. N. Martin, Dr. T. Perceval Gerson, Allen C. Blach, and C. E. Toberman. In 1924, the organization re-incorporated under the name of The Hollywood Bowl Association. In 1926, Allan C. Balch became president of the Association and Mrs. Leiland Atherton Irish was made chairman of the summer concert committee.

The first series of summer concerts at the Bowl were given in 1922, Alfred Hertz conducting. Since those early days, when music lovers sat on blankets or lap robes on the dusty hillsides, down to the present when 20,000 seats accommodate the audience, a total of more than 8,000,000 have attended Bowl presentations. The distinguished conductors who occupied the Bowl's podium include Walter Henry Rothwell, Eugene Goossens, William Van Hoogstraten, Howard Hanson, Pierre Monteux, Bruno Walter, Bernardino Molinari, Albert Coates, Sir Henry Wood, Sir Hamilton Harty.

Today L.A. ranks as the music-center of the world. Outstanding composers, conductors, instrumentalists and singers, too numerous to mention, have been summoned here by the motion picture industry. And from the sound-track of Hollywood pictures, some of the best and finest melodies come pouring through.

Opera On Its Toes

win their audiences immediately. Their position, though envied by every other dancer, is far from being an easy one, for they seldom have a second opportunity to redeem themselves in the event of error. In opera they rarely have the stage to themselves, and always must interpret someone else's ideas.

Ballet gives the much needed "lift" to opera, and is eagerly awaited by the audience. At the Paris Opera House, operas are not accepted for presentation unless they include an outstanding ballet sequence. It was for this famous house that Wagner added the Venusberg ballet to *Tannhaeuser*, and Verdi inserted the large gypsy ballet into the third act of *Il Trovatore*.

Ballet always will have a definite and important place in opera as long as it fills the function for which it was intended, and does not merely use the opera as an excuse for virtuose display. And its popularity is attested anew at every performance.

All Means To an End

uncontrollable rigidity will appear. He should continue concentrating upon weight, and weight only, until such playing is basic with the student.

Assuming that a weight technic has now become second nature to the pianist, he may examine the multitude of approaches in which arm weight is absent or only incidental. Here we must recognize that even absolute rigidity will have its instantaneous moments. Bravura playing often demands it. Very rapid light staccato passages may be played with finger stroke only. Light octaves may be played from the wrist. Every possibility must be explored.

So-called finger technic is concerned primarily with articulation of the individual digits. The forearm is carried along while the elbow is flexed about ninety degrees. The upper arm hangs loose or adjusts the position of the forearm. With this technic, the wrist may be relaxed so that the hand weight assists the fingers in tone production, or the hand itself may be suspended with the minimum requisite wrist tension so that tone is solely the result of finger stroke. When the pianist is ready to include this technic in his equipment, his concern becomes that of the older schools—the strengthening of finger attack and, with this, the development of speed in flexion and retraction.

This may be the place to employ some of the multitude of finger studies written in the past, but the goal must be not merely the striking of the keys, but rather the mastery of a controlled stroke ranging from staccato to legato, with absolute evenness between the fingers. Matthay describes this technic admirably under the heading "Added Impetus".

Another phase of practice will be concerned with acquisition of a wrist and a forearm technic in which single tones, octaves, or chords are produced by a muscular stroke of the hand or forearm. Here, particularly, stiffness in muscles which should remain relaxed must be avoided. If hand stroke is practiced, the forearm must be suspended with as little effort as possible and the upper arm must hang loose much of the time. Of course, the ability to relax one set of muscles while exerting others is a prime essential in all technic. Wrist and forearm technics seem to be outstanding offenders in the matter of unnecessary tension. The forearm stroke will be used less often than the hand stroke, but it has its place in a comprehensive technic.

The last technical category—and it should be last —deals with those applications of rigidity which

Liszt termed "Vibrato". Thomas Fielden describes them thoroughly in his *Science of Pianoforte Technic*. These include many states of resilient muscular tension during which the force of the whole arm, or of the body, is applied to the key. They are too numerous to detail here, but they embrace all those attacks during which one key is struck, not only for its own sake, but also as a springboard for the playing of following tones.

These are the technics of "bravura". Without them no pianist can reach the top. They are not only very hard to master, but their premature practice may break the student down entirely. It must also be pointed out that their injudicious application will make the playing sound noisy and unmusical. They are to be reserved for moments when they are clearly required for musical reasons.

In reviewing the subject of pianoforte technic within so short a space, it is clear that no attempt can be made to indicate the suitability of any particular technical approach. Such consideration must always be predicated upon the nature of each work played. Also, it is impossible to cover such important matters as fingering and practice routines. I only wish to emphasize that the great technician is great because every imaginable device is under his command, so that he can always select that which will best serve his interpretation.

When every manner of technical approach has been mastered and can be employed with limitless facility, we say that the pianist is a "virtuoso". Unfortunately, every virtuoso is not a true artist. Some are concerned with showing off their virtuosity rather than with artistic fidelity. On the other hand, there are many pianists whose musical results suffer through technical inadequacy.

Technic is the "means" of performance. Interpretation is the end. One must not only be technically equipped to do all, but one must possess a high degree of musicianship to properly employ a great technic.

Keep Your Tools Sharp

composer that he is afraid to study music theory for fear it will destroy his originality, I am reminded of a cartoon I once saw of a bored young woman and a worried and perspiring music professor: the student, lightly waving aside the notes on the blackboard, remarking,—"I didn't come to you to learn how to *read* music; I just wanta know how to write it!"

The Attitude Counts

the possibility of artistry or skilled craftmanship from such a comparatively superficial experience. A careful start to preclude errors is the cheapest and shortest way in artistic training. The private teacher, properly chosen, is more highly and specially equipped. Conversely, public school teachers are required to be more versatile. The same personal attention is not received by the child in class work. In private lessons he may progress in proportion to his ability, and subject matter is more comprehensive, intensive and complete. The private teacher can direct and promote preparation for concerts with intelligence, experience and without being criticized for favoritism.

What are the elementary evidences of talent by which a parent may be guided if a career is desired? The greatest and least recognized is again attitude. Success can only happen through the will to express it—through the great enjoyment of projecting musical beauty and sharing it by adequate performance for others. The person who really wants a career will find a way and discipline himself for it to materialize. The need is for guidance as to the best medium, whether voice, instrument, composition, etc.

A child who wants music has the first evidence of talent. A good ear, natural coordination in physical skills, ease and enjoyment of public performance or appearance—these are the obvious signs, but ambition is the most practical of all the indications. The great assets of musical, social and educational heritages, like inherited wealth, are of invaluable help if used and not abused; but these are not essential to one who wills to succeed. Talent is a great asset, but not necessarily the whole principal.

Earnest parents who lack the advantage of a musical education ask us, "What can I do to help?" For them as well as for those musically trained there are responsibilities and ideals that are equally applicable:

1. To encourage listening to good music enthusiastically, and on a par with other family activities.

2. A definite scheduled routine for practice adjusted to family conditions.

3. Attendance at studio or public recitals, which are a type of examination, except that they are performed for parents and friends and depend upon the appearance of both parent and child for vitality and effect.

4. Not to assume the teacher's duty at home.

5. To respect and trust the music teacher.

6. To encourage music at home. Help the child to respond to requests for his performance, and listen attentively as though it were not the thousandth time.

7. To provide the best possible music library. The great mass of this literature is barely touched at lesson time and must be sought by the pupil himself. Sight reading is largely a matter of practice. Phonographs and records can do much to add enthusiasm and musical morale.

What then must the music teacher contribute to all this?

1. Recognizable progress by the student in performance, artistry and attitude toward real study.

2. Sincere attention to his combined needs. "To the pupil according to his needs, from him according to his ability."

3. Opportunities for semi-public and public performances.

4. Encouragement to the student to broaden his musical interests and activities, coordinating music with his daily life.

5. Promptness and regularity in appointments. A standardized business policy.

In short, the whole attitude of teacher, parent and student toward music study may be expressed by again quoting David Patterson: "A music teacher is not a court jester engaged once or twice a week to entertain your child, but an educator dealing in jewels of the mind so precious as to have won and deserve reverence in the hearts of mankind and in the deeds of great composers."

Music By the Yard

in the thick of it. Few composers of concert music have the benefit of the ready-made audition of their works that accrues to the composer of filmusic, and in no other field can a composer experiment almost endlessly with new and unusual musical effects as he can in this field, where those effects are needed and wanted.

The next time you see a movie, listen to the music too, and maybe you will notice a thing or two that will interest you, especially if you are a musician or composer yourself—perhaps you will even want to trace the thematic material in its development with the plot. At any rate, quite a bit of it makes nice listening, whether you permit it to distract your attention from the story or not.

New Sounds on the Air

ly" has no comic section and that "Superman Comics" is unconcerned with world affairs, does not materially affect the circulation of either periodical. In other words, there is not only room for, there is a need for specialization.

I envision the day when the several million persons living in and about an area such as Los Angeles will have their choice of not one dozen but three or four dozen radio stations. To be sure, there will still be the large networks, with the Jack Bennys, the Bob Hopes, and the high Hoopers. But at the same time, the alternatives to the Hopes and the Bennys will be more than just carbon copy shows that are budgeted at five instead of fifteen thousand dollars.

And the alternatives will be more than just a couple of hours of recorded symphony music a day. Or a couple of hours of jazz. The alternatives will be found on those dozens of specialized stations.

There will be, perhaps, two or three stations that play nothing but classical music. Not just an hour here, an hour there, but all day. And not just the familiar "Pathetiques" and "Eroicas", but the equally pathetic and heroic compositions of less well known composers.

There's a reason why we don't hear all the performances of the Los Angeles Philharmonic Orchestra, the Hollywood Bowl concerts, the local operas, the multitude of other musical events. Quite simply, the large stations either cannot afford or do not choose to cancel out their commercial shows for such cultural events. The smaller stations, grabbing what's left of the live shows, and making their fortunes on spot announcements, similarly cannot afford or do not choose to be so esoteric in their programming.

Think, however, how all that available music would appeal to a small station which was keyed to that type of presentation. Here would be no cause of sandwiching in a couple of hours of "public service". Here would be the small station with its own Jack Bennys and Bob Hopes—only their names would be Wallenstein, Pinza, Rubinstein, et al.

Other stations could specialize, as many of them do now, on the popular tunes of the day. By records and remote control, the Freddy Martins and Frankie Carles could continue to entertain as backdrops to the morning's wash or the evening's beer.

The jazz devotee, now sharing the same plight as his longer haired brother, would not have to wait patiently for a once-a-week Eddie Condon show. Nor would he have to listen through hours of unhep disc jockeys and records before digging the duke for a few minutes. No, he would have at the flick of his dial stations which could be depended upon for "le jazz hot" and undiluted.

And so it should go. More stations: more music: more different kinds of music. And concurrently, more listeners: more music lovers.

The increased competition of more stations, more programs, and more and increasingly varied music will undoubtedly have a salutary effect on commercial broadcasting. It's the rule rather than the exception for the agency and network producers to be guided by "what has been done" rather than "what should or might be done".

One of the results of this type of thinking has been that the orchestras on most commercial radio shows sound alike. (Indeed, too often are the same men playing the same arrangements.)

My guess is that in the future, the sounds will be different. The music behind Jean Sablon will not be the same as the music between Fred Allen and Mrs. Nussbaum. And the musical cues for *Suspense* will differ from the musical cues for *Ma Perkins*.

Admittedly I'm drawing the picture in broad lines. But the resemblance is still there. That's why I am so confident that the future will bring forth increased originality in composition, arrangement and orchestration. That's why I'm so confident that music on the air will be increasingly organic to the individual program, and will have new vitality, new sounds to enchant the listener.

The Initial Adventure

the treasures to be found in chamber works, for example, which unfailingly bring a new consciousness of musical values, or neglecting the study of lieder which will be of such an illuminating character that its musical influence will be felt permanently.

Specialists in any particular musical field will be primarily mechanicians unless their experience has extended over widely varied phases of musical literature, thus attaining musical understanding, artistic convictions and maturity. It is not a suitable field for those of limited vision, those who are readily discouraged, those who lack an adventuring spirit or those who consider it a means of projecting their own ego. However, if a musical life be entered with complete devotion, artistic integrity and love for music itself, the inner rewards are unbounded.

Scherzo

nature. In a letter Mozart writes, "Not a day passes but I think of death"—and "I suffer from fits of melancholy". Does this sound like bubbling happiness in the key of C major?

The tragic and the humorous are indeed often welded into artistic natures. Beethoven as well as Shakespeare were prevented from a fatal solemnity by their genius for humor. It is therefore no accident that Beethoven was the inventor of the "modern" scherzo—the jazzed-up minuet. This movement, created out of his tragic nature, is a sort of symbol of his indestructible spirit which spoke the language of humanity.

Do not, however, search for humor in a Chopin scherzo. Perhaps someone might discover a sort of grim humor in his four scherzi, but even Niecks, the Chopin authority, admits "There is in them neither frolicsomeness nor humor". Chopin, by a strange process of morbid assimilation, created the jokeless scherzo.

Romanticism, Impressionism and other isms took the academic kinks out of music and exerted their own special influence upon the technique of humor. Thus we see Wagner's Romanticism, with all its Teutonic and philosophic magnificence, counterbalanced by his humorous masterpiece *Die Meistersinger*, and Debussy's exquisite humor emerge out of the shadowy clouds of Impressionism.

And, last but not least, Jazz gave humor a new voice with its original rhythm, color and improvizational spirit. The classes as well as the masses were fascinated. Serious composers also "caught on" and stole from the Jazzics. They composed sonatas, concertos, suites and even fugues that seem to laugh as they lost their academic seriousness in syncopation. Among those who fell under the spell are the Who's Who of music from Debussy to Stravinsky.

Some examples are; Debussy's *Golliwog's Cakewalk* and *Minstrels*, Ravel's *Violin Sonata*, Honegger's *Concertino*, Milhaud's *Creation of the World*, Carpenter's *Skyscrapers*, Copland's *Music for the Theater*, Gruenberg's *Daniel Jazz*, Hindemith's *Klavieruebung*, Tansman's *Concerto*, Antheil's *Jazz Symphony*, Weill's *Three-Penny Opera*, Krenek's *Jonny spielt auf*, Stravinsky's *Ragtime* and *Story of a Soldier*. Jazz has helped liberate the modern "classical" composer from the tendency towards intellectual mystification, too much Schopenhauer and atonal counterpoint.

A sense of humor as well as technical considerations are often back of the sophisticated simplicity of composers of the modern school. This is a healthy sign, for the direct and simple style with its optimistic coloring has done much to rid the public of the idea that good music must be dry, sad and unintelligibly weighted with learning. Now a light and graceful work by a first rate composer has a chance of appreciation without the stigma of triviality.

Humor, as well as tragedy, is necessary to music's completeness because it is a part of the record of human emotions. Without it the composer, as well as the listener, is lost in the solemnity of too much profundity.

Music Flows With the Tide

tions with the music of the composer, they will turn to him for relief and mental diversion. Such must be the mold into which the present-day musical idiom must be cast.

It is noteworthy that an overwhelmingly large part of our concert and radio programs is still devoted to the idioms of the past. It must be assumed then that that idiom still ministers to the emotional needs of our audiences. Evidently, there must be a need to wander away from the present into the soothing world of a bygone era. Even a program consisting entirely of compositions of the old masters still appears to satisfy the most fastidious.

If a composer feels that it is more natural for him to express himself in the idiom of the past, let him do so by all means. Outstanding works of the old masters are replayed until they are almost worn threadbare, yet the audience wants more and more of them. Even some of their lesser works are revived perennially. However, the compositions of our present-day idioms are entitled to first consideration. They are nearest to us. They are typical of our age; they represent the idiom of the present day.

In the past, man lived close to nature. The composer's heartbeat swayed in sympathetic resonance with the billowing of the ripening wheat, the rustle of the foliage caressed by the breeze, the babble of the meadowbrook. As time went on, cities developed in number and in size. Vast industrial plants supplanted the pastoral scenes. Workers today carry the clattering pulsation of the machine from their shops to their homes. Passing through streets, they are engulfed by a noise-carnival, by the whistling, honking, shrieking and screeching. This tumult gives rise to a new musical idiom. This confusion of uncoordinated sound is jazz in its first crude form. It is the musical idiom of the Twentieth Century.

The Inside Story

painting and sculpture use form and matter seen through the human eye. Some comparatively new schools make an exception. They are obviously and most interestingly striving to reach the absolute also in their own realms. Architecture, more closely related to music through elements of form, is yet strongly dependent on matter. Poetry, prose and drama need the word.

Music, on the other hand, speaks a language which can never be everyday's and everybody's language; it uses material out of which no houses can be built, with which no pictures can be painted. Why then see its foremost purpose in achieving descriptive, that is, material effects? Why try to imitate other arts instead of rejoicing in music's transcendental qualities in which it is equaled by no other art?

Music's foremost task is bringing messages to its listeners which cannot be expressed in words, in stone or marble, or on canvas. Only pure music can do that, music in which no thought associations of a material nature are forced upon the listener's mind, but on whose immaterialized waves his soul can escape to regions of spiritual beauty.

During the first quarter of this century it seemed as if in the art of the Dance a trend towards emphasizing the absolute, though of course of a different nature than that of music, had gained enough momentum to make this kind of dancing the prevailing one. The later development, however, has taken a different turn. Today, both the dancers and the public seem to favor performances providing for "stories", dramatic action in the longer ballets, pantomimes of some sort in the shorter dance compositions.

It seems that the sheer beauty of motion and formal structure for which the dance is so very fit does not suffice to satisfy either the performers or the public. This is to be regretted, because it deprives us of some splendid opportunities and enjoyments in the field of the arts. Absolute dance, that is dance based on motion and form only, not on dramatic action of any kind, has a powerful and extraordinary quality, particularly if it allies itself with music written especially for this purpose, music that is absolute in all but the purpose to serve as a guide to the dancers in form and mood only.

We live in a materialistic age. Materialism brought the "story-music" into existence in the still more materialistic period before the first World War and keeps it alive today. It is so much easier to cling to a "meaning" in music, or to see a story acted on the dance stage, than to try to penetrate the realms of thought by way of the beauty of tones, or through the beauty of harmonic motions of trained human bodies, or through both.

This endeavor to write absolute music, however, has at all times brought forth music of a much deeper and more lasting kind. Serious young composers, aware of the decline of materialism, which is bound to come soon, will strive therefore to write mostly music of this higher kind.

A Song For Everyone

two months after the Burbank Civic Chorus was organized, the group performed from memory the entire *Polovetzian Dances* from Borodin's *Prince Igor* with symphony orchestra. These people had never sung music of this type previously. An appreciation of the minor wistfulness of the Caucasian melodies and a knowledge of the story of the opera so stirred their imaginations that each one of the ninety people gave his best efforts to creating a commendable performance. With careful planning and proper presentation, every director will find that his chorus can enjoy singing all music from Bach to Gershwin.

Since responsibility stimulates interest, there is no doubt that people work more compatibly when they have jobs to perform for the benefit of the chorus. The officers elected from the group should attend to all business and personnel questions, while the director should have the choosing, rehearsing, and the performance of the music as his duties. When all obligations of the organization are in the director's hands, the result is so often a musical dictatorship. The active business-like functioning of a group of officers will do much to promote an active, satisfied, and hard-working choir.

Music is an unselfish art to be enjoyed by all, whether they be professional musician, amateur, or auditor. If a conductor can help through this intangible and powerful force, to create a means of escape from material interests, he is then, in reality, fulfilling his rightful duty. None of us can ever know the effect of our group's music, both upon the individual performer and the listener, for the living personality perpetuated through beautiful sound never perishes, and the result of music's repeated hearings is always new.

The Library Lends a Hand

the singing societies indigenous to each foreign group, the small halls and intimate theatres, arrangers, transcribers and songwriters. Another aid that grows in value the more it is used is a calendar of musical events. For months ahead we fill out each season's musical schedule to the extent of our knowledge, checking off holidays, feast days and noting anything that might interfere with the size of an audience.

All these grew directly from the requests of the public. A stranger in town wants to join a friendly choral group or study club, a teacher is trying to find where blackboards with the staff on them are sold, a hobbyist desires to reach others interested in his speciality, or the local artist is picking a date for her once-a-year recital to avoid finding that everyone has gone to hear the visiting celebrity.

We have a collection of American popular songs ranging from early 19th century to the present. What our people have whistled, hummed and sung in the collective bathtubs of the nation is a matter of interest to the curious and necessity to novelists, playwrights and program makers.

On the local scene every library should collect its own records. This we have done for San Francisco, resulting in a representative collection of music played, heard and published locally. Augmented by a huge program collection, this permits us to illustrate any decade of the city's musical life. Many are of the early 1850's when Kate Hayes and Anna Bishop were the popular song birds and music halls were full of revelry. Included are hundreds of Tivoli programs from beer garden days to the period that ended with the disaster of 1906. San Francisco's early love of opera is reflected in the programs of one company after another from the first opera performance in 1852. (Incidentally, the opera was *La Sonnambula*, produced by the Pelligrini Opera Company).

This work continues, saving many a long hour of research for the historian of tomorrow and the day after tomorrow. Announcements, bulletins, programs and the critics' reviews, year after year since 1917, give a graphic picture and tell a vivid story of music in San Francisco.

Not so important perhaps, but an inevitable outcome of librarians' interest and the public's curiosity, is a sizeable and lively collection of autographs. These have been scribbled on programs, scrawled on pictures inscribed to the department or to the good friends who have given them to us, or the autograph may be in the form of an interesting letter. These are carefully preserved and grow in affectionate and sentimental value as they become older.

There seems to be an ever wider horizon before the music department; ideas and ideals we never quite reach, but that in working for and sharing with the public we push ever farther ahead of us.

Drastic Decade

thing thrown together in haste, just to make a background of a sort against the development of the story on the screen. Today careful planning and thought is given to every small detail. A great deal of effort is made by the composer to see that his music fits every action and every mood. The best way to achieve this is to have music that has a message in itself. And whenever music has something to say in itself, it becomes an artistic expression and a work of art.

No longer do serious composers consider motion picture music as something beneath their dignity. Composers well known in the concert hall are more and more willing to accept this new field as another medium for their self-expression. Prokofiev, among others, has written scores for several pictures, and two of them, *Lieutenant Kije* and *Alexandre Nevsky* have since been performed by many symphony orchestras and have become a part of standard repertory.

That more and more film scores are bound to find their way to the concert hall, is only a matter of time. There is no doubt that some of the finest contemporary music is being written here in Hollywood. Most of it unfortunately is lost in the background of the story on the screen, or forgotten once the picture has had its run. A work of art, to live on, must be performed, and performed continuously as years go by. The concert hall is naturally the right answer to that.

The motion picture composer is well equipped to give an excellent account of his capabilities as a musician. He has ample opportunities to experiment, and under the most favorable and remunerative conditions. All sorts of tricks, devices and orchestral effects used in scoring pictures have added immeasurably to his knowledge of orchestral coloring.

And when we add to this tremendous technique a natural flair for showmanship and inspiration, we have all the elements necessary for the making of good concert music.

Let us not forget that music, whether it is for the theatre, motion picture or concert hall, is primarily a matter of showmanship. Wagner and Beethoven were well aware of this long ago.

The Growing Art

ly artistic music disappeared from the screen, and the musical background was supplied by cheap, sentimental theme songs. Popular musical numbers filled every picture, regardless of plot or theme.

Several years passed before the films divested themselves of such banal musical accompaniments and restored their dignity by approaching the Wagnerian ideal of the *Gesamtkunstwerk,* wherein music of high standard is an integral part of acting and drama.

Although I regard *Gesamtkunstwerk* as ideal for the screen, I am fully conscious that few attend the movies just to listen to the background music. The music is to the photoplay what the Greek chorus was to the Greek tragedies—a psychological and emotional accentuation of the dramatic story. Scenes lacking dramatic conflict, or having commonplace dialogue, do not need musical accompaniment. In such instances, music would only jar or mar the story sequences. There are, however, dramatic scenes which can be heightened with music by accentuating the rhythm of the picture and underlining the particular idea the story tries to convey pictorially, thus focusing the attention of the audience on its significant scenes. Music has become an indispensable adjunct of the screen, specifically written for it.

Movie music styles still are replete with musical imitation and puerile exerpts from familiar compositions. If modern film music is to achieve any degree of permanence it will have to shed its swaddling clothes. That it will succeed in doing so is evidenced by the adult musical scores turned out now and then—scores in which the music is as vital to the story as its dramatic sequences.

Despite all criticism, it is undeniable that enormous strides have been made in cinema music. While here and there we can still detect the *Hearts and Flowers* and *Poet and Peasant* flavor in scores, there are signs that this tendency sooner or later will vanish completely.

European films, notably those of France and Russia, have gained remarkable dramatic effects through the scoring of modern music, but composers of Hollywood still cling to the romanticism of the Nineteenth Century, regardless of the picture's subject matter. The reasons for this are simple. In the first place, a very limited number of contemporary distinguished composers have been given the opportunity to write music for the screen. And those who were called in by the studios were either obliged to change their style of composition, or their music was exchanged for a more conventional pattern. Secondly, there is the commercial angle, which cannot be ignored.

Every new art form, including contemporary music, is seldom understood by the masses, and the making of pictures is a commercial enterprise which involves fabulous expenditures. Naturally, the industry endeavors to satisfy the greatest number of movie-goers and it cannot afford to take risks with radical innovations. For this reason the industry prefers both story treatments and musical scores of conventional type. However, it is my belief that a musical language of the Twentieth Century will gradually replace the Nineteenth Century as movie-goers grow accustomed to the new musical idiom, and are weaned away from the post-Tchaikovsky period.

The tasks and responsibilities of the modern screen composer are enormous. Film music reverberates throughout the four corners of the world and its listeners are legion. Its educational value is immeasurable. The musically untutored person receives an unconscious musical education in the picture house, and his appreciation for better music can be developed by these means. The modern film composer has it in his power to shape a new musical idiom for a new generation.

Triad Out Of Tune

by displaying a general interest in their child's study of music rather than a specific interest in the kind of compositions the child should be assigned by the teacher.

They can best assist the teacher by seeing that his rules of practice are followed by the child. This does not necessarily mean the use of pressure or force. They only need to manifest a genuine interest in his work, make him feel that they are entertained by his performance of his lessons, thus developing his ego and a desire to perfect his playing so as to gain more of their plaudits. They should keep an eye on the child's practicing rather than on the teacher's teaching.

If teacher and parent are in accord as to the objective they seek—that is, to instill in the child a love of and appreciation for good musicianship, then the third and most important member of the triad, the child itself, will reach the desired goal.

Thus the triad out of tune will become a harmonious entity.

Choreographic Beginnings

have drawn their rarest steps and attitudes anymore than musicians were to publish their musical scores complete with all parts written and the richness of chord content fully written out. More often we find the melodic line for voice and violin, a brass part or two and the rest of the work left for the individual musician or orchestrator.

Before leaving the 17th Century in this brief survey, we should cite the work of Pere Mestrier, *Ballets Anciennes et Modernes*, published by Rene Guignard in 1682. We owe a great deal of our historical knowledge to this author, who, in addition to his information, also sets a pattern which future historians will rather faithfully follow, namely—the dance before the Christian era, the impact of the Church on the Dance, and the modern day ballet.

In 1699, permission was given to Raoul Auger Feuillet to publish his work on dance notation called, *Choregraphic, ou l'Art d'ecrire la Dance*. The first edition followed in 1700. This method, the authorship of which has been disputed, became the first full and comprehensive method of writing dances by signs and symbols and until the actual skeleton line figure was used by various inventors such as Blasis—(who merely indicated the way and unless some of his claimed manuscripts are found, it must be assumed he never completed his project)—Alexandre Saint Leon, and Albert Zorn.

Again, as in the study of the other works of Caroso and Negri, the results do not yield themselves easily. The section of the detached pas of single steps each set against their symbol and explained, are very clear and it seems as if no better choice of symbol could possibly be made. After a concentrated study they evoke the step and with the same degree of justness that the term *jete* or *assemble* brings to mind either step in all its detail. The difficulty begins with compound movement such as *grand jete en tournant,* which comprises roughly the elements of *battement, coupe, saute* and *retomber*. It is not easy to record by draft the succession of each movement and the exact planes in which they function. However, I am certain that without a great deal of publicity about it, it has been the mainstay of various teachers' methods and the source of constant search by ballet masters. It could not be otherwise. Certain of its tables contain dozens of examples of involved steps, simple and compound, which constitute a rich mine of information to be constantly drawn upon. Basically the steps are mechanically sound and present complexities difficult for even our modern technicians.

The method of Raoul Auger Feuillet lasted roughly over a full century. It certainly was in use before its printing and various authors such as Pierre Rameau, Malpied and Magny did little more than offer slight clarifications and modifications.

Here again with Feuillet the tables promise much more than the actual dances written down by himself and Pecourt. Like Caroso, Feuillet wrote about intricate and difficult steps and explained them in his rules. In his dances, however, he employs largely the steps appropriate to dances of the court and salon. These are rather limited in variety and on the whole are repetitious. It is rather a pity the very great wealth of separate steps was not fully incorporated into the dances left for posterity.

The citation of Feuillet's *Choregraphie* brings us to the dawn of the 18th century, one of the richest periods in the history of dancing. Works of Pierre Rameau, de Chausac, Jean Georges Noverre, Lambranzi and Magny follow and add greatly to the store of rare books on the dance.

Every Detail Counts

task is not unlike that of a composer. It must stand on its own value. Frequently, a skilled dancer will rise above poor choreography, and achieve great personal success. But this is no credit to the choreographer.

Three indispensable factors enter into an artistic ballet:

1. The choreographer should have a wide education, be proficient in the technique of the ballet, conversant with the different periods and styles of national dances, well versed in music and painting, and above all, he must have imagination.
2. The dancer must possess technique and personality and be musically inclined.
3. The teacher must be a master of the ballet, possess discernment and the power of analysis, coupled with patience.

These requirements are rarely found in one person. We hope that the public will become more and more educated in the art of the ballet so that they will be able to differentiate between the dignified and the vulgar. Only then can we hope to see again a dancer keeping in the style and the period of the play, and not just grabbing the ballerina in the most inappropriate places with the sole aim of executing gymnastic stunts to gain plaudits through a manifestation of prowess rather than artistry.

A Cobblestone Road

Young aspirants must realize that the American public demands of its performers more versatility in interpretation, vocalization, languages and personal charm, than most other audiences in the European and Latin American countries. To satisfy this demand, one must have first class vocal material and be willing to give up many years to study the technic necessary for the delivery of arias, songs and lieder, and many more years to acquire musicianship, style, language, technic and personality—not to speak of the bankroll needed.

Musical education is a blessing and helps one to appreciate and enjoy one of God's greatest gifts. The American singer, however, cannot claim the same high standard in vocalization as he can in versatility. Considering the rich vocal material in this country, this fact is very disappointing, but the deficiency is due primarily to the approach of most of our young singers toward the profession.

It is unfortunate that singing is looked upon as a lucrative business. Why wait five or ten years to become a perfect vocalist when there is money to be had immediately? Naturally, most singers would like to attain perfection. But the process is too long and too costly. Who will support them and their families during this long period of preparation? Why not earn money now and study later? Why give up everyday comforts for perfect singing? Others with less artistry accumulated fortunes. Why immolate oneself on the altar of bel canto?

My father often said, "A voice is a gift from God, and we should not capitalize on it." Perhaps he was old-fashioned, but there was a time when only those with a specially gifted voice and with a genuine love of music adopted singing as a profession. Today with the radio engineers manipulating gadgets that makes one's voice big or small, light or heavy, and with the films dubbing, cutting and connecting high and low notes, why waste five or ten years on vocal study? And as for the love of music, why bother? Is it necessary to love a profession in order to support oneself or his family? Why not make hay while the sun shines?

The potential artist who assumes such an attitude is not apt to go places. The notion that after a year or two of singing lessons one is ready to mount the concert stage, and that all one needs is a good manager and a still better publicity man, is entirely erroneous. To get your picture posted on billboards or printed in the newspapers may bring you a lot of fan mail, boost your ego, and even pad your pockets with greenbacks temporarily. But unless you have the stuff in you of which great singers are made, you are doomed to bitter disappointment.

There never before has been such a widespread study of singing in this country as in the present day. If you can afford to take up singing as an avocation or as a diversion, you never will regret it. But if you wish to acquire fame and fortune, my advice is to think it over before you take the plunge.

A New Field Opens

performers to produce, but of original compositions of serious musical merit, created directly for concert perfomance. Were such a repertory available, it would be a challenge to every accordionist to master it, and the large demand of today would snowball to ever increasing proportions.

The serious composers of today, who are now struggling fervently to make their work better known in the fields of orchestra, chamber music, voice, or piano, must face the tremendous competition presented by the accumulated masterworks of the past 200 years. Were they to turn some portion of their attention to the accordion, they would find, instead, an eagerly awaiting public.

Doubtless some have considered the accordion beneath their dignity, not realizing its comprehensive scope nor its inherent possibilities. Others may have hesitated to make the necessary effort of mastering the instrument's technicalities. Yet a few consultations or lessons with a skilled accordionist could smooth these paths with ease. There is nothing derogatory in asking technical advice. Brahms did not hesitate to seek Joachim's aid before completing his great *Violin Concerto*, and musical history bristles with similar examples.

The accordion is ready to take its place in the concert sun. It will benefit composers by granting them a large new outlet for their creative powers and adding materially to their financial rewards. It will benefit publishers through expanding sales. It will benefit performers by augmenting their professional activities. It will benefit impresarios by giving them many new and interesting artists to present.

And lastly, but far from least, it will benefit the public by offering new musical enjoyment.

The Distaff Side

The most promising start cannot be fulfilled if the periods of interruption are too prolonged. The responsibilities of fulfilling the cycle of life fall irrevocably upon the woman more than on the man. If a woman can hold to her work through the more hectic years when her children are very young, if her professional standing survives the slowed-down activity during these extremely full years, then she is in a sound position to do her best work as time becomes more available and maturity and experience augment her understanding.

There is an increasing number of men who do not view with alarm a wife who maintains an interest in a profession of her own, and who believe that a woman's career can bring something additional to a marriage in the way of ideas and interests.

There are hundreds of talented young women today, full of enthusiasm and determination, on the threshold of musical careers. Theirs are more than dreamy-eyed ambitions of a career-life. Fully aware of the responsibilities and qualifications that were less fully understood by preceding generations,—along with continuously expanding opportunities open to them, major achievement by women in the world of music will be increasingly realized.

Form Makes the Symphony

symphonic construction) yet fail in my esteem because, finally, it is too academic. A modern composer must press on the boundaries of the great form which he has inherited; Beethoven expanded the development section; Brahms added a second development after the recapitulation in the sonata-allegro movements; Sibelius exchanged the functions of the statement and development sections, showed them to be successfully interchangeable. And so, further, it must go. We must forever avoid academic manholes, for herein lies musical death, starvation. Twenty years ago, when I was a mere lad, all of the surrounding critics seemed to insist upon our writing purely academic symphonies. Today, seeing that they were so wrong yesterday, they have swung to the opposite extreme; they seem to approve only those "symphonies" which now break every rule, indeed do not even express or outline the barest necessities of true symphony form. The inevitable result will be—tomorrow—that composers will fly back to academic symphonic form as a drowning man clutches a straw. Absolute primitivism, or absolute academicism are both equally bad.

The form of the modern symphony must forever be an advance upon all that we have known before, yet utilizing all that we have known before. Rules may be broken with utmost daring, but it must also forever be apparent that the composer broke them because he knew them all too well; likewise, and equally important, ancient rules may be closely followed if, in the doing, the composer has demonstrated that he is master of them, and not that they are his absolute master, his one guide in an otherwise fluid and utterly incomprehensible world of music creation.

To sum up: we must write symphonies today, tomorrow and forever as they have always been written (1) with heart and conscience (2) with a complete mastery of the rules which have not been compiled by one master, but by a hundred great minds, and (3) we must have enough confidence in our own talent to break these rules whenever necessary. Conscience, Mastery, Audacity!

The Past Once Was New

at the expense of the present which is entitled to the same fair and unbiased appreciation. There are some people who would indulge in the beauties of old music as an antidote against the alleged confusion and ugliness of modern art. Intentionally or not, they overlook the fact that those beauties always have been the result of the daring efforts of the creative imagination of artists reaching out into new, unexplored territories. We must not use history as an escape from our own problems, but derive from it courage and inspiration for the solution of those problems.

One of the most wholesome effects of historical studies is the revelation that there are incredible amounts of most impressive music which does not sound like nineteenth century material. This does not imply a reflection upon nineteenth century music as such. But through the peculiar structure of our concert life, not only the public at large, but also many professional musicians are so conditioned to that type of music that they are shocked when they hear contemporary music of a different flavor. To many it is a great surprise to experience exactly the same shock when they are exposed for the first time to the sounds of the thirteenth and fourteenth centuries.

The study of music history, if properly conducted, should open the student's mind to the amazing varieties of musical expression and make him eventually more tolerant and appreciative of the creative efforts of our own time.

Mirthful Melody

with a working knowledge of the stage. Some smattering of this latter the composer should have acquired himself through close observation of performances he has witnessed. Care must be taken in the choice of an associate, however, for much good music since the beginnings of opera has been wasted through failures due to bad plots and bad dialogue. Marketing a complete work is in the realm of business and follows much the same lines as introducing a new product or an invention: the money of a backer and the interest of a producer.

The foregoing requirements need not seem insurmountable. There must be many of the younger generation already partially or wholly equipped to satisfy the desire of a large public, longing for a rebirth of the merry, mirthful musical. May the bright standards relinquished by recent and earlier melody makers be born aloft again by this new generation in the renaissance of an art wherein gloom and sorrow take flight and happiness and mirth take the stage.

Little Town's Big Music

America. A psalm with narrator, to text by Morax, the work has been widely performed in Europe, on several occasions under Sirpo's direction, but in the United States only once, so far as is known, in 1925 in New York. A favorite with Sirpo, he has termed it without qualification "one of the greatest musical compositions of the twentieth century." The work established Honegger's international reputation overnight, and probably remains his most significant achievement. *Le Roi David*, wrote critic Gilbert Chase, "is an object lesson on 'how to be successful though modern.' "

Sunday, the final day of the festival, an unusual children's musical play, *We Build a Town*, by Paul Hindemith, will be presented in the afternoon, and in the evening Ezio Pinza, Italian basso and star of the Metropolitan, will appear as guest soloist with the Hood River Symphony Orchestra.

Two prizes will be offered in connection with this festival. One prize of $1,000.00 will be given to the person composing the winning festival overture and $100.00 will be given to the young boy selected to take the part of the young boy in *"King David."*

Nothing of so vast a scope has ever been planned

or projected in any Northwest community before. Hood River is fully alive to the importance and significance of what it has undertaken. It has entered upon this great program with a dedicated confidence. Music lovers from the length of the Coast and all parts of the nation are expected to attend in great numbers. The town of Hood River is well aware that the eyes of the nation will be upon it. And knowing well the energy and genius of their conductor, the town will again draw upon the inspiration of his leadership and know the undertaking with succeed.

As for Boris Sirpo, he will continue to give freely of his time and of his spirit with a sense of deep-felt gratitude "for everything wonderful America has done for me and for my family."

Opera With a Suitcase

able, often after a decade. Great composers have wasted fine music on impossible texts which cry for revision.

It is high time for the American composers to learn to write for and in a simpler medium. It is time that they become more practical. Let them look to the *Barber* (Rossini) or *Don Pasquale* (Donizetti) or *Falstaff* (Verdi) for their models; let their harmonies be ever so modern, if the voices are handled in bel canto style. If the opera has theatrical value the opera can become a success. But let them write for small casts and inexpensive productions so their works can be performed easily.

Goethe says somewhere that "in limitation there is mastery" and this applies especially to the field of opera. The beginnings of opera in English should not be endangered by costly experiments in extreme modernity, or by works which repel the public by needlessly tragic content, by symbolism, futurism and what not.

Let the operas be in opera style, in bel canto, written to be sung, and in good taste. If comic, let us remember that Moliere and Beaumarchais gave deep messages in the guise of humor and entertainment. Menotti's operas, as well as *Porgy and Bess* are first class entertainment. Their musical value thereby is not curtailed.

I repeat: we need many groups working for new audiences with a new repertory . . . . and on small budgets.

OPERA MUST LEARN TO TRAVEL WITH LIGHT BAGGAGE.

Free For the Asking

recorded music are deeply appreciated by music lovers living near the Library, many of whom cannot afford to attend paid performances. Through gifts and purchases the collection of records is now over 1600.

During the war requests for greater listening facilities became insistent. Despite inadequate space and staff, a table phonograph was installed in the Music Room by the end of 1945. From the moment the Library opens until closing time it is rarely idle. Many students follow the music with a copy of the miniature score, borrowed from the Library's collection of over one thousand.

Listening to records in the Library is far from meeting the needs of a music conscious community, however. "Do you circulate records"? is a constant and insistent question. To do so would require the establishment of what is known as an Audio-Visual Aids Department, the dream of all forward looking librarians.

And what, you ask, would you find in such a place? Ideally speaking, an auditorium equipped with a stage, a motion-picture screen, a grand piano, and a collection of films, slides and records for both reference and home use; also soundproof booths for listening to records. With such equipment, educational programs of vital interest to the community would give the Library its rightful place as the dynamic center of the cultural life of the city.

Stranger In His Own Land

fine music in our country today if the opportunity for sustained work could be provided for those composers who are capable of demonstrating their abilities. The worldwide interest and prestige that the music of Sibelius has brought to Finland has amply repaid that country for the money which has enabled him to pursue his lifetime in creative activities.

A concert artist can not develop exclusively in the studio, and by the same token, a creative artist must come in contact with an intelligent audience if he is to attain his full stature. This presents a problem to the American composer which is often as baffling as it is exasperating. A great deal of new music is presented to the public each year, but that by American composers comes in homeopathic doses, infinitesimal quantities. The public is thus led to believe that Americans can't compose good music

and the composer himself is made to feel he has no part in the musical development of his own country.

The situation will not materially improve until those who are aware of it are willing to devote more time and effort in bringing the facts of the case to general attention.

The two remedies attempted most frequently thus far have been the contest, and the slogan "an American composition on every program". While both of them have produced some good results, their total effect still has been very slight. The winner of a contest receives a performance and a certain amount of publicity, but the lasting value is usually not very great. In attempting to put an American work on every program, the conductor is apt to do more harm than good if the work happens to be inferior. The emphasis should rather be the search for good American works and frequently repeat performances of those which have proved themselves worthy.

Another device which might prove extremely valuable would be the establishment of a fund to provide rehearsal time for the purpose of reading new works. If every major orchestra in the country had such a fund and could devote an afternoon a month to this purpose, the results, over a period of time, would probably be most gratifying. It would enable the composer to hear his work and thus greatly aid him in the composition of future works, and it would give the program committee a chance to make an intelligent decision regarding worthwhile works to be included on regular programs.

By pursuing realistic and vigorous methods it is to be hoped that the time is not far off when the American composer will have an audience and that his time can be spent in creative pursuits and not in the cultivation of the social and political graces already mentioned. On this happy day, he will cease to be a stranger in his own country.

Where Now?

last named, most prolific of contemporaries, and the least performed, reveals a tropical richness, an individual style, and novel combinations which merit consideration of a few more of his numerous compositions, among them twenty-five chamber works, symphonies, and five operas.

We hear now of an obscure composer living in our midst who heralds the future of a New Music, by means of an electrical invention, which eliminates all known instruments and forms. Speed the day!

Off With His Head!

printed word, like lead, possesses weight out of all proportion to its value, and when it is irresponsibly used its potentials for mischief are terrific.

No critical bias can permanently subvert the sovereign fact of genius. Wagner survived Hanslick's personal boycott, Bach and Mozart emerged in all their shining strength from critical evaluations that found the one "pedantic" and the other "precious." However wrong a critic may be in his estimate of the music of his contemporaries, his disapproval can merely delay, not prevent, the eventual recognition of a genuinely original talent. What his opprobrium may do, however, is discourage contemporary interest in works that a later age may quite possibly come to cherish more tenderly.

One of the modern critic's hardest tasks is to appraise the music of his own era fairly, without pre-judgment, and without demanding that it conform to whatever style, period or school he may personally espouse. The only criterion of its permanent worth is the validity with which any work of art reflects and draws strength from the shaping forces of its own time. The critic aware of those forces will be more likely to assess the music of his contemporaries accurately than one inclined to judge it wholly by standards forged in the crucible of an earlier generation's own struggle against bigotry.

To justify his office, in any age, the critic must be something more than a parasite living off the creative efforts of those he presumes to judge. At its worst, criticism can sink to abysmal levels of triteness and venality. At its finest, it becomes itself an act of creation, by that degree to which it illuminates, extends and enriches the subject with which it deals.

The California Plan

tion and the various music teachers' certification systems in Europe are obvious. In pre-war Central Europe, every private music teacher was obliged to join the professional organization, which was government controlled. But he could not do so without passing an examination before a Board usually consisting of the professors of the State Conservatories. This dreaded examination decided whether the candidate would be able to follow his vocation. It took usually two years of compulsory studies for this ordeal and the outline of the curriculum was cut and dried. Often nervousness caused failures and

hardly ever was the creative or pedagogic ability of the teacher considered an important factor. The California Plan is entirely voluntary and allows leeway for individual development and for group studies, though its general scope is outlined by the association.

The organization of this project is well administered. It is headed by a central executive committee which appoints advisory committees in the various branches. These in turn provide for local Plan chairmen who establish the contacts between the candidates and the central committees. These officers as well as the leaders of local branches know the members very well; therefore, they show understanding for the individual candidates and are able to give them valuable help.

Annual examinations are conducted in spring. They are quite comprehensive and consist not only of tests in oral or written form but also of advisory conferences and student-demonstrations. The teachers keenly enjoy the challenge of those contests. Not only the teachers of San Francisco and Los Angeles but also those in Sacramento, Glendale, San Diego, Long Beach and many other cities have established study groups for the California Plan.

It is to be hoped that this project will be an ever increasing source of artistic inspiration for the teachers and a stimulus for their continuous self-education. It will make music teaching in California more efficient and contribute to the growth of musical culture.

Repetition Spells Success

lapping. This overlap does away with pauses between notes and makes the playing smoother and more rapid. Later on, overlap goes to much greater lengths. When reading by sight, an expert keeps his eyes several beats ahead of his fingers thus reacting to four or five beats at the same time. A good sight reader is somewhat like a machine which receives raw material, performs a series of operations upon it and then turns out a finished product. Such a combination of simple movements, combined into an organized action pattern, requires practice and repetition.

This emphasis on repetition is, without doubt, a "carry-over" from my own music study in Germany. We know that it is important to do a thing well; furthermore, pupils should be made to see the importance of a good weekly performance. And intelligent repetition, when practicing, is quite an aid.

Let the Music Dance

The last thing to be affected by good or bad dance music is the old fashioned ballet (still alive today) in which pirouettes and steps have to be executed within two, three or more measures, while melody and even rhythm, quite unaffected, run in virtually opposite ways! The modern ballet comes far closer to musical language and intentions, and the true pantomime (Stravinsky, Prokofiev) travels practically "hand in hand" with music.

Such an intimate amalgam is far more likely to be achieved when composer and dance group work in close accord from the beginning. When I composed for the Danish Royal Ballet Company, the choreographer, Gaubier, and I studied the manuscript until we were in complete agreement about the dance treatment. The important episodes, moods, cues and the like were agreed upon; after that, the rest was my own work and my own judgment. I was told later that the company had never danced so easily to a piece of music. If this was true, it was because I composed it as a dancer would have—music for the dancer.

Distinctly Different

rangers. The rate of compensation for both arranging and orchestrating is considerably higher.

Composers employed by the motion picture studios usually present the orchestrator with a complete score, even indicating instrumentation; others give a complete sketch in form, but leave the instrumentation to the orchestrators; still others merely present an outline of what they want and leave it to the arranger to complete the sketch and to orchestrate it.

Some studios employ both arrangers and orchestrators besides composers; others require arranging and orchestrating to be done by the same individual. In isolated cases the composer is required to make his own arranging and orchestrations, but time seldom permits this practice inasmuch as the composer usually conducts the orchestra when scoring for a picture.

The arranger-orchestrator is a member of a respected and well-established profession. To become a qualified member of this profession the individual must have a complete knowledge of solfeggio—not the movable Do System. He must be acquainted with the range of all instruments, with a special understanding of the harp, the French horn and percussion. He also should be equipped with a thorough background of harmony and counterpoint. He should familarize himself and be able to analyze the various forms of compositions, old and new, classical and popular.

In addition, if the arranger-orchestrator aspirant then is willing to work under pressure and take severe criticism, with little praise, he may apply for membership in the American Society of Music Arrangers. And God help him!

What Price Culture?

that the winning of an Academy Award should immediately raise the price of a composer to three and four times the salary he received previously.

This, of course, is supply and demand, but where does the art come in? What has happened to all this money that Mr. Public has paid for his musical enlightenment? What actual value has Mr. Public received for what he has spent?

Brahms, Beethoven, Tchaikovsky—their work is of great value, but the culture these composers have instilled in their music never can be bought. You learn that by a deep appreciation of the great music these men have set down on paper. You prove this by being tolerant of all music and by a sincere attempt to seriously understand all music.

You do not necessarily believe all the publicity about that foreign composer just because of his press campaign. You do not take for granted that this or that great symphony conductor is above criticism when all the while he refuses to play American works. You are not swayed by the sensationalism employed by many artists. You do not take for granted a situation in an opera house where complete stagnation of repertory is caused by the sponsors who are wealthy enough to demand performances of only such works as they are able to understand or deem socially correct.

You give back to music, in return for what it gives you, not dollars but wholehearted effort to develop and preserve our great talent in this country. You pay back what you owe to music by encouraging that talent. You use every means at your disposal, moral, physical and financial, to help that talent progress and blossom, because only in this way do we find true music culture.

Music is capricious and nebulous. She touches only one in millions with genius and even so, greatness never appears until helped and encouraged by mortals. Brahms, Beethoven and Tchaikovsky need no encouragement now, but that young ambitious composer who has just graduated from Juilliard certainly does. He needs it from the conductor and he needs it from the producer, but mostly he needs it from the public. His auditors are the ones who will preserve his art, if they ever find it, and they are the only ones to demand ways of finding it.

Well Tempered Musician

permit ourselves a surprising laxity at the opposite or purely musical end of the scale.

We affirm that "popular" music is cheap and in bad taste because its emotionalism and its childish structure overbalance any other pretensions it may have. Yet we, as musicians, berate the public for not immediately accepting music of purely technical import at first hearing. Certainly we should not "play down" to our auditors, but we must be chary of asking too much of them without proper preparation.

In this respect, pianists might take a lesson from vocalists, who often explain a new or extremely modern song before presenting it. The dignity of the pianist would not suffer were he to break the traditional stony (and often stodgy) silence on the platform and offer a few carefully prepared words of explanation calculated to arouse interest in the coming work. Nor is it fair to let the majority of the auditors guess at the encores, even assuming that the musically erudite will recognize them at hearing.

Every concert artist realizes the necessity of balancing a program with respect to contrast, color, rhythm, key, tempo, and other pertinent factors. Yet this important matter is seldom dwelt upon by the teacher, who too often makes up the program himself and assumes that the pupil somehow will learn the art offhand.

When two music critics evaluate a performer in a diametrically opposite manner, it should not be assumed that one (the worst one, of course) is merely venting spite. The performer must ask himself if there is not some hidden factor, some contributing cause rather than a direct one, which has led to that adverse opinion. For some degree of imbalance must exist somewhere along the line.

The teacher, too, must preserve a state of balance in all his dealings with his pupils. The days of the excitable Herr Professor, armed with a ruler and a terrible temper, are happily past. The instructor of today must realize his responsibility in the development of a human being, and see that his musical education is well grounded in a full appreciation of the various steps during his training.

That music is a great art has been said by poets and plain people in many descriptive ways. For music and true musicians strive always to attain the ideal state of perfect balance.

Inspired Instruments

in some churches are often made up of persons who know little or nothing about music. Often they make it very difficult for the organist to maintain a standard of musical excellence by demanding music of an inferior sort. The organist is not always in a position to "take his stand" and therefore comes under unjust criticism. Yet, with proper co-operation it is possible for the music to increase the appreciation and understanding of the audience or congregation.

It is always safe for a mediocre organist to cover his own shortcomings by placing the works of well known masters on his program. Whereas, if he were required to perform works by contemporary composers, he would have to "sell" an unfamiliar work. One does not have to sell Bach.

All music in the church should glorify God. It would seem that at times this is forgotten or overlooked. Most organists have learned that self-glorification has no place in their work. Would it not be well to consider the words of Apostle Paul in I Corinthians 10:31, 32, and apply them to the instrumental music in the church?

"Whether therefore ye eat, or drink, or whatsoever ye do, do all to the glory of God. Give none offence, neither to Jews, nor to the Gentiles, nor to the church of God."

The Vocal Flight

French liaison. This produces the straight line in singing where all words came from the same "take off", lip, tongue, or teeth.

The onward pulse is produced by using the native stress of the consonants. Here is its life and power. Just as in poetry the metric beat must underlie the interpretation and be subordinate to it, so in singing, freedom to express any emotion and thought must be built on the rhythmic beat of the words. This is the power that enthralls both singer and listener, caught in the exquisite form of musical and poetic rhythm.

New Times, New Rules

why. There is an explanation for all progressions, chord formations and musical effects even in the wildest turmoil of sounds.

If our musical instructors today would only pledge themselves to the art of analysis, the same progress could be made in Modern Music as has been made in other fields.

Unbalanced Symphony

women have by necessity participated in the casts of drama and opera for many centuries. Women in opera choruses and stellar roles have long been accepted without controversy. In opera, the power and discipline of an emotional and mental Isolde has been respected for years, while her instrument-playing counterpart in the orchestra pit still remains a doubtful minority.

Entire organizations of women players have been successful in concert and radio for more than two decades. Notable among these are the Chicago, Cleveland, Boston, and New York Women's Symphonies. The oldest continuous women's group, organized fifty-five years ago, is the Los Angeles Women's Symphony. With a background of fine traditions, it has played many good seasons, a few bad ones, depending upon its budget. These players, dedicated to the service of great music, naturally contribute much time to committees raising funds for the continued existence of the major local symphony. Women's symphonies no longer "prove a point," but they may become more prominent again as women are discriminated against in major orchestras.

Women symphony conductors are still a curiosity in some localities. There seems to be no great prejudice against them, but there are not very many open opportunities in the field. However, they will be heard from with more frequency because they are studying constantly, and many are proving themselves in educational ensembles.

Educators believe that as both men and women are developed to the greatest extent of their talents, total civilization of man increases more rapidly. Our only real concern lies with making greater and greater music. Music is an expression that rises above the barriers of color, creed, age, or sex. It is immaterial whether a man or a woman is the physical medium through which the finest of symphonic literature is presented. Undergirded by a certain amount of technical proficiency, the artist is no longer a man or woman, but a human soul lifted into the realm of understanding, expression, and appreciation in the presence of great music.

No Par For the Course

study and argue the merits of this grip or that grip, shoulder action, wrist action, and slight deviations. The moment a player is off his game, back to the pro he goes for a check up. The pro goes over the whole range of movements again, analyzing the faults, explaining, demonstrating until the player regains his swing and confidence.

Does the average teacher of a musical instrument do this for his students? Do many professional instrumentalists go back for a checkup? New students have come to the writer with literature supposed to have been studied. In looking over the studies assumed to have been absorbed, one is astounded to find in many instances that page after page is void of any instructive editing by the previous teacher. The dates of the lessons, however, are most carefully inscribed.

This is not to infer that the original editings are always incorrect, but with ever growing ideas for improvement of fingerings and bowings, and with due consideration for the peculiar hands of every individual, it is impossible to consider most editions efficient in every detail, nor can a teacher ignore these facts.

When the technical equipment of an instrumentalist can be taught on a par with the teachings and analysis of an athletic instructor or coach, more students will be ready to cope with the real problems of musical interpretation.

Conducting On Cue

separately and very difficult sequences are "broken down" into several parts.

The music cutter and his staff cut in all the music tracks in the consecutive order of their respective reels and then they are "dubbed" with the dialogue sound effects at the necessary level or volume control in relation to each other.

Music for motion pictures is usually composed after the picture has been completed, as dissolves or inserts are frequently missing and additional sound effects are "dubbed" in at the same time that the music and dialogue are being transferred on to the final composite track.   ,

One wonders, when viewing a film, how many of the audience realize the effort and the many people who have had part in giving them their evening's entertainment. As one of the fortunate few to follow the "vagaries of music in pictures" from its inception to the preesnt day, I wish to doff my hat to the many composers whose scores I have had the pleasure of conducting.

Select For Yourself

music critics has pointedly asked in print why you, who are presumably an intelligent musician, have thus far neglected to employ the compositional talents of the famous Mr. Zee (who scorns formal symphonies, and only indites tone poems for orchestras of 150 or more players).

Meanwhile, don't forget that a million dollars is at stake. It's your job to protect that million dollars, to see that it is a good investment, as far as you can. No one will object if you advance the cause of serious music incidentally; on the contrary, all concerned will be gratified if you do. But your *first* duty is to the investment, and anything else must be secondary or incidental.

That investment probably is not yours, personally, but neither is it the producer's individual investment, either. If it is the studio's money, that only means that it represents the investment of thousands of ordinary folk like (or perhaps even including) yourself, who have bought the studio's securities or those of companies holding the studio's securities.

You can't afford to make a mistake because, quite literally, there will not be time to retrieve it. There's just time to do the underscoring, and no more. In fact, the longer you ponder the less time remains of your precious two weeks.

If this is your position, not merely once, but every time the studio makes a new picture, then you are the titular head of the music department and official music director of a major film company. The responsibility is yours, and yours alone.

Come on, Mr. Reader. *Whom would you select?*

———————◆◆◆———————

Flamenco and Castanets

dancer. At times it is even timid and given to under- rather than overstatement. Grace is always preferable to violent motion.

In the case of the woman dancer, the skirts are worn very long, therefore the greatest part of the performance is done from the waist up—a delicacy like that of lace.

Of all the dance arts, I consider that which belongs to Spain as the most poetic. One cannot help re-

sponding to this wonderful expression; for it is said that dancing influences the soul the most. Spanish dancing influences one's life.

Where Seldom Is Heard

What they don't know is that statistics have shown that once someone enters at the bottom, unprepared, he will stay at the bottom, still unprepared. There is no disgrace, however, in starting with a small band or with a small radio station somewhere in the sticks *after* gaining a thorough musical education, because this education will pay off. It will produce in them a pattern of thinking which will lead them out of the morass of mediocrity. If their ideas are strikingly novel, somewhere someone will remark, "What's this guy doing playing in this dive?" and there will be a new piano star on the firmament of show business. In the same manner the style and sound of an unknown orchestra will attract attention, and a new arranger will go to the top along with the band whose style he has created.

And here's where the studios come in. No sooner. Because they naturally can afford to buy the best on the market of American show business. So can the sponsor of a radio show. Each picture is an investment of a million dollars or more. A radio show sells millions of dollars worth of cigarettes or soap. Can its musical score be entrusted to someone who might still be experimenting, still be learning? Of course, we all learn up to the day where we either pass on, or stagnate, and we all experiment with new ideas, if we are worth anything as creative artists. But the words "learning" and "experimenting" are here used in the sense: not as yet having attained ultimate mastery of the craft. And this is where someone with a fine musical education will have the edge over anyone with an inadequate one.

So I tell the kids: stay in school, get all the musical education you can. You'll forget some of it later, but it will have broadened your horizon.

And yet I am certain that any day now the first batch of these eager beavers will be at the various studio gates and radio stations, shouting: "We're here. Where is the score paper? Where do you keep the pencils?" Right at a time when Crosby is doing two repeats on every show, and the major studios are cutting their production 50%. So that's where I discourage them. Futile motion No. 17. See what I mean?

Let's wish them luck, though.

Scissors Save the Score

their proper accompaniments in music.

One of the foremost screen composers has an interesting method of procedure wherein he uses a different orchestral combination in each sequence. An extremely effective one was the use of two harps, two celestas and several sets of bells for the music accompanying a sleigh ride. Another blended the sweet tones of a pipe organ and strings for a pastoral scene. Many times the string section was left out entirely and only woodwinds and horns were used.

In these days, when each studio has a contract orchestra (meaning that the same men play every recording) it is well for the composer to know the drawbacks as well as the merits of each player. In this way he can write beautiful cadenzas for a fine violinist or leave out involved passages which a less proficient musician might find difficult to perform. Many fine effects may be missed if the player is not taken into consideration.

A film composer's task is a unique one and his craft a specialized art. Any music writer entering this field would do well to study the varied treatments of music which have been developed in this trade. He will save himself much grief by using the experience of others for his own benefit.

Heard But Not Seen

tion as commercial fare on national networks with the tariff happily paid by the sponsor. It is to be hoped that the days when serious music on the air was a program manager's sustaining stepchild are past for good.

Radio orchestras have a happy facility for introducing new works by contemporary composers which never has been shown by the symphonies of the nation. Radio, with its microphones, acoustically treated studios and master mixers at the controls, can make music come out of your loudspeaker as it was intended to.

New tone colors, voicings, and instruments with small voices can now be written-in by experimenting orchestrators to novel advantage. Were microphones and skilled monitors in all large auditoriums, new music written for films and radio with the microphone in mind could be heard in correct proportions.

For this encouragement of musicians to play, composers to write, conductors to perform, orchestras to

be sponsored, the radio industry deserves credit. American public taste is rising through insatiable desire for better music and more of it; a more desirable way than if an American B.B.C. (with a rather sticky board of directors with very conservative tastes) served out a regulated sample of what they think listeners *ought* to hear. Credit also should be given to the Federal Communications Commission in Washington, which examines the schedules of all stations to see that a percentage of serious music is presented in the public interest.

A cross section of important new music, heard on U. S. broadcasts in the past two years, was taken by this writer through examination of titles re-recorded for overseas broadcast to troops. Some of the selections are an encouraging example of good music on the air:

> *Concertino* (N. Lopotnikov); movie score: *How Green Was My Valley* (A. Newman); *In Memoriam* (Wm. Grant Still); *Paradise Garden* (Delius); *Adagio For Strings* (Samuel Barber); *Metamorphosis of Themes of Carl M. von Weber* (Paul Hindemith); *Bachianas Brasileiras No. 7. Prelude for Eight 'Cellos* (Villa-Lobos); *Second Symphony* (David Diamond); *Pinocchio* (E. Toch); *Concerto For Orchestra* (Bela Bartok); *Symphonies No. 1, 5, 6, 7, 8,* (Shostokovich); *Elegie* (L. Barrymore); *Brazilian Samba* (Milhaud); *Porgy and Bess* (Gershwin); *Merry Overture* (Korngold); *First Piano Concerto* (Roy Harris); *Burlesque* (Stravinsky); *William Billings Overture* (Wm. Schuman); *Taming of the Shrew* (Tedesco); *Ballerina* (M. Gould).

When you listen to great music or new music in your home free of charge or in the theatre for a balcony fee—or perhaps to fine recordings of this music engendered by the film and radio industries—remember it is proof that music is an ever-expanding art of expression, a truly fine art no matter what field it invades.

Background To Foreground

Psychological problems are always present, it seems, to complicate relations between the artist and his pianist. There are the temperamental exhibitions and moody periods in which most artists eventually indulge, that the accompanist somehow is expected to offset.

Yet even with endless problems and ceaseless labor, accompanying can be made a truly fascinating business. There are compensations that can come from a feeling of solid "teamwork", a sincere attempt at producing the best humanly attainable result.

All in all, a career in the background can be moved to the foreground, if one makes it so.

Why Not Say It?

baritone, mezzo, etc.) before the singer has become stabilized in his tone production for the same reason. There is rarely any immediate need of classifying a voice, though certainly a teacher should formulate an accurate diagnosis as quickly as possible.

The question arises as to the extent pupils should be made conscious of physical activities that occur in tone production. Many successful teachers, with a fine working knowledge of the contributions science has made, rarely discuss problems of diagnosis with their pupils; nor does this fact minimize the effectiveness of their application of corrective procedure. However, the analytical student in his class may expect an answer to his problems in factual explanation. The teacher, properly equipped, can give this information to the satisfaction of this student. Most certainly, in his use of imagery with any of his students, he will use descriptive terms which conform to logic and common knowledge.

With these examples before us, we should consider their implications for vocal pedagogy. Certainly, voice teachers should be familiar with scientific research. If they were, a change of methods would not be as necessary as a change of viewpoint. Every other field of human knowledge is being constantly broadened. Why should our attitudes toward the teaching of voice remain static? Some teachers actually believe great volume of tone comes from a contraction of the diaphragm, but do not know that the singing act calls for a relaxing of the diaphragm and that its contraction is the thing that *fills* the lungs.

Voice teachers should also know enough of the science of acoustics to realize that it is impossible for a "soundboard" action of the hard palate or teeth to take place, and sound cannot arbitrarily be directed or "placed" anywhere, except as these concepts have a certain psychological value. The "chest register" and "head register" are not actually generated in chest nor head but always in the larynx. The unification of these two "registers" is accomplished by each being strengthed past the point of break with the other. This process will then enable the quality to be changed gradually. One adjustment, or "register" will take over the work as the other releases its tension. An understanding of the anatomy of the mouth and throat should be had sufficiently to know the principles of vowel and consonant modification and what sounds to use to correct faulty tone quality and enunciation.

An understanding of these physiological factors cannot conceivably limit the aesthetic horizons of any teacher. Rather, by building on the solid foundation of factual principles, he can more perfectly help to produce a superstructure of beauty and permanence.

Mozart vs. Mayhem

not the slightest help from the network or anybody else

Here was a case where the program was plenty absorbing if it had been properly "sold" to the listeners

I think the Saturday afternoon opera could also be "sold" as an absorbing afternoon's entertainment providing of course that somebody with a little imagination would take hold of the commentary and the ghastly ghastly ghastly intermission "studies in affectation"

And while we're on the subject of the Crosby program Bing's show is one hunk of musical entertainment that has the absorbing quality

If you were to divide the elements of the show you would probably end up with a good eighteen minutes of music and about seven minutes of talk with the rest of the time going for commercials

In other words it is possible with the proper selection of music and six or seven minutes of imaginative presentation to make eighteen minutes of music absorbing

Considering the magnetic Crosby personality I realize that that is a bigger challenge than it sounds but at least it is reducing the problems to fundamentals

so come on you music-ers let's quit being pushed around by screams in the night and organ glissandos

The Speeding Hour

as it gives him a chance to make necessary changes before proceeding with the orchestration.

Much effective orchestral background is lost to the radio listener by careless microphone placement and inadequate studio acoustics. It is hoped that future broadcasting studios will emulate the film industry in the science of sound reproduction.

Thanks to the interest displayed by writers, producers, sponsors, and the discerning radio audience, radio underscoring is destined to emerge with many new and interesting artistic qualities.

Pianists In Retrospect

the philosopher, the writer, the DaVinci of the piano. How well one perceived these traits in Busoni when one had the good fortune to meet him and speak with him! He was thoroughly at home in all the arts because his mind and interests embraced all culture.

While Busoni's style of playing was unlike Paderewski's, they had one trait in common—a genuine respect for art. When Paderewski played, the error of mere virtuosity was exposed and the listeners were entranced by his entirely subjective approach to the piano. Although he had a set pattern for the works he was about to perform, he relied on the actual mood of the moment. He created that mood by playing in a dimly-lighted auditorium—thereby establishing perfect communion between the audience and himself. We who have heard him at various times will agree that his playing never was twice the same. Nevertheless, a Paderewski performance invariably abounded in emotional charm, tenderness, pathos and passion. He appealed equally to the musician and layman. His public always was aroused to delirious enthusiasm. One had to see as well as hear him in order to appreciate the man who seemed to build a stairway to the sky.

Although some critics argued that Paderewski's Bach or Beethoven departed from accepted tradition, all agreed that here was bigness of style, based upon intellectual understanding and unique individuality. Musicians might not have agreed with his performance of the *"Waldstein"* Sonata of Beethoven, arguing that he took undue liberties with phrasing and tempi, even changing the text in some spots. Yet he made you forget tradition by the new beauties he revealed. It is not difficult to understand Paderewski's hold upon the public in the past generation.

Leopold Godowsky was revered in like manner by his colleagues. DePachmann spoke of him as "a God." Rachmaninoff declared, "All of us pianists sit at Godowsky's feet." Huneker said, "The superman of the piano!" Josef Hofmann added, "I doubt it there are many pianists today who have not learned something from Godowsky. I know that I did, and I am thankful for it." In fact, every worthy pianist during Godowsky's lifetime was his adorer and friend and looked upon him as their prophet.

Paradoxical as it may seem, Godowsky's towering genius did not have that power over the public. He made no bid for popular appeal. His music and his playing, like the writings of the great philosophers, was beyond the comprehension and appreciation of the average mind. Here was a contrapuntal genius who combined the spirit of Bach and Chopin. This trait was so gloriously displayed in his fifty-three masterful transcriptions of the Chopin Etudes, which eclipsed anything of the kind previously attempted. Only Godowsky, the transcendental pianist, could successfully perform all of them.

He had a special zest in tackling and mastering the most formidable mechanical difficulties. As a master of polyphonic style and independence of finger work, he was unrivalled. Here was the superman of the piano who could well afford to approach his pianistic task objectively because he deliberately developed it as a distinctive art in itself. No other pianist could master this manner of delineation so extraordinarily. To quote Huneker, "The violet ray, dramatic passion, flame and fury are not present; they would be intruders on his palette." His piano tone was always legitimate, never forced. In every attribute he was "a pianist for pianists."

Personal acquaintance with Godowsky gave me ample cause to revere him for his genuine humbleness, soulful character and keen sense of humor. His accomplishments were varied. He possessed intellect and culture. He was as much at home in literature, history, philosophy, and science as he was in music. He understood people and life. He had a warm heart and a generous soul. His door was open to all young artists who sought his advice and encouragement.

Godowsky transcended all who came before him and his piano playing will echo in the ears of every living artist. His contribution to music has advanced piano art immeasureably.

"If God played the piano, He couldn't play much better than I do." Thus spoke Vladimir DePachmann of himself. Bold as this may sound, one must forgive him, for with his eccentricities he was a man of genius. This man of many moods and affectations was entirely transformed the moment he began to play. As Ruskin said: "A man may hide himself from you, or misrepresent himself to you every other way; but he cannot in his work; there, be sure you have him to the inmost." It is not given to all to feel intensely, nor to play Chopin as he should be played, but DePachmann possessed a gift for penetrating to the very soul of this poet of composers.

DePachmann's Chopin differed in every essential from that of others. He was so fastidious in his playing and his ideals were so great, that after one successful tour, re retired for eight years in order to delve into the intricacies and penetrate more deeply into the inner sanctum of Chopin's soul. To quote him: "I retired for eight years after one of my tours because I felt that I played like a pig. Then after the public accepted me wholeheartedly, I decided I still needed another two years to perfect my art. Now I play like a God!" Remarks such as these were accepted by his auditors for he redeemed himself of all his caprices by his superb artistry. His title "The Chopinzee" was honorably earned.

Some artists pass like a swift blown breeze—while others leave us with unforgettable memories. The world of art goes on, though these geniuses have departed, but they left their music and their art as a heritage to be cherished as "A thing of beauty and a joy forever."

The Commercial Scarecrow

be judged if he would discontinue his bad habit of meddling with the abilities of those entrusted to carry through. The sponsor should place enough confidence in the well educated people he hires of his own choice, to *seek* their advice in matters of taste and not continue in the stagnant, plodden path of forcing his personal tastes on everybody. For in this practice, I believe he is more often wrong and consequently the final loser by his own tampering. Naturally, he should have his say, but if his objections are too frequent to allow sincere effort, then he should hire new talent. In any case, for the benefit of the listeners as well as for his own gain, he should abide in the judgment of those trained for the task.

I believe the public is far overdue for new material. I believe that they are as tired of the stereotyped movies and radio programs as they are of the stereotyped singing commercials. I believe that we can freshen the air waves and movies by taking down or at least subduing our "scarecrow".

Earlier history reveals that musicians and writers usually starved to death. Not so today, for which I am sure we are, all of us, more than grateful. For the sustaining force of American music is paid advertising. Yet this same sustaining force harbors a crushing element—commercialism, and too much commercialism crushes initiative. Progress thrives on initiative.

It will be a great day when we can put to practice a successful antidote for the "Commercial Scarecrow".

Every Trick Is Needed

ranger must consider technical facility as well as sound and acoustics, harmonic treatment, or voicing to bring out the leading parts. Every trick of counterpoint or composition must be at the arranger's fingertips.

A special device often used for the microphone is an "echo chamber," a measured box to augment sound which will make a small group sound as though more musicians were playing. Separate boxes often are used to enclose vocal groups, improving tonality and group coordination, especially where the vocal parts are arranged in odd or unusual intervals.

An interesting subject for speculation is whether or not such composers as Tchaikovsky or Debussy or composers of the still older school would follow these new trends were they with us in the present day. Personally, I think their records show that they were quick to utilize all technical advancements, adapting them through the media of their own genius.

Let Them Shine

We all have heard young performers who have excelled seasoned artists. As Karl Wecker, manager of the Hollywood Bowl, remarked to the guests at a symphony association banquet, some of the young soloists who appeared in the Bowl last summer gave more inspiring performances than did certain of the top ranking artists.

Suppose they have all the necessary qualifications; then what? They still are not established artists and are likely to remain so without the necessary pull or financial backing even though they may surpass some better known pianists now before the public.

Let the public demand the excitement of technical display. Let our younger pianists strive for superb technical proficiency. It never fails to win admiration and recognition and perhaps will insure that elusive backing necessary to guarantee a successful concert career.

The spark of real artistry and musical insight which the few possess cannot be smothered or dampened but only enhanced by fine technical equipment; and to have enriched their palette of flexibility and control of artistic expression, enables pianists to give and receive more joy and satisfaction in their chosen work of recreating music.

Together We Sing

8. To promote knowledge of repertory and principles of interpretation.
9. To properly classify voices (Usually the second or third semester).
10. To promote knowledge of class voice teaching methods and materials (For teacher training classes).

The objectives above naturally suggest the nature of activities expected in voice class work. The following basic theory and practice content have been characteristic of classes taught by the author in the past:

1. Principles of how to practice.
2. Posture.
3. Principles of breathing and of breath control development; inhalation, suspension, exhalation, and recovery.
4. Articulation—Vowels and consonants.
5. Vocal exercises—How to obtain relaxation; legato, increase beauty, resonance and control of tone, smooth the registers and increase the range and flexibility of the voice.
6. How to reduce or eliminate fear and self-consciousness.
7. Principles of thought coordination in relation to correct singing.
8. How to study a song.
9. How to memorize songs.
10. Principles of interpretation.
11. Singing facts and helpful suggestions.
12. How to speed up vocal learning.
13. How to sing high and low tones easily and properly.
14. The principles of singing in downward and in upward scale progressions.
15. Stage deportment—Walking, holding music or notebook, use of hands, facial expression, acknowledging applause, acknowledging accompanist.
16. How to classify voices (For teacher training classes).
17. Analysis of class voice texts; suggestion of supplementary song material (For teacher training classes).

The Printed Page Lives

ing a lesson, Godowsky once remarked to me, "You should not be conscious of arms or elbows."

Brilliant, accurate, technical playing can be developed through the thorough knowledge and practice of Czerny, Liszt, Clementi, Chopin, and Henselt studies. I have found the practicing of Hanon most beneficial, transposing the exercises in all keys.

There is nothing of greater importance musically and technically than the study and daily practice of the works of Bach—particularly the preludes and fugues.

One of the greatest assets of the serious pianist is the playing of chamber music—in blending the tone of the piano with the quality of the string tones. In balancing the color values of the instruments in the climaxes and nuances, one learns to measure one's own effects with the instruments.

The development of one's personality, the culture of one's mind, gives one a broader understanding of music itself and the ability to make the printed page live for the audience. To that end one should read good literature, study history and all the arts.

The piano is a great instrument, capable of evoking all moods and emotions, enabling the artist to express his or her individuality.

Stresses Stop the Song

hours"? Beauty does not mix with strain and physical discomfort. Loveliness is not akin to ugliness.

I should like to applaud the Society of Singing Teachers, Inc., for their efforts on behalf of the student of singing. One reads with great interest, the Statement of Laws and Precepts, released through their editorial committee, upon which vocal pedagogy should be based. I am going to quote but one, to me, vital point, something taught me as a beginner and with which I am substantially in agreement: "Vowels are properly formed and resonated in the laryngeal and oral areas of the pharynx supplemented to some extent, by the mouth cavity. Excessive lip-shaping of vowels should be avoided as much as possible. Formation and resonation of vowel tones in the laryngeal and oral areas of the pharynx will not cause them to sound 'throaty' or guttural. All free tone sounds 'in front' to the listener."

To me the final test for the young singer is the ability to sing from pianissimo to forte and the more difficult transition of forte to pianissimo without losing command of the breath, changing the pronunciation or altering the expression.

A saner approach to the art of singing is needed. Teachers should be giving these young, eager seekers of careers truths, facts, instead of fanciful absurdities. I could never forget one charming, well-meaning teacher, who was seated beside me at a Sunday afternoon recital and who turned to me at its close to say—"Do you know, Madame Cutter, that the longer I teach, the more certain I am that all the beauty of the voice is to be found under the upper lip!" How ridiculous!

Singing is not complex, but rather, very simple. Singing is a joyful and natural expression. It is speech put on pitch—the art of sustaining, and prolonging the vowel sound, plus normal diaphragmatic breathing and a relaxed jaw and throat. It is freedom of tone and charm of manner instead of stress and strain—tonal beauty instead of noise, for it is the quality of a voice that gives its distinction. Not how big, but how beautiful. Let us get better acquainted with "bel canto".

That Terrible Child

write in a polyphonic style which no other instrument can as successfully employ.

The great masters of the past, realizing the shortcomings of piano tone in composing for that instrument, tried to hide its weakness by constant movement of the sound, filling up the spaces between melodic lines with harmonized accompaniment or moving counterpoint.

A large tone is of paramount importance to a pianist, aiding him to perform contrasting melodies and figurations. He will have no difficulty in playing a polyvoiced composition, performing each voice in a slightly different volume of tone.

The great Titans of the past, Liszt, Anton Rubinstein and Rachmaninoff and great masters of the present, Horowitz, Artur Rubinstein, Serkin and Casadesus, always are likened in their interpretations to the symphony orchestra because their tonal qualities are so great.

It would be well for every young pianist to get acquainted with the structure and mechanics of the instrument and find out for himself what makes it "tick". The benefits and experience derived from such a study will greatly help the young pianist to muzzle *l'enfant terrible*.

Music Also Serves

possible. Almost any song which has "God" or "Lord" or even expresses what is considered a high ideal is accepted as a "sacred song." Students of sacred music who look forward to singing solos in church should examine most carefully the context and musical value of every solo which they select for final presentation. Likewise, directors and ministers of music should be continually vigilant that they do not allow their soloists to use unsuitable materials. Probably the greatest error in this regard is the adaption of secular music to sacred words. This is especially flagrant with the music in the "public domain" (free from copyright restrictions) and therefore familiar to the general public as a secular number. For the careful singer, director, minister of music, or minister, these will have no place.

The relationship of church music to worship is in-

separable. Assuredly, a successful service, one which conveys to the worshipper the highest expression of the three elements—adoration, praise, petition—will include the greatest in church music, executed in an appropriate manner.

How Does It Sound?

of art. You might just as well say that for a poet to express himself grammatically would detract from his powers of imagination. If you have not had a sufficient drill in music so that you can sing the music accurately, as it is written, then you are hopelessly handicapped, no matter how good your natural voice may be, nor how much feeling you may have for music. Vocally, you may be equipped to sing the music, but in musicianship, you are so weak that you cannot cope with the complex rhythms of modern expression. When you sing with an orchestra, your musical training will spell success or failure. Singing is a profession in which only those well equipped succeed.

Don't be afraid to sing. Like everything else in the world, singing is best learned through the actual doing. Almost all the distinguished artists have done a tremendous amount of singing, and what they know is based on practical experience. Of course they had to have basic theories, but they have worked out these theories into facts through long practice in actual singing. Don't be afraid that your voice will wear out, for nature constructed it of the toughest material she knew how to create and it will stand a lot of work. As soon as you can sing anything at all, do so. Not with the idea that it is perfect, or even good, but with the view of gaining the understanding which only comes through actual experience. You learn to swim, by swimming; to skate, by skating. You will learn to sing in the same manner, by singing.

DON'T use exercises that tend to tighten the muscles surrounding the larynx.

DON'T use exercises that lead to exhaustion.

DON'T sing any songs that employ more than one note outside of the most comfortable range of the voice.

DON'T use eccentric vocal methods.

DON'T use remedies for throat troubles which are liable to prove more violent irritants than the trouble itself.

BEWARE of straining your voice while singing in a choir or chorus. Choir singing forms the best kind of practice, but must not be overdone.

BEWARE of teachers who tell you that a complete vocal training may be secured in one or two years.

Oratorio Carries On

added several fine works to the repertory including *St. Paul* and *Elijah*.

Modern composers have made few attempts but fortunately these have been fine contributions. Pierne's *Children's Crusade* is an example as are Honneger's *King David*, Kodaly's *Hungarian Psalm*, Albert Roussel's *Psalm 80* and William Walton's stirring *Belshazzar's Feast*. Vaughn Williams deserves mention for his *Dona Nobis Pacem*. In our own country there has been less activity since the turn of the century and the only sacred work of major proportions that comes to mind is the *Sacred Service* of Ernest Bloch, a deeply contemplative and truly beautiful composition which this writer had the good fortune to premier in Cleveland.

It is to be hoped that some of America's top composers may endeavor to produce major choral works in oratorio style, for there is no doubt that oratorio is here to stay.

Vocal Millionaires

Bidu Sayao who can give us both a splendid Rosina and a convincing Mimi.

Many others, also magnificent singers, may be better actresses yet they have not been gifted with exceptional "resonance chambers" and they had to acquire with study and struggle what Mother Nature did not endow them. Because of this we should appreciate their accomplishments the more.

Therefore, I consider the 17 singers above mentioned the vocal millionaires, in a privileged position to distribute their riches lavishly and calmly. And those riches rest on the tremendous sensitivity of their "soundingboards."

The male millionaires?

Tenors: Caruso, Zenatello, DeMuro, Lauri Volpi, Johnson, Gigli, Fleta, Lazaro, Muratore, Crimi, Bonci and Schipa. The last two had a peculiar rich resonance particularly in their sublime "mezza voce". When they attempted to force their voices the beautiful resonance was lost. Baritones: Ruffo, Borghese, Battistini, John Charles Thomas, Dufranne, Stracciari, Galeffi, Benedetti and Sammarco. Bassos: Mardones, Pinza and (unknown to this country) Sibiriakoff.

What about Chaliapin? Well, Chaliapin was a great singing actor, the best of the past generation, but with a mediocre voice: I might say the noisiest voice I have ever heard.

My modest suggestion to the young singers is to pay special attention to resonance, which will give to their voices power, beauty and, above all, the carrying quality which will project easily regardless of the amplitude of the theatres.

Volume without resonance is only noise, and noise disappears rapidly. That's why many voices do not last long!

Simplicity In Song

It's not a question of simple things for simple people. I have found that the majority of people who study voice possess fine minds and unusual ability. The fact that they are working with a subject that is complex, and unfortunately steeped in traditional musts and must-nots, is enough to guarantee that only those with extreme talent will have even a fighting chance, unless teachers begin their instruction with clear, concise, and simple explanations.

In singing, as in acting, lack of naturalness is to be deplored. Naturalness can be achieved only by the singer's absolute control mentally and physically, of every phase of his technique. To sing one's song without imagination and instinctive melodic line, is to convey to the listener a colorless pattern of words and music, even if the technic, physiologically speaking, is flawless.

Let us assume that correct tone production has become automatic though natural, and that the singer can concentrate his faculties on the interpretation of the musical offering.

The teacher then should simplify the situation by "breaking down" the text to achieve a clear and interesting reading, thus helping the student to convey the full meaning of the words to his audience. If the singer adds color as well as real inner feeling, the song becomes a vital living experience for audience and artist.

The real difficulty in achieving beauty and simplicity in singing, would seem to be the desire of teacher and pupil to exaggerate every natural sequence to an abnormal degree, disdaining anyone who mentions simplicity with the words; "That is for simple people!"

150

Poise Means Freedom

expression. The power to do this comes through relaxation.

The mature artist is much more apt to have emotional poise. In young artists, the sheer exuberance of youth often carries them completely out of the realm of artistry into dramatic display, gusty, uncontrolled, and confusing. Vital enthusiasm and spontaneity there must be, but in well molded effort bringing the right effect at the right moment. Grace and economy of force bring smoothness, dignity, and authority to a rendition, while quiet and calm bring more ease and agility.

Every artist must penetrate his songs with healthy enthusiasm, flooding his consciousness with its meaning, but never sing more than he feels. Fighting force must never be substituted for emotional intensity gained through study, experience, and maturity. All imaginary situations must be made real with simple, sincere truthfulness, and must be vitally expressed. This takes inborn desire, acquired technic, creative ability, generosity, warmth and courage. These are displayed with poise.

With poise, the artist rightly uses his individuality to create personality. He outwardly displays with vital dignity his inner feelings for his audience to grasp. He must show his natural love for his work.

Poise is not afraid of extremes, nor does it pour the artist into a mold. Rather, it leaves him free and flexible enough to work less and accomplish more with his right to create, provided he is already well grounded in technic and musicianship.

Singing For Fun

that he enjoys singing, that he have a sense of pitch, a sense of rhythm, and a memory for melody.

If he has a beautiful voice as well, and has studied music to the point where he can read it easily, he is indeed of great value. A few seasons of singing under a good director may find him qualified as a professional and he can begin singing for money. However, I do not believe he will ever again be as happy with his achievement as he was when he was singing for fun!

Is The World Sick Vocally?

or the point of absolute balance and harmony. Could we turn the pages of history back to the studios of the famous Manuel Garcia in London or Paris, and hear Malibran or Jenny Lind singing the beautiful bel canto—the perfect voice—we would listen entranced, thrilled, and realize that for these brief, golden moments God and man meet in supreme union.

Why Not Sing?

sult equals the sum and substance of our mental and emotional capacity.

The physical reaction, which entails the principle of sound when applied to our bodies as our instrument of vocal release, is actually the smallest consideration in speaking or singing. Yet since it is so little understood by most people, it has become a "bug-a-boo", and its importance magnified to ridiculous proportions.

Just a little understanding can give the freedom required in good singing, and leave more time for the development of the more important factors, namely— the mental and emotional energies or the psychological and philosophical capacities, in which lie the real power of beautiful and interpretative singing.

Your body is your instrument; your emotional energy is the power that drives; your mind is the motivating force that directs the energies, and your reasoning power is the balancing point.

The mind carries the knowledge of all the details, such as pitch, rhythm, tempo, pronunciation, articulation, tone and finesse. The heart carries the sympathetic understanding of all the human emotions. When these two factors are set in harmonious motion, with a definite purpose in mind, the body becomes a willing servant. With an understanding of the physical reactions and a little practice, the body responses become habitual and work subconsciously.

Then singing becomes not only a beautiful art but also a healthy, stimulating activity as every muscle and every nerve is set into easy, vibrant, harmonious motion. Singing is a joy and your voice the most satisfactory medium of self-expression yet discovered for human use.

Subjective and Objective

Further evidences of a subjective and objective balance can be found in those of Stravinsky's works which are based on the music of others. This includes the early ballets based on Russian folk themes and many later works which use excerpts from Pergolesi, Tchaikovsky, Rossini and others. There was an original subjective need to use the music which he enjoyed.

In writing the *Pulcinella* ballet, Stravinsky, ". . . . feeling certain sympathetic affinities with the music of Pergolesi, reverted in imagination to the environment of the Neapolitan music makers of the early eighteenth century and produced . . . 'a portrait' of Pergolesi and his times." That the music sounds original and is therefore more than a transcription is a tribute to his ability to blend characteristic styles of the old and new, a feat impossible with the pure "objective" method.

Speaking of *Dances Concertantes* (1942) which gently parodies the ballet music of the last century, he says: "After studying many pages of a certain composer, I begin to sense his musical personality and signature. Like a detective I reconstruct his musical experience." Having been influenced by the composer, Stravinsky begins to influence the composer with his own composing. In this interplay between the old music and the modern ear, a new music is born.

Ingolf Dahl quotes Stravinsky in *Modern Music* (Summer 1946): "I do not have any ultimate viewpoint of composition, and when I write my next symphony it will then be an expression of my will at that moment. And what that will is going to be I do not know now. I wish people would let me have the privilege of being at least a little bit unconscious. It is so nice sometimes to go blind just with the feeling for the right thing."

Why Sing?

shaped and polished, it becomes a gem of rare beauty.

So it is with your voice. You may have a voice that is quite listenable in its natural state; but with expert training and coaching, your voice will become doubly beautiful, even as the polished jade.

The rules for good singing are really simple: humility, sincerity of purpose, the ability to "stick," a willingness to co-operate and work with your teacher, the correct mental approach, and a large portion of good humor! Your voice is the product you are working to perfect; the rules are the tools you work with. You are the "factory"; so if you really want to become a singer, let's roll up our sleeves and get into production!

Tune To the Times

Among the modern composers whose works I have had the privilege of introducing are the Americans: Robert Russell Bennett, Aaron Copland, Charles Martin Loeffler, Everett Helm, Charles Jones, Harold Triggs, Gardner Read, Gail Kubik and William Grant Still; Russia's Khatchaturian, Achron and Knipper; Austria's Schoenberg and Toch; Poland's Tansman; Italy's Rieti and Castelnuovo Tedesco; Brazil's Guarneri; France's Milhaud; and Hungary's Kodaly. However, the list of contemporary composers is as endless as the waves Gustav Mahler mentioned at the beginning of this article. Even a passing glance at the musical scene will disclose a galaxy of living composers such as the Americans: Samuel Barber, Ernest Bloch, Paul Creston, Vladimir Dukelsky, Bernard Wagenaar, Henry Cowell, Charles Ives, David Diamond, Quincy Porter, Virgil Thomson, Bernard Herrmann, Roger Sessions, Kent Kennan, Douglas Moore, Leo Sowerby, Marion Bauer; Russia's Stravinsky, Prokofiev, Shebalin and Miaskovsky; Czechoslovakia's Martinu; England's Vaughn-Williams, Walton, Benjamin Britten and Gerald Finzi; Austria's Alban Berg; Hungary's Dohnanyi, Bartok and Miklos Rozsa; Mexico's Carlos Chavez, Silvestre Revueltas, Blas Galindo, and Pablo Moncayo; Spain's Rudolpho Halffter; France's Francaix, Jacques de Menasce and Manuel Rosenthal, and Brazil's Villa Lobos. As any list is always incomplete—so this one must also be, due to space limitations and the wonderful creative fresh springs of music that are continually welling up to refresh mankind.

Hollywood–Los Angeles

The Hollywood Bowl has long held pre-eminence in the field of summer concerts throughout the world, because of the caliber and scope of its presentations and the fact that among some thousand performances of its *Symphonies Under the Stars* since 1922, there has been but one postponement because of rain.

Occupying a canyon in the Hollywood Hills, the Bowl's acoustical properties were discovered by William Reed and his son, H. Ellis Reed, in 1919. After desultory theatrical and musical performances, the season of symphonies were instituted and have continued for eight weeks each summer since that time.

The Bowl property of 69 acres includes the surrounding hills so that the natural beauty of the amphitheater is preserved. It belongs to Los Angeles County, and is leased to the Hollywood Bowl Assn. which operates the property and attends to its upkeep. It was purchased by donations from patrons, including pennies tossed into a huge bowl in Pepper Tree Lane, the entrance. Such donations today are applied to upkeep.

Heading the campaign to preserve and develop the Bowl was Mrs. J. J. Carter, whose dynamic personality engendered enthusiastic support from the entire Hollywood community. Continuance of the Bowl, even during the trying war years, was largely due to the energy and business acumen of Mrs. Leiland Atherton Irish in the capacity of general manager.

First conductor in the Bowl was Alfred Hertz. Since that time virtually every famous conductor of the world has led the orchestra, and practically every distinguished artist has appeared as soloist or in one of the grand opera performances given.

Karl Wecker, now general manager, cites plans of the Bowl Assn. for a school of music, school of the theater, and school of ballet. The association also leases the Pilgrimage Play Bowl, a smaller amphitheater nearby where the life of Jesus has been draamatized for two decades. It is suitable for musical or theatrical performances of smaller scope.

The Philharmonic Orchestra of Los Angeles was founded in 1919 by William Andrews Clark Jr., who contributed largely to its support until his death in 1934. It displaced the earlier Los Angeles Symphony, of which Adolph Tandler was the last conductor. Apart from one season at a Hollywood theater, and for special events in the large Shrine Auditorium, the orchestra has played in the Philharmonic Auditorium, a former theater renamed to honor the organization. Since Clark's demise the orchestra has been operated by the Southern California Symphony Assn, organized by a group of public spirited citizens, with Harvey S. Mudd as president and Mrs. Leiland Atherton Irish as executive vice-president and general manager. Since 1946 Mudd has been chairman of the executive board, with Henry L. Duque as president, with the active leadership in the hands of Conductor Alfred Wallenstein and Manager Wilfrid L. Davis.

In addition to its regular symphony pair concerts in Los Angeles, the orchestra regularly visits a score of Southern California communities to present series that vary in length according to the local support. The orchestra also has appeared in San Francisco and Sacramento, and participated in the centennial celebration in Provo, Utah.

The orchestra's first conductor was Walter Henry Rothwell, who built the original ensemble and led it until his sudden demise in 1927. He was followed on the podium by George Schneevoigt, Artur Rodzinski and Otto Klemperer as perma-

nent conductors, with later seasons divided between Bruno Walter, Leopold Stokowski, Albert Coates, John Barbirolli and George Szell. Since the 1944-45 season it has been under the leadership of its first American director, Alfred Wallenstein, who endeavored immediately to create active public interest and wider support of the organization.

Wallenstein launched an annual series of *Symphonies for Youth* concerts broadcast coast-to-coast, which twice won first place in a national radio poll as an outstanding educational program. Wallenstein conducts and acts as commentator on the programs, which are worked out in cooperation with William C. Hartshorn, music supervisor of the Los Angeles City School System. The programs are coordinated with regular school instructions, and reinforced by a weekly local radio broadcast. An intermission feature is a quiz on musical subjects. The repertory of the regular adult concerts is made available to school music teachers and studied by the pupils, who then are permitted to attend rehearsals. At the concerts, the regular staff of ushers is augmented by members of the Women's Committee, an organization which originally sponsored such concerts under the leadership of Mrs. Cecil Frankel.

Junior Philharmonic Clubs and College Forums have been active, the latter started by Cornelia Clark Davis, who previously had instituted the system in San Francisco. Pension Fund concerts have been directed by Arturo Toscanini, Eugene Ormandy and Otto Klemperer.

The most famous of all youth orchestras is Peter Meremblum's California Junior Symphony, which has appeared in several feature pictures and film short subjects. It has played in Hollywood Bowl, sharing the podium with the Los Angeles Philharmonic, and in the Philharmonic Auditorium, Shrine Auditorium and various concert halls of the vicinity. Former members now are sprinkled through the leading symphony orchestras of the country.

Founded as the Meremblum String Ensemble in 1936, it became a full orchestra a year later and rapidly expanded to number over 100 capable young performers. Some come a distance of thirty miles to attend the regular Saturday morning and Wednesday night rehearsals under Meremblum's baton. Guest conductors include many of the world's most eminent, Walter, Stokowski, Steinberg, Coates, Barbirolli, Rodzinski, Iturbi, Szell and the Bakaleinikoffs, to name but a few. The players average of high school age, but their musicianship has won the unanimous praise of visiting musical celebrities.

The orchestra won world renown when it appeared in the film, *They Shall Have Music*, with Jascha Heifetz, later appearing in *There is Magic in Music*. Several short films featuring the orchestra alone have been released. The entire group of young players has professional status as members of the Musicians Union. Aspirants too young to join the major group play in the Pioneer Orchestra, under the direction of Joseph Oroop, until they attain the requisite age and experience.

The orchestra has given first readings of a number of important scores, including Kern's *Scenario* and Barrymore's *Russian Suite*. Its alumnae include Dorothy Wade, concert violinist, and Dolly Loehr, pianist, better known as Diana Lynn, screen star.

The Janssen Symphony Orchestra was founded in 1940 by Werner Janssen and functioned until 1946 when the conductor assumed the post of musical director of the Portland Symphony. Its activities may be resumed later. During its operation, it presented several concerts annually

(Continued on page 282)

Burbank

Music in Burbank centers about the Burbank Symphony Orchestra and the Burbank Civic Chorus. Both organizations receive civic support through the park and recreation department of the city and give both individual and joint concerts during the winter season, and a summer series in the Burbank Bowl.

The symphony orchestra was founded by Leo Damiani who has been its conductor since its inception, and though still a semi-professional group is aspiring to fully professional status. It has premiered a number of works by resident composers and has broadcast over major radio networks.

The civic chorus was founded by John H. Ellis, who remains its permanent conductor and also is assistant conductor of the symphony orchestra. An organization of some ninety singers, it participates in many gala events of the community. The city also has a community concert series which presents well-known touring artists.

Glendale

The Glendale Symphony Orchestra, which has just completed its 23rd season, is sponsored by the Glendale College and the Parks-Recreation Department of the City of Glendale, under the auspices of the Glendale Symphony Assn. Concerts are given in the high school auditorium and are free to the public. Its membership is made up of both professionals and amateurs who rehearse once a week, and the programs presented are comparable with those offered by other symphony orchestras of the country.

Some former conductors of the Glendale Symphony Orchestra were J. Arthur Myers, Modest Altschuler, Adolph Tandler, Liborius Hauptman, and William Ulrich. The present conductor, Scipione Guidi, has just completed two years as musical director.

The Glendale Oratorio Society has been in existence over twenty years, rehearsing once a week to present three concerts each season. It has had several eminent conductors, including John Smallman. Its present conductor, Benjamin Edwards, has completed three seasons.

For its fourth season, the Glendale Philharmonic and Artists Assn. is presenting a series of five concerts, including the Philharmonic Orchestra and leading artists.

—Edna Crowell Levy

Pasadena

Pasadena's chief musical asset is the Civic Music Assn., with Richard Lert as musical director, which sponsors the Pasadena Civic Orchestra of 100 and Civic Chorus of 250, performing eight to ten Civic Auditorium concerts annually, all open to the public. The association has completed its 19th year, highlighted by the annual Spring Music Festival, a month-long series of more than a dozen events in which 2000 musicians participated before audience totaling some 21,000.

The semi-professional orchestra also serves as a training ground for major symphony work, and the chorus, too, has graduated members to concert or opera stage and radio. Competent young artists of the vicinity are given opportunity as soloists, and among those so helped to win still wider success are Eula Beal, Leonard Pennario, Harold Keel, Emery Darcy, Mona Paulee, Lillian Steuber, Alexander Murray, John Raitt, Nan Merriman, Douglas Beattie, Virginia Card, Lillian Fawcett, Olive Mae Beach, Jane McGowan, Peggy Turnley, Phyllis Moffett, George Burnson, and John Shafer.

Lert's policy is to include at least one work by an American composer on each program, with preference to those residing in Southern California. A newsworthy "scoop" was the recent premiere of a long-lost *Rondo* by Mozart, which records declared never had been played before. As an authority on Handel, Lert also has presented seldom heard Handelian works. The association is financed partly by an annual fund from the city and largely by membership dues from some 1000 members. The Junior League also cooperates in presentation of special events for children.

Pasadena is considered one of the world's leading centers for chamber music. The Coleman Chamber Music Assn., founded by Alice Coleman Batchelder, who still is its musical director, has just completed its 42nd season, and this year has launched a chamber music competion. The organization has had to increase its series, and repeat each program in the Pasadena Playhouse twice or thrice.

The 3000-seat Civic Auditorium accommodates the Elmer Wilson concert series, which has brought leading artists for the past 13 years, and the visits of the Los Angeles Philharmonic Orchestra. The city shows lack of appreciation for only one type of musical event—the dance.

Of special interest is the American Music Theater, which has presented "opera in the American way" for six consecutive seasons under Lert and the late George Houston, with excellent English texts.

Other organizations include the Bach Society, the Cauldron Singers, and the noted Pasadena Boy Choir, led by John Henry Lyons. The city schools system is credited with an exceptional music department, and there is a great deal of church music, since Pasadena has one and one-quarter churches to every 990 persons. Broadway this year has had four operetta stars who "graduated" from Pasadena church positions.

—Charles D. Perlee

Santa Monica

The city of Santa Monica is rapidly becoming a musical mecca. It sponsors its own professional symphony orchestra, a civic (amateur) orchestra, and an annual season by the Philharmonic Orchestra of Los Angeles, as well as numerous concerts and musical events.

The Santa Monica Symphony Orchestra, whose records and broadcasts have brought to international attention, was founded in 1945 by Jacques Rachmilovich, who remains its permanent conductor, under the auspices of the Santa Monica Civic Music Guild, founded by Mmes. Cecil Frankel and Leiland Atherton Irish. It has introduced a number of new works, both American and foreign, and Conductor Rachmilovich makes a practice of performing at least one work by an American composer on each program.

The Santa Monica Civic Orchestra was founded in 1947 and Arthur Lange engaged as conductor. The amateur group rehearses weekly and plans occasional concerts. Both orchestras receive some financial aid from the city.

The Continental Artists Series is designed to highlight the local artists, giving them opportunities to perform in concert in their own community. The Civic Music Guild sponsors a regular series of events for children, with music played by leading artists.

Programs are presented by the Music Arts Society, Junior Music Arts Society, Theater Guild, and Recreation and Playground Department of the city. A summer series is known as Symphonies by the Sea.

In the field of dance, the newly organized Ballet Association of America makes its home in Santa Monica. It has given several local and Los Angeles presentations, and plans a series of dance attractions up and down the Coast.

—Raoul Gripenwaldt.

Fresno

Music in Fresno is promulgated largely by the Fresno Musical Club which presents a philharmonic course of six to eight concerts annually, and stimulates music appreciation through contests for children and resident concerts. Fresno State College sponsors a series of programs by guest artists on the campus, in addition to public performances given by its own concert organizations. These include a symphonic orchestra, a concert band, male, female, and a cappella choirs. Annual activities include five orchestral concerts, a performance of the *Messiah* and various faculty, student and other programs.

—Bell T. Ritchie

San Francisco Bay Region

The San Francisco Opera Association celebrated its 25th anniversary with the 1947 season. Gaetano Merola, its founder-conductor, can well be credited with a magnificent achievement. Five hundred and forty-eight performances of seventy-four operas, the statistics read at the close of the 1947 season. The roster of artists and conductors includes every name of musical importance throughout the singing world, as well as famous conductors, stage directors and ballet masters.

Kenneth Monteagle, president, and Paul Posz, manager since 1940 and now secretary, are responsible for the touring engagements of the company, inaugurated in 1941, which have bolstered financial support to such an extent that it has operated for the past seven years without having to call upon the guarantors for assistance. Armando Agnini, with the association since its inception, bears the title of stage and technical director, and the multiplicity of activities and responsibilities entrusted to him call for unlimited imagination and artistic taste. Curran Swint has been publicity director for fifteen years. The opera chorus is directed by Kurt Herbert Adler, and the ballet by William and Howard Christensen.

The Opera Guild, organized in 1938, with Mrs. Stanley Powell as chairman, has done its share in developing wider public interest in opera, largely by student performances which have been offered each season except during war years. Mrs. Thomas Carr Howe, Jr., is the present chairman.

The San Francisco Symphony Orchestra is recognized from coast to coast as "one of the top orchestras" (Life Magazine, May 5, 1947) and Pierre Monteux, versatile, authoritative conductor, "one of the great men of music." Its nation-wide tour (March-April-May, 1947) with a schedule of 58 concerts in 59 days in major cities of the United States and Canada commanded the artistic approval of critics far and wide.

The real beginning of the present San Francisco Symphony followed the earthquake and fire. The first regular season in 1911-12 was conducted by the American composer, Henry Hadley. Then followed fifteen years of leadership by Alfred Hertz. Issay Dobrowen and Basil Cameron shared the podium one year. The symphony finally ceased its regular series for an entire season until an amendment to the city's charter was inserted in the ballot, and by popular vote a tax of one-half of one percent of property valuation began pouring into symphony coffers. This sum meant then as now, a stable assurance for the symphony. The orchestra also plays for the entire opera season.

Monteux's 13th season finds the San Francisco Symphony in its 36th year at the height of its career. For the 1947-48 season 88 concerts in 22 weeks are planned, including a "triple subscription series" at the Opera House, with the same program played on Thursday nights, Friday afternoons and Saturday nights. This particular arrangement, inaugurated in 1946, accommodates some 10,000 listeners. The Young People's Series of six concerts led by Rudolph Ganz, also will be continued. Out-of-town concerts will again take the orchestra to Berkeley, Palo Alto, San Jose, Sacramento, Redlands and Beverly Hills.

The Symphony Forum, comprising members of the various Bay Region college and university forums, whose chairman is Mrs. Harold D. Pischel, is an active, stimulating group of young people whose members compose most of the Thursday night subscription series audiences. No mention of the symphony would be complete without laudatory citation of Mrs. Leonora Wood Armsby, president and managing director, and Howard Skinner, secretary-business manager.

The Art Commission Symphony Series, always held at the Civic Auditorium, frequently draws a capacity audience of 7,000. These popularly-priced concerts are administered by Edward D. Keil, president, and members of the Art Commission. Many local artists have in the past been introduced through this series recently including Florence Quarteraro, soprano, and Solveig Lunde, pianist (in debut). Honegger's *King David* and Verdi's *Requiem* included local soloists Verna Osborne, Herta Glaz, Carl Hague, and the Municipal Chorus.

Perhaps the most ambitious offering under Art Commission auspices was premiere of the San Francisco Civic Ballet in November, 1947, assisted by the Markova-Dolin Ensemble and the San Francisco Symphony. This organization succeeds the San Francisco Ballet founded by Adolph Bolm, and now may be recognized as a permanent organization on equal footing with the San Francisco Symphony and Opera Associations.

In Oakland cultural life centers around a symphonic group and an outstanding annual program. The Oakland Symphony, under the leadership of Orley See (14th year), sponsored by a large civic group of several hundred music-minded citizens (E. W. Ehmann, president), gives an annual subscription concert series. Made up of professionals and semi-professionals, this live-wire organization has a progressive policy of "American soloists and American compositions." A stimulating feature is presentation of young artists in solo appearances through a series of competitions sponsored by the music teachers of the Oakland Public Schools. Soloists who appeared in the regular subscription series recently were Wanda Krasoff, Arpine McKenna and Robert Brereton, Bay Region pianists.

The University of California Symphony, Albert Elkus and William Denny, conductors, is the oldest symphonic organization in the whole Bay Region. Drawing its nucleus of players for the most part from University enrollments, as well as featuring talented young University students as soloists, the concerts each year at the Men's Gymnasium and Wheeler Hall are important features in East Bay musical life.

The Young People's Symphony, managed by William E. Chamberlin, commands interest in its service to youthful players under 18 years of age; gifted young soloists are presented in debut appearances. Standard symphonic repertory is always programmed and the group, some 90 strong, receives musical training under the leadership of Jessica Marcelli. Monthly broadcasts are scheduled for the 1947-48 season, besides concerts on the U. C. campus and appearances in Oakland, San Francisco and Marin County.

North of San Francisco, across Golden Gate Bridge, is the Sonoma County Symphony, George F. Barr, conductor. Inland, to the east of the Oakland vicinity, are the Stockton Symphony, Manlio Carlos Silva, conductor; and the Sacramento Philharmonic, George Barr, conductor. Down the peninsula, Nathan Koblick is manager-conductor of the Peninsula Symphony.

Still farther south at Carmel, each summer (for the past ten), Dene Denney and Hazel Watrous present a Bach Festival, lasting an entire week. A local orchestra and chorus composed of amateurs and professionals of the Monterey Peninsula, under the leadership of Gastone Usigli, who commutes to and from Hollywood for rehearsals, are augmented by outstanding soloists during Festival Week. Under Denney-Watrous management touring artists also are brought to Carmel and San Jose.

(Continued on page 283)

San Diego

The San Diego Symphony Assn., inactive during the war, soon will resume its summer series concerts at the Ford Bowl in Balboa Park.

The San Diego Light Opera Assn. has had two successful seasons under Manager William Dean. It has presented light opera under Julius Leib with Charles Cannon directing the chorus. Leo Scheer conducted this organization in several operas including Rossini's *Barber of Seville*.

The Community Symphony, organized and conducted by Nino Marcelli, provides symphonic experience for its members as well as fine music for the public.

The San Diego Symphonetta, comprised of 42 professional musicians conducted by John Metzger, has given several successful concerts in its first season just completed.

A new group doing much for music in San Diego is the Friends of Music, sponsoring concerts of chamber music under the general direction of Arnold Small.

Headed by Conductor Nikolai Sokoloff, the Musical Arts Society of La Jolla has presented series of concerts and recitals each season.

The Youth Symphony of San Diego, founded and conducted by Leo Scheer, is now in its third year and is sponsored partially by the Recreation Department. During its brief history the Youth Symphony gave concerts for military personnel during the war, as well as the public at home.

Among choral societies there is Polyphonia, now in its fifteenth year, founded and directed by Earl Rosenberg. The San Diego Community Chorus, organized and directed by Carl Dewse has been presenting, among its many programs, a performance of Handel's *Messiah* each year. There are also several school groups of unusual merit. These include the Treble Clef Women's Chorus of San Diego State College led by L. Deborah Smith, and the A Cappella Choirs of the Hoover and Grossmont High Schools directed by Myron Green and Meryle Donahue respectively, both prize winning organizations.

Two philanthropic organizations of San Diego which have done much to provide opportunities for young talented musicians are the Society of Associated Arts, which provides scholarships with local teachers for qualifying students who cannot afford lessons, and the Musical Merit Foundation, which offers yearly awards of scholarships to well known conservatories and schools of music, and prizes for outstanding achievement by music students.

Several concert series bring the touring artists to San Diego's music lovers yearly. These include the Master Art Series, the Clifford Ellison Series and last, but surely far from least, the Amphion Club of San Diego, reputed to be the oldest organization of its kind in America. This club has brought to San Diego a series of concerts on a non-profit basis for an uninterrupted period of 54 years.

—Leo Scheer

Orange County

Musical Arts Club, an organization of professional musicians, singers, artists and teachers, was organized in 1932 to further interest and direct public attention to the cultural and practical value of music and art. Under President Ethel Lynn Mansfield it presents an artist course, bringing artists to Orange County each year. It also conducts an annual contest for young musicians and singers.

The Fullerton Community Concert Assn. organized in 1946, has Mrs. J. J. Alexander as president. Cantando Club, a male chorus, was organized in 1927. President Carter H. Lane, Director Leland Auer, and Accompanist Christine Rees present three concerts yearly, engaging guest soloists. The Cecilian Singers, a women's choral group, was organized 1929. Now president is Florence Markwood, director Mary Batten Steffenson, accompanist Esther Vogtt Gordon. Two concerts are presented each year.

Orange County Youth Symphony, organized 1940, is conducted by Norma L. Perkins. The orchestra is supported by the Anaheim Kiwanis Club, and is composed of youths from all of Orange County. Four concerts are given each season in different cities of Southern California.

The Annual Music Festival held at various high school auditoriums is an outstanding feature of Orange County. Its program includes band, orchestra, girls' and boys' glee clubs and mixed chorus.

Anaheim Dance Pageant is one of the most popular and outstanding attractions given in Orange County each year. It was organized in 1935 and is directed by Lenoir Richards Martin, assisted by Mrs. Anna L. Richards, her mother. Mrs. Richards is known for her pageantry through California and Nevada from 1890 to 1942. During the past twelve years, sixteen pageants have been staged in Orange County and two in Los Angeles, with all proceeds going to charity. These pageants have been sponsored by Anaheim Council of Parents and Teachers, Anaheim Elks Drum Corps and Band, and The Childrens Welfare Club of Los Angeles.

—Albert M. Cranston

Santa Barbara

Musical activities have undergone a renaissance in Santa Barbara since the war years. The Opera Guild, under the chairmanship of Mrs. Wallace Blair, has produced a number of light operas and is to produce a series of summer events in the Santa Barbara County Bowl.

The former Santa Barbara State College is now a branch of the University of California. Its augmented musical department has presented a number of musical events. Josephine Murray, supervisor of music in the public schools has offered a number of concerts by pupils. Gladys Moorhead continues to develop creative expression and musical understanding in the very young.

The newly-organized Music Academy of the West presented several concerts during its first season and promised more in the coming years.

Well-known artists are brought to Santa Barbara music lovers by the Lobero Foundation, under the chairmanship of Mrs. H. O. Koefod, and the Santa Barbara Music Society under the presidency of Clarence Graff. A series of choral events is presented by the Santa Barbara Music Society Chorus.

—Mildred Couper

Stockton

Stockton is fast becoming one of California's better known cultural centers. Aside from the nationally recognized music conservatory of the local College of the Pacific, Stockton boasts an excellent public schools music program. Instrumental and voice training are stressed on all educational levels from first grade through junior college and specialized conservatory studies. A civic music program is making rapid strides through the medium of the Metropolitan Recreation Department. A privately subscribed symphony of some years standing adds to the city's musical enjoyment.

The City Metropolitan Recreation Program attempts to cover those phases of musical activity not covered by public school music, acting as an adjunct to the latter. Activities include a baton twirling and precision drill corps of elementary age girls known as the "Recreaettes". These youngsters have appeared in numerous local, San Francisco and Lodi parades, and have won several prizes assisted by the boys drum corps, another unit of training.

The Stockton Community Band is sponsored by the Metropolitan Recreation Department, Stockton's Musicians's Assn. (A. F. of M.), and the Adult Division of Stockton City Schools. A completely adult unit of fifty local musicians, this concert band has progressed rapidly and in less than one year's time has played a highly successful series of summer concerts and will be a featured attraction in the Community Christmas Pageant. The summer concerts are presented, free to the public, on various city parks.

The Stockton Symphony Orchestra, under the direction of Manlio Silva, presents a winter concert series which includes two symphony ballet programs directed by Mrs. Helen Moore Roberts. In early spring, the Northern California High School Music Festival is presented in the Civic Auditorium. Composed of music groups of many high schools, this event draws widespread interest and features "name" conductors as well as the hundreds of juvenile

(Continued on page 159)

Puget Sound Area

The nine seaport cities on Puget Sound, even the Seattle-Tacoma section where population is densest, are to a high degree dependent on imported artists for musical performances. Climax of the musical year in Seattle, the largest city and the one with the greatest musical resources, is the annual "season" of three to five performances of the San Francisco Opera Co., sponsored by the Seattle Symphony organizat.ion, which attracts some 4,500 persons each evening to the barn-like Civic Auditorium.

Forty or more "attractions" are listed in a year by the town's leading impresario, Cecilia Schultz, for her Moore Theater, and several other concert series rely on imported talent.

The largest and most noteworthy musical venture of the Puget Sound region's communities is the newly-named Pacific Northwest Symphony Orchestra, under the leadership of Musical Director Carl Bricken and Associate Conductor Eugene Linden, now engaged in its first season of concerts in the sponsoring cities of Seattle, Tacoma, and Olympia. It had been the custom for the Tacoma Philharmonic Orchestra's concert season to follow the Seattle Symphony's for the personnel of the two organizations were as high as seven-eighths identical. The new Pacific Northwest Symphony recognizes this state of affairs, and its boast is that all of its nearly 80 members are year-round residents of the region they serve.

The Seattle Symphony existed in varying degrees of prosperity for 43 seasons under such eminent conductors as Henry Hadley (1909-11), Karl Krueger (1926-31), Basil Cameron (1932-38), Nikolai Sokoloff (1938-41), Sir Thomas Beecham and a succession of guest-conductors (1941-44). Its last three seasons were conducted by Carl Bricken, who came to Seattle from the University of Wisconsin, and who has become musical director of the Pacific Northwest Symphony. The Seattle Symphony community organization continues, under the old name, to sponsor eight pairs of subscription concerts to be given during the 1947-48 season in the Moore Theater, a popular concert series in the Civic Auditorium, and other activities, musical and educational. G. Baltzer Peterson is president, Phil Hart manager, and Vera White, office manager.

The Tacoma Philharmonic was founded in 1933 by its only conductor, Eugene Linden, then a young graduate of the Portland Junior Symphony. From a modest beginning, it gradually expanded to a membership of over 70, which included many Seattle Symphony players. It normally played four or five evening concerts and two or three children's concerts each season, plus a concert or two in nearby Olympia. The sponsoring organization in Tacoma is headed by Mrs. Everett Griggs, II, while that in Olympia, the Fine Arts Guild, has Mrs. Peter Schmidt as its president.

Linden, now associate conductor of the Pacific Northwest Symphony, will conduct two of its eight braces of Seattle subscription concerts, two of its four Tacoma engagements, and its solitary Olympia appearance during the 1947-48 season, Bricken leading all the other programs. Though a slight reduction in scope and number of programs for the region, compared with previous seasons, it is hoped other cities of the region and State will underwrite concerts, to provide longer seasons now that the foundation has been laid for a first-rate regional orchestra.

A second important symphonic ensemble, with over 80 members was founded by George M. Ross, an accountant, in 1944-45, with Don Bushell as musical director, a position he still occupies. The first season produced one orchestral concert; the next two, two each. The second season saw

also development of a 90-voice mixed chorus, which now has performed oratorios of Mendelssohn and Elgar, as well as works for chorus and orchestra by Brahms and Vaughan Williams. Affairs of the society are in the hands of committees elected by the dues-paying membership, and the venture has had broad community support.

Civic non-professional orchestras of lesser size and achievements exist in several of the smaller cities. The Bremerton Symphonic Orchestra was founded in 1942 under Ernest Fitzsimmons, who led it in three programs. It was taken over, the following spring, by Walter C. Welke of the University of Washington Music School, the present conductor. The Bremerton city government contributes materially to the upkeep of this 55-member orchestra. Rachel Swarner is associate conductor; president of the Symphonic Association is Ralph Canfield. Policy of the orchestra is to present resident soloists and to include contemporary American compositions on each program.

Port Angeles, on the Olympic Peninsula, has a "Little Symphony" under A. Lee Freeman which gives one concert a year, usually importing a handful of professionals from Seattle. An annual performance of *The Messiah* is also given there. Bellingham, near the Canadian border, has a Civic Orchestra conducted by Frank d'Andrea, head of the Music Department of the city's Western Washington College of Education. There is also a Bellingham Concert Band, led by Harry Pond of the public school system. Olympia, at the other extreme of Puget Sound, has its own Symphony, now in its second year, conducted by Leslie Armstrong, the public school music supervisor.

The Youth Symphony Orchestra of the Pacific Northwest (not to be confused with the Pacific Northwest Symphony Orchestra), was founded in 1942 by its present musical director, Francis Aranyi. This full-sized orchestra is maintained and managed by a board representing the parents of its members, and it plays mature, classical programs several times each year both for the general public and before student assemblies in the public schools. The organization also operates a summer music camp, Camp Waskowitz, under Aranyi's direction.

Two instrumental ensembles engage many of Seattle's professional musicians during the summer. The larger of these, directed by Jules Radinsky with Don Bushell as associate conductor, is the 70-member orchestra presented free to the public by the Seattle Park Department in Sunday afternoon concerts in Volunteer Park. About half of this orchestra consists of regular Symphony players, and its programs are divided between popular tunes of the day, conducted by Radinsky, and lighter concert works, conducted by Bushell. The smaller orchestra of approximately 45 members, gives week-day evening concerts in various parks paid for by funds derived from recording royalties received by Local 76 from the American Federation of Musicians. Conductorship rotates among its members.

It has been the custom in Seattle since the advent of Carl Bricken in 1944, to broadcast (locally) one of each pair of Symphony concerts. During the 1946-47 seasons, the Seattle symphony was twice among those heard on the regular Sunday evening sponsored symphonic program of the NBC Pacific Coast network. Beyond such sporadic appearances, however, there is little work for musicians in radio stations of the Puget Sound area.

The Division of Adult Education and Extension Services of the State University sponsors conferences, lectures, plays and concerts. In collaboration with the School of Music, it

(Continued on page 284)

Portland and Vicinity

Revival of the Portland Symphony Orchestra after nine years of inactivity is infusing new vitality into the musical life of the city. Sponsored by the Symphony Society of Portland, the orchestra announced the most comprehensive concert series it has ever undertaken for its 1947 gala silver anniversary season.

Planned are 10 Monday evening concerts beginning in November and ending in March, some with internationally known soloists, and 10 Sunday "twilight" concerts, also a series of morning children's concerts in cooperation with the Portland Junior Symphony Orchestra.

John A. Laing, who was president of the symphony society when it suspended activities and has been active in getting the orchestra started again on a sound financial basis, has been re-elected president for the present fiscal year. Werner Janssen is the conductor and James S. Hart, manager.

The Portland Junior Symphony Orchestra, a non-professional ensemble of about 100 young musicians from 10 to 20 years of age, opened its 24th consecutive season in November. It gives three evening concerts each year and shortened morning programs for young people; this year it is collaborating with the senior orchestra in the children's series. It presents one young pianist, chosen in a contest, as soloist and also one violinist, violist or 'cellist as soloist each season. Jacques Gershkovitch has been conductor since the orchestra's founding. Moe M. Tonkon is president of the Portland Junior Symphony Orchestra Association, and Helen Erskine is executive secretary.

Organized in 1946, the Portland Opera Assn. has as its object the promotion of grand opera performances in Portland. It is a non-profit organization. This season the association sponsored a short season of opera by the San Francisco Opera Company in September. Kurt H. Koehler is president and E. B. MacNaughton is vice president and treasurer.

The 10th annual chamber music series by famous ensembles and artists opened in October with a concert by the Paganini String Quartet. This series is guaranteed by Friends of Chamber Music, R. F. Arragon, chairman, and by Reed College. Booked also on the series are the Albeneri Trio and the Pascal Quartet. The Budapest String Quartet usually gives a short series in June under the same auspices.

The Portland Chamber Orchestra, a string ensemble of about 50 professional and semi-professional musicians, was organized in 1946 and gave one concert last season. It plans two, possibly three concerts for 1947-1948. Boris Sirpo is conductor. The orchestra is sponsored by its own association of which D. C. Burkes is president.

Another small symphonic group, non-professional, is the Portland Hobby Orchestra, Bert Harris, conductor.

Among the city's choral ensembles, the Apollo club of Portland is the oldest and best established. This chorus of about 50 men's voices is now in its 57th consecutive season. It is non-professional, but with professional standards. In addition to civic singing activities, the chorus gives two formal concerts each season and for several years now has presented outstanding young American singers as soloists. Albert E. Jones is director and Conn B. Williams is president.

The Portland Symphonic Choir is a large mixed chorus directed by Karl Ernst. C. Herald Campbell is president. The choir plans major radio broadcasts this season and a special Christmas music event. It is scheduled to appear twice during the season with the Portland Symphony Orchestra.

A new men's chorus, the Portland Men's Glee Club, was organized this year by John Stark Evans, former director of the famous Eugene Gleemen. Portland boasts also excellent Norwegian, Swedish and Swiss singing groups. Two fine women's choruses are the Monday Musical Club chorus, William Bradley, director, and the Crescendo Club, Juanita Kilbourn Clauss, director. Both are non-professional.

Two concert series by internationally famous artists are scheduled for presentation by Ellison-White bureau, Frank E. Andrews, president, also special concerts and a short season by the San Carlo Opera company. The Record Shop, Phil Hart, manager, will bring the Ballet Russe de Monte Carlo and the Philadelphia Orchestra.

The American Guild of Organists has a strong Oregon chapter with headquarters in Portland. Paul Bentley is Dean. Last season the local organists raised funds through an organ concert to purchase chimes for the great organ at the Portland Municipal Auditorium (a little musical matter neglected for the past 30 years by the City Fathers) and presented a set of chimes to the City of Portland.

During the war the Portland Art museum started a series of informal Sunday afternoon concerts by local musicians and artists from nearby universities which proved so popular the concerts are being continued. The museum is sponsoring also a second series of Wednesday night concerts. Henri Arcand, Portland pianist, is in charge.

Organized in the autumn of 1947 is the Portland Ballet Guild, which plans to promote programs by local dancers.

In addition to its annual competitive music festival in the Spring, the Oregon Music Teachers Assn. presents nationally known artists in concert at its annual convention in June.

National Music Week in Portland is sponsored by the Oregon Federation of Music Clubs. The main event is a Collegiate Choral Festival with choruses from seven Oregon universities and colleges taking part. The University of Portland is co-sponsor and the Rev. George L. Dum of the University faculty is chairman.

—Susie Aubrey Smith

Salem

Choral presentations during National Music Week and annual performance of the *Messiah* at Christmas time comprise the schedule of the Salem Oratorio Society.

The Crescendo Club, organized at Salem High School in 1929 by a student group, has given opportunity to numerous young artists, and for the past ten years has sponsored a concert series bringing artists of renown to the community. Well-known artists also are brought under the auspices of the local Community Concert Assn., at present headed by Silas Gaiser.

Musical activities of Willamette University also aid the city and the surrounding communities in maintaining a musical consciousness exceptional for the population.

—Melvin H. Geist

Tacoma

The Tacoma Philharmonic, which presents four concerts each spring with well known guest artists, is now united with the Pacific Northwest Symphony Orchestra, formerly the Seattle Symphony. Founded in 1933, its president is Mrs. Everett Griggs, and its conductor Eugene Linden.

The Orpheus Club, founded 1904, presents concerts at Christmas and in the Spring. Arthur O. Hansen is president and Clyde H. Keutzer, conductor.

Ladies Musical Club holds afternoon concerts in which young artists from the community and surrounding area

(Continued on page 284)

Arizona

Though Arizona is still in its musical infancy, its culture each year is becoming richer, with higher ideals and standards of performance apparent in the programs presented by musical organizations in the various communities.

Phoenix, the capital of the State, has an extensive musical life. It has just organized a Symphony Orchestra under the direction of the young American conductor, John Barnett, who also serves as associate conductor with the Los Angeles Philharmonic Orchestra.

The Musicians Club programs are held twice monthly from October through May, featuring soloists in voice, piano, violin, 'cello, flute, and other instruments, as well as dancing and readings. Besides the Musicians Club Little Symphony, ensemble groups give concerts each season. Among special programs during the year are one for winter visitors, held in the lounge of Hotel Westward Ho; an organ program in one of the churches, and a program of Arizona composers. The Dorian, B Natural, St. Cecilia, and Young Musicians clubs are affiliated and afford opportunities for musical expression and growth to musicians of all ages. The Musicians Club sponsors the Lyric Singers, a women's choral club, and has a study group available to all its members.

The Piano Teachers Assn. each season sponsors an outstanding Arizona musician in concert and presents one of its own members in recital monthly. It contributes toward musical scholarships at the various colleges of the State and has, in the Phoenix Public Library, a room containing books on music and musicians, piano compositions, recordings, and music magazines available to the public.

The Oratorio Society of the Phoenix Union High School is one of the leading choral organizations of the State and has many times sung on nation-wide broadcasts such works as the *Requiem* of Mozart and the *St. Matthew's Passion* of Bach. Other musical organizations include the Community, Linde, and Town Hall artist series. The Lion's Club presents an outdoor summer series in the Encanto Shell in Encanto Park, and here Sunday evening concerts are given by the Phoenix Band. The Orpheus Club, a choral group consisting of business and professional men, presents annual concerts.

As a winter resort and the home of the State University, Tucson is probably the most highly developed musical center in Arizona. Though presented primarily for students, the faculty recitals and artist and lecture series of the University of Arizona are available to, and well supported by, the people of Tucson. The Symphonic Choir of the University, in addition to annually presenting the *Messiah* during the Christmas season, in which Pacific Coast soloists participate, has in past seasons presented the *Requiems* of Faure and Brahms, plus other large choral works. The University Concert Band, abandoned during the war, is resuming its place as one of the most popular musical organizations.

The Tucson Symphony Orchestra several years ago came under the directorship of the University. It continues to grow in personnel and to improve in quality but presents only faculty members as soloists.

The Tucson Boys' Choir has appeared many times on national radio hook-ups, and each season makes an extended concert tour which has included Pacific Coast cities. The Junior Choral Society, one of the many organizations sponsored by the Saturday Morning Musical Club, has in its short history taken its place as one of the leading youth choirs in this part of the country, thanks to the presence of one of America's outstanding young choral directors at its head.

The Saturday Morning Musical Club, the oldest musical organization in Tucson, has given many years of service to the community, and has grown until today it is a highly developed institution. Junior branches of the club include the Rhythm, B Sharp, Harmony, and La Campanella clubs, together with a children's orchestra and the La Campanella Trio. The adult groups include the Temple Singers, Civic Oratorio Society, and Lyric String Ensemble. With these many groups forming the nucleus of the institution, the Saturday Morning Musical Club also sponsors a regular artist series each season as well as numerous civic concerts.

The Society of Arizona Composers presents concerts consisting entirely of music by resident composers and offers annual awards for outstanding compositions written during the current year to encourage further production. These prize-winning works are presented at special programs in Tucson and Phoenix.

In the northern section of the State musical life is centered around the Arizona State College at Flagstaff. The a cappella choir of this school is well known through its annual appearance in the Easter sunrise services from the rim of the Grand Canyon. Sponsored by the college is an annual music festival, the highlight of the season for all young musicians in northern Arizona.

The Globe Community Chorus, comprising people from all walks of life, presents several concerts each season, on one of which is presented an oratorio—the major study of the year. This city also has a Woman's Music Club organized on a district basis and including membership from the nearby towns of Miami and Inspiration. Many localities such as Safford, Ajo, and Douglas have active Music Clubs, encouraging high standards in musical development and performance through the presentation in recital of local and State-wide talent.

A few miles east of Phoenix is the Arizona State College at Tempe. Its small but proficient music department, in addition to offering musical activities usually found in colleges, holds each summer a music camp for qualified students. Designed especially for high school students of serious intent, the camp, through its course of study, does much to raise musical standards of young Arizona musicians.

—Harry Rickel

Idaho

Though Idaho is somewhat away from the beaten path of music, it must not be forgotten that the concept of Music Week was instituted in the capital city of Boise, where it still remains an outstanding annual feature.

Twin Falls supports an artist series, sponsored by the Junior Chamber of Commerce, which also sponsors a community choir. The Soroptomist Club sponsors concerts of resident and touring artists.

Semi-professional orchestras are maintained in Moscow and Pocatello under the auspices of the two divisions of the University of Idaho.

—Teala Bellini

Stockton

performers. It is fostered by Frank Thornton Smith and Harold Heisinger of Stockton High School. Orchestras, bands and choral groups of high caliber are featured. Also, at this time of year, elementary age youngsters are busy rehearsing for the all-city public schools orchestra. Only the best instrumentalists are chosen and many participate in the elementary solo contest.

An innovation of two years ago for summer musical activity is the Pacific Music Camp. Fashioned after the famous Interlochen, Michigan, school, it features the best of conductors and students from all over the nation. It is held on the campus of the College of the Pacific which also houses the students during the session.

Starting this year, with the intention of becoming an annual affair, is the Community Christmas Pageant. Conceived and directed by Gene Rotsch, music director, it is truly a community pageant of the yuletide season. All the service clubs, labor unions, private merchants, schools, city government, and individuals with special talents contribute their time, money and efforts to make a success of the pageant. Featuring the Community Band, a ballet on the holiday theme, special dances and the Monday Nighters, a choral group directed by F. T. Smith, this may well become a musical event of statewide interest.

—V. E. Gene Rotsch

Academic Activities

GEORGE PEPPERDINE COLLEGE

George Pepperdine College offers a major in music, including courses in applied music, and work in theory, music history and music education.

For individual students, arrangements with properly recommended artist teachers, make possible artist-teaching of all orchestral and solo instruments and singing. In the music organizations stress is laid upon preparing music for public performance. "Special achievement award" students, "music major" students, and other advanced music students including those who have studied conducting, assist the music faculty in directing the music organizations.

Musical groups providing professional training for the students are: the College Chorus, Men's Chorus, Women's Chorus, men's quartets, instrumental ensembles, band, and orchestra. Membership in these groups is on a competitive basis and in some of the more advanced organizations is considered honorary and highly valuable as experience for all participants. The Euterpean Society, a student organization sponsored by the Department of Music, correlates the activities of the music organization with those of other student organizations on the campus.

The Department of Music also offers classes in training for the opera. The aspirant receives a thorough and practical training in acting, in foreign languages, and participates in the preparation and public performance of operas given under the direction of experienced conductors in a modern and fully equipped theatre.

The department includes considerable emphasis in training for church musicians and in musical training for ministers. Important courses in the history and analysis of religious developments in music, performance of musical works of religious significance, and participation in the planning and execution of daily volunteer religious assemblies are offered and supported by the department.

SO. CALIFORNIA SCHOOL OF MUSIC

Southern California School of Music and Arts, founded in 1945 by Lily D. and Hal D. Crain and Walter H. Chase, is devoted to serious purposes in music from beginning to fully developed artistry, and offers graded courses, diplomas, certificates and degrees through affiliation with Fremont University. Its teaching staff includes Ernst Krenek, composer; Simon R. Stein, pianist; Erik Zeisl, composer and conductor; Charles Follett, Ruth Widenham, pianists; and others. It is approved under the G. I. Bill of Rights.

IMMACULATE HEART COLLEGE

Immaculate Heart College offers courses in music taken in conjunction with the academic work offered by the College leading to the degrees of Bachelor of Arts, Bachelor of Music, Bachelor of Music Education, and a special secondary credential in music. Also diploma courses in applied music and selective courses for students who desire only the theoretic or applied work.

An Institute of Sacred Music has been founded under the direction of Rev. Robert E. Brennan, director of music of the Archdiocese of Los Angeles. Its curriculum provides for the thorough training of organists, choirmasters and teachers, and offers a major in ecclesiastical music to students working for degrees and credentials.

MOUNT ST. MARY'S COLLEGE

Mount Saint Mary's College, founded in 1925, is conducted by the Sisters of St. Joseph of Carondelet with Mother Marie de Lourdes as president and Sister Rose de Lima as dean. Courses in music include participation in string ensemble, orchestra, choral group, and choir, affording opportunity for public appearances. Art courses include water color techniques, painting in oil or pastel. landscape, figure or portrait drawing, study of interiors, theory of design, and applied design in ceramics and leather.

The college is empowered to confer honors, degrees, and diplomas in the arts and sciences. It is a member of the National Catholic Education Assn., the Assn. of American Colleges, the American Council on Education, the Northwest Assn. of Secondary and Higher Schools, the Western College Assn., and is affiliated with the Catholic University of America. Its students are admitted on transcript of credit to the University of California and other universities and colleges in the State and elsewhere. The college is approved by the California State Department of Education for training and recommending candidates for the General Elementary Credential, the General Secondary Credential, and the General Secondary Credential with music major.

AMERICAN OPERATIC LABORATORY

The American Operatic Laboratory was founded in 1945 by Hugh H. Edwards, who now functions as General Director. Approved under the G. I. Bill of Rights, it has offered a series of operatic presentations in English, and plans to give regular performances with graduate students and guest artists, as well as numerous student opera presentations. Faculty includes Val Rosing, artistic director; Robert O. Brink, technical director; Curtis Stearns, musical director. Its primary purpose is teaching light and grand opera in a practical manner. The organization presented forty public performances during its first season.

SAN FRANCISCO CONSERVATORY

The San Francisco Conservatory of Music, now entering its thirty-first year, was founded by Ada Clement and Lillian Hodghead. Accredited under the G. I. Bill of Rights, the Conservatory closely cooperates with the University of California Music Department and receives credit through the University of California Extension Division. It has all departments of instrumental and vocal music, and students may enter the preparatory department, register for diploma courses (after fulfilling requirements) or enter as special students at any time. From 1925 to 1930, Ernest Bloch was artistic director of the Conservatory and still remains an honorary director.

SAMOILOFF BEL CANTO STUDIOS

The Samoiloff Bel Canto Studios and Opera Academy was founded in 1907 in New York City by Lazar S. Samoiloff, and opened in Los Angeles, California, in 1929. Since Dr. Samoiloff's death in 1945, it has been continued under the direction of his daughter, Zepha Samoiloff Bogert, at 3150 West 6th St. Some of its outstanding students include Isa Kremer, Rosa Raisa, Jules Bledsoe, George Houston, Claire Dux, Bianca Saroya, Dimitri Onofrei, Juila Claussen, Nelson Eddy, Robert Brink, Margaret Phelan, Gudmundur Ronolfsson. Its faculty includes Rose Ough, Lucia O'Brien Liverette, voice; Ernest Gebert and Florence Hart, coaching; Norma Stuart, acting.

Personalities

of

Music & Dance

SAUNDERS, RICHARD DRAKE

Musicologist, critic, composer, conductor, pianist. b. Chicago, Ill. St. piano w. mother, Irene Daura Saunders, D. Murray, Chicago; A. Polk, Valparaiso; piano, theory w. Henry Edmond Earle, Pasadena, Alexis Kall, Los Angeles. Mus. M. Zoellner Cons. Concertized, cond. in U.S. Western representative, Hollywood correspondent Musical Courier since 1935; music editor Hollywood Citizen-News (daily) 1930-44; Valley Times (daily) 1945-46. Program annotator Janssen Sym. Orch., Santa Monica Sym. Orch. Prof. mus. Woodbury Coll. 1935-38, Dean, Zoellner Cons. 1938-39. Founder, prop. Saunders Publications, 1928-42, RDS Publications since 1942. Editor *Things Worth Knowing in Music and Art,* 1927. Consultant editor *Music and Dance in California,* 1940; editor-in-chief *Music and Dance in California and the West,* 1948. President Drake-William, Inc.; editor-in-chief, Bureau of Musical Research, Inc. Inventor *Danscore* method of dance notation. Prop. Danscore Co. Comp. incl. several orch. works, *Mass in E* (mss.), *Desir* (pf) (Schirmer), *Songs of the Months* (cycle) (RDS Pub.), numerous songs, piano pieces. Member Phi Beta (hon.). Hobbies: sports; coll. railroad working timetables. Wife, Ann Wardell, pianist, author. 5617 Hollywood Blvd., Hollywood 28, Calif.

PERLMAN, WILLIAM J.

Director, Bureau of Musical Research, Inc.; author, playwright, producer. Author of *My Country* (produced N.Y.C., 1926), *When Ignorance is Bliss* (prod. N.Y.C., 1927), *The Broken Chain* (1929), *The King's Pleasure* (L. A., 1937), *If it Please the Court* (L. A., 1937); co-author, *The Bottom of the Cup* (N.Y.C., 1928), *The House of Remsen* (N.Y.C., Editor, *Movies on Trial* (MacMillan, 1937). Collaborator, *Einstein* (Doubleday-Doran, 1944). Part owner and manager, Mayfair Theatre, N.Y.C. (1924-1928). Co-producer Sean O'Casey's *Juno and the Paycock* (1926). Publisher *Who's Who in Music and Dance in Sou. Calif.* 1933; *Music and Dance in Calif.* 1940; *Music and Dance in Calif. and the West* 1948. Secretary-Treasurer Drake-William, Inc. 5617 Hollywood Blvd., Hollywood, 28, Calif.

ADLAM, BASIL G.

Music director, western div., American Broadcasting Co. b. Chelmsford, England. Arr. U. S., 1923; citizen, 1930. St. comp., theory w. Herman Genss, San Francisco. Played sax. w. Phil Harris, Ozzie Nelson bands. Arr., cond. w. Horace Heidt's orch. (4 yrs.); arr. MGM (1 yr.). Cond. ABC's *Mr. President, Music by Adlam, Opie Oates Show*. Comp. incl. *The House Is Haunted, Poor Robinson Crusoe, Pin Marin*, others. Member ASCAP. American Broadcasting Co., Inc., 6285 Sunset Blvd., Hollywood 28, Calif.

AGNINI, ARMANDO

Stage director. b. Naples, Italy, July 11, 1890. St. Royal Cons. of Naples: 'cello w. Giara, theory w. Sarasate; technical school in Paris; expert in piano construction w. Jacob & Doll Piano Co. Stage director for leading opera companies throughout world, incl. Metropolitan Opera, New York; San Francisco Opera Co. (25 yrs.); Montreal Opera; Boston Opera; Hollywood Bowl; Covent Garden; Paris Opera; Opera Comique; Buenos Aires, St. Louis, Ravinia Park, New Orleans, Trenton, Newark Festival, Pittsburgh, Mexico, Italy, etc. Designed special modern stage of San Francisco Memorial Opera House. Teaches acting, stage design in San Francisco, New York, St. Louis. Hobby: painting. San Francisco Memorial Opera House, San Francisco, Calif.

AGUILAR, JUAN

Pianist, teacher, composer, arranger. b. Zacatecas, Mexico. Grad. Coll. of Our Lady of Guadalupe. Comp. incl. *Arcades de Roma Reverie, Two Masses* (a cappella), *Valse Brillante*. Concertized Mexico, U. S. 3854 East Blvd., Culver City, Calif.

ALBANESE, NINO MARIO

Concert pianist, composer, teacher. b. Castiglione-Salentino, Italy, 1911. Att. Davis Music Coll., 1923. St. piano w. Frank Nagel, Marguerite D'Aleria, Richard Buhlig, Los Angeles. Awarded Music Scholarship, Royal Conservatory, Naples and Palermo, Italy; grad. 1931; st. w. Italian masters Finizio, Respighi, Longo. Concertized Naples, Palermo, Rome, Paris, elsewhere in Europe; returned to U.S. 1931. Soloist w. L.A. Philharmonic, Glendale Civic, CBS orch. Comp. include *Two Masks, Mechanical Man, Romanza, Fandanguillo, Cante Hondo, Viva Tu Madre, Tango, Flamenco, Iberian Themes Suite, Sonata* (pf & vn) *Ballad*, two pfs.; songs: *Bocca Dolorosa, Withered Flower, Perche*. Asst. cond. Chamber Opera Co. seven nat'l. concert tours w. Columbia Concerts Corp. and w. S. Hurok since 1937. Two years U.S. Army Inf. and special service as soloist Army hospitals, broadcasts. Wife, Nina (Pinto) pianist, teacher; son, Claude Pierluigi, (age 11) pianist, 10231 Silverton Ave., Tujunga, Calif.

ALBERTI, HELEN NOLDI

Teacher of voice. Widow of Achille Alberti, teacher of L. A. St. voice w. Alexander Busi, Bologna, Italy; Matilda Marchesi, Mme. Laborde; French diction w. Yersin Sisters, Paris. Operatic debut w. Sophie Scalchi. Sang leading roles, Metropolitan Opera, 1908-09. Soloist London Symphony Orch. at Royal Albert Hall w. Sir Landon Ronald and w. Carl Rosa Co., England, 1910, in Queen's Hall w. Sir Henry Wood. Made eight tours of U. S. in English opera. 197 S. Los Robles Ave., Pasadena, California.

ALDRICH, ADELINE G.

Dancer, teacher of dance. b. Gallup, New Mexico. Grad. Belcher Studio, L. A., st. piano w. Sherwood Music School, Chicago; voice w. Louise Heinecke; grad. Normal course of dancing. Many concert, solo appearances in U. S. Choreographer of numerous ballets, esp. for children. Member Whittier Chamber of Commerce. Hobbies: art work, drawing, painting, singing. Organizer of many special civic programs for Whittier and nearby cities. 217 No. Greenleaf Ave., Whittier, Calif.

ALLAN, KEITH CHRISTIE

Singer-actor, librettist, stage director. b. Berkeley, Calif., Oct. 7, 1911. Att. Stanford Univ. Spec. in comic opera, basso-buffo roles, esp. Gilbert and Sullivan, incl. Dr. Daly (*Sorcerer*), Sergeant (*Pirates*), Sir Despard (*Ruddigore*), Dick Dead-Eye (*Pinafore*), Don Alhambra (*Gondoliers*), Pvt. Willis (*Iolanthe*), Pooh-Bah (*Mikado*), Grosvenor (*Patience*), Judge (*Trial By Jury*); also Bartolo (*Barber*), Dulcamara (*L'Elisir*), Osmin (*Seraglio*), Geronimo (*Secret Marriage*), Bruschino (*Bruschino*), Jupiter (*Orpheus in Hades*), Kezal (*Bartered Bride*). Radio producer, anonuncer; w. OWI during war, Pacific, Far East, Southeast Asia. Now prod. supervisor, ldg. basso buffo San Francisco Comedy Opera Guild. Hobbies: sculpture, mask making, verse, short stories. Mgmt. Larry Allen, Inc., San Francisco, Calif. Res. 2954 Avalon Ave., Berkeley 5, Calif.

ALLER, ELEANOR (Mrs. Felix Slatkin)

Solo 'cellist. b. New York City, 1917. St. 'cello w. father, Gregory Aller, Felix Salmond; scholarship at Juilliard School of Music; grad. 1935. Premiered Frederick Jacoby's *'Cello Concerto* under Albert Stoessel; toured w. Jacoby East and West coasts. Soloist w. El Paso Symphony, Hartford Symphony, N. Y. and L. A. WPA Orchestras, Standard Hour (Svedrofsky) (Korngold *Concerto*, written especially for her by comp.), motion picture *Deception*. Member Chamber Group of Hollywood Theater Alliance, Hollywood String Quartet, Juilliard Alumni Assn. 125 South Swall Dr., Beverly Hills, Calif.

ALLER, VICTOR

Pianist. b. N.Y.C., 1905. Att. Juilliard Sch., N.Y. St. piano w. Josef Lhevinne. Soloist N. Y. Orch., El Paso Sym. Concertized throughout U. S., Canada. 502 N. Plymouth Blvd., Los Angeles, Calif.

ALLINGHAM, CAROLYN

Teacher of voice. St. voice w. Vittorino Moratti, Berlin, Germany; May Scheyder Stone and Ethel Parke Brownrigg of Metropolitan Opera, N. Y.; theory, sight reading w. Max Botki, Stern Cons., Berlin; also Boston (Mass.) Cons. Fellowship award, Curtis Inst. Philadelphia where st. w. Mme. Sembrich (1928); coached w. Conraad B Bos, Berlin, and Willem van Giesen, Berlin, Paris, Italy. Concert, church work in New York, Berlin, Paris. 139 So. Los Robles Ave., Pasadena, Calif.

ALVARY, LORENZO

Opera and concert singer; leading basso, Metropolitan Opera Co. b. Hungary, Feb. 20, 1909. Grad. in law. St. voice in Europe. Sang leading roles w. principal opera companies of Europe, North and South America, under Toscanini, Bruno Walter, Steinberg, Szell, Merola, etc. Repertory incl. all standard basso roles, many in several languages. Concertized extensively throughout world. Recordings w. RCA-Victor. Mgmt. Columbia Concerts, Arthur Judson, Steinway Hall, 113 W. 57th St., New York, N.Y .

AMFITHEATROF, DANIELE

Conductor, composer, pianist. b. St. Petersburg, Russia, 1901. Att. Cons. at St. Cecilia and Pontifical High School at Vatican. St. cond. w. Bernardino Molinari. Assoc. cond. Minneapolis Symph.; guest cond. Boston Symph. Comp. incl. *Poema del Mare, Miracolo delle Rose, Preludio ad una Messa da Requiem, American Panorama, Concerto for piano and orchestra*. 1465 Monaco Dr., Pac. Palisades, Calif.

ANDERSON, LENNARD

Concert pianist, teacher of piano. b. Tacoma, Wash., 1916. Began study of piano, age 6. Advance study w. Paul Pierre McNeely, Seattle. B.A. Pacific Lutheran Coll.; M.A. New York Univ. Staff pianist KUI (5 yrs.). Played two Coast Network programs. Official pianist Tacoma Philharmonic. Assoc. w. Tacoma Public Schools. Appeared w. Puget Sound Philharmonic; solo recitals in Seattle, Tacoma, Yakima, Aberdeen, Bellingham, Everett, Shelton. Comp. several small piano pieces. 503-4 Bernice Bldg., Tacoma 2, Wash.

Armando Agnini

Nino Mario Albanese

Basil J. Adlam

Helen Noldi Alberti

Adeline G. Aldrich

Keith Christie Allan

Eleanor Aller

Carolyn Allingham

Lorenzo Alvary

Lennard Anderson

165

ANDERSON, ROBERT ERIC

Pianist, teacher, music-educator, practitioner of music therapy. b. Aspen, Colo., Nov. 27, 1908. St. w. Nellie Lawrence Witter, Aspen; Mrs. P. O. Perkens, Salt Lake City; Mrs. Z. B. Brown, Hugo Mansfeldt, Pierre Douillet; master classes, pvt. work w. Jonas, Godowsky, Stojowski, E. Robert Schmitz. Normal training, San Francisco State Tchrs. Coll. Affil. w. Nat'l Academy of Music, N. Y. Dir. Robert E. Anderson Piano School, San Francisco; member of faculty, Sherman Clay School of Music. Comp. *Woodland Sprites, Introspection and Retrospection, Lullaby,* (left hand alone), *Pinwheel, Tau Nu, Valse Impromptu.* Inventor of topographical visual method scale patterns and keyboard harmony charts. Member S. F. MTA, Marin County MTA, Local No. 6. AFM. 340 Waller St., San Francisco 7, Calif.

ANTHEIL, GEORGE

Composer, conductor, pianist. b. Trenton, N. J., July 8, 1900. St. piano w. Constantin Sternberg, Philadelphia, theory w. Uselma Clark Smith; comp. w. Ernest Bloch, New York. Concertized extensively as pianist, U. S., Europe; soloist w. all leading symphonies. Asst. cond. Berlin State Th. Comp. incl. 6 *Symphonies,* 7 *Overtures,* short orch. pieces (*Decatur in Algiers, Over the Plains, The Golden Spike,* others); *Violin Concerto, Piano Concerto,* 2 *Violin Sonatas,* 3 *Piano Sonatas,* 4 *String Quartets, Quintet* (4 w. w., vla.) *Octet,* songs, piano pieces. Author: *Bad Boy of Music* (autobiography); contr. to many mags. etc. Scored films for Republic, Paramount, Columbia, Eagle-Lion, DeMille, Hecht, incl.: *Specter of the Rose, Plainsman and the Lady, Plainsman, That Brennan Girl, Repeat Performance, Buccaneer, Once In a Blue Moon, Angels On Broadway.* Member: ASCAP, Screen Comp. Assn. Hobby, research. Film agent, Wm. Morris, Beverly Hills. 2711 Laurel Canyon Blvd., Hollywood 46, Calif.

ARLOVA, LYDIA

Ballet dancer, prima ballerina. b. Chicago, Ill. St. w. Andreas Pavley, Serge Oukrainsky, Bronislava Nijinska, Alexander Kotchetovsky, Vincenzo Celli, Vera Trefilova. Prima Ballerina, Pavley-Oukrainsky Ballet. Danced in U. S., Canada, Mexico, South America, Europe. Headed own concert company w. partner, Lucien Prideaux. Leading danseuse, prima ballerina, Chicago Opera Co., San Carlo Opera Co., Cincinnati Summer Opera Co. Hobbies: cooking, making quilts, collecting cameos. Mgmt. Fortune Gallo, 1697 Broadway, New York City. Studio 62-A, 1425 Broadway, New York, N. Y.

ARMSBY, LEONORA WOOD

President and managing director, The Musical Assn. of San Francisco. War Memorial Opera House, San Francisco, Calif.

ARMSTRONG, FRANCIS J.

Concert violinist, teacher of violin. b. St. John, New Brunswick, Canada. Naturalized citizen, 1918. Grad. Royal Cons. of Music, Leipsig, Germany; att. Univ. of Leipsig. Dir. violin dept., Cornish School, 1917-1922. Founded Seattle Orchestral Soc. 1922. Many times soloist w. Seattle Symphony orch. and Yakima Philharmonic. Chairman violin committee, Washington State Board of Ed. Dir., violin dept., Seattle Coll. Dir. Art Museum, Chamber Music Concerts 1946-47, 1947-48. M.C. for Seattle Symphony broadcast concerts since 1944. Member advisory board, Music & Art Foundation, Washington State Press Club. Mgmt. Joan Mosberg, 522 No. 84th, Seattle, Wash.

ARNAUD, LEO N.

Composer, arranger. b. Couzon, Rhone, France. Att. Cons. Lyons, France. St. solfege w. Jean Vauchant; theory w. A. Savard, P. Vidal; 'cello w. H. Bedetti; cond. w. Staram. Perf. under Stravinsky, Ravel, Milhaud, Doyen, Paray, Vitowsky, others. Arr. Hollywood 1936; American citizen 1939. Scoring, arranging for leading film studios since 1936. 628 N. Canon Dr., Beverly Hills, Calif.

ARNO, VICTOR

Concert violinist; radio concertmaster, soloist. b. Savannah, Ga., 1907. Started violin age 6; st. w. Alexander Bloch, Leopold Auer (2 yrs.), Caesar Thomson, Brussels (1 yr.), Willy Hess, Berlin (2 yrs.). Diploma (w. grand distinction) from Le Jury Central de Musique de Bruxelles. Soloist w. Berlin Phil., Leipsig Phil., Dresden Phil., other European symphonies; recitals in major European cities and capitals of Belgium, Holland, Germany, Norway, Denmark, Rumania, England. U.S. concerts in Carnegie Hall, N.Y., etc.; Havana, Cuba (ausp. Pro Arte Musical Soc.). Assoc. mus. dir. Paramount Theatre, N.Y.; mus. dir. Buffalo Theatre, Buffalo. Cond., presented music programs w. himself as soloist. Concertmaster radio programs incl. *Texaco Star Theatre, Big Town, Birdseye, Westinghouse, Academy Award, Cresta Blanca, The Doctor Fights, Bell Telephone, Chase and Sanborn, General Motors Frigidaire, The Borden Show, Mobilgas,* many others. Recordings for RCA-Victor, Columbia, Decca, Capitol. 4517 Ledge Ave., North Hollywood, Calif.

ARVEY, VERNA (Mrs. William Grant Still)

Pianist; writer. b. Los Angeles, Calif., Feb. 16, 1910. St. piano w. Rose Cooper Vinez, Alexander Kosloff, Marguerite d'Aleria, Ann Eachus. Concertized in U. S., Latin America; soloist w. L. A. Philharmonic Orch. (Klemperer), CBS (Paige), others. Contributor to Musical Courier, Opera and Concert, Etude, Musical America, Musical Digest, Dance, Chesterian (London), N. Y. Times (music sec.), other magazines. Author monograph on life and work of William Grant Still; several libretti (Still music); Choreographic Music (E. P. Dutton). 3670 Cimarron St., Los Angeles 7, Calif.

ARVIDSON, DELIA

Pianist, accompanist, teacher of piano. b. Des Moines, Iowa. St. w. Frank Nagel (3 yrs.), Paul van Katwick (2 yrs.), Paul Stoye (5 yrs.). Grad. Highland Park Coll., Des Moines, Iowa. Post-grad. work Drake Univ. (2 yrs.). Concertized throughout Middle West and South. Soloist w. Des Moines Symphony Orch. at age 15. Member: Delia Quartette, Cornelius Van Vliet trio. Hobby: traveling. 1187 Longwood Ave., Los Angeles, Calif.

ASPER, FRANK W.

Organist. b. Logan, Utah, 1892. Att. Stern's Cons., Boston Univ., Univ. of Utah, New England Cons. Mus. D. (hon) Bates Coll. 1938. Concertized in U. S., Mexico. Organist w. Tabernacle Choir, Salt Lake City. Comp. incl. organ music. Member: Rotary, AGO, Kappa Gamma Psi, Pi Kappa Lambda, Nat'l Assn. for Am. Comp. and Cond., S.A.R. Mgmt. Willard Matthews, New York City. 61 Laurel St., Salt Lake City, Utah.

AVIRETT, ABBY de
(See: de AVIRETT)

AVIRETT, ELIZABETH de
(See: de AVIRETT)

BABITZ, SOL

Violinist, writer, teacher of violin. b. Brooklyn, N. Y., Oct. 11, 1911. St. violin w. Alexander Roman, Carl Flesch; att. Berlin Hochschule fuer Musik. Concertized in U. S., Europe; soloist Santa Barbara Bowl, Evenings on the Roof, Redlands Bowl, La Jolla Sym. First vn. w. L. A. Philharmonic, Hollywood Bowl orchs. 1933-37; concertmaster various radio orchs.; Mus. Guild Chamber Players (Klemperer), Ojai Fest. Orch. (Johnson). Lecturer Mills Coll. 1939, UCLA 1940, USC, L. A. City Coll., etc. on *Dance Writing, History of Violin, History of Jazz.* Editor vn. dept. International Musician since 1940. Pub. incl. *Dance Writing,* 1939; *Stravinsky Symphony in C,* 1940; *Mus. Quarterly,* 1941; *Schoenberg Violin Concerto,* Strad (London) 1942; program notes for Stravinsky works; *Circus Polka* (Stravinsky) (arr. vn. and pf.) (Assoc. Mus. Pub.). Comp. inc. *Rhythm in Time and Motion Study* (Adv. Mgmt.), *Principles of Extensions in Violin Fingering* (Delkas). Recordings incl. Ives' *Second Sonata, Mvt. 2* (Alco). Hobby, coll. jazz records. Member AFM, Local 47. 1970 Cheremoya Ave., Hollywood 28, Calif.

Victor Arno

BACHMANN, BARTON

Pianist, conductor, composer; teacher piano, theory, organ. b. Charlotte, Mich., Sept. 10, 1898. European, American tours as concert pianist; cond. Nelson Opera Co; first cond. and gen. music dir. Riverside Opera Assn. since inception; organist-choirmaster, Church of the Ascension; New Haven; All Saints Episcopal Church, Riverside. Prof. Piano and Theory, Southwestern College, Univ. of Redlands, Chicago Musical College, Riverside College. St. Dessauer-Troostwyk School, New Haven; piano, theory, conducting, Max Dessauer; organ, Walter Earle Hartley; Chi. Mus. College; piano, Alexander Raab; theory, Louis Victor Saar; comp., Felix Borowski; degrees, Mus.M., Mus.M., Chic. Mus. College; post-grad. Diamond Medal; foreign study, Vienna. Comp. *Suite in the Old Style.* (pf); *Six Tonal Portraits* (pf); smaller piano works, chorals, songs. Member: AGO, Sinfonia Frat. (Phi Mu Alpha); MTA. Hobby, pictorial photography. 4223 Twelfth St., Riverside, Calif.

BAFFA, EMIL

Conductor, pianist. b. Philadelphia, Pa. St. piano and theory w. Homer Simmons, Homer Grunn (L.A.). Piano concerts throughout West. Music Dir. Hollywood Playhouse. Cond. numerous operas and Columbia broadcasts; Del Mar Club (2 yrs.). Mus. Dir. Florentine Gardens (7 yrs.). Cond. recordings, series of short subjects for RCM Productions. Orchestrated many musical shows and operettas. Member Local 47, AFM. Hobby: golf. 2265 Panorama Dr., Hollywood, Calif.

BAILEY, MARIAN (RICK)

Pianist, organist, teacher. b. Colton, Calif., Nov. 25, 1913. Ed. Univ. of Redlands; st. organ w. Heaps, Poister, Spellman, piano w. Bachmann; comp. w. Leach; choral w. Olds. Mus. B. (organ) Univ. of Redlands, post-grad. (organ). Concert tours as pianist throughout West incl. Fed. of Music Clubs conventions, L.A. and Riverside. Comp. *Seven Last Words* (organ suite); song cycle (Japanese songs); choral works; piano trans. Tchaikovsky's *Waltz of Flowers*; numerous songs incl. *Rendezvous with Destiny.* Member: MTA, Nat'l Guild of Org.; Nat'l Choral Dir. Assn.; San Bernardino Valley Music Assn.; Phi Kappa Lambda; Calif. Fed. of Music Clubs; Redlands Music Assn. Hobbies: collecting music boxes, phonograph records. Minister of Music, First Pres. Church; organist, Knopsnyder Mortuary. 197 W. Olive Street, Colton, Calif.

BAKALEINIKOFF, CONSTANTIN

Conductor. b. Moscow, Russia, 1896. Entered Moscow Cons. of Music at age 9. Grad. from Cons. as cellist and composer, 1916. Organized, toured w. Chamber Music Group, The Moscow Trio, through Siberia and Orient, 1918. Came to L. A. 1920. Mus. cond. for Grauman theatres until 1928, Paramount Studios, Columbia Studio, 1935, MGM, 1935-41, RKO Radio Pictures since 1941. Cond. San Diego Symphony Orch., Ford Bowl, San Diego, San Francisco Symphony, All Russian program w. New York Philharmonic, Carnegie Hall, N. Y., Hollywood Bwl, 1943-47. Awarded Sheffeld Silver Bowl for playing to largest audience at Hollywood Bowl, 1944. Guest cond. two *Command Performances*; musical dir. RKO's *Hollywood Star-Time, A Date With Judy.* Guest cond. and speaker, Pacific Music Camp, Stockton, Calif., 1947. Hobbies: stamp collecting, golf, horseback riding, football. RKO Radio Pictures, Inc., 780 Gower St., Hollywood, Calif. Agent: Martin Music Management, Hollywood, Calif.

BAKER, ISRAEL

Violinist. b. Chicago, Feb. 11, 1920. Began st. of violin at 4; first pub. appearance at 6. Teachers incl., Adolph Pick, Louis Persinger, Jacques Gordon, Bronislaw Huberman. Winner of Nat'l. High School Violin Contest, Chicago Women's Music Club Contest, Young Artist Contest of Society of American Musicians, Chicagoland Music Festival Contest. All-American Orch. (Stokowski); chosen as soloist in Scheher-

azade, 1941. After tour joined NBC Symphony (Toscanini); soloist NBC Coast-to-Coast Artist Recital Period. After discharge from Army Air Forces, became concertmaster Indianapolis Symphony and Hollywood Bowl Symphony. Soloist w. Dayton Philharmonic, Illinois, Indianapolis, Terre Haute, Hollywood Bowl, Chicago Summer Symphonies. 1478½ W. Vernon, Los Angeles, Calif.

BAKER, MARJORIE DUNCAN

Piano teacher, diseuse. b. Springville, Calif., Oct. 20, 1897. St. w. Ruby Duncan Hicks, Abby DeAvirett, U.S.C. College of Music, Los Angeles; Cornish School, Seattle; Sherwood School, Chicago; Isidor Philipp, Olga Samaroff, Guy Maier. Toured West as pianist, also diseuse, singing American folk songs. Five years judge at Nat'l Piano Tournament. Colleague and Fellow Calif. MTA. Member: Dominant Club, Opera Guild of So. Calif., Sigma Alpha Iota, Pan-American League, Glendale Art Assn., Women's Committee Philharmonic Assn.; board member Glendale Philharmonic Assn.; life member Club San Moritz, Native Daughters. Hobbies: raising flowers, collecting authentic early American costumes. Pupils incl. Carol Mae Clint, June Presho. 1646 Highland Ave., Glendale 2, Calif.

BALL, AMORETTA

Teacher of voice; conductor; coach. Att. Minneapolis Sch. of Mus.; Univ. of Utah. St. voice w. Mme. Papova, Stella Paul Bradford, Lazar Samoiloff; piano, theory w. Gustavos Johnson; dramatic art w. Louise Meade Holt. Assoc. tchr. w. Samoiloff (3 yrs.). Toured U. S., Canada w. theat. cos. 11 yrs. Early radio artist. Org., dir. choral socs. Seattle, Oakland, San Diego. Staged, dir. mass choral groups, Calif. Pac. Intern. Expos. 1935-36. Founder-dir. Bel Canto Choral Club. Member MTA. Studio, 640 Broadway, San Diego, Calif. Res. 3762 Van Dyke Ave., San Diego, Calif.

BALL, SAMUEL

Concert pianist; teacher of piano. b. Sherman, Texas. Att. Austin Coll., Cincinnati Cons .of Music. St. piano w. Pettis Pipes, Hans Rischard, Leopold Godowsky. Concertized throughout U.S., especially in West and Southwest. Soloist w. major symphonies, incl. Chicago Sym. (von Fielitz), Detroit Sym. (Gabrilowitch), others. Radio series, CBS, etc. Dean of Mus. Guy Bates Sch. of Theatre Arts (1 yr.); L.A. studio since 1928. Students incl. Leonard Pennario, Roy Cooper, Edward Earle, Lillian Rose, Jo Anne Connor, Einar Markusson, Corryn Kiehl, Georgia Nicklett. 4013 W. 2nd St., Los Angeles 4, Calif.

BALLARD, ROBERT H.

Arranger. b. Nyack, N. Y., 1913. Music major Occidental Coll. St. harmony, comp., counterpoint w. Edmund Ross. Comp. of *Brazilian Bogie, I Knew What I Wanted.* Arr. Gus Arnheim Orch., 1934-37, Phil Harris, 1938-42, NBC, Hollywood staff, 1944-47, Freddy Martin Orch. Member ASMA. Hobby: horseback riding. 18821 Erwin St., Reseda, Calif.

BALOGH, STEPHAN

Pianist, teacher of piano, theory; dean of education, director music dept. Cornish School, Seattle, Wash. b. Budapest, Hungary, 1900. St. piano, comp. w. Dohnanyi, Bela Bartok, Kodaly, Arpad Szendy, Debussy. Assoc. w. Eugene d'Albert, Frederick Lamond. Performing artist and teachers' degrees Royal Hungarian Cons. of Music, Vienna Hochschule; post-grad., Columbia Univ., New York Univ. Europe, U.S.A. solo recitals. Radio perf. 32 Beethoven *Sonatas* in series. Two-piano recital appearances w. wife, Patricia Balogh. Comp. incl. piano pieces, three suites for orch., string quartets, several songs, canons and fugues. Analysis records for educational use; all radio appearances printed for schools. Hobbies: chess, tennis. Wife, Patricia, collaborator, partner two-piano team *The Baloghs.* Member Cornish School Faculty. Cornish School, 710 East Roy St., Seattle 2, Wash.

Robert Eric Anderson

Lydia Arlova

Leonora Wood Armsby

Francis J. Armstrong

Leo N. Arnaud

Constantin Bakaleinikoff

George Antheil

Delia Arvidson

Sol Babitz

Barton Bachmann

Emil Baffa

Marian Bailey

Marjorie Duncan Baker

Samuel Ball

Nicholas E. Barabe

Amoretta Ball

Robert H. Ballard

Stephan Balogh

Gennaro Barbieri

Helen M. Barnett

Gilbert Barrios

Vera Barstow

LeRoy Bartholomew

Mebane Beasley

BARABE, NICHOLAS E.

Voice teacher, lyric tenor. b. Dayton, Ohio, 1904. St. voice w. Verna C. Blythe, L. A. High School and pvt., 3 yrs.; Charles Hammer, 6 yrs. Sang ballads w. Harry Owens, 1927; tour w. West Coast circuit, Fanchon & Marco; tour around world as soloist on ship, 1930; soloist in prologue to *Carmen* at Carthay Circle, other theaters; leading role in operetta, *The Days of the Dons*, Phil. Aud. 1930. Concert recitals, L. A. and environs; soloist KFI, KNX and KHJ. Recordings of ballads w. Jack Taylor Orch. Wife, Averil Barabe, piano tchr.; st. Univ. of Calif. Berkeley. 4707 Beverly Blvd., Los Angeles, Calif.

BARBIERI, GENNARO

Vocal teacher, coach. b. Messina, Italy, 1893. St. piano at 8; concertized at 10, nicknamed *Little Mozart;* st. mus. school, Catania, Naples Cons. Machine gunner World War 1, wounded. Arr. U. S. 1927; priv. secy. and asst. art dir. to Gennaro Papi, Metr. Opera House; asst. dir. Phila. Academy; Cincinnati Zoo Opera, Nat'l Grand Opera Co., New York; artistic dir. Musical Retreat Club (Giovanni Martinelli, Pres.) Presented grand opera w. students incl., Selma Kaye (Chi. Opera Co.), Laura Triggiani, Stella Hughes. 1728 No. Orange Dr., Hollywood, Calif.

BARBOUR, LYELL

Pianist, teacher. b. Bloomington, Ill., 1896. St. piano w. Edgar Nelson, Josef Lhevinne, Tobias Matthay. Soloist w. Minneapolis, Chicago, Cleveland, L. A. Symphonies. Member Budapest Trio (Europe). 640 Broadway, San Diego, Calif.

BARENE, ROBERT

Violinist. b. Cincinnati, Ohio, 1912. Attended Cincinnati College of Music, Cincinnati Cons. of Music, Juilliard Graduate School. St. w. Emil Heerman, Eugene Ysaye, Robert Perutz, Leopold Auer, Paul Kochanski. Played under dir. of Fritz Reiner, Ralph Lyford, Rudolph Thomas, Leopold Stokowski, Walter Damrosch, Albert Stoessel, Vladimar Bakaleinikoff, Max Steiner, David Broeckman; on NBC, CBS, Chase & Sanborn, Texaco, Kellogg, etc. Soloist Cincinnati Symph., Beethoven Assn., Town Hall, N.Y.C., 1930. 336 N. Palm Dr., Beverly Hills, Calif.

BARNETT, ALICE (Mrs. George Roy Stevenson)

Composer. b. Lewiston, Ill. St. w. father, Orrin Barnett; Chi. Mus. Coll.; comp. w. Felix Borowski, Adolf Weidig; Middleschulte, Hugo Kaun, Berlin; piano w. Rudolph Ganz. Taught theory, hist. appre. San Diego H.S. Comp. incl. many songs pub. Schirmer, Ditson, C. Fischer, Boston Mus. Co. Mus. chairman San Diego Sym. (14 yrs.). Member: ASCAP, Allied Artists Council (charter). Hobbies: fishing, gardening 4310 Randolph St., San Diego, Calif.

BARNETT, JOHN

Conductor. b. New York City. Grad. Manhattan Sch. of Music, N. Y.; Mozarteum, Salzburg. St. w. Walter, Weingartner, Enesco. Won scholarship from N. Y. Phil.-Sym. Soc. Cond. Stamford (Conn.), Brooklyn, N.Y.C. Symphonies. Assoc. cond. L. A. Phil. Orch., Cond. Phoenix Sym. Orch. Philharmonic Aud., Los Angeles 13, Calif.

BARNETT, HELEN M.

Assoc. Prof. of Music, U. of C. Santa Barbara College; teacher of voice and music ed. b. Toronto, Canada. St. piano w. Mrs. Hubbard, Chicago; voice w. Thomas McBurney, Chicago; William Shakespeare, London; John Smallman, Los Angeles. A.B. Univ. of Calif. at Berkeley; M.A. at U.S.C. Grad. study at Columbia. Toured throughout U.S. in concerts. Soloist, choral dir. First Methodist Woodlawn Ch. Chicago; Vermont Square Methodist Ch.., Los Angeles; First Congregational Ch., Chicago; Church of Christ, Scientist, Santa Barbara (6 yrs.); Presbyterian, Methodist choirs, Orpheus Club, Santa Barbara. Comp. *The Brook* (publ. M.C.A.), *Hail Delta Kappa Gamma* (publ. by fraternity), *Two Parts Song* in collaboration w. Dorritt. Member: Pi Lambda Theta, Phi Kappa Phi, Delta Kappa Gamma, Pi Beta, Music and Speech, Assn. of Univ. Women, Strollers' Club, Players' Club. Hobbies: collecting bells, gardening. Univ. of Caif., Santa Barbara, Calif.

BARRIOS, GILBERT R.

Arranger, composer. b. Oakland, Calif., Sept. 25, 1928. St. piano w. Karl Troutman; comp., orch., theory w. Julius Toldi; trumpet w. E. M. Hiner. App. at Avadon, Meadowbrook, Palladium, etc. Arranger for three local orchs. Comp. incl. pieces for small orch. Hobbies: riding, shooting. 1733 W. 24th St., Los Angeles 7, Calif.

BARRYMORE, LIONEL

Composer, actor. b. April 28, 1878. St. theory w. Henry Hadley, New York; comp. w. Eugene Zador, Hollywood; pf. w. Agnes Morgan; also competent oboist. Orchestral works perf. by Hollywood Bowl (Stokowski), New York Philharmonic-Symphony (Rodzinski), Santa Monica Sym. (Rachmilovich), Los Angeles Phil. (Finston), Federal Sym. (Sample), others. Comp. (orch.) incl.: *Partita, Fugue Fantasia, Nos. 1, 2, Tableaux Russes, Valse Fantasia, In Memoriam*. Recordings incl. *Tableaux Russes*. Member ASCAP. Hobbies: art, etching. Under contract to MGM Studios, 10202 Washington Blvd., Culver City, Calif. Res. Chatsworth, Calif.

BARSTOW, VERA

Concert violinist, teacher. b. Celina, Ohio. Att. Pittsburgh Cons. of Music. St. violin w. Luigi von Kunits. Performed under dir. Stokowski, Muck, Oberhoffer, Rothwell, Goossens and many others. Concertized Europe and U. S. Living and teaching in Pasadena for past twenty years. Pupils incl. Eunice Wennermark, Alexander Murray, Roderick Krohn, Elizabeth Mills, 1939 Rose Villa St., Pasadena, Calif.

BARTHOLOMEW, LeROY

Voice teacher, coach, concert singer. b. Missouri, 1907. B.Mus. Wisc. Cons. of Mus. 1935; post-grad. work Chic. Music Coll. (3 yrs.); st. voice w. Verna Lean, Cameron McLian, Cincinnati Cons.; Roland Pease, Univ. of Ariz.; Graham Reed, New York; cond. w. Rudolph Ganz; theory w. Gustave Dunkleberger; comp. w. Louis Gruenberg. Leading tenor Milwaukee Municipal Opera Co., 1933-34; soloist tenor Milwaukee Municipal Opera Co., 1933-34; soloist First Baptist Ch., Oak Park; First Methodist Ch., Evanston; staff soloist WTMJ, Milwaukee; WGN, WMAO, Chicago, Faculty, Wisc. Cons. of Music 1936-37. Sang w. Chicago American Opera Co.; concertized throughout Middle West; sang *Messiah* for many churches, organizations. Pupils incl. William Strom, (first award, Chicago Festival Land Contest). Wife, Alma Land, concert pianist, st. w. Rudolph Ganz; Richard Buhlig, Olga Steeb, Ethel Leginska, Mme. Altman; soloist w. orch. Wilshire Ebell Theater, 1944; grad. Wisc. Cons. of Music, (organ, piano) Chicago Musical Coll. 3 yrs. 522 No. Brand Blvd., Glendale 3, Calif.

BASKERVILLE, GAIL HAROLDSON

Music educator. b. Brookings, S. D. B.S., S.D. State Coll.; M.A., Univ. of Wash. St. comp. w. W. A. Peterson, George McKay; cond. w. Carl Christensen; piano w. W. A. Peterson, Harry Krinke, Lucile Vogel Cole, Irving Humber; voice w. Harry L. Kohler, George Peckham; 'cello, wood-winds, Don Bushell. West Coast concert tours. Pianist, organist, soloist, accomp. for soloists, orchestras, choirs, choral groups. Dir. church choirs, orch., school operettas, vaudevilles, plays, orch., ensembles in Oregon and Seattle. Supervisor of Music Kent Public Schools; teacher in King County and Seattle Public Schools. Now teaching str. instr. classes, orch., a cappella choirs in public high school. 605 Paramount Theatre Bldg., Seattle, Wash.

BATTRAM, FLORENCE COLBY

Composer. Four yrs. p.g. Univ. of Calif. at Berkeley, Music Dept. Orchestrations of Joaquin Miller Day, Woodminster Amphitheater, Oakland, Sept. 1943, 1944. Comp. *Four Preludes on Themes from the Chinese, Two Songs for April* (Hartwich and Gordon), *Five Christmas Carols, Thirteenth Century Italian Laude, Two Christmas Carols, Thirteenth Century Italian Laude, Darest Thou Now, O Soul* (Walt Whitman), *Psalm C* (all mss.). 1176 Sunnyhills Rd., Oakland 10, Calif.

BAY, EMANUEL

Pianist. b. Crimea, Russia. Grad. Petrograd Cons. of Music w. first prize, and Leopold Godowsky's master school in Vienna. Concertized and appeared as soloist w. orchs. in Europe. Accomp. to Zimbalist, Elman, Milstein in U.S.A.; Heifetz since 1934. Recordings of Beethoven's Sonatas, Brahms, Grieg, Faure, Mozart w. Jascha Heifetz. Hobby: painting. Mgmt.: Columbia Concerts, Inc., Steinway Bldg., N.Y. Res. 5640 Franklin Ave., Los Angeles, Calif.

BEAL, EULA

Concert, radio singer, contralto. b. Riverside, Calif. St. voice w. H. Norman Spohr (5 yrs.), Arthur Alexander (2 yrs.), Homer Samuels (4 yrs.); coached w. Shibley Boyes (6 yrs.). Concert debut at 17 in Riverside; operatic debut as Mignon (Riverside, 1939). Soloist w. Pasadena Civic Orchestra (Lert) 1939; won contest Nat'l. Fed. Mus. Clubs, 1941, U.C.L.A. Young Artist Contest, Occidental College Young Artist Audition; soloist w. L.A. Philharmonic (Bruno Walter) 1942, (Wallenstein) 1946 and 1947; soloist with San Francisco Symphony 1947; soloist C.B.S. prog. *Melodies America Loves* (1942 to date); N.B.C. w. L.A. Philharmonic Orch. (KHJ) 1947; Mgmt, Nat'l Concert and Artists Corp, New York. 1780 No. Los Robles Ave., Pasadena, Calif.

BEASLEY, MEBANE

Concert and opera baritone; teacher of singing. b. Fayetteville, N. C., Aug. 9, 1890. Att. Wake Forest Coll., N. C. St. piano, violin, theory w. Jules Hugelet, Greenville, S. C. St. voice 4 yrs. w. George Sweet (pupil Lamperti, Garcia), 5 yrs. w. Guiseppe Campanari, 3 yrs. w. Louise von Fielitzsch (pupil Marchesi, DeLucca). Boy soprano, church, oratorio. Sang leading baritone roles in major opera houses of world, incl. Metropolitan Opera, Manhattan Opera, N. Y., also light opera, musical comedy, oratorio, 1907-1927. Concertized extensively in U. S. Two decades scholastic, professional career; two decades teaching. Vocal studios in New York (2 yrs.), Santa Barbara, Hollywood (20 yrs.). Founded Hollywood Grand Opera Co. 1935 to give opportunity to young singers; produced, conducted, directed, sang in over 275 performances grand, light operas, given 68,000 voice lessons to date. Students incl.: Felix Knight (7 yrs.) (Ld. ten. Metropolitan Opera), Barbara Patton (6 yrs.) (Brooklyn Opera), Anne Jeffreys (4 yrs.) (opera, mus. com., RKO Pict. star), Hugh Edwards (3 yrs.) (dir. Amer. Operatic Labr.), Robert Marks (6 yrs.), Harold Reed (3 yrs.) (Pacific Opera), Joyce Gray (5 yrs.) (Santa Monica Opera), Betty Grable, Virginia Bruce, Ruth Gillette, Richard Dennis. Member MacDowell Club, Phi Beta. Hobbies: fishing, hunting. 1930 N. Vine St. Hollywood 28, Calif.

BEAUCHAMP, LILLAH

Soprano, opera and concert. b. Augusta, Texas. St. voice, roles w. Gennaro Curci, Los Angeles. Concertized in U. S., esp. in West. Sang opera, chorals, oratorios under L. Walker, others. Roles incl. *Cavalleria Rusticana, I Pagliacci, Il Trovatore, Aida, Butterfly, Tosca, La Boheme, Otello, Faust.* Hobbies: gardening, fishing, hunting, swimming. Member board of dirs., Palo Verdes Coll.; Opera Guild. Rolling Hills, Calif.

BEAUDOIN, HESTON M. and FLORA E.

Dancers, teachers of dancing. Heston, b. Ogden, Utah. Flora, b. Alberta, Canada. Both st. w. Fanchon and Marco, Eduardo Cansino, Johnny Mattison, Olga Ziceva, San Francisco Ballet School, Johnny Plaza, Aggie Auld, Walton Biggerstaff. Danced throughout U.S. App. in many benefits, hospitals, local organizations, etc. Opened Palo Alto school in 1932. Members: Dancing Masters of America; Dancing Masters of Calif. 464 Colorado Ave., Palo Alto, Calif.

BECKER, OTIE CHEW

Violinist, teacher. b. London, England. Grad. Royal Coll. of Music, London. St. w. Emil Sauret, Joseph Joachim. Soloist Berlin Phil., N. Y. Phil., L. A., Phil. 431 S. Alvarado, L. A., Calif.

BEHAN, GLOANAH BALL

Teacher of piano, organ, voice, theory. St. Notre Dame de Lourdes Academy, Ft. Scott, Kans. Normal training St. Louis Inst. of Music w. Harriet Husted Stuart, L. M. Dodd, Louis Victor Saar, Ellis Griffis, Gottfried Galston; harmony w. Arthur Edward Johnstone, Univ. Extension Cons., Chicago; organ w. Chas. E. Galloway. Child specialist coll. degree, MTA of Calif. Grad. teacher. Pres. Kern County Branch, MTA. Member Pi Mu, AGO, Choral Conductors' Guild, Past Presidents Club. 1720 Sixteenth St., Bakersfield, Calif.

BELL, WAUNEVA

Mezzo soprano. b. Hartshorne, Okla. Voice production, repertory w. Feodor Gontzoff. B.S. Okla. A&M Coll. Soloist Beethoven's *Ninth Symphony* (Leopold Stokowski), Hollywood Bowl, 1945. Principal American-Savoy Gilbert & Sullivan Repertory Co. Sang Amneris in *Aida*, Marina in *Boris Godunov*, Hollywood Opera Reading Club, Delilah, Euterpe Opera Reading Club; overseas tour as soloist USO, 1946; soloist *Ice Follies of 1946.* Member Phi Kappa Phi. Hobbies: swimming, dancing, horseback riding. 1938 No. Vine St., Hollywood, Calif.

BELLINI, TEALA

Concert pianist, teacher of piano. b. Collinsville, Mass. Piano w. Julius Hartt (12 yrs.), Wyllys B. Watterman (Leschetizky exponent) (5 yrs.). Early study w. Dore Grafton Nye, Edward Noyes; harmony w. Ernest Bloch. New York debut Aeolian Hall, 1920. Concertized throughout U.S. Taught piano in Hollywood, Torrance, Twin Falls. On faculty of Julius Hartt Foundation, Hartford, Conn. from 1916-1921. Member Nat'l Business & Prof. Women; Soroptomist Club. Hobbies: collecting teapots, jugs, perfumes, doing fine handwork. 511 Second Avenue West, Twin Falls, Idaho.

BERCOVITZ, ABE

Violinist; musical director KGW. b. Philadelphia, Pa. 1904. St. violin w. father, Carl Denton, Walter Bacon, Louis Sobelman, Boris Sirpo. Concertized in U. S., esp. in Pennsylvania, Oregon. Member Portland Symphony 15 yrs.; played under Van Hoogstratten, Rodzinski, Iturbi, Kurtz, Goossens. First violin, staff orch. KGW. Dir. KGW since 1926. Program dir. *Musical Soiree.* Hobby, fishing. Wife: Pauline Bercovitz, pianist. b. Boston, Mass. St. w. Edgar Courson. Vice-pres. General Music Service (Music by Wire). Member Fed. of Wom. Mus. Clubs. KGW, Portland, Ore.

BERDAHL, ARTHUR C.

Director of Music, Fresno State Coll. b. Canton, S.D., Sept. 26, 1906. A.B., M.A., Ph.D. Att. Augostana Coll. Univ. of Iowa. Cond. State Coll. Orch. Comp. incl. *Judas Iscariot* (cho., orch., soli), *Str. Quartet*, songs. Member: MTA, MENC, Phi Mu Alpha Sinfonia; Amer. Sym. Orch. Lgs., NEA, CTA, CSEA, ACSI. Hobbies: sports, theatre. Fresno State College, Fresno 4, Calif.

BERMAN, PAULA (POLLY)

Composer. b. Brusilov, Russia. In America since childhood. St. piano, harmony w. Rosmarin, Montreal; voice w. Lazar Samoiloff, Los Angeles; theory, comp. w. Richard Drake Saunders, Hollywood. Comp. incl. *Rhapsody* (violin and orch.), *Mazurka* (str. quartet), *A Distant Land, Hebrew Lullaby, Do You Know? Fight to Victory, President's Ball* (RDS Publ.), numerous songs, piano pieces. Organized Wom. Con. for youth sym. orchs. 1946. Member: Mailamm (first vice-pres.), Jewish Congress, Wom. Div (prog. chairm. 3 yrs.). Hobbies: inventing, interior decorating. 132 N. Formosa Ave., Los Angeles 36, Calif.

BIBBINS, FREALON C.

Clarinet and E-flat Clarinet. b. Santa Cruz, Calif. St. w. George Hastings, Henry Bossert, Harold Randall; harmony and comp. w. August Hinrich. Principal cl. w. NBC in San Francisco 1932-1935; first cl. Federal Symphony S.F.; second and E-flat cl. S.F. Symphony under Pierre Monteux since 1943. Recordings w. S.F. Symphony (Monteux). Son. Frealon N., cl. alternate w. S.F. Symphony and S.F. Opera. Hobby: student of accountancy. 4032 Irving St., San Francisco, Calif.

BIGGS, RICHARD KEYES

Organist, choirmaster, composer. b. Glendale, Ohio. Att. Cincinnati Coll. of Music, Univ. of Michigan. Comp. incl. *Sunset, Mass of St. Joseph, Veni Sancte Spiritus, Mass of St. Anthony.* Concertized U. S., France, England. 1201 N. Las Palmas Ave., Hollywood, Calif.

Lionel Barrymore

Emanuel Bay

Gail H. Baskerville

Florence Colby Battram

Eula Beal

Heston M. and
Flora E. Beaudoin

Gloanah Ball Behan

Wauneva Bell

Teala Bellini

Abe Bercovitz

Gregory I. Blarowski

BIRMINGHAM, ALMA

Pianist, teacher of piano. b. San Francisco, Calif. St. piano in Europe, San Francisco, Chicago, New York, France, Germany. Appeared as soloist and accomp. for mother, Lillian Birmingham, contralto; other artists. Taught in Chicago; dir. Hull-House Music School, Chicago. At present in own studio. 3299 Washington St., San Francisco, Calif.

BITTER, MARGUERITE IRENE

Concert pianist, teacher. b. New York City. Att. UCLA, USC, Juilliard Grad. Sch. N. Y. Fellowship at Juilliard, scholarship w. Stojowski; pvt. st. w. Ann Eachus, L. A., Alberto Jonas, N. Y., Olga Samaroff. Coll., Fellow Degree Calif. MTA. Concert tours throughout Calif., Southwestern, Midwest states, Canada. Soloist w. Federal Sym. (Sample), Valley Dist. (Robinson), Little Sym. (Svedrofsky), Hollywood Bowl (Iturbi); many two-piano recitals w. Chas. Wakefield Cadman; soloist Redlands Bowl. Annual solo recitals USC. Recordings: *Dark Dancers of the Mardi Gras* (Co-Art) w. Cadman; pictures at MGM, RKO, Warner Bros. Coast to coast broadcasts CBS, Mutual. Students incl. James Shomate, Gloria Roberts, Elizabeth Garott, Eleanor Freeman, Maurice Tauzin, Carol Johnston, Evelyn Strum, Dianne Rogers, Pauline Harutunian, others. Pres. Dominant Club 1943-44; vice-pres., L. A. MTA, 1942-44. At present dir. state board Calif. MTA. Faculty USC Coll. of Music since 1945. Member Mu Phi Epsilon, advisor bd. of dir., Dominant Club. .2823 Ellendale Pl., Los Angeles, Calif.

BLADES, IRENE

Teacher of voice. b. McLeansboro, Ill. Att. Forest Park Univ., St. Louis; degree in voice, piano; Chicago Mus. Coll.; American Cons. of Mus. A.B. Indiana Univ. Church soloist; choir dir. Dir. Principia Mothers Choral Club, St. Louis; St. Louis School of the Theatre; also *Stars of Tomorrow* on on KSD. Pupils John Lake (1939), Priscilla Armbruster (1941) won Young Artists Contest, St. Louis Symphony Soc. Est. Los Angeles voice studio 1941. Students incl. Harry Babbitt, Ginny Simms, Louanne Hogan, Trudy Erwin, the Todds, James Lennon, Pay Hyatt, James Holt, Richard Krueger, Robert Lawton, Dorothy Larsen, Byron Palmer. Member: MTA; Delta Gamma. 3475 W. Sixth St., Los Angeles, Calif.

BLAKESLEE, S. EARLE

Conductor, composer. b. Oberlin, Ohio. Att. Denver Univ. Coll. of Mus. (B.Mus.); Pomona Coll. (B.A. 1908). Postgrad. st. voice w. Wm. Shakespeare, London, Oscar Saenger, N.Y., Franco Cannone, Rome, 1926-37. Comp. inc. *Red Cloud* (Amer. Indian gr. opera), *Hickory, Dickory, Dock* (lt. opera), *Flute of the Gods* (sym. poem). Comp., dir. incidental music of historical pageant *First Californians*, prod. Inter-Comm. Civic. Assn. Chairm. Dept. of Music, Chaffey Jr. Coll.; dir. a cappella choir (100 voices); dir. L.A. First Meth. Ch. Choir. Pres. Calif.-Wn. Mus. Eds. Conf.; chairm. Nat'l Comm. on Jr. Colls. Dir. J. Coll. Fest. Chorus, L.A. Nat'l Conv. MENC 1940. Wife, teacher, cond. Chaffey Jr. Coll.; son, Bevington, tenor. 805 w. 16th St., Upland, Calif.

BLAROWSKI, GREGORY I.

President, National Society of Music and Art. b. San Francisco, Calif. St. piano, theory, comp. w. pvt. tchrs. in New York, Leipzig, Chicago, Los Angeles. Concertized as pianist, U.S., Europe. Founded Nat'l. Soc. of Music and Art, 1946, as active organizer of all chapters throughout U.S. Hobbies: collecting programs, old editions of music. National Society of Music and Art, Roosevelt Bldg., 727 W. 7th St., Los Angeles 13, Calif.

BLINDER, BORIS

Principal violoncellist, San Francisco Symphony Orch. and Opera Co. b. Crimea, Russia, 1900. St. 'cello w. father, Samuel Blinder, Jacques van Lier, Berlin, Joseph Salmond, Paris. Won Amati 'cello in contest for all Russian 'cellists (in Odessa). Concert tours throughout U. S., Europe, Asia, North and South America. Soloist w. major sym. orchs. throughout world. First 'cellist, Paris Sym. (Monteux) 1926-37, San Francisco Sym. (Monteux), San Francisco Opera, since 1937, Hollywood Bowl (Stokowski, others) 1936-47. Member Paris, San Francisco Str. Quartets. Member AFM Locals 6 and 47. Hobby, coll. 'cello bows. 2367 Green St., San Francisco, Calif.

BLINDER, NAOUM

Violinist, violin pedagog. b. Lutzk, Russia, 1891. Grad. Imperial Cons. Odessa. Violin prof. Imperial Cons. Odessa, 1911 - 1920. Soloist w. Moscow, Leningrad, Odessa, other Russian orchs. under Glazunov, Klemperer, Fried. Recitals Carnegie Hall, Town Hall, 1928-29-30-31. Former prof. Inst. Musical Art (now Juilliard School, N. Y.) Concert-master S. F. Symphony Orch. Founder S. F. String Quartet. Faculty Mills Coll. Made Officer d' Academie by French Government, 1939. Tchr. of Isaac Stern, 1944 Green St., San Francisco, Calif.

BLOOMFIELD, THEODORE

Conductor. b. Cleveland, Ohio, June 14, 1923. St. Overland Cons. (B.M.), Berkshire Music Center, Juilliard Grad. Sch. (diploma). Guest cond., N. Y. Little Sym., others. Founder-cond. Cleveland Little Sym. Hobbies: bridge, fishing, ping pong. 2001 Pinehurst Rd., Hollywood 28, Calif.

BLOCH, ERNEST

Composer. b. Geneva, Switzerland, July 24, 1880. St. w. Jacques-Dalcroze, Rasse, Ysaye, Knorr. Prof. Geneva Cons. 1911-15. Cond. Lausanne concerts. Comp. incl. several symphonies, tone-poems, major works for soli and orch., chamber music, songs, piano pieces. Gold Beach, Ore.

BOERSMA, JAMES

Arranger, conductor, trombonist. b. Kalamazoo, Mich., 1910. Grad. Pasadena H.S. music course; Southwestern Cons. Dallas; special music courses USC. St. symphony and opera conducting w. Bruno Walter, Albert Coates; band conducting, arranging, trombone w. Joseph DeLuca. Taught instrumental music Dallas Public Schools. Pres. S.C. Bandmaster's Assn (2 yrs.). Dir. Angelus Temple Silver Band, since 1934; symphony orchestra since 1937. Head Music Dept. Angelus Temple since 1944. Teacher of adv. harm., orchestration, conducting Angelus Cons. of Music. Arr., dir. Angelus Hour, other radio programs; dir. annual presentations of sacred operas, Angelus Temple. Arr. over 200 numbers for orch., band, instr. solos and ens., hymn fantasies for voices with orch. and band acc. Author of *Songleader's Handbook* (for religious services). 4545 Morse Ave., North Hollywood, Calif.

BOLM, ADOLPH

Dancer, choreographer, teacher of dance. b. St. Petersburg (Leningrad) Russia. Att. Imperial Ballet Sch. Organized first European tour of Russian Ballet (w. Pavlova) 1908. Member original Diaghilev Ballet. Founded Bolm Ballet Intime. Regisseur general, Ballet Theatre, 1942. Choreographed numerous films, stage ballets incl. new version *Firebird, Mephisto.* 2061 No. Sycamore Ave., Hollywood 28, Calif.

BONANOVA, FORTUNIO

Baritone, concert and opera; dramatic actor. b. Mallorca, Spain. Att. Univ. of Madrid; protege of Chaliapin. Debut as Valentin (*Faust*), Barcelona Opera. Concertized, sang in opera in Europe, North, Central, South America. American dramatic debut w. Katherine Cornell in *Dishonored Lady.* Leading roles in numerous films, stage plays. Comp. incl. songs, arr. of Mallorcan folk melodies. Producer: film concerts in color. Hobby, gardening. 13016 Chandler Blvd., Van Nuys, Calif.

BONELLI, RICHARD

Baritone. b. Port Byron, N. Y. Att. Syracuse Univ. St. voice w. Alexander, de Reszke, Vilonat. Member Metropolitan Opera Co. Sang opera, concerts, radio throughout world. c/o L. E. Behymer, 427 W. 5th St., Los Angeles 13, Calif.

Polly Berman

Frealon C. Bibbins

Alma Birmingham

Marguerite Irene Bitter

Irene Blades

Yascha Borowsky

S. Earle Blakeslee

Boris Blinder

James Boersma

Fortunio Bonanova

Wiliam Robinson Boone

Lillian Bowles

Sylvan Breyn

177

BOONE, WILLIAM ROBINSON

Organist, pianist, musical director. b. Newport, R. I. St. piano w. Hans Schneider, Providence, R. I.; theory w. Homer Norris, New York; choir training w. G. Edward Stubbs, New York; organ w. S. B. Whitney, Everett E. Truette, Boston. Came to Oregon in 1910. Reorganized Piano School of Oregon State Coll. 1910. Managed Godowsky Master Classes, Portland. At present organist, musical dir. First Methodist Church and Temple Beth Israel; organist and dir. Scottish Rite Bodies and Al Kader Shrine Chanters. 1530 N. E. Stanton St., Portland, Ore.

BORISOFF, ALEXANDER

Concert 'cellist, composer, teacher. b. Odessa, Russia, 1900. St. 'cello w. Joseph Phess, comp. w. Malishewsky; Master's Degree, Russian Royal Conserv.; debut at age 16 w. Odessa Symph. Orch. Later first 'cellist same orch.; instructor Govn't. Cons. Member Odessa Art Quartet (5 yrs.). Concertized Europe and U. S.; soloist Hollywood Bowl, 1929 (Walter); joint recital w. John McCormack; soloist w. L. A. Phil. Orch., (Rodzinski); principal 'cellist L. A. Phil., Hollywood Bowl Orchs.; soloist world premier Bloch's *Voice in the Wilderness*, own arr. Haydn 'Cello Concerto No. 2 in D-major; own comp. *Allegrettino*, from *Suite in Olden Style*, (Klemperer). Comp. of *String Quartet, Suite* (orch.), *Spanish Suite, Poem Ancien* ('cello and orch.), Suite Burlesque (violin and 'cello). Commissioned by Standard Symphony for comp. for symphony based on Song *America*, perf. by L. A. Philharmonic on Standard Hour and Hollywood Bowl. Recordings for Decca, Capitol. Pupils incl. Robert La Marchina, Gilbert Reese, Elizabeth Greenschpoon, Helen Gertmenian, Joseph DiTullio, Alfred Broadbent. 340 So. Cloverdale Ave., Los Angeles, Calif.

BOROWSKY, YASCHA

Concert violinist. b. Odessa, Russia. Grad. St. Petersburg (Leningrad) Cons.; st. violin w. Auer, Kargueff; theory w. Glazunov. Concertized Europe, America, Hawaii, all major mus. centers; plays Magini violin once owned by De Beriot; soloist w. various orchs. Violinist in numerous feature films (Hollywood) during past decade. Comp. incl. transcriptions, arrangements of various masterworks. Recordings w. all major film studios. Member AFM, Local 47. Hobby, coll. violin bows. 1610 N. Normandie Ave., Hollywood 27, Calif.

BOWLES, LILLIAN

Opera, concert soprano. b. Indianapolis, Ind. Att. Indianapolis Cons., N. Y. Conservatory. St. w. Wm. Francis Parsons; oratorio w. Arthur Mees; opera w. Herbert Witherspoon; coaching w. Bruno Huhn; theory w. Fredrick Stevenson. Soloist w. Los Angeles Philharmonic Orchestra, Buffalo Symphony, Greek Theatre at Berkeley; soprano role in *Messiah* w. Long Beach Choral Oratorio Society. Also Los Angeles Bible Institute Chorus. Sang *Nedda, Leonora* and *Joan of Arc* w. Allied Grand Opera Co., N.Y.; prima donna w. Manhattan Light Opera Co. singing leading roles in twelve light operas, *Robin Hood, Bohemian Girl, Mikado, Said Pasha*, etc.; w. Western Concert Artists League in an Arabian song cycle. Return eng. w. Shakespeare Club, Pasadena; Clerbois Little Symphony, Santa Barbara. Presented and managed own concerts; wrote, directed, produced musical pageant, *America Singing* w. herself in leading role. Now soloist Church of Christ, Scientist, Los Angeles. Mgt. L. E. Behymer, Phil. Aud., Los Angeles. 400 North Serrano Ave., Los Angeles, 4, Calif.

BOYD, EUNICE

Violinist, pianist; teacher of violin, piano. b. Los Angeles, Calif. St. violin w. Hess, Peck, Altschuler, Persinger, Halleux; piano w. Larmer, McDonald, Linne; theory, Grinnell Coll. Concertized in U. S., Europe, North, South America; soloist w. various leading sym. orchs. Founder, first cond. annual Los Angeles Mozart Festival 1941. Member: Amer. Red Cross (6524 hrs. during war), Hollywood Opera Rdg. Club. Hobbies: drama, French poodles. Pupils incl. Eloise Roessler, Constance Ruddick, Winifred Wick, John Strauss, Lucille Hunt, Eda Schlatter, Virginia Tharaldson. 7315 Sunset Blvd., Hollywood 46, Calif.

BRAN, MARY

Impresario, concert manager. b. Kiev., Russia. In U. S. since 1939; citizen 1946. Manager concerts throughout Europe; Sou. Calif. since 1940. 1031 N. Clark Dr., Hollywood 46, Calif.

BREYN, SYLVAN

Concert pianist, teacher. b. Philadelphia, Pa. Started piano at age of 5. First recital in Phila. at 10. St. w. Heinze, Sowerby, Godowsky. Protege of Frederick Neil Innes, appearing as soloist w. him in Denver and on tour. Gave many concerts in Colorado at 15 under sponsorship of Univ. of Colo. Coartist w. Spanish cellist, Antoni Sala, throughout U.S., England, Australia & New Zealand. Coach-accomp. w. Charles Dalmores, tenor of Metropolitan & Manhattan Opera Companies. Radio recitals over NBC. Contributor of articles to Music and Dance in California, 1940, 1948, The Musician, (N.Y.), others. Revised, edited many piano works. Member Spa. Country Club. 1717 No. Vine St., Hollywood, Calif.

BRICKEN, CARL

Conductor, pianist. b. Shelbyville, Ky., Dec. 28, 1898. Att. Phillips Acad., Andover, Mass., Yale Univ.; B. A. cum laude 1922. Cond. college orch., Yale Glee Club. Piano recitals Town Hall 1928-29. Guest cond. Chicago, Illinois, Univ of Wisc. Sym., others; cond. English premiere opera *Schwanda* (Weinberger). Now permanent cond. Seattle Symphony Orch. Comp. incl. two *Symphonies, Prelude, Suite* (orch.), *Piano Quintet, Str. Qartet, Violin Sonata, 'Cello Sonata, Variations* (2 pfs.), piano pieces, songs. Seattle Symphony Orch., 620 Seaboard Bldg., Seattle, Wash. Res. 1019, 39th North, Seattle, Wash.

BRINKMAN, MARJORIE

Soprano. b. Kansas City, Mo. Concert, radio appearances in U. S. 866 So. Westgate Ave., Los Angeles, Calif.

BRODETSKY, JULIAN

Violinist. b. Russia, 1894. Grad. Petrograd Cons. of Music, 1916. Tchr. S. F. Music Cons. of Riga, 1916-1919. Concertmaster State Grand Opera Theatre, Moscow. Member Bruler String Quartet, Koln, eGrmany. Asst. concertmaster S. F. Symph. Orch.; 1st violin w. L. A. Phil. Orch. 444 N. Alfred St., Los Angeles, Calif.

BROWDA, MORRIS

Concert pianist, composer, teacher of piano, critic. b. Wilmington, Del., 1908. B. M., USC, 1930. St. piano w. Erwin Brynicki, Vienna; theory, comp. w. Charles Pemberton (USC); piano w. W. J. Anderson. Concertized in U.S., Europe. Comp. incl. *Prelude and Fugue* (orch.), several preludes and fugues, other works for piano, chamber music, songs. Music critic, Calif. Jewish Voice. Wife, Rae Fink Browda, concert pianist. B.M., USC. St. piano w. Swarthout. 1808 No. Kenmore Ave., Los Angeles 27, Calif.

BROWN, IRENE (Mrs. J. Urner)

Piano teacher. b. Walla Walla, Wash. Grad. Walla Walla Coll. Cons. Music. St. piano w .Dent Mowrey, Olga Steeb, Rae Robertson. Duo-piano work w. sister Vivian under Gastone Usigli, Hollywood, San Diego Symphony under Modest Altschuler, Ford Bowl, Nino Marcelli; played at women's clubs, colleges. On faculty of piano dept., Walla Walla Coll. Cons. of Music (3 yrs.). Member MTA, NGPT. 640 Broadway, San Diego, Calif.

BROWN, VIVIAN

Pianist, teacher. b. Walla Walla, Wash. Grad. Walla Walla College Cons. of Music; post-grad. piano work w. Malen Burnett, Dent Mowrey, Ethel Bartlett and Rae Robertson. Duo-piano work w. sister Irene under Gastone Usigli, Hollywood, San Diego Symphony under Modest Altschuler, Ford Bowl under Nino Marcelli; played two-piano concerts woman's clubs, colleges, churches. On faculty of Malen Burnett School of Music (2 yrs.); head Piano Dept. Walla Walla College Cons. of Music (4 yrs.). Member Calif. State MTA, NGPT, NGO. 640 Broadway, San Diego, Calif.

178

Alexander Borisoff

BRUNI, FRANK R.

Producer, director, singer. b. New York City. St. voice w. Eduardo Petri; art, theater. Toured U. S. in stage revues; Produced numerous stage shows and revues. Pres. and General Director of Florentine Gardens where he has presented in musical productions, Paul Whiteman, Sophie Tucker, Harry Richman, Gertrude Niesen, Carmen Armaya, Allan Jones, Betty Jaynes, others. Hobbies: art, theater. Florentine Gardens, 5955 Hollywood Blvd., Los Angeles, Calif.

BRUNS, GEORGE E.

Musical director, conductor KEX. b. Sandy, Ore. 1914. St. piano w. Emil Enna; piano, theory, comp. w. Dent Mowrey; plays bass fiddle, trombone, tuba. Member Sterling Young, Paul Pendarvis orch. Arr., bass fiddle w. Harry Owens orch. Arr., trombone w. Teagarden orch. Musical dir. KEX since 1945. Comp. incl. *Rainbow River* (Bergman, Vocco & Conn) Hobby: fishing. KEX, Portland, Ore.

BRYON, ARTHUR J.

Violinist, composer, teacher. b. London, Eng., 1910. Att. Royal Acad. of Music, London. Grad. S. F. Cons. of Music. A. B. Fresno State Coll. Concertmaster Fresno Symph. Orch. 937 T St., Fresno, Calif.

BUCHAROFF, SIMON

Composer, concert pianist. b. Kiev, Russia, 1881. St. Vienna Cons. of Music, 1902: piano w. Julius Epstein, Emil Sauer; comp. w. Stephan Stocker, Robert Fuchs. Piano recitals, 1905-1916 in Europe, America. Head Piano Dept., Wichita Coll. of Music, 1907. Master classes piano comp., 1931-36. Operas incl.: *Drama of Exile*, 1912, *A Lover's Knot* (Chicago Opera, Campanini) 1916, *Sakahra* (Frankfort State Opera, Germany) 1924, *Addio*, 1936, *Jewel*, 1941. Orchestral works: *Four Tone Poems, Scene de Ballet*, (Phil. Soc., N.Y. Mengelberg), *The Wanderer's Song*, 1928, *Death Scene* (*Sakahra*), 1928, *The Trumpeter's Death*, 1928, *America*, 1929, *Moses*, tone poem, 1940, *Das sterbe Gloeklein*, 1942, *Capriccio*, 1942. Cantatas: *Hear My Voice, Oh Lord, Jerusalem*. Chorus and orch.: *The Four Freedoms*, 1943, *Salute to a Free World*, 1943; numerous works for piano, voice, violin, various combinations. Won David Bispaham Memorial Medal, American Opera Soc. of Chicago. 1456 So. Cardiff Ave., Los Angeles 35, Calif.

BUHLIG, RICHARD

Pianist, pedagog. b. Chicago, Ill., 1880. St. piano w. Leschetizky. Played w. leading orchs., Europe and America. Soloist Los Angeles Phil. Orch., Hollywood Bowl. Recitals throughout Europe. Taught in Berlin, Vienna, Paris, N. Y. Ed. Bach *Kunst der Fuge*. 114 S. Carondelet St., Los Angeles Calif.

BURG, WILLIAM van den

(*See*: van den BURG)

BURT, HELEN McCARTHY

Teacher of voice; coach, coloratura soprano. b. Los Angeles, Calif. Started singing in Catholic children-choirs at age of 4. St. voice w. Queena Mario, Rosina Heeder. Maria Lanfranchi, Leon Rothier, Ellen Beach Yaw; coached w. Isidore Luckstone, Emilio A. Roxas. Appeared in operatic and musical productions; soloist on radio; concertized throughout U. S. Teacher of George Formes, Carrol Eaton, Fiama Scafati, Kenneth Donner, Evelyn Baker, and her daughters Jean & Cathleen Burt. Hobby: writes songs and poetry, many items published. Member Kappa Alpha Pheta. 433 S. Westmoreland Ave., Los Angeles, Calif.

BURTON, DOROTHY

Teacher of piano. b. Alhambra, Calif. Secondary mus. cred. UCLA; A.B., 1930. St. w. de Zielinski, Alfred Butler, Francis Wright, Carolyn Alchin, Abby de Averitt; Godowsky master class 1933; I. Phillip master class 1939; Tarnowsky master class 1945. Delegated by UCLA to organize music dept. Amer. School in Tokyo, Japan. Head mus. dept. Holtville H.S.; seven years experimental work w. children at UCLA Elementary School in application of progressive methods to class and private piano; associated w. Univ. Elem.

School since 1930; taught adult piano classes Univ. Extension UCLA campus; gave teacher training courses to Raula Lampi, Emily Bell, LaVerne Scott, Eva Tossava, Myrla Smith, Gratia Lazier, Melina Morley, others. 625 Warner Ave., Los Angeles, Calif.

BUSHELL, DON

'Cellist, teacher, conductor. b. Seattle, Wash., Jan. 16, 1908. St. w. George Rogovoy, Kolia Levienne, Mischa Schneider, Peter Meremblum, Alex Schneider. B.A., 1931; M.A., 1941 Univ. of Wash. Soloist w. Bremerton Symphony, Western Washington Symphony, Univ. of Wash. Symphony. Sonata recitals w. Andor Foldes (Bellingham, (Seattle) Bellingham String Quartet (5 yrs.), Seattle String Quartet (2 yrs.), various solo appearances in Seattle, Everett, Bellingham, Wenatchee, Longview, Ellensburg, Portland, Victoria. Musical dir., Seattle Philharmonic and Choral Soc.; teacher of 'cello and dir. of chorus, Cornish School; co-conductor, Seattle "Pops" Orch.; formerly instruc. Western Washington College, Bellingham 1932-1945; chairman of Music Dept., 1944-1945; conductor, Western Washington Symphony, 1938-42; Nat'l Adjudicator, Music Educators Nat'l Conference. Member: Seattle Symphony, Tacoma Philharmonic. Pres., Seattle Chapter, Washington State MTA. 411 Smith St., Seattle 9, Wash.

BUTTOLPH, DAVID

Composer, conductor, b. N. Y. C., 1903. Grad. Inst. of Musical Art. Cond. NBC Studios, N. Y. C., 6 yrs. w. 20th-Century-Fox since 1933. 20th-Century-Fox, Los Angeles, Calif.

BUTTREE, MARGARET

Teacher of piano. b. St. Paul, Minn. Grad. Dakota Cons. of Music, Fargo, N. Dak. St. piano American Cons. of Music, Chicago, w. Silvio Scionti, Josef Lhevinne; harmony w. A. Anderson, Adolf Weidig; normal training w. Louise Robyn. Dir. Dept. of Normal Training (11 yrs.) of Dak. Cons. of Music; later, Dir. of Cons. Secondary Cred. Calif. MTA. Ex-pres. Musical Arts Club, Orange Co., Calif. 427 N. Palm, Anaheim, Calif.

BYERS, ROXANA WEIHE

Concert pianist, teacher. b. San Francisco, Calif. First piano lessons w. mother; st. w. Wagner Swayne, San Francisco, Fannie Bloomfield Zeisler, Chicago, Lazare Levy, Cons. Nationale de Paris, Alfred Cortot and Ecole Normale de Musique, Paris; harmony, counterpoint w. Edw. Strickland, Univ. of Calif., Adolph Weidig, Amer. Cons., Chicago. Prof. Mus. American Exp. Forces Univ., Beaune, Cote d' Or France; member Army Ed. Corps, France, 1919; org. dept. music for reconstruction in Letterman Gen. Hospital, San Francisco. Soloist w. Honolulu Symph. Orch. Founder and dir. Hawaii Cons. of Mus., Honolulu. Comp. incl: *Reverie in D flat* (organ) (Oliver Ditson); *Song Cycle, Woodland Scenes, My Aim*. Vice-pres. Dominant Club, Recording Secy. MTA, State Colleagues Degree; Dir. Piano Faculty Bev. Hills Cons. of Music. 6171 Barrows Dr., Los Angeles, Calif.

BYRENS, FLORENCE COOLES

Violinist, music educator. b. Ft. Worth, Texas, 1910. B. Ed. UCLA, 1930; M. Sci., USC, 1933. Research psychology of music Univ. of Iowa. Form. instr. Compton Jr. Coll. Music superv. Artesia, Calif. 1345 S. Burnside Ave., Los Angeles, Calif.

CAILLIET, LUCIEN

Conductor. b. France, 1891. Att. Cons. Dijon, France. Member Phila. Orch. (Stokowski, Ormandy) 20 yrs. Tchr. comp., orch., Nat'l. Music Camp, Interlochen, Mich., 1939, USC. Comps. publ. by Witmark, C. Fischer, Elkan-Vogel, Sam Fox. Recorded for RCA Victor. Made Officer d'Academie, 1937. 7327 Rindge Ave., Playa Del Rey, Calif.

CALDWELL, GLADYS

Librarian Art and Music Department, Los Angeles Public Library. b. Boston, Mass. B.A., UC at Berkeley. St. piano w. private tchrs. here and Europe; private music sch. Came to L.A. 1922. Los Angeles Public Library, 630 W. 5th St., Los Angeles, Calif.

Irene Brown

Vivian Brown

Frank R. Bruni

George E. Bruns

Simon Bucharoff

Helen McCarthy Burt

Dorothy Burton

Don Bushell

Margaret Buttree

Roxana Weihe Byers

CALKER, DARRELL W.

Composer, conductor. b. Washington, D. C. Att. Epsicopal Cathedral Sch., Curtis Sch., Philadelphia. St. orch., comp. w. Victor Young. Mus. dir. Walter Lantz cartoons for past 7 yrs. Comp. incl. *Penguin Island*, orch. suite, chamber music, smaller works, numerous film scores for Paramount, 20th-Century Fox, Columbia studios. Musical Courier Citation 1947 for best cartoon score. Walter Lantz Cartoon Co., 861 No. Seward, Hollywood 38, Calif.

CALL, AUDREY

Concert violinist; composer. b. Marion, Ind. Att. Nat'l. Cons., Paris; st. w. d'Indy, Roussel, Capet, Touche, Nadaud, Hayot; violin, comp. w. J. Walter Keller, P. Marinus Paulsen (U. S.). Mus. B., Mus. M., Paris Cons. Debut as child prodigy w. Chicago Symp. (Stock), then toured Midwest. Won Soc. of Amer. Musicians competition, Chicago, Nat'l. Young Artists Contest (Amer. Music Fest.) New York, scol. Paris Cons. Concertized extensively in Europe, U. S. Featured on radio programs; staff artist 5 yrs. NBC and CBS, Chicago. Comp. incl. *Elegy* (orch.; premiere Chicago Wom. Symp.), *Lapis Lazuli* (Violin Concerto), *Boomer the Bass Drum* (child. story), numerous violin soli (pub. C. Fischer), songs. Rec. *Boomer the Bass Drum* (Mercury). Member AFM (N. Y., Chicago, L. A.). Hobby, writing children's stories. 10253 Sunland Blvd., Roscoe, Calif.

CALLIN, OWEN

Music critic, Los Angeles Evening Herald and Express; music, record critic, International News Service. b. Fostoria, Ohio, Dec. 4, 1911. Att. Ohio State Univ.; B.S. in Journalism. Active in music as singer and w. own small orch.; also plays guitar. Hobbies: records, amateur radio, cards. Los Angeles Evening Herald and Express, 1243 Trenton St., Los Angeles 15, Calif.

CANDELL, THOMAS P.

Composer, arranger; president Candell Music Pub., Inc.; director Candell Studios of Modern Music. b. Buffalo, N. Y., 1909. Att. East Sch. of Mus.; st. comp., theory, cond. w. Otto Cesana; Colby Cons. of Mus.; piano at Lockwood Sch. of Mus.; grad. degrees. Soloist Carnegie Hall, Town Hall, Strand Theatre, Paramount Theatre, others in New York City. Affil. w. Carol Mus. Co., Red Star, Mus. Corp. of Amer., Republic Mus. Co.; CBS, NBC. Radio work in New York. Author books on music theory, modern harmony. Founder: Candell Studios of Modern Music, Candell Music. Pub., Inc. Comp. (many pub.) incl. *Anywhere Girl* (musical show), *You'll Never Know, Dreaming Again, Shadows, My Day, Zingarella, If You Were Busy*. Recordnigs incl. *Concerto for Guitar, Nola, Dizzy Fingers* (Carol Rec.). Member Oakland Cham. of Com.; AFM Local 6; Veterans Bus. and Prof. Men's Assn. Hobbies: tennis, golf, music research. Candell Music Pub., Inc., Candell Studios of Modern Music, 518, 17th St., Oakland, Calif. Res. Rt. 3, Box 499, Walnut Creek, Calif.

CARPENTER, ESTELLE

Music educator. b. Brooklyn, N. Y. Grad. Wililam L. Tomlins Cons .of Music, Chicago. Att. Chicago, Northwestern, Columbia, Boston Universities. St. w. William C. Stadtfeld, Kate Douglas Wiggin, Walter Damrosch, William Piutti, Humphrey J. Sewart, Stanley Hall, Frederic Burk, Paul Steindorf, Fred N. Innes, Father William Finn. Music supervisor, San Francisco Public Schools (1899-1945). Formerly mus. dir., San Francisco State Normal Sch., San Francisco Tchrs'. Coll. (21 yrs.) Arr. first series of Young People's symphony concerts, San Francisco Civic Aud. Dir. huge choruses for S.F. Civic Armistice Day celebration. Introduced music appreciation in S. F. schools; Pres. radio school broadcasts. Lectured on *The Child Voice*, and var. phases mus. ed. Nat'l. Education Assn., Nat'l. Music Supervisor Conf., Calif. Western Educators Conf., Calif. Fed. Music Clubs conv. Certificate of merit from mayor of San Francisco. Chairman, public school committee music week (10 yrs.); education, civic music for Calif. Fed. of Music Club. Hon. memb. S. F. music clubs. First life-memb. of West Coast Nat'l. Educa-

tion Assn. Member: Nat'l. Congress of Parents and Tchrs.; MTA; Nat'l. League for Women's Service and Women's City Clubs; DAR; S. F. Opera Guild; board of governors, Loring Club. Founder-guarantor S. F. Opera Ass'n. Fairmont Hotel, San Francisco, Calif.

CARR, ALMA

Voice teacher. b. Versailles, Ohio. St. piano w. pvt. tutors. Became piano teacher and accomp. Protegee of Georgia Frost Newcomer, voice tchr. Phoenix, Ariz. St. voice, vocal pedagogy w. Andres de Segurola. Member MTA. Former local treas., former dir. Youth Choir, Orch. of First Christian Ch., San Bernardino, mus. dir. First English Lutheran Ch. Hobby, pipe-organ. Pupils incl. Herbert George Kruis, boy-soprano. 116 East Temple St., San Bernardnio, Calif.

CARR, ARTHUR GEORGE

Pianist, composer, organist, conductor, teacher. b. Pontiac, Mich., Feb. 29, 1908. Att. Albion Coll., Yale Univ., Zoellner Cons., UCS Army Bandmasters Sch. Mus. B. 1932, Mus. M. 1939, Mus. D. (hon.) 1941, Zoellner Cons. U. S., European concert tours; soloist w. New Haven Sym., Yale Glee Club, Los Angeles Fed. Sym. Concert app. w. Hans Kindler, Felix Knight, Mary Garden, Lanny Ross, Francesca Braggiotti, Serge Oukrainsky, Zoellner Str. Quar., Anne Jamison, Patricia Bowman, Doris Doe, Sydney Rayner. Vice-pres., prof. of piano, theory, Zoellner Cons. 1935-41. Chief W. O. Bandleader U. S. Army 1942-46 (bronze star). Organist, choirmaster St. Thomas Epis. Ch. of Hollywood. Comp. incl. symphonic poems, *Rondo* (pf. and orch.), operetta, chamber music, chorals, *The Mountain* (wom. cho.), piano pieces incl. *Mariwari Nautch*, songs incl. *As On the Night, Hosanna to the Son of David, Riding to Lenham, Summer Night, White Swan on the Lake*, etc. (pub. Schirmer, Webster, Galaxy). Member: Mary Carr Moor Mss. Club, AFM Local 47, Soc. of Amer. Comp., AGO. Hobbies: tennis, golf. 642 S. La Brea Ave., Los Angeles, Calif.

CARTER, ARTIE MASON (Mrs. J. J. Carter)

Founder Hollywood Bowl concerts. b. Salisbury, Mo. Grad. Christian Coll., Columbia, Mo., 1906. A.B., B.M. St. w. A. E. Guerne, Xaver Scharwenka. Grad. Kansas City Cons., 1911. St. Vienna w. Marguerite Liszniewska, Leschetizsky, 1911-13.

CARTER, PAULENA ELIZABETH

Pianist. b. San Francisco, Calif., 1930. St. w. mother at age of 3, James Woodward King (4 to 6); coached w. Olga Samaroff under two-yr. Hood Scholarship at Phila. Cons. of Music, w. Allison R. Drake (ages 9-10), Mme. Raissa Kaufman, Max Rabinowitsh; harmony, orch., comp., w. Mary Carr Moore. Soloist w. Sacramento Jr. Coll. Symphony Orch., Stockton Municipal Symphony (at 7), Sacramento Muncipal Symphony, Santa Rosa Symphony, Modesto Symphony. Played at World Fairs, San Francisco, N. Y.; appeared many times on Behymer matinees; on KPAS; w. Meremblum Jr. Symphony Orch. Soloist w. All Southern Calif. High School Orch. (Santa Barbara). Many concerts for USO, hospitals & camps. Awarded 3 citations for this work and Hollywood Canteen work. First winner KFI-Los Angeles Philharmonic Orch. Young Artists Competition at 13 (1944). Appeared on Packard Program under Claude Sweeten KFI, (20 weeks). Grad. from Senior High School at 13. Soloist w. L. A. Philharmonic (Wallenstein) at 15., ABC Radio Hall of Fame, summer season of Ford Sunday Evening Hour, *Sparkle Time Program* under Meredith Willson CBS (24 wks.), Kern Memorial Program, Hollywood Bowl, Redlands Bowl, Pacific Music Camp, Stockton (C. Bakaleinikoff), Command Performance for Armed Forces overseas, KFI Twenty-fifth anniversary. Broadcasts w. San Francisco Standard Symphony Orch (S. F.), KFI (James Sample), Ford Showroom CBS (Willson), California Jr. Symphony Orch. (Meremblum, Steinberg, Previn, Ormandy, etc.) Comp. *Cinderella Suite, Fantasy* (prize winners). Member AFM. Hobbies: horseback riding, fishing, drawing. Management: MCA—Abe Meyer, personal representative. 5959 Franklin Ave., Hollywood 28, Calif.

Thomas P. Candell

Paulena Elizabeth Carter

Audrey Call

Darrel W. Calker

Estelle Carpenter

Alma Carr

Arthur George Carr

183

CASIGLIA, ARTURO VITTORIO

Musical director, teacher of voice. b. Palermo, Sicily, 1891. Grad. Palermo Cons. of Music; Mus. D. Asst. cond. La Scala Opera, 1921. U. S. since 1922. Prod. opera in Boston, 1922, w. local artists. Choral dir. Mexico City Opera House, 1923; first choral dir. San Francisco Opera Assn. Organized Pacific Opera Co., 1925 (Mme. Butterfly, mem. to Puccini). 2643 Baker St., San Francisco, Calif.

CASO, EDUARDO

Choir director, founder Tucson Boys' Choir. b. London, England, July 3, 1901. Educated Westminister School, London w. Gabriel Paulet (Conservatoire, Paris). Faculty Memb. Eton College, Windsor, England; Aiken's Prep. School for Boys, South Carolina. Concert tours, radio appearances and recordings w. Tucson Boys' Choir. Founder Blind Choir; School for Deaf and Blind; colored choir for boys; in charge of Tucson community sing. Hobby, sports, especially soccer as amateur and semi-pro. Martin Music Management, Hollywood, Calif.; res: 549 No. Mountain, Tucson, Ariz.

CASTELNUOVO-TEDESCO, MARIO

Composer, pianist. b. Florence, Italy, 1895. Att. Royal Cons., Florence. St. piano w. Del Valle; comp. w. Pizzetti. Comp. incl. La Mandragola, Violin Concerto, piano works, orch. chamber music, songs, piano pieces. Now scoring, orchestrating film scores. 209 So. Clark Dr., Beverly Hills, Calif.

CEPPARO, LEON

Teacher of voice. b. Venice, Italy, March 22, 1890. St. voice, teaching, theory in Milano, Trieste, Paris, w. Mario Ancona, Alessandro Bonci, Giovanni Sbriglia. Taught in Italy, U. S. Comp. numerous songs, incl. Dorme la Notte, Barcarolla, Non baciar mi piu. Students incl. Tamaki Miura, Angelo Minghetti, Claudio Frigerio, Tandy MacKenzie, Lodovico Tomarchio, Raffaele Moscocci. Hobbies: hunting, horseback riding. 3216 Club Dr., Los Angeles 34, Calif .

CHAMLEE, MARIO

Tenor. b. Los Angeles, Calif., 1892. Att. USC; st. voice w. Achille Alberti. Debut w. Nat'l Grand Opera Co., Los Angeles, 1916. Sang w. Metropolitan Opera Co., 1920-28, 1936-37, opera in Paris, Vienna, Prague ,Brussels, other music centers; concertized in Europe, U. S. 8118 Hollywood Blvd., Hollywood 46, Calif.

CHAMLEE, RUTH MILLER (Mme. Mario Chamlee)

Soprano, opera and concert; teacher of voice. b. Portland, Ore. St. in Spokane, Seattle; piano w. Alfred Venino (Leschetizky pupil); voice w. Elizabeth Richmond Miller (de Reszke pupil); in Paris, also Spain (5 yrs.) w. d'Aubigny, Emil Bourjois, Giovanni Sbriglia. Debut w. Cosmopolitan Opera Co. New York City, 1917, as Gilda (Rigoletto); leading roles w. Aborn Opera Co.; debut w. Metropolitan Opera Co. as Micaela (Carmen w. Farrar). Concertized throughout U. S., sang leading roles w. Chicago Civic, Ravinia, Cincinnati, other opera comps., Soc. of American Singers, N. Y., etc. Repertory Inc. leading soprano roles in Rigoletto, La Boheme, Lucia, Lakme, Martha, Maid Mistress, La Traviata, Carmen, Romeo and Juliet, Faust, Mignon, Manon, others. Numerous concerts w. husband, Mario Chamlee. Co-organizer, artist w. Chamlee USO Camp Entert. Unit, during war; home service, Los Angeles Red Cross. Pres. Dominant Club, L. A. Reg. gov. Calif.-Western Div., NATS 1945-48. Member preview committee for music in films, Nat. Fed of Mus. Clubs. 8118 Hollywood Blvd., Hollywood 46, Calif.

CHASHOUDIAN, MARSHALL G.

Concert violinist, conductor, teacher of violin. b. Boston, Mass. 1901. St. violin w. Jacques Hoffman, Anton Shedlovsky, Fr. Kneisal (N. Y.), Albert Vertchamp, Louis Kaufman, Sylvain Noack; comp., theory w. Frank Grundy (Boston). Julius Gold, Julius Toldi; cond. w. Albert Coates. Played w. People's Symphony (Mollenhauer, Mason, Hadley) Philharmonic Quartet, Boston Orch., Players, Cond. theater orchestra, Boston. Concertmaster Santa Barbara Symphony (Clerbois) 1928, Radio, screen work in Hollywood since 1926. Scored picture Anoush; Arr. chorals, Armenian dances for symphony. Comp. incl. etudes for violin, piano pieces, songs. Numerous radio, film recordings with Hugo Reisenfeld, Raymond Paige, Felix Mills, etc. Member AFM, Local 47. Pres., Armenian Allied Arts Assn. Hobby: woodcarving. Teaching in L. A. since 1926. 103 N. Harvard Blvd., Los Angeles 4, Calif.

CHAUDET, ALLENE

Teacher of piano and harmony. b. Vermont. St. w. von Liebich (pupil of Anton Rubinstein) (6 yrs.), Bloomfield Zeisler, Frank Damrosch, Myrtle Ellwin. Soloist Boston Festival Orchestra (at age 14) under Gustave Mahler, Hollywood Bowl under Adolph Tandler. Concertized throughout U. S. Started teaching Chicago 1916; opened Hollywood Studio 1919. Pupils include Lynette Altabet, Sandra and Ronnie Burns, Joan Benny, Edna and Janet Cantor, Jackie Cooper, Douglas Fairbanks, Jr., Annie Power (daughter of Annabella), Gwynn Pickford, Gloria Swanson, Shirley Temple, Yolanda, other screen, radio celebrities. Hobby, golf. 2000 Las Palmas Ave., Hollywood, Calif.

CHENOWETH, WILBUR

Composer, pianist, organist. b. Tecumseh, Nebr. Scholarship Lincoln Mus. Coll. and Univ. of Nebr. Sch. of Music; B. Mus. St. piano, organ, comp. w. Sigismond Stojowski, Alexander Lambert, Pietro Yon. Soloist w. orchestras U. S., Europe. Radio programs, NBC, Mutual. Prof. of piano, organ, comp. Univ. of Nebr. 1932-38; head piano dept. Occidental Coll. (L. A.) 1939-45. Choirmaster, organist, Neighborhood Ch., Pasadena. Comp. incl. works for orch., piano and orch., piano, violin, organ, chorus, songs, pub. by Schirmer, C. Fischer, Boston Mus. Co., Flammer, Witmark, Chappell. Recordings Ampico piano, Duo-Art organ. Lecturer on mus. Westlake Sch. for Girls, Los Angeles. Member, ASCAP. 12828 Marlboro St., Brentwood, Los Angeles, Calif.

CHERKASSKY, SHURA

Concert pianist. b. Odessa, Rusia, 1911. Att. Walden Sch. N. Y., Park Sch. Baltimore, Curtis Inst. of Mus. Philadelphia; st. piano w. Josef Hofmann. Concertized in Europe, U. S. 1418½ N. Sierra Bonita Ave., Hollywood, Calif.

CHERRIER, ALEXANDRE

Voice teacher, choral conductor, dramatic tenor. b. Montreal, Canada, 1897. Pupil of Jean De Reszke, Mario Marafioti, Madame Ver Trees. Soloist w. L. A. Philharmonic Orch., 1926; Carmen, Faust, Turandot, Andrea Chenier, Tosca, Cavalleria Rusticana (Merola), Los Angeles Grand Opera, 1927. Radio soloist KFI, KMTR, KFVD, KGFJ. Motion Picture work (recent) Song of Bernadette (20th Century-Fox), French versions Walt Disney. Choir director, soloist St. James Church and Our Lady of Loretta, (25 yrs.). Soloist Elk's Lodge Redondo Beach (6 yrs.). Calif. repr. Alfred Dixon school of speech and phonetics of New York. Member MTA. Hobby: electrifying voice production (electronics). 732 So. Norton Ave., Los Angeles 5, Calif.

CHESNUT, LORA PERRY

Organist. b. Beloit, Kans. Grad. Harrisburg Cons. of Music, Pa. Att. Kansas State Coll. (taught there one year); taught Pendleton Acad., Pendleton, Ore. St. w. Wm. Leonard Hofer, Wm. J. Decevee, Percy Shaul Hallett, Mary Carr Moore, Jas. H. Rogers, Alex. Schreiner, Clarence Mader, Norman Coke-Jephcott. Comp. cantata, choral music, secular compositions. Choral arr. of Sons, and The Common Fate sung at S.F. World's Fair. Arr. Wind Song by James H. Rogers (pub. Schirmer). Fellow AGO, 1940. Organist, Second Church of Christ, Scientist, Pasadena. 1818 Navarro Ave., Pasadena, Calif.

Arturo Vittorio Casiglia

Eduardo Caso

Leon Cepparo

Marshall Chasdoudian

Allene Chaudet

Ruth Miler Chamlee

Wilbur Chenoweth

Alexandre Cherrier

Lora Perry Chesnut

Van A. Christy

Mario Cimino

Ada Clement

Gertrud Cleophas

185

CHOATE, ROBERT A.

Director of Music Education, Oakland Public Schools. b. Anna, Ill., Oct. 22, 1910. Att. Univ. of Illinois, Cornell Coll.; Northwestern Coll. B.S.M. 1935, M.M. 1939. Pres. Washington Music Ed. Assn. 1940-41; board of dir. Music Ed. Nat'l Conf. 1945-50; Music Chairm. Calif. School Supervisors Assn. 1945-48; Asst. Dean Sch. of Music, Northwestern Univ. 1938-39; dir. of mus. Spokane pub. schls. 1939-41. Faculty Northwestern Univ. summers 1940-42, 1946-47; Univ. of Calif. summers 1944-45. Author numerous magazine articles. Member: Pi Kappa Lambda, Phi Mu Alpha. Oakland Public Schools, 1025, 2nd Ave., Oakland, Calif. Res. 5426 Brann St., Oakland, Calif.

CHRISTY, VAN A.

Chairman, Music Dept., Santa Barbara Coll., instructor of voice, choral conducting, secondary music methods. b. Revere, Mo., 1900. Ph.D., M.A. Teachers Coll. Columbia Univ.; B.A., Missouri Univ. Composer, arranger, lecturer, adjudicator music contests, festivals. Arr., edited songs: *The Dove and the Lily* (Swedish Folk), *The Old Woman and the Peddler* (English Folk), *Pilgrims Song* (Tchaikovsky), *The Virgin by the Manger* (Franck), *Shenandoah* (American Folk) *Nelly Was A Lady* (Foster), *Lithuanian Song* (Chopin), others. (G. Schirmer) *Joshua Fit de Battle ob Jericho* (4 and 8 parts), *Vale of Tuoni* (Sibelius) *Panis Angelicus* (Franck) *A Legend* (Tchaikovsky) others. (Hall & McCreary Co.). Books incl. *Glee Club and Chorus* (Schirmer, 1940). Lectures incl. *Selection of Choral Material* (Calif. Wn. Music Ed. Conf., Salt Lake City, 1947), *Music Integration* (Nat'l Ed. Assoc. Yearbook for 1940). Vice-pres. Calif. Western Music Ed. Conf., So. Sec. (1945-47). Member Phi Mu Alpha Sinfonia, Kappa Delta Pi, Phi Delta Kappa. Hobbies: travel, fishing, hunting, athletics. 527 De la Vista, Santa Barbara, Calif.

CHUDNOW, DAVID

Musical director. b. Milwaukee, Wisc., June 29, 1902. St. piano, theory, private teachers; Univ. of Wisc. B. A. Univ. of Wisc. Toured in vaudeville w. orchestras. Universal Studios (2 yrs.); Warner Bros. (3 yrs.). Established own organization to supply music for independent film companies. Recordings of over 300 films include: *Miracles Can Happen, Personal Column, Sleep, My Love, Atlantis.* Member Local 47 A.F. M., Masons, Phi Sigma Delta. Hobbies: theater, traveling. 8913 Sunset Blvd., Los Angeles, Calif.

CIMINO, MARIO

Operatic tenor; coach. b. Italy. Att. San Pietro Maillo Cons., Naples; Santa Cecilia Cons., Rome. Sang opera and concerts Europe, North, South America. Res. of U. S. since 1935. Hobbies: fishing, hunting. Studio: 8118 Sunset Blvd., Hollywood 46, Calif.

CLAUSEN, LESLIE P.

Instructor in theory and piano. b. Ferndale, Calif., 1907. Grad. Univ. of Calif. St. w. Arnold Schoenberg, Arne Oldberg, Alfred Mirovitch. Accomp. UC Glee Club European tour, 1928. Cond. US Band, 1929. Instr. theory, piano L. A. City Coll. since 1931. Pres. So. Calif. Jr. Coll. Assn., 1936-37; pres. Calif. Wn. Music Edu. Conf. So. Dist., 1939-1940. 2039 Ivar Ave., Hollywood, Calif.

CLEMENT, ADA

Director, San Francisco Conservatory of Music. b. San Francisco, 1877. St. piano w. Ina Griffin, Oscar Weil, Josef Lhevinne, Berlin; Harold Bauer, Paris; special work w. Wanda Landowska; theory w. Wallace Sabin, Albert Elkus, Ernest Bloch. Played w. San Francisco Symphony under Henry Hadley; heard frequently in solo and ensemble concerts. Founded Ada Clement Piano School together w. Nettiemae Felder and Lillian Hodghead; later incorporated under name of The San Francisco Conservatory of Music. 3435 Sacramento St., San Francisco 18, Calif.

CLEOPHAS, GERTRUD

Concert pianist, teacher. b. Iowa. Mother, Kirsti Cleophas, teacher of piano & voice. St. w. Fannie Bloomfield Zeisler,

Chicago, Theodor Leschetizky, Vienna. Appeared w. Berlin Philharmonic, (Kunwald), Minn. Symphony, (Oberhoffer) Hollywood Bowl (Oberhoffer, thrice under Altschuler) MacDowell *Second Concerto* nine times w. orch. Played on stations KHJ, KFAC, others; concertized leading cities Europe and America. Played before Crown Prince Olav and Crown Princess Martha of Norway at banquet held at USC. Member: Leschitzky Assoc. of America, Dominant Club. 1215 No. Louise St., Glendale, Calif.

COE, MINNA PELZ

Soprano, teacher, mus. dir. b. New York City. Prima donna Portland Opera Assn.; Pres. Portland Opera Club, 1922-35; title role in world premiere *Winona*; head voice dept. Ellison White Cons. Portland, Ore. 1933-37; sang at Opera Comique, Paris, under Eli Cohen; prod. Chinese Opera *Kuan-Yin* (Avsholomoff) w. 40 Chinese pupils, 1930. Several former pupils w. Metropolitan and Mexico Opera Houses. Organized, dir. The Melodians, Police Glee Club, The Fifty Fifty Club Chorus, Business and Prof. Women's Club Chorus, Minna Pelz Singers. Sang in Hollywood Bowl Concerts. Mus. dir. Temple Emmanuel, Beverly Hills. Husband, Willard Coe, baritone, former pupil. 1939 N. Franklin Cir., Hollywood, Calif.

COLLINS, ANTHONY VINCENT

Conductor, composer. b. Hastings, Eng., 1893. Grad. Royal Coll. of Music, London, 1922. First viola w. London Symphony Orch., Royal Opera, Covent Garden, Scottish Orch., others. Cond. London Symph. Orch., B.B.C. Orch., London Phil. Orch., Sadlers Wells Opera, London Mozart Opera. Comp. two operas, *Catherine Parr, Perseus and Andromeda*, two cantatas, six chamber works, *Quartet* (flute, violin, viola, harp). Motion picture scores incl. *Victoria the Great, Nurse Edith Cavell, Queen of Destiny*, many others. Member: AFM Local 47. 4778 Bonvue Ave., Los Angeles, Calif.

COMEL, NINO

Conductor, composer, voice teacher. b. Trieste, Italy, July 10, 1902. Ed. Trieste Cons. of Music; theory, harmony, comp. w. Maestro Smareglia; grad. diploma in piano. Mus. D., Trieste Cons. of Music. Cond. numerous operas, concerts in Europe and U. S.; cond. San Francisco Opera Assn. Comp. include: *Symphony in A major*; comic opera *Conquest of Percy*; numerous chorales and songs. Lecturer on musical subjects, especially in West. Has made English translations of many operatic librettos, incl. *Barber of Seville, Don Pasquale*. Teacher of Josephine Tuminia and Claramae Turner, both of Metropolitan Opera Co. Hobby: astronomy. 45 Maiden Lane, San Francisco, Calif.

CONKLIN, SIBYL

Contralto, opera singer, teacher of voice. b. San Diego, Calif. Member Prize Chor. Soc. England. Sang w. Carl Rosa Co. England, opera in Germany, Austria, Interstate, N. Y., Creatore, International Opera Cos. Tournee of Mexico. Member Music Makers Club. 3329 First Ave., San Diego, Calif.

CONNOR, JO ANNE

Concert pianist. b. Des Moines, Iowa, July 1, 1923. Att. Northwestern Univ., Evanston, Ill. Mus. B. St. piano w. Samuel Ball, Los Angeles. Also proficient accompanist, organist, violinist, singer. Concertized in U. S., especially in Middle West and California. Member: Pi Kappa Lambda, Delta Omricron, Tuesday Musicale (Pasadena). Hobbies: sports, gardening, outdoor activities. 1106 Okoboji Dr., Arcadia, Calif.

CONWAY, CARUTHERS

Composer, pianist. b. Los Angeles, 1921. St. piano w. Gertrude Diehl Turnell, Ariz. (2 yrs.); Thilo Becker, Los Angeles (7 yrs.); Harry Kaufman (1 yr.); comp. w. Mary Carr Moore (1½ yrs.); comp., orchestra w. Ernest Kanitz; counterpoint w. Wesley Kuhnle (2 yrs.); Comp. incl. preludes and fugues for organ; songs for organ and soprano; piano, violin works; songs *The Wanderer*, (words by Zoe Akins) and to Ernst Dowson texts. 341 So. Lafayette Park Pl., Los Angeles, Calif.

Jo Anne Connor

Caruthurs Conway

Shirley Cornell

May MacDonald Hope
Coryell

Minna Pelz Coe

Hal Davisson Crain

Mildred Couper

Marcella Craft

Albert M. Cranston

Edith Cunningham

187

COOL, HAZEL

Pianist, organist; teacher of piano and organ. Concertized in U.S. esp. w. Hammond organ. 715 Laurel St., Modesto, Calif.

CORNELL, SHIRLEY

Concert violinist. b. Santa Monica, Calif., Dec. 28, 1923. St. w. Joseph Achron, Henri Temianka, Sascha Jacobsen. Radio, motion pictures w. recording orchs. Played w. Hollywood Bowl Symphony Orch.; youngest member. Janssen Symphony, Los Angeles. Toured Europe, Central America, Australia, Southwest Pacific. Recitals in Southern and Northern Calif. Won Young Artists contest at Univ. of California at Los Angeles. Member Pro Musica Trio. Mgmt. L. E. Behymer, L. A. 236½ So. Poinsettia Pl., Los Angeles, Calif.

CORYELL, MAY MacDONALD HOPE

Concert pianist; teacher of piano. b. Leavenworth, Kan. St. piano w. Teresa Carreno, Berlin, Leopold Godowsky, Los Angeles; theory, comp. w. Carl Busch, Kansas City, Ernst Becker, Berlin, Frederick Stevenson, Los Angeles; voice w. Schoen-Rene, Berlin. Concertized extensively in Europe, U. S.; special attention to chamber music. Soloist w. Kansas City Sym., other orchs., Los Angeles Philharmonic Quartet, Coolidge Libr. chamber concerts. Intro. to U. S. new works by Bloch, Goossens, Enesco, Brescia, Bossi, Kaun, Strauss. Founder, pianist, Los Angeles Trio, 1916-28. Dir. church choirs; sp. courses mus. apprec. Hobbies: books, history. Studios: Sherman, Clay Co., Sacramento; St. George's Hall, San Mateo. Res. studio: 3771 Clay St., San Francisco, Calif.

COUPER, MILDRED

Pianist, teacher, composer, lecturer, critic. b. Buenos Aires; arrived U. S. 1915. Att. Williams Cons. Buenos Aires. Grad. Karlsruhe Baden Cons; st. w. Moszkowski, Sgambati, Cortot. Taught piano Mannes Music School, New York (9 yrs.). Now teacher piano, harmony Music Academy of the West, Santa Barbara, Calif. Comp. *Children's Pieces*, *Children's Songs*, two sets of songs to verses by Ogden Nash—*Barnyard Cogitations* and *Fur and Feathers* (sung by Radiana Pazmor); *Irish Washerwoman*, (variations for piano) played by Simmons, Cherkassky, Adele Marcus; orchestral version played by Werner Janssen Symphony, *Piano Quintet* played by Simmons Chamber Music Group, Los Angeles, Music Lovers' Soc., San Francisco. Formerly experimented and concertized in quarter-tone music, primary work in this medium *Dirge*, (publ. by New Music) 1937. 780 Mission Canyon, Santa Barbara, Calif.

COWELL, HENRY DIXON

Composer; pianist. b. Menlo Park, Calif., March 11, 1897. St. UC; Inst. of App. Mus.; w. Seeger, Wood. Guggenheim Fellow. 1931. Concertized U. S., Europe. Faculty Stanford Univ., UC, Mills Coll. Comps. incl. orch., ballet, chamber music, piano pieces, chorals. Inventor new system of Mus. notation. Rt. 10, Box 126, Fresno, Calif.

CRAFT, MARCELLA

Lyric soprano, teacher of voice. b. Indianapolis, Ind. St. w. Chas. R. Adams, Boston; Alessandro Guagni, Milan; Jacques Stueckgold, Munich; Wm. S. Brady. Sang opera in Italy, Mainz, Kiel; w. Royal Opera of Munich (5 yrs.). Concertized U.S. 1914-22, Germany 1922-32. Soloist w. Chicago, Phila., N.Y., L.A., S.F., Minneapolis, St. Louis, New Haven, Cincinnati Sym. Orch., under Stransky, Stock, Stokowski, Sir Henry Wood, Alfred Hertz, Oberhoffer, Zoch, Horatio Parker. Taught in Munich, Germany. Coaches opera, concert, oratorio. Gen. dir. of Riverside Opera Assn. for past 8 yrs. 4539 Main St., Riverside, Calif.

CRAIN, HAL DAVISSON

Baritone, teacher of singing. b. Ottawa, Kansas, Sept. 10, 1891. Att. Ottawa Univ. St. voice w. Herbert Witherspoon, Adelin Fermin, Louise von Feilitzsch. B.M., Ottawa Univ. Concerts, appearances as soloist w. various orchs., organizations. Church soloist; cond. various church choirs. Founded-cond. L. A. first Bach Cantata Soc. (3 yrs.). Managed master classes L. A. for Olga Samaroff-Stokowski and Louis Persinger. Music critic Musical America staff, both in N. Y. and L. A. (20 yrs.); reviewer for Christian Science Monitor. Dir. L. A. Conservatory (5 yrs.). Founder Southern Calif.

School of Music and Arts., L. A. Prominent students incl. William Matchan. Studio: 3173 Wilshire Blvd., L. A., Calif. Res.: 25 So. Orange Grove Ave., Pasadena, Calif.

CRANSTON, ALBERT M.

Opera basso, teacher of voice. b. Cleveland, No. Dak., Jan. 22, 1904. B.A. Jamestown Coll., N. D.; Perfect Voice Inst., Chicago, grad., post-grad., grad.-teacher. St. voice w. Eugene Fenchtinger, Sr.; opera repertory w. Pietro Cimini. Member San Carlo, San Francisco, Los Angeles, Chicago, Metropolitan Civic Opera Cos., Hollywood Bowl, others; roles incl. Zuniga, Morales, Escamillo (*Carmen*), Plunkett (*Martha*), Samuel (*Masked Ball*), Fiorello, Basilia (*Barber of Seville*), Herald, King Henry (*Lohengrin*), Ferrando (*Il Trovatore*), King, High Priest (*Aida*). Repertory of sixty operas. Concertized throughout U. S. and Canada. Sang on NBC and CBS. Appeared in motion pictures *Anthony Adverse, Night at the Opera, Rosalie, Nurse Edith Cavell, Mr. Smith Goes to Washington, Gone With the Wind, This Is The Army, The More the Merrier, Diary of a Chambermaid, Duel in the Sun*, others. Students incl. first prizewinner Orange County Musical Arts Club, 1946, 1947, many active professionals. Representative of Perfect Voice Inst. for So. Calif. Member NATS. Studio: 206 So. Rose Street, Anaheim, Calif.; res. 626 So. Vermont Ave., Los Angeles, Calif.

CRITTENDEN, RAY

Baritone, teacher of singing. b. Walnut Grove, Ill., April 19, 1892. Att. Drake Univ. Coll. of Fine Arts. St. voice w. William Shakespeare, Achille Alberti, Percy Rector Stephens, John C. Wilcox; conducting w. Father Finn; languages w. Louis Dreyfus. Mus. D., Chapman Coll., 1940. Dir. Fine Arts, Chapman Coll., 1933-43. Music Rotary Int'l Calif., Nevada, Hawaii. Concertized extensively on West Coast; repertory incls. all standard baritone operatic, oratorio roles. Lectures throughout U. S. on vocal pedagogy; clinics for voice teachers. Chairman of vocal forums Nat'l MTA, NATS, St. Louis Conventions, 1947. Member Musicians' Guild of So. Calif. (pres. four times), Western Concert Artist's League; one of three charter members NATS selected from Calif. and Nevada. 525 No. New Hampshire Ave., Los Angeles, Calif.

CROW, MARY HOBSON

Contralto, concert singer, vocal teacher. b. Salt Lake City, Utah. Started piano at early age; st. piano Univ. of Utah (normal); Univ. of Nevada (normal). Grad. Indianapolis Cons. of Music, 1918; grad. in piano and voice New England Cons. of Music, 1923. St. theory and harmony w. George Chadwick, Arthur Foote, Frederick Converse; voice w. Chas. Bennett Blickfeldt; opera w. Cunella, Carducci; mis-en-scene w. Mme. Wenschenk. Mus.B., 1935, Mus.M., 1936, U.S.C. Sang Amneris, Delilah, Countess, Azucena, Witch, Siskadee and Waskema (*Narcissa*). Taught music and art, Roseville H.S. (2 yrs.), head of music dept., Hanford H.S. (5 yrs.), Glendale H.S. (2 yrs.), Pacific Inst. of Music & Fine Arts (3 yrs.), voice, Chapman Coll. (1 yr.), Glendale schools, and pvt. studio. Member: Mu Pi Epsilon, Pi Kappa Lambda; music chairman Kiwanis Club, Tijunga. Studio: 642 No. LaBrea Ave., Los Angeles; res. 1628 Irving Ave., Glendale, Calif.

CROWN, JOHN

Pianist, teacher. b. Hove. England, 1912. Att. Hoch's Cons., Germany, Academy of Vienna. St. w. Moritz Rosenthal, Rich Stoehr. Concertized England, Australia, Germany, U. S. 1333 N. Orange Grove Ave., Los Angeles 46, Calif.

CUNNINGHAM, EDITH

Pianist, composer. b. Virginia City, Nev. Att. Coll. of Notre Dame. Grad. Coll. of the Pacific, Stockton. St. piano w. Pierre Douillet, Wallace Sabin; comp. w. William J. McCoy, Domenico Brescia, Mills College. Former member Athenian Trio. Organized-cond. Richmond Trio (3 yrs.). Comp. incl.: *Gifts, Remembrance*, sung World's Fair, 1938, Treasure Island by Armand Girard, *Exile, When Love Passed By, A Prayer for Peace, Supplication, Misunderstood*, trios, quartets for strings. Won San Francisco Musical Club Contest w. song, *Gifts*. Member Calif. Composers and Writers Club, S. F. Musical Society, MTA. 428 28th St., Richmond, Calif.

Gennaro M. Curci

CURCI, GENNARO MARIO

Basso, teacher of voice, opera coach. b. Trani, Italy, 1889. Grad Royal Acad. of Santa Cecelia, Rome (degree, tchr.); st. voice w. Antonio Cotogni, piano w. Bernardino Molinari. Operatic debut 1910. App. as leading basso in 69 operas throughout Europe, South, Central America, under Toscanini, Mignone, Serafin, other cond. Tchr., coach several Metropolitan Opera singers. Comp. incl. numerous songs (pub. Ricordi; Hinds, Hayden & Eldredge; Cardilli), sung by Gigli, Schipa, Tokatyan, Stracciari, Besanzoni, etc. Song *One Night in Venice* sung by Gigli in UFA film. Studios in New York several years; recent years in Los Angeles. 300 N. Citrus Ave., Los Angeles, Calif.

CURTIS, GRACE SPELLACY

Teacher of piano. b. Lima, Ohio. St. piano w. mother, Mrs. Simon Spellacy, concert pianist. Att. Cincinnati Cons. of Music w. Fred Shaler Evans (3 yrs.), Hugo Masfield, San Francisco, Oscar Kinsey, John Garroway, Sister Celestine (St. Mary's Academy), Helen Curtis, Helen Miller (L. A.). Comp. *Yankee Boy*, (Miller Mus.), *Nocturne and Caprice* (pf.) (mss). Teacher of Leslie Scott. Member MTA. Hobby: flowers. 613 Woodrow St. Taft, Calif.

CUTTER, BELLE FORBES

Voice consultant; b. Harbor Springs, Mich. St. w. Proschowski (Paris), Lamperti, Eva Wilke (Berlin). Music dir. at Chicago Musical Coll. (10 yrs.); sang in opera in Germany, sang for Kaiser Wilhelm of Germany and Queen of Holland; on radio U. S. coast to coast (13 yrs.); first woman on staff of WGN (Chicago Tribune); starred on sponsored programs, Chicago-Buick, Manor House Coffee, Thompsons' Malted Milk; appearances with Chicago Edison Symph., N. Y. Symph. Orch., etc.; concertized in Europe and U. S. A. Teacher of Evabelle Tanner, Claudia Wirsen, Mme. Emma Roe, Melita Kreig, Stephen Whitford (all teachers), Gina Vandeveer (Vienna Opera), Dorothy Herman, Mildred Gerber (both w. Chicago Opera), Eleanor Phelps, (formerly leading lady for Maurice Evans), Zelma Smithpeter (twice winner of largest scholarship for voice given by Chi. Mus. Col.), Nathan Cherney, Mary Jane Walsh (leading lady of *I'd Rather Be Right* and other B'way productions) Lillian Cornell, Paramount Pictures, Joseph Williams (w. *Winged Victory*), Faye Marlowe (20th Cent.-Fox); Robert Franklin, (Columbia Broadcasting System); Jeannette Rollins (L. A. Civic Light Opera), Mervin Allan (*The Desert Song*). 7526 Fountain Ave., Hollywood, Calif.

CUTTER, MURRAY

Arranger, orchestrator, composer. b. Nice, France, 1902. Organist Cath. Ch., Nice, France. Pianist w. salon and concert orchs. Toured Europe w. American dance bands. Music supervisor Warner Bros. Theater, Phila., Roxy Theatre, N. Y. Arr. radio, Paul Whiteman Orch. Billy Rose shows, 1933-36. 426 Bonhill Rd., Los Angeles 24, Calif.

CYKLER, EDMUND A.

Pedagog, conductor. b. San Jose, Calif. Ph.D. Univ. of Prague. B.A. Univ. of Calif. St. w. J. Feld, Prague. Cond. L. A. All-City Sr. H.S. Orch., Jr. Coll. Orch. Faculty Sacramento Jr. Coll., L. A. Jr. Coll. (spec. in mus. hist.); Univ. Calif., summer session, 1931-33. Faculty Univ. of Oregon, Eugene, Ore.

DAMIANI, LEO GEORGE

Conductor: founder, music director Burbank Symphony. b. St. Paul, Minn., July 29, 1914. St. violin w. Chester Campbell, McPhail School of Music, Robert Pollack. Juilliard School of Music, New York, conducting, score analysis harmony w. Mary Carr Moore. Violinist w. Twin Cities Civic Symphony, and Minneapolis Symphony Orch. Formerly teacher of violin, cond. various instru. ensembles. To date cond 26 symphony concerts Burbank Symphony Orch.; guest cond. Beverly Hills Symphony. Comp. works for strings; tone poem, *Quest*. Member Jr. Chamber of Commerce, Burbank; AFM Local 47. Hobbies: golf, swimming, riding. Cond.,

trained symphony orch. in motion picture, *Humoresque*. Music Department, Warner Bros. Studio, Burbank, Calif.

DANIELS, MARK

Baritone, teacher of voice, radio artist. b. Griggsville, Ill. St. voice w. Sara Glance Bowman, Geo. Taglieri (6 yrs.), Adelin Fermin (Rochester, N.Y.). Soloist church choir at age 16. Toured U.S. as memb. of Male Quartet. Concertized; app. in opera w. Portland Opera Assn.; Rochester American Co.; Eastman Theater; American Opera Co., in *Pagliacci*, *Faust*, *Butterfly*, *Martha*, *Marriage of Figaro*, w. Chicago Civic Opera in *Bohemian Girl*, *Chimes of Normandy*, *Gondoliers*, *Yeomen of the Guard*; two seasons w. Central City Opera Assn., Denver; M.C. KEX Concert program for Lipman-Wolf Concert Hour. Soloist, cantor Temple Israel; First Church Christ Sci., Portland, Ore. Hobby: dogs. Studio: Ainsworth Bldg., Portland, Ore.

DANZ, LOUIS

Lecturer on music and art, author, composer. b. St. Paul, Minn., 1887. St. music privately in U. S. and abroad. Publ. comp. for piano. Author many articles and books, incl. *Zarathustra, Jr.* (Brentano), *The Psychologist Looks at Art*, *Personal Revolution and Picasso* (Longmans, Green) *It is Still the Morning*, (novel) (Morrow) *There is a Rebel in the Arts*, *Not Always Hero*, *Art, Man and Wonder*—books dealing w. interrelation of music and art as mirrors of their period and subject of music and art from viewpoint of structure, color, general symbolism w. ref. to social conditions. 510 S. Main St., Santa Ana, Calif.

DARVAS, FRANZ

Concert pianist; teacher of piano, French, German. b. Vienna, Austria, March 14, 1889. St. piano, theory w. Adolf Kraus, Vienna; Louis Victor Saar, Rafael Joseffy (5 yrs.), Percy Goetschius (5 yrs.), Frank Damrosch, Franklin W. Robinson, New York; Vincent d'Indy, Paul Vidal, Paris. B.S. Coll. of the City of New York 1909; grad. study Columbia Univ. 1912-13; Mus. M. Immaculate Heart Coll. 1935; M.A. Univ. of So. Calif. 1941; working on Ph.D. USC. Diploma in prac. comp., Inst. of Musical Art, N. Y. 1912. Piano and lecture recitals in New York, Arizona, California. Faculty Inst. of Musical Art, N. Y.; Arizona Sch. of Mus., Phoenix; Orange County Sch. of Fine Arts, Anaheim, Calif.; Immaculate Heart Coll., Los Angeles, Calif. Comp. incl. *La Belle Dame Sans Merci* (orch.), *Piano Concerto*, piano pieces, songs. 5662 Fernwood Ave., Los Angeles 28, Calif.

DAUN, HELEN ADELE (Mrs. Leo Joseph)

Pianist, organist, teacher. b. Los Angeles, Calif., April 24, 1897. St. piano w. Olga Steeb, Guy Bevier Williams; organ w. Edith Rounds Smith; L.A. Cons.; voice w. Russell E. Booker, Arthur Babcock at L.A. Cons. of Mus., Affil. tchr. Sherwood Music School, L.A. Cons.; mus. dir. Redlands Preparatory School 1928-1936. Chamber music appearances. Colleague member Spinet, MTA; state board, CMTA. Hobbies: art, child psychology and education. 1329 No. Chrysolite Ave., Mentone, Calif.

DAVID, ANNE LOUISE

Concert harpist, pianist, composer, accompanist. b. Boston, Mass. St. theory w. Arthur Foote, Edward MacDowell, Heinrich Gebhardt; pf. accomp. w. Emil Mollenhauer; harp. w. Schuecker, Sassoli. Concertized since age nine; toured U.S., Europe as soloist, also collab. w. Sarah Bernhardt, Alma Gluck, Eddy, others. Studio accomp. (pf) for Nordica, the DeReszkes, Melba, Plancon. At age 13 taught harp, pf. in New York, San Francisco. During the two world wars gave over 4000 concerts for USO, Army, Navy, Air Bases and 525 hospital concerts. Many compositions, arrangements (Bach *Preludes*, *Fugues*, etc.) for harp, pub. by G. Schirmer, Boston Mus. Co. Recordings of Debussy, Brahms, Beethoven, Wagner, other works. Plays specially made harp, designed in lavender, gold. Hobby, aviation. Studio: Fairmont Hotel, San Francisco, Calif.

Belle Forbes Cutter

Ray Critenden

Bain Dayman

Leo George Damiani

Mark Daniels

Louis Danz

Franz Darvas

Helen Adele Daun

Anne Louise David

Frederick Davis

Verner D. Delaney

192

Abby De Avirett

DAVIS, FREDERICK

Teacher of voice, chorus; choral conductor. b. Neiafu, Vavau, Tonga (Friendly Is.), Jan. 15, 1909. Att. Auckland Univ. Coll., New Zealand; st. theory, comp. w. William E. Thomas, violin w. Henry C. Engel, voice w. William Gard, Mario Constantini, Lazar S. Samoiloff. Cond. Latvian Singers transcontinental tour, 1934-35; mus. dir. Salt Lake City Civic Opera.; cond. Salt Lake Philharmonic Choir, Swanee Singers Male Chorus (Utah, Los Angeles, San Francisco), Greek Orthodox Church choir, Salt Lake City. Comp. of choral and vocal music. Member; NATS Nat'l Assn. for American Conductors and Composers; Salt Lake City Lions Club; Chairman, Choral Dept. Utah Fed. of Music Clubs; dir. (board) Cambrian Assn., Salt Lake City. Hobbies: reading, tennis, hiking. Res. 233 Fourth Ave., Salt Lake City 3, Utah; studio: 606 Templeton Bldg., Salt Lake City 1, Utah.

DAVISE, HUGO

Composer, pianist. b. L. A., Calif., 1907. Att. Univ. of Calif.; B.E., M.A. in philos. St. w. Henry Schoenefeld, Arnold J. Gantvoort, Leonard Walker. Comp. of *Four Preludes, Music Box, Woodwind Quintet, Piano Concerto, String Quartet, Four M Suite* (orch.) Member Amer. Comp. Alliance, N. Y., 2507 Wellington Rd., Los Angeles, Calif.

DAYMAN, BAIN

Teacher of voice, singer; vocal coach. b. Konotop, Russia. St. w. father and European teachers during childhood. Grad. Broadview Coll. (USA). St. w. Herbert Witherspoon, Louis Arthur Russell, Frederic Warren, J. C. Malatesta, Albert E. Ruff, Edwin J. Meyer. Anatomy and physiology of the throat Calif. Lutheran Hospital under Dr. George McCoy. A.B., Ph.D. degrees. Concert appearances New York, Canada, Chicago, San Francisco and L. A. Special artist, MGM Studios. Former member Apollo Club, Chicago. Hobbies: swimming, ice-skating, hiking, reading. Studio: 6087 Sunset Blvd., Hollywood, Calif.

De AVIRETT, ABBY.

Pianist; teacher of piano. b. Austin, Texas, Nov. 16, 1882; d. Los Angeles, Calif., May 31, 1947. Early studies w. mother. St. piano w. William Mason, Carl G. Schmidt, New York; pvt. and master classes w. Busoni, Godowsky in Europe, 1900, 1910, 1924; comp. w. Wolff, Hoshschule, Berlin. Prof. pupils incl.: Elizabeth O'Neil (Mrs. Abby de Avirett), Emil Danenberg, Earle Voorhies, Shirley Ross, Kathreen Reime, Adeline Ostrowsky, Amelia Hester, Yvette Wilcox, Warren Langlie, Betty Hain Lewin, Barbara Sheldon, Jack Crossan, Nancy Joy Currie, Bess Daniels, Alice S. Durham, Raymond McFeeters, Irene Trepanier, Julia Howell, John Garth, Reta Mitchell; also accompanists and pvt. and public school tchrs. Studio: 267 S. Arden Blvd., Los Angeles, Calif.

Editor's Note:

Abby De Avirett, who passed away while this volume was being compiled, was one of the outstanding pedagogs of Southern California, whose untimely demise was mourned by all his colleagues. Through his individual efforts he contributed much to the advancement of music in Los Angeles, where he was a pioneer. He trained a host of pupils who also added to the progress of music locally, some of them internationally.

De AVIRETT, ELIZABETH

Concert pianist; teacher of piano. b. near Sioux Falls, S. D. (nee Elizabeth O'Neil). St. piano w. Abby de Avirett, Los Angeles; Edwin Hughes, Josef Lhevinne, New York and Chicago (pvt. and master classes). Concertized throughout U. S.; app. as soloist w. orchs., recitals, club programs in Sou. Calif. Asst., later co-teacher w. Abby de Avirett. Studio: 267 S. Arden Blvd., Los Angeles, Calif.

de GRASSI, ANTONIO JOACHIM

(*See:* GRASSI)

de JAHN, AGNES EYRE

(*See:* JAHN)

de KEREKJARTO, DUCI

(*See:* KEREKJARTO)

DELANEY, VERNER D.

Ass't. Prof. of Music, Fresno State College. b. Waterbury, Nebr., Dec. 7, 1898. Att. Lawrence Cons. of Music. B.A., M.A., Univ. of Washington. Grad. work Univ. of Calif., Berkeley; Columbia Tchrs. Coll., New York City, Westminster Choir School, Princeton, N. J. Voice w. August Werner, Seattle; Mme. Melanie Guttman Rice, Chas. Baker, Eva Gauthier, N.Y.C. Concertized throughout midwest w. Univ. of Wash. Symphony, Virginia Sym., Duluth Sym., Iowa State Tchrs. Coll. Sym. and Chor., Pacific Philharmonic Chorus, Oakland, San Jose Municipal Chorus. Dir. St. James Episcopal Cathedral Choir, Fresno; Fresno Male Chorus; Cecilian Singers of Fresno. Taught in Seattle public schools. Head of voice, Choral dept. Fresno State Coll. past six yrs. Member: Amer. Assn. of Univ. Prof., NATS, Mus. Edu. Nat'l. Conf., Phi Mu Alpha Sinfonia, Sigma Chapter, Fresno Rotary Club, Executive Club. Hobbies: collecting records, gardening. Fresno State College, Fresno, Calif.

de la VEGA, MARIA

Soprano, concert and opera. b. Ocotlan, Jalisco. St. voice, theory w. Francisco Camacho Vega, Justino Camacho Vega, L. A. Prima donna, Los Angeles Civic Grand Opera Assn. Roles incl. Violetta (*La Traviata*), Nedda (*Pagliacci*), Butterfly, Mimi (*La Boheme*), etc. Numerous concerts and recitals throughout Southern Calif. Member AGVA. Hobby: costume design. 510 No. Commonwealth Ave., Hollywood, Calif.

DELMAR, DEZSO

Pianist, composer. b. Hungary, 1891. St. Royal Acad. of Music, Budapest, w. Bela Bartok, Arpad Szendy (pupil of Liszt), Zoltan Kodaly. Grad. Univ. of Budapest, accredited professor of music. Solo and chamber music recitals in Europe, U.S. under mgt. of Nat'l Music League. Comp. Symphony in c-minor (mss), String Quartet in g-minor (mss), 15 Fugues and Inventions (mss), *Berceuse, Toccata, Kompon,* and others (pub. Moravety Freres, Leipsig, Timisoara, Budapest). Member MTA. 1622¼ No. Alvarado St., Los Angeles, Calif.

DEMING, ROGER

Pianist, accompanist, coach of piano and voice repertory. Piano w. Egon Petri (Europe). Assoc. w. D'Alvarez, Louis Graveure, Schumann-Heink, Leonore Sparks, Ellen Beach Yaw. Concertized throughout U.S. Studio in New York City for 20 years. Member Nat'l Ass'n for American Composers and Conductors. Hobby, composing. 1943 Rose Villa, Pasadena, Calif.

de RIMANOCZY, JEAN

Prof. of violin and chamber music, Cornish School of Music. b. Vienna, Austria, Feb. 4, 1904. Ed. in Budapest; att. Royal Hungarian Acad. of Music. Artist's Diploma Extraordinare Degree from Royal Academy. St. w. Eugene Hubay, Zoltan Kodaly, Bela Bartok. Concert tour of Europe, 1924-25. Came to America, 1925. Member Minneapolis Symphony; prof. Duluth School of Music, 1926-27. Toured western U.S. as soloist, 1927-28. Soloist w. Toronto, Winnipeg, Calgary, Vancouver, Seattle, Tacoma, Symphony orchs. Cond. radio orchs., chamber music groups for Canadian Broadcasting Corp. Founded and cond. Calgary Philharmonic; lectured for Carnegie Foundation. Concertmaster Vancouver Symphony Orch. 1933-43; concertmaster and assoc. cond., Seattle Symphony since 1944; conductor, soloist Canadian Broadcasting Corp. Hobbies: target shooting, flying, racing-cars. Cornish School of Music, Seattle, Wash.

DER ZAKARIAN, ARAM G.

Concert violinist; teacher of violin. b. Providence, R. I. Att. San Francisco Cons. of Mus. St. violin w. Cesar Thompson, Robert Pollak, Samuel Gardner; comp. w. Ernest Bloch. Gave talks on violin for MTA Conv. 1933, 1938; leader round table disc. Students incl. Nancy Rosenthal, Irene Balasis, Vasken Chakmakjian. Member board of dir. Kern Philharmonic Soc. Hobby, photography. Wife, Katherine Franck, pianist, singer; st. piano w. Agnes de Jahn, Mary Geerts; voice w. Otto Morando, Bell T. Ritchie. Dir of instr. music dept., Bakersfield City Schools. 2881 N. Inyo St., Bakersfield, Calif.

Elizabeth De Avirett

Madge de Witt

Maria de la Vega

Aram G. and
Catherine Der Zakarian

Tilli Dieterle

Dezso Delmar

Rudy de Saxe

195

DE SAXE, RUDY

Composer, conductor. b. Cairo, Egypt. St. comp., theory in Bologna, Rome, Italy. Faculty: Southwestern Coll., Columbia Univ. Comp. incl. two *Symphonies*, *Aurora* (sym. poem), *Prayer for a Soldier* (orch.), *Paumanok* (sym. poem on Whitman's *Sea Drift*), *Trees* (orch.), *Concerto* (piano and orch.), *Monastero* (str. quartet), *Hail, My Native Land* (march), *Rhapsody* (pf.), *Parodiette* (pf.), *A toi mon bien aimee* (vocal), piano pieces, songs, film scores. Member: Nat'l. Assn. of Amer. Comp. and Cond.; ASMA. Editor *The Score*. official organ ASMA Reviewer film music for Hollywood Review. Now scoring motion pictures at various Hollywood studios. 3838 Ventura Canyon, Sherman Oaks, Calif.

de SEGUROLA, ANDRES
(*See:* SEGUROLA)

DETERMANN, JEANNE TURPIN

Concert singer, lyric soprano. b. New York City, 1918. St. voice, piano, harmony, Venice H.S.; voice w. Coster-Hewlett Studios, Wm. Tyroler, Sutro-Seyler Studio (Alice Mock) Soloist *Messiah*, *Creation* at leading churches in Los Angeles, Hollywood, Santa Monica. Guest soloist Tabernacle, Salt Lake City; Composer's Forum, Santa Barbara, 1941; Santa Barbara Summer Fiesta; Santa Monica Symphony series, 1947; light opera series KFI (Claude Sweeten), 1946; sang for U.S.O. and Red Cross Shows, 1943-47; permanent soloist Trinity Baptist Church, Santa Monica. Recorded *Lullaby* by Florence Olds LaGatta (Co-Art). 4th Prize winner 1947 Atwater Kent auditions. 12516 Pacific Ave., Mar Vista, Calif.

DEUTSCH, ADOLPH

Composer, conductor, pianist. b. London, England, 1897. Grad. Royal Acad. of Music, London. Comp. incl. *Scottish Suite* (orch. and bagpipes), *Essay on Waltzes* (orch.). *The Great Garrick, They Won't Forget, Swing Your Lady, Espionage Agent, Years Without Days*, others. 1010 Moraga Dr., Los Angeles, Calif.

de WITT, MADGE

Vocal teacher; concert, opera singer; radio artist. b. Utah. Grad. State Normal School, Albion, Idaho, and National Academy of Music, N. Y. St. voice w. David Bispham, McKenzie Gordon, others; protegee of Mme. Schumann-Heink. Concertized in U. S. for Nat'l Fed. of Women's Clubs; appeared on programs with Antonio Scotti and Schumann-Heink; soloist KPO, KGO. Teacher of Grace Fettes, soprano, 1st prize winner Talent Parade, Golden Gate International Exposition, 1939; Peggy Denning, contralto, prize winner Eisteddfod Musical Festival, 1939, also Exposition winner; and Anita Aguerra, coloratura, concertizing in South America (decorated with gold medal by President of Nicaragua in 1946) Studio: 1698 Portola Dr., San Francisco, Calif.

DEWSE, CARL W.

Baritone, teacher of singing, choral conductor. b. Lawrence, Kans., 1906. Att. Cons. of Music, Hays, Kans.; Univ. of Redlands; won $2,000 Marion Talley Scholarship, 1928; st. voice w. Enrico Rosati (N.Y.); languages w. Matilda Trucco; piano, theory w. Eduardo Trucco. Soloist WRNY, WDAF, WIBW, KFSD, KSDJ; sang leading roles in *Faust*, *Bartered Bride, Pygmalion*, in Riverside, Redlands, San Diego; light opera at Jolson Theatre, N.Y. 1929-30; toured w. *The Great European Passion Play* 1935; Redpath Chautauqua (middle west); founder-director San Diego Community Chorus; co-founder Musical Merit Foundation; dir. church choir, San Diego; cond. Handel's *Messiah* annually for last 10 yrs.; chorus dir. *Black Hills Passion Play* 1947; Verdi *Requiem* 1947. Member: Phi Mu Alpha, MTA. Hobby: painting. Wife, Charlotte Dewse, teacher of piano and organ; st. at Univ. of Redlands w. Arthur Poister; member AGO, MTA. 4305 Hortensia St., San Diego, Calif.

de ZUNIGA, JULIA BAL
(*See:* ZUNIGA)

DIETERLE, TILLI

Accompanist, teacher. Faculty Beverly Hills Cons. of Music since 1943. b. Austria, 1923. St. piano age five w. Louise Mardiros (10 yrs.); Samuel Ball, Pauline Cohn (4½ yrs.); theory, harmony, comp. at UCLA w. Schoenberg. Mus.B. UCLA. Won award at Festival Allied Arts (Calif., 1935); Music War Council of America award (Chicago, 1945) Toured Pac. Coast, Canada as accomp. w. Mary Tiffany, Fred Martel, Murice Reva. Soloist KMTR, now KLAC. Pupils include Larry Day, Cyrene Epstein (on KPAS *Pianists of the Future*. 1937 Greenfield Ave., Los Angeles 24, Calif.

DOBBS, RALPH

Concert pianist, teacher. b. Chicago, Ill., 1908. Att. Chicago Musical Coll., American Cons. of Music. St. piano w. Alexander Raab, Maurice Aronson, Laura Harris; theory, comp., chamber music w. Adolf Weidig. Master class w. Percy Grainger (3 summers). App. in Hollywood Bowl (Grainger), Los Angeles Philharmonic (Rodzinski), Chicago Symphony (Stock). Toured w. Paul Robeson. Over 60 appearances in Northwest since affil. w. Willamette Univ. Three seasons w. Columbia Concerts Corp. Willamette University, Salem, Ore.

DONAHUE, LESTER

Concert pianist. b. Los Angeles, Calif. St. piano w. Thilo Becker, L. A.; Krause, Berlin; Egon Petri, Rudolph Ganz. Berlin debut, Beethoven Saal, 1913; London, Sterning Hall, 1914; New York, Aeolian Hall, 1915. Concertized throughout the world. U.S. tours incl. Boston, Chicago, Phila., Detroit, Wash., San Francisco, Los Angeles. Soloist, Hollywood Bowl its first year (1922); thrice since. Made ten appearances w. Stokowski, Phila., orch., 1926-27. Soloist w. most major symphony orchestras of the world. Introduced Hammond Piano in U.S., European Tour, 1928. Vice-pres. Municipal Art Comm., L. A., last three years. Res.: 2181 West 25th St., Los Angeles, Calif.

DOUGLASS, SADIE

Teacher of piano. b. LaCrosse, Wisc. Piano w. Ida Schumann, Thilo Becker; organ w. Chas. Demarest; harmony w. Chas. Demarest, Carolyn Alchin; voice w. Catherine Collette, Monnie Hayes Hastings. Soloist Fourth Church of Christ, Scientist (9 yrs.). Past-Pres. Dominant Club. Member MTA. 324 So. Kenmore Ave., Los Angeles, Calif.

DRUCKER, VLADIMIR

Trumpeter. b. Russia, 1898. Grad Moscow Cons. in trumpet, violin, tympani. Arr. U. S., 1919. Soloist Los Angeles Symphony (Rothwell). Solo trumpeter New York, San Francisco, Cleveland, Hollywood Bowl Symphonies. Invited to play solo trumpet in opera and symphony in U.S.S.R. and to teach at Moscow Cons. 1932. Invited by Toscanini to join New York Philharmonic. First trumpet w. Werner Janssen Symph., Santa Monica Symphony, Columbia Studio Orch. Daughter Valeska (10 yrs.) talented pianist. Wife, Virginia Strong, concert singer, soloist w. Seattle Symphony and Artur Rodzinski. 2177 Hollyridge Dr., Los Angeles, Calif.

DULEY, GEORGE TOWER

Teacher of voice and piano. b. Upland, Calif., June 12, 1905. St. w. Elsie Duley Hess, Vinal Frederickson, Edward Horton, Ernest Douglas, S. Earle Blakeslee, others. Appeared as pianist, organist, singer throughout Calif., Mexico until 1931. Pres. Civic Concert Assn.; board of dir. of Chaffey Art Assn. Sponsor of Civic Concert Assn. Wife, Dorothy Williams, teacher of dance. b. Phila., Penna., Sept. 13, 1909. St. w. Florence Cowanova, Theo. Kosloff, Stefano Mascagno, Elisa Cansino, Jose Fernandez, Harold Kreutzburg. D. M. of A. Degree. Appeared throughout U. S., Mexico. Choreographed many ballets for schools, clubs, some w. symphony orch. Member: So. Calif. Dancing Tchrs. Assn. Club No. 1; Sponsor Civic Concert Assn. Hobby, gardening. Studio: 222 East B. St., Ontario, Calif. Res.: 511 Princeton St., Ontario, Calif.

Carl W. Dewse

DUNHAM, ROWLAND W.

Dean, Coll. of Music, Univ. of Colorado. b. Melrose, Mass., April 18, 1885. St. New England Cons.; Amer. Cons., Fontainebleau w. Widor, Farnam. Fellow, AGO. Concert organist, music lecturer. Comp. of church music. Member Phi Mu Alpha; AGO (examiner). Assoc. Ed. American Organist; contrib. Etude, Consumers' Research. Hobbies: bridge, billiards, baseball. 789 15th St., Boulder, Colo.

DUNING, GEORGE WILLIAM

Conductor, composer, arranger. b. Richmond, Ind., 1908. Majored in theory Cincinnati Cons. of Music; comp. w. Mario Castlenuevo-Tedesco. Musical dir. and supervisor radio programs Kollege of Musical Knowledge, (7½ yrs.). Recording arrangements for Victor, Columbia and Graphic Records. Arranged, conducted Command Performances for Navy Armed Forces Radio Services. Mus. Supervisor of Eddie Cantor's picture Show Business. Arranged production numbers for Tonight and Every Night, Tars and Spars, Thousand and One Nights, Jolson Story. Screen credits for Down to Earth, Johnny O'Clock, The Guilt of Janet Ames, The Corpse Came C.O.D., Her Husband's Affairs. Comp. of theme and variations, St. James Infirmary. Charter member Screen Composers Guild; member ASMA, SWPA. Hobbies: cameras and guns. Columbia Pictures Corp., Hollywood, Calif. Management Burr G. Blair, Beverly Hills, Calif.

DUNNING, OWEN C.

Trumpeter, Mus. Director KOIN. b. Hoquaim, Wash., 1904. St. trumpet w. Nicholas and Frank Heric; violin, viola, bass, Fisher School of Music ,Walla Walla, Wash. Toured Orpheum Circuit on West Coast w. Herman Kenin Orch. Played w. Columbia Theatre Concert Orch., Portland. First trumpet Portland Symphony under Lemay. Staff musician and arr. KOIN (14 yrs.). Music dir. since 1944. Comp., arr. music for White Fires of Inspiration and other radio dramatic shows. Hobbies: fishing, hunting. KOIN, Portland, Ore .

DURHAM, ALICE S.

Teacher of piano. b. Malvern, Iowa. Grad. Galesburg H.S. (Ill.), harmony, extension dept. USC. Asst. Tchr. to Abby DeAvirett (1920-35); normal and master classes w. Dr. Guy Maier (1940-45); Colleague-child specialist degree, MTA; accredited tchr. Progressive Series of Piano Lessons. Advisor Eta Chapter Nat'l Soc. of Pi Mu; past-pres. Long Beach Mus. Arts Club; member: MTA; Woman's Music Club, artist's chair; Long Beach Phil. Orch. Assn. Pupils incl. Mary Louise Williams Smith and Dorothy Woodruff Archer. Hobby, flower gardening. 234 Ximeno Ave., Long Beach, Calif.

EAMES, HENRY PURMORT

Prof. of musical art and aesthetics, Claremont Grad. College. b. Chicago, Ill., 1872. St. theory, piano w. W.S.B. Matthews; piano, William Sherwood, Ignace Paderewski; comp. Ivan Knorr. B. A., L.L.B., and Mus. D. Prof. musical art, aesthetics Scripps Coll., Claremont, 1927-41; now Prof. Emeritus, Scripps Coll.; Claremont Grad. Coll. 1929 to present. Lectured many summer courses at various colleges: i.e. U.C. at Berkeley, U.C.L.A., Univ. of Hawaii, Honolulu, Univ. of New Mexico, Imperial Univ., Tokyo, Japan, Claremont Grad. Coll., Comp. opera seria (1 act); 5 pageants; light (3-act) opera; two orch. suites, 30 publ. songs, piano teaching pieces. Member: Soc. of Amer. Mus. (Pres. 1914-18); Cliff Dwellers, Philosophical Soc., American Soc. for Aesthetics (Pres. So. Calif. Div. 1944-46), Native Composers, etc. Claremont Graduate College, Claremont, Calif. Res.: 137 W. 7th St., Claremont, Calif.

EDWARDS, HUGH H.

General director, founder, American Operatic Laboratory; baritone. b. Mineola, Texas. Won local Atwater Kent contest. Concertized in U. S., esp. Los Angeles and vicinity. Sang w. Los Angeles Civic Light Opera Assn., various other local opera prods. Served w. Air Forces (Capt.) incl. India, China, 1942-45. Organized American Operatic Lab. 1945; gave 40 perf. in first year. American Operatic Laboratory. 4705½ Elmwood Ave., Hollywood 4, Calif.

EICHENLAUB, FRANCK AND BEATRICE

Franck, Teacher. b. Vancouver, Wash., 1886. Att. St. Mary's Coll., Oakland. St. w. Karl Markees, Royal Sch. of Music, Berlin, 1903-4, Otokar Sevcik, Prague, 1904-8, Ovide Musin, Brussels, 1908-9. Concertized in Germany, Belgium. Played before King Albert of Belgium, 1908. Organized Portland Concert Trio, Portland String Quartet. Pres. Portland Symphony Orch. several yrs. Member MTA. Hobbies: gardening, sketching. Wife, Beatrice. b. Craftsbury, Vt. St. w. Marie Bender, Royal Sch. of Music, Berlin, 1903, Xaver Scharwenka, Berlin, 1904, Mme. Eylau, Berlin, 1908-9. Assoc. w. husband in sonata recitals, concerts. Research in pedagogical work. Member MTA. Hobby, experiments in kitchen. Pythian Bldg., 918 S.W. Yamhill St., Portland, Ore.

ELKUS, ALBERT I.

Prof. of music, composer. b. Sacramento, Calif., 1884. B.L. Univ. Calif., 1906, M.L. 1907. St. piano w. Hugo Mansfeldt, Harold Bauer, Josef Lhevinne; comp. w. Oscar Weil, Carl Prohaska, Robert Fuchs. Head theory dept. S. F. Cons. of Music 1923-25, 1930-37; tchr. theory, comp. Dominican Coll., San Rafael, Calif., 1924-31; Lecturer Mills Coll. 1929-33; Univ. Calif. 1931-35; dir. Univ. Orch. since 1934; prof. music since 1935; chairman music dept. since 1937. Comp. incl. I Am The Reaper (male cho.), Concertino on Lezione III of Ariosti (chamber orch.), On a Merry Folk Tune (orch.), Impressions from a Greek Tragedy (orch.), songs, piano pieces. Juilliard publ. award 1935; co-editor The Letters and Papers of Oscar Weil. 1209 Shattuck Ave., Berkeley, Calif.

ELLIS, CAROL WEISKOPF

Soprano, teacher of voice. b. Los Angeles, Dec. 16, 1913. Att. L. A. City College, Zoellner Cons. St. piano w. William Killgrove, Mme Marie Bal; voice w. John D. Nield, Louise Gude, Lillian Flickinger, Menotti Frascona, Chas. Dalmores, Hans Blechschmidt. Soloist Burbank Symphony, Redlands Bowl. Prima donna, Lyric Light Opera Co., L.A. Light Opera Co. Solo work in film studios, radio, oratorio, churches, First Baptist Ch. of Hollywood, Temple Israel. Numerous choral arrangements of church music. Film recordings, Anthony Adverse, Midsummer Night's Dream, others. Hobby: ceramics. 919 No. Lamer St., Burbank, Calif.

ELLIS, DOROTHY

Concert pianist, teacher of piano. b. Detroit, Mich. St. piano w. Alexis Kall, coached w. Gretchaninov, Prokofiev. Concert tours, recitals throughout U. S., app. Los Angeles, New Orleans, Chicago, other centers. Concert soli, films, radio; made one of first piano recordings in sound pictures in The Valiant (Paul Muni). Comp. incl.: Concerto (piano and orch.), Color Suite, piano pieces, songs. Member: Phi Beta; Sherman Oaks Woman's Club, AFM Local 47. Hobbies: gardening, painting, sports. 15100 Sutton Ave., Sherman Oaks, Calif.

ELLIS, JOHN

Choral director, arranger, teacher of voice, baritone. b. Washington, D. C., July 15, 1915. Att. L. A. City College, Occidental College Seminars. Voice w. Pietro Cimini. (6 yrs.). Debut as Dancairo (Carmen). Sang w. San Francisco Opera, 1935-36. Hollywood Bowl, 1933-38. Also Bowl sound consultant. Staff soloist KFWB (2 yrs.); Burbank Symphony, others. Dir. and founder Burbank Civic Chorus; asst. cond. Burbank Orch. Soloist-dir. of church choirs. Lecturer on chorus music. Music editor, Burbank Evening Review. Forty opera roles in repertory. Film studio vocal scoring for 7 yrs. Sec. Treas., San Fernando Chapter Choral Conds. Guild. Memb. Lions Club. Hobbies: collecting historical records, deep sea fishing. 919 No. Lamer St., Burbank, Calif.

ELMASSIAN, ZARUHI

Lyric soprano. b. Lynn, Mass. Att. Fresno State Coll., Univ. of Calif., scholarship New England Cons., Boston, 1939-41. Voice w. Louise Gude-Funk, Mme. Sundelius. Scholarship Eastman School of Music, New York. Winner State & Nat'l Fed. Music Clubs competition, 1931. Appeared w. Los Angeles-San Francisco Civic Opera in Carmen, Tannhauser, Lucia, Traviata, Hansel and Gretel, Manon. Oratorio soloist, Messiah, Elijah, St. Paul. Soloist Los Angeles Phil. Orch. (Rodzinski), 1932; in Ninth Symphony (Klemperer), 1935. Soloist churches, radio, motion pictures. Member Repertoire Club, Phi Beta. Hobby, gardening. 2224 Fourth Ave., Los Angeles, Calif.

Jeanne Turpin Determann

Ralph Dobbs

Lester Donahue

Sadie Douglas

Vladimir Drucker

Owen C. Dunning

George W. Duning

Mr. & Mrs. George Tower
Duley

Alice Durham

Henry Purmort Eames

Hugh H. Edwards

Dorothy Ellis

John Ellis

EPS, ROBERT van
(*See*: VAN EPS)

ETTINGER, LEON
Concert manager; teacher of singing. b. Washington. St. voice w. mother, Wallace Sabin, Frederick Blickfelt, Achille Alberti, Lazar Samoiloff, Landseer MacKenzie. Concerts, oratorio, church soloist, U. S., esp. Pac. Coast. Co-organizer, manager Pasadena Music Fest. Assn. (4 yrs.), bus. mgr. American Music Theatre (4 yrs.); mgr. Bartlett-Frankel Str. Quartet. Now mgr. Coleman Chamber Mus. Assn. (15 yrs.); dir. Thorne Hall, Occidental Coll. Wife, Nouvart Ettinger, tchr. of piano. 802 S. Arroyo Blvd., Pasadena, Calif.

EVANS, JOHN STARK
Organist, conductor. b. Hampton, Iowa, Feb. 27, 1891. Att. Grinnell College, Iowa Univ.; private st. New York, Paris, piano w. Ganz, Casadesus; organ w. Widor, Courboin; comp. w. Goldmark. B.A. 1913; Diploma Fontainebleau 1924; Mus.D. 1947. Many recitals, choral concerts. Conductor Eugene Glee Men (16 yrs.). Assoc. dean of School of Music at Univ. of Oregon (12 yrs.). Now dir. of music, Lewis and Clark College; organist, choirmaster First Presbyterian Church, Portland. Comp. *Solemn Mass*, many songs, organ compositions, violin solos. Member: Rotary, Mason, AGO., A.A.U.P. Knife and Fork. Lewis and Clark College, Portland, Ore.

EVANTI, LILLIAN
Coloratura soprano; composer. b. Washington, D.C. St. w. Ritta Chiampi, Paris; Mme. Battero Alexandrina, Rosina Storchio, Italy. Mus. D., Howard Univ. Many world tours in concert; app. w. leading symphony orchs.; featured in operas Europe and U.S. Comp. incl. *Twenty-Third Psalm*, numerous songs. Member Zeta Phi Beta. Hobbies: chess, pastel painting, making fruit cakes. Mgmt. (pers. repr.) Leo Steen, 1910 Vermont Ave., Washington, D.C.

EVERETT, SUZANNE
Teacher of voice. b. Santa Cruz, Calif. Mus. major San Francisco Coll. Voice and pedagogy at San Francisco Cons. of Music (5½ yrs.). Asst. teacher to Rena Lazelle, San Francisco Cons. of Music. Own vocal studio in Burlingame, Calif., several years; Hollywood studio since 1938. Pres. of Peninsula Music Society 1936-38. 1592 Cross Roads of the World, Hollywood 28, Calif.

FARRELLE, VITOLD
Violinist, teacher, conductor orchestra and chamber music. b. Pomona, Calif., 1903. Attended Bruxelles Cons. St. w. A. Saslavsky, Edouard Deru, Ysaye, Alfred du Bois, others. Played w. Bruxelles, Sacramento, San Francisco Symphony Orchs. under Mengelberg, Weingartner, Ansermet, Defauw, Hertz. Member Farrelle Quartette, Entre-Nous Quartette, Pro-Musica Quartette. Concerts over KFBK; recitals, Bruxelles, London, Paris (1932), S.F. (1933), L.A., Sacramento (1933-34), toured Northern Calif. (1937-38); cond. Sacramento YWCA Phil. Orch. (1925-26-27), Sacramento Phil. Orch. (1933-34), Westminster Phil. Orch. (1934-37), Chi. Symph. Orch. (1935-40); many pupils now well known professionals. Comp. cadenzas for Brahms, Beethoven, Viotti, Paganini Concertos, Tartini's *Devil's Trill* Sonata; three sets of etudes: studies in 1st position; development of the position; advanced; *Basic Principles of Bowing*; *Harmony for Instrumentalists* (White Smith Co.), *Violin Method*. Hobbies: target shooting (winner of national competitions); coll. rare Colt revolvers; coll. rare books on California. 2620 P St., Sacramento 16, Calif.

FERGUSON, MARION J.
Singer, teacher of singing. b. San Francisco. St. New England Conservatory; voice w. John O'Neil, Esther Mundell (de Reszke exponent). Concertized in U. S. especially in West; soloist in various churches San Francisco, Denver, other cities. Also competent pianist, appearing often as accompanist. Member; San Mateo County MTA (Music Committee), Country Concert Assn., Denver Ladies Choral. Hobby: cooking. Taught voice 30 years in San Francisco, Denver, San Mateo. Studio: 434 San Mateo Dr., San Mateo, Calif.

FERIR, EMILE
Violinist, violist, composer. b. Brussels, 1873. St. Brussels Cons. w. Ysaye, Firket. Princ. violist Scottish Orch., Glasgow, Phil. Orch., London; solo viola Boston Symph. Orch., L. A. Symph. Orch. Comp. incl. *Songe, Caprice Basque, Crepusle d'Orient*. Appeared w. Joachim, Ysaye, Casals. San Clemente, Calif.

FERLAZZO, BALDASSARE
Concert violinist, teacher of violin, concertmaster, Burbank Symphony Orch. b. Boston, Mass., Grad. New England Cons. of Mus. St. violin w. Harrison Keller, Leopold Auer; theory, comp. w. Frederick Converse; solf. w. LeNom. Won first prize at 14; scholarships held 5 yrs. Concertized throughout U. S., Canada; 3 seas. Colby Concs. Maine; pl. for Prince of Wales (Lake Louise, Can.); radio w. Werrenrath Hour, others; much chamber music. Soloist with Standard Sym. (Shepherd), 20th Century Sym. (Martini), Sinfonietta (Fiedler), Burbank Sym. (Damiani), others. Illus. lectures with E. B. Hill, Harvard Univ. St. philosophy Harvard. Comp. incl. concert trans. of masterworks. Member AFM Local 47. Hobbies: philosophy, sports, swimming, tennis. 1333 Valley Heart Drive, Burbank, Calif.

FERRAHIAN, EUNICE
Pianist, composer, teacher. b. Armenia, 1887. Ed. Univ. of Sou. Calif. Coll. of Music. Mus. B. 1930; Mus. M. 1932. Piano w. Sigismund Stojowski, Olga Steeb; comp. w. Henry Schoenefeld. Comp. symphonic poem *Enchanted Castle*, premiere by USC Orchestra (Alexander Stewart) *Trio Nocturne* (violin, 'cello, piano), choral Cantata (mss.), various songs, piano works. 1924 Westview St., Los Angeles, Calif.

FERRARO, FLORA
Concert pianist, teacher of piano. b. Utah. St. piano w. Fanny Bloomfield Zeisler (several years), theory, comp. w. Adolph Weidig, modern technic w. Paolo Gallico, New York City. Concertized in Los Angeles several years. Studio: 614 Templeton Bldg., Salt Lake City, Utah.

FERRY, CHARLES
Composer, organist, teacher. b. Eureka, Ill., Dec. 5, 1890. Att. Augustine Coll., Rock Island, Ill.; St. w. Wilhelm Middelschulte, Chicago, Charles Marie Widor, Paul Le Flem, Paris; A. M. Allen, Boston. Concertized throughout U.S.; plays piano, organ. Radio over WQAM, Miami; KMPC, L.A. Comp. of over 100 songs, piano, violin, organ; grand opera *Prince Ivan* (1935); Oratorio *Judgment*; six sonatas, quintets, quartets, trio for strings and piano, organ numbers. Comp. pub. by Presser, Ditson, Boosey, Flammer. Teacher of Robert McDonald, Catherine Mills. 912½ W. 20th St., Los Angeles, Calif.

FINSTON, NATHANIEL W.
Violinist, conductor, film producer. b. New York City, 1895. Att. City College of N. Y. St. w. Elin and Sam Franko, Pietro Floridia. Guest cond., mus. dir. Rialto Theatre, N. Y.; organized first orchestra of Capitol Theatre, N. Y.; former memb. Russian Symphony of N. Y.; N. Y. Philharmonic Symphony, Boston Opera Orch.; former musical director and head of music dept. M.G.M. Studios. Member Adv. Committee on Music, Dept of State. President, Symphony Films, Inc. since 1946. Recordings for Victor, Columbia. Just completed *Song of My Heart* based on life of Tchaikovsky (Symphony Films, Inc., Allied Artists, Inc. release) Hobbies: collecting rare music, books, phonograph records. 838 N. Orlando, Hollywood 46, Calif.

FISHER, MARJORY M.
Music critic, San Francisco News. b. San Jose, Calif. Att. Coll. of the Pacific; st. violin, theory w. Louis Persinger, San Francisco, Albert Stoessel, New York. Mus. B. Concertized in U.S. as violinist, violist; played with quartets, orchestras. Correspondent for Musical America, Pacific Coast Musician; author numerous magazine articles U.S., England. Member, Mu Phi Epsilon. Hobbies: theater, horseback riding. San Francisco News, San Francisco, Calif. Res. Alexander Hamilton Hotel, San Francisco, Calif.

Zaruhi Elmassian

John Stark Evans

Suzanne Everett

Vitold Farrelle

Marion J. Ferguson

Eunice Ferrahian

Nathaniel W. Finston

Baldassare Ferlazzo

Flora Ferraro

Charles Ferry

John L. Fitzer

Loretta B. Foote

Philip Mauro Foote

FITZER, JOHN L.

Arranger, pianist. b. Phoenix, Arizona, 1913. St. theory, comp. w. Gerald Strang, Ernest Camp, Hollywood Cons. of Music. Arranger for 717th AAF concert and dance orch. (France, Belgium, Germany); Radio Concert Orch. broadcast from Gulfport, Miss. Command piano concerts for American Army's High Command in the E.T.O. Comp. *Les Delices, Lament to a Profligate* (mss). Hobby book collecting. 2343 E. Pacific Coast Highway, Long Beach, Calif.

FOOTE, LORETTA B.

Pianist, teacher of piano. b. Berkeley, Calif., Jan. 14, 1917. New York State Regents Diploma. Member of two-piano team of *Loretta and Phil.*, *Can You Write a Song* program radio station KFRC, WHDL. Composer of popular songs. Recordings: *Loretta and Phil*, Music-Mart Label. Member AFM., Local 6. Hobbies: flying, swimming. 510, 15th St., Oakland 12, Calif.

FOOTE, PHILIP MAURO

Teacher, pianist, composer. b. Kewanee, Ill., July 18, 1920. B. Sc. Ch. E.; L. A. G. (licentiate of Assoc. Board, Royal Coll. and Royal Acad. of Music, London, Eng.). Sang Ch. of Good Shepherd, Columbus, Ohio; accomp. Columbus Pub. Sch. Orch., Ohio State Univ. Choral Soc., Ohio State Univ. Men's Glee Club. Cond. Symphony and Choral, Madras (India) Musical Assn. Member of hammond organ, two-piano team *Loretta and Phil, Can You Write A Song* program, radio KFRC, KMPC, KRE, KLY, etc. Owner and head of Modern Music (teaching) and Music-Mart, music publishers, record manuf. Comp. incl.; *Omar Khayyam Suite* (piano), *Concert Valse* (violin, piano), *Idyll* (piano), *Ming Hoy* (operetta), *Dark Emperor* (musical comedy), *Dos Bailes Flamencos* (orch.), *Symphony in F Major* (*The Leaf Shower*), (orch.), *The Buckle of Isis* (grand opera), *I Give To You My Heart, A Red, Red Rose, Shadow Tones*, others. Recordings: *Loretta and Phil*, Music-Mart label. Vice-Pres. Calif. Comp. and Writers Soc.; Amer. Fed. of Musicians, Masons, Eagles, Kappa Sigma, Past Comm. Amer. Legion Post, etc. Hobbies: flying, sailing, swimming. 510, 15th Street, Oakland 12, Calif.

FORTHMANN, MADELAINE (Mrs. Harold Boyer)

Concert pianist, teacher of piano. b. L. A., Calif. Att. Hamlin Univ., St. Paul, Minn. St. piano w. Thilo Becker, L. A., Sigismund Stojowski, N. Y., Johanna Graudan, Minneapolis; comp. w. Russell Harris. Concertized in U. S. Los Angeles debut, 1939. Recitals, radio performances, esp. Minn., So. Calif. Duo-piano appearances w. Mildred Titcomb Rains, others. Comp. incl. piano pieces. Hobbies: skiing, horseback riding, swimming. 435 S. Lafayette Park Pl., Los Angeles, Calif.

FRAGALE, FRANK D.

Composer, clarinetist. b. Sciara (prov. Palermo) Italy, Dec. 1, 1894. Att. Bellini Cons., Palermo. Theory, comp. w. Julius Gold, L.A. Appeared w. leading symphony orchs. in U.S., Italy. Comps. incl.: *Fantasia* (cello and orch.), *Passacaglia*, several suites for orch.; opera, *Dr. Jekyl and Mr. Hyde*, numerous chamber music works, esp. for wind instruments. Recordings w. orch. under Hertz, Monteux, Reiner, others. Hobby: gardening. Member San Francisco Symphony Orch., Municipal Opera of San Francisco, Res. 1925 Belmont Ave., San Carlos, Calif.

FRANCHETTI, ALDO

Conductor, composer. b. Mantua, Italy, May 15, 1892. St. in Mantua; att. Royal Conservatory, Milano, age 10: diploma in comp. Cond. first performance age 16. Cond. opera, concerts throughout Italy; *Aida* before pyramids in Egypt, 1912, Cairo Opera, Spain, So. America, U. S., Japan; world tours w. Alessandro Bonci. Cond. first sound picture Vienna (Kinotophone Co., 1913); Chicago Civic Opera, San Carlo Opera, Boston Opera, Philadelphia, Pittsburgh, Los Angeles Opera Fest. (1935). Comp. six grand operas including *Na-Miko-San* (Japanese) (David Bispham Gold Medal), *Tiao Ch'an* (Chinese), *Reginella Triste* (Italian), *Prince of Dreams*; seven orchestral tone poems: *Life, Odys-*

sea, The Sunken Belfry, Vineta, Rake, Bertha at the Hedge, Italia; opera sequences for *Anthony Adverse* (Warner Bros.); chorals, cantatas, songs, piano pieces, etc. Recorded numerous songs w. Italian Columbia, Phonotipia. Member Warner Bros.-First Nat'l Pictures Corp. musical staff. Hobbies: chess, crossword puzzles. 6691 Emmett Ter., Hollywood 28, Calif.

FRANKENSTEIN, ALFRED

Musicologist, writer, music and art editor, critic, San Francisco Chronicle. b. Chicago, Ill., 1906. Grad. Univ. of Chicago; st. Yale Univ. Instructor, Univ. of Chicago, Univ. of Calif. Exten. Reviewer: Musical Courier, Chicago Tribune, Chicago American, Review of Reviews. Music editor San Francisco Chronicle since 1934. Contrib. to various journals; lecturer on music. Program annotator, San Francisco Symphony. San Francisco Chronicle, San Francisco, Calif.

FRASER, EARL

Teacher of voice, piano. b. Cedar Rapids, Iowa. St. piano w. Julian Pascal, Arthur Friedheim, Abby Whiteside, Karl Leimer; voice w. Mme. Ragna-Linne, Heywood Winters, Frank Carroll Giffen, Florence Lee Holzman, Gateman Griffith, J. H. Campbell; theory w. Alchin; comp. w. Allard de Ridder, Howard Hansen. Comp of 20 songs to Sara Teasdale poems, *Fantasy* (String orch. and pf.) Six pupils selected for leading roles in Riverside Opera prods. 401 So. Sycamore Ave., Santa Ana, Calif.

FREDERICK, KURT

Violinist, conductor. b. Vienna, Austria. Grad. State Coll. of Mus., Vienna. Cond. Albuquerque Sym. Orch. Assoc. prof. of mus., University of New Mexico, Albuquerque, N. M.

FREDRICKS, JESSICA M. (Mrs. Harry Schaff)

Head Music Librarian, Music Dept., S. F. Public Library. b. San Francisco, Calif. Musical edu. w. Eleanor Drew; Ada Clement, Lillian Hodghead of S. F. Conservatory of Music; Univ. of Calif. Given many club and radio talks. Compiled bibliography *California Composers*; articles in prof. magazines. Hobbies: Musical San Franciciana, gardening, traveling. San Francisco Library, San Francisco, Calif.

FREEMAN, THOMAS FREDERICK

Teacher of piano, organ, theory. b. Bothwell, Ontario, Canada, Dec. 26, 1883. St. organ w. W. F. Skeele; piano w. Thilo Becker, Leopold Godowsky; theory w. Chas. Pemberton, Herman Dutra, Hugo Leichtentritt. Assoc. AGO; Fellow AGO. Concertized in U. S., Europe, incl. Bechstein Saal; Berlin; recital own comp. in Greek Theatre, Berkeley. Comp. incl. three High School operettas, songs, piano and organ pieces. Studio equipped w. 3-manual organ, two pfs. Member: AGO, Amer. Leg., Rotary. Hobbies: leather craft, weaving, bookbinding. Homestead Ave. and Walnut Blvd., P. O. Box 514, Walnut Creek, Calif.

FREESE, RALPH

Tenor, teacher of voice, choral conductor. b. Norwich, Kans., 1900. St. Cincinnati Cons. of Music (2 yrs.); voice w. Dan Beddoe (Beddoe Scholarship 2 yrs.); Florence Lamont Hinman (4 yrs.), William S. Brady, N.Y. (1 yr.). Coached w. Ricardo Martin, Lazar Samoiloff, John C. Wilcox, Franz Hoffman: choral conducting American Cons., Chicago. Asst. Dir. KOA Denver, 1924-28; NBC announcer N.Y. 1929-30. Member: Kiwanis, Choral Cond. Guild. Hobby: writing. 439 Gaviota Ave., Long Beach 12, Calif.

FRIED, ALEXANDER

Music editor, San Francisco Examiner, since 1934. b. New York City, 1902. Began st. of piano age 8. A.B., Columbia Univ, 1923; won Mosenthal Fellowship in music criticism; M.A. 1924. Joined staff of The Musical Digest, later became managing editor. Music Editor of San Francisco Chronicle, 1926. Contributed articles on music to other publications. Wife, Audrey Farncroft Fried, former opera and concert soprano. San Francisco Examiner, Third and Market Sts. San Francisco 19, Calif.

Madelaine Forthmann

Frank Fragale

Aldo Franchetti

Jessica Fredricks

Thomas Frederick Freeman

Anthony Galla-Rini

Ralph Freese

Alexander Fried

Malcolm Frost

Carl Fuerstner

Eugene Fulton

Ruth Ellen Gannon

Robert M. Garretson

FRIEDHOFER, HUGO W.

Composer, orchestrator. b. San Francisco, Calif., 1901. St. w. Domenico Brescia, S. F. Warner Bros Studio, 1936. Orch. for over 50 major films incl. *Anthony Adverse, Prince and Pauper, Charge of the Light Brigade, Dr. Erlich, Dark Victory.* 7974 Woodrow Wilson Dr., Los Angeles 46, Calif.

FROST, MALCOLM

Teacher of piano. b. Marshfield, Wisc., 1909. St. piano w. David Campbell (3 yrs.), I. Philipp (Paris, 1 yr.); theory, comp, Univ. of Oregon (2 yrs.). Teacher of Skitch Henderson, pianist on Bing Crosby's program (1947). Faculty member, NGPT. Hobby, playing the piano. Studio: 308 Fine Arts Bldg., Portland, Oregon.

FROST, ROBERT R.

Oboist; manager. b. Oroville, Calif. St. piano w. mother, Faith Orton Frost, later w. Thomas Giles; clarinet w. Clarence Hawkins; oboe w. William Lym, Henri de Busscher; won schol. 3 successive yrs. LDS Cons., Utah. Clarinetist, oboist w. Salt Lake Sym. (12 yrs) (Freber, Shepherd), Los Angeles Philharmonic 1924-46 (Rothwell, Klemperer, Barbirolli, Wallenstein, others), Hollywood Bowl 1923-45 (all leading conds.). First oboist Vitaphone Orch. 1927-32, Enterprise Studios since 1945. Also now first oboist, manager Sen Fernando Valley Sym. (Ronka). Concertized extensively in U. S. Radio work w. NBC, CBS, Mutual, Westinghouse Program 4 yrs., etc. Recordings w. Hollywood Bowl, LA Phil., various studios. Member AFM Local 47. Hobbies, hunting, fishing. 1519 Thompson Ave., Glendale, Calif.

FUERSTNER, CARL

Conductor, composer, pianist. b. Strasbourg, Alsace-Lorraine, June 16, 1912. St. Staatliche Hochschule fuer Musik, Cologne, Germany. Many years of tours throughout country as pianist, accompanist. Now dir. opera dept., Eastman School of Music, Rochester, N.Y. Guest pianist Annual Music Festival, Brigham Young Univ., Provo, Utah. Numerous radio appearances. Cond. Service Men's Symphony Orch., San Francisco. Cond. first American performance Boccherini's *Stabat Mater;* NBC Univ. of the Air broadcast, oratorio *Jephte* by Carissimi. Sonata recital w. Jacques Gordon, American Festival at Nat'l Gallery, Washington, D. C. Comp. *Concerto* (orch.), *Concerto Rapsodico* ('cello & orch.), *Clarinet Quintet, Divertimento* (str. quartet), *Sonata* for four violins, *Pavane and Marcetta* (violin, piano), songs, piano pieces. Hobbies: hiking, bicycling. Mgmt.: Jean Ancona, Concert Bureau, Eastman School of Music, Rochester, New York. 575 Averill Ave., Rochester 7, N .Y.

FULTON, EUGENE

Teacher of voice, choral conductor, concert singer. b. San Francisco. St. voice w. Lazar Samoiloff, Louis Graveure, Leandro Campanari, Giulio Silva; theory, Julius Gold. Winner first Atwater Kent scholarship contest for S.F. Cond. Loring Club Male chorus, Bel Canto Chorus of Redwood City (prizewinning chorus at World's Fair, Treasure Island, 1939), Fulton A Cappella Chorus and Ebenezer Lutheran Church Choir. Dir. Fulton School of Music. 2810 Clay St., San Francisco 15, Calif.

GAINES, BERNICE van LOAN

Composer, pianist, organist. b. Milwaukee, Wisc. Ed. Univ. Minn.; Duggenheim (Paris); Willard Patton (Minn.). Concertized throughout East, Mid-West on Chatauqua, other circuits; taught at Univ. of Minn. for 16 yrs. Comp. *The Brotherhood of Man* (text, Olive Schreiner) (soloists, chorus, & orch.) (organ arr.); *Majalla* (used annually at Ramona Fest.) *Little Songs for Little People, Song of Today;* many children's songs, art songs, ballads, piano pieces. Recording: *Brotherhood of Man.* Member: Composer's Soc.; Nat'l Assn. for Music and Related Arts, Inc. 10584 Wellworth Ave., Los Angeles 24, Calif.

GALLA-RINI, ANTHONY

Concert accordionist, teacher of accordion. b. Hartford, Conn., Jan. 18, 1904. St. accordion, other wind and brass instr. w. father, John Galla-Rini; theory, comp. w. Van

Broekhaven, New York, Gastone Usigli, San Francisco. Annual concert tours incl. all major centers; soloist w. Denver Symphony (Caston), Oklahoma Symphony, other orchs. Comps. incl. *Concerto* (accor. and orch.), many original short pieces for accordion, standard methods, exercises, and transc. of several hundred masterworks, (pub. Fischer, Schirmer, Summy, etc.) Victor recordings of Brahms, Schubert, Gossec, Strauss, Gounod, Galla-Rini, other works. Inventor of numerous improvements, attachments for accordion. Perf. accordion soli in various films, incl. *A Bell For Adano, Dragonwyck, Laura, State Fair, Rhapsody in Blue, Mr. Skeffington, Mask of Dimitrios.* Member AFM. Hobbies: hunting, fishing, swimming. Mgmt. Martin Music Management, Hollywood, Calif. Res. 4572 Ellenwood Dr., Los Angeles 41, Calif.

GANNON, RUTH ELLEN

Composer, arranger, pianist, teacher of instrumental, choral music. b. San Francisco. Mus. B. Univ. of Chicago, School of Music; grad. Chicago School of Nursing, Imperial Technical Inst. Contributed musical services during war. Orch. pianist Humboldt Evening H.S., San Francisco. Various radio appearances. Comp. for orch.: *March Symphonic* (5 numbers), *Leisure Moments;* Opera: *Drusilla & Orestes;* Chorals: *Tribute to Music and Song, The Lord Was Seen In His Glory, Glorious Tamalpais;* numerous instrumental works incl. *La Jorgiana de Faro, Love is Waiting, Maypole Rehearsal, Nimrod, Saturnalia,* etudes, variations, etc., many songs. Master Craftsman, Fireside Ind. Inc., Adrian, Michigan. Member Nat'l Academy of Music, N.Y. Hobbies: painting, laces, applied arts, writing. 4558 19th Street, San Francisco, Calif.

GARRETSON, ROBERT M.

Pianist, arranger. b. Portland, Oregon, 1915. Grad. Ellison-White Cons. St. piano w. S. Stojowski, Frances Striegel Burke, Myron Jacobson, George Hopkins, Lillian Steuber, Olga Steeb. B.A. Univ. of Oregon, major in music. Postgrad. work USC, UCLA. Orch. w. Lucien Gaillet, Arnold Schoenberg; musicology w. Walter Rubsamen, George McManus. Concertized So. Calif. and Pacific Northwest. Soloist Univ. of Oregon Orch., Portland Junior Symphony. Duopianist w. Katherine Dunham *Blackouts,* Veloz & Yolanda, *Musical Portraits,* Blue Network, 1944. Mus. dir. Virginia-Johnson dancers. Coach, pianist for L.A. Civic Light Opera, 1946-47. Recordings for Columbia, MGM, 20th-Century Fox Studios. 5401 Brynhurst Avenue, Los Angeles, Calif.

GATCH, PHILIP MILTON and ALICE

Director of music; teacher of singing, public speaking; concert tenor. b. Los Angeles, Calif., July 25, 1907. Att. Pacific Coll., Newberg, Ore. St. voice w. Mary Adele Vann, Mark Daniels, Nicola Zann, Elizabeth Thesloff, Robert Warwick Sr. Staff tenor, C.B.S. radio KOIN (2½ yrs.), KWJJ, Portland (1 yr.), KXL (1 yr.), KTBR, Portland (1 yr.), Baronets Male Quartet (76 concerts). Recordings w. Enterprise Records; transcriptions, CBS. Member: MTA, B.P.O. Elks 1497, Native Sons of the Golden West, Ramona Parlor, L. A. Hobbies: swimming, tennis, sports, concerts. Wife, Alice, organist, pianist, accompanist. b. Gresham, Ore., June 16, 1907. St. piano, organ w. Nellie Kennedy, Mme. Wood, Randolph Howard. 409 So. Hobart Blvd., Los Angeles 5, Calif.

GEERTS, MARY E.

Teacher of piano; accompanist, member Fresno Trio. b. Buffalo, N.Y. St. piano w. Theckla Adam (pupil Ethel Newcomb, Mme. Moskowska), Agnes de Jahn (pupil Leschetizky), Fresno. Concertized before women's clubs in Calif. At present Pres. of Fresno Musical Club; associate memb. of Leschetizky Assn. of America. 740 Roosevelt Ave., Fresno, Calif.

GEIST, MELVIN H.

Dean of music, prof. of voice, Willamette Univ. b. Morganville, Kans. Att. Univ. of Kansas (B.M.), Univ. of Mich. (Mus. M.), Juilliard Sch. of Music, Columbia Univ. Soloist w. Salem Sym. Orch., others; Winfield Oratorio Soc., Eugene Oratorio Soc., McPherson Oratorio Soc. Regional governor, NATS, Northwest dist. Member Phi Kappa Lambda, Phi Mu Alpha, Beta Theta Pi, Salem Rotary Club. Hobby, golf. Coll. of Music, Willamette Univ., Salem, Oregon. Res. 160 W. Lefelle, Salem, Oregon.

GERSHKOVITCH, JACQUES

Conductor. b. Irkutsk, Siberia, Russia. St. w. Rimsky-Korsakov, Tcherepnin, Glazunov, at Imperial Cons. of Music, from which grad. w. honors, 1913. Won Schubert schol. under Nikish. Cond. symphony military orch. during World War I. Member Pavlova Orch. on tour through Orient. Cond. Tokyo Symphony Orch. Arrived U. S., 1922. Cond., Portland Jr. Symphony Orch. since 1923. Portland, Ore.

GERTS, POLLY

Teacher of ballet, tap, Spanish Dance. b. Chicago, Ill. Grad. from Holton Arms School, Washington, D. C., Teacher's Certif. in piano, harmony, mus. hist. Knupfer Studios; St. folk dancing w. Mary Wood Hinman; interpretative dance w. Doris Humphrey; ballroom dancing w. Eugene Bournique and William Crocket Perrin; ballet w. Adolph Bolm, (5 yrs.); w. Olga Preobrajenskya, Paris; Muriel Stuart, Chicago; Spanish dance w. Maria Escudero, Paris; Jose Otero, Seville; Jose Alvarez, Marijo Mentero, Chicago. Member of Bolm Ballet Intime in Chicago; app. in stage productions Balaban & Katz Theaters. Taught ballet Bush Cons. Chicago; Nashville Cons. of Music, Nashville, Tenn. Dance Studio: 71 W. Colorado, Pasadena, Calif.

GIFFEN, FRANK CARROLL

Tenor, teacher of voice. b. Truckee, Calif., 1874. St. in California w. Hiram Gage; in Europe guided by Etelka Gerstin: w. Von Dulong, Berlin; DeSales, Munich; Vivarelli and Panzani, Florence; Dousette, Paris. Recitals in London, Switzerland, Florence. Sang tenor lead with Bach Choir in Berlin. Taught singing in Florence, Italy (2 yrs.). Long established in San Francisco. Originator of movement which made San Francisco Opera Co. under Merola. Pupils include Georgianna Strauss, Douglas Beattie, Elsa Behlow Trautner, William Eddy. 976 Chestnut St., San Francisco, Calif.

GIFFORD, CLEMENCE (Mrs. Norman Sherwood)

Concert singer, teacher of voice. b. in California. Att. Mills Coll.; st. voice w. Achille Alberti. Appeared in opera, concert, oratorio and with major orchestras. Many appearances at Hollywood Bowl with leading conductors. At present contralto at two churches, Los Angeles. 1230 So. Camden Dr., Los Angeles, Calif.

GILLAM, JEANNE

Concert violinist. b. Sayville, New York, May 14, 1928. Scholarship, Brooklyn Cons. under Jacques Malkin; further st. w. Joseph Oroop, Henri Temianka (first violinist Paganini Quartet). Soloist Steinway Hall, New York, at age 10. Memb. of Meremblum and Women's Symphonies, Brodetsky Ensemble. Prize winner Glendale Symphony Auditions; scholarship Immaculate Heart H.S. Soloist KNX, KFWB, Long Beach Municipal Concert Hall and Pepperdine College. Participant in Bach Festival, Carmel, 1947. 4761 Melrose, Los Angeles, Calif.

GLASSER, ALBERT

Composer, conductor. b. Chicago, Ill., 1916. Musical ed. Univ. of So. Calif. Composer of Concerto (violin and orch.) (prize winner USC Alchin Foundation), Suite for Strings, Suite for Orchestra, Two Preludes for Orch. (prize winner Calif. Composer's Contest, 1937), Sonata (viola and piano) tone poem for orch. and narrator, The Pied Piper, tone poem for orch., The Raven. Comp., orchestrated, cond. scores for following motion pictures: Killer at Large, Philo Vance Returns, Abilene Town, Gas House Kids in Hollywood, Cisco Kid Series, Meet Your Navy, others. Recordings: Danny Boy (string orch.), For He Is A Jolly Good Fellow, Salute to Vincent Youmans, others. Charter member ASMA, SCA. Hobbies: photography, recording. 506 No. Edinburgs Ave., Los Angeles 36, Calif.

GOHL, JEANNETTA

Teacher of piano. b. St. Paul, Minn. St. piano w. Ernest Walker, Grace Leach, Frank Weltner, Lee C. Miller, St. Louis; sp. courses w. Guy Maier, Mme. Lhevienne, Richard Buhlig, L.A.; harmony, comp., organ w. Chas. Galloway, Oxford Piano Course, Chicago; Ward Method w. Mother Stevens, N.Y. Accr. tchr. Effa Ellis Perfield (N.Y.); progressive series, St. Louis

Inst. of Mus. Faculty summer 1947, St. Louis Inst. of Mus., Acad. Sacred Heart, St. Louis, (13 yrs.); Colleague, Child Spee. Calif. MTA, Corr. sec. L.A. MTA. Hobby: philosophy. 3127 Liberty Ave., South Gate, Calif.

GOLD, JULIUS

Theorist, musicologist, pedagog. b. St. Joseph, Mo., 1884. St. violin w. Sir Henry Heyman, Henry Holmes, Bernhard Listemann, Emile Sauret; spec. courses w. Bernhard Ziehn. Att. Chic. Musical Coll. (scholarship). Former memb. S. F. Symph. Orch. and Opera Assn. Lecturer Stanford Univ. (summer 1931), Dominican Coll. (summer 1932). Prof. counterpoint and comp. Dominican Coll. 1931-35. Students incl. Otto Cesana, Lajos Fenster, Isaac Stern, Chas. Dalmores, Meredith Willson, Frank Fragale, Nathan Firestone, Ray Kimbell. Contributor to Hans Joachim Moser's Musiklexikon (Berlin, 1905). 1811 Whitley Ave., Hollywood 28, Calif.

GOLDBERG, ALBERT

Music editor, critic, Los Angeles Times. b. Shenandoah, Iowa. Att. Univ. of Nebraska, Chicago Musical Coll., Gunn School of Music. Mus. M. Faculty Chicago Musical Coll., Gunn School of Music 1922-1935; asst. music critic Chicago Herald Examiner 1925-1935; State dir. Fed. Music Project (Illinois) 1935-43; co-cond. Illinois Sym. Orch. 1936-1942; music critic Chicago Tribune 1943-47; music critic Los Angeles Times since 1947. Los Angeles Times, 202 W. First St., Los Angeles 53, Calif.

GOLDMAN, MAURICE

Composer, conductor. b. Philadelphia, 1910. B.S. Western Reserve Univ., B.M. Cleveland Inst. of Music. Assoc. Cond. L.A. Oratorio Society; Opera Coach L.A. Cons. Conducted at Severance Hall, Cleveland, Town Hall, New York, Orchestra Hall, Pittsburgh. Head Opera Dept., Cleveland Inst. of Music; dir. Akron Civic Opera Guild; dir. Cleveland Light Opera Theater; choral dir. Western Reserve Univ, Cleveland; dir. Negro choir Wings Over Jordan. Comp. Sound Pictures (winner International Choral Competition); Sacred Service (Witmark); collaborator and cond. musical background for Lady in the Lake. Hobbies, tennis, recordings. 6313 Weidlake Dr., Hollywood, Calif.

GONTZOFF, FEODOR

Singer, voice teacher; b. Tobolsk, Siberia. Grad. Divinity Acad., Kiev, Russia (Bach. of Theology); grad Univ. Moscow (Candidate of Law). St. voice w. Umberto Vidal, Milan, Italy; grad. Imperial Cons. Moscow w. Diploma of Free Arts. Sang leading baritone roles w. Moscow Grand Opera until 1923; faculty Imperial Cons. 1920-23; toured Russia w. Alexander Gretchaninoff in recitals of composer's songs 1922, also 1925. Toured Baltic, Scandinavian countries, France, Germany, 1923. Faculty Russian Cons. of Paris, (Rachmaninoff, dir. 1926). App. in Riga w. Latvian Nat'l Orch., Helsingfors w. Nat'l Symphony Orch., Marseilles, Cologne w. Symphony Orch.; soloist in Elijah (Mendelssohn Fest.) Riga; Messiah (Prot. Cathedral), Paris; soloist Saint Sulpice. Soloist funeral of Marshal Foch, Notre Dame de Paris. Head Voice Dept. Kidd-Key Coll. and Cons. Sherman, Tex. 1929; taught Memphis Coll. of Mus., Bush Cons. Dallas, Chicago Cons. In L. A. since 1938. Pupils incl. Maria Kurenko, Alexander Vesselovsky, Maria Ullman, Eloise MacDonald. Harold Stambaugh, Wauneva Bell, Joan Leslie, Irene Dunne. Studio: 1938 Vine St., Hollywood 28, Calif.

GOODMAN, LILLIAN ROSEDALE

Vocal teacher, singer, pianist, composer, linguist. Mus. D. Boguslawsky College, 1943. Grad. Juilliard School of Music, N. Y.; additional study in Europe. St. piano w. Alexander Lambert; comp. w. Percy Goetchius; Julius Gold; voice w. Buzzi-Peccia; comp., cond. w. Emil Fuchs. Faculty memb. and head vocal dept., Boguslawski Coll. of Music, Chicago. Staff member Federal Theater Project, Chicago. Concert performances, stage presentations, radio appearances. Victor Recording artist. Comp. of classical and popular songs incl. Cherie je t'aime, My Heart Is Sad, Pour toi, musical settings to Carl Sandburg's American Song Bag, music to poems of Theodore Dreiser. Member ASCAP, MTA, League of American Pen Women. 2415 Pilgrimage Trail, Hollywood, Calif.

GOULD, NORMA

Dancer; teacher of dance. b. L. A., 1888. St. w. Kiralfy, Chalif, Rosetta O'Neill, Tina Flade, Adolph Bolm, Kreutsberg. Toured as solo dancer w. Philippini Symph. Orch.; Calif. Little Symph. (Tandler). Several productions w. own comp. at Phil. Aud., L. A.; soloist Hollywood Bowl. Founder L. A. Dance Theatre. 7213 Beverly Blvd., Los Angeles, Calif.

GRASSI, ANTONIO JOACHIM de

Violinist, composer. b. Trieste, Italy, 1885. St. Milan Cons., Leipzig Cons., Royal Acad., Berlin, w. Joachim, Sevcik, Ysaye, Firket. Played under Mahler, Nikisch, Max Bruch. Concertized Trieste, Berlin, Finland, Prague London, Amsterdam. Comp. incl. *Berceuse and Scherzo, The Night is Nigh, Valse-Serenade, Rhapsodic Prelude*. Wife, violinist, son, Antonio Jr., pianist. 2030 Lyon St., San Francisco, Calif.

GREEN, HELEN HENNESSY

Voice and choral director. Ed. Cincinnati Coll. of Music, Metropolitan Coll. St. voice, violin, piano, theory, harmony, comp., languages, chorus, orch. w. Frank Van der Stucken, Richard Schliewen, Winthrop Sterling, Sidney Durst; later st. w. Esparanza Garrigue, New York Wm. Shakespeare, London. Taught music in Ohio, Indiana colleges. Dir. choirs, choruses in San Francisco Bay District, presenting oratorios, concerts. Pupils incl. Marion George, Elizabeth Wills, Edna May Wonacott, Joan Carroll. Studios: 6019 Hollywood Blvd.; 5012 Beverly Blvd., Los Angeles, 919 Bushnell at Huntington Dr., South Pasadena, Calif.

GREENE, PATTERSON

Music critic, music editor, drama editor, Los Angeles Examiner; writer; playwright. b. Superior, Wisc. St. piano, comp. Washington State Coll.; comp. at Harvard Univ. w. E. B. Hill. A. B., Harvard Univ. Plays incl.: *Papa Is All, The Closed Room* (prod. w. Peggy Wood), *Music in the Distance*. Hobby collecting records. Music critic, Los Angeles Examiner since 1927. Los Angeles Examiner, 1111 S. Broadway, Los Angeles 54, Calif.

GRIFFIS, ELLIOT

Composer, pianist, teacher of piano, composition. b. Boston, Jan. 28, 1893. Att. Ithaca Coll., Yale Univ., New England Cons. of Mus.; st. w. Horatio Parker, George W. Chadwick, Stuart Mason, Lee Pattison. Won Juilliard Schol.; Pulitzer Prize 1931. Mus. D. New York Coll. of Mus. 1937. Faculty Grinnell Coll., Iowa, Brooklyn Settlement Sch., St. Louis Inst. of Mus.; dir. Westchester Cons. Taught in New York, Vienna (2 yrs.), Los Angeles. Comp. incl.: *Symphony, Paul Bunyan—Colossus* (sym. poem), *A Persian Fable* (orch. ballade), *Yon Green Mountain* (orch. suite), two *String Quartets, Montevallo* (conc. gr., str. org. pf.), *Trio* (vn. vcl. pf.), *Sonata* (vn. pf.), *Letters from a Maine Farm, A Set of Eight, Miniatures, Studies*, other piano works, *Sunlight and Shadow* (song cycle), other songs. Hobby: painting, art. 141 N. Swall Dr., Los Angeles 36, Calif.

GRIPENWALDT, RAOUL

Impresario, music critic, lecturer, author. b. Glasgow, Scotland, June 21, 1912. In U. S. since 1931. Founder Santa Monica concert series, co-manager Continental Artists series, manag. dir. Ballet Assn. of America, pro. chairm. Jr. Santa Monica Mus. Arts Soc., mgr. Santa Monica Sym. Orch. (1945), Editor Music and Arts Mag., mus. reviewer Santa Monica Evening Outlook (daily), contributor to Musical Courier, Clef Mag., Beverly Hills Citizen, others. Commentator Hollywood Bowl, Rose Bowl (Pasadena), Greek Theatre (Santa Monica) prods., numerous radio programs. Member bd. of dir. Santa Monica Civic Music Guild. Hobby, coll. historical recordings. Santa Monica Evening Outlook, 1245, 4th St., Santa Monica, Calif. Res. 2313 Oak St., Santa Monica, Calif.

GROFE, FERDE

Composer, conductor, arranger. b. N. Y. C., 1892. St. theory, harmony w. Chas. Pemberton; orch. Pietro Floridia. Performed under Tandler, Hamilton, Rothwell. Cond. radio programs incl. *Philip Morris, Seal Test, Sal-Hepatica, Best Foods*, Phila. Sym., Nat'l. Sym., Washington, Phil. Soc. of N. Y., NBC Sym. Scored Paul Whiteman's *King of Jazz, Rhapsody in Blue* for symphonic and radio orch. Comp. incl. *Grand Canyon Suite, Mississippi Suite, Three Shades of Blue, Tabloid Suite, Hollywood Ballet, Cafe Society Ballet, Symphony in Steel, Wheels, Trylon and Perisphere, March for Americans*, 710 Adelaide Place, Santa Monica, Calif.

GROW, ALEXANDRA

Teacher of piano, pianist. b. San Bernardino, Calif. St. piano w. Alex Kosloff (5 yrs.), Motte La Croix (Wolley Found. Scholarship in Paris, 2½ yrs.); history of music, Nadia Boulanger; schol. to Fontainebleau Sch. of Mus. and Art w. Camille de Creax, Robert Casadesus; summer courses Mills Coll. w. Marcel Maas, Claremont Coll. w. Henry P. Eames, Lee Pattison; master class w. Alfred Cortot. B. A., Occidental Coll. App. Cite' Univ., Paris San Bernardino Jr. Coll., San Bernardino Woman's Club, Occidental Coll., Univ. Woman's Club, State Conv. Program of Calif. MTA, Beverly Hills Hotel, Benevolent Tea of San Bernardino MTA, Rialto Woman's Club. Member MTA, Sigma Alpha Iota, Business and Prof. Women's Club, San Bernardino Opera Assn. Taught piano, theory San Bernardino Jr. Coll. (7 yrs.). Two yrs. England, France w. American Red Cross (Club Program Chairman). Hobbies: gardening, reading. 591 Ninth St., San Bernardino, Calif.

GUIDI, SCIPIONE

Violinist, conductor. b. Venice, Italy, 1890. Grad. Cons. of Milan, Italy. Diploma magistri. St. violin, piano, harmony, counterpoint, orchestration. First recital at age 12, touring Italy, France, England. Arrived U. S. 1916. Recitals New York, Baltimore, Washington, Providence, Holyoke, Delaware, Hastings, Springfield, Topeka. Concertmaster N.Y. Philharmonic (12 yrs.). Soloist w. Bodanzky, Mengelberg, Furtwangler, Toscanini, Stokowski. Founder Phil. String Quartet. Concertm., cond., soloist, St. Louis Symphony Orch. Now cond. Glendale Symphony Orch. Recordings: Edison, Victor. Hobby: motorboating. 1260 No. Harper Ave., Hollywood 46, Calif.

HAAS, ALEXANDER F.

Concert manager. b. New Milford, N. J., Feb. 24, 1892. Early training w. Wolfsohn Musical Bureau. Att. New York Univ. Asst. Mgr. N. Y. Symphony (Walter Damrosch), for several yrs. Personal representative of Mme. Ernestine Schumann-Heink (15 yrs.); toured w. many artists, among them Chaliapin and Pavlova. Since 1939 Pacific Coast concert manager of Nat'l. Concert and Artist Corp. 79 Post St., San Francisco 4, Calif.

HALL, ETTADELL

Pianist, teacher of harmony, piano. b. Clay Center, Kans. St. w. parents, Martin A. and Mary Jones, G. S. Rice Inter. Coll. of Music, and Sherwood Music School, Chicago; harmony, theory w. Will Harding, Chicago; rhythm, orchestra w. Sam Pryor, St. Joseph, Mo., w. Leon Rosenbloom 1943-47; theory, comp. w. Francis Keyser 1947. Taught piano Intern. Cons., St. Joseph Mo., (10 yrs.). Rep. Sherwood School of Music for last 17 yrs. Conducted own dance bands Oakland, Modesto, San Bernardino. Played over KFMI, KFWM, KLX, Oakland. Comp. musical plays, travelogues. Concerts w. Claier Trio in Bay Area, 1924-29; Italian Quartet, 1913. Sponsored Leo Podolsky programs, Berkeley, Oakland, 1939. Member MTA. Daughters, Etta Louise Carson, pianist; Mary Josephine Hunt, pianist. 2591 61st Ave., Oakland, Calif.

HANCOX, MILDRED M.

Vocal teacher. b. Newark, N. J. St. organ w. Middleshulte, Chicago at age 13; organ soloist in churches; st. voice w. Sophie Friedman, Chicago; protegee of Schumann-Heink (2½ yrs.) w. Jean de Reszke (Paris, 3 yrs.); sang Ortrud, Azucena, other roles in La Scala, Milano, Haensel at Covent Garden; Amneris in Berlin, etc. Sang for soldiers overseas during World War I; wounded in action. Teacher of Mana Zucca, Mary Hatcher, the Merry Macs, Franz Imhof, Harriet Brooks. Member Mana Zucca Mus. Club, Miami; Amateur and Artist Music Club, N.Y. 2932 Wilshire Blvd., Los Angeles, Calif.

Philip Milton Gatch Mary E. Geerts Melvin H. Geist Polly Gerts

Clemence Gifford Jeanne Gillam Albert Glasser Jeannetta Gohl

Maurice Goldman Feodor Gontzoff Lillian Rosedale Goodman Helen Hennessey Green

Elliot Griffis Raoul Gripenwaldt Alexandra Grow Scipione Guidi

207

HANSEN, TONIA DREW (Antonia D.)

Singer; teacher of voice. b. Eidsvold, Norway. Early training piano, voice w. father, pvt. tchrs. in Copenhagen, Paris. St. voice w. Frantz Proschowski, New York; repr. Proschowski sch. for Bay Area. Concertized in Europe, U. S., Orient; also song lectures spec. in Scandinavian and French songs. Soloist church choirs, Larchmont, Pelham, N. Y., Manila, Kobe, Batavia. Now soloist St. Peter's Epis. Ch., Oakland. Taught voice, dramatics Highlands Sch., Kaban Djabia, Sumatra. Studio: College Music Center, 5830 College Ave., Oakland 18, Calif. Res. 6340 Chelton Dr., Oakland 11, Calif.

HARELSON, HARRY BOONE

Head Music Dept., Arizona State Coll.; teacher of voice, theory. b. Bardwell, Ky., 1892. Att. Chicago Mus. Coll., Columbia Sch. of Mus., Chicago. B.S.M., Mus. M. Taught Heath H.S. (Ky.), Mesa Union H.S. (Ariz.). Comp. incl. *April Song* (3-pt. fem. vc.) (FitzSimons). Member: Ariz. Ed. Assn., Mus. Ed. Nat'l Conf., Assn. of Univ. Profs., Soc. of Ariz. Composers, others. Hobby, gardening. Arizona State College, Tempe, Ariz. Res. 1015 Van Ness Ave., Tempe, Ariz.

HARFORD, MARGARET

Music editor, Hollywood Citizen-News. b. Los Angeles, Calif. Att. Zoellner Cons. of Mus., Univ. of Calif. B.A. Univ. of Calif. St. piano w. Joseph Zoellner Sr., Grace Lovejoy, Margaret Rose Sheet (pupil Arnold Wagner); voice w. pvt. tchrs. Feature writer, film reviewer Hollywood Citizen-News; music editor since 1944. Hobbies: reading; research. Hollywood Citizen-News, 1545 N. Wilcox Ave., Hollywood 28, Calif.

HARLINE, LEIGH

Composer, arranger, conductor. b. Salt Lake City, 1907. St. w. J. Spencer Cornwell; comp. and arranging self-taught. Comp. background scores for *Snow White, Pinocchio*, other Disney shorts, various feature films, R.K.O. Studios, 780 N. Gower St., Hollywood 28, Calif.

HAROLDSON, RUTH

Conductor, violinist. b. South Dakota. Prof. of Violin, Whittier Coll.; cond. Los Angeles Women's Symphony, Whittier Symphony, Los Angeles Women's Symphonietta. Att. MacPhail Sch. of Mus., Minneapolis; Amer. Cons., Chicago; summers at Music Mountain, Conn. St. violin, theory w. Jacques Gordon, Mischa Mischakoff, Sascha Jacobsen, Modest Altschuler, Leo Sowerby. Won 3 Juilliard scholarships. Concertized extensively throughout U.S. Soloist w. Chicago, other leading symphonies, as violinist, guest cond. Member: Sigma Alpha Iota, Dominant Club. Hobbies: motoring, ice skating, color movies. Mgmt. Fred Blackburn. Studio: Whittier College, Whittier, Calif. Res. 124 N. Painter Ave., Whittier, Calif.

HARRIS, ALBERT

Composer, conductor. b. London, England. St. piano w. Belinfante; harmony w. Mary Carr Moore; theory, comp. w. Eugene Zador; cond. w. Albert Coates, Richard Lert. Asst. mus. dir., NBC (Hollywood) Cond. *Storehouse of Music*. Comp. String Quartet in A-minor (Los Angeles MacDowell award), Cycle of *Maiden* songs for soprano (Richard Pauloo award). *Overture, Waltz, and Rondo* (perf. by Pasadena Civic Orch., w. composer as guest cond.). Orchestrator for *Song of Norway* (Grieg Operetta). 1660 No. Western Ave., Hollywood, Calif.

HARRIS, ROY

Composer. b. Lincoln County, Nebr., 1898. St. piano w. mother, Arthur Farwell, Bliss, Altschuler, Scalero, Nadia Boulanger, Guggenheim fellowship 1927-28; Creative Fellowship Pasadena Music & Arts Assn., 1930. Head comp. dept. Westminster Choir Sch. at Princeton, N. J.; dir. Princeton Festival of Amer. Music. Member exec. committee of American Comp. Alliance. Comp. incl. works for orch., chorus, chamber music, piano. Colorado College, Colorado Springs, Colo.

HART, JAMES

Manager, Portland Symphony Orch. b. Portland, Ore., 1917. A.B. Amherst College, Amherst, Mass. Instr. of Music, Amherst College, 1939-41. Bus., 507 Fenton Bldg., Portland 4, Ore.; Res.: 3738 S.W. Council Crest Dr., Portland, Ore.

HART, MARY MARTHA

Teacher, pianist. St. piano w. Olga Steeb, Lillian Steuber; master classes w. Guy Maier; diploma, Olga Steeb Piano School. Soloist Behymer Matinee Series at Barker Bros. Recitals Calif. and Okla. Member MTA, Business & Prof. Women's Club. 735 So. St. Andrews, Los Angeles, Calif.

HEADLEY, HUBERT KLYNE

Pianist, conductor. b. Parkersburg, W. Va., 1906. Att. Coll. of Pac. Cons. Dir. music, Montezuma Sch. for Boys, Los Gatos; public schs. Red Bluff, Calif. Sup. of Music., Redwood City, 1930. Asst. prof. mus., Fresno State Coll., 1935. Mus. M. Eastman Sch. of Mus., N. Y., 1937. Dir. instr., Univ. of Calif. at Santa Barbara. Comp. incl. *California Suite, Argentango, Piano Concerto, Symphony*, others. Awarded Edward McDowell Fellowship in comp. Peterborough, N. H. Univ. of Calif., Santa Barbara, Calif.

HEALY, ELIZABETH

Personal representative of Robert O'Connor, pianist, Nicholas Vasilieff, tenor, and secretary-manager of Saturday Morning Musical Club and Temple of Music and Art. b. Pittsburg, Calif. Studied St. Joseph Academy at Tucson. Voice w. Carl Bronson, Angela O'Byrne. Appeared as soloist in churches, Tucson, Women's Club, Camaguey, Cuba. Member Saturday Morning Musical Club. Formerly music critic and society editor of Havana Post and Times, of Cuba, Havana, Cuba. Hobby: painting. 324 South Sixth Ave., Tucson, Ariz.

HEEDER, ROSE LEAVES

Teacher of voice and piano. b. Canada. St. piano, organ w. father, late Matthew Leaves, choral cond.; also w. late James Hamilton Howe, Hugo Mansfelt, Hans T. Seifert, N.Y.C.; coached w. Epstein. St. methods of vocal teaching w. Louis Graveure. Creator of new scientific voice method known as Heeder Method. Accomp. Metropolitan Concert Co., N. Y. Pianist, Philharmonic Quartet, Orpheus Trio. Member MTA. Hobby, interior decorating. Studio: 1801 Grove St., Berkeley, Calif.

HEGEDUS, MARGIT (Marget Hegedus Cave)

Violinist. b. Nagybanya, Hungary. Att. Acad. of Music, Budapest. St. w. Sevcik. Performed under Meredith Willson, David Broekman, Raymond Paige, Felix Mills, Joseph Pasternack; KHJ, NBC. Concertized Europe. P. O. Box 433, Moorpark, Calif.

HEIFETZ, EMANUEL R.

Violinist, teacher, composer. b. New York City, 1914. St. violin w. uncle, David Heifetz, E. P. Delavanti, George Mulford, A. Zaslavsky, Calmon Luboviski, Peter Meremblum, Robert Pollak. Soloist KFI, KGER. Played in Heifetz Trio w. Irwin Coster, 'cellist, Benno Rubinyi, pianist. NBC, CBS broadcasts (Meredith Willson); violin soloist KSL on "Melodic Flight." Entert. dir. Hill Field during war. Past pres. San Bernardino MTA; concertmaster San Bernardino Symphony (Karel Shultis). Comp. incl. *Little Dutch Dolls* (C. Fisher); *Comprehensive Violin Method* (Bronson Pub.) songs. Wife coll. as lyricist. 1370 Arrowhead Ave., San Bernardino, Calif.

HEIFETZ, JASCHA

Violinist. b. Vilna, Russia, 1901. Att. Royal Cons. of Music, St. Petersburg. St. violin w. Auer. Concerts, soloist w. leading symphonies throughout world. In film *They Shall Have Music*. Chevalier of the Legion of Honor, France. Comp. incl. transcriptions, arrangements of masterworks. Management: Columbia Concerts, New York City. Res. Balboa, Calif.

Rose Leaves Heeder

HEINDORF, RAY

Composer, arranger, orchestrator. b. New York City, 1908. With Warner Bros. since 1931; prior to then w. MGM, Sam Goldwyn. Among numerous pictures scored are *Up In Arms*, and *The Wonder Man*, w. Danny Kaye, *The Time, The Place, The Girl, My Wild Irish Rose, Rhapsody in Blue, Night and Day* (last two nom. for Academy Award), *Two Guys From Texas, Romance in High C., April Showers*; in prep. *Life of Marilyn Miller*. Scored Warner Bros. musical pictures 16 yrs. Won Academy Award two successive yrs. for *Yankee Doodle Dandy*, 1942; *This Is The Army*, 1943. Warner Bros. Studios, Burbank, Calif.

HESS, ELSIE DULEY

Teacher of voice, piano; pianist. St. piano w. Claude Gotthelf, Arthur Friedheim, Wilma Souvageol. Teachers training w. Irene Carter Oates, Constance Beauer; master classes, Noah Steinberg; voice w. C. M. Hall, Harriet Gill. Fresno repr. of Burrows School. Comp. of: *Hush-a-Bye My Baby*, (publ. Quincke) *Indian Suite, Reminiscence, Among My Souvenirs* (a pageant) (mss.). 520 Brown Ave., Fresno, Calif.

HICKMAN, C. SHARPLESS

Music critic, reviewer, editor. b. Seattle, Wash. Reviewer, Christian Science Monitor; editor, Note, Chamber of Comm. music bulletin. Former critic, Los Angeles Times 1943-47, San Fernando Valley Times, 1947. Contrib. articles to various music journals. 701 Ocean Ave., Santa Monica, Calif.

HILSBERG, IGNACE

Pianist, pedagog. b. Warsaw, Poland, July 8, 1894. St. Petersburg Cons. (Essipoff, Sauer); Laureate Petersburg Cons. Concertized throughout world, appearing w. major symphony orchestras in Poland, Russia, Siberia, Greece, Orient, Europe and USA. Soloist. w. Boston Symph., New York Philharmonic-Symphony, Los Angeles Philharmonic, Hollywood Bowl orchestras. Professor Royal Cons., Athens, Greece (2 yrs.); faculty Juilliard School of Music, N. Y. (10 yrs.). Recordings w. Brunswick. Member Bohemian Club (N.Y.). Hobby, fishing. 135 N. Anita Ave., Brentwood, Los Angeles 24, Calif.

HINES, JEROME

Basso. b. Hollywood, Calif., 1921. St. Gennaro M. Curci. B.S., UCLA. Won Hollywood Bowl auditions, 1942. At 17 app. in light opera Los Angeles, San Francisco. App. w. San Francisco Opera Co. in *Tannhauser, Rigoletto, Aida*; *Faust* for Opera Assn. of Golden West; San Carlo Opera Co., on tours. Starred in five operas w. New Orleans Opera Assn. At present w. Metropolitan Opera Co. Concerts in U.S., Hollywood Bowl, etc. Taught chemistry during war at UCLA. Comp. several songs. Hobbies: deep-sea fishing, ice skating. Metropolitan Opera Co., New York City.

HIRT, CHARLES C.

Director of choral organizations; Director Department of Sacred Music, Univ. of So. Calif.; Minister of Music, First Pres. Church of Hollywood. b. Nov. 4, 1911. B.A., Occidental Coll.; M.S., Ph.D., Univ. of So. Calif. Coached w. John Smallman, others. Instructor public school music, 1934-1942. Since 1943 w. Univ. of So. Calif. Travels extensively as guest conductor choral festivals and lecturer on choral music and Russian liturgical song. Founder-cond. Cathedral Choir; recorded (Columbia) w. Dennis Morgan. Member: Sigma Alpha Epsilon, Phi Kappa Phi, Phi Mu Alpha Sinfonia, Pi Kappa Lambda, Phi Beta Kappa, Choral Conductors' Guild of So. Calif., So. Calif. Vocal Assn. College of Music, Univ. of So. California, Los Angeles, Calif.

HOFFMAN, FRANS

Choral conductor, coach, teacher of voice; lieder, oratorio singer. b. Holland. Grad. Royal Dutch Soc. of Mus. Concertized in Europe, U.S., Orient. Arr. Los Angeles 1924. Head voice dept. Westminster Choir Coll. Princeton, N.J., 1934-42; min. of mus. Immanuel Pres. Ch., 1942; Prof. of voice, Univ. of So. Cal. 1027 S. Doran St., South Pasadena, Calif.

HOFMANN, JOSEF

Pianist. b. Podgorze, Poland, 1876. St. piano w. father, Urban, and A. Rubinstein. Concerts throughout world; soloist w. all leading sym. orchs. Dir. Curtis Inst. of Music, 1924-38. c/o L. E. Behymer, 427 W. 5th St., Los Angeles, Calif.

HOFFMEISTER, HALESIA, D.

Teacher of piano, theory, harmony. b. Iowa. St. piano w. Vallie Beck, Roessler, May MacDonald Hope Coryell; harmony w. Carolyn Alchin, Doris Moon, Vincent Jones, Frank Anderson. Pupils incl. radio performers and music supervisors in public schools. Author of *Contracts and Graphs* for sight reading and keyboard correlation (publ. 1929): *Magic Note Text*. Member MTA, Alchin Club. 5434 Hillcrest Dr., Los Angeles, Calif.

HOLLENBECK, WILLIAM H.

Trumpeter, musical director, choral and instrumental. b. Los Angeles, 1917. B.M. Univ. of Southern Calif. St. w. Lillian B. Wilson, Lucien Cailliet, Harold Mitchell, Philip Memoli, Former dir. Southwest Boys Band, South Gate Boys and Girls Band, Huntington Park Elks Band, Southern Calif. Boys Band. Organized children's orch. for Shirley Temple picture *Little Miss Broadway* (1937). Dir. Army Air Forces band training school, Greensboro, N.C. under Capt. Glenn Miller. Dir. of Music, Woodbury Coll. since 1940. Asst. dir. Music Dept., Loyola Univ. since 1938, acting dir. 1946. Appeared w. Loyola Univ. Band; trumpet, asst. cond. L.A. Rams Band. Hobby: tennis. 145 La Villa, Downey, Calif.

HOLMELUND, ESTELLE ZINK

Musical therapist. b. Brookfield, Mo. St. flute, played in choirs, orchestras, bands; won state honors as soloist. Founder of Parents' Assn. for Physically Handicapped Children of San Mateo County, Calif. Started summer schools and physiotherapy classes that have developed into semi-public local schools for spastics and two state institutions in Calif. Active flutist in amateur symphony orchestras. At present engaged in music therapy work in psychiatric wards of hospitals. Chairman of Peninsula Music Work Shops for Music in Hospitals. Address: 134 Elm Street, San Mateo, Calif.

HOLT, HARRIET

Teacher of voice, piano, drama. b. Hanford, Wash., 1910. Ed. Lasell Coll., Auburndale, Mass., 1929; won Henry Dunham Scholarship from New England Cons.; Sherwood Music School, Chicago; Leonid Snegoff (drama); voice w. Gennaro Curci. Concert tours, dramatic stage, radio appearances. Taught public school music, drama, Conway, S. C.; tchr. Zoellner Cons. of Music, L.A.; Allington-Pratt Music School, Van Nuys; own studios since 1939. Prod. and directed radio sketches KMPR, KECA, KMPC. Member Van Nuys Cultural Arts Committee; rep. for music Van Nuys Chamber of Commerce; Mus. Dir. Church of the Vespers; Junior and Adult Church Choirs; Valley Vespers Choir; concerts at Edward Everett Horton home; dir. Children's Choir, Studio City Episcopal Church 1934-44; Sherman Oaks Presbyterian Adult Choir 1943-44; G.I. Metropolitan Air Base Choir 1943. Program dir. Van Nuys Christmas Season Broadcasts; drama dir. Glendale Tuesday Afternoon Club; won first place, 15th Annual So. Calif. Tournament of One Act Plays, Santa Ana (1941). Comp. of plays, monologues, operetta *Palmetto Moon*; libretto to *Drums* (Prince Parkhurst). Hobbies: swimming, walking. 17013 Otsego Street, Encino, Calif.

HOOD, EVELYN

Concert pianist, teacher of piano. b. Bogard, Mo. St. w. Joseph Lhevinne; coached w. Isidore Phillip, Sergei Tarnowsky. Mus. B. American Cons. Chicago (1937). Concertized throughout U. S. Soloist w. Tulsa Symphony, San Gabriel Symphony, Calif. Artist Series, Pasadena (1944) w. San Marino Women's Club, KVGO, KXLA, Pasadena. Teacher of Margaret Frese, Mary Margaret Poole. Member: Sigma Alpha Iota; Tuesday Music Club, Pasadena. Hobbies: skating, swimming. 936 Huntington Dr., San Marino, Calif.

Ray Heindorf

HORODAS, MARTIN

Basso, concert and opera; teacher of voice. b. Pskov, Russia. St. voice w. Billari, Hageman, Cesare Sodero, New York. Sang leading bass roles w. Aborn, Boston, San Carlo, New York Civic, other opera cos.; concertized in U. S., Europe, incl. Lewissohn Stadium. Comps. incl songs, piano pieces. Hobby, fishing. Member AGMA. 109 N. Whitnall Hwy., Burbank, Calif.

HOUSER, FRANK

Violinist, teacher of violin. b. San Francisco, 1916. St. violin w. Argiewicz (10 yrs.); Univ. of Calif. Member NBC staff orchestra, 1936; San Francisco Symphony since 1936. Violinist for Music Lovers Soc.; second violin, San Francisco String Quartet. Asst. concertmaster, San Francisco Opera Orch. Played under Hertz, Stokowski, Walter, Barbirolli, Goossens, Monteux. Recordings w. S.F. Symphony (Monteux). Member San Francisco Music Club. Hobbies: fencing, swimming. Wife, Frances La Vergne, pianist. 1969 Green St., San Francisco, Calif.

HOUSINGER, EUNICE

Hammond organist, pianist, conductor; teacher of Hammond organ, piano, voice. b. Stamford, Conn. St. piano w. Sherwood Sch. of Mus. (diploma), Miracle Series (diploma); voice w. Edmund G. Myers; organ w. Jack Callahan. Concerts in U. S., particularly in West; numerous radio app. incl. program KVOS (2 yrs.), soloist KGO, KPO, others. Cond. Merced Orch. since 1946. Spec. in Hammond organ w. all devices. Comp. incl. songs, piano, organ pieces. Member AFM Local 454. Hobbies: sports, esp. swimming, boating. Studio: Shaffer Bldg., Merced, Calif.

HOWE, ZOULA COCKERILL

Teacher of piano. b. Shell City, Mo. St. piano Boarding Cons., Shelbina, Mo. w. Nora Naetor at age 7; Megquire Cons., Booneville, Mo. w. Edward Baxter Perry (3 yrs.); Cottey Coll. and Cons., Nevada, Mo. (P.E.O. Sisterhood) (3 yrs.) w. Mr. and Mrs. Edouard Blitz; w. Marie Pabereskin (Pittsburgh, Pa.); organ w. Albert S. Tufts, L. A. Organist motion picture houses, vaudeville (10 yrs.). Member, Colleague MTA. Assoc. tchr. Sherwood Music School (Chicago). Tchr. of Billy Turley. 216 No. Orange St., Glendale 3, Calif.

HOWELL, JULIA

Instruc. in harmony, dictation. b. Los Gatos, Calif. Mus. B. Univ. So. Calif. Music M. Eastman Sch. of Music, Rochester, N.Y. Spec. sec. credential, diploma, L.A. State Normal Sch. St. theory, comp. w. Carolyn Alchin, Vincent Jones; piano w. Abby de Avirett. Dir. mus. Redondo Union H.S., Supt. mus. Redondo Beach City Schls., 1917-20. Summer faculty N.Y. Univ., 1926, 1930. Harmony class demonstration, Nat'l Mus. Supervisors Conf. Chicago, 1929, Calif. Conf. in L.A. Comp. of songs, *Suite* (piano & organ), incidental mus. to two *Three Minute Plays* by Thornton Wilder. Organist Long Beach, L.A. churches, since 1914. Chairman harmony, dictation dept. School of Music, Univ. So. Calif., since 1920. 5321 Mt. Helena Ave., Eagle Rock, Calif.

HOWELL, RUTH

Singer, teacher. b. Nauvoo, Ill. Att. Carter Cons., L. A. St. piano w. Grace Hilgen, Hans Blechschmidt, Arthur Alexander, Josef Schmid, Richard Hageman; voice w. de Segurola, Gilbert, Mrs. Jones-Simmons, George Wilbur Ried. Sang for motion pictures, radio. Toured southwest. Hollywood Bowl as Orthlinde in *Die Walkure.* Head voice dept., Hollywood Conserv. (5 yrs.). 1559 N. Kingsley Dr., Hollywood, Calif.

HUBBELL, FRANK ALLEN

Conductor, composer, arranger, trumpet player. b. Denver, Colo., 1907. Att. Boguslawski Coll. of Music, Chicago. St. harmony, theory, orch., comp. w. Edmund Ross (pupil of Saint-Saens); symphonic score reading, conducting w. Albert Coates, Vladimir Bakaleinikoff. In Hollywood studio, radio, recording field since 1936. Among founders of Santa Monica Symphony Orch. Comp. *Mother Nature's Children* (prod. 1937) *French Suite* (string quartet) *Theme and Variations* (chamber orch.) *Pasacaglia and Scherzo, Cortege (Vers la*

Tombeau). Procession Kismet, (full orch.) *California Suite* (based on Calif. history). Currently w. KFI staff Hollywood Bowl Young Artists program, Lux Radio Theater. Music dir. of Belda Recording Co., mus. dir., cond. Ballet Assn. of America. Hobby: collecting first editions and old manuscripts of early Calif. history. 4242 McFarlane Ave., Burbank, Calif.

HUGHSON, GLORIA NASSI

Concert violinist, teacher of violin. b. Sacramento, Calif. St. violin w. Emily Rulison Smith, Sacramento, Naoum Blinder, San Francisco; theory, comp. Sacramento Coll. Concertized in California. First violin Sacramento Philharmonic Orch. Radio KFBK. Soloist and concertmistress Sacramento Coll. Symphony; concertmistress, Sacramento Youth Orch. First violinist, soloist w. Sacramento Convention Ensemble. Member M.N.S. violin trio, various string quartets. Also competent pianist, accompanist. Member Sacramento Saturday Club. Hobbies: knitting, collecting personality clippings. Teacher in Sacramento since 1944. 864 36th St., Sacramento, Calif.

HULTMAN, PAUL

Pianist. b. Omaha, Nebr. Father, Rev. J. A. Hultman, first teacher. Pupil of Emil Liebling, Arthur Foote. Att. Worcester Academy, Williams Coll. Coached w. Xaver Scharwenka, Berlin (2 yrs.), Robert Lortat, Paris. Toured Sweden w. father (baritone); joint concert tour w. Gustave Holmquist. Establ. music conservatory in Worcester, Mass., faculty incl. membs. of Boston Symphony Orch. After ten yrs. returned to concertizing w. Julia Clausen, Gustave Holmquist, H. William Nordin, Northland Trio. Faculty Bush Cons. Choirmaster, organist, Messiah Lutheran Church, Chicago since 1930, choir dir. organist Los Angeles, Pasadena churches. 1022 Cacique St., Santa Barbara, Calif.

HUNT, MINABEL

Accompanist, coach, organist. Att. Franklin Coll., Denison Univ., Metropolitan School of Music, Indianapolis. St. w. Frank La Forge, Edwin Hughes, R. Huntington Woodman, New York City. Accomp. People's Chorus (oratorio) Indianapolis (3 yrs.), Brooklyn Morning Choral (10 yrs.); studio accompanist-coach for Franz Prochowsky, Oscar Seagle, Adelaide Gescheidt, New York. Toured as accomp. w. Opera Group under National Music League and Junior League, New York. Accomp. program chairman New York Matinee Musicale (7 yrs.); director-organist Richmond Hill Cong. Church, Long Island (5 yrs.). Now repertoire coach Herbert Wall Vocal Studios; organist Wilshire Methodist Church. Mother of Marsha Hunt, screen actress. 7950 Sunset Blvd., Hollywood, Calif.

INESITA

Spanish concert dancer (soloist). b. New York, 1925. Featured solo dancer Civic Light Opera Productions of *Rio Rita, Meet the People.* Appeared as solo dancer at War Memorial Opera House, San Francisco; concertized all over West Coast in leading theaters, auditoriums. Gave complete concert program at Long Beach Municipal Auditorium. Solo dancer leading night clubs, Mexico City, N.Y.C. Member: AGVA., Actors' Equity, Screen Actors Guild. 828 No. Laurel Ave., Los Angeles, Calif.

IRISH, MRS. LEILAND ATHERTON

Music educator. St. piano, theory w. Edna Schwartz; public speaking w. Eula Beans. Off. organist Fraternal Brotherhood, 1910. Exec. vice-pres., gen. mgr., So. Calif. Sym. Assn., Hollywood Bowl (14 yrs.). Vice-pres. Greater Los Angeles Plans, Inc. Bus. dir. Los Angeles County Art Assn. Hon. pres. Santa Monica Music Civic Guild (sponsoring Santa Monica Sym.). Member: Dominant Club (hon.), Centennial Committee, Daughters of the Golden West, Sigma Alpha Iota, Delta Kappa Gamma, Chi Omega, Euterpe Opera Reading Club. 5733 Virginia Ave., Hollywood 38, Calif.

ITURBI, AMPARO

Concert pianist. b. Valencia, Spain. St. piano w. brother, Jose. Concertized, appearances w. leading sym. orchs. throughout world. Duo-piano concerts w. brother, Jose. Victor records. 729 No. Rodeo Dr., Beverly Hills, Calif.

Alexander F. Haas   Ettadell Hall   Mildred M. Hancox   Tonia Drew Hansen

Ruth Haroldson   James Hart   Mary Martha Hart   Emanuel R. Heifetz

Elsie Duley Hess   Ignace Hilsberg   Jerome Hines   Charles C. Hirt

Frans Hoffman   Halesia D. Hoffmeister   William H. Hollenbeck   Estelle Zink Holmelund

213

Harriet Holt

Evelyn Hood

Frank Houser

Eunice Housinger

Zoula Cockerill Howe

Frank Allen Hubbell

Gloria Nassi Hughson

Minabel Hunt

Paul Hultman

Inesita

Peter Jarrett

Gertrude L. Johnson

Alta Johnstead

Werner Janssen

ITURBI, JOSE

Concert pianist, conductor, actor. b. Valencia, Spain, 1895. Att. Valencia Cons., Paris Cons. St. piano w. Malats, Staub. Concerts and soloist w. leading sym. orchs. throughout U. S. Cond. Rochester Phil., Mexico City, Hollywood Bowl, other orchs. Duo-piano concerts w. sister, Amparo. Numerous film recordings, Victor records. Under contract MGM studios, Culver City, Calif.

JACKSON, GRACE EMMONS

Teacher of piano, theory, harmony, history of music. Piano w. Lillian B. Pomeroy, Emil Liebling, Archibald Sessions; organ w. Harrison Wilde, Alfred J. Chaplin, Archibald Sessions; piano normal, Adelaide Trobridge Perry, Vernon Spencer, Marguerite Hauber O'Leary, Batchellor-Landon Musical Kindergarten Method, Sherwood Music School Normal Course. Colleague Degree, MTA of Calif. Treas. Calif. Federation of Music Clubs, financial secretary, MTA of Calif. Hobbies: dancing, young children. 419 W. Glenoaks Blvd., Glendale, Calif.

JACKSON, NANCY

Dancer, teacher of dancing. b. Colorado Springs, Colo. St. dancing w. Denishawn, also in London; Doris Humphries, Martha Graham, New York; Harold Kreutzeberg, Salzburg; Mary Wigman, Dresden; Spanish, Mexican in those countries. Toured U.S., Europe (London, Paris, Madrid, Monte Carlo, etc.); danced for former King and Queen of Spain, Prince of Wales. Lectured for numerous clubs. Instr. for Assoc. Dncg. Tchrs. of Am., So. Calif. conven. 1943-46. Choreographed numerous ballets, dances. Member Assoc. Dncg, Tchrs. of Am. Hobbies: art, painting, gardening. 1330 Winston St., San Marino, Calif.

JACOBS, ARTHUR LESLIE

Director, music dept., Church Federation of Los Angeles. b. Ft. Wayne, Ind., 1896. St. w. Christian, Delamarter, Decaux, Bonnet, Philipp; cho. w. Williamson. Dir. Bach Festivals; founded Fest. of Modern Music, First Cong. Ch., Los Angeles. Church Federation, 3330 W. Adams, Los Angeles, Calif.

JAHN, AGNES EYRE de

Pianist, teacher. b. Ortonville, Minn. Hon. grad., won schol. New England Cons. of Music. St. harmony, comp. w. George W. Chadwick, Edward Shippen Barnes; piano w. Leschetizky (4 yrs.), Vienna. Toured as solo pianist w. Jan Kubelik in England, Scotland, Wales, U. S., Canada. Played w. the London Symphony. Concert appearances in Vienna, Berlin, Lausanne, London. Comp. piano pieces, songs. Judge of Nat'l Piano Playing Tourn., Oakland div. (2 yrs. in succession). Faculty member Inst. Mus. Art, N. Y. (4 yrs.). Active member Leschetizky Assn. of America. Pupils incl. Jeanne Pollack, Minnie Sasahara, Gladys Schorling, of Fresno, Calif. 702 Peralta Way, Fresno 4, Calif.

JANSSEN, WERNER

Conductor, composer; music director, Portland Symphony Orch. b. New York City, 1900. Grad. Dartmouth Coll., 1921; hon. mus. degree, 1934. Fellow of Amer. Acad. in Rome; Prix de Rome, 1930-34. Cond. under Toscanini, first native New Yorker to cond. N.Y. Philharmonic-Symphony. 1934-35. Cond. Chicago, Cleveland, Detroit, St. Louis, Rochester, Los Angeles, other leading orchs., all major European symphonies. Cond. many commercial radio hours, Standard Symphony broadcasts, etc. Founded Janssen Symphony of Los Angeles, directed 1941-46; cond. Baltimore Symphony 1938-39; Utah Symphony 1946-47, Portland Symphony since 1947. Comp. New Year's Eve in New York, many chamber works, film scores, incl. General Died at Dawn, Blockade, etc. Victor records of many standard works, also moderns commissioned for perf. w. Janssen Symphony, incl. Genesis, comp. by Schoenberg, Shilkret, Toch, others. Decorated Knight, first class, Order of White Rose (Finland) for interp. of Sibelius Symphonies. Mgmt. Arthur Judson, 113 W. 57th St., New York 19, N.Y. Portland Symphony Orch., 507 Fulton Bldg., Portland, Ore.

JARRETT, PETER

Concert pianist. b. Honolulu, Hawaii, June 29, 1918. St. piano, theory w. Alexander Raab, Berkeley, Calif. Concertized throughout the U.S. incl. Honolulu, L.A., San Francisco, eastern cities. New York Town Hall debut 1946. 2516 Warring St., Berkeley, Calif.

JOHNSON, GERTRUDE L.

Teacher of singing. b. Indianapolis, Ind. St. piano four years w. private teachers. Att. Cincinnati Cons. of Music. Voice w. Tecla Vigna, Dan Beddoe, Frantz Proschowski. Taught voice and piano Atlanta Cons. of Music, Presbyterian College, Williamsburg, Va., Methodist Female College, Millersburg, Ky. Soloist First Church of Christ, Scientist, Atlanta, Ga. Teacher of voice for thirty yrs. Member MTA. 15 So. Raymond Ave., Pasadena, Calif.

JOHNSTEAD, ALTA

Pianist, teacher of piano. b. Tacoma, Wash. Began piano study at age 8. Piano, harmony w. Paul Pierre McNeely, Seattle. Public appearances in Tacoma, Seattle, Spokane; radio appearances in Seattle over KOL; Tacoma, KMO, KVI, KTBI. Member Washington State, Tacoma MTA, Tacoma's Ladies Music Club, Junior Ladies Music Club. Studio: 606 No. Anderson St., Tacoma, Wash.

JONES, EDWIN

Violin teacher: faculty member, Santa Barbara State College, Univ. of Calif.

JONES, ISABEL MORSE

Music educator. b. Cleveland, Ohio. Att. Los Angeles H.S., UCLA. St. violin, piano, comp. w. pvt. tchrs Cleveland, Sierra Madre, Los Angeles; orch. w. Walter Henry Rothwell; comp. w. Shaul-Hallet, Thilo Becker, Fanny Dillon. Member Los Angeles Women's Orch.; app. under Harley Hamilton, Adolph Tandler, Henry Schoenefeld. Concertized in So. Calif.; taught violin 10 yrs. Music editor, critic Los Angeles Times 1925-47, Daily News 1924-25; gen. news Fresno Bee, 1922-23. Correspondent Musical America 1940-47. Founder-dir. Music Academy of the West, 1947. 814 Philharmonic Auditorium Bldg., 427 W. 5th St., Los Angeles 13, Calif.

JORY, MRS. JOHN HOWARD (Laura Olschewski White)

Teacher of piano, theory, composition. b. Seattle, Wash. St. piano w. Mrs. Clement J. Challar, Louis Dimond, Henry Squire (Univ. of Washington), Sigismund Stojowski; priv. and master classes w. Noah Steinberg, theory w. Ada Deighton Hilling, Univ. of Wash. Past-pres. Fresno County MTA. Member Fresno Musical Club, Fed. Music Clubs. Pupil, Mary Kim, form. teacher Peabody Inst. Baltimore, Md. Hobby: gardening. 3464 Kerchoff, Fresno, Calif.

KANITZ, ERNEST

Composer, teacher of comp., conductor. b. Vienna, Austria, April 9, 1894. St. Univ. of Vienna, theory, comp, w. Franz Schreker. Fur.D., Vienna, 1918. Cond. Vienna' Women's Chamber Choir; concerts throughout Europe. American citizen since 1944. Prof. of theory Winthrop College (1838-41). Head, Music Dept., Erskine College (1941-44); professor comp., counterpoint, Univ. of So. Calif. since 1945. Comp. performed in leading music centers of Europe, U. S. incl. Hollywood Bowl, (Stokowski), Los Angeles Philharmonic (Wallenstein), St. Louis Symphony (Golschmann). Comp.: Gay Overture, four songs for soprano, Orch., Ballet Music, for orch. and women's chorus (Univ. Edition), Motion Picture (three orch. fantasies) (C. Fischer), Evening Festival for Radio, Serenade (wind instr. pf. percuss.), Concerto for theremin and orchestra, Concerto Grosso, Sonata (vn. and pf.) (Univ. Edition), Suite (vn. and pf.), String Quartet in D, String Trio, Dance Sonata for 4 wind instr. and pf., Trio (fl. vn. pf), Two Pieces (clarinet, pf.), Two Pieces (trumpet, pf.), Sonata California (alto sax., pf.) (C. Fischer), Quintettino (wind instr., pf.), Suite (fl., 2 vns., pf.); Opera, Wunder Wilan, Liberation (school orch.); numerous choral works, chamber music, songs, piano pieces. Author of: A. Counterpoint Workbook. Member: Austrian League of Composers (secretary), American Assn. of Univ. Professors, Phi Mu Alpha Sinfonia (hon.). Hobbies: ping-pong, chess. 2907 So. Normandie Ave., Los Angeles, Calif.

Mrs. John Howard Jory

Philip J. Karp

Agnes Eyre de Jahn

Ernest Kanitz

Jody Kay

Bernard Katz

Louis Kaufman

217

KARP, PHILIP J.

Principal bass, San Francisco Symphony (Pierre Monteux), San Francisco Opera Co. (Gaetano Merola). b. Knoxville, Tenn., 1915. St. violin, piano w. father, Maurice Karp (pupil of Kneisel), piano w. Earl Fraser; theory, harmony Univ. of Miami; bass w. I. Schull Lipschutz. Member: Miami Symphony (Arnold Volpe) Bach Society, Oratorio Society, Pasadena Civic Orch. (Richard Lert), Los Angeles Philharmonic, Hollywood Bowl, National Phil. Symphony, Pittsburgh Symphony (Fritz Reiner), staff Radio City, San Francisco. Recordings for Victor w. S.F. Symphony (Pierre Monteux). Faculty member, Academy of Music, San Francisco. Wife, Jane Davis Harris, contralto, soloist in churches, a cappella choirs. Hobby: collecting pipes, antique autos, firearms. 1431 Cole St., San Francisco, Calif.

KATZ, BERNARD

Conductor, composer, arranger. b. San Francisco, Calif., 1909. Began piano age 10 w. Louis Felix Raynaud, San Francisco. First major recital Berkeley Greek Theatre, at age 12. Soloist w. San Francisco Symphony Orchestra, Pacific Coast premiere Gershwin *Rhapsody in Blue*, 1931; Gershwin *Concerto*, 1932. Toured Pacific Coast in piano recitals. Official pianist, organist Mutual Broad. System, 1936, and Natl. Broad. Co., 1938. Music dir., comp., arr. for radio: *Union Oil Program*, since 1941; *The Mayor of the Town*, Lionel Barrymore, since 1942; *Cresta Blanca Hollywood Players*, since 1943. Library of original music exclusively composed for dramatic radio programs considered largest, most complete on Pacific Coast. Recordings of transcribed 15-minute piano and organ recitals played on major networks. Hobbies: hunting, fishing. 1706 Garth Ave., Los Angeles, Calif.

KAUFMAN, ANNETTE (Mrs. Louis Kaufman)

Concert pianist, accompanist. b. Chicago, Ill. Att. Institute of Musical Art; st. piano w. James Friskin, New York, Mme. Jeanne Blancard, Ecole Normale, Paris. Accompanist to Louis Kaufman in concert tours of U.S., Europe, Mexico, Premiered, recorded many new works of American contemporary composers. Recorded *American Album* w. Louis Kaufman (Vox Prod.). Cf. Louis Kaufman biography. Member AFM Local 47. Hobby: coll. American antiques, art, books. c/o Louis Kaufman, National Concert and Artists Corp., 711 Fifth Ave., New York 22, N.Y.

KAUFMAN, LOUIS

Concert violinist. b. Portland, Ore. St. violin w. Kneisel; Inst. of Musical Art, N.Y.; grad. Artists Course w. highest honors. Won Loeb $1000 prize; Naumburg Award, N.Y. Concert tours throughout U.S., Europe, Mexico. Introduced new works (some commissioned) by Bennett, Copland, Loeffler, Helm, Jones, Triggs, Read, Kubik, Still, Khatchaturian, Achron, Knipper, Toch, Tansman, Rieti, Castelnuovo-Tedesco, Guarnieri, Milhaud, Kodaly, others. Played violin soli for over 400 feature films for Warner Bros., 20th Century-Fox, M-G-M, R.K.O., Paramount, Selznick, other studios. Won Musical Courier citation 1926 for best instr. solo in films. Recordings incl. Khatchaturian *Concerto* (w. Santa Monica Symphony; Rachmilovich), Copland *Sonata* (w. composer) (Concert Hall Soc.); Bennett *Hexapoda* (Five Studies in Jitteroptera) (w. composer), Toch *Quintet* (Kaufman String Quartet w. composer) (Columbia Masterworks); Saint-Saens *Concerto, b-minor, Op. 61* (w. Santa Monica Symphony; Rachmilovich), J. S. Bach *Concerto II, E-major* (w. Santa Monica Chamber Orch.; Rachmilovich), Bach *Partita, d-minor* (vn. alone); Respighi *Sonata, b-minor*, Bennett *Song Sonata*, Delius *First Sonata* (all w. T. Saidenberg), Tchaikovsky *Trio, Op. 50* (w. T. Saidenberg, pf. Kurt Reher, vc), *Contemporary Violin Recital* (modern works) (Disc. Rec. Co.); *Americana Album* (w. Annette Kaufman) (Copland, Still, McBride, Helm, Triggs works), Toch *Serenade* (2 vns. vla. w. Monasevitch, Menhennick), Smetana *Trio* (w. Firkusny, pf. Van den Burg, vc.) (Vox. Prod.); Vivaldi *4 Concerti* (Swoboda, orch. dir.; Nies-Berger, organ) (Concert Hall). Member: AGMA, AFM Local 47, Amer. Archaeological Soc. Hobby, coll. Amer. antiques, art, books. Mgmt. National Concert and Artists Corp. 711 Fifth Ave., New York 22, N.Y.

KAY, JODY (Mrs. Josephine Lux Kagy)

Dramatic soprano, composer, author, poet, artist. b. Peru, Indiana. Sang w. family trio as child artist. St. voice w. Clifford Lott, Miss Chaney. Concertized in U.S. Soloist Christian Science Church, L.A. (8 yrs.); Soloist other churches. Comp. incl. *Love's Great Ecstasy, Today, Sing, America, Sing, Be Not Weary in Well Doing* (sac.). Author many song lyrics, poems. Contributor of articles to various papers, magazines. Member Hollywood Women's Club. Hobby: horseback riding. 2148 Beechwood Ter., Hollywood 28, Calif.

KEGL, JOSEPHINE GERIN

Teacher of piano, theory. b. McCartney, Pa. St. at Oberlin Cons., Oberlin, Ohio. Mus.B., Bush Cons., Chicago, 1925. Mus.M., under Philip Borowski, Gunn School of Music, Chicago, 1927. Asst. to Leo Sowerby, Gunn School of Music (5 yrs.). Head Theory Dept., Columbus Cons., Aurora, Ill. (5 yrs.). Pupil of Ethel Leginska; protegee of Gina Vandeveer (singer, Berlin Staats Opera, Vienna Hof Opera). Assoc. Kreig-Gerin Music Studios, North Hollywood, Calif. (1930-1942). Studio, 10861 Moorpark St., North Hollywood, Calif.

KELLER, ALFRED

Violinist, teacher. b. Waterbury, Conn., Sept. 20, 1904. St. violin w. Albert Stoessel, Institute of Musical Art, N.Y.; w. Sevcik, Chicago and Pisek, Bohemia; w. Jeno Hubay, Budapest, Hungary; w. Carl Flesch, Berlin and Curtis Institute of Music, Phila.; w. Paul Kochanski, Juilliard Graduate School of Music, N.Y. A.B., Univ. of Cincinnati, Cinn. Ohio. Concertmaster, Portland Symphony Orch. (Willem Van Hoogstraten) 1925-1927; first violinist, New York Symphony (Walter Damrosch) 1927-1928; first violinist, Cincinnati Symphony (Fritz Reiner, Eugene Goossens) 1929-1935. Taught at Univ. of Wyoming summer 1945; taught at Willamette Univ., Salem, Ore., 1945-46. 2205 N.E. 50th Ave., Portland 13, Oregon.

KELLER, WILLIAM

Accompanist, pianist, teacher. b. San Francisco, 1919. St. piano w. Ada Clement, Carl Friedberg; theory w. George A. Wedge; harmony w. Lillian Hodghead; comp. w. Raymond White. Master classes w. Josef Lhevinne, Albert Elkus. Grad. S.F. Cons. of Music, 1937; Juilliard School of Music, 1942. Accomp. to Kayton Nesbitt, Romalda Stetsky, Paul Walti, Anna Rene, Olga Christiani: Instructor, S.F. Cons. of Music. Hobby: travel. S.F. Conservatory of Music, 3435 Sacramento St., San Francisco, Calif.

KENDALL, EDITH FORD

Teacher of singing. b. Ogden, Utah. Began violin at age 8. St. w. Enoch Ford (father), Henry Irwin (pupil of Wirch, Berlin), Louis W. Ford, (brother). Played professionally for ten yrs.; traveled w. family concert group. St. voice w. Chevalier Alberto L. Guelli (2 yrs.), Amelia Chellia (N.Y.C.) (3 yrs.), Alberto Alanso, (Valencia, Spain) (2 yrs.), Hubbard (N.Y.C.). Toured Keith-Orpheum Circuit as memb. of Pla Operatic Trio (4 yrs.). Concertized throughout U.S., Canada, Hawaii. Taught voice in Los Angeles (10 yrs.); estab. in San Francisco (18 yrs.). Pupils in leading roles, opera, concert, radio. Member MTA. Studio: 990 Geary St., San Francisco, Calif.

KERBY, MARION

Singing character-actress. b. Streator, Ill. Att .Annah Morgan Drama Sch., Chicago. Many years acting, Broadway, Legitimate stage. Acted-dir. all girls' cast of *Hamlet*, Powers Theater, Chicago, patronage Southern and Marlowe. First recital Aeolian Hall, London, patronage Ellen Terry, Sir James Barrie, Bernard Shaw, etc. Returned to America, app. in *The Traveling Salesman, The Country Boy, Third Degree, Pals First, Miss Ananias, The Real Thing, The Proper Spirit, Her Country, The Easiest Way* (revival), *Seventh Heaven*, others. Recitals in N.Y., London, Newport, Palm Beach, Canada; Library of Congress, Elizabeth Sprague Coolidge Festival w. John Jacob Niles; Town Hall, N.Y. w. Raymond McFeeters, 1947. Broadcasts BBC London, Hilversum, Holland. *For You I Die*, motion picture, 1947, Collector of negro songs, stories; singer of American folklore. 1722 No. Stanley Ave., Hollywood 46, California.

Josephine Gerin Kegl

William Keller

Edith Ford Kendall

Marion Kerby

Duci de Kerekjarto

Clyde Keutzer

William T. Killgrove

Ray Kimbell

Edith Knox

Rudolph Kopp

Theodore Kolline

Gladys Koven

Wanda Krasoff

219

KEREKJARTO, DUCI de

Concert violinist, composer, conductor. b. Ruttka, Hungary. St. Royal Acad. of Mus. Budapest; violin w. Jeno Hubay, theory, comp. w. Zoltan Kodaly. Diploma, Royal Acad. of Mus. Concertized throughout world; soloist w. all leading orchs. under Nikisch, Walter, Bodansky, Reiner, Iturbi, Hertz, Rodzinski, others. Comp. incl.: *Symphony, Prelude to Peace* (sym. poem), *Concerto* (violin and orch.), numerous violin pieces and transcr. of masterworks. Recordings w. Columbia, Decca Cos. Member, AFM Local 47. Hobbies: chess, gardening. Now under contract to Universal-International Pictures, Universal City, Calif. Mgmt. Music Corp. of America, Beverly Hills, Calif. Res. 12149 Oxnard St., North Hollywood, Calif.

KEUTZER, CLYDE

Concert tenor, dir. of music. b. Peru, Ill. M.A., Ph.B. Att. Univ. of Chicago, Columbia Univ. Town Hall concerts, 1937, 1940. Former member Phila. Civic Opera Co.; concerts in U. S. Soloist in oratorios. U.S.O. dir. 1943-45. Head voice dept., Univ. of North Carolina; Baldwin-Wallin Cons. of Music. At present, dir. dept. of music, College of Puget Sound. Member: Beta Theta Pi, Phi Mu Alpha-Sinfonia. College of Puget Sound, Dept. of Music, Tacoma, Wash.

KILLGROVE, LIEUT. WILLIAM T.

Musical director, organist. b. Kansas City, Kans. 1895. Att. Coll. of Mus., Univ. So. Calif., Western Inst. Music, Denver, Colo. St. w. Adelaide Perry Trowbridge, Charles E. Pemberton, Walter F. Skeele, John Smallman, John Finley Williamson, Ernest Douglas, Henry Housely, Lillian Backstrand Wilson. Comp. of musical play, *Dawning*, marches, choir music. Cond. band, orch., opera, oratorio. Mus. dir. several prominent L. A. churches incl. First Pres. Ch. of L.A., First Pres. Ch. of Hollywood, Calvary Pres. Ch. of So. Pasadena, Knox Pres. Ch. of L. A. Mus. dir. San Gabriel Drum and Bugle Corps. (nat'l champions Amer. Legion 1935-37), (won State champ. 9 yrs.). Pres. So. Calif. Band Masters' Assn. (3 yrs.); formerly officer AGO. Commission U. S. Navy, 1938, Line Lieut (highest rank given any musician in Navy except John Phillip Sousa). Concertized L.A. city parks, radio, etc. Plays keyboard instruments, brass instruments. 1141 Windsor Pl., Pasadena, Calif.

KIMBELL, RAY

Composer, pianist, teacher of theory, composition, piano. b. Sterling, Colo., Jan. 28, 1917. St. theory, orch., comp. w. Julius Gold, piano w. Adrian Vermaas, trpt. w. Will Bickett; also att. San Francisco Cons. of Music. Perf. w. various prof. orchs. in Western U.S. Lecturer on theoretical, allied subjects. Faculty Music and Arts Inst. 1946-47. Comp. incl. *Suite in the Classic Forms* (sym. orch.), other orch. works, chamber music, piano pieces, songs. Member AFM Local 6. Hobby, skiing. 263-G Clinton Park, San Francisco, Calif.

KING, ELEANOR CAMPBELL

Dancer. b. Middletown, Pa. Att. Theatre Guild School, Clare Tree Major's School of Theatre, Doris Humphrey-Charles Weidman Dance Group. Fellow, Bennington School of the Dance, Bennington, Vt. '38. Choreography for group: *Icaro, Ode to Freedom, American Folk Suite, Paradisms* (with Elizabeth Colman), *Beasts and Saints, Ascendence and Agonistæ, She, Tempest on Olympus.* Solo Choreography: *Characters of the Annunciation, Roads to Hell, Song for Heaven, Song of Earth, Mother of Tears, Moon Dances, Spirit Dance, To the West, Soliloquy in the Morning, Peace—an Allegory,* others. Dir. Seattle Dance Theatre. Hobbies: drawing, Bach, reading. 908 Madison, Seattle 22, Wash.

KLEIN, EMANUEL

Trumpeter. b. N.Y.C., 1908. Att. Inst. of Musical Art on scholarship. St. trumpet w. Max Schlossberg. Played solo trumpet under Kostelanetz, Shilkret, Black, Rappe, Romberg, Noble, Matty Malneck, Comp. incl. *Tiger Fantasy.* 10647 Camarillo St., No. Hollywood, Calif.

KNOX, EDITH

Concert pianist, teacher. b. Los Angeles, Calif. Scholarship w. Olga Steeb (3 yrs.), Albert Elkus (4 yrs.), Josef Lhevinne 1925, Sigismund Stojowski 1926; Fellowship Juilliard Grad. School (5 yrs.) w. Alexander Siloti; also taught secondary scholarship students in Juilliard. Played w. Nat'l Orchestral Assn. New York City; Portland Phil. (Vladimir Bakaleinikoff), Hollywood Bowl (Kurtz), San Diego Sym. (C. Bakaleinikoff), Vancouver Orch. (deRidder), Glendale Sym. (Altschuler), Sinfonietta Soc., San Francisco, Berkeley Univ. Orch. (Elkus), Appearances in Berkeley, Redlands Bowls; Morning Musical Salon Series, Los Angeles, Beverly Hills (6 yrs.). Concertized extensively in Central Europe 1931-33. Nat'l hon. member, Sigma Alpha Iota; member MTA. Hobbies: swimming, drawing, painting. Mgmt. Dorothy Huttenbach, 513 No. Rodeo Dr., Beverly Hills, Calif. Studio: 1547 So. Gramercy Pl., Los Angeles 6, Calif .

KOLLINE, THEODORE (Kolin, Feodor)

Composer, musical director, coach. b. Warsaw, Poland. Choir boy Westminster Chapel (age 11). St. piano w. Busoni (Vienna) (debut, age 13); voice w. Raymond von zur Muellen (debut as composer, age 17, conductor, 19). Cond. International Orchestra, London; mus. dir. Isis Cons., San Diego. Mus. D., Washington, D.C. Ph.D., Societe des Beaux Arts, Paris. Comp. of Hindu opera, *Harischandra*, four operettas: *The Concubine Drinks* (Chinese), *Lafayette* (French), *Last Night of the Fiesta* (Spanish), *The Man in the Moon* (Viennese); three symphonies; three ballets: *Primavera, Radium, Tchort*; orch suite *Voice of India*; symphonic poem *Gengis Khan*; *Preludes Romantique, Preludes Primitives, The Dance of Life* (dance forms of 12 nations); *Homage to the Masters*; incidental music for Wilde's *Salome*, songs, piano trio, piano quintet, quartet. Author: *Secrets of Music* (1927); *A New Music* (1937), *Poems* (1947), *The Divine Conflict* (3 act musical drama, Life of Liszt) (1947); *Life and Work of Beethoven* (1947). Medal of Pan-American Inst. for Hispanic music. Teaching method, John Dewey School. Coll. Michio Ito, Elise Dufor. Pres., Beethoven Society of America. Founder, Academy of Esthetic Synthesis (Regd.). Lecturer on music, art. Teacher of Lionel Barrymore (comp.), Lew Ayres (comp.), Ginger Rogers (voice, piano), John Carroll (voice, drama), Cathy Downs (drama), Lloyd Brooks (drama), Jackie Horner (piano). Freelance comp. for motion picture background music. 119 So. Detroit Ave., Los Angeles 36, Calif.

KOPP, RUDOLPH G.

Composer, conductor. b. Austria, March 22, 1887. Grad. Cons. of Vienna w. honors at 16. St. violin w. Karl Prill; theory, harmony, counterpoint w. Herrman Graedener; comp. w. Robert Fuchs, Richard Henberger. Concertmaster, asst. Kapellmeister military orch., Vienna. First violinist Folk Opera House. Traveled throughout Germany, France, Italy, U. S. Solo violist in Los Angeles Symphony. Member: Brahms Quintet. Music dir. Million Dollar Theater, L. A., Balaban & Katz, Chicago. Cond. symphony concerts in Mid-West. Co-founder, mus. dir. Young People's Orch. of Milwaukee. Formerly w. Paramount, now w. Metro-Goldwyn-Mayer. Amang pictures are: *The Sign of the Cross, Cleopatra, The Crusades,* for Cecil B. DeMille; *Gallant Bess, My Brother Talks to Horses, Tenth Avenue Angel,* others; many short subjects. Metro-Goldwyn-Mayer Pictures, Culver City, Calif.

KORNGOLD, ERICH WOLFGANG

Composer. b. Bruenn, Austria-Moravia, 1897. St. w. Robert Fuchs, Alex. V. Zemlinsky. At age 10 comp. *Fairy Tale Contata* (perf. Mahler), at 11, *The Snowman, Don Quichotte, Piano Sonata d-min.* Comp. incl. *Die Tote Stadt, The Ring of Polycrates, Violanta, Die Kathrin* (opera), *A Winter's Tale* (overture), *Sinfonietta, Much Ado About Nothing, Das Winder der Heliane* (orch.) adaptions of Strauss, Offenbach works; *Piano Trio, Piano Sonata C-maj.,* chamber music, songs, piano pieces, numerous film scores incl. *Midsummer Night's Dream, Captain Blood, Give Us This Night, Anthony Adverse, Prince and Pauper.* 9936 Toluca Lake Ave., North Hollywood, Calif.

Theodore Kratt   Melita Krieg   Gretchen Kuehny   Lorraine Laliberte

Alexander Laszlo   William Lava

Rena Lazelle   Rowland Leach   Vladimir Lenski   Richard Lert

KOVEN, GLADYS

Concert pianist, teacher. b. Cincinnati O. St. w. Thilo Becker (3 yrs.); Juilliard, w. Josef Lhevinne (5 yrs.), harmony, theory, comp. w. Reuben Goldmark. Joint recital w. Marion Talley at Biltmore; soloist at Roxy's N. Y. under Erno Rappee; joint recital w. Nina Koshetz; soloist w. David Broekman Orch. over NBC.; concertized thru U.S. 1919 Argyle St., Hollywood, Calif.

KRASOFF, WANDA

Concert pianist, teacher of piano. b. San Francisco, Calif. Father, Alexander, opera singer. St. piano w. Adolph Ryss, Alexander Raab. Won award from Gainsborough Music Found. Concert tours of U.S., particularly in West. Soloist w. Bach Festival, Carmel (Usigli); Standard Symphony (Monteux); Oakland Symphony (See); Bay Region Symphony, Oakland, San Francisco (Reiser, Brico); Northern California Symphony (Abas); etc. Member Berkeley Piano Club, MTA., Pacific Musical Soc. Hobbies: photography, travel, hiking. Studio: 2741 College Ave., Berkeley, Calif.

KRATT, THEODORE

Dean, School of Music, University of Oregon; choral, orchestral conductor. b. Portland, Ore., 1897. Mus. B., Mus. M., Mus. D. Chicago Mus. Coll.; Mus. D. Cincinnati Cons. of Mus. St. w. Felix Weingartner, Vienna. Examiner Nat'l Assn. of School of Music. Member: MTA, Mus. Ed. Conf., Rotary Intern. School of Music, University of Oregon, Eugene, Ore.

KRENEK, ERNST

Composer. b. Vienna, Austria, Aug. 23, 1900. Att. Humanistic H. S., Vienna; Univ. of Vienna; Imp. Acad. of Mus. Vienna; State Acad. of Mus., Berlin. Mus. D. Comp. incl. 12 operas, 4 symphonies, 7 string quartets, 3 piano concerti, 3 piano sonatas, other orchestral works, song cycles, chorals, piano suites, pieces. Member: MTA; Amer. Musicol. Soc.; Soc. for Aesthetics; League of Composers, Intern. Soc. for Contemp. Mus., etc. Faculty Sou. Calif. School of Music and Arts. 1450 Belfast Dr., Hollywood 46, Calif.

KRIEG, MELITA

Concert pianist, teacher of piano and voice. Mus. B., Mus. M., Mus. D. St. piano w. Harry R. Detweiler, Harold von Mickwitz, Edgar Nelson, Ella Spravka, Jan Chiapusso, Glenn Dillard Gunn; voice w. Lamuel W. Kilby, Charles W. Clark; comp. w. Harry R. Detweiler, Edgar Brazelton, Henry Schoenfeld, Felix Borowski, Leo Sowerby; coached w. Franz Prochowski, Frank LaForge, Burton Thatcher, Herman DeVries, Arthur Dunham. Faculty Columbia Cons., Ill. (10 yrs.), Bush Cons. (5 yrs.) Glenn Dillard Gunn Sch. (5 yrs.). Concertized throughout U.S. as soloist, accompanist, soloist w. orch. under Richard Czerwonky, Chicago, Raymond Paige, L.A. Radio KNX, KFAC, KMTR; mus. dir. WSWS, Chicago. Cond. women's, men's chorus; lecturer North Hollywood Woman's Club (10 yrs.) Comp. incl.: Lady with the Moonbeam Slippers, Song of the Guitars, I Am A Soldier, My Dream Caballero, The Jubilee Dance, The Dancer, (piano); A Psalm of Praise, (anthem); Button Tree, (operetta); numerous mss. Member Illinois MTA, charter member Omega Chapter, Sigma Alpha Iota; San Fernando Valley Music Club, Zonta International 11163 Moorpark St., North Hollywood, Calif.

KROELL, CECILIE

Pianist, teacher of piano. b. in Germany. St. piano w. Xaver Scharwenka, Rudolph Maria Breithaupt, Berlin. Concert degree Cons. Cologne. Taught Bonn Cons. Concertized Germany, Europe, U.S. Exponent of Breithaupt piano technique of weight control. 738 Burnside Ave., Los Angeles, Calif.

KUEHNY, GRETCHEN

Concert 'cellist, teacher. b. Los Angeles, Calif., 1914. St. 'cello w. Julius Herner, Axel Simonsen, Stephen De'ak. Awarded Hancock Schol., U.S.C. Concertized throughout So. Calif. as soloist. First 'cellist w. Brodetsky Chamber Music Ensemble. Former member Hollywood Bowl Orch. At present recording for motion pictures, transcriptions and radio w. Meredith Willson, Victor Young, David Rose, Irving Fried-

man, others. Founder-director Kuehny 'Cello Club; originated Kuehny 'cello quartet. Faculty Pepperdine College; Fine Arts Cons. of Music. Students incl. memb. of L. A. Philharmonic, Hollywood Bowl Orch. Hobby: writing. Husband, Edwin Geber, 'cellist w. L. A. Philharmonic Orch. 3302 Griffith Park Blvd., Los Angeles 27, Calif.

LALIBERTE, LORRAINE

Pianist, teacher. b. McGregor, Iowa. Childhood training under Kate P. Calvin of Montana State College. B.M. Montana State College at 14. Advanced st. Berlin and Paris, w. Godowsky, Teresa Carreno, Rudolph Ganz, Isidor Philipp; harmony, comp. w. Edgar Stillman Kelley. Public appearances in Berlin, Leipzig, Halle, Paris. Founder-dir. Conservatory of Music and Dramatic Art, Great Falls, Mont.; chairman, League for Advancement of Music (radio); dir. Twelve Piano Ensemble. Member Board of Directors, Community Concert Assn. Pianist w. Chicago Symphony String Quartet. Concerts in Middle West cities. Pupils incl. scholarship winners at Chicago Musical Coll., Cincinnati Cons., Northwestern Univ., Whitman Coll., Univ. of Washington. Studio: No. 400, Fischer Studio Bldg., Seattle, Wash.

LANGE, ARTHUR

Composer, conductor, teacher of theory, orchestration. b. Philadelphia, Pa., 1889. St. piano, violin, theory w. pvt. tchrs. in U.S. Cond. Hollywood Bowl, NBC Orch. (N.Y.); KFI Aud.; numerous mus. plays, operettas, N.Y. Now mus. dir. Santa Monica Civic Orch. Arr. var. operettas in N.Y. Comp., arr., cond. many film scores since 1929 for all major studios; headed mus. depts. M-G-M, Fox, International Studios. Founded Co-Art Rec. Co 1936; superv. all recording since. Comp. incl. A Gosling in Gotham, Big Trees, Antelope Valley (symp. poems), The Fisherman and His Soul (cham. orch.), two quartets, piano Sonata, many short piano pieces, over 500 pub. songs. Author: Arranging for the Modern Dance Orch.; Theory of Harmonic Structure and Progression. Nat'l. Pres. NSMA. Member: AFM, Screen Comp. Assn.; Bohemians. Hobby, research on new theories of music. 9076 St. Ives Dr., Hollywood 46, Calif.

LASZLO, ALEXANDER

Composer, conductor, concert pianist. b. Budapest, Hungary. Att. Franz Liszt Hungarian Royal Academy of Music, Univ. of Munich. Ph.D. in Art. Former Professor Hamburg, Munich. Constructed machine to create Colorlight-music, medium blending sound and color. Concert tours in Europe, U. S.; soloist Hollywood Bowl. Comp. incl.: Praeludii, Dreams, Sonatina, Fantasia for Colorlight-music (Breitkopf & Haertel), songs, film, stage and radio music; Improvisations on 'Oh Susannah' (orch. & band, Guild Publ.), Mechanized Forces (orch. & band), 4D-122 (piano concerto), Hollywood Concerto (piano concerto, recorded by Hollywood Symphony Orch. (Constantine Bakaleinikoff), The Ghost Train of Marshall Pass (piano and orch.), motion picture scores for Paramount, RKO, Republic Studios. Member: Academy of Motion Picture Arts and Sciences, ASCAP, SCA. Mgmt. MCA. Dir., first conductor new Hollywood Symphony Orch. 2784 La Cuesta Dr., Hollywood 46, Calif .

LAVA, WILLIAM

Composer, conductor. b. St. Paul, Minn., March 18, 1911. St. Northwestern Univ.; later theory, comp. w. Gerardo Castillo; conducting w. Albert Coates. Composer, conductor, arranger w. RKO, Republic, Warner Bros. Studios. Comp. incl.: Moonrise (suite for orchestra), various songs, piano pieces; numerous original film scores incl.: Destination Tokyo, Horn Blows at Midnight. Scored Academy winner short subjects, I Won't Play, 1944, Star In The Night, 1945, Hitler Lives, 1945, A Boy and His Dog, 1946. Member Screen Composers Assn., ASMA. Hobby: tracing the history of music, esp. among primitive peoples. Warner Bros. Studios, 4000 So. Olive Ave., Burbank, Calif.

LAWRENCE, RAYMOND

Singer, playwright; drama director Rennay Shry-Ock School of Music-Arts and Drama. App. throughout U.S. in stage, opera, films, radio. Author: Alexander the Great (epic drama). Also competent painter, stage designer. Rennay Shry-Ock School of Music-Arts and Drama, 1353 Post St., San Francisco, Calif.

LAZELLE, RENA

Singer, teacher, coach. b. Boston, Mass. St. w. Mme. Elena Varesi, Chicago; Ross David, Oscar Saenger, Victor Maurel, Louis Graveure, N. Y. Church, concert work, Chicago, 1905-06; church, concert, light opera, grand opera, N.Y., 1906-15; concert tours throughout U.S., Canada, 1906-15; middle West, 1915-22; Pacific Coast, 1922-30. Member S.F. Opera Company, 1923-25. Author of musical plays: *An Evening With Mr. Pepys; Soiree at the Burneys.* Head vocal dept., MacMurray Coll., Jacksonville, Ill., Tiffany School of Music, Springfield, Ill., 1915-20. Assoc. Prof. of Voice, Univ. of Kansas, 1920-22. Head vocal dept., San Francisco Cons. of Music since 1922. Member: S.F. MTA, Calif. State MTA, Nat'l MTA; Mayflower Descendants; S.F. Women's City Club. San Francisco Conservatory of Music, 3435 Sacramento St., San Francisco, Calif.

LEACH, ROWLAND

Violinist, composer, dir. School of Music, Redlands Univ. b. Haverhill, Mass., April 26, 1885. Att. New England Cons., Yale Univ. A.B., Beloit, 1908, Mus.B. Yale, 1910. App. as violinist Chicago, L. A., Calgary Symphony, Indianapolis, others; conductor of Rockford, Ill. Symphony, Riverside Community Opera Assn., DePauw Symphony, Comp. incl.: *Sonata* (vn. and pf.), *Concert Overture,* Sym, poem *Aucassin and Nicolette, Seven Casual Brevities* organ (Gray), *Etude Caprice* (piano) (Summy), *Reveille* (male cho.) (Hall and McCreary), *Impromptu* (song) (Fischer), others. Lecturer on music and art. Wrote *University Harmony* (Edwards Bros.). Member: American Comp. All., Phi Beta Kappa, Pi Kappa Lambda, Phi Mu Alpha Sinfonia, Am. Musicological Soc., A.A.U.P., Beta Theta Pi. Hobbies: painting, boxing. University of Redlands, Redlands, Calif.

LEGINSKA, ETHEL

Concert pianist, composer, conductor, teacher of piano. b. Hull, England, 1886. Att. Hoch Cons. Frankfort. St. piano w. Leschetizky; theory w. Rubin Goldmark; comp. w. Ernest Bloch. World concert tours as pianist. First woman to conduct major symp. orchs. Comp. incl. *Gale* (opera), *Beyond the Fields We Know* (orch.), *From a Life* (orch.), numerous songs, piano pieces. Founded *New Venture In Music* 1943 to aid young artists. 254 S. Hobart Ave., Los Angeles 4, Calif.

LEHMANN, LOTTE

Soprano. b. Perleberg, Germany, 1885. Att. Gerster Sch., Berlin. St. w. Tiedke, Jordan, Teinhold, Mallinger. Sang leading roles opera, concert throughout U. S., Europe incl. Metropolitan Opera, Covent Garden, Salzburg Festivals. Radio appearances under Toscanini, others. Author, *Midway In My Song, Eternal Flight.* Victor recordings. Hope Ranch, Santa Barbara, Calif.

LEIB, JULIUS

Director instrumental music, San Diego State College; director San Diego Light Opera Assn. b. Hamburg, Germany, 1886. Grad. Wittenberg Cons., Leipsig Cons. (2 yrs.). St. French horn w. Spangler; 'cello w. T. Burger. Arr. U. S., 1907. Played 'cello, French horn w. Kansas City Symphony (Bush). Program dir. WGBW; cond. of band and orchestra for Exposition, 1935; cond. San Diego Symphony Orch. Assn., 1936-37 in Ford Bowl. Faculty, Music Dept., San Diego State Coll., 1938. Son, Robert Lieb, concertmaster San Diego Sinfonetta (Sokoloff). Hobby: woodworking. 332 I Ave., San Diego, Calif.

LENSKI, VLADIMIR

Violinist, teacher. b. Paola, Kans., Feb. 25, 1894. St. violin w. Jan Colberg, London, at Hochschule w. Joseph Joachim, Andreas Moser, Berlin; Cons. of Paris w. Emile Sauret; harmony and composition w. Adolf F. Weidig. Grad. American Cons., Chicago. Concerts in principal cities of Europe and U.S. Gave first violin concert on the air over KFI; first soloist for sound pictures at Universal. Pupils incl. John Hart Stout, Delores Watson. Head, violin dept., Southwestern College of Music, Los Angeles. 5374 Irvine Ave., North Hollywood, Calif.

LERT, RICHARD

Conductor. b. Vienna, Austria, 1885. Att. Vienna Acad. of Music; st. w. Richard Heuberger, others. Mus. D. Regular cond. opera, concerts Frankfurt, Mannheim, Hannover, Berlin, Vienna; guest cond. Copenhagen, Oslo, Haag, Paris, other music centers. In U. S. cond. Los Angeles Philharmonic Orch., Hollywood Bowl Orch., San Francisco Opera, Washington Opera, others; dir. L. A. Oratorio Soc. At present permanent cond. Pasadena Civic Orch., Pasadena Festival Ass., dir. American Music Theatre. Pasadena Civic Music Assn., 16 N. Marengo Ave., Pasadena 1, Calif. Res. 2477 Canyon Oak Dr., Hollywood 28, Calif.

LESLIE, SERGE

Dancer. b. Fremont, Nebr. Began dancing w. Edna McRae; St. dance w. Chester Hale, New York; later associate, soloist Capitol Theatre, 1926. St. w. Alexandre Volinine, Bronislava Nijinska, Paris, 1929. European debut Palace Theatre (9 mos. engagement). Partner of Doris Niles since 1932. Theater, concert appearances major centers Europe, U. S. Bibliophile; collector of important dance library. Hobby, bookbinding and gilding. Cf. biography of Doris Niles. 557 S. Coronado St., Los Angeles, Calif.

LEVIENNE, KOLIA

Violoncellist. Grad. Leipzig and Petrograd Imperial Cons. St. 'cello w. Julius Klengel. Played w. Nikisch, Winderstein, Glaznuov, Newmark, Hessin, Orlov, Cherepnin, others. Toured w. Chaliapin, 1922-23. Concertized Leipzig, Berlin, Munich, London, Petrograd, Moscow, Esthonia, Manchuria and throughout U. S. 274 Chiquita St., Laguna Beach, Calif. Calif.

LEVIENNE, MISCHA (MICHAEL)

Concert violinist, composer, arranger, teacher. b. Lithuania, grad. Imperial Petrograd Cons. under Leopold Auer (1913); classmates were Jascha Heifetz, Toscha Seidel, Cecilia Hansen. Also grad. in law, Petrograd Imperial Univ. Arrived U. S. 1922. Concertmaster, soloist w. Anna Pavlova (2 yrs.). Concertized since age 13 throughout Russia, Europe; tour of Siberia, 1917, Baltic States 1918, 1921. Joint recitals w. Tenor Dimitri Smiknoff in Germany, 1922. Wife, Lola Bori, Lyric-dramatic soprano; toured w. Golden West Opera Co. 1943 as Nedda (*Pagliacci*) Micaela (*Carmen*); soloist Greek Theaters (C. Bakaleinikoff 1943; two years soloist w. USO overseas. 6046 Rodgerton Dr., Hollywood, Calif.

LEVY, EDNA CROWELL

Concert violinist. b. Massachusetts. Piano w. father, William Crowell; violin at New England Cons. of Music, Boston, w. Felix Winternitz, Sylvian Noack, Alfred Megerlin, Davol Sanders. A.B., U.C.L.A.; M.A., S.C. Concertized throughout U.S. Concertmaster Glendale Symphony Orch. since 1933. Member Dominant Club, Tuesday Afternoon Club. Hobby: books. 1970 Verdugo Knolls Dr., Glendale, Calif.

LEWIS, BERNIE K.

Composer, arranger, orchestrator, conductor. b. U.S. B.A. Chic. Cons. of Music. St. harmony w. Busch, comp., arr. w. Nutting. Comp. of *Fantasie Simplice* (publ.), *Beautiful Carnation, Polynesian Lament, Aloha-Lanii, Kona-Trail, Polynesian Rhythms* (So. Music Publ. Co.); popular songs, *I've Changed, Things Are Going to Come My Way; California Symphony* (mss). Hobby: boating, surfing, fishing. 136 No. Rampart Blvd., Los Angeles, Calif.

LEWIS, J. ARTHUR

Music educator. b. Hinsdale, Ill. Att. USC. St. voice, cho. w. father, J. J. Lewis, Chicago. Coordinator, Bureau of Music, City of Los Angeles, since inception. Organized cho. (1200 voices) Tenth Inter. Olympics, Hollywood Bowl Cho. (1000 voices) (Stokowski, Ormandy), other L. A. groups. Dir. Music festivals, Kern County. Cho. dir. UCLA (9 yrs.). Toured Pacific Coast w. cho. ensembles. Hobby, golf. Bureau of Music, City of Los Angeles, Calif.

LEWIS, KAROLYN KING

Concert pianist, teacher of piano. b. Pasadena, Calif., Nov. 4, 1904. St. piano w. Isidor Philipp, Alfred Cortot, Paris, Alfred Mirovich, Alexis Kall, Carl Leimer, U.S. Concert tours throughout western U.S. Comp. incl. ballet music, songs, piano pieces. Member: Redlands Spinet; MTA. Hobbies: riding, swimming. Knoll Road, Redlands, Calif.

LEWYN, HELENA

Concert pianist; teacher of piano. b. Houston, Texas. St. piano w. Blanche O'Donnell, Houston; Fanny Bloomfield-Zeisler, Chicago; Leopold Godowsky, Conrad Ansorge, Berlin; Richard Buhlig, Los Angeles; theory, comp. w. Edgar Stillman-Kelley, Frederick Stock. Debut age 16 as soloist w. Berlin Philharmonic Orch.; Amer. debut w. New York Symphony (Damrosch); soloist w. Hollywood Bowl (thrice) (Oberhoffer, Stokowski), St. Louis Sym., other orchs. Concertized extensively in U. S., Europe. App. in numerous sonata recitals, chamber mus. events. Comp. incl. songs (Shelley poems). Hobby, painting. 6683 Sunset Blvd., Hollywood 28, Calif.

LINDEN, ANTHONY

Flutist. b. Helena, Mont. St. w. Alfred Queusal. Principal flutist Minneapolis Symph. (Oberhofer), S. F. Symph. Orch., (Hertz), L. A. Symph. Princ. flutist under Stokowski, Walter, Coates, Toscanini, Monteux. 6689 Emmet Terr., Hollywood 28, Calif.

LINDEN, EUGENE

Conductor. b. Chicago, Ill., Feb. 3, 1912. Cond. Seattle Mozart Theatre; assoc. cond., Pacific Northwest Symphony; dir. Opera Workshop, Univ. of Washington. 4520 Myrtle St., Seattle 8, Wash.

LINDOFT, HAROLD G.

Arranger, orchestrator, copyist. b. Galesburg, Ill. St. violin w. father, Chas. A. (6 yrs.), Francois Bouchett (3 yrs.). Violinist, arr. for Loew's State, Los Angeles (9 yrs.), Warfield Theater, San Francisco (3 yrs.), Fox, Oakland (1 yr.), Hal Roach (7 yrs.). Arr., copyist for Ferde Grofe, orchestrated for symphony, Grofe's comp. Member San Diego Symphony Orch. (2 yrs.). Concertmaster, arr. Desert Song Company, 1945-46. Radio w. Felix Mills on *Mr. X. Studebaker Strings, Burns & Allen, Pepsodent Show, Old Gold Comedy Theater.* Comp. of *Suite Leclere,* (mss.), *String Quartet* (mss.). Hobby: photography. 12358 Bromwich St., Pacoima, Calif.

LIVINGSTON, GERTRUDE

Pianist, teacher of piano and organ. b. San Francisco, Calif., 1886. Att. Univ. of Calif., Univ. of Chicago, Mills Coll. St. harmony, organ, piano w. Chas. Seeger, Wm. Carruth, Wm. McCoy, Robert Tolmie, Robert Elkus. Mus. B. Univ. of Calif. Piano comp. incl. *Firelight Waltz, Elfen Dance.* Member: Pacific Musical Club, MTA, East Bay Opera Lg., Nat'l Guild of Piano Teachers, Nat'l Fed. of Music Teachers, Oakland Symphony Orch. Hobbies: piano ensemble, gardens. Teacher of Nanette Matthews, Douglas Kyle, Deanna Faust. 40 Jerome Ave., Piedmont, Calif.

LOCKER, MARTHA DAUGHN

Soprano, concert and opera. b. Chicago, Ill. Att. Chicago Musical Coll.; st. voice with Edith Gaudenzi, various pvt. tchrs. Concertized extensively in U. S., Alaska. Spec. in unusual programs incl. Aramaic works, songs by women comp., etc. Concerts in Town Hall, Carnegie Hall; Broadway shows, operettas. Comp. numerous songs, incl. *Gentle Mary* (Schirmer). Hobbies: painting, sculpture, sewing, designing, inventing, swimming, hiking. Mgmt. Annie Friedberg Concert Bureau, New York. 6500 Yucca Ave., Hollywood 28, Calif.

LOVE, EDNA BARR

Head music dept., Modesto Jr. Coll. b. Holdrege, Nebr. B.M., M.M. Amer. Cons. of Music; New England Cons. of Mus., Boston; grad. State Tchrs. Coll., L. A.; Univ. of Calif.; Columbia Univ. St. voice w. Karleton Hackett, Lawrence Strauss, Wm. Cooper; piano w. Edwin Clahre, Thilo Becker, George McManus, Silvio Scionti, Albert Elkus; theory, comp. w. Wm. McCoy, Rossetter Cole, Domenica Brescia, Arthur

Anderson, Adolph Weidig, Leo Sowerby; pipe organ w. Henry Dunham, Morton Mason. Dir. of mus. Modesto City Schools, 1920-24; instr. Alex, Hamilton J. H. S., Oakland, 1924-25; instr. Amer. Cons. of Mus., summers 1929-31-35; instr. in music Modesto Jr. College 1922-24 and since 1925. Comp. *Suite for Orchestra, Te Deum,* songs, piano pieces. Modesto Jr. College, Modesto, Calif.

LURWICK, GALEN

Pianist, teacher, accompanist. b. Joplin, Mo. St. piano w. Mrs. George Winter (scol. Joplin) Lester Donahue, Richard Buhlig, Lois Lynn Rogers, Sergei Tarnovsky; harmony, comp. Chapman College w. Mary Carr Moore (extension course). Guest soloist w. major symphony orchs. Accomp. singers of Metropolitan Opera Co. on tour. Comp. *Embers* (mss), *Prayer* (mss), others. Member MTA, AFM. Hobbies: swimming, antique furniture refinishing. 232 So. Serrano Ave., Los Angeles 4, Calif.

LYDICK, MAUD HOLCOMB

Teacher of piano. b. Denton, Texas. Diploma Cincinnati Cons. of Mus. St. piano w. Theodore Bohlman, Wm. Kraupner, Arthur Friedheim (pupil of Franz Liszt); harmony, theory w. Edgar Stillman Kelley. Sec. certif. for piano, harmony, history of music from U.C. Faculty Cincinnati Cons. of Mus. 1916-1918; taught harmony, piano Toledo Cons.; inaugurated Children's Hour on KFSD, 1926. Member MTA. Studio: No. 8, Silvergate Studios, 1039, 7th Ave., San Diego 1, Calif.

MAASKOFF, ANTON

Violinist. b. N. Y. C., 1896. Grad. Royal Manchester Coll. of Music, England. St. violin w. Adolph Brodsky. Soloist w. London Sym., Halle, Scottish, Vienna Phil. Orchs. Concertized Europe, So. Amer., So. Africa. 9415 Oakmore Rd., Los Angeles 35, Calif.

MacDONALD, JEANETTE

Soprano; opera, film, radio, prima donna-actress. b. Philadelphia, Pa. St. voice w. Grace Adele Newell; dancing w. Ned Wayburn. App. in numerous Broadway shows, pictures incl.: *The Love Parade, The Vagabond King, Naughty Marietta, New Moon, Bittersweet, Maytime, Girl of the Golden West.* Operas: Chicago, Montreal, other companies. Soloist w. leading symphonies; concert tours in U. S., Europe. Numerous recordings for RCA, Victor incl. *Cinderella,* several Victor Herbert albums. Hobbies: walking, swimming, riding. c/o Helen Ferguson, 321 So. Beverly Dr., Beverly Hills, Calif.

MACKENZIE, MARTHA ALICE

Teacher of singing. b. Falls City, Nebr., Nov. 25, 1889. Att. Franklin Sch. of Music, Chicago Musical Coll., Royal Cons. of Music (Germany), Austro-American Cons. St. voice w. Yeatman Griffith, N.Y.C. Prima donna Herald Square Opera Co. Soloist choirs in Germany, Canada, U.S. Recitalist Germany, Canada, Prince Edward Islands, Panama, Canal Zone, U. S. Prod. and entertainer Prologues in film theatres Canada, Newfoundland. Prod. 25 operas and operettas. Pvt. studios Omaha, Nebr., Santa Monica, Calif., Canal Zone. Comp. incl. *An Irish Lullaby, A Love-lit Canoe.* Member: San Bernardino MTA; Valley Concert Assn.; San Bernardino Opera Assn.; Romany Club; YWCA Y-Teen Com. Hobbies: sports, bridge. At present w. Brush Studios of Music. 440, 17th St., San Bernardino, Calif.

MADER, CLARENCE

Organist composer, teacher of organ. b. Easton, Pa., 1904. St. piano w. Charles Davis, Homer Grunn, Henry Levey; organ w. Perry Hallett, Lynnwood Farnam; comp. w. Percy Hallett. Soloist 5 nat'l Organ Conv., Bach Festivals L. A. and Carmel; recital tours throughout U. S., Canada. Organist Immanuel Presby. Ch. since 1929. Comps. incl. *Christmas Oratorio, Make We Merry,* scores for small orch., 6 Trios, Quartet, Suites (organ), sets of piano pieces, numerous songs. Students incl. David Craighead. Member: AGO (post-Dean, So. Calif. Chapter), So. Calif. Choral Cond. Guild (first pres.). Immanuel Presbyterian Church, 663 S. Berendo St., Los Angeles 5, Calif.

Mischa Levienne

Edna Crowell Levy

Bernie K. Lewis

Karolyn King Lewis

Helena Lewyn

Harold G. Lindoft

Martha Daughn Locker

Galen Lurwick

Maud Holcomb Lydick

Clarence Mader

Ulderico Marcelli

Blanche Wayne Marfield

Frederick Marvin

William Matchan

Iona Maxwell

225

MAHOOD, FELICIA

News editor, music critic Westwood Villager. b. Santa Monica, Calif., Oct. 16, 1920. Ed. Santa Monica City Coll. Associate of Arts Degree. Co-manager, Continental Artists Series; Secretary Ballet Assn. of America; Beverly Hills Junior Women's Club; Beverly Hills Young Republicans; Westwood Hills Women's Club; Patron's Assn. S. M. City College, etc. Hobbies: collecting records, making plastic picture frames and plastic desk name plates. Music reviews for Musical America, other mags. 218, 16th St., Santa Monica, Calif.

MALMIN, GUNNAR J.

Teacher. b. Thompson, Iowa, April 9, 1903. B.A. Luther Coll. Decorah, Ia., Mus.B., St. Olaf Coll., Northfield, Minn.; Mus.M., Univ. of Michigan. Grad. work, Univ. of Minn., Northwestern. Comp. *Bethlehem* (Xmas cantata), *Songs and Hymns for Treble Voices*, *Songs and Anthems for Treble Voices*, others. Protestant mus. dir. Post Chapel, Fort Lewis; asst. dir., Pacific Coast Norwegian Singers' Assn., dir. Norwanna Male Chorus, Tacoma; mus. dir. Pacific Lutheran Coll, Parkland, Wash. 952 Wheeler St., Parkland ,Wash.

MALOTTE, ALBERT HAY

Composer. b. Philadelphia, Pa. 1895. St. w. William S. Stansfield, Georges Jacob, Eugene Sizes. Theatre organ concerts England, U. S. Mus. dir. Disney Studios (4 yrs.); scored various films. Comp. incl. two ballets: *Carnival in Venice* (prem. Hollywood Bowl 1934), *Little Red Riding Hood*, two light operas, over 80 songs (pub. Schirmer). Hobbies: boxing, judo. Member ASCAP, Nat'l. Assn. of Judo. c/o G. Schirmer, 3 E. 43rd St., New York, N. Y.

MARCELLI, NINO

Composer, conductor. Grad. Nat'l. Cons. Music, Chile. St. theory, w. Soro; 'cello w. Brighenti; comp. w. Brescia. Cond. Santiago, Chile, Symph. Soc.; So. Amer. Opera Co.; Santa Monica, Calif., Municipal Orch., Opera Co.; S. F., L. A., Hollywood Bowl orchs. Founder-cond. S. D. Symph. Orch., Oratorio Soc. Comp. *The Rout of the Philistines, Suite Araucana, Ode to a Hero, Solitude, Carmelita, Song of the Andes,* others. 2740 1st Ave., San Diego, Calif.

MARCELLI, ULDERICO (RICO)

Composer, conductor. b. Rome, Italy, 1888. Grad. Nat'l Cons., Santiago, Chile. St. theory, orch., comp. w. Domenico Brescia, violin w. Georvino, piano w. de Paoli, horn w. Zanzani. Hornist Teatro Marin, Santiago, at age 14. Won Prix de Rome. Prof. of music Nat'l Cons. of Ecuador; artistic dir. Teatro Sucre de Quito. Cond. Grant Park, Chicago (9 seasons); guest cond. (incl. own comp.) Panama Pac. Exp., Pan-Amer. Exp. (S. F.), Hollywood Bowl, S. F. Symphony, Ford Bowl (San Diego). Radio cond. Chicago, L. A., S. F., Detroit, Mexico City, etc.; orig. cond. Fibber McGee and Molly, Carnation Hour. Comp. incl. *La Marseillaise, Ilya of Marom, Liefkronan* (music dramas), *Daniera* (grand opera), *Water Colors* (symp. sketches), *Immortal Light* (cho. soli, organ, orch.), two quartets, short pieces for strings, various chamber music, ensembles, songs. Member: Bohemian Club, Palette and Chisel Club (Chicago), AFM (N. Y., Chicago, Detroit, S. F., L. A.). Hobby: painting, sculpture. 10253 Sunland Blvd., Roscoe, Calif.

MARCHANT, LUTHER BRUSIE

Professor of voice, dean of School of Music, Mills Coll. (since 1922). B. A. Univ. of Calif. St. voice w. Marie Withrow (S. F.), Francis Walker, Oscar Seagle, Chas. Bowes (N. Y.), Jules Algier (Paris). Faculty State Coll. of Wash., Spokane Sch. of Music. Mills College, Oakland, Calif.

MARFIELD, BLANCHE WAYNE

Soprano, teacher of singing. b. Okolona, Miss. St. Cosmopolitan Sch. of Mus., w. L. A. Torrens, Chicago; Augusta Renard, N.Y.; Cincinnati Cons. w. Minnie Tracy; coached w. Claudio Muzio (Metropolitan Opera); Paul Longoni (dir. Chic. Civic Opera); diction, Clare Kellogg (N.Y.); languages, Buccini School of Languages (N.Y.); piano, Mme. Edmund Severn (N.Y.). Toured U.S. and Canada in concert and light opera; soloist w. Pittsburg Symphony, Ravinia Park; N.Y. churches, Shubert opera. Member: MTA (Board); Pasadena Fine Arts; Tuesday Musicale (Pasadena); Matinee Musicale (N.Y.). Hobby: antiques (china, glass, furniture). Taught in N.Y., Chicago, Hollywood, Pasadena. 730 No. Hill Ave., Pasadena, Calif.

MARGULIS, SYLVIA WEINSTEIN

Concert violinist. b. Portland, Ore. Grad., post-graduate Damrosch Inst. of Musical Art, New York City. St. violin w. Kneisel, Sevcik, Leopold Auer. Soloist w. Portland Symphony Orchestra (Van Hoogstraten). Concertized principal cities Northwest, New York and Chicago. 2966 N.W. Cornell Road, Portland, Ore.

MARTIN, WILLIAM McKELVY

Artists representative, concert manager. b. Rochester, N.Y. Att. Univ. of Mich., USC (A.B.); Univ. Cruise 1927-28. Assoc. manager Sou. Calif. Sym. Assn. (Los Angeles Philharmonic Orch., Hollywood Bowl) 1936-43; concert mgr. MCA (Beverly Hills) 1945. Bus. mgr. Greater Los Angeles Opera Assn. 1948 L.A. Metropolitan (New York) opera season. Mgr. Beverly Hills Music Fest. 1947. Founded Martin Music Management 1946. Member: Betha Theta Pi; dir. L.A. Jr. Ch. of Comm. 1941-41, dir. Mus. Found. Jr. Ch. of Comm.; dir. Opera Guild of L.A. Martin Music Management, 746 N. Cahuenga Ave., Hollywood 38, Calif.

MARVIN, FREDERICK

Concert pianist, head piano dept. Occidental College. b. Los Angeles, Calif., June 11, 1920. St. w. Milan Blanchet, L.A.; Curtis Inst. of Music, Philadelphia. Concertized throughout U. S. in recitals and as soloist w. symphony orchestras incl. Miami, Pasadena, Glendale, Phoenix. Piano solos in film *Voice in the Wind*. Citations for musical therary during war, (Air Corps, 3 yrs.). Mgmt. L. E. Behymer, Los Angeles, Calif.

MATCHAN, WILLIAM

Concert baritone. b. Zumbrota, Minn. Att. Pomona Coll., Univ. of So. Calif. St. w. Borghild Jansen, Berlin, Ralph Lyman, Pomona Coll., Theodore Schroeder, Boston, Hal Crain, Los Angeles. Concert tours in the U.S., esp. Pacific Coast. Sang world premiere of Malotte's *91st Psalm* w. L.A. Philharmonic Orch., composer cond. Soloist w. Hollywood Bowl, Vancouver, Pasadena, other orchs., Redlands Bowl. App. in oratorios *St. Matthew's Passion, Christmas Oratorio, Messiah, Elijah, Seven Last Words,* Verdi *Requiem,* CBS Nat'l Broadcasts, KFI, KNX, etc. Member Screen Guild, AFRA. Hobbies: horseback riding, swimming. Mgmt. Gertrude Purple Gorham, 125 No. Le Doux Rd., Beverly Hills, Calif. Res. 1735 No. Gramercy Pl., Hollywood 28, Calif.

MAXWELL, CHARLES

Composer, arranger. b. Leipzig, Germany. Att .Leipzig Cons., Teachers' Coll. St. comp., piano, violin. Arr., orch. for Morris, Leo Feist, Waterson, Berlin & Snyder, music publ., N. Y. Comp., mus. dir. for Morris and Green vaudeville and musical comedy prod. Assoc. w. Arthur Lange in arr. musical scores for Erlanger, Shuberts, Eddie Dowling. Comp., arr. M.G.M., 1929-36; freelanced 20th Century-Fox, Columbia, Universal, Paramount; now w. Warner Bros. Comp. incl.: *Ode to a Hobo* (1941), *Three Miniatures* (flute, violin, viola) (1942), *Suite for Small Orchestras* (1944), *Toccata and Coda Religioso* for Symphony (1946), first perf. by Burbank Symphony (Damiani) (1947). Member Bohemian Club of L. A., ASMA, Screen Comp. Assn. Hobbies: gardening, hiking, reading. 475 N. Bowling Green Way, Los Angeles, Calif.

MAXWELL, IONA

Piano teacher; pres. MTA, Fresno. b. Fresno, Calif. St. w. Elsie Christie, Thyra Aerstrup; master courses w. Noah Steinberg, John Williams, Frederick Lyons; organ w. Mrs. Chas. Williams; theory, harmony w. Earl Towner. Pupils incl. Allan Harkins (music supervisor, Stockton schls.). Affiliated w. Sherwood Music Extension School, Chicago. Member Fed. Music Clubs; ex-pres. of MTA. 2695 Blackstone Ave., Fresno, Calif.

Marguerite May

Charles Maxwell

Francesco Mazzi

Raymond McFeeters

Ross McKee

J. Chas. McNeil

Chas. A. and
Robaline J. Meacham

Marguerite Meadows

Jack Meakin

Ivar Melander

Ray Meany

John and Viva Metzger

Sergei Mihailoff

MAY, MARGUERITE

Teacher of voice, arranger, composer. b. Salt Lake City, Utah. Att. Drake Univ. St. piano w. Edith Packard Davis, Schleur-Doshe, Margaret Lane, Shesby; voice w. Chas. Roach, Dean Couper, Genevieve Wheat Ball, Ross Vernon Miller, Talbot McRae; comp., arr. w. L. S. Gerberick. Concerts w. Mme. Wagner Shaube, 1924. Many musical shows incl.: *Blossom Time, Gingham Girl*; Keith Orpheum w. Gus Edwards, Joe E. Howard, Jack DeWinter, others. Radio app. WCFL Chicago; WCAU Phila.; WMCA N.Y.; WJB New Orleans; KMPC L.A. (2 yrs.). Last concert tour w. own company through West Indies and South America, 1932. Students incl. Shirley Mills, Mrs. James Cruze, C. A. Palmer, John King, Alex Morrison, Kay Coulter, Marilyn and Janet May (daughters). Hobbies: horseback riding, swimming. Member West Hollywood Ch. of Com., others. Former pres., co-founder SAMC, amateur song writers' club. 7710 Sunset Blvd., Los Angeles, Calif.

MAZZI, FRANCESCO

Concert violinist. b. Italy. Student Belgian School. St. w. Adolfo Betti; Edouard de Thier; Mario Frosali, Remo Bolognini. Winner of Harris Schol. Concertized in France, Italy, 1938; in U.S.A. since 1939. App. w. New York City Symphony in concerti of Beethoven, Mendelssohn, Brahms. Taught master class violin, chamber music Brooklyn Cons. of Music. Leader of string quartet in N.Y. under patronage Adolfo Betti. Now affil. w. American Broadcasting Co. Numerous arrangements, editions of concert selections by Brahms, Dvorak, Debussy, Rimsky-Korsakov, etc. (pub. by C. Fischer). Member AFM San Francisco, N.Y. Hobby: swimming. Mgmt. Jeannette & Myra Gause, 15 Park Way, Piedmont, Calif.

McDOWELL, ANN THOMPSON

Pianist, accompanist. b. Ardmore, Okla. B.Mus. Bush Cons. Chicago. St. w. Godowsky, Bachaus, Fraemcke, von Mickwitz, Demorest, Russell. App. w. Bush Temple Orch. Accomp. for Ruth St. Denis on western tour, incl. Phil. Aud. (Los Angeles), San Francisco Opera House, 1946; Acc. Royal Dadmun, Guy Herbert Woodward in piano programs of American composers, and original pianologues. 522 No. Mariposa Ave., Los Angeles, Calif.

McFEETERS, RAYMOND

Pianist, accompanist, teacher, composer. St. piano w. Abby DeAvirett, Paolo Gallico, Rudolph Reuter, Carl Friedberg (Juilliard Scholarship). Coached w. Richard Hageman; organ w. Charles Demorest; harmony w. Carolyn Alchin. Appeared as pianist and accompanist throughout U. S., Canada. Comp. include songs, works for piano, organ, violin. *A Psalm of Praise*, sacred song, awarded Kimball Prize (Chic. Council of Teachers of Singing, 1940). Coll. w. Marion Kerby (singing character-actress) in arrangements of Kentucky Mountain Folk Tunes and Negro Exultations. Organist, Hollywood Inst. of Religious Science. 1825½ No. Argyle Ave., Hollywood 28, Calif.

McKAY, GEORGE FREDERICK

Composer. b. Harrington, Wash., 1899. Att. Univ. of Wash., Eastman Sch. of Music. St. w. Wood, Sinding, Palmgren. Comp. incl. orch., chamber music, piano pieces. Univ. of Wash.. Seattle, Wash.

McKEE, ROSS

Pianist. b. Seattle, Wash. Founder and dir. Music and Arts Inst. of S. F. (affil. w. Golden Gate Coll.). St. piano w. Wager Swayne, Paul Pierre McNeely, John C. Manning; pipe organ w. Theo. Strong. Network broadcasts and concerts throughout Calif. and western states. Dir. all activities of Sch. of Music, Drama & Opera incl. curriculum, concert series in S.F. and Oakland, app. of faculty and student artists of Music & Arts Inst. as guest artists throughout Calif. Contr. to Pacific Coast Musician, Southwestern Mus.; spec. articles for newspapers. 2622 Jackson St., San Francisco, Calif.

McMANUS, GEORGE STEWART

Prof. of music, UCLA. b. Phila., Pa. Grad. Edinburgh Univ. Mus. Doc. St. w. Godowsky, Lhevinne, Hopekirk, Hazell, Van Ogle. Perf. w. Reid Orch., Edinburgh, New England Conserv. Orch., L. A. Phil., Boston People's Sym., others. Concertized Europe, U. S., Canada, Australia, New Zealand, Hawaii. Comp *Fountain of Youth*. Lectures Harvard Univ., New England Cons. of Music, Mills Coll. 216 Tavistock Ave., Los Angeles, Calif.

McNEELY, PAUL PIERRE

Concert pianist, composer, lecturer, teacher of piano, theory. b. Marshall, Mo. St. piano w. Blanche Ragsdale, Marshall, at age 5; Bertha Kirby, Robert E. Wadell, Kansas City; Eduard Scherubel, Alf Klingenberg, Washburn Coll., Topeka, Kan.; Melville Liszniewski, Rudolph Ganz, Josef Lhevinne, Phila., New York, Berlin. St. theory, comp., orch. w. Eduard Scherubel, George Barlow Penny, Washburn Coll.; Cornelius Rubner (3 yrs.) Columbia Univ.; Hugh A. Clark, Penna. State Univ.; orch. cond. w. Gilbert Raynolds Combs, Combs Cons. of Mus., Philadelphia. B. A. (liberal arts), B. Mus. (piano) Washburn Coll.; B. Mus. (adv. comp., orch.) Penna. State Univ. Concertized in U. S., especially East, Middle West, Northwest, also in musicales featuring own comp. Lecturer on music appreciation, psychology, opera, other phases, Washington, Montana. Dir. School of Music, head piano dept. Montana State Coll. (5 yrs.), pvt. studios Seattle since then. Comp. incl. orch. works, chamber music, cantatas, sonatas, fugues, miscl. piano pieces. Member: State Program Com. MTA 1921; State Piano Contest Com. 1923; chairman State Glee Club Com. 1926; Revision Com. for State H. S. Syllabus (for music study under pvt. tchrs.) 1927-29; technical board Pro-Musica Soc. (Seattle) 1928-30; chairman Seattle Exam. Com. for Bellingham Schools (music) 2 yrs.); chairman Exam. Board for outside mus. study Bremerton H. Schls. 1920-29. Faculty member Nat'l. Guild of Piano Tchrs. Member: Washington MTA, Seattle MTA, Univ. of Penna. Club, Kansas Univ. Club, Washburn Coll. Club, Phi Delta Nu, Kappa Sigma, Masonic Frat.; life accred. tchr. State of Washington. Res. studio: Paramount Theatre Bldg., 907 Pine St., Seattle 1, Wash.

McNEIL, J. CHAS.

Composer, arranger, pianist, organist. b. Columbia, S. C., 1902. Att. Chicora Coll., Columbia, Amer. Cons. of Music, Chicago, UCLA, USC, Chapman Coll., Los Angeles. St. comp. w. Mary Carr Moore, Henry Bellaman, Arthur Lange, Arnold Schoenberg, A.B. (mus. maj.) USC 1933; Mus. B. Chicago Univ. 1931; Mus M. Chapman Coll. 1938. Works perf. by Sou. Calif. Symp. Orch. (Sample), Schubert Club, Golden Gate World's Fair, Mary Carr Moore Mss. Club, etc. Comp. incl. *Mojave, In the Mist, Judith* (w. choreogr.), several other symphonic tone poems; *South Carolina Suite* (orch.), *Suite for Strings, String Quartet, Prelude and Fugue, Sonata*, numerous other piano pieces. *Song Cycle*, over 600 published songs. Contrib. articles to music mag. incl. Etude, Melody. Gives annual trophy for outstanding comp. Mary Carr Moore Mss. Club. Member: Mary Carr Moore Mss. Club; Native Amer. Comp. Hobby, golf. 510 S. Alexandria Ave., Los Angeles, Calif.

MEACHAM, CHAS. ALLEN

Violinist, arranger, teacher. b. Belton, Mass., 1920. Att. Univ. of So. Calif., Univ. of Calif., (Berkeley), U. S. Army Mus. Sch. St. violin w. Naoum Blinder; theory w. Walter Klein, Lucien Cailliet, Ernest Toch. Staff artist McClatchy Broadcasting Co., 1937-41. Memb. 2nd A.F. Radio Prod. Unit (Major Glenn Miller); W/O Bandleader U. S. A.A.F. 1943-46 670th, 37th, 709th, AAF Bands. Violinist on series of armed forces broadcasts KGMB Honolulu, T. H. Memb. theatre, hotel orchs. Sacramento, San Francisco; San Francisco Symphony, 1946 to present. Life alumni memb. Phi Mu Alpha-Sinfonia. Opera House, San Francisco, Calif.

Paul Pierre McNeely

MEADOWS, MARGUERITE

Mezzo-soprano, concert and opera; teacher of voice. b. Brooklyn, N. Y. St. voice w. Marcella Sembrich, Juanita Pruett,. Jeanotte; coached w. Herbert Braham; theory w. Albert Stoessel, Juilliard Sch. of Mus.; att. Feagin Sch. of Drama, N. Y. Soloist w. New York Oratorio Soc.; Riverside Ch.; various opera cos. Concertized, radio work in U. S. Repertory in 8 languages; opera roles incl. Mignon, Delilah, Carmen, etc. Created, directed, produced series of children's records (Music Box Rec.), numerous children's radio scripts. Co-founder, first pres. San Fernando Valley Sym. Assn. Coll. on music apprec. records for Houston Educational Sym. Member: AFRA, L.A. Women's Lyric Club, Swedish Cultural Soc., Scandinavian-American Foundation. Hobby, cooking. 6125 Yucca St., Hollywood 28, Calif.

MEAKIN, JACK

Musical director, composer, arranger. b. Salt Lake City, Utah, Sept. 1906. Pre-med. Stanford Univ. (2 yrs.), A.B. in economics, Stanford 1928. Began piano age 7. Worked way through Stanford playing piano, arr. for dance bands. Staff pianist, arr. NBC, San Francisco (9 yrs.) mus. dir. NBC (S.F. 1936-37). mus. dir. CBS (since 1938). Asst. cond. Bohemian Club Symphony 1937-38. Comp. arr. for Meredith Willson, Al Goodman, Larry Clinton, Mark Warnow, Ted Fio Rito. Radio Producer, 1940-44: *Basin Street, Luncheon Date With Ilka Chase,* Norman Corwin's *This Is War,* Phil Spitalny's *Hour of Charm, Cugat for Camels, Thanks To The Yanks, Kay Kyser's Kollege, Hit Parade.* Comp. popular, piano, instr. works. Comp-cond. Mutual's *Arch Oboler Plays* 1944, *Silver Theatre* 1946. Now comp-cond. *The Great Gildersleeve* and *Joan Davis Show.* 9116¼ Sunset Blvd., Hollywood 46, Calif.

MEANY, RAY

Hawaiian guitarist, poet, world traveler, adventurer; founder, manager Honolulu Cons. of Music, Golden Gate Publ. Hawaiian, standard, popular music for Hawaiian steel guitar, other str. instr. Played over WGBK, Evansville (3 yrs.), KFBK, Sacramento; daily radio program KGDM, Stockton; KWBR, Oakland (4 yrs.). Hawaiian guitar orchestrations. Pres. recitals Treasure Island during Golden Gate Intern. also annual Hawaiian concerts at Woodminster Amphitheater. Comp.-writer numerous songs published here and abroad. Contributor to newspapers, magazines. Songs, transcr. recorded by Capitol, Majestic, Bluebird, Oliver Records, others. Founder, publisher Music Studio News, internat'l monthly magazine. Served in U. S. Army during the war. Member: American Guild of Banjoists, Mandolinists, & Guitarists, Nat'l Assn. of Music, Merchants, Oakland Chamber of Commerce, American Legion. 15,000 guitar students; branch studios in several California cities. 5464 Foothill Blvd., Oakland, Calif.

MELANDER, IVAR

Pianist, teacher. b. Moscow, Idaho, 1907. Att. State Coll. of Wash., Teachers Coll. of Columbia Univ., Juilliard, N. Y. City. St. piano w. Herbert Kimbrough, Mary Cameron, James Friskin, Paul Pisk. App. Bach Festival, First Congreg. Ch., (L.A.), MTA State Conv. (Riverside). Comp. piano solos, two-piano choral, light operatic, numerous recorder ensembles. Pupils won first, other prizes in Allied Arts Festival, L.A., KFI Young Artists Compet., Riverside County Piano-playing Compet., current annual schol. Riverside Community Chorus. Past Pres. Riverside Br. MTA. Member Phi Mu Alpha. Hobbies: ensemble and recorder playing, sketching. Res. 4670 Rubidoux Lane, Riverside, Calif.; studio 4287 Lime St., Riverside, Calif.

MENUHIN, YEHUDI

Violinist. b. N. Y. C., 1917. Started violin age 4 yrs. w. Sigmund Anker, Louis Persinger. Debut age 7 yrs. as soloist w. S.F. Orch.; three yrs. later, Manhattan Opera House. St. in Europe w. Adolph Busch and Georges Enesco. App. w. Lamoureux Orch; debut w. N. Y. Phil. Sym. Orch., 1927. Concertized extensively, U. S., Europe. c/o L. E. Behymer, Phil. Aud. Bldg., 427 W. 5th St., Los Angeles 13, Calif.

MEREMBLUM, PETER

Violinist, conductor, founder-director California Junior Symphony Orch. b. Batum, Russia, 1891. Att. Imperial Conserv., Petrograd. St. violin w. Leopold Auer; theory w. Glazounov. Played under Koussevitzky, Schneevoight, Stokowski. Member Petrograd String Quartet, Bruhler Schloss Quartet. Head violin dept. Cornish Sch., Seattle, Wash. Concertized throughout world, incl. Berlin, Moscow, N.Y. Cond. symph. orch. in Russia, Cornish Orch., Seattle, Meremblum String Ensemble, Meremblum Jr. Orch., L.A. 720 N. Spaulding Ave., Los Angeles, Calif.

MEROLA, GAETANO

Conductor. b. Naples, Italy, 1881. Ed. technical schools, Jesuit Coll.; grad. in piano, comp. Conserv. of San Pietro, Majella, Naples. Asst. to Machinelli, Met. Opera, N. Y. 1900; cond. Savage American Opera Co. 1902-05; cond. w. Oscar Hammerstein, Manhattan Opera House, N. Y. and London 1907-12; mus. dir w. Arthur Hammerstein and Shuberts 1912-18. Produced *Firefly, Peasant Girl, Alone at Last, Katinka, Maytime and Star Gazer.* w. San Carlo Opera Co. 1918-22; dir. Gen. L. A. Opera Assn. 1926-32; dir. Gen S. F. Opera Assn. since 1922. Chevalier Legion of Honor, France; Commendatore, Order of Crown of Italy. Member Italy-Amer. Soc.; Bohemian Family, Cenacolo, Olympic, Japanese Amer. (S. F.) clubs. Hobby, study of medicine. War Memorial Opera House, San Francisco, Calif.

METZGER, JOHN F.

Conductor, violinist, teacher. b. Chatanika, Alaska, 1910. St. New England Cons. of Music (2 yrs.); violin w. Calmon Luboviski, Harrison Keller; B. A. San Diego State Coll. Dir. adult evening class orch. (10 yrs.); San Diego County H.S. (4 yrs.). Founder-cond. San Diego Sinfonietta, 1947. Sonata recitals w. William Strong, and wife, Viva Crise. Member: Kappa Gamma Psi, MTA, Music Makers, Board Member Music Merit Found., San Diego Tchrs.' Assn. Hobbies: travel, books, swimming. 1009 Madison Ave., San Diego, Calif.

METZGER, VIVA CRISE

Pianist, teacher, composer. b. Escondido, Calif., 1910. St. harmony at Berkeley; theory w. Catherine Urner; piano w. Dolce Grossmayer (10 yrs.), Lyle Barbour (1 yr.). Comp incl.: *Happy Little Fingers, Happy Fingers No. 2* (publ. Belwin). Secy. MTA, Music Makers. Hobbies: reading, swimming. 1009 Madison Ave., San Diego, Calif.

MIHAILOFF, SERGEI

Concert pianist, composer, lecturer, teacher of piano. b. Moscow, Russia, Sept. 10, 1898. Att. Imperial Cons. Moscow. St. piano w. Leon Conus, Sergei Rachmaninoff, Albert Elkus, Willem Harmans, Alexander Raab. Concertized in U. S. Cond. normal classes, lectures for piano tchrs. 1930-34. Concerts, lectures on Russian music at Principia Coll., Ill., others. Playwright, *How to Become a Successful Piano Teacher,* 1934; author *A Journey to Freedom,* (autobiography), articles, music criticisms for Novaya Zarya (newspaper). Invented, patented music device for studying scales. Comp. incl. *Symphony, String Quartet,* songs, numerous piano pieces: *Minstrels, Village Festival, A Lullaby* (Robbins), *Gitanillo, Chica* (Summy). Hobbies: book collecting, reading. Wife, Frances Mihailoff, interior designer. Son, Dmitri Mihailoff, teacher of piano. 2820 Baker St., San Francisco 23, Calif.

MILLS, ESTELLE BROWN

Teacher of voice. b. Nebraska City, Nebr. Cousin of Louise Homer and Jane Osborne Hannah. St. voice w. Chas. W. Clark (2 yrs.), Jane Osborne Hannah (Chicago and Leipzig Grand Opera) (10 yrs.). Concertized in N.Y. City, Middle West; had studios in Omaha, New York, Leipzig. Pupils incl. Frances Lehnerts, Mrs. Seifert, The Rounders, Hazel Eden. Hobby: gardening. 428 So. Mariposa Ave., Los Angeles, Calif.

Gaetano Merola

Pierre Monteux

Lucien Moraweck

MITCHELL, ROBERT BOSTWICK

Conductor, composer. b. Los Angeles, Calif. St. Eastman Sch. of Music, N.Y. Coll. of Music. Won Eastman Scholarship. Fellow, AGO at age 18. Radio dir., KFI Staff Orch. Comp., dir. *Conquest* radio show. Founder-dir. Mitchell Boy Choir. Dir. Mitchell Boy Choir School. Comps. incl. several masses, orch. works, religious and popular songs, piano pieces, chorals. Numerous recordings (United Artists). Member AGO, AFRA, AFM Local 47. Mitchell Boy Choir School, 1757 No. Western Ave., Los Angeles, Calif.

MOCKRIDGE, CYRIL

Composer. b. London, England, 1896. Grad. Royal Coll. of Music, Royal Acad., London. St. piano, theory w. Landon Ronald. Accomp. Maggie Teyte, Elsa de Narcki. Comp film scores. 1836 Benedict Canyon Dr., Beverly Hills, Calif.

MONTEMEZZI, ITALO

Composer. b. Vigasio, Italy, 1875. St. Milan Cons. w. Saldaino and Ferroni. Comps. incl. *The Love of Three Kings, Giovanni Gallurese, Hellera, La Nave, Principezza Lontana* (operas), tone poems for orch., chamber music, etc. 714 No. Walden Dr., Beverly Hills, Calif.

MONTEUX, PIERRE

Conductor, music director San Francisco Symphony. b. Paris, 1875. Trained Paris Cons. St. solfeggio, harmony w. Lavignac; counterpoint, fugue w. Lenepveu; violin w. Berthelier. From 1849 cond. concerts in Paris founding series at Casino de Paris for ultra-modern French music. Cond. Theatre des Champs-Elysees, Chatelet, Odeon, Paris; Covent Garden, Drury Lane, London; also Berlin, Vienna, Budapest. Came to U. S. as cond. Russian Ballet, 1916; led concerts Civic Orch. Soc., 1917; cond. at Met., 1917-19; Cond. Boston Sym. Orch. 1918-19; Cond. S. F. Sym. since 1935; guest L. A. Phil. Hollywood Bowl, etc. Cond. NBC Sym. Hour; Cond. first performances of Stravinsky's *Le Rossignol, Petrouchka, Le Sacre du Printemps,* Debussy's *Jeux,* Ravel's *Daphnis et Chloe,* Roger Ducasse's *Le Joli Jeu du Furet.* Tour of U. S. w. S. F. Symphony 1947. Memorial Auditorium, San Francisco, Calif.

MOORE, MARY CARR

Composer, music director, soprano. b. Memphis, Tenn. Aug. 6, 1873. St. theory w. John Haraden Pratt, Leipzig Cons., voice w. H. B. Pasmore. Mus. D., Chapman Coll. Sang in public since age 12, opera, concerts, recitals, U. S., Europe. Cond. own operas, orch. works in Los Angeles, San Francisco, Seattle, San Diego, other mus. centers. Prof. of music and theory, Chapman Coll. (18 yrs.); Olga Steeb Piano School. Comp. incl. 10 operas: *The Oracle, The Cost of Empire, The Leper, Memories, Harmony, The Flaming Arrow, David Rizzio, Los Rubios, Flutes of Jade Happiness, Legende Provencale; Indian Idyll* (orch.), *Saul* (orch. suite), *Kidnap* (orch.), *Concerto* (piano and orch.), *Suite* (str. orch.), *Brief Furlough* (quintet, also orch.), *Piano Quintet, Clarinet Quintet, String Quartet, Trio* (vn. and pf.), chorals, works for violin and piano, 'cello and piano, piano solo, numerous songs; pub. Schirmer, Webster, Robbins, Ditson, C. Fischer, Quincke, Witmark. Founder, hon. pres. Mary Carr Moore Mss. Club. Member: Womens' Press (hon. life), MacDowell (hon. life), Euterpe, Matinee Mus., L. A. Opera and Fine Arts, Schubert, other clubs; founder-memb. Native Amer. Comp. Soc.; Pen Women; P.E.O. Sisterhood. Res. studio: 4037 Leeward Ave., Los Angeles, Calif.

MORAWECK, LUCIEN

Composer, arranger, pianist. b. Belfort, France, 1901. St. piano w. father, Alfred Moraweck, (cond., teacher), Alfred Cortot, Helene Kastler (4 yrs.); harmony w. Georges Caussade, (tchr. Paris Conservatory) (2 yrs.). Arr. for Lud Gluskin on German tour; cond., arr. Paramount theatre, Paris. Arr. in U.S. 1935. Arr. for CBS N.Y., 1935-36; CBS L.A., 1937. Academy Award for scoring *The Man in the Iron Mask,* 1939; *The Lady in Question* (Columbia). Film scores incl. *International Lady, Friendly Enemies, Avalanche, The Return of Monte Cristo, High Conquest.* Radio scores for *Suspense* (since 1943); *Through the Iron Curtain* (1946), *Passport for*

Adams (Corwin), Orson Welles programs. Comp. incl.: *The Girl at a Spinning Wheel* (harp), *Habanera in the Night* (vn. and pf.), *Improvisation on a Theme, Mermaid* (piano). Soloist *Pan-American Program, Masquers,* Radio Mexico City, La Hora Nacional. Recitals San Jose, Costa Rica. 4149 Wilkinson Ave., No. Hollywood, Calif.

MOSS, EMANUEL

Violinist, conductor. b. Odessa ,Russia, 1909. St. violin w. Leopold Lichtenberg; harmony, comp. w. Alfred Sendrey; cond. w. Vladimir Bakaleinikoff, Albert Coates. Member: Cleveland Symphony Orch., Janssen Symphony; asst. cond. Los Angeles Pops Orch.; principal violin Santa Monica Symphony. Recordings for Victor, Columbia, motion pictures, radio. Under contract to MGM. Hobbies: rare bows, philosophy, paintings. 610 So. Kenmore Ave., Los Angeles, Calif.

MOWREY, DENT

Pianist, composer. b. New York City, June 11, 1889. St. w. Reger, Bauer. Comp. include piano pieces, songs. 1062 S.W. Douglas Pl., Portland, Ore.

MOYER, NANCY CAROL

Tympanist; percussionist. b. Los Angeles, Calif. St. University H.S.; Univ. of So. Calif. Only woman tympani player in a major symphony orchestra. Played w. Hollywood Bowl Sym. (Stokowski), Santa Monica Sym. (Rachmilovich), Werner Janssen Sym. (Janssen), Beverly Hills Orch. (Waxman), Sou. Calif. Opera Orch., Pasadena Civic Orch. (Lert), Pan-Pacific Woman's Orch., Hollywood Canteen Sym., All-City H.S. Orch., 17th Dist. Amer. Leg. Girls Band, Southwest Boys and Girls Band, others. Featured on stage w. Ken Murray's *Blackouts of 1947.* Recordings w. Janssen Sym., Santa Monica Sym., incl. *Tchaikovsky Sym. I and II,* Khatchaturian *Masquerade Suite,* De Falla *El Amor Brujo,* others (Victor, Concert Hall, Disc, etc.). Member: Hollywood Opera Rd. Club, Bib and Tuckers, Mannequins of Asst. Lg., Sigma Alpha Iota, Sigma Xi, Hollywood Models Guild, AFM Local 47. Hobbies: writing, art, drama, modeling. Mgmt. Paul R. Moyer, Paramount Studios, Hollywood, Calif. 6700 Franklin Ave., Hollywood 28, Calif.

MURRAY, LYN

Composer, conductor. b. London, England, 1909. Ed. Barrow-in-Furness, Lancs., Eng. Cond. various radio programs. Comp. *Camptown, Cromer, Variations on a Children's Tune, Esther,* (opera) (libretto by Norman Corwin); incidental music for Columbia Workshop prod., radio dramas. Recording: *The Lonesome Train* (chorus,, orch., soloists) (Decca), *Music from Snow White and the Seven Dwarfs* (Decca), *Christmas Carols* (Lyn Murray Singers) (Columbia). Member: ASCAP, ASMA, Songwriters Prot. Assn., League of Composers. Mgmt. Wm. Morris Agency, Beverly Hills, Calif.

MURTEY, EMERIE RUDLAND

Concert pianist, teacher of piano. b. Sacramento, Calif., Sept. 1, 1910. St. piano w. Constance Mering, Mrs. Noah Brandt, Alexander Raab, Frederic Saatman, Richard Buhlig; harmony and theory w. Vitold Farrelle. Soloist KFBK String Ensemble; Sacramento Phil. Orch.; Calif. Fed. of Music Clubs. Joint concert tours w. Lucille Ehorn; Vitold Farrelle. Recitals Sacramento H. S., Allied Arts Breakfast Club, Chicago Art Club, others. Dir. Placerville Choral Society (3 yrs.). Organist choir dir. Episcopal Ch. Member: Calif. Fed. of Music Clubs, Saturday Club, MTA. Hobby: collecting antique glassware. 3125 3rd Ave., Sacramento, Calif.

MUSE, CLARENCE

Composer, singer, lyricist. Grad. Dickerson Univ., Pa. Singing waiter Hudson pleasure boats. Dir. music school, Chicago. Founder Lafayette Theatre, Harlem. Concertized throughout U. S. Motion pictures incl. *Hearts in Dixie, Rain or Shine, The Wet Parade, Huckleberry Finn.* Comp. incl. *When It's Sleepy Time Down South, Liberty Road, Alleyway of My Dreams.* Author, *Way Down South.* 2135 Clinton St., Los Angeles, Calif.

Estelle Brown Mills

Robert Bostwick Mitchell

Mary Carr Moore

Lyn Murray

Emanuel Moss

Nancy Carol Moyer

Emerie Rudland Murtey

MYLES, MARGARET

Concert pianist, teacher of piano. b. Hamilton, Ontario, Canada, July 1, 1913. Private tchrs. in Tacoma, Seattle, Chicago. Canadian Festival Winner. App. in concerts, radio, oratorio, churches. Soloist w. Ralston Club, Treble Clef Club. Hobby: collecting records. At present teaching at College of Puget Sound, Tacoma, Wash.

NATHAN, ROBERTA

Teacher of Voice. 1717 No. Vine St., Hollywood 28, Calif.

NEMETH-SAUNDERS, LAUREL

Soprano, opera and concert; teacher of voice. b. Hazelton, Pa. St. voice w. Wronski, Milano; Seagle, N. Y.; Samoiloff, Walker, Michaud, L. A. Opera prima donna U. S., Europe, incl. Hollywood Bowl, Los Angeles Grand Opera, Sou. Calif. Opera Assn., Carcano Opera, Milano; light opera w. Schubert. Concertized in U. S.; twice soloist San Francisco Pan-Pacific Exposition; radio series; soloist with leading orchs. under Usigli, Samoussoud, Sample, Tandler, Saunders, Cimini, others. Faculty, Zoellner Cons., Guy Bates Post Theatre Arts. Comp. incl. song *My Wish*. 5456 Sierra Vista Ave., Hollywood 38, Calif.

NETHERY, MARGERY

Teacher of piano. b. Kearney, Nebr. St. piano w. Florence M. Hole, London, Eng. (T. Matthay pupil, licentiate Royal Acad. of Music, Trinity Coll. of Music); theory, harmony w. Incorporated Society of Musicians; in America w. Fanchon and Birt Summers, Ed. Baxter Perry (pupil of Franz Liszt), Olga Steeb. Concertized extensively, specializing in ensemble work and accompanying; pianist, Riverside Opera Assn. Past-pres. MTA, Riverside Branch. Member Los Angeles Fed. of Music Clubs, Nat'l Fed. of Music, Nat'l Guild of Piano Teachers, Exponents of Swedish Music. Affiliated Sherwood School of Music. Teacher of Mildred Erickson Kammeyer, others. 3690 Elmwood Dr., Riverside, Calif.

NEWELL, CHARLES N. W.

Pianist, teacher of piano. b. San Francisco, 1892. St. piano w. Frank Moss, Guyla Ormay, Pierre Douillet, Hugo Mansfeldt, San Francisco; Moritz Moszkowski, Isidore Philipp, Paris; Cecile Chaminade, London; Tina Lerner, Vladimir Schavitch, San Francisco. Teaching in San Francisco since 1923; master classes in Hollywood, Honolulu, other cities. Member MTA. Hobbies: gardening, goldfish. Studio: 408 Stockton St., San Francisco, Calif.

NEWMAN, ALFRED

Conductor, composer. b. New Haven, Conn., 1901. St. piano w. Alexander Lambert, Sigismund Stojowski. Comp. w. Reuben Goldmark, George Wedge; piano-vaudeville w. La Rue and Bordoni. Two gold medals, Fonanda Cons. (Paderewski, Busoni, Muck, judges). App. w. N. Y. Phil. Piano recitals. Comp. of piano quintet, piano sonata, orch. suites, *Lithographs*, *Street Scene*, several piano pieces. Member Hobbie Quartet. Guest cond. Cincinnati Sym. Orch. 1926, Amer. Orch. Soc. N. Y., Hollywood Bowl 1932, L. A. Phil. Orch. 1933; soloist w. U. Parks, New Haven, (1911). Mus. Dir. Twentieth-Century Fox, Studios, Los Angeles, Calif.

NEWMAN, PAULINE

Pianist, teacher of piano. b. San Francisco, Calif. St. piano w. Marcell Ciampi (8 yrs. pupil and asst.), Paris, France. Spec. courses Univ. of Calif. in teaching, pedagogy, pub. sch. music. Recitals in U.S., France. Spec. in children's chorals. Faculty MacJannet Sch., St. Cloud, France; Chateau de Bures Sch., St. Germain, France; Sunset Sch., Carmel, Calif. Member MTA, rec. secy. San Francisco chapter since 1946. Studio in San Francisco for several years. 1904 Franklin St., San Francisco, Calif.

NIJINSKA, BRONISLAVA

Choreographer, dancer. St. dance w. Cecchetti. Att. Imperial Sch., St. Petersburg. Appeared w. Diaghilev Ballet,

Vienna Opera Ballet, Polish Nat'l Ballet, others. Choreographed numerous ballets. 1553 No. Stanley Ave., Hollywood 46, Calif.

NILES, DORIS

Concert artist; classic, interpretative, character dancing. b. Redlands, Calif. St. w. Michel Fokine, Jose Otero of Spain. Classic training w. Vera Trefilova, Alexandre Volinine. First appearance, Capitol Theater, N. Y. C. (remained seven yrs.). Concerts in Carnegie Hall, 1927-28-29. App. before Alphonso XIII of Spain in Madrid, also twice at Santander, summer palace. Danced in Paris Paramount Theaters (5 yrs.) 1929-34; w. Raquel Meller, Palace Theater, 9 mos. Extensive tour for Paramount 1933: Bordeaux, Toulouse, Marseille, Rome, Streatham, Brighton, others. Nine mos. tour in Italy w. Schwarz Co.: Rome, Milano, Turino, Livorno, Spezia, Naples, Genoa, San Remo. Tour 6 mos. w. Raquel Meller, 1934: Manrreaa, Angelsola, Puigcerda, Tarragona, Reus, Barcelona, Gerona, Palma de Mallorca, Gandia, Madrid, Cordova, Malaga, Spanish No. Africa, Jerez, Cadiz, Sevilla. Six mos. Grosvenor House, London, 1935. Recital Fortune Theater, 1936. Sixteen wks. Olympia Theater, Paris, 1937; First concerts Salle Pleyel 1937; same year incl. Provence, Le Havre, Nancy, Lyon, Rheims, Deauville, Ostende, Cannes, Nice, Biarritz. During Word War II app. for units of Belgium Army and hospitals. Concert at Royale du Parc, Brussels, February, 1940; Theatre Royale du Gymnase, March, 1940; Luxembourg, March 1940. Danced w. Serge Leslie in Massenet ballet, *Le Cid*, before Pres. Lebrun of France at PreCatalan. Created several ballet-divertissements for three dancers: *Les Ambulantes*, *Les Forces Errantes*, *Le Corbeau* and *Le Tragedie de la Horloge*. Special music comp. for her dances by Tullio Carloni, Ernesto Lecuona, Pierre Kolpokoff, Tito Schipa, Edw. Kilyeni, Eugene Goossens, Henry Purmort Eames. 557 So. Coronado St., Los Angeles, Calif.

NILSON, EINAR

Conductor, composer. b. Kristianstad, Sweden, Feb. 21, 1881. St. Royal Cons., Stockholm; Hochschule fuer Musik, Berlin; violin w. Josef Joachim; comp. w. Max Bruch and Paul Juon; grad. 1907. Cond., comp., Max Reinhardt's Theater, Berlin 1908-33. Co-cond. Salzburg Festivals 1920-33. Cond. European, American performances Reinhardt-Humperdinck spectacle *The Miracle*; Hollywood Bowl performances *A Midsummer Night's Dream*, 1934, world premiere of Richard Strauss' *Country Gentleman*, Berlin 1918; inaugurated Salzburg Festival as musical advisor, cond. to Reinhardt and Hofmannsthal, 1920. Comp. *Three Ballets* w. Hugo von Hofmannsthal (prod. by Reinhardt,, Vienna, Stockholm Operas, many other theaters); incidental music to Hofmannsthal's version of Calderon's *The Great World Theater* and *Everyman* (Hollywood Bowl, 1936); incidental music for plays by Shakespeare, the German classics, Tolstoy, Strindberg, etc. Member ASMA. Hobby, preparing smorgasbord. American citizen since 1937: w. Warner Bros. First Nat'l since 1941. 8519 Nash Dr., Hollywood, Calif.

NOACK, SYLVAIN

Violinist. b. Rotterdam, Netherlands. Att. Cons. Amsterdam, Holland. St. w. Andre Spoor, Leopold Kramer, Bram Eldering. Member Amsterdam Concertgebouw, Aix-La-Chapelle Municipal, Boston Sym., St. Louis Sym., L. A. Phil., Hollywood Bowl orchs. Concertized in U. S., Europe. Cond. Aix-La-Chapelle Sym., L. A. Phil., Hollywood Bowl Orch. Member Carl Flesch String Quartet (4 seasons). Founder Noack String Quartet, 1919; Boston String Quartet. 341 N. Van Ness Ave., Los Angeles, Calif.

NORRIS, PAULINE DAHL

Pianist, teacher of piano, ensemble coach. b. Seattle, Wash. St. piano w. mother, Ethel Gertrude Cannon, Glen Dillard Gunn, Rudolph Ganz; comp. w. Arthur Olaf Andersen. Assoc. of Glen Dillard Gunn (Chicago); head of musical dept., Starrett School, affiliated w. Univ. of Chicago. Non-resident member Musicians Club of Women, Chicago. Hobby: viewing sunsets. Address: 742 S.W. Vista, Portland 5, Ore.

Doris Niles and Serge Leslie

NORTON, MILDRED

Music editor, critic Los Angeles Daily News. b. Missouri. Att. UCLA. St. violin, piano, voice w. pvt. teachers. Author numerous articles on music; contributor to various musical journals. Los Angeles Daily News, 1257 S. Los Angeles St., Los Angeles 15, Calif.

NOVIKOFF, IVAN F.

Balletmaster. b. Kazan, Russia, August 24, 1899. Att. Russian Imperial Theatrical School, St. Petersburg. Balletmaster, choreographer, composer degrees. App. in Russia, China, Japan, Canada, Europe and U.S. Comp.: *Swan Queen and the Prince* (classical ballet), *Cossack Revels* (ballet). Choreography, *Fifth Symphony*, Beethoven; *Fourth Symphony*, Tchaikovsky; *Russian Revels, Enchanted Princess*, others. Founder, Novikoff Junior Ballet Co., Novikoff Civic Ballet. Hobbies: ice skating, fishing, skiing. Balletmaster and dir. The Novikoff School of Russian American Ballet, Pacific Coast st. 1924. Studios: Holyoke Bldg., 111 Spring St., Seattle, Wash.; 431 Broadway, Tacoma, Wash. Res.: 2531 26th Ave. North, Seattle, Wash.

O'CONNOR, ROBERT

Concert pianist, teacher of piano. b. New York City. St. w. Paolo Gallico, I. Phillip, Egon Petri, Paris Conservatoire. Mus. M. European debut: Salle Erard, Paris. Tours in Europe, U. S.; recitals and appearances w. orchestras in Wigmore Hall, London; Bechstein Salle, Berlin; Vichy, France; Town Hall, New York, etc. Member Pi Delta Phi, Phi Mu Alpha. Hobby: rose growing on Nantucket Island. Management: Elizabeth Healy, Temple of Music, Tucson, Arizona. Res. 324 So. Sixth Ave., Tucson, Arizona; bus.: Univ. of Arizona, Tucson, Arizona.

OLDS, W. B.

Conductor, teacher. b. Clinton, Wis., 1874. Att. Beloit Coll., Oberlin Cons., Amer. Cons. St. voice w. Allen, Heacox, Weidig, Kimball, Hackett, Seagle. Comp. incl. numerous songs, chorals. Faculty Grinnell Coll., Illinois Coll., James Millikin Univ., Univ. of Redlands. 805 N. University St., Redlands, Calif.

OLSON, MRS. FRED L.

Teacher of voice. b. San Francisco, Calif. St. piano at early age. Voice w. Yeatman Griffith; repertory w. Richard Hageman. Concertized as singer on Pacific Coast. Began teaching voice in 1910. Among her pupils are: Jane Powell, David Brooks, Murry D. Carter, Olga Ruff Carter, Dorothy Fisher, Harry Steele, Violet Eterno Raschio, Corinna Mura, Sylvia Horenstein, Civilla Allyn, Jean Howard. Member Nat'l Fed. of Music Clubs, Oregon MTA; past-pres. Tuesday Afternoon Club; charter memb. Portland Women's Club. Hobby: collecting music. 208 Fine Arts Bldg., Portland. Ore.

OUKRAINSKY, SERGE

Choreographer, dancer; teacher of dance and choreography. b. Odessa, Russia (Leonide Orlay de Carva). St. dancing Lycee Condorcet, Lycee Carnot, Acad. Julian, Paris. Mime in French Mus. Fest., Paris. Partner, solo dancer w. Anna Pavlova, Pavlova Ballet Russe 1913-15; guest artist Chicago Opera Assn. 1915-16, first dancer 1916-17. Co-founder Pavley-Oukrainsky Ballet which became official ballet of Chicago Opera. Tours solo and with own ballet throughout Europe, North and South America, all music centers. Ballet master Los Angeles and South America, all music centers. Balletmaster Los Angeles and San Francisco Opera Cos. 1927-30. Dance dir. Warner Bros., Fox, Tec-Art Studios 1927-30. Dir. Oukrainsky Ballet since 1931; staged ballets in Hollywood Bowl 1934-37, Chicago Exposition 1938, etc. Created *Videballeton*, synchron. of dance, film, music. Choreographed 20 full ballets, incl. *La Fete a Robinson, Boudour, Dance Macabre, Gates of Redemption, Captive Princess, Temple of the Sun, Trianon, Aztec Sacrifice, Les Elements*, 47 opera ballets, 80 divertissements. Known as only dancer able to perf. barefoot toe dance. Member, AGMA. Hobbies: scene design, costumes, decorating. Perry Studio, 1753 N. Highland Ave., Hollywood 28, Calif. Res. 5538 Barton Ave., Hollywood 38, Calif.

PARNES, IRVING

Concert manager. b. Milwaukee, Wisc., Dec. 9, 1918. Att. L. A. City Coll., USC. Music publicity since 1940; presented concerts in L.A. since 1944, esp. of Amer. folk music, dancing. Prod. recording *Calypso Carnival* (Sir Lancelot) (Crest Label). Hobbies: theater, horseback riding, swimming. 707 Philharmonic Auditorium Bldg., Los Angeles 13, Calif.

PARSONS, GIEHL IRVING

Concert violinist, teacher. b. Omaha, Nebr .St. violin w. Moritz Rosen; theoretical subjects w. Chas. Lagourge, E. Murray, both of The Music Conservatory of the Northwest. Concertized throughout U.S., Canada, Mexico; soloist, concertmaster, conductor, theater and radio. Composer of several violin text books. Member, past president, MTA of San Francisco; AFM, Local 6. Hobby: violin making. Studio: 844, 33rd Ave., San Francisco, Calif.

PASCARELLA, ENZO

Director Sou. Calif. Inst. of Music. b. Naples, Italy .St. Royal Cons. Mus., (awarded Gold Medal) and Univ. of Naples. A.B., B.S., Mus. D., Prof. Music Lyceum of Naples: Member Naples String Quartet, founder member Pascarella Trio, N.Y.C. Concertmaster Naples San Carlo Royal Opera, Naples Symphony Orch., New York Opera Comique, Faculty, Naples Lyceum at 17; coached w. Cesar Thomson; app. w. orch. and solo recitals in Europe and U. S. Comp. incl. *Habanera* (voice and orch.,) *Spanish Dance* (string trio), *Lyric and Dance a La Gavotte*, (orch), *Lullaby* (voice, chorus, orch.). Cond. N.B.C., C.B.S. orchestras, N.B.C. Musical Guild programs, Beethoven Fest. 1938 (coll. w. Weingartner). Member AFM. N.Y.C., L.A., San Diego; Verdi Club (hon.), Inter. Soc. of Composers, City Island Yacht Club. 848 Beech St., San Diego, Calif.

PATTERSON, JESSIE McDONALD

Vocal teacher, soprano, musical director. b. Highnore, So. Dakota. Att. Dakota Wesleyan Univ.; grad. Highland Park Coll., Des Moines, Iowa. St. voice, w. John Smallman, Yeatman Griffith; oratorio w. Sir Henry Wood, London. Concertized in U.S. and Europe. Musical dir., soprano soloist *The Pilgrimage Play* (15 yrs.) ; mus. dir., soloist in L. A. churches. Member: NATS, MTA, L. A. Dominant Club, Euterpe Opera Reading Club. Management: Seth S. Patterson, same address. 6632 Cahuenga Ter., Hollywood 28, Calif.

PEARSON, EVA

Teacher of piano. 542½ No. Harvard Ave., Los Angeles, Calif.

PEARSON, RUTH

Asst. voice, drama coach, Rennay Shry-Ock School of Music-Arts and Drama. St. dance McCune Sch., Salt Lake City; piano w. Beckstrand, Fogelberg, Jenson, Shepherd, Jolas, Reid. B.A., Univ. of Utah. St. drama w. Koch, Banff Sch. of F.A.; voice w. Lucie De Vienne, Mme. Rennay Shry-Ock; radio prod. Stanford NBC Radio Inst. App. in dramatic roles KDYL (3 yrs.), Rennay Shry-Ock School of Music-Arts and Drama, 1353 Post St., San Francisco, Calif.

PEIRCE, RUTH

Teacher of piano, theory. b. South Dakota. Enrolled in Coll. music dept. when in elementary school; later student assistant. B.S. South Dakota State Coll.; A.B. Univ. of Michigan; two summer quarters at Stanford to qualify for secon. teaching cred. in Calif.; grad. American Cons., Chicago. St. piano w. Allen Spencer (American Cons.), harmony, comp. w. Adolf Weidig; children's methods w. Louise Robyn. A tpresent teaches secondary schools, pvt. piano. Member MTA, CTA, PTA, Women's Guild of Presbyt. Ch. Hobbies: flowers, books, snapshots. 3429 Rosemary Ave., Glendale 8, Calif.

PELLICCIOTTI, QUIRINO

Teacher of voice. b. Italy. St. piano, theory w. Maestro Salerno Phila., voice w. Ettore Martini, Achille Alberti, Los Angeles, Parola in *La Scala*; theory w. Ghidotti. Among his pupils are Ann Ayras (N.Y. Civic Opera, Glyndebourne Fest.), Alexander Serbaroli (1947 Atwater Kent Award), Norma Larson (Capitol Rec.), Carmen Prietto (rec. *The Bells*), Aurora Miranda. 610 So. Berendo Ave., Los Angeles, Calif.

238

Margery Nethery

Charles N. W. Newell

Pauline Newman

Einar Nilson

Pauline Dahl Norris

Ivan F. Novikoff

Robert O'Connor

Mrs. Fred L. Olson

Giehl Irving Parsons

Serge Oukrainsky

Enzo Pascarella

Jessie McDonald Patterson

Ruth Peirce

PENDLETON, EMMET

Concert pianist, composer; teacher of piano, composition. b. Red Bluff, Calif., May 30, 1887. Att. State Coll., Chico; Univ. of Calif., Berkeley. St. piano w. Hugo Mansfeldt, *San Francisco*; theory, comp. w. Florence Guppy, Arthur Farwell, Arthur Foote, others. Concertized extensively in U. S., Europe. Sp. program in Liszt House, Weimar, Germany, 1922. Numerous club, other recitals, Northern Calif.; instr. in piano 25 yrs. Weekly broadcasts KHSL, Chico; KVCV, Redding, 1935-37. Comp. incl. *Pendeltonia* (5 pf. pcs.), *Excerpts California* (pf. pcs. on themes of Maidu Indians of Nor. Calif.), *Miniatures* (25 songs), *Lieder von Schnenden Seelen* (song cycle), *Light of the Lord* (sac. song cycle), *Among the Lillies* (4 songs), *From Moon-Filled Sky* (6 songs), chamber music, chorals, songs, piano pieces; many pub. in England, U. S. 1038 Oak St., Red Bluff, Calif.

PENNARIO, LEONARD

Concert pianist, composer. b. Buffalo, N. Y., July 9, 1924. St. piano w. Edward Fischer, Buffalo, Samuel Ball, Olga Steeb, Guy Maier, Los Angeles; comp. w. Ernest Toch; orch. w. Lucien Cailliet. Concertized throughout U. S., Europe, Asia; soloist w. leading symphony orchestras incl. New York, Los Angeles, Chicago, Cincinnati, Indianapolis, San Francisco, Dallas, Denver, Minneapolis. War service (3 yrs. Air Force) India, Burma, China; three bronze stars. Resumed career in 1946-47 season, playing over sixty engagements and as featured artist, Nelson Eddy Radio Show (NBC). Comp. *Piano Concerto in D-Flat*, *Fireflies* (2 pfs.) (Summy), *March of the Lunatics* (Sprague-Coleman), *Ballade*, other piano pieces. Member AGMA. Management NCAC. Res. 306 So. Westminster Ave., Los Angeles, Calif.

PERLEE, CHARLES D.

Music critic. b. Pasadena, Calif., 1907. St. piano, theory, voice w. private tchrs. Music reviewer, Pacific Coast Musician, 1933-39; music reviews, comments, various articles for Pasadena Star News since 1939. Contributor to Etude, other music magazines. Editor, The Baton, Pasadena Civic Music Assn. monthly mag. Vice-pres., Amer. Music Theatre; Assoc. mgr. Pasadena Civic Orch. and Civic Chorus. Hobbies: record collecting, mountain climbing. Pasadena Star News, 525 East Colorado St., Pasadena 1, Calif.

PERLMAN, WILLIAM J.

See page 163.

PERRIERE, MICHEL

Musical director AFRS, Universal recorders. b. Nice, France. St. violin, viola at Paris Cons. Harmony, counterpoint, composition w. Louis Fourestier and Ribollet. Played w. Paris Symphony, Concerts Gervasio, opera, chamber music. Cond. Royal Theatre, Lutetia Theatre, Paris, Little Carnegie Playhouse, N. Y., 1927, Martin Beck Theater, N. Y. Toured Eastern cities w. musical shows. Cond. KFI-KECA for sponsored shows, 1930. Worked at MGM, other major studios as violist. Band leader of 370th AAF Orch. 1942; Asst. to Meredith Willson of AFRS Shows, 1943. Member AFM, Local 147. 2030 Linnington Ave., West Los Angeles, Calif.

PETERSON, EDNA GUNNAR

Concert pianist, teacher of piano. b. Chicago, Ill. St. piano w. Rudolph Ganz, Chicago Musical College and Berlin; August Spanuth, Berlin, Arthur Farwell, Edgar Stillman-Kelly, Adolf Weidig. Debut in Berlin w. Berlin Philharmonic Orch.; American debut w. Chicago Symphony Orch. Soloist w. Minneapolis, St. Louis Symphony Orch. four times w. Los Angeles Philharmonic. Joint recitals w. Mary Garden, Tetrazzini, others. Member: Mu Phi Epsilon Musical Sorority; Dominant Club, MTA, Local 47 AFM. 229 So. Harvard Blvd., Los Angeles, Calif.

PETRI, EGON

Concert pianist; teacher of piano. b. Hanover, Germany, 1881 (citizen of The Netherlands). Att. Dresden Kreuzschule. St. violin w. father, Henri Petri; comp. w. Kretzschmar, Draeseke; piano w. Richard Buchmayer, Teresa Carreno, Feruccio Busoni; organ, French horn, philosophy in Berlin. Mus. D. Manchester Univ., England. Decorations: Phoenix and Redeemer, Greece; Polonia Restituta, Poland. Debut as pianist, Holland, 1902. Concertized extensively throughout Europe (1911-32), U. S. (since 1932); soloist w. all major orchestras of Europe, U. S., under leading conductors. Violinist, Dresden Royal Orch. 1889-91; Professor, Manchester Royal Coll. of Music. 1905-11, Basle Cons., Berlin Hochschule fuer Musik, Mills Coll., Oakland, Calif. Cond. master classes Zakopane, Poland, Colorado Springs, Colo., Los Angeles, Washington, D. C., Boston, New York City, Cornell Univ., Ithaca, N. Y. Visiting lecturer in music, Cornell Univ. 1940-46. Chosen by Busoni to arr. for piano his *Indian Phantasy*, *Piano Concerto*, and operas *Die Brautwahl*, *Dr. Faust*. Editor complete works of J. S. Bach (coll. w. Busoni, Muggellini) (pub. Breitkopf). Recordings of Franck, Brahms, Busoni, Liszt, Chopin, other works (Columbia). Now pianist in residence, Mills College, Oakland, Calif. Res. 4684 Reinhardt Dr., Oakland 2, Calif.

PETTIBONE, LILLIAN

Pianist, teacher. b. Wapakeneta, Ohio. B. A., Washington State Coll. St. piano w. Mme. Marguerite Melville Liszniewska, Ruth Bradley, Arthur Loesser, Alfred Mirovitch. Soloist w. Portland Symphony Orch. (Van Hoogstraten), Portland Phil. Orch., Federal Symphony Orch. Numerous concert appearances in the East and West, and radio. Member: Mu Phi Epsilon, Oregon MTA, Alpha Chi Omega. Hobby, Collector of miniature pianos. Ainsworth Bldg., Portland, Ore.

PHILLIPS, MADALYN (AKERS)

Composer, organist. b. Hutchinson, Kan. St. Knox Coll.; post-grad. American Cons., Chicago; pvt. instr. Mus. B., Mus.. M. (Summa cum laude); Comp. incl. *Clouds in the Moonlight* (organ) (orch.); Easter number, *He is Risen as He Said,* (featured 3 yrs. Forest Lawn Sunrise Services); *Abraham Lincoln Walks at Midnight* (Vachel Lindsay); religious drama for soprano, contralto, 13 males voices, chorus, narrator, ballet; *Suite* (vn. and pf.); several organ suites; chorals; piano solos, and songs. Latter perf. by Tibbett, Thomas, Giannini, Marshall, Morgan, Sweetland. Member: Soroptimist Club, Dominant Club, Sigma Alpha Iota (hon.). Hobbies: coll. musical novelties; aiding young talent. 355 First Ave, Chula Vista, Calif.

PHILLIPS, RONALD

Clarinetist. St. w. Perrier, DiBusscher, Bonade. Played w. Seattle Symphony under Karl Krueger, Basil Cameron Nikolai Sokoloff, Sir Thomas Beecham, Carl Bricken. Soloist w. Beecham in three performances of Mozart *Clarinet Concerto*, 1942; w. Bricken 1946. Assisting artist w. Coolidge Quartet in Mozart *Quintet* 1942; w. Dorothy Maynor 1946. Toured w. Martha Graham, dancer, two seasons. Instructor of clarinet, Univ. of Washington. Wife, Gladyce Bezeau Phillips, pianist, teacher. St. piano w. Alexandre Sklarevski, Maurice Dumesnil, Leopold Godowsky. With Seattle Symphony, 6 yrs. Concertized in Pacific Northwest; w. concert orchs .in theatres, radio, hotels. 4532 4th Avenue, N.E. Seattle, Wash.

PIASTRO, JOSEF (Borisoff)

Violinist, teacher, composer, conductor; mus. dir. Palos Verdes Community Art Assn. Sym. Orch. b. Kertch, Crimea, Russia, March 1, 1890. St. w. Sarasate, Auer, Liadov, Glazunov, Rimsky-Korsakov. Att. St. Petersburg Cons. App. w. Saint-Saens, 1919. Decorated by King Alexander of Greece, Russian Czar Nicolas II, Sultan of Arabia. Recitals throughout world. Played under Nikisch, Coates, Safonoff, Fried, Glazunov, Koussevitsky, others. Comp. for violin, orch., piano, songs, symphonies, string quartets, opera, violin method. 5500 W. 118th St., Inglewood, Calif.

PISK, PAUL AMADEUS

Composer, pianist. b. Vienna, Austria, 1893. Grad. Univ. of Vienna Cons. Ph.D. in musicology, state tchrs. diploma, cond.'s diploma. Traveled throughout Europe and U.S.A. as comp., lecturer, pianist. Comp. for orch., piano, vocal, chamber music. Several recordings. Member Amer. Musicological Society, League of Composers, American Composer's Alliance, Pi Kappa Lambda, MTA. Univ. of Redlands, Redlands, Calif.

Quirino Pellicciotti

Emmet Pendleton

Leonard Pennario

Michel Perriere

Egon Petri

Madalyn Phillips

Lillian Pettibone

Ronald and Gladyce Phillips

Joan B. Powers

Lucien Prideaux

Bert Prival

Frank Pursell

Del Purves

POLLACK, ROBERT

Violinist, conductor. b. Vienna, Austria. Att. Cons. Leipzig, Germany. St. w. Sitt, Marteau, Flesch. Concertized Europe, Orient, U. S., Canada. Cond. Tokio, Jr. Sym., S. F. Chapman Orch., L. A. Prof. violin Geneva, Moscow, Vienna, San Francisco, Tokio. 1860 N. Wilton Pl., Hollywood 28, Calif.

POWELL, EDWARD B.

Orchestrator, conductor, composer. b. Savanna, Ill., 1909. St. theory w. Wilson, Schillinger; music analysis w. Schoenberg. Orch. musical comedies by Schwartz, Berlin, Duke, Warren, others incl. *Let 'Em Eat Cake*, (Gershwin); also ballet *Union Pacific* (Nabokov) for Monte Carlo Ballet Russe. Orch. incl. *Broadway Melody, Top Hat, Born to Dance, Goldwyn Follies*, 614 Hillcrest Rd., Beverly Hills, Calif.

POWERS, JOAN B.

Teacher of piano, organ, harmony. b. York, Nebr. St. piano w. Herbert Kinner (grad. Boston Cons.), Mary Hilsabeck; organ w. LeRoy Rogers, Univ. of Denver; harmony w. Barton Bachmann, master classes W. Karl W. Gherkens. Theater organist, Brighton, Colo. Sec. MTA San Bernardino Br. Member San Bernardino Valley Concert Assn.: Civic Opera Assn. Resident teacher The Brush Studio of Music. 497-17th St., San Bernardino. Husband. Joseph F. Powers; arranger, percussion, marimba. Children's Marimba band. Res. 833 Colima Rd., San Bernardino.

PRIDEAUX, MEREDITH (LUCIEN)

Choreographer, ballet dancer. b. Mineral Point, Wisc. St. drama Houston, Tex. at age 8 played parts in *Penrod, Daddies, Daddy Longlegs*, other plays. St. dance, choreog. w. Andreas Pavley, Serge Oukrainsky, Bronislava Nijinska, Alexander Kotchetovsky, Vincenzo Celli, others. Premier danseur Pavley-Oukrainsky Ballet; guest choreographer Chicago Opera; headed own concert company (Intern. Concert Corp. mgmt.); guest choreographer Polish Opera Co. Choreographer, leading dancer San Carlo Opera Co. (14 yrs.); choreographer Cincinnati Summer Opera Co. Hobbies: costume designing for opera, period plays; decorating. Mgmt. Fortune Gallo, 1697 Broadway, New York City. Studio 62-A, 1425 Broadway, New York, N. Y.

PRIVAL, BERT

Dancer, choreographer, teacher of ballet. b. Englewood, N. J., Sept. 14, 1905. Att. Gymnasium, also Amer. H. S., Berlin, Germany, 1912-18. St. ballet at Berlin Opera, Metropolitan Opera Ballet Sch., N. Y.; also w. Alexis Kosloff, Martin Ferrari, Luigi Alberteri, others. Premier danseur Winthrop Amer. Gilbert & Sullivan Opera Co., Musical Opera, St. Louis, Hollywood Bowl, L. A. Civic Light Opera Co., S. F. Golden Gate Inter. Expos., Hollywood Ballet Co. (tour), Metropolitan Opera Ballet; solo app. throughout U. S. Dance soloist various films, incl. *Emperor's Waltz*, ets. Choreographed numerous ballets, ensemble dances. Member: Equity, Screen Actors Guild, Ch. of Comm. Maitre de ballet, owner, three San Fernando Valley ballet schools: 12546 Ventura Blvd., Studio City; 5267 Bakman, North Hollywood; 14418 Victory Blvd., Van Nuys. Res. 4932 Medina Rd., Woodland Hills, Calif.

PRO MUSICA TRIO

Pro Musica Trio consists of Tanya Gould, pianist, Shirley Cornell, violinist, Eleanor Kessler, cellist. Tanya Gould, b. Canada, 1924. St. piano w. Boris Berlin of Toronto Cons. of Music, from which grad. at age 15. Scholarship w. Mme. Olga Samaroff-Stokowski, N. Y.; w. Richard Buhlig, L. A. Att. Phila. Cons. of Music. Shirley Cornell,—for full biography, see Cornell. Eleanor Kessler, b. San Francisco, Calif., 1926. St. violin w. Boris Blinder, S. F., Carl Stern, N. Y. Won Gainsborough Foundation Award. Soloist San Francisco Sym. (Rudolph Ganz), String Symphonia (Roy Harris). Pro Musica Trio toured extensively through Canada, Mexico, Italy, France, Germany and leading cities of Central and So. America. Management: Behymer Artist Bureau, 415 Auditorium Bldg., Los Angeles, Calif.

PURSELL, FRANK

Concert singer, choral conductor, teacher of voice. b. Tulare, Calif., 1904. St. voice w. Edward Pease, George Walker, John C. Wilcox, Chicago; repertory, lieder Conraad V. Bos (New York); opera roles w. Ernest Knoch; choral conducting w. Father Finn, Alexander Stewart, John Smallman. Soloist St. Bartholomew's Church, N. Y. Oratorio roles w. Brooklyn Oratorio Society, Philadelphia, Bach Festival, Los Angeles Oratorio Society. Cond. Whittier College A Cappella Choir, Whittier Oratorio Society, 1936-42. Founder-director Bach Society of Sacramento, Director Trinity Episcopal Church Choir. Cantor B'Nai Israel Temple, Sacramento. Member NATS. Hobbies: mountain climbing, stamp collecting. Pease Conservatory of Music, 2130 L Street, Sacramento, Calif.

PURVES, DEL.

Concert pianist, violinist. Legal name Purves-Smith. b. Boise, Idaho. St. piano, harmony w. C. Purves-Smith; violin w. Beth Lackey-Barron, Ellis Levy. Concertized in U. S. on both piano and violin. Member MTA; Etude Club, Berkeley; Tuesday Musicale, Pasadena. Mgmt. Larry Allen Inc., 79 Post St., San Francisco. 172 Highland Blvd., CCC, Berkeley 8, Calif.

PURVES-SMITH, C.

Pianist, teacher, musicologist. b. St. Leonards, Sussex, England. St. w. Alice Purves-Smith, Frederick Mariner, Alexander Raab, others. Concertized in U. S. and China. Dir. School of Music, Peking Inst. of Fine Arts (1924-1926). Author numerous articles on music in Musical Observer, Etude, Pacific Coast Musician; regular contributor Music of the West; formerly editor Pianists Dept. Musical West. Taught piano Pasadena, 1927-1939. Now teaching, Berkeley, Calif. Member MTA; Past Pres. L. A. County MTA; member American Society of Mechanical Engineers. Developed gunnery control mechanisms used in aircraft during war; numerous other mechanical devices. Comp. incl. numerous piano pieces and songs. 172 Highland Blvd., CCC, Berkeley 8, keley 8, Calif.

PURVIS, RICHARD IRVEN

Organist, choir director, composer. b. San Francisco, Calif., August 25, 1915. Debut as organist age 13. First public perf. age 4. St. organ w. Wallace Sabin, Sir Edward Baristow, England. Won Curtis Memorial Scholarship, Curtis Institute, 1935. Organist, First Bapt. Ch., San Francisco, 1933-35; St. James Epis. Ch., Philadelphia, 1939-42. Head, mus. dept., Episcopal Acad., Overbrook, Pa., 1940-42. U. S. Army, Combat Service, 1942-45. Organist, choirmaster, St. Mark's Luth. Ch., San Francisco, 1946-47. Dir. Wednesday Morning Choir, Oakland. Choral master, Hamlin Sch., San Francisco. Now organist, master of choristers, Grace Cathedral, San Francisco. Concertized extensively throughout U. S., British Isles. Plays monthly series of organ recitals. Comps. incl. *The Ballad of Judas Iscariot* (oratorio), *Mass of St. Nicholas, Mass of the Nativity* (Anglican comm.), anthems, songs, chorals, works for organ, piano. Recordings w. Phila. Symphony (Toscanini). Colleague, AGO. Grace Cathedral, 1055 Taylor St., San Francisco 8, Calif.

PUTNAM, ETHEL WILLARD (Mrs. Clyde Willard)

Piano instructor. b. South Dakota, Jan. 18, 1888. St. theory, piano w. Grace G. Goodykoontz (Mitchell, S. D.); piano, theory under Waldo F. Chase (L. A.); master classes, Sigismond Stojowski, Harold Bauer, Richard Buhlig; research on pedagogy w. Edith Rhetts, Univ. of So. Calif. Teacher of Edith Caroline Hart, Jimmie Marsh, Dorothy Judy Klein. 1411 Elm Ave., Long Beach, Calif.

QUAID, MRS. HAZEL HARVEY

Pianist, music educator. b. Cincinnatus, N. Y., June 18, 1892. Att. Grinnell Academy, 1908, Grinnell Coll., 1909-11. St. piano w. Claude Gotthelf, 1915, Franz Darvas, 1916-17 at Arizona Sch. of Mus.; Gail Martin Haake, 1935, American Cons. B. A. Arizona S.T.C., Tempe, 1932; M.A. Northwestern Univ., August, 1937. St. w. Richard McClanahan, (N. Y. repr. Tobias Matthay) 1939. Est. piano studio Tempe, Ariz. 1919. Choirmaster, organist, Tempe Cong. Ch., 1925-35. Dir. of Glee Clubs, Tempe Union H. S., 1932-34. Affili. w. Arizona State Tchrs. Coll., 1932. Pres. Phoenix Piano Tchrs. Assn., 1940. Pres., Arizona State MTA, 1941-43. Comp. incl. *By the Brook, A Child and I, The Lord Is My Shepherd.* Now asst. professor, Music Dept., Arizona State College, Tempe, Arizona.

QUALEN, EDWARD N.

Choral conductor, teacher of voice, b. Iowa, 1907. B.B.A. degrees at University of Minn; B.A. Occidental Coll. Studied composition, harmony, voice, Occidental; choral work, voice w. Father Finn, J. F. Williamson, Robert Shaw; voice w. Carl Guggisberg, St. Paul, Mme. Gallbeck, Chicago; Dir. mus. First Baptist Church, Pasadena; soloist at church; member AGO; former pres. Choral Conductor's Guild of Southern California. Wife Elizabeth A., pianist; st. w. Carl Jansen, St. Paul. 75 North Marengo Ave., Pasadena, Calif.

QUENZER, ARTHUR

Director, Calif. Academy of Music; bassoonist. b. New York City, 1905. Att. Columbia Univ. Appeared on radio programs incl. Nelson Eddy, Amos 'n Andy, Rise Stevens, Joan Davis, Herbert Marshall, Dick Haymes, Phil Harris. Comp. music for motion pictures, *Fun and Fancy Free, Cowboy and the Lady, Merrily We Live, Swiss Miss, You're A Sweetheart.* Recordings all major companies. Organized Calif. Academy of Music, faculty of active radio and motion picture studio musicians. Member: ASCAP, Song-writers Prot. Assn., AFM Local 47, Chamber of Commerce. 5267 Bakman Ave., North Hollywood, Calif.

QUINN, ALFRED PRICE

Music critic, teacher of piano. b. Atlantic City, N. J. St. w. Emil Held, Phila.; Leipzig Cons.; st. w. Teichmuller, Sitt, Schrechk, Krehl. Taught Epworth Univ., Oklahoma Mus. Acad., Brooklyn Cons. of Mus., asst. to Teichmuller, Leipzig. Comp. incl. salon mus. and teaching material. Music critic, B'nai B'rith Messenger, 759 S. Hope St., Los Angeles, Calif.

RAAB, ALEXANDER

Pianist, b. Raab, Hungary. Arr. U. S., 1915. Att. Vienna Cons. St. w. Hans Schmidt, Robert Fuchs, Prosnitz, Leschetizky. Soloist w. Wiener Tonkunstler, Chicago Sym. Orch., Minneapolis Sym. Orch., London Sym. Orch., others. Annual concerts; recitals w. Kubelik in Eng., Russia, Germany, France. Head piano dept., Chicago Musical Coll. 2516 Warring St., Berkeley, Calif.

RABINOWITSH, MAX

Pianist. b. Libau, Latvia, 1893; arr. U. S., 1922. Grad. Imperial Univ. of Petrograd. St. piano w. Essipov, Barinova, Imperial Cons. of Petrograd. Several world concert tours. Traveled U. S. and Europe as soloist and accomp. w.. Chaliapin, Jeritza, Anna Case, Isadora Duncan, Anna, Elise and Margo Duncan. Soloist w. leading Russian orchs., Europe, America. Comp. numerous songs, piano pieces. Piano synchronization for various film studios; under contract to RKO Prod. (past 4 yrs.). Hobbies: cards, football. Teacher of Pauline Carter, Andre Previn. RKO Productions, 780 Gower St., Hollywood 38, Calif.

RACHMILOVICH, JACQUES

Conductor; founder-musical director Santa Monica Symphony Orch. b. Odessa, Russia. Att. St. Petersburg (Leningrad) Cons. Concertized as pianist, U. S., Europe. Cond. U. S., Europe. Recordings w. Concert Hall, Disc, others. Member AFM Local 47. 2426 Aspen Dr., Hollywood 28, Calif.

RADAMSKY, SERGEI

Singer; teacher of singing. b. Kharkov, Russia, 1895. St. voice w. Leoparti, Alexandria, Egypt; New England Cons. of Mus. (2 yrs.), Ramon Blanchart, Boston (3 yrs.); Giovanni Gravina, New York (1 yr.), Vita, Milano. Arr. U. S. 1910; concertized, sang opera 1918-23 Europe 1923 (*Lucia, Carmen, Boheme, Butterfly* (in Italy); toured w. New Manhattan Opera in U. S.; toured Russia 1937; sang *Wozzek* (Berg) under Stokowski, 1932-33. Asst. to Blanchart, 3 yrs.; lectured; wrote articles on music for N.Y. Times. Prod. opera, *Hansel and Gretel,* others, Los Angeles. Students incl. Sadomoff, leading basso, Moscow Gr. Opera. Mgmt. Behymer Artist Bureau, 427 W. 5th St., Los Angeles 13, Calif. Studio: 702 Crenshaw Blvd., Los Angeles, Calif.

RADERMAN, LOU

Concert violinist. b. N.Y.C., 1903. Grad. Damrosch Sch. of Music. St. violin w. Kneisel, Spearing, Tranka. First violinist Volpe Sym.; asst. concertmaster Russian Sym., Victor Sym., NBC Sym. (Black, Kostelanetz). Victor Red Seal Records. Solos for MGM pictures, radio. Recitals London, N. Y. Organized Modern Sextet Ensemble. 4051 Sawtelle Blvd., Culver City, Calif.

RALSTON, FRANCES MARION

Composer, pianist, teacher of piano, harmony, composition. b. St. Louis, Mo. St. New England Cons., Boston, grad. piano course. St. piano w. Carl Faelten, Boston; comp. w. E. R. Kroeger, St. Louis; Adolph Weidig, Chicago; Arthur Foote, Boston. Recitals of original comp. in St. Louis, Denver, Charlestown, Rockford (Ill.), Wellesley (Mass.), Petersboro (N.H.), Bellingham (Wash.), San Francisco, Los Angeles, Pasadena. Faculty Central Coll., Lexington, Mo.; Rockford College, Ill.; Wellesley College, Mass. Comp. incl. *The Awakening* (wom. cho.) teaching pieces, *Piano Sonata c sharp m., Musical Ideas For Beginners, Theme and Variations* (pf); *Sonata* (Vn. and pf.) *Scotch Idyl* (organ) *Trio* (pf. org. vc) (mss); operetta, *End of the Rainbow,* twenty songs, *Sonata* ('cello), short pieces for 'cello; *String Quartet, Quintet* (voice, fl. vn. vc. pf) perf. 1933; *Song of the Singers* (wom. cho.), piano concerto *Dixie,* (mss.) *Saul* (oratorio) (mss.) (text, Robert Browning) also *First Piano Concerto* given 40 perf. full orchestras. Studio: 35 So. Raymond Ave., Pasadena, Calif.

RAY, JOHN MENSFORTH

Concert violinist, teacher of violin, harmony. b. South Shields, County Durham, England. St. w John Nicholls, A. Brodsky, Manchester Royal Coll., Leon Sametini, Chicago. Teacher's Certificate from Chicago Musical Coll. Colleague Degree, Calif. MTA., San Francisco Convention 1947. Toured England w. Carl Rosa Grand Opera. Concertmaster D'Oyly Carte Opera Co. Concertized in England, Canada, United States. First chair Montreal Symphony Orch. Faculty, San Francisco Conservatory of Music, 1935-1947. Pvt. studio, also Assoc.Teacher, Music & Arts Inst. of San Francisco. Wrote two books: *Elementary Theory and Harmony for the Violin* and *Modern Scales for the Violin,* (mss). Chairman Violin Forum, M.T.A. Convention at Riverside, Calif., 1946; Pres., San Francisco of Music Teachers' Assn. of Calif. 1946-47-48. 2147, 34th Ave., San Francisco 16, Calif.

RAYMOND, GENE

Composer, actor. b. New York City. St. Professional Children's School. Composer of musical comedy, *The Gold Brickers;* adaptation, *Concerto of Death.* Numerous songs incl. *Release, Let Me Always Sing, Please, Will You.* Several songs recorded by Jeannette MacDonald. Hobby: golf, riding, dog breeding. Care of Helen Ferguson, 321 So. Beverly Dr., Beverly Hills, Calif.

REDEWILL, HELENA MUNN (Mrs. Francis H.)

Musicologist, critic, lecturer, pianist, organist. b. Ohio. St. piano, organ, theory, Univ. School of Music, Ann Arbor; Charles Marie Widor, Wagar Swayne, Paris; Arthur Schnabel, Berlin. A.B., A.M. Univ. of Michigan. Organist American churches, Paris, Berlin, Vienna. Concert programs, costume recitals, lectures Europe and U.S. Many pub. poems, articles, short stories. Natnl. ed. The Triangle (Mu Phi Epsilon) 1930-40. Cited for distinction, Univ. of Mich., 1937. Faculty Univ. of Calif. Dept. of Journalism. San Francisco Bay Area repr. for Musical Courier. Member: Calif. Writers' Club; Lg. of Amer. Pen Women; Pac. Mus. and Berkeley Piano Clubs; Pub. Rel. and Wom. Fin. Com. San Francisco Symphony Orch. University of California, Berkeley, Calif.; res. 1675 Euclid Ave., Berkeley 9, Calif.

REID, C. W.

Pianist teacher of piano. St. piano w. John Hasler, A. C. Smythe, Joseph MacIntyre, A. C. Lund; New England Cons. w. Edwin Khlare. Taught at Brigham Young Univ. (16 yrs.), McCune Sch. of Mus. (10 yrs.), head piano dept. Rennay Shry-Ock School of Music-Arts and Drama (2 yrs.). Comp. incl. C. W. Reid System of Piano Study, teaching pieces, etudes for piano. Rennay Shry-Ock School of Music-Arts and Drama, 1353 Post St., San Francisco, Calif.

243

REINBERG, HERMAN

Solo 'cellist, instructor of 'cello and chamber-music, Mills College, Oakland. First desk. S. F. Symphony Orchestra and Opera Assn. b. Lodz, Poland, 1898, Nephew of Josef Lhevinne. St. w. Klengel, Leipzig and Ludwig at Dr. Hoch's Cons. of Music, Frankfurt am Main. Played with Frankfurter, Basle, Switzerland and other leading orchestras under most well-known conductors. Concertized in Poland Germany, Holland, Switzerland, San Francisco. Played over NBC, KFRC (S.F.). Member of Krefelder and Basle String Quartets. Member Music Lovers Society of San Francisco. 312 Maple St., San Francisco, Calif.

REINBURG, ANNABELLE

Lyric-coloratura soprano; teacher of voice; repetiteur. Att. Royal Acad. of Mus., London; Hochschule fuer Musik, Berlin. St. w. Johnstone, Douglas, Weber, London; Felia Letvine, Paris; Levandowsky, Heydenreich, Rosenstein, Wilcks, Berlin. Soprano soloist, British Broadc. Corp. and Baird Television, London. Won Mozart scholarship, Salzburg, Austria. Prod., dir. Band Box Theatre, Berlin; asst. dir. Windmill Theatre, London. Spec. in voice, phonetics, stage deportment. 8118 Sunset Blvd., Hollywood 46, Calif.

RHINES, HOWARD M.

Radio announcer, writer, producer. b. Hoquiam, Wash. St. arts, letters, Bradley Coll, Ill. Spec. in preparation classical recorded programs for radio. Member, AFRA. Hobby, coll. records, esp. vocal artists of past. KMPC, 5939 Sunset Blvd., Hollywood, Calif. Res. 8558 Holloway Dr., Hollywood, Calif.

RICKEL, HARRY

Concert pianist; teacher of piano. b. Winslow, Ariz., May 3, 1914. Grad. Univ. of Ariz., 1937. Mus. B., Mus. M., Univ. of Ariz. St. piano, theory w. Richard Buhlig. Annual concert tours of Arizona. Head piano dept., Tucson Sr. H.S. Member: Phi Mu Alpha, Phi Kappa Phi, Phi Delta Kappa. 1317 E. Helen St., Tucson, Ariz.

RICKMAN, EDWIN T.

Pianist, choral director, teacher of piano. b. Missouri, Aug. 25, 1903. Grad. San Francisco State Coll. St. cond. w. Hans Leschke; comp. w. Ernst Bacon; piano w. Lincoln Batchelder, Jeanne Farrow Kimes, others. B.A., San Francisco State Coll. Pres., San Francisco Municipal Chorus, Calif. MTA, San Francisco Choirmasters and Organists Assn. Minister of Music, First Baptist Ch., San Francisco. Address: 360, 23rd Avenue, San Francisco, Calif.

RIHERD, GUSTAVE

Concert pianist, teacher of piano. 12 So. Fair Oaks Ave., Altadena, Calif.

RILEY, IRVING R.

Teacher-pianist, arranger. b. Pawtucket, R. I. St. piano at 10 w. Eliz. Watt (2 yrs.), John M. Foy (5 yrs.); harmony, comp. UC; Colleague Degree State MTA. Solo pianist 8 yrs. w. Fox West Coast Theaters. Alternate soloist first performance *Rhapsody in Blue*, Melbourne, Australia, 1928; soloist San Diego Symphony Orch. (Marcelli), accompanied schumann-Heink in San Diego. Member Kiwanis; Past-Pres. MTA of San Diego. 640 Broadway, San Diego, Calif.

RIMANOCZY, JEAN de

(*See:* de RIMANOCZY)

RINQUEST, E. H. BAXTER

Teacher of voice. b. Salina, Kans. St. voice, Chicago Musical Coll., theory w. Henry Housley; coached w. John Dennis Mahan, David Bispham, Percy Rector Stephans, William S. Brady, Herbert Witherspoon. Soloist, choir director, teacher in Denver, Colo. Author, *How to Develop Your Speaking Voice.* 4250 Livingston Dr., Long Beach, Calif.

RITCHIE, BELL T.

Teacher of voice, concert singer. b. Glasgow, Scotland. St. voice w. Walter John Hall, N.Y.C., (3 yrs.), William Shakespeare, Yeatman Griffith, Percy Rector Stevens, N.Y.C. (3 yrs.), Plunkett Greene, London (6 seasons). Traveled through British Isles and The Hebrides, making special study of folk songs. Appeared throughout Calif. in program of folk songs, also soloist modern English songs. Presented opera readings, musical readings for Red Cross benefits. Charter member and Pres. of Fresno Music Club, (19 yrs.). Central Regional Vice-Pres. State Fed. of Music Clubs. Hobby: reading of poetry, Shakespeare. 1415 Wishon Ave., Fresno, Calif.

RITTIGSTEIN, EVA

Teacher of piano. b. San Francisco. St. piano w. Paolo Gallico, Alexander Raab; shortly w. Wagner Swayne; master classes, private lessons w. Josef Lhevinne. At present w. Alexander Raab; exponent of his teaching principles. Long established teacher in San Francisco. Member MTA. 683 Sutter St., San Francisco, Calif.

RIZOR, RUTH

Concert pianist, teacher of piano. b. Santa Barbara, Calif. Att. Santa Barbara Coll. St. piano w. Henry T. Polk (pupil Leschetizky), Harold Smythe, Guy Maier. B. A., Santa Barbara Coll. in mus. ed. Concertized in U. S., princ. in West. Soloist w. Burbank Sym. (Damiani), other orchs. Radio KFI, KFWB, KWIK, etc. Taught in L. A. public schs., 2 yrs. Comp. incl. *Alma Mater*, used by Santa Barbara High School. Member: Soroptomists; Bus. & Prof. Women's Club, Glendale. Hobby, collecting rare books, esp. antique cook books. 1227 Viscano Dr., Glendale, Calif.

ROBB, JOHN DONALD

Dean of Music, Univ. of New Mexico. b. Minneapolis, Minn., 1892. Att. Yale Univ. (B.A.), Minn. Law Sch., Harvard Law Sch. St. theory w. Horatio Parker, David Stanley Smith; comp. w. Juilliard Sch., Nadia Boulanger, Paul Hindemith, Roy Harris. Comp. incl.: *Symphony for Strings, Piano Sonata, Violin Sonata, An Orchestral Excursion, String Quartet*, chamber music, songs, chorals, pieces for piano, organ. Recordings of Indian tribal music. Member: Nat'l Assn. of Mus. Exec. in State Univ.; Yale Club (N.Y.). Hobby, golf. Univ. of New Mexico, Albuquerque, N. M. Res. 1623 Sigma Chi Rd., Albuquerque, N. M.

ROBINSON, DELLA HOWELL

Dramatic soprano, teacher, director. b. Kansas City, Mo, St. w. Mme. Green, N. Y.; Phyllis Wolf, Boston Cons.; Constantino, F. X. Arens, Arthur Alexander, Los Angeles; coached w. Richard Hageman. Sang for Browning Club, other Pasadena Clubs; oratorio w. Wm. Tyroler, John Smallman; w. Boston Montana Band, Butte, Mont. (5 yrs.). Soloist, dir., Presbyt., Methodist, Episcopal Churches, Anaconda, Mont.; soloist 1st Methodist Church (3½ yrs.), 1st Presbyt. Ch., Pasadena, Neighborhood Church, (1½ yrs.), Church of Truth (1 yr.), concert soloist, Women's Choral Club. Concerts Pacific Coast, Middle West. Soloist KNAX, KFI, KHJ, KWKW, KLAC. Gives one day a week to recording voices of boys at McCornack General Hospital to be sent to relatives. Pres. Serbiolian Club, Pasadena; Pres. Fine Arts Club (2 yrs.). 999 No. Hill Ave., Pasadena, Calif.

ROBINSON, GRACE THAYER

Teacher of piano and violin. b. Keams Canon, Ariz. St. violin w. Aram der Zakarian (9 yrs.); piano w. Mary Geerts, Agnes de Jahn; theory, piano w. Barton Bachmann. Att. Fresno State Coll.; grad. from University of Redlands 1937 with B.M. in piano and public school music. Vice-pres., program chairman Fresno County MTA; sponsor Treble Clef Musical Club; sec'y. Fresno Musical Club. Plays viola in Fresno State Coll. Symphony Orch. Tchr. instrumental and vocal music, Fresno County Schools (8 yrs.). 4045 Iowa Ave., Fresno, Calif.

RODETSKY, SAMUEL

Concert pianist, teacher. b. Sevastopol, Russia, March 9, 1906. Holder Colleague's Degree, Calif. MTA. St. w. teachers in Siberia, China, Japan; Jos. Geo. Jacobson, S. F. Numerous appearances as soloist w. Nat'l Broadcasting Co. orchs., others. Repeated appearances as soloist at MTA Conventions, etc. Past- pres. of S. F. MTA (3 yrs.); past pres. of Haskalah Club (2 yrs.); State vice-pres. of Calif. MTA (3 yrs.). Member Doric Lodge, F & A Masons, other org. 144 Parker Ave., San Francisco, Calif.

C. Purves-Smith

Hazel Harvey Quaid

Edward N. Qualen

Arthur Quenzer

Sergei Radamsky

Frances Marian Ralston

John Mensforth Ray

Herman Reinberg

Annabelle Reinburg

Harry Rickel

Edwin T. Rickman

Irving R. Riley

Bell T. Ritchie

Eva Rittigstein

Ruth Rizor

Della Howell Robinson

RODGERS, IRENE

Teacher of piano, composer. b. Bothell, Wash. St. piano w. John J. Blackmore, S. Stojowski, Frank LaForge; specialized in accompanying (N.Y.); various music courses Univ. of Washington. Writes mainly for children. Comps. incl.: *Piano Book for Little Jacks and Jills* (*Bks. I, II, III*), *A Treasury of Tunes and Rhymes*, other beginner's and supplementary books; piano numbers incl.: *A Balalaika Serenade, The Dream Weaver, Moon Mist, Valse Melodie, Etude Fantastique*; songs incl.: *Teach Me Thy Way, Negro Lemant.* Member Ladies Musical Club. Studio 301 Paramount Theatre Studio Bldg., Seattle, Wash. Res. 409, 16th North, Seattle, Wash.

RODRIGUEZ, JOSE

Editor, 1940 edition of *Music and Dance in California.* b. Guatemala City, Nov. 18, 1898. St. piano w. Bree, Pugno, in Europe. Cond. in England and Canada. Former reporter, city editor Los Angeles Record, Los Angeles Herald; correspondent various wire services; numerous critical articles newspapers and magazines. Monographs on Stravinsky and Schoenberg. Comp. *Piano Concerto, Symphonic Variations,* piano pieces, songs. Pioneered serious music in radio; edited many critical and technical books. 216 So. Almont Dr., Beverly Hills, Calif.

ROGERS, LOIS LYNN

Concert pianist, teacher, coach. b. Emporia, Kan. D. of Laura McClure, pianist; B. M. Grinnell Coll., grad. Amer. Cons. Music, Chicago; piano instr. Busch Cons. Chicago; att. Stern's Cons., Berlin; piano, pipe organ w. Scheve, Heniot Levy, Rudolph Maria Breithaupt, Adele aus der Ohe, Serge Tarnowsky; comp. w. Adolf Weidig. Weekly piano radio broadcasts WGN, Chicago, KBW, Buffalo. Concertized Berlin, London (1927-1928), other European cities; Brooklyn, Philadelphia, Chicago, Minneapolis, Rochester, Buffalo, other Eastern cities; soloist Minneapolis, Chicago orchs. (Verbrugghen, Cherwonky) concertized through Southern states (1937-1938). 945 Afton Road, San Marino, Calif.

ROMBERG, SIGMUND

Composer. b. Hungary, July 29, 1887. St. w. Victor Heuberger. Comp. music for films, incl, *Maytime, Desert Song, New Moon, Viennese Nights, Children of Dreams, The Night is Young, Girl of the Golden West*; operettas incl. *Student Prince, My Maryland, Nina Rosa, Maytime, Desert Song, New Moon*, others. Plays piano, organ, violin, 'cello, bass. Collector of musical scores of operas and operettas. 1023 N. Roxbury Dr., Beverly Hills, Calif.

RONKA, ILMARI

Conductor; composer; music director San Fernando Valley Symphony Orch. b. Ely, Minn., May 14, 1905. St. theory, comp., violin, piano, Inst. of Musical Art, N. Y.; comp., interpretation w. Jean Sibelius, Jarvenpaa, Finland, 1936-38. Played w. Cleveland Sym. (Sokoloff) 1928-30; Cincinnati Sym. (Goossens) solo trb. 1934-43; NBC Sym. Orch. (Toscanini, Black) solo trb. 1942-45; San Francisco Sym. (Hertz), Cincinnati Summer Gr. Opera; Pryor Band, Asbury P., N. J. solo trb. 1930; Goldman Band, N. Y. euphon. 1928. Cond. Helsinki Radio Orch., Hollywood Bowl Easter 1946, Los Angeles County Sym. Band orch. radio series 1946-47. Comp. incl. two symphonic suites, *Fantasette* (trpt. and tromb.) (Fillmore); *Daily Studies for Brass Instr.* (C. Fischer), chamber music, songs, etc. Recorded Brahms *Hung. Dances* w. own Sinfonietta (Columbia) w. trb. solo on reverse. Founder-cond. San Fernando Valley Symphony Orch. 1946, San Fernando Valley Junior Symphony 1947. Cond. perf. numerous film recordings. Contract w. RKO Studios, 1945-46; now under contract Enterprise Pictures. 6217 Elmer Ave., North Hollywood, Calif.

ROSS, JOSEPH

Music copyist and librarian. b. Hartford, Conn., 1901. Att. New England Cons.; st. viola w. Paul Whiteman, Vincent Lopez, Roger Wolfekann, B. A. Rolfe. Member Masonic Shrine. Hobby fishing. 1558 No. Vine St., Hollywood, Calif.

ROTSCH, V. E. (GENE)

Conductor, music director, educator. b. Cortez, Colo., April 1, 1917. Grad. Whittier (Calif.) Union H. S.; att. Miramonte J.C., Stockton J.C., Coll. of the Pacific. A.B. (music) Coll. of the Pacific, 1941. St. trombone w. Hy Lammers. Soloist Long Beach Mun. Band at age 12; San Francisco World's Fair; stage, radio in Los Angeles; w. boys' band in film *Sunny Side Up* (Fox). Now mus. dir. Stockton Metropolitan Recreation Program; founder-cond. 50-piece Stockton Community Band; orig., gen. dir. Community Christmas Pageant; dir. orig. *Recreaettes* (100-piece juv. girls baton, drill corps); band instr. Adult Div. Stockton City Schools, summer high schools; tchr. Stockton H. S. Comp. songs incl. *Dream Girl of Rho Lambda Phi, Hail to Stagg, Down the Ways.* Member: Stockton Jr. Chamb. of Com., Elks Club, Stockton Mus. Assn., Rho Lambda Phi, Amer. Legion. Hobby, coll. smoking pipes. Bus.: Mus. Dir., Recreation Dept., Room 207, City Hall, Stockton, Calif. Res.: 2377 Vail Ave., Stockton, Calif.

ROY, GEORGE V.

Music educator. b. Denver, Colo., 1901. Dir. Olinger-Highlander Boys Band, 1917-22; tchr. St. Vincent's Home for Orphans, 1916, National Jewish Home 1936-42, Adams City H.S. 1938-42), Central City H.S.; Blackhawk school 1937-48. Dir. of Music, Westwood H.S., Denver P.S., 1947, St. Joseph Par. Sch., J. K. Mullen Home for Boys, Colorado Mil. Sch., El Jebel Shrine Band. Faculty (head brass inst.) Colorado Coll. of Ed. Greeley, 1945-48. Dir. Denver Junior Police Bands, 1937-47. Played under cond. Horace E. Tureman, Henry E. Sachs, John S. Seick, Rudolph Ganz. Three years trumpet w. Denver Symphony Orch. (Caston). Member: AFM, Denver Lions Club, Denver Masonic Order, Rocky Mtn. Consistory, El Jebel Shrine, Footprinters, Elks, Colorado Music Edu. Assn. Hobby: teaching youngsters to play well. 969 So. Vine St., Denver, Colo.

ROZSA, MIKLOS

Composer, conductor. b. Budapest, Hungary, April 18, 1907. Grad. (hon.) Leipzig Cons. of Music; st. comp. w. Hermann Grabner. Mus. D. Orch. works perf. by all leading symphonies, Europe, U.S. under Walter, Monteux, Coates, Ormandy, Lange, Stokowski, Munch, Wallenstein, von Dohnanyi, Straube, Weisbach, others, incl.: *Serenade; Scherzo; Theme, Variations and Finale; Capriccio, Pastorale and Danza; Concerto; Jungle Book Suite, Thief of Bagdad Suite.* Also comp. *Trio* (Serenade) (vn.va.vc.), *Quintet* (pf.2 vn.va.vc.), *Rhapsody* (vc.orch.), *Variations on Hungarian Peasant Song, North Hungarian Songs and Dances Suite, Duo* (vn.pf.), *Duo* (vc.pf.), *Sonata* (2 vns.), *Variations, Bagatelles, Kaleidoscope* (pf.), songs, madrigals (fem.voices), *Motet* for mxd. ch. Feature film scores incl. *Thunder in the City, Divorce of Lady X., Four Feathers, U-Boat 29, Thief of Bagdad, That Hamilton Woman, Lydia, Sundown, The Jungle Book, Jacare, Five Graves to Cairo, Sahara, Dark Waters, Song to Remember* (arr.), *Blood on the Sun, Double Indemnity, Spellbound* (Academy Award, 1945), *The Lost Week End, The Killers* (Musical Courier Citation, 1947), *The Red House, Macomber Affair, The Other Love*, etc. RCA-Victor recordings *The Jungle Book Suite*, music from *Spellbound, The Red House.* Lecturer on film music, U.S.C. Universal-International Studios, Universal City, Calif.

RUBSTEIN, ARIEL

Pianist, composer. b. Kiev, Russia. Grad. Russ. Imp. Cons. w. title of Free Artist. St. comp. w. Gliere, piano w. Busoni, Vienna, Berlin. At fourteen engaged as coach Municipal Opera House Kiev. Appeared in concerts and w. orchs. in Europe. Dir. Community Center Cons. of Music, New York (7 yrs.). Invited to Pacific Northwest to direct the Ellison-White Cons. of Portland, (now Portland School of Music), which position he still holds. Comp. musical pantomime *Mademoiselle Bluebeard*, prod. by late Florenz Ziegfield. Among radio activities, has directed chamber music programs for two yrs. over Columbia Network. Portland School of Music, Portland, Ore.

Grace Thayer Robinson

Samuel Rodetsky

Irene Rodgers

Lois Lyn Rogers

Ilmari Ronka

Miklos Rozsa

Joseph Ross

Gene Rotsch

George V. Roy

Morris Hutchens Ruger

RUGER, MORRIS HUTCHINS

Teacher of music, composer. b. Superior, Wisc. Dec. 2, 1902. A.B., Columbia Univ.; M.S., Northwestern Univ.; two yrs. on doctorate, Columbia Univ. Eight years professional singer, concert, opera, oratorio. Comp. incl.: *Symphony,* 3 operas, *String Quartet, Quintet* (piano, strings), *I Hear America Singing* (cantata), *Piano Sonata, Variations* (piano, orch.), numerous songs, piano pieces. Text book, *Harmony, A Creative Approach to Four-part Writing,* (pub. Delkas). Hobbies: tennis, mountain climbing. 1627 Virginia Rd., Los Angeles, Calif.

RUNYAN, CHARLES MERTON

Conductor, pianist, organist, composer. b. Spencer, Iowa, 1896. Att. U. of Oregon; st. w. J. J. Landsbury, Jane Thacher; comp. w. Dominico Brescia. Played on radio programs *Dr. Kate, Hawthorne House, Women's Magazine,* etc. Cond. Eugene Municipal Band, various theatre orch.; Gilbert & Sullivan operettas for Beden-Savoy Opera Co., 1947. Composed *Crater Lake Suite, Rhapsody* (saxophone), *Janet, Stitches, Darkness, Drinking Song, In Heaven We'll All Be Free* (mss.); *When I Am Gone, Hoofbeats* (songs) (comp. Pub. Club). 1025 Post Street, San Francisco, Calif.

RUSSELL, FLORENCE

Singer, pianist; teacher of voice; coach. b. Hanford, Calif., Nov. 16, 1895. Training in piano from childhood; voice from age 13. Grad. Pomona Coll. (1913-17). St. piano w. Leopold Godowsky; organ w. Walter Earle Hartley; voice w. William Shakespeare, Louis Graveure; coaching w. Richard Hageman, Pietro Cimini, Arthur Alexander. Sang w. Los Angeles Opera Co. (Merola, Cimini, Hageman), others; concertized in U. S. Faculty Pomona Coll. (2 yrs.), Sutro-Seyler Studio (5 yrs.); head Russell Studios (15 yrs.). Dir. *Caroleers* (10 yrs.). Married Smith Russell, tenor, actor; former dir. UC Glee Club; w. Pasadena Comm. Theatre. Dir. Russell Little Theatre and Studio Operas. Children: Patricia Russell Baker, pianist, soprano, teacher; Smith Russell Jr., tenor; Wilfred Russell, tenor, guitarist. Students incl. Dana Andrews, Joe Baker, Dorothy Brockman, Frank Cornwell, Esther Brady, Elizabeth Walberg, Manya Nova, Nina Lissauer Rudolf, Olive Pontiz. Studios: 424 N. Larchmont Ave., Los Angeles 4, Calif.

RUSSELL, HENRY

Music director, composer, conductor. b. Moorhead, Minn., Sept. 4, 1913. Att. Concordia Cons. St. theory, comp. w. Modeste Altschuler, Joseph Schillinger, Eugene Zador. Tours w. name bands, incl. Ted Fio Rito, Ted Weems, George Ohlsson, Horace Heidt. Cond. choirs, orchs. on radio shows: Andy Devine, Fitch Bandwagon (2 yrs.), Dick Powell (1 yr.), Cass Dailey (1 yr.), Victor Borga, U.S. Army show *Front and Center* (w. Dorothy Lamour). Scored numerous films; now scoring, comp., cond. *Lulubelle* (Benedict Bogeaus). Many recordings w. Decca, Brunswick, Okay, Vocalion, Coast record cos. Since 1946 dir. of mus. NBC Western Div. National Broadcasting Co., Sunset and Vine Sts., Hollywood 28, Calif.

RUSSO, S. EDWARD

Director, Russo School of Music and Dance; conductor, composer. b. Pittsburg, Calif. Att. San Jose State Coll.; st. piano, theory, band instr., tchr. course. A. B., San Jose State Coll. App. w. San Jose Symphonic and Marching Bands. During war cond. cadet choirs, bands, Yale Univ., Boca Raton, Fla., Maxwell Field, Ala., Amarillo, Tex. Active war service, flight engineer. Comp. incl. chamber music (several trios, quartets), piano, instrumental pieces, songs. Numerous radio, other arrangements. Member: American Legion, Phi Mu Alpha (life), Kappa Delta Pi (life), San Jose State Alumni Assn. Hobby, fishing. Founded Russo School of Music and Dance, Sept., 1946; branches in Antioch, Brentwood, other towns. Russo School of Music and Dance, 30 W. 5th St., Pittsburg, Calif.

ST. DENIS, RUTH

Dancer; choreographer. b. Newark, N. J., Jan. 20, 1880. Toured U. S., Europe, Orient since 1906. Founded Denishawn Sch. w. husband, Ted Shawn; Spiritual Arts Soc. 1931. Author, books, poems. 3433 N. Cahuenga Ave., Hollywood, Calif.

ST. PIERRE, JOSEPH

Violinist; violin maker, repairer. 3651 Wilshire Blvd., Los Angeles, Calif.

SAMPLE, JAMES

Conductor. b. Minneapolis, Minn. Att. MacPhail School of Music, Mozarteum, Austria, Ecole des Chefs, Paris. B.M.; B.P.S.M.; Doctor of Music Degrees. Appeared Austria, France, Canada; New York, Chicago, Los Angeles, other principal cities of U. S. cond. opera, symphony, radio. Cond. KFI, Hollywood Bowl Aud. Hobbies: music, flying, motion pictures. Mgmt. Martin Music Management, Hollywood, Calif.

SAUNDERS, RICHARD DRAKE

See page 163.

SAVITSKY, ALEXANDER

Violinist. b. Baku, Russia, 1890. Grad. Tiflis Cons. of Music (Caucasus), Petrograd Univ. (Russia). Dr. of Natural Sciences. Violin w. L. Auer, 1904-1907, Prof. Marsick, Paris (2 yrs.). First violinist Imperial Court Orch., 1907-1912 under H. Warlich, Rimsky-Korsakov, Glazunov, Rachmaninov, Ziloti, Mahler, Weingartner, others; concerts in Russia. In U. S. since 1923. Asst. concertmaster Capitol Theater Orch. (Ormandy, Mendoza) N. Y. C., 1923-30; concertmaster 1930-35. Concertmaster KFI, KHJ w. C. Sweeten, D. Brockman, F. Stark. Now w. L. A. Philharmonic (Wallenstein). Recordings radio, motion pictures. Member Silver Trowel Lodge No. 415 of F.A.M. Hobby, photography. Mgmt. S. C. Symphony Assn. 1359 No. Ridgewood Pl., Hollywood 28, Calif.

SAWTELL, PAUL

Composer, conductor. b. Gilve, Poland, 1906. St. Conservatories of Music at Essen, Berlin, Munich, Chicago. Guest cond. various symphony orchestras. Cond. major motion picture studios. Comp. and cond. *The Fighting Guardsman, Secret Command, Mr. Winkle Goes to War, Tarzan and the Amazons, Tarzan and the Leopard Woman, Tarzan and the Huntress, Desperate, Trail Street, Born to Kill.* Now scoring *Renegades* (Columbia), *Design for Death* (RKO), *New Mexico* (Harry Sherman Prod.). Mus. dir., comp. several Army, Navy training films. Member: Academy of Motion Pictures, Screen Composers. Hobbies: cooking, hunting, photography. 4055 Kraft Ave., North Hollywood, Calif.

SAXE, RUDY de

(*See:* DE SAXE)

SCHALLERT, EDWIN

Drama, film editor, Los Angeles Times. b. Los Angeles, Calif., 1890. St. piano w. Katie M. Strassberger (Strassberger Cons. of Mus., St. Louis, Mo.); voice w. William Lott. M.A., St. Vincent's Coll. Music editor, Los Angeles Times (10 yrs.). Wife, Elza B. Schallert, singer, writer. Los Angeles Times, 202 1st St., Los Angeles, Calif.

SCHARF, WALTER

Composer, conductor, pianist. b. New York City. Att. N. Y. Univ. Comp., arr. Warner Bros., Paramount, 20th-Century Fox Republic studios (mus. dir., 4 yrs.). Now comp. Universal-Internat'l studios. Cond. Phil Harris radio show, others. Comps. incl. *Palestine Suite,* performed in Hollywood Bowl (Stokowski), Standard Hour (Janssen), other orch., small works, numerous feature film scores. Hobbies: golf, fishing. Universal-Internat'l Studios, Universal City, Calif.

SCHAUB, ARDELLA

Teacher of piano, pianist, accompanist. b. Minnesota. Grad. MacPhail Sch. of Music, Minneapolis, Minn. St. pub. sch. mus. w. T. P. Giddings; theory w. Berquist, Glen Dillard Gunn, John Mokrejs; Columbia Univ. Dykerna, Wood, Mahler; piano, Louise Albee, Adelaide T. Perry, Hans Blechschmidt; piano normal w. Louise Robyn, Gail Haake, Adelaide T. Perry, Carolyn Bowen; voice repertory, radio w. Eleanor Poehler, Beatrice Thurston; improvisation w. David Patterson; creative work, Wm. O'Toole; tchrs' classes, Leo Podolsky, Guy Maier, Richard Buhlig. Sup. of Pub. Sch. Music (7 yrs.); private teaching L. A. (15 yrs.). Colleagues, Fellows Degrees, Calif. MTA. Member Nat'l. Guild of Piano Tchrs., Mu Phi Epsilon. First pres., jr. sec., Hollywood Opera Reading Club; past-pres. L. A. Branch MTA; now first v.p. Calif. MTA. Hobbies: records, books, antiques. 6227 W. 5th St., Los Angeles 38, Calif.

Ariel Rubstein

Arnold Schoenberg

Charles Merton Runyan

Florence Russell

Henry Russell

S. Edward Russo

Joseph St. Pierre

Walter Scharf

James Sample

Alexander Savitsky

Paul Sawtell

Ardella Schaub

Leo Scheer

Eda Schlatter

Josef Schnelker

SCHEER, LEO

Conductor, composer. b. Jersey City, N.J., 1909. St. Inst. of Mus. Art, N.Y. C. w. Mischa Mischakoff, Naoum Blinder, Otto Meyer, Morris Hutchins Ruger, Pierre Monteux. Cond. Federal Symphony; asst. cond. San Diego Symphony; dir. mus., San Diego County Schools; cond.-founder San Diego Youth Symphony Orch.; assoc. cond. San Diego Civic Light Opera Co. Comp. incl. *Los Cargadores* (orch. suite), *From Haiti* (orch. fantasy), *Hands Across the Isthmus*, (chamber orch.), *A Soldier on Leave* (overture), *Three Moods* (viola, chamber orch.), *Lament* (Engl. hrn. or viola, pf.), (won Composer's Press Award, 1945); *Scheer Violin Method* (Belwin). Member: Soc. of Amer. Comp. and Cond.; MTA. Wife, Ruth Jenner Scheer, Mus.B. Yale, pianist, organist. Now w. Los Angeles Cons. of Music, cond. sym. orch., prof. of violin, viola. 3911 Roderick Road, Los Angeles 41.

SCHLATTER, EDA

Concert pianist. b. Grabill, Ind. St. theory, comp. UCLA; piano w. Norman Soreng Wright. B.A. UCLA. Concertized throughout U.S., especially California. Soloist w. Santa Monica Sym. (Rachmilovich); annual Franck Festivals, L. A.; Mozart Festivals, L. A.; Redlands Bowl; UCLA Concert Series; Riverside Mission Inn concerts; Los Angeles Ebell, and w. various other orchs., etc. Made tour of U. S. during war, playing in hospitals. Won Mu Phi Epsilon perf. contest 1940; Phi Beta plaque 1941. Member: Mu Phi Epsilon (pres. Phi Nu Chapter 1941-42; Schol. Chm. L. A. Alumnae Chap. 1947-48); Phi Beta Kappa; Pi Lambda Theta; AFM Local 47. Arroyo Corrido, Pala, Calif.

SCHNELKER, JOSEF

Organist, teacher. b. Fort Wayne, Ind. 1911. Mus. B., Oberlin Cons., Mus. M., Univ. of Michigan. Graduate study, New York City. Organist, music dir. large churches in Fort Wayne, Detroit, Cleveland. Frequent appearances organ recitalist, piano accomp. from coast to coast. Faculty, Central Coll., Iowa, 1944-46. Present head of theory, organ depts., Willamette Univ. Assoc. member AGO, Pi Kappa Lambda, Phi Kappa Phi. Hobby photography. College of Music, Willamette Univ., Salem, Oregon.

SCHOENBERG, ARNOLD

Composer. b. Vienna, Austria, 1874. St. theory w. Zemlinsky; largely self-taught. Cond. orchs. in performances of own works. Faculty Sternsches Cons., Berlin; Academy of Arts, Berlin, Amsterdam; UCLA, USC. Comp. incl. *Verklaerte Nacht*, two chamber syms., *Violin Concerto*, *'Cello Concerto* (str. quartet, orch), *Theme and Variations* (orch.), *Pelleas and Melisande* (sym. poem), *Pierrot Lunaire* (melodrama), *Die gluckliche Hand* (musical drama), *Von heute auf morgen* (opera), *Guerre-Lieder, Erwartung, Quintet for Winds*, several string quartets. Author of *A Manual of Counterpoint, Style and Idea, Structural Functions of Harmony* (Philosophical Library). 116 N. Rockingham Ave., Los Angeles 24, Calif.

SCHOOP, PAUL

Composer, concert pianist. b. Zurich, Switzerland, 1909. Grad. Zurich Cons., diploma at age 17. St. piano w. Frey, Cortot, Casadesus, Schnabel, Kreutzer; comp., theory w. Dukas, Boulanger, Hindemith, Schoenberg; mus. sci. w. Schuenemann; musicology w. Sachs; elec. instr., television w. Trautwein. Accomp. sister, Trudi Schoop, at age 12. Concertized U.S., Europe, also w. two-piano team; soloist w. leading orchestras. During war formed Schoop Co., toured for USO. Comp. incl. mus. com. *Three Apple Trees, Schoolmaster's Journey Through Hell, Everything New* (comm. by Swiss Govt.), *Obsi, The Enchanted Trumpet, The Merchant of Yonkers*; ballet mus. for Danish Royal Ballet; *Fridolin, Blonde Marie, Ringelreihen, Want Ads*, others for Trudi Schoop Comic Ballet; *Trio* (fl. ob.cl.) (Berlin w. Hindemith); *Dance Suite* (orch.); *Satire on Radetzky, Tango Symphonic, Imp's Holiday, Impressions* (pf) (3 books), *Ballade, Songs Without Words, Sonatas, Suites, Songs for Children*, miscl. songs, piano pieces. Scored

numerous films, U.S. and Europe, incl. *Truth Is Trouble, All Good Things Come from Heaven, Here Comes Mr. Jordan*, features, cartoons. Music for European radio versions *Adventures of Tom Sawyer, Huckleberry Finn*. Wife, Bonnie Vallarini, dancer, instr. 2478 Hollyridge Dr., Hollywood 28, Calif.

SCHOOP, TRUDI

Dancer, choreographer. b. Zurich, Switzerland. St. ballet in Vienna. Created Trudi Schoop Comic Ballet. Tours throughout world. Choreographed *Barbara, Want Ads, Fridolin on the Road, Blond Marie, Underworld, Servant Girl Goes to Town*, others. Hobbies: painting, art. Mgmt., Sol Hurok, 30 Rockefeller Plaza, New York; c/o Paul Schoop, 2478 Hollyridge Dr., Hollywood 28, Calif.

SCHULTZ, CECILIA

Impresario. b. Cincinnati, Ohio. Grad. Illinois Wesleyan Coll. of Music. St. piano w. private tchrs. in Chicago. Head of piano dept., Kansas State Coll. (3 yrs.). Promoted chamber music concerts, matinee musicales. Estab. Moore Theatre as center of musical activities in Seattle. Now leading impresario of Northwest, after having entered the field with a chamber music series, presenting principal concert artists in Seattle and vicinity. Moore Theatre, 1932, 2nd St., Seattle, Wash.

SEE, ORLEY

Violinist, conductor, Oakland, Vallejo Symphony Orchs. b. Galion, Ohio. Mus. D. Denison Univ. St. violin w. Col Marcosson, Hugo Herman, Theodore Spiering. Asst., concertmaster Chautauqua, N. Y. Orch. Member Cincinnati, San Francisco symphonies. Organized-directed Philharmonic Trio, Philharmonic String Quartet. Faculty Denison Univ.; Central Tchrs. College, Mo.; Tchrs. College, Indiana, Penna. Member AFM, Phi Gamma Delta, Rotary Club. Hobby: mountain life. 48 Wildwood Ave., Piedmont, Calif.

SEGUROLA, ANDRES de

Teacher of voice; formerly operatic singer. b. Valencia, Spain. St. law, Univ. Valencia and Barcelona—piano, harmony, singing at same time; 1896 to 1908 sang at opera houses in Rome, Madrid, Lisbon, Salzburg, Milan, Naples, Paris, London, Buenos Aires, Mexico. Engaged by Oscar Hammerstein for Manhattan Opera House, N. Y., 1908. Joined Met. Opera Co., 1909; remained twelve consec. yrs. Sang in world premieres of *Girl of the Golden West, Gianni Schicci, Le Donne Curiose, Madeleine*. Sang gala performance at Metropolitan in honor of King and Queen of Belgium, 1919. Vocal teacher, coach of Deanna Durbin, Orvil Harold, Anna Fitziu, Marion Talley, Rosemary Lane, Edith Fellows, many others. Recordings for Victor, Columbia. Knight Commander of Alfonso XII of Spain, Knight Commander of the Crown of Italy, of Santiago of Portugal, of the Mediiidie of Turkey, Knight of the Order of Cristo of the Vatican, Rome, Officer of Academy from France; Silver medal from King Edward VII. Lecturer on Arts of Singing, Mills College, Oakland, Cumnock School, etc. 1545 N. Laurel Ave., Hollywood, Calif.

SEIDEL, TOSCHA

Concert violinist. b. Odessa, Russia, 1899. Grad. Imperial Cons. of Music, Petrograd. St. violin w. Alexander Fieldemann, Sternisches Cons., Berlin, Leopold Auer. Concert debut Christiania, Norway, 1914; Carnegie Hall, N.Y., 1918. Transcontinental and European tours. World tour, 1922. Soloist w. leading orchs. Played entire historic development of violin literature CBS, 1930-32. Violin trans: *Eli-Eli* (trad'l Hebrew), *Anitra's Dance* (Grieg) *L'Amour de Moir* (17th Cent.), *Troika* (Tchaikovsky) *Syrian Berceuse*. Recordings Columbia Masterworks, Victor Red Seal: *Intermezzo, Brahms Hungarian Dance No 1, Minuet and Gavotte*, (Mozart), *Brahmsiana* (Bakaleinikoff), *Albumblatt*, (Wagner). Now under contract w. Paramount Studios. Member Sierra Club, Bohemians (N.Y.). Pres., Bohemians (L.A.). Hobbies: astronomy, bacteriology, photography, chess, hiking. 259 Veteran Ave., Los Angeles, Calif.

Cecilia Schultz

Toscha Seidel

Leah Dana Seykora

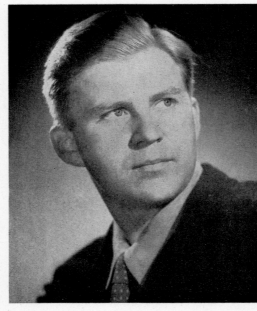

Paul Schoop

Albert Sendrey

Eudice Shapiro

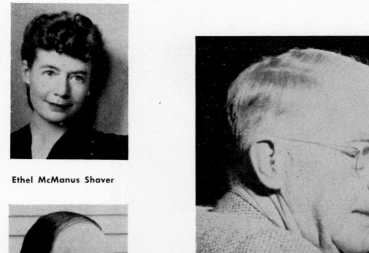

Ethel McManus Shaver

Raymond Shry-Ock

Constance Jeanette Shirley

Lev Shorr

Dilworth Simmons

Rennay Shry-Ock

SENDREY, ALBERT

Composer, arranger, orchestrator. b. Chicago, Ill., 1911. Att. Leipzig Cons., Paris Cons., Trinity Coll. of Mus., London. St. 'cello w. Kinkulkin, Klengel; piano w. Teichmuller; orch. w. Geehl; cond. w. Barbirolli, Coates. Won Chicago Sym. Award 1940, Reichhold Award 1947. Comp. incl. Ballet Suite, three symphonies, Sinfonietta, Viola Sonata (pub. Elkan-Vogel), 'Cello Divertimento, Woodwind Quintet, Grande Chaconne (piano), chamber music, piano pieces. Recording: Ballet Suite (Pathe). Scored film Whirlpool, Paris, 1934. Arr., orch. Korda Films: Thunder in the City, Men Are Not Gods, Thief of Bagdad, That Hamilton Woman, Lydia, New Wine, Jungle Book; M-G-M films: The Yearling, Sea of Grass, High Barbaree, Undercurrent, The Unfinished Dance, Desire Me, If Winter Comes, others. Member: ASCAP, Screen Comp. Assn., ASMA. Hobbies: fishing, coll. rare modern mus. records. 5939 W. Lindenhurst Ave., Los Angeles, Calif.

SESSIONS, ROGER

Composer, teacher. b. Brooklyn, N. Y., Dec. 28, 1896. St. comp. Harvard Univ. (A.B.), Yale Sch. of Mus. (Mus.B.); w. Horatio Parker, Ernest Bloch. Faculty Princeton Univ. 1935-45, New Jersey Coll. for Women 1935-39; Univ. of Calif. since 1945. Comps. incl.: three symphonies, two operas (The Trial of Lucullus, Montezuma), violin concerto, The Black Maskers (orch.), duo (vn. pf.), two sonatas (pf.). Hobbies: travel, languages. 107 Tamalpais Rd., Berkeley 8, Calif.

SEYKORA, LEAH DANA

Violinist, teacher. b. Florence, Colo., 1906. Grad. Schwinger School of Music, Pueblo, Colo. St. violin w. Alexander Roman, Joseph Rosenfeld, Vera Barstow; harmony, theory w. Frances Frothingham. Programs for Women's Music Club, Musical Arts Club, City Club. Soloist w. St. Luke's Choristers and various other churches, organizations. Pres. Long Beach MTA 1946-47. Member Women's Music Club of Long Beach, Musical Arts Club of Long Beach. Playing viola w. string ensemble. Pupils incl. Eunice Wennermark, William Heffernan, Orla Rees, Judith Ayer, Edward Acosta, Paul Benedick, Mary-Anne Reynolds. 271 Junipero Ave., Long Beach, Calif.

SHAPIRO, EUDICE

Concert violinist. b. Buffalo, N. Y. St. violin w. father; won scholarships Eastman Sch. of Mus. and w. Efrem Zimbalist, Curtis Inst. of Mus. Won $1000 award Nat'l Fed. of Mus. Clubs 1937. First violinist Amer. Art Quartet. Concertized throughout U. S. Soloist w. sym. orchs. under Stokowski, Goossens, Reiner, Klemperer, Barzin, Janssen, Black, others. Former concertmistress Paramount Studio Orch.; now concertmistress RKO Studio Orch. Judge in KFI Young Artists Aud. Numerous film recordings. Husband, Victor Gottlieb, 'cellist; former member Coolidge Quartet, 'cellist Amer. Art Quartet; now first 'cellist RKO Studio Orch. Music Dept., RKO Studios, 780 Gower St., Hollywood 38, Calif.

SHAVER, ETHEL McMANUS (Ethel Bacon McManus)

Pianist, teacher. b. Chattanooga, Tenn. B.M. Oxford Coll. (Miami Univ.), Oxford, Ohio. Teacher's certif. Hamilton Coll. Lexington, Ky.; choral, orch. cond. Univ. of Calif., Berkeley; master classes, pvt. lessons Richard Buhlig; master classes Guy Maier; Colleague Calif. MTA. Faculty member, chairman Nat'l Guild Piano Tchrs., American Coll. of Mus. Past-Pres. Kern County MTA, Kern County Musical Assn. Member board of directors Kern County Philharmonic Assn. Pupils incl. Robert Haag, Doris Davis, Marcia McKee. 2004 Verde St., Bakersfield, Calif.

SHIRLEY, CONSTANCE JEANETTE

Concert pianist, composer, teacher of piano. b. Los Angeles, Calif. St. piano w. mother, Jo Anne Shirley; trio w. father, Samuel Taylor Shirley baritone. Debut age 4, radio perf. age 5, reg. soloist KHJ age 6, also concerts. Played violin 8 yrs. sch., coll. orchs (age 15); A.A. (music) L. A. Jr. Coll.; Mus. B. Chapman Coll.; att. USC, UCLA; Mus. M. Chapman Coll. (age 20); Mus. D. Temple Hall Coll. and Sem., Ill. St. Theory, comp., orch. w. Mary Carr Moore (2 yrs.), Arnold Schoenberg (3 yrs.); orch.

w. Lucien Cailliet (3-yr. course in 2 yrs.), piano master class w. Guy Maier. str. quartet, fugue w. Charles Pemberton; comp., anal. w. Howard Hanson; Schillinger Sys. w. David Holguin; two-pfs. class w. Leslie Clausen, L. A. Jr. Coll. Scholarships Eastman Sch. of Mus., Coll. of Pacific, Chapman Coll. Won So. Calif. Wonder Child Contest (age 6), radio contests, State and Tri-State piano contests, UCLA Young Artists Aud. (1944), Glendale Symphony Aud., others. Concerts, recitals in U. S., especially California; played own comp. intro. Mary Carr Moore Piano Concerto on 3 Amer. Comp. programs Pan-Pac. Expos. (S.F.) (1939). Concerto app. under Marcelli, Cykler, Sample, Vincent, Guidi, Petran, others. Guest Collegium Musicum (Alexis Kall). Comp. won USC annual Apolliad (1st place 3 consec. yrs.), J. Chas. McNeil Trophy, Olga Steeb Award, Mary Carr Moore Mss. Club, L. A. Fest. of Allied Arts contests, Charles Wakefield Cadman Award (two-piano work), others. Comp. incl. Poem in Retrospect (orch.), Fantasie (pf. and orch.); Piano Sonata, Art Gallery (ballet); two string quartets; Elephantasia (pf. suite); Ghosts on Plantation Legree, Flight of Wild Geese, Caprice Brilliante, Double Fugue (pf.); Double Fugue (4-pt. voc.), numerous songs, piano pieces. Member: Schubert Club (hon. life), Theta Sigma Gamma, Mary Carr Moore Mss. Club (secy. 3 yrs.; pres. 2 yrs.), Hollywood Creative Club (mus. chairman), L. A. Opera and Fine Arts Juns. (vice-pres.). Hobbies: gardening, art sewing. 5822 Lexington Ave., Hollywood 38, Calif.

SHIRLEY, JO ANNE

Concert pianist, soprano, teacher of piano. b. Orange City, Iowa. St. voice w. father, grandfather; piano w. Jessie Councilman; child prodigy, ch. organist, solo, choir singer age 8 to 18. Att. Morningside Cons. (st. w. Barbour), Drake Univ. (w. Nourse); st. piano w. Ella Free (pupil Jedliczka, Moszkowski), Leopold Godowsky (master class). Tchrs. diploma (piano. harm.) Sherwood Sch. of Mus. (also 2 yrs. voice). Concertized in U.S. as pianist, soprano. Founder-director Shirley Cons. of Music and Allied Arts, first comprehensive cons. in Hollywood. Pupils incl. daughter, Constance Jeanette Shirley. 5822 Lexington Ave., Hollywood 38, Calif.

SHRY-OCK, RAYMOND FRANKLIN

Violinist; associate director, Rennay Shry-Ock School of Music-Arts and Drama. b. Minneapolis, Minn. St. violin w. father, grandfather; later violin, theory in Chicago, Europe. Child prodigy at age 5; concert tours in Middle West: asst. concertmaster w. touring operetta companies. Toured w. Henry W. Savage (Parsifal), English Grand Repertoire Cos. Member: Minneapolis Symphony (Oberhoffer) 20 yrs.; Los Angeles Philharmonic (Rothwell) and Hollywood Bowl (all leading cond.) 18 yrs.; opera, ballet seasons in addition. Comp. incl. operettas, violin soli, songs. Rennay Shry-Ock School of Music-Arts and Drama, 1353 Post St., San Francisco, Calif.

SHRY-OCK, RENNAY

Singer, actress, teacher of voice and drama; founder-director Rennay Shry-Ock School of Music-Arts and Drama. b. Duluth, Minn. St. piano w. Mme. Ostergren; early recitals as pianist. St. voice w. Walter Leon, Katharine Hart Bibb, Frank Bibb, Wilmont Goodwin, New York City; Frantz Proschowsky (4 yrs.). Concertized extensively in U.S., especially East, Middle-West; recital, opera, oratorio, church appearances. Vocal studio, also Little Theatre in Los Angeles 1926-1942. Head of music dept., Cumnock School; film work MGM Studios (3 yrs.); contributed programs to Hollywood Bowl. Founded Rennay Shry-Ock School of Music-Arts and Drama, 1942. Rennay Shry-Ock School of Music-Arts and Drama, 1353 Post St., San Francisco, Calif.

SIMMONS, DILWORTH

Concert pianist, teacher of piano; Prof. of Piano, Pease Conservatory of Music, Sacramento, Calif. b. Provo, Utah, 1915. Att. Brigham Young Univ., De Paul Univ. St. piano w. C. W. Reid, Sergei Tarnowsky. Concertized in U. S.; recitals Chicago, midwest cities; lecture recitals. Member: Saturday Club, MTA. Hobby, cartooning. Mgmt. Bertha Ott, Chicago (1939). Pease Conservatory of Music, 2130 L St., Sacramento, Calif.

Boris Sirpo

SIMMONS, HOMER

Concert pianist, composer. b. Evansville, Ind. St. piano w. Grunn, Paderewski, Respighi; theory w. Nadia Boulanger. Performed at Hollywood Bowl (Goossens, Svedrovsky). Concertized in U. S., France, Switzerland, England. Comp. incl. *Phantasmania, Stairways, Three Waltz Vignettes, Scherzino, Tango at Midnight*. Martin Music Management., 746 N. Cahuenga Blvd., Hollywood 38, Calif.

SHORR, LEV

Concert pianist; teacher of piano. b. Russia, 1896. St. piano w. father, Vladimir Shorr. Won scholarship Petrograd (Leningrad) Imperial Cons. 1912; st. theory w. Glazunov, piano w. Essipova (wife of Leschetizky); grad. (hon.) 1917. Concert tours through Russia, Siberia; later U. S. Orient. Faculty Vladivostok Mus. Acad. Co-artist w. Yehudi Menuhin, Gregor Piatigorsky, Mishel Piastro, Raya Garbousova, others; guest artist San Francisco String Quartet; official pianist San Francisco Sym. Orch. (Monteux). Soloist w. San Francisco Sym. Orch., radio programs. Joint sonata, solo recitals w. wife, Frances Wiener. Member AFM Local 6. Students incl. Hepzibah Menuhin, Samuel Lipman, Leon Fleisher. Studio 532 Geary St., San Francisco, Calif.

SIMPKINS, WINIFRED HANFORD

Pianist, teacher of piano. b. Oakesdale, Wash. B.A., M.A. State Coll. of Wash. St. piano w. Harriet Scholder, Mme. Marguerite Liszniewska of Cincinnati Cons. of Mus., Arthur Friedheim, Harold Logan, Egon Petri. Program for national convention, Mu Phi Epsilon. Concertized in U. S. incl. appearances w. music clubs in Portland, Seattle, Spokane, Burlingame, Stockton, others. Member Mu Phi Epsilon, Stockton Piano Club. On board of directors, Modesto Symphony Orch. 415 Myrtle Ave., Modesto, Calif.

SIMPSON, ELIZABETH

Teacher of piano, coach, lecturer. b. Alamo, Mich. St. w. Wager Swayne, Heinrich Barth, Artur Schnabel, Tobias Matthay, Alfredo Casella, Thomas Fielden, Wanda Landowska, Nadia Boulanger. Lectured before 5 state conventions. Concertized throughout Calif. Accomp., member of Bach Choir, Amateur Musical Club. Author of *Basic Pianoforte Technique*. Contributor to *The Etude, Musical Courier, Pacific Coast Musician*. 2833 Webster St., Berkeley, Calif.

SIRPO, BORIS

Composer, conductor, teacher. b. Viipuri, Finland, 1893. St. w. Hrimaly and Ippolitov-Ivanov. Att. Petersburg Cons. 1907-11. St. w. Sevcik, Jacobsen, Kulenkampff, Schrecker, others in Berlin, Prague, Vienna; cond. w. Felix Weingartner, Basel. Granted Finnish State Music Stipendium scholarship 1932. Founder-dir. Viipuri Cons. 1918-1939, Viipuri String Quartette, Viipuri Chamber Orch. 1920. Cond. Viipuri Symphony 1928, Nat'l Singing Festivals 1932, Symphony Chorus of Viipuri 1939. Founder-cond. Hood River Music Assn. chorus and orch., Portland Chamber Orch. Assoc. prof. of music Lewis and Clark Coll. Comp. *Symphony No. 1 (F major), Slavic Symphony (A major), Symphony No. 2 (e minor), Chamber Symphony*, three orchestral suites, piano quintet, string sextet, songs and violin solos, music and story for motion picture *The Little Fiddler* (prod. in Finland). Knight (First Class) of the Order of the White Rose, Commander of the Order of Stanislaw. Member Nat'l League of Finnish Composers, Accademia Musiche Contemporance at Milan (hon). 3635 S. E. Ankeny, Portland, Ore.

SKILES, MARLIN

Composer, conductor. b. Harrisburg, Pa., 1906. St. Froehlich Cons. of Music, Harrisburg and w. Ernest Toch; cond. w. Albert Coates. Arr. for leading dance orchestras. Musical settings of symphonic music for *The Play's The Thing* (Hamlet), *Ballade of the Duel* (Cyrano de Bergerac), *Grass* (Sandburg), *The Children's Hour* (Longfellow), *Life Has Loveliness To Sell* (Teasdale). Recordings by Columbia and Victor.

Member ASCAP, SCA, AFM, ASMA. Hobbies: photography and scale model miniature trains. 369 Homewood Rd., Los Angeles 24, Calif.

SKINNER, FRANK

Composer, orchestrator. b. Meredosia, Ill. St. first w. father. Later Chic. Musical Coll. Arr. for N.Y. music publishers (15 yrs.). Orch. for MGM, *The Great Ziegfeld*, 1935; Universal Studios, 1936. Written scores for motion pictures incl. *Backstreet, The Egg and I, Tap Roots, The Exile, Arabian Nights, Smash Up, I'll Be Yours, Ride the Pink Horse*, etc. 724 No. Rodeo Dr., Beverly Hills, Calif.

SLATKIN, FELIX

Concert violinist, teacher. b. St. Louis, Mo., 1915. St. violin w. Sylvan Noack, Michel Gusikoff, Ephrem Zimbalist; cond. w. Fritz Reiner (Curtis Inst.); grad. Curtis Inst, 1933. Asst. concertmaster St. Louis Symphony, 1934-37; concertmaster Warner Bros. (5 yrs.); concertmaster Fox Studios since 1940. Soloist w. St. Louis Symphony (Molinari, Ganz), Hollywood Bowl (Iturbi) 1935. Gen. concert tour throughout U. S. Member Chamber Group of Hollywood Theater Alliance; Hollywood String Quartet. Solo recordings for Co-Art Recording Co. Cond. Beverly Hills Symphony, Army Air Forces, Santa Ana, and N Y. during World War II. 125 South Swall Dr., Beverly Hills, Calif.

SLOANE, LILLIAN

Teacher of voice. b. New York City. St. w. father in Hungary and N. Y.; Inst. of Musical Arts, N. Y. w. Damrosch, etc. Taught voice N.Y.C., assoc. w. Albert Jeannotte. Specializes in voice correction in collaboration w. throat specialists. Hobbies: art, cooking. Teacher of many operatic, radio, stage, film artists from advent of talking pictures to present incl. Bessie Love, Leatrice Joy, Blanche Sweet, Norma Talmadge, Mae Murray, Patsy Ruth Miller, Buddy Rogers, Mary Astor, Evelyn Laye, Peggy Wood, Jan Clayton, Robert Arthur, Gloria Warren, Walter Kent. 8241 DeLongpre Ave., Los Angeles 46, Calif.

SMITH, SUSIE AUBREY

Music editor and critic Oregon Journal. b. Portland, Ore. Grad. Portland Academy. St. voice w. Frank King Clark, Paris, Berlin; violin w. Karl Markees, Berlin. Member Professional Women's League, Alliance Francaise of Portland, Portland Symphony Society, Oregon Press Club. Hobbies: swimming, legitimate drama, foreign moives. 1731 N.W. Everett St., Portland, Ore.

SNELL, DAVID L.

Composer, conductor, pianist. b. Milwaukee, Wisc., 1897. Att. Wisc. Cons. of Music, Meyer Cons., Milwaukee. St. harmony w. Meyer. Concertized at age 11. Member MGM music staff (16 yrs.). Scored following motion pictures: all *Hardy* pictures, *Dr. Kildare* (coll. w. Edward Ward), *The Women, Thunder Afloat, Blackmail, Glamour Girl, Dancing Co-Ed*. Comp. *Under the Stars, Out of the Deep, Downstream Drifter, Song of the Thin Man, Bad Bascomb, Up Goes Maizie, Under Cover Maizie, The Cockeyed Miracle, Lady of the Lake, Between Two Women, Mighty McGurk, Merton of the Movies, See Here, Private Hargrove, What Next, Corporal Hargrove?* 1212 No. Isabel St., Glendale, Calif.

SOLLOWAY, GLORIA MICHELE

Bassoonist, pianist. b. Budapest, Hungary, July, 1923. Scholarship bassoon, piano Juilliard School of Music; st. w. Frederick Moritz, Achille Heynen, Simon Kovar. Diploma Nat'l Orchestral Assn. (Leon Barzin) N. Y. First bassoonist Oklahoma State Symphony (Victor Alessandro) 1944-45; New York City Center Symphony (Leonard Bernstein) 1945-46; Ballet Russe de Monte Carlo, Bach Festival, Carmel (Gastone Usigli) 1946; Utah State Symphony, Salt Lake City (Werner Janssen) 1946-47; Hollywood Bowl Symphony 1947; Portland Symphony (Werner Janssen) 1947-48. Hobbies: traveling, reading, swimming, badminton. 569 No. Rossmore Ave., Hollywood 4, Calif.

Frank Skinner

Felix Slatkin

Winifred Hanford
Simpkins

David Snell

Marlin Skiles

Lillian Sloane

Susie Aubrey Smith

259

SOLLOWAY, HARRY

Concert violinist. b. Riga, Latvia, 1899. St. violin w. Henri Berthelier at Conservatoire Nationale, Paris; scholarship winner w. June Hubay, Royal Hungarian Academy of Music, Budapest (grad. w. honors). Concertized throughout Italy where awarded title of Cavalier; recitals in Great Britain. Featured soloist International Celebrity Concerts, 1927-29; soloist w. Sir Henry Wood; on return to America, concert-master under Walter Damrosch, NBC program; soloist, concert-master, conductor Paramount Theater, N. Y.; soloist, concert-master w. Werner Janssen, Joseph Pasternak in Calif. Solo recordings for "Grammaphone" Berlin. Collector of paintings, antiques. Inventor musical educational toy *Pick-A-Note*. Now affiliated w. motion picture studios in L.A., as soloist, concertmaster. Grandfather Movshe Chait, condutcor Imperial Symph. Orch., Riga. Wife, June, vocal coach-pianist. Daughter, Gloria, bassoonist-pianist. Son, Carleton, non-professional 'cellist, Lt. Marine Corps (4 yrs.); student Calif. Institute of Tech. 569 No. Rossmore Ave., Hollywood 4, Calif.

SOLLOWAY, JUNE (June Starr)

Vocal coach, pianist, arranger, piano-accordion. b. Pittsburgh, Penna., 1903. Att. Carnegie Tech School of Music. St. w. Maestro Schiavoni, Milan, Italy; Laura Hilgerman, Budapest, Hungary. Coached Shubert operettas, collaborator of motion picture scores, arrangements for records and transcriptions. Arr. for Capitol Records and L. A. Board of Education. Hobbies: collecting paintings, etchings, antiques, swimming, badminton, golf. 569 No. Rossmore Ave., Hollywood 4, Calif.

SORENSEN, FERDINAND

Teacher of 'cello and violin. Studio: 315 Fine Arts Bldg., Portland, Oregon.

SPRENGLE, MARTHA FRANCES

Teacher of piano, pipe organ. b. Ashland, Ohio. St. piano, pipe organ, Cleveland School of Music w. James H. Rogers; piano w. Richard Buhlig; composition, theory w. Benjamin Blodgett, Stanford Univ. also w. Elsie Cook Laraia, Royal Academy of Music, London, England. Charter member Fresno Music Club, MTA; lecturer State Convention, MTA. Hobby: study of philosophy, especially that of George Santayana. 1115 T Street, Fresno, Calif.

SQUIRE, RUSSEL NELSON

Prof. of Music and Hd. Div. of Fine Arts, George Pepperdine Coll. b. Sept. 21, 1908, Cleveland, Ohio. B.S.M., Oberlin Coll.; M.A., Western Reserve Univ.; Ph.D., N.Y. Univ. Dir., Oberlin Summer Music Schl. ,dir. instrumental music, public schools., Chillicothe, Ohio; Prof. of Music, hd. dept., 1937; hd. div. of Fine Arts, George Pepperdine Coll., L. A., Calif., since 1942; visiting tchr., Western Reserve Univ., summer, 1945. Member Ohio Mus. Edn. Assn.; Mus. Educators Nat'l Conf.; Rotary Internat'l. Who's Who in Music, Who's Important in Music, Who's Who in American Education. George Pepperdine College, 1121 West 79th St., Los Angeles, Calif.

STANHAM, LOUIE MAE

Teacher of piano, harmony, theory. b. Pasadena, Calif. St. piano w. Harold Gleason, Leo Ochnler; comp. w. Charles Wakefield Cadman, Percy Shaul Hallett. Soloist Church of Religious Science. Teacher of Douglas Moffet, radio soloist. Comp. incl. *Gavotte* (mss); arr. of James H. Rogers' *Giants* for two pianos (mss). Member Exec. Board, Pasadena Fine Arts Club, Music Arts Club, Sierra Madre Art Guild, Musicians' Club. 830 Alameda St., Altadena, Calif.

STANLEY, JANE

Pianist, accompanist, teacher of piano and harmony. Grad. Dakota Cons. of Music, Coll. of Music, Univ. So. Calif., Postgrad. work at Univ. So. Calif., Univ. Washington, Univ. of Calif.; colleague-degree Calif. MTA. St. w. Carolyn Alchin, Abby Whiteside, Alfred Mirovitch, Milan Blanchet. Pres. Student Body, College of Music, U.S.C.; teacher, res. dir. Anaheim Branch, of College of Music ,U.S.C.; faculty member Kern County Union H.S.; teacher Dept. of Adult Education, Long Beach (7 yrs.); organized, directed concert course for Adult Dept.; teacher, dir. Creative Section, Women's Music Club of Long Beach (5 yrs.); mus. dir. Junior Ebell Club; founder, executive chairman Pianists Assn. of Long Beach; Music Chairman, city-wide Music Week (1940); Pres. Long Beach Women's Committee for Sou. Calif. (1945-46). Teacher of Doyle Henderson, Jane Gluth, Dee Green, Harold Redick, Edison Heniford. Eunice Womack, May Wunder. 132 Pine Ave., Long Beach, Calif.

STAUFFER, PAUL

Teacher of piano. b. Luray, Mo. St. w. W. Gifford Nash, A. K. Virgil, A. M. Jewett, Henry Kloman Schmidt, Henry Houseley, Horace Tureman, Rossiter G. Cole, Marx Oberndofer. B. Mus. Denver Cons. Music. Appointed by Gov. Sweet of Colorado to French-American Cons. at Fontainebleau, France where st. w. Isidor Phillip, Silva Erard, Mott-Lecroix, Camille Decreus. Concertized throughout Western U. S. State Pres. MTA, Pres. Southwest District, Nat'l Fed. of Music Clubs; past-Pres. Colorado MTA., Colorado Fed. of Music Clubs. Member San Diego Rotary Club. Pupils awarded scholarships to Juilliard, Eastman, Curtis, Phila. Cons. 640 Broadway, San Diego, Calif.

STEARNS, CURTIS L.

Conductor, composer, pianist. b. Coburg, Germany, 1904. Att. Academy of Tonal Arts, Munich, Sternsches Conserv., Berlin, Germany. St. cond. w. Siegm. v. Haussegger, Alex v. Fielitz, piano w. Pembar, comp .w. Josef Haas. First cond. State Opera House, Karlsruhe, Germany, cond. Phil. Orch. Karlsruhe 1925-33, choir dir. State Opera House, Coburg, Bavaria, 1924-25; on radio Berlin, Munich, Stuttgart, Frankfort, NBC. Accompanist and coach to Anne Jamison, Mona Paulee, Frederick Jagel, Vivian della Chiesa, Mario Berini, Jan Kiepura, Marta Eggerth, Anne Brown. Concertized Germany, France, Italy, Switzerland. Comp. light opera *Land of Wonders* 1933, cycle of songs to lyrics by Tagore 1935, string quartet 1935. Mus. dir. Amer. Operatic Laboratory, Los Angeles. 760 North Wilton Pl. Los Angeles, Calif.

STEELE, R. VERNON

Writer, composer, conductor, lecturer, critic. b. Walnut Grove, Ala., 1885. Editor and publisher Pacific Coast Musician. St. voice w. Siegfried Brutkeiwicz, Frederick Dunster, Glenn Friermood, A. Howard Garrett; comp. w. Walter Edward Howe. Organized and cond. (4 yrs.) El Paso Sym. Orch. (honorary life cond.), Orlando (Fla.), Santa Monica Sym. Orchs. Pacific Coast Musician, Philharmonic Auditorium Bldg., 427 W. 5th St., Los Angeles 13, Calif.

STEGNER, NELL L.

Teacher of piano, accompanist, organist. b. St. Paul, Minn. St. piano w. C. G. Titcomb, Sansone College of Music, St. Paul; piano, pipe organ w. George Fairclough, harmony w. Rhys-Herbert, piano w. May MacDonald Hope Coryell, Organist, First Methodist Church, L. A. (4½ yrs.), Westlake Presby. Church (3 yrs.), First Presby. Church (1 yr.), Methodist Church, St. Paul (4 yrs.), Evangelical Church, St. Paul (3 yrs.). Formerly accomp. to Ellen Beach Yaw, Mme. Pasquali, others. Member MTA. Hobby: painting. 623 No. Seward St., Los Angeles, Calif.

STEINER, MAXIMILIAN RAOUL

Composer, conductor. b. Vienna, Austria. Ed. Imperial Academy of Music; theory, orch. w. Fuchs, Graedner, Mahler, Rose; organ w. Schenner. Gold Medal at grad. Cond. extensively in England, France, U. S. Music director RKO Studios (10 yrs.), Selznick Intern. Pictures (2 yrs.), now under contract to Warner Bros. American citizen since 1920. Winner Academy Awards 1935, 1937, 1945. Comp. over 200 film scores incl. *The Informer, Now Voyager, Since You Went Away, Garden of Allah, A Star Is Born, Little Lord Fauntleroy, Gone With The Wind, Tomorrow Is Forever, Charge of the Light Brigade, Four Wives, The Letter, Casablanca, Saratoga Trunk, The Corn Is Green, San Antonio, Mildred Pierce, The Stolen Life, Beast With Five Fingers*. Hobbies: photography, model boats, collecting antique and modern guns, expert target shot. Member ASCAP, AFM, SCA. Decorations from French, Italian, Belgian governments. Warner Bros. Studios, Burbank, Calif.

Harry Solloway

June Solloway

Gloria Michele Solloway

STEINERT, ALEXANDER

Conductor, composer, pianist. b. Boston, Mass., 1900. Grad. magna cum laude Harvard Univ., 1922. Att. Paris Cons., 1923. St. w. Gedalge; d'Indy, Koechlin. Piano soloist Boston Sym. (Koussevitsky), 1925. Comp. incl. *Southern Night, Leggenda Sinfonica,* chamber music, *Two Poems by Shelley* (soprano and orch.), *Concerto Sinfonico* (piano and orch.). Cond. Amer. premiere Tcherepnin's opera 01-01, Casino Theatre, N. Y., Rimsky-Korsakov's *Coq. d'Or,* Gershwin's *Porgy & Bess* in N. Y. and on tour, Gershwin Memorial Concert, Hollywood Bowl. Won Amer. Prix de Rome, 1927. 477 Homewood Rd., Los Angeles 24, Calif.

STERN, CLARA TESTER

Composer, conductor. b. Vienna, Austria. Ed. Imperial Switzerland w. Oscar Schulz, voice w. Mme. Linnee, Chicago; American Cons. of Music, piano w. Luening Cons., Milwaukee Cons., Milwaukee. Honor grad. American Cons. of Music. Concertized in U. S. Soloist, Chicago Marine Band; church soloist Chicago, Seattle, Milwaukee. Song comp. incl.: *Take Care, If Just Remembering, Sweetheart.* Member Amphion Club, San Diego. Hobbies, child welfare, organization of music benefits. 614 So. St .Andrews Pl., Los Angeles, Calif.

STEUBER, LILLIAN

Concert pianist, teacher. b. Los Angeles, Calif. St. w. Julian Pascal, L. A.; Josef Lhevinne, N. Y.; coached w. Harold Bauer, Egon Petri. Soloist w. Los Angeles Philharmonic Orch., (Rodzinski, Klemperer), Hollywood Bowl (Slonimsky), four times w. Werner Janssen Symphony incl. Standard Symphony broadcasts, five times under Richard Lert, thrice soloist Carmel Bach Festival (Usigli), San Diego Bowl (Sokoloff, Marcelli), Santa Monica Symphony (Rachmilovich), also solo appearances w. orch. under Barrere, Dahl, others. Sonata concerts w. John Pennington of London String Quartet, Anton Maaskoff, trio concerts as member of Penstemur Trio, guest appearances w. London String Quartet, Weiss Woodwind Ensemble, seven times guest artist Coleman Chamber Series, Pasadena. Gave numerous first performances in West of works by Hindemith, Bartok, Achron, Weiss, Toch, Villa-Lobos, Mignone, Szymanowski. Concerts, recitals in Mexico City, Eastern cities, Europe. Pupils incl.: Lillian Magidow, William Teaford, John Manken, John Latimer, Daniel Pollack, Dorothy Zeigler, David Bacon. Member Artist-Faculty USC. 571 No. Mariposa Ave., Los Angeles, Calif.

STEVENS, HALSEY

Composer. b. Scott, N. Y., Dec. 3, 1908. Att. Syracuse Univ., Univ. of Calif.; st. w. William Berwald, Ernest Bloch. Faculty Syracuse Univ. 1935-37; Dakota Wesleyan Univ. 1937-41; dir. Coll. of Mus. Bradly Polyt. Inst. (now Bradley Univ.) 1941-46; Univ. of Redlands, 1946; Univ. of So. Calif. since 1946. In U.S. Naval Reserve 1943-45. Program annotator, L.A. Phil. Orch. since 1946, Phoenix Sym. Orch. since 1947. Music critic newspapers Syracuse, N. Y., Mitchell, S. D., Peoria, Ill.; corresp. Musical Courier, Musical America, etc. Staff Middlebury Coll. Comp. Conf. 1947. Comp. incl. three *Symphonies,* two *Trios, Quintet* (fl. pf. str.), *Suite* (clar. and pf.), *Sonata* (vn. and pf.), *Sonatina* (fl. and pf.), *Sonatina* (pf.) (pub. Broude Bros.), *Serenade* (viola or clar. and pf.) (Music Press), *When I Am Dead, My Dearest* (mxd. cho.) (Arrow Mus. Pr.), four trans. of Handel arias (Schirmer). Awards incl. Phi Mu Alpha Sinfonia (national) 1943, 1946; Nat'l Fed. of Mus. Clubs chamber music 1945; Middlebury Coll. Comp. Conf. Publ. Prize 1946, others. Member: Amer. Comp. Alliance; Phi Mu Alpha, Phi Kappa Phi; League of Composers; MTNA; Amer. Assn. of Univ. Professors; Mus. Library Assn. Institute of the Arts, University of Southern California, Los Angeles 7, Calif.

STEVENS, THOMAS J.

Head Music Dept., Taft Junior College. b. Fresno, Calif., 1907. A.B. Fresno State Coll. (music major); M.A. College of Pacific. St. violin w. Will Hays; double bass w. Olney Rudd; tuba w. Leonard's Band, Golden Gate Park Band, San Francisco, Earl Towners Orchestra, Islam Temple Shrine Band. Member San Francisco a capella choir. Dir. Taft H.S. and Junior Coll. Symphony Orch., Taft Oratorio Soc. Member MENC, Pres. Taft Community Concerts. Hobby: baseball. 210 W. Woodrow Ave., Taft, Calif.

STEWARD, LUTHER MRS.

Teacher of piano, harmony. b. Maxinkuckee, Ind., Nov. 11, 1878. Grad. Teachers' Coll. in Pub. School Music and Education; B.M. Degree, piano major. Special certificates from Sherwood Inst. of Mus. Ed., Perfield, Oxford, etc. St. U. of Ariz., USG and w. pvt. tchrs. of piano. Has been largely responsible for placing applied music course in Arizona High Schools and certification of private music teachers. Certified by State Board of Ed. for Applied Music, Public School Music. Past vice-pres. Ariz. State Music Tchrs. Assn., past Pres. of PPTA, Sec. of Phoenix Piano Tchrs. Assn.; member Phoenix Musicians Club, Eastern Star No. 5. Hobby: applied music for secondary schools. 51 Mitchell Dr., Phoenix, Ariz.

STIDHAM, EVERTON E.

Teacher of voice, coach, baritone. b. Lafayette, Ind., 1897. St. voice w. James Murray, New York City (6 yrs.), Mme. Seymour Hodgson, coached w. Lester Hodges (5 yrs.). Soloist in church choirs, radio and light opera. Choir director. Soloist w. symphony orchs. New York City, Indianapolis, El Paso, San Bernardino, Los Angeles. Opera w. Riverside Opera Co. and Adohr *Operas of the Air.* Roles of Figaro in *Barber of Seville,* Valentine and Mephistopheles in *Faust,* Escamillo in *Carmen,* Bumerli in *Chocolate Soldier;* other roles in *Tales of Hoffman, Fledermaus, Blonde Donna.* State Dir. and Second Vice-Pres., MTA; dir. San Bernardino Light Opera Assn., San Bernardino Valley Concert Assn., chairman Perris Hill Bowl Assn. (10 yrs.). 427 Magnolia Ave., San Bernardino, Calif.

STILL, WILLIAM GRANT

Composer, conductor. b. Woodville, Miss., May 11, 1895. Att. Wilberforce Univ., Oberlin Cons. of Mus. St. theory, comp. (scholarships) w. George W. Chadwick, Edgar Varese. Mus. M. Wilberforce Univ., Mus. D. Oberlin Coll., Mus. D. Howard Univ. Guggenheim, Rosenwald Fellowships. Won Harmon Award, 1927; AFM Trophy, Local 767; Cincinnati Sym. Orch. prize for overture. First colored man to conduct major symphony orch. in U. S. when dir. Hollywood Bowl Orch. in own comps., 1936. Cond., arr. *Deep River Hour* CBS, WOR. Commissions from N. Y. World's Fair, CBS, Paul Whiteman, League of Composers, Cleveland Orch., etc. Comps. incl. four ballets: *Troubled Island, A Southern Interlude, A Bayou Legend, Blue Steel;* four ballets: *Lenox Avenue, La Guiablesse, Sahdji, Miss Sally's Party;* works for large orch.: *Afro-American Symphony, Symphony in g-minor, Darker America, Dismal Swamp, Song of a City* (w. cho.), *Kaintuck'* (piano, orch.), *Africa, Plain-Chant for America* (bar., orch.), *In Memoriam The Colored Soldiers Who Died for Democracy, Old California, Bells, Poem, From the Black Belt, Festive Overture, Fanfare for the 99th Fighter Squadron, Can'tchs Line 'Em, Fanfare for American Heroes, Archaic Ritual, Western Hemisphere* (Symphony No. 3), *Wood Notes,* works for small orchestra, band, violin, oboe, organ, voice, chorus, piano solo. Member: League of Composers; ASCAP. Hobby, making children's toys. 3670 Cimarron St., Los Angeles 7, Calif.

STOKOWSKI, LEOPOLD

Conductor. b. London, Eng., 1882. St. organ, violin, piano in England, France, Germany. Mus. D. (hon) Univ. of Pa. Organist St. James, London; St. Bartholomew's Ch., N. Y. Con. Cincinnati Sym. 1909-12; Philadelphia Orch. 1912-36; guest cond. Los Angeles Phil., San Francisco Sym. other leading orchs.; mus. dir. Hollywood Bowl 1945-46. Formed All-American Youth Orch. touring South America. Film app. in *Big Broadcast of 1937 Fantasia,, Carnegie Hall.* Comp. incl. *Dithyrambe* (fl. vc. harp), numerous transc. of Bach works. 9330 Beverly Crest Dr. Beverly Hills, Calif.

Morris Stoloff

Igor Stravinsky

Fred Sorenson

Russel N. Squire

Louie Mae Stanham

Jane Stanley

Paul Clarke Stauffer

Curtis L. Stearns

Nell Stegner

Clara Tester Stern

Lillian Steuber

Halsey Stevens

Mrs. Luther Steward

Everton E. Stidham

William Grant Still

Lawrence Strauss

Glen Strayer

Dorothy Studebaker

STOLOFF, MORRIS

Musical director, Columbia Pictures Corp. b. Philadelphia, Penna. Protege of W. A. Clark, Jr. Violin w. Leopold Auer. Memb. L. A. Philharmonic Orch. Concertmaster Paramount Pictures (8 yrs.); musical director Columbia Pictures since 1936. Cond., supervised musical scores written by Gruenberg, Toch, Collins, Rosza, Tiomkin, Friedhofer, other equally prominent composers. Guest cond., Philharmonic Orch. (1946) other symphonies. Won Academy Award 1944 for musical score of *Cover Girl*; in 1946 for *The Jolson Story*. Columbia Pictures, Hollywood, Calif.

STRAUSS, LAWRENCE

Singer, teacher of singing. b. Portland, Ore. General musical education in piano and singing in America and Europe. St. w. Jean de Reszke, Raymond Von Zur Muehlen, and Sir George Henschel. Appearances in Paris, London, New York, Boston, and Universities throughout United States. Authority on French and German song literature. Hobby; Philately. 3221 Washington St., San Francisco 15, Calif.

STRAVINSKY, IGOR

Composer, pianist, conductor. b. Oranienbaum, Russia, 1882. St. w. Kalfati, Rimsky-Korsakov. Guest cond. w. leading sym. orchs. of world. Concertized as pianist, lecturer. Comp. incl. several ballets, *Rossignol, Fire Bird, Petrouchka, Rite of Spring, Les Noces, Pulcinella, Fairy's Kiss*, several symphonies, numerous works for theater, large and small orchs., and all combinations of instruments, songs, chors., etc. Author, *Chronicle of My Life*. Member AFM, Local 47. 1260 No. Wetherly Dr., Hollywood, Calif.

STRAYER, GLEN

Voice teacher, school director. b. Wagner, S.D., 1910. St. Morningside Coll., Sioux City, Iowa (2 yrs.); Drake Univ. School of Mus. (1 yr.); MacPhail School of Mus., Minn. (1 yr.). Head Fine Arts Dept., Wasatch, Mt. Pleasant, Utah (6 yrs.); taught voice, drama, Salt Lake City, 1935; instr. voice, drama, Hollywood Cons. (5 yrs.). Hd. Dept. of voice and drama Fox Studios, Huntington Park (5 yrs.) Hd. Hollywood Musical Coll. Recitals for clubs and organizations in Minn. Dir. Spring Mus. Fest., Des Moines, Iowa 1931. Plays piano and organ. Hobby, oil painting. 5605 Hollywood Blvd. Hollywood 28, Calif.

STUDEBAKER, DOROTHY

Voice coach. b. Chicago, Ill. St. voice w. Warren Shaw, Philadelphia; Helen Chase, New York; Harold Hurlbut, Hollywood. Soloist First Church of Christ, Scientist, Freeport, L. I., New York, Sixth Church of Christ, Scientist, Kansas City, Mo., *Musical Comedy Hour*, WABC (CBS), New York, Helen Harrison String Ensemble, Hotel Mayfair, L. A., *Musical Intime* L. A. Staff soprano KEHE (1½ yrs.), special engagements as soloist KFWB, KNX. Since 1938 voice coach w. Radio Enterprises, Inc., 1746 No. Cherokee Ave., Hollywood 28, Calif.

SULLIVAN, BRIAN

Tenor, concert and opera. b. Oakland, Calif. St. Univ. of Sou. Calif. music scholarship. Debut in *Barber of Seville* (w. John Charles Thomas), Long Beach, 1940. Leading tenor w. Central City Opera, St. Louis Municipal Opera, Hollywood Greek Theatre (two seasons) (*Rose Marie, Rosalie, Desert Song*). Soloist w. Hollywood Bowl Easter Serv., Pasadena Mus. Fest.; toured w. Ice Follies. Sang *Show Boat* on Broadway. Recording: complete score from *Street Scene*. Member: AGMA, Equity, AFRA, AGVA, SAG. Hobbies: woodcarving, photography. Mgmt. Sylvia Hahlo, New York, N. Y.

SUNDSTEN, JOHN

Pianist, accompanist, teacher. b. Munsala, Finland, October 11, 1899. Toured Norway summer of 1926 as piano soloist w. male chorus of 50 voices. Toured Finland, summer of 1938 in piano recitals. Accompanist on Pacific Coast to many well-known artists. Studio: 206 Paramount Theatre Bldg., Seattle; Res.: 2212 Everett Ave., No. Seattle, Wash.

SWARTHOUT, MAX van LEWEN

Pianist, teacher; Dean, College of Music Univ. of Sou. Calif. b. Pawpaw, Ill., 1880 Att. Royal Cons. Music, Leipzig, Germany; Cons. at Gottschalk, Balatka and Chicago, Ill. Perf. w. Leipzig Gewandhaus Orch. (Nikisch), Leipzig Cons. Orch. (Sitt). Plays violin, pipe organ. Univ. of So. Calif.,

SWAYNE, WAGER

Pianist; teacher of piano. b. Toledo, Ohio. St. piano w. Theodore Leschetizky, Vienna; comp. w. Jean Gallon, Paris. Honorary Mus. D., Detroit Foundation of Music; decorated w. Palmes Academiques for musical work in Paris. Taught piano in Vienna, Paris, New York, Boston, San Francisco. Pupils incl. Genia Nemenoff, Marie Mikova, Emile Baume, Jacques Fevrier, Anatole Kitain, Kathleen Lockhart Manning, Dene Denny, Elizabeth Simpson, Ruth Finley. Studio: 20, 21st Ave., San Francisco, Calif.

SYKES, LAUREN B.

Organist-Choral Conductor. b. Newberg, Ore., Dec. 31, 1905. St. organ, w. T. S. Roberts of Williamette Univ.; Lucien E. Becker, F.A.G.O., Portland; theory, comp. w. Frank Wright, Brooklyn. Assoc. of American Guild of Organists Degree. Organ soloist w. Victoria, B. C., Canada Symphony Orch. Organ recitals, choir concerts at 1939 San Francisco Fair. Organ soloist w. Northwestern Regional Conventions of American Guild of Organists. Organist Portland Symphonic Choir in major oratorio works. Comp. nine works for organ. Member: Soc. of Oregon Composers; AGO. Hobbies: gardening, colored movies. Now organist-choirmaster, First Christian Church, dir. of mus. at Multnomah School of the Bible, Cond. a cappella choir Pacific Bible College, Head Organ Dept. Cascade College. Studio: 1122 S.E. 60th Ave., Portland 15, Ore.

SZIGETI, JOSEPH

Violinist. b. Budapest, Hungary. St. violin w. Hubay. Concerts, soloist w. leading symphony orchs. throughout world. Management, Arthur Judson, Inc., 113 W. 57th St., N.Y.C. Res. Palos Verdes, Calif.

TALBOT, IRVIN

Conductor. b. St. Louis, Mo., Jan. 27, 1896. Musical Dir., New York Paramount, Rivoli Theaters, Radio City, Paramount Studios. Guest appearances Hollywood Bowl. Cond. many motion picture scores. Member The Bohemians. Hobby: collecting biographies, musical scores. Mgmt. Music Corp. of America. Paramount Pictures, Inc., 5451 Marathon St., Hollywood 38, Calif.

TANDLER, ADOLPH

Conductor, composer, violist L. A. Phil. Orch. b. Vienna, 1875. Grad. Royal Music Academy, Vienna. Inaug. cond. school, children's concerts, L. A.; Public Prize Memory contests L. A. Founder, cond. (5 yrs.) Little Symphony, L. A. Comp. incl. *Symphony for Chamber Orch., Remember the Alamo, Viola Concerta*, others. Guest cond. Hollywood Bowl, L. A. Phil. Orch. 1442 Ridgeway Ave., Los Angeles, Calif.

THOLEN, NELLIE

Music teacher. b. Kansas. Att. St. Louis Inst. of Music. St. piano w. Gottfried Galston, Arthur Edward Johnstone, Ernest R. Kroeger. Comp. *Progressive Series Teachers' Manual*, in collaboration w. Jean Williams. Pupils incl. Lamar Crowson, Tana Bawden, Wayne DeMott. Member: Mu Phi Epsilon; Education Chairman Oregon MTA; Nat'l. Federation of Music Clubs; State Junior Counselor (4 yrs.). Hobbies: photography, hiking, golf. Studio: 315 N.E. 41st Ave., Portland, Ore.

Brian Sullivan

John Sundsten

Wager Swayne

Lauren B. Sykes

Nellie Tholen

Irvin Talbot

Jane Stewart Thomas

Douglas Thompson

Forrest Thornburg

Margaret Tilly

Monica Ting Weaver

Byron I. Tipton

Leonora C. Tompkins

267

THOMAS, JANE STEWART

Violinist, pianist, teacher. b. Birmingham, Ala., April 6, 1909. Ed. Santa Ana Junior College; Univ. of Arizona in violin, piano, voice. Mus. B., Univ. of Arizona. Concertmaster Univ. of Arizona Orch., Tucson Symphony Orchestra, Phoenix Little Symphony, Junior College Orchestra. Toured in West in ensemble work. Choir dir. Mesa Methodist Church. Organist Phoenix Encanto Community Church. Comp. *Sonatinas, Nocturnes,* other works for piano; several orchestrations. Member Phoenix Mus. Club, Mesa Mus. Club (past pres.), Phoenix Woman's Club, MTA (State Secretary), Phoenix Piano Tchrs.' Assn. 2807 No. 8th Ave., Phoenix, Ariz.

THOMAS, JOHN CHARLES

Baritone, opera and concert. b. Meyersdale, Penna., 1891. Attt. Peabody Cons. St. voice w. Blackman, Fermin. Sang concerts, opera, radio, throughout world; leading roles w. Metropolitan, Covent Garden, Chicago, San Francisco, other operas. 1093 Broxton Avenue, Los Angeles 24, Calif.

THOMPSON, DOUGLAS

Pianist. b. San Francisco, Calif., 1910. St. piano w. Chas. Hart, Gunnar Johansen. Pianist for S. F. Symphony Orch. (Monteux) 1939-1942, soloist for Junior Civic Symph. Orch. (Pollak) 1938; Federal Symph. Orch. (Bacon, 1937, Gunderson, 1938); programs over KRE, KPO, KGO, KFRC, 1928-30; concert accompanist for Tito Schipa, Arnold Schoenberg, Sally Rand, May O'Donnell, Vivian Wall, Radiana Pazmor, Robert Pollak, S. F. Opera Ballet, Jeanette MacDonald, Ballet Russe, Julius Huehn, Katherine Dunham, Agnes DeMille, Henri Temianka, Sascha Jacobinoff, others. Official pianist Bach Festival, Carmel, 1936. Concertized through Idaho, Washington, Utah, Arizona, Oklahoma, Texas, 1937; toured world twice w. jazz bands and to Orient and N. Y. 1931-33; toured Mexico, 1947. Played many first performances of modern composers in S. F. incl. works of Chavez, Ray Green, Stravinsky, Schoenberg, Hindemith, Ives, Lou Harrison, Ruggles. 630A Filbert St., San Francisco 11, California.

THORNBURG, FORREST

Dancer, dance teacher. b. Cambridge, Mass., April 16, 1906. St. dance w. Whitten; Denishawn School. Appeared w. Miriam Winslow Dance Group; Nashville Civic Ballet (3 seasons). Solo appearances w. Boston Pops Orch., Providence Symphony, Boston Hall, Los Angeles, and various tours. Soloist w. Ruth St. Denis in concerts, etc. Dance Dir. Ariz. School of Music. Choreography to many dances and ballets. Member: D.M. of A.; Chic. Nat'l D.M. of A., So. Calif. Dancing Teachers Assn., Arizona State Fed. of Music Clubs (vice-pres.), Phoenix Mus. Club. Now directing Church of the Divine Dance. 230 E. McDowell Rd., Phoenix, Ariz.

TILLY, MARGARET

Pianist. b. Maidenhead, England, 1900. St. piano w. Harold Samuel, Harold Bauer, Frank Wickman. Won gold medal Assoc. Board of Royal Acad., Royal Coll. of Music, London, Eng. (4 consec. yrs.); debut New York 1917. Concertized in England (4 yrs.). Soloist w. symph. orch. and London Chamber Society; Bach recitals in London and Edinburgh; guest artist 18 times w. Stradivarius Quartet, N. Y.; sonata recitals w. Kathleen Parlow, John Pennington; first to perform in the West Roy Harris' *Piano Sonata* at request of composer, also first perf. Harris' *When Johnny Comes Marching Home* w. L. A. Phil. Orch. Lecture-recitals w. Roy Harris, Redfern Mason at Stanford Univ., Mills Coll., L. A. Public Library, S. F. Public Library, Dominican Coll., etc. Head music dept. Katherine Branson School (10 yrs.). Lecturer for Univ. Calif. Ext. Division. Member faculty Dominican Convent (7 yrs.). Founder of Music Lovers Society, 1933. Head Music Therapist, Langley Porter Clinic, S. F. 2208 Steiner St., San Francisco, Calif.

TING (WEAVER), MONICA

Teacher of voice and violin. b. Santa Monica, Calif. St. piano w. mother, Mrs. Bessie von H. Ting; violin w. Don

Pardee Riggs, Oskar Seiling, Edwin F. Jones; voice w. Horatio Cogswell. Piano accomp. U.S.C. School of Music. Public school music cred. U.S.C., Redlands; music supervisor (7 schools) Coachella Valley (1 yr.), Exeter and Orosi Schools (4 yrs.), Inglewood Schools (1 yr.). Council Music Chairman, Tulare-King's County District P.T.A. Choral director Visalia Mother's Chorus (2 yrs.). A.B., U.C. at Santa Barbara. Member Santa Barbara Community Symphony Orch. Comp. *Sequoia Suite, Spirits of Spring* (orch.), numerous songs, piano pieces. 1511 De La Vina, Santa Barbara, Calif.

TIPTON, BYRON I.

Teaching of singing, dramatic tenor. b. Selma, Calif., 1907. St. voice w. Franz Volckers, Berlin; Dora Pease, Iowa; Mrs. Gilbert Doyle, Berkeley. Choir Manager, Memorial Methodist Ch., San Francisco; soloist So. Methodist Ch., Oakland; Epworth Ch., Los Angeles; choir dir. and soloist St. Paul's Methodist Ch., Fresno (6 yrs.); dir. and second tenor w. Lisle Quartet, Fresno (12 yrs.). Toured western states as tenor soloist Messenger Quartet (2 yrs.). Member NATS. 904 Roosevelt Ave., Fresno, Calif.

TOCH, ERNST

Composer. b. Vienna, Austria, 1887. Att. Univ. of Vienna; Ph. D.; st. piano w. Willy Rehberg; comp. self-taught. Won Mozart, Mendelssohn schols., Austrian State Prize in comp. Toured U. S.; lectures USC. Author: *The Shaping Forces in Music.* Comp. incl. numerous symphonic works, overtures, chamber music, works for voice and piano; also scores for various films. Member AFM Local 47. Hobby, chess. 811 Franklin St., Santa Monica, Calif.

TODD, TOM T.

Pianist, composer. b. Portland, Ore., 1923. St. piano w. Dent Mowrey (2 yrs.) Sylvan Breyn; comp. w. Ernst Toch, George Tremblay. Arranger for Benny Goodman orch. Staff pianist MGM. Piano in pictures *Make Mine Music, The Killers.* Comp. *Clarinet Concerto* played by Benny Goodman, *Trumpet Concerto*, misc. piano pieces. 3870 Avenida del Sol, North Hollywood, Calif.

TOLLEFSON, MAUDE A.

Singer, teacher of voice. b. near Elkpoint, So. Dak. Early studies in both violin and voice. Mus. B. American Cons. of Music, Chicago. Concertized in U. S. as violinist (Redpath Mgmt). Vocal appearances in concerts, recitals, churches. Member: S.F. Branch, CMTA, (Colleagues degree), San Francisco Musical Club. Hobby: gardening. Studio and program dir. for WEVD, N.Y. City. Taught in San Francisco since 1939. 2100 Divisadero Street, San Francisco, Calif.

TOMPKINS, LEONORA C.

Pianist, teacher of piano. b. Aberdeen, S.D. Grad. Sherwood School of Music (Chicago). St. piano w. Wm. H. Sherwood (2 yrs.), Georgia Kober (1 yr.), Ernest Hutcheson (Pres. of Juilliard Foundation N.Y.) (3 seasons), A. Mirovitch (3 seasons) Olga Steeb, Abbie Whiteside (8 summers), Guy B. Williams, Milan Blanchet (4 yrs.), Mrs. Thilo Becker; harmony, comp. w. Daniel Protheroe, Chicago; Wm. McCoy, S. F.; Carolyn Alchin, Vincent Jones, Julia Howell (USC) Howard Hanson, Arne Oldberg (3 summers), Arnold Schoenberg (2 summers). Pupils winners in Allied Arts & Eisteddfod (L. A. 9 successive yrs.) William Ruoff, Olive Schweitzer (winner 3 yrs.) Lois Allen, Barbara Boose, Marcile Shanafelt, Agnes Hanson, Harriet Stolte. Pres. of Alchin Harmony Assn. of L. A. (1940-41), pianist for Ebell Club (Santa Ana), Ebell Music Section Leader (3 yrs.). Member of S. A. Women's Club (hon.), Music Chairman for Orange County Fed. Women's Clubs, 1945-47. Piano teacher State Teacher's College, Aberdeen, S. D., Polytechnic-John Francis H. S., Brea-Olinda H.S. Comp, string quartette, violin sonata, many piano pieces, songs. Hobbies: singing and composing. 711 So. Sycamore St., Santa Ana, Calif.

Frederick Tooley

Clem and Bernice Towner

Alice Trau-Fischer

Irene Trepanier

Alta Turk

Edward C. Truman

Antonio Triana

Elthea Snider Turner

Belle Udell

Robert Van Eps

Caroline Unruh

David P. Unruh

Gastone Usigli

269

TOOLEY, FREDERICK

Teacher of voice, baritone soloist. b. Columbus, Ind. 1908. B.M. Eastman School of Music, M.M. Northwestern Univ.; voice w. Grace Gauthier, Louis Graveure, Adelin Fermin, Jessie Fenner Hill, Claude Warford, Loyal Phillips Shaw. Appeared in opera, oratorio, recitals in Rochester (N.Y.), New York City, Denver, Colorado Springs. Asst. professor of voice Colorado College since 1937. Choirmaster Shove Memorial Chapel, Colorado Springs. In Army Air Forces 1942-1945. 605 No. Neveda Ave., Colorado Springs, Colo.

TOUMANOVA, TAMARA

Danseuse; prima ballerina. b. Russia. Featured with Ballet Russe, Ballet Theatre, Paris Opera Ballet, other leading ballets. 524 N. Bedford Dr., Beverly Hills, Calif.

TOWNER, CLEM A.

Teacher of theory and composition, choral conductor. b. Ulysses, Nebr. B. Mus. Wesleyan Cons., Lincoln, Nebr.; M. Mus. Cincinnati Cons. Cincinnati, Ohio. St. piano w. Vernon Spencer, Nebr. Wesleyan Cons.; Martin Krause, Stern's Cons. Berlin, Germany; theory, comp. w. Edgar Stillman Kelly. Head Music Dept., Oxford (Ohio) Coll. 1914-1929. Organizer and Head, Dept. of Music, Hendrix Coll., Conway, Ark. 1929-1939. Comp. *Prelude for the Piano, Suite* (two pf), *Star of the East, Christmas Song, My Dreams*, etc (mss.). Member Phi Mu Alpha (Sinfonia). Wife, Bernice Horrlee, pianist, organist, accompanist. B.S., Major Music Ed., Miami Univ., Oxford, Ohio. Taught piano, organ and music theory, Miami, Univ., Oxford, Coll., Hendrix Coll. Formerly accompanist for Lambert Murphy, Marjorie Maxwell, Cecil Burleigh. Member Delta Omicron. 2145 North Allen Ave., Altadena, Calif.

TOWNER, EARL

Conductor. b. Latah, Wash. Att. Coll. of Pac.; New England Cons. st. comp., theory w. G. W. Chadwick. Mus. B., Coll. of Pac. Dir. Inglewood Hour KNX (9 yrs.); St. Matthias Epis. Ch. male choir. Comp. chorals, songs, organ, piano pieces. Hobby, carpentry. Mgmt. Columbia Broadcasting System, Columbia Sq., Hollywood 28, Calif.

TOWNSEND, NORMA

Concert pianist, teacher of piano. 504 E. MacDowell Road, Phoenix, Arizona.

TRAU-FISCHER, ALICE

Opera singer, lyric soprano, teacher of voice. b. Praha (Prague), Czecho-Slovakia. St. voice w. Wallerstein, Praha; Elise Elizza, Franz Steiner, Vienna . Sang principal roles, Chamber Opera, Volksopera, Vienna. State Opera, Bayrouth (3 yrs.). Mozart Festival. Repertory of 33 roles incl. Cherubino, Zerlina, Blondchen, Nuri, Marcelline, Lola, Nedda, Mme. Butterfly, Aennchen, concert tours. U. S. since 1934. Hobby, astrology. Studio: 1141 Post St., San Francisco, Calif.

TREPANIER, IRENE

Pianist, teacher. b. Canada (Amer. citizen). St. violin w. Carlton Wood, Leah Seykora; harmony, comp. w. Frances Frothingham; piano w. Morris Wolfson, Olga Steeb, Elizabeth and Abby DeAvirett. Accomp. and soloist for churches, clubs, educational organizations. Member MTA, Musical Arts Club, Woman's Music Club. Hobby: collecting phonograph albums (records). Teacher of Carole Gene Davis (13 yr. old pianist). 132 Pine Ave., Long Beach, Calif.

TRIANA, ANTONIO

Dancer, choreographer. Debut at age nine at Teatro Imperial, Sevilla. Toured Spain w. Velasco Co. Engaged w. Argentinita for *El Amor Brujo* (de Falla), 1933; w. Laura de Santelmo for *La Vida Breve* at Lyceo Theatre, Barcelona, 1934. Opened dance academy in Madrid, 1935. Toured w. Argentinita through France, Belgium, England, Holland, So. America, Mexico, U. S., 1937-40. Commissioned by Mexican govt. to present *Amor Brujo* at Bellas Artes w. own company, 1940. Danced eight consecutive seasons at Carnegie Hall,

N. Y. Appeared at Hollywood Bowl in *El Amor Brujo, Bolero, Carmen* (Stokowski). At present preparing company for South American tour. 1242 No. New Hampshire Ave., Los Angeles, Calif.

TRUMAN, EDWARD C.

Music director, composer. b. Des Moines, Iowa, 1918. Drake Univ. (1936-38). St. piano w. Alexander Raab, Moissaye Boguslawski, Chicago; Ernest Toch, Miklos Rosza (U.S.C.). Piano soloist WGN, Chicago, 1927-28. Comp.-cond. MBS, origination *Radio Comes of Age*. Comp. *Broadcast Mood Music* (Van Brunt Publ. Co.), piano suite *Tabloid Edition*, (mss.). Transcriptions: Armed Forces Radio Service; *Dramatic Cues, Soap Opera Themes, Familiar Tags and Endings*. Prod. supervisor KSO, KRNT, Des Moines, 1938-44. Member Music Staff MBS (KHJ) 1946-47. Assoc. Editor *Pacific Theater* magazine. Member Assoc. for Education by Radio, Radio Writers' Guild, American Veterans Committee. Management Sue Clark, Hollywood. 314 N. Mission Dr., San Gabriel, Calif.

TURK, ALTA (Mrs. E. A. Everett)

Singer; teacher of voice. b. Hillsboro, Texas. St. voice w. Edward Rowdon, Gypsy Ted Wylie (MacMurray Coll.), Abilene, Tex.; Ollie Guthrie Egert, Waco, Tex.; Walter Golde, Frank La Forge, Franco Autori, New York. Concertized in U. S., especially Southwest. Won first hon. 6 cons. yrs. Texas Fed. of Mus. Clubs cont. App. on sym. programs; San Diego Expos.; Dallas Centennial, etc. Soloist Inst. of Religious Science (3 yrs.). First pres. mus. unit, Woman's Forum, Abilene; pres. 6th Dist., 1st vice-pres. Texas Fed. of Mus. Clubs; curator mus., lecturer Calif. Women of Golden West. Member: MTA, Wilshire Junto Club, Woman's Club of Inst. of Rel. Sc. Mgmt. Dorothy Huttenbach, Behymer Artist Bureau, 427 W. 5th St., Los Angeles 13, Calif. Res. 170 N. Highland Ave., Los Angeles, Calif.

TURNER, ELTHEA SNIDER

Organist, composer, teacher. b. Sanborn, Iowa. B.M. Northwestern Univ. 1918; M. Mus. U.S.C. 1931. St. piano w. Alexander Wurtzburger (pupil of Leschetizky); organ, theory w. Gilbert Piaggi (Royal Academy of Music); voice w. Lillian Ellis (pupil of de Reszke), Walter Allen Etults; comp. w. Arne Oldberg, Carl Beecher, Peter C. Lutkin, Charles Pemberton, Lucien Cailliet, Miklos Rosza. Dir. of Cons. Junior College Nevada, Mo.; Inst. of Music Los Angeles City Schools. Organist University and Wilshire Methodist Churches. Comp. incl. sacred and secular works for piano, organ, violin, voice, ensemble, string quartet, orchestra, operettas, (publ. by G. Schirmer, Silver Burdette, O. Ditson). Member: Pi Kappa Lambda, Alpha Chi Omega, Dominant Club, resident colonist MacDowell Colony, Peterboro, A.G.O., Society of Native American Composers. 859 Mullen Ave., Los Angeles.

UDELL, BELLE

Dramatic soprano, opera, concert, oratorio. b. New York City. St. voice, theory w. Martin Horodas, New York and Los Angeles. App. w. San Carlo, other opera comps. Leonora (*Il Trovatore, Forza del Destino*), Aida, Santuzza, Elsa, Tosca, Mimi, Butterfly, other roles. Concert tours, oratorio app. in U.S. Member San Fernando Valley Mus. Assn. First soloist, San Fernando Valley Sym. Orch. (Ronka). Hobby, gardening. 109 N. Whitnall Ave., North Hollywood, Calif.

UNRUH, CAROLINE M.

Concert pianist, teacher, coach. b. Oklahoma City, Okla. Grad. Southern Methodist Univ. St. piano w. Rudolph Ganz, Rudolph Klepzig, Hans Richard, Leon Sampaix, Bess Daniels, Abby DeAvirett, Walter Scott . Mus.B. Advanced study, Chicago Musical Coll. Concert appearances, Midwest and Pacific Coast. Recordings: *Messiah* album, California Nightingales. Member: Soroptimist Club, Alameda MTA. Hobbies: gardening, counseling. Official accompanist and coach for Unruh Philharmonic Chorus; First Methodist Ch., Children's Chorus. 742 Wesley Ave., Oakland 10, Calif.

Henry J. Vajcner

William Van den Burg

Nicholas Vasilieff

Francisco C. Vega

Genevieve Vekroff

Jeanette Sonia Violin

Mischa Violin

Dorothy Marie Wade

Elisabeth Waldo

Herbert Wall

George Walker

Claude A. Ward

Louise Stiles Ware

UNRUH, DAVID P.

Teacher of voice, choral conductor, composer. b. Nebr. Father, Peter Unruh, singer and choral conductor. Grad. Lawrence Coll. Mus. B., Chicago Musical Coll. Mus. D. Concert appearances, Middlewest, Pacific Coast. Comp. dozen choral numbers. Recordings: *Messiah* album, California Nightingales. Cond. of Unruh Philharmonic Chorus. Dir. ladies', men's and mixed choruses (32 yrs.). Presented numerous light operas. Member: Kiwanis Club, Public Speakers' Club, Music Club, NATS. Hobbies: musical research, tennis. Studio: 478 Santa Clara Ave., Oakland 10, Calif.

USIGLI, GASTONE

Conductor, composer, pianist; teacher of conducting, theory, opera, voice, piano. b. Venice, Italy, Nov. 25, 1899. Att. Venice Cons., Berlin Cons., Univ. of Turin. Mus. D. (degrees in music, letters, philosophy, languages). In America since 1928. Cond. operas Venice, Verona, Treviso (It.) Philadelphia, Chicago, San Francisco, Los Angeles, etc. Cond. New York City Sym., San Francisco Sym., Los Angeles Phil., other leading symphonies. Cond. Bach Festival, Carmel (8 yrs., since inception), Venice Internat'l. Mus. Festival. State dir. (3 yrs.) Sou. Calif. Fed. Music Project. Now cond. San Jose Sym. Orch. Founded (1932) San Francisco Chamber Sym. to present young soloists, American works. Cond. over 100 American works, 2 American operas, presented over 150 young American artists. Repertory incl. over 500 sym. works, 35 operas, 100 oratorios, cantatas. Won Ricordi Prize 1924 (Toscanini judge) w. symp. poem, *Don Quixote*. Comp. incl.: two symphonies, one grand opera, ten symphonic poems, two string serenades, chamber music, chorals, numerous songs, piano pieces. Hobbies: chess, mountain climbing, swimming. Mgmt. L. E. Behymer, Philharmonic Aud. Bldg., 427 W. 5th St., Los Angeles 13, Calif. Res. 2245 Sacramento St., San Francisco 15, Calif.

USSHER, BRUNO DAVID

Music critic, writer. b. Fuerth, Bavaria, 1889. St. Oxford, Leipsig Univ., Leipsig Cons. Western reg. dir. Federal Mus. Project, 1938. Program annotator L. A. Phil. Orch. in Hollywood Bowl, 1923-45. Lecturer USC. Music critic, L. A. Express, L. A. Daily News, Pasadena Star News, other papers. Editor, *Music and Dance in Southern Calif.*, 1933. Hotel Ocean Village, Ocean Beach, San Diego, Calif.

VAJCNER, HENRY J.

Arranger, composer, teacher, director. b. Chicago, June, 1918. St. orch., theory w. Walter Dellers, Chicago; comp., theory w. Leo Sowerby, American Cons., Chicago. In U. S. Coast Guard arr., scored numerous recruiting programs. Dir. of entertainment unit South Pacific bases and hospitals. Arr., scored for dramatic radio shows, vocal units, orchestras, bands. Arr. and soloist Armed Forces Radio Show. War service citation Secretary of Treasury. Accordion soloist Roxy Theater, New York City. Music supervisor (Music Center Studio), Long Beach. Music Center Studio, 1120 American Ave., Long Beach, Calif.

Van den BURG, WILLIAM

Conductor, violoncellist. b. Hague, Holland, Sept. 18, 1901. Hon. grad. Royal Cons. of Hague, 1920. Dutch Gov't. scholarship at Ecole Normale de Music, Paris w. Pablo Casals, Diran Alexanian. Asst. to Casals, Alexanian, 1921. St. comp. Curtis Inst. w. Fritz Reiner, diploma 1933. Assisting artist, tours w. John McCormack throughout U.S. 1925. Solo 'cellist Phila. Orch. (Stokowski) (9 yrs.). Asst. to Stokowski. 1934. Soloist Hollywood Bowl w. Monteux 1935. Assoc. cond., first 'cellist San Francisco Symph. (Monteux). Cond. Sacramento, San Jose Symphonies; head 'cello, orch. depts. Mills Coll. (Oakland) 1936. Cond. many radio programs. Organized Nat'l Youth Orch., S.F. Concerts for soldiers during war; awarded Officer d'Academie by France, 1937. Prof., orch., cond. Univ. of City of L.A. in LaHabra. Now w. MGM Studios. Arr. album for 'cello, piano; various concert pieces. Recorded Grieg *Sonata*, Bach *Concerto* (oboe and orch.) (Alco), Smetana *Trio* (Vox). Hobbies: books, photography, tennis, bridge. 3122 Patricia Ave., Los Angeles 34, Calif.

VAN EPS, ROBERT

Pianist, composer, arranger. b. No. Plainfield, N.J., March 10, 1909. St. piano, theory w. William L. Calhoun, New York (4 yrs.); Vernon Spencer, Los Angeles (5 yrs.); composition, self-taught. Radio, motion pictures (MGM), concert appearances. Comp. *Piano Concerto Nos. 1, 2, Wind and the Chimney, Concert Fugue No. 5, Arabesque, g-sharp minor, Reverie, Etude in F-sharp*. Commercial recordings w. all companies. Hobbies: woodcrafts, metal crafts, badminton. 426 Sonora Ave., Glendale 1, Calif.

VAN VLIET, CORNELIUS

'Cellist. b. Holland, 1886. St. w. Eberle, Rotterdam; Mossel, Amsterdam. Soloist age 12 w. Leipsig Philharmonic. Toured Europe w. Prague Philharmonic. Soloist Vienna Philharmonic (Mahler). Concert tours in U. S. Mgmt. Florence Smith, 2007 Vista Del Mar, Hollywood 28, Calif.

VASILIEFF, NICHOLAS

Dancer, ballet, character, concert; teacher of dancing. Seing-Hirsch Bldg., 918 S. W. Washington Blvd., Portland, Ore.

VEGA, FRANCISCO CAMACHO

Conductor, composer, pianist, teacher. b. Guadalajara, Jalisco, Mexico. St. piano w. father, Juan de la Cruz, Guadalajara; theory, comp., conducting w. Juan Aguilar, Nat'l Cons. of Mexico; Rafael Tello; Alba Herrera y Ogazon. Prof. of music, Nat'l Cons. of Mexico. Cond. Palacio de Belles Artes, Mexico City, Cuba, South America, New York, Chicago, Los Angeles, other music centers. Tours throughout North, Central, South America. Comp. *Los Volcanes* (symp. poem), *Spanish Gypsy Suite*, string quartet, chorals, songs, piano pieces. Recordings w. Victor, Columbia, Azteca Co., L. A.; Peerless Co., Mexico City. Numerous arr., comp. for Hugo Riesenfeld; Music dir., symphonic conductor, Radio XEW, Mexico City. Member AFM. Hobby: collecting scores. 510 No. Commonwealth Ave., Hollywood, Calif.

VEGA, MARIA de la

(*See*: De la VEGA)

VEKROFF, GENEVIEVE

Teacher of voice, coach. b. Ashland, Wisc. Grad. Chicago Mus. Coll.; st. voice w. Herman de Vries, Ernst Knoch, Emma Roe. Soloist Sinai, Isaiah KAM Temples, Chicago; sang EverReady Radio Hour, N. Y. In Los Angeles since 1931. Teacher of Dorothy Speights, (*Carmen Jones*); Lois Lee (*Red Mill*). Studio: 5300 La Cresta Court, Los Angeles, Calif.

VIOLIN, JEANETTE SONIA

Concert violinist. b. Chicago, Ill. Att. American Cons. Chicago; Chicago Mus. Coll. St. violin w. Leon Sametini. Debut playing Paganini *Concerto*, Chicago. Concerts in U. S. World premiere perf. Clifford Vaughn *Concerto*, Los Angeles, repeat perf. San Francisco. Under contract RKO Studios. Member AFM. Hobby: oil painting. 176 So. Gardner St., Los Angeles, Calif.

VIOLIN, MISCHA

Concert violinist, conductor. b. Odessa, Russia. St. w. mother; won scholarship age 8 w. Stern Cons., Berlin; st. violin w. Alexander Fiedeman. Debut age 12 w. Berlin Philharmonic (Nikisch). Concerts, app. w. symphony orchestras throughout world, incl. command perf. for British Royal Family. Gold palm from La Prensa, Brazil. Amer. debut Carnegie Hall, 1920. Cond. numerous orchestras, incl. Hollywood. Concert transcriptions of various masterworks. Member AFM. Hobby: fishing. 176 S. Gardner Ave., Los Angeles, Calif. Mgmt. Martin Music Management, Hollywood, Calif.

WADE, DOROTHY

Concert violinist; film studio recording musician. b. Eureka, Calif., Oct. 11, 1923. St. violin w. Oskar Seiling (10 yrs.), Peter Meremblum (7 yrs.). Concert tours in U.S.: soloist w. Los Angeles Philharmonic Orch. (Ernest Schelling), Redlands Bowl, etc. Concertmistress Calif. Junior Sym. Orch. under Meremblum, Mitropoulos, Kindler, Dorati, Kurtz, Iturbi, etc. Recordings in numerous films. Hobbies: swimming, horseback riding, coll. Heifetz recordings. Member AFM. Local 47. Mgmt.: Hollywood Artist Bureau (Mae Norton), 159 S. Beverly Dr., Beverly Hills, Calif. Res. 2567 Armacost, West Los Angeles 34, Calif.

Mark Warnow

WALDO, ELISABETH

Concert violinist. b. Tacoma, Wash. St. violin w. W. R. Hedley, Seattle; scholarship Curtis Inst. of Music, Phila. Twice gold-medal winner Northwest Music Meet, Seattle. Soloist leading clubs of Northwest incl. Music & Art Found. Toured w. Leopold Stokowski All-American Youth Orch. So. America, U.S.A., Canada (2 seasons). First violin sec. L.A. Philharmonic (1 season) (Stokowski, Barbirolli, Steinberg, Iturbi, Hageman). Soloist L.A. concerts incl. broadcasts to So. America; concerts Coordinator of Inter-American Affairs office. Soloist L.A. County Museum Radio Program (Mutual) (Rozsa, cond.). Solo tours to Central, So. America incl. Guatemala, Panama, Cuba, Colombia, Peru, Chile, Mexico. App. on leading radio networks of these countries; XEW (Mexico) w. Augustin Lara, Ernesto Lecuona. Featured Film *Clasa Studios* (Mexico). Concerts for G.I.'s in Caribbean area. Violin soloist for Xaxier Cugat first nat'l. concert tour incl. performances Chicago Civic Opera. Now giving own concerts specializing in Latin American music. 1141 Tremaine Ave., Los Angeles, Calif. Mgmt. Martin Music Management, 746 N. Cahuenga Ave., Hollywood, Calif.

WALDROP, UDA

Composer, organist, pianist, choral director. b. Berryville, Ark., 1886. Att. London Royal Academy. St. piano w. Matthay, Verne; theory, pipe-organ w. Chas. W. Pierce, Royal Coll. of Organists, London. Organist, choral dir. St. Luke's Epis. Ch., 1st Cong. Ch., San Francisco. Comp. music for Bohemian Club Plays *Nec Netama*, 1914, *Golden Feather*, 1939. Accomp. Kreisler, Melba, Calve, Clauson, etc. 30 McLaren St., San Francisco, Calif.

WALKER, GEORGE

Teacher of singing. b. Fox Lake, Wisc., 1874. Att. Univ. of Chicago, Univ. of Wisconsin. St. voice w. Manuel Garcia, London, Viardot-Garcia, Paris, Heinrich Feinhaus, Berlin; Klindworth-Scharwenka Conservatorium, Berlin. Had active singing career of thirty-five years (twenty-five years in opera and concert in Europe), singing under Nikisch, Mahler, Muck, Moerike, Mengelberg, Weingartner and Siegfried Ochs. Since 1941 Dir. Voice Dept., Cornish School, Seattle. 710 East Roy St., Seattle, Wash.

WALL, HERBERT

Singer, teacher of voice; director Herbert Wall School of Music. b. Texas. Att. Univ. of Chicago Med. Sch.; st. voice w. Charles W. Clark, Oscar Seagle, N.Y.; Jean de Reszke, Paris 1920-25; Sorbonne; Oxford Univ. (w. Fellows) 1934. U. S. Army 1917, song leader 98th Div.; later Mus. Dir. U. S. Army, Washington, 1917-20. Concertized, sang opera roles in U. S., Europe, incl. Don Giovanni, other ldg. roles Nice, 1943, soloist w. Weingartner, Vienna 1924, various orchs. Chairm. Dept. of Fine Arts, Univ. of Missouri, Ohio State Univ.; dir. of opera, faculty Univ. of Texas 1936 while maint. New York studio. Estab. Herbert Wall Sch. of Music 1942. 7950 Sunset Blvd., Hollywood 46, Calif.

WALLENSTEIN, ALFRED

Conductor, violoncellist. b. Chicago, Ill., 1898. St. 'cello w. Klengel. Soloist w. Chicago Sym., N .Y. Phil. Sym., others. Concertized in U. S., So. America. Cond. Wallenstein Sinfonietta, other radio orchs. Permanent cond., L. A. Phil. Orch. since 1944. Philharmonic Orch., 427 W. 5th St., Los Angeles 13, Calif.

WARD, CLAUDE A.

Baritone soloist, choral conductor, vocal instructor. b. Portland, Ore., Oct 2, 1911. Att. (4 yrs.) Cons. of Music, Coll. of the Pacific. Master classes in voice w. Radiana Pazmor, Frederick Haywood; summer sessions Juilliard School of Music, N.Y.C.; coaching in choral cond. w. Peter J. Wilhousky; vocal methods w. Bernard Taylor. Att. Choral Cond. Inst., Occidental Coll., Prof. Sch. Westminister Choir Coll., Princeton, N. J. w. John Finley Williamson. Soloist *St Paul*, *Messiah* w. Stanislaus Co. Oratorio Soc., Modesto, Turlock,

Calif.; San Jose Mun. Chorus in *Elijah, Messiah, Rose Maiden*; S. F. Bach Soc., Coll. of the Pacific cho. and orch.; Santa Cruz Oratorio Soc. and Orch.; *Faure Requiem* w. St. Luke's Epic. S. F.; w. Loring Club Male Chorus, S. F.; Chr. Sci., Cath. Churches, Synagogues, Stockton and San Francisco. Min. of Music First Congr. Ch., S. F. Religious Music Chr. Calif. Fed. of Music Clubs. Treas. S. F. Choirmasters and Organists Assn. Music chr. California Cong. of Parents and Teachers, 2nd Dist. Org. and dir. S. F. Oratorio Soc.; dir. Bell Choral Club at Pac. Tel. and Tel. Co., S. F. Fire Dept. Glee Club. 264 Dolores St., San Francisco 3, Calif.

WARE, LOUISE STILES

Teacher of piano, pianist, organist. b. San Bernardino, Calif., Nov. 26, 1920. Grad. Sherwood Music Sch., Chicago. St. piano w. Rowena Bishop, Leo Podolsky, Ethel Leginska. Former organist, Trinity Luth. Ch., St. John's Epis. Ch. Colleague Calif. MTA. Past-pres. San Bernardino Branch MTA. Member: San Bernardino Valley Concert Assn. gov. bd. Del Rosa, Calif.

WARNOW, MARK

Conductor, composer. b. Russia. Arr. U.S. at age 6. St. violin w. Franz Kneisel, Arthur Hartman, comp., cond. w. Mortimer Wilson, Arnold Volpe. Debut as concert violinist Town Hall 1924. Cond. Massel Opera Co. at age 18. Staff cond. for CBS since 1933. Mus. dir. for radio shows of *We the People, Helen Hayes Theatre of the Air, March of Time, John Charles Thomas Westinghouse Program, Ed Wynn Borden Show, Vick's Matinee Theatre, Norman Corwin's Pursuit of Happiness, All Time Hit Parade, Blue Velvet Music, The Instrumentalists, Columbia Workshop, Saturday Night Swing Session, Your Hit Parade,* and U.S. Army *Sound Off.* Guest cond. N.Y. Philharmonic-Symphony Orch. Lewisohn Stadium, 1940, pres. premier *Ballad for Americans* w. Robeson. Cond. Carnegie Hall *Pop* Concert, Rochester Symphony, 1946. Prod. musical comedy 1943. Numerous trans. for U.S. Treasury during war. Comp. *You're Mine, Love Time, Hail America, Princess Anaesthesia* (radio operetta), *Jazz Bacchanale* (ballet), *The Miss That Eloped with the Swiss* (radio operetta). Columbia Broadcasting System, Columbia Square, Hollywood, Calif.

WARREN, ELINOR REMICK

Composer, pianist. b. Los Angeles, Calif. St. music since age 5; pvt. tchrs. Los Angeles, New York. Att. Westlake Sch. for Girls, Los Angeles, Mills Coll., Oakland. Concertized extensively as pianist, also as accomp. to leading artists. Soloist w. Los Angeles Philharmonic, Hollywood Bowl, other principal orchs. Over 200 pub. comps. incl. *The Passing of King Arthur* (orch., soloists, cho.); *The Fountain, The Dark Hills, The Frolic of the Elves, The Crystal Lake* (orch.); *The Harp Weaver* (cantata; bar., wom. cho., harp, orch.), *The Sleeping Beauty* (cantata; sop., bar., mxd. cho., orch.), *Quintet* (woodwinds, horn), numerous sac., secular chorals, songs, piano pieces. Member: AGMA, ASCAP, Dominant Club, Native Comp. Soc., Sigma Alpha Iota (hon.). 179 S. McCadden Pl., Los Angeles 4, Calif.

WAXMAN, FRANZ

Composer, conductor. b. Germany. St. Berlin, Dresden. Comp. film music scores, U.F.A. Studios, Berlin, 1930, Paris, London; mus. dir. Universal Studios, Hollywood, 1934-35. Comp.-cond. MGM Studios, 1935-42; Warner Bros. Studio 1943-47. Comp. Overture, *Athaneal the Trumpeter, Elegy for Strings, Concerto for 'Cello, Carmen Fantasy,* commissioned, played by Heifetz. Numerous feature film scores include: *Captains Courageous, Rebecca, Objective Burma, Humoresque, The Two Mrs. Carrolls, Dr. Jekyl and Mr. Hyde, Possessed.* Recordings include: *Carmen Fantasy* (Heifetz) (Victor), selections from *Humoresque* (Isaac Stern and Oscar Levant) (Columbia), *Bach Concerto* (Heifetz) (Victor). Cond. Hollywood Bowl Symphony, 1944-46. Cond., mus. dir. Beverly Hills Music Fest., 1947. Film mgmt. Music Corp. of America, Beverly Hills, Calif.; concert mgmt. Martin Music Management, 746 N. Cahuenga Blvd., Hollywood 38, Calif.

Elinor Remick Warren

John Roy Weber

Eunice Wennermark

Frances Wiener

Franz Waxman

Lillian Hinkle Williams

Roy Webb

Erich Weiler

Lee Whitney

Jean Williams

WEBB, ROY

Composer, conductor. b. New York City, 1888. Att. Columbia Univ. St. theory, orch. w. Julius Vogler; orch., assisted in prod. musical comedies: *Wild Flower, Stepping Stones, Connecticut Yankee, Peggy Ann.* Arr. orch. for RKO, N.Y.; comp.) arr. music for *Japanese Bowl, Art's Rejuvenation* in coll. w. brother, Kenneth Webb (radio, stage playwright), Lambs Club, *Gambols;* comp. many music scores RKO-Radio, incl. *Alice Adams, Quality Street, Love Affair, Last Days of Pompeii, Sylvia Scarlett, Plough and the Stars, A Woman Rebels, The Woman I Love, Kitty Foyle, Tom, Dick and Harry, Stage Door, Abe Lincoln, A Man to Remember, In Name Only, Vivacious Lady, My Favorite Wife, Flight for Freedom, Hitler's Children, Mr. Lucky, Murder My Sweet, Fallen Sparrow, Experiment Perilous, Enchanted Cottage, Cornered, Spiral Staircase, Notorious, Sinbad the Sailor, The Locket, They Won't Believe Me, Magic Town.* 10677 Somma Way, Bel Air, Calif.

WEBER, JOHN ROY

Composer, conductor, violinist. b. Fond Du Lac, Wisc., 1899. St. w. Ludvig Wrangall; grad. (B.M.) Wisconsin Univ. School of Music. Violin soloist on tour U.S. and Orient. Toured W. Edward Grieg and Royal Grand Opera. Violinist. w. Milwaukee, Minneapolis, Seattle, Los Angeles Orch. Prof. violin, comp. w. Cons. in Middle West. Founded Little String Symphony Orch., (children 2½ yrs. to 10 yrs.) app. Fiesta de Los Angeles, 1932. Traveled in Europe, Orient w. own orch. Founder-director Hollywood Symphony Orch. Managed Hollywood Canteen Symphony Orch. during war. Comp. 12 songs, *Symphony, Suite* (orch.), piano solos, violin pieces. Charter member Amer. Soc. of Music Arr. Member Wisc. MTA. Hobbies: mountain climbing, tennis, horseback riding, psychology, philosophy. 1558 No. Vine St., Studio 216, Hollywood, Calif.

WECKER, KARL

Conductor; manager of Hollywood Bowl. b. Norwalk, Ohio. St. violin w. Wm. E. Simpkinson (7 yrs.), Jean ten Haze (2 yrs.), master classes w. Eugene Ysaye. Att. Cincinnati Cons. of Music (5 yrs.); st. cond., comp. w. Ralph Lyford. Mus. B., Mus. M., Mus. D., Cincinnati Cons. Concertized as violinist in U.S. Mus. dir. University of Cincinnati; founder-cond. Univ. of Cincinnati Student Orch. Assn. Founder-cond. Grand Rapids Sym. Orch (17 yrs.); mus. dir. Grand Rapids Jr. Coll. State dir. Federal Music Proj. Michigan, California. Guest lecturer, Univ. of Ga., Univ. of Mich., Mich. State Coll., USC., UCLA, others. Manager, Hollywood Bowl since 1945. Contributor to various publications. Comp. incl. violin ped. works, pub. C. Fischer. Member: MTA, Nat'l Assn. of Mus. and Rel. Arts. Hobby, gardening. Hollywood Bowl, 2301 N. Highland Ave., Hollywood 28, Calif.

WEILER, ERICH

Violinist, violist, conductor, librettist; founder Comedy Opera Guild. b. Germany. St. violin, theory, cond. w. pvt. tchrs. Europe, U. S. Spec. study history of opera; owns large library of recondite, forgotten opera scores, both pub. and mss. Member San Francisco Symphony (27 yrs.), San Francisco Opera Orch. (25 yrs.). Chamber music, solo concerts in U. S., Europe. Revised libretti, orch., made English trans., and cond. over 80 pref. of seldom-heard operas for Comedy Opera Guild, incl. *Bruschino the Grouch* (Rossini), *Two Misers* (Gretry), *Village Singers* (Fioravanti), *Secret Marriage* (Cimarosa), *Kalif of Bagdad* (Boieldieu), others. Member, Family Club of San Francisco. Hobby: to produce unjustly forgotten operas in new English translations, creating new operatic repertory. Mgmt., Larry Allen, Inc. 79 Post St., San Francisco, Calif. Res. 276, 25th Ave., San Francisco, Calif.

WENNERMARK, EUNICE

Concert violinist. b. Pueblo, Colo. St. violin w. Leah Seykora, Francis Schwinger, David Eisenberg, Joseph Achron, Vera Barstow; coached w. Louis Persinger. Concertized throughout U.S.; toured w. John Charles Thomas; soloist w. Denver Sym., Pueblo Sym., Carmel Bach Festival (Usigli),

L.A. Federal Orch. (Usigli, Altschuler), L.A. Orch., Occidental Coll, UCLA, Hollywood Bowl, Hollywood Mem. Aud., leading women's clubs, orgs., esp. in Sou. Calif. Winner several first awards Nat'l. Fed. of Mus. Clubs. Concertmistress w. Sokoloff, Usigli, Schoenberg, Altschuler, Samoussoud, Coates, Lert; KFI-KECA staff orch. Film rec. w. major studios, incl. Warner Bros., RKO, Paramount, Columbia, Republic, 20th Century-Fox, Universal-International, MGM, General Service, Disney, PRC, Eagle-Lion. Radio programs w. John Charles Thomas (Westinghouse) (3½ yrs.); Dave Rose, *Holiday for Music, Request Performance;* Bell Tel.; Red Skelton; Ford Sunday Eve.; Eddie Bracken; Victor Borge; Wm. Gargan; Hollywood Mystery Time; Tony Martin; Victor Young, others. Music dir. KMPC, cond. *Symphonettes* (str. ensem.). Rec. for Decca. RCA-Victor, MGM, Capitol. Violinist-dir. Wennermark Violin Choir (own students). Pupils incl. June Howard, UCLA Young Artist winner. 236 S. Clark Dr., Beverly Hills; 1213 S. Ridgeley Dr., Los Angeles, Calif.

WHITNEY, LEE

Soprano, opera and concert. b. Catawissa, Pa., nee Greta Altpeter. Grad. Thiel Cons. of Music, Greenville, Pa. Att. Juilliard (Fellowship), N.Y. St. voice, repertory w. Marcella Sembrich (Juilliard), Frank La Forge, Kurt Schindler, Eleanor McClelland, New York; Camille Decreuse, Blanche Weinschenk, Paris. Concertized, sang leading opera roles in Rouen, Tours, Rennes, Amiens, France; throughout U.S. in New York, Boston, St. Louis, Central City, Ford Bowl, San Diego, Louisville, other centers. Repertory incl. Manon (*Manon*), Micaela (*Carmen*), Traviata (*Traviata*), Gilda (*Rigoletto*), Louise (*Louise*), Butterfly (*Butterfly*), Juliet (*Romeo and Juliet*), Mimi (*Boheme*), Thais (*Thais*), Marguerite (*Faust*), Philine (*Mignon*), Nedda (*Pagliacci*), Doll (*Tales of Hoffman*), Eunice (*Quo Vadis*), Mireille (*Mireille*), Adele (*Fledermaus*); also lt. operas. *Maytime, One Wonderful Night, Blossom Time, Three Little Girls, Three Musketeers, Merry Widow, Gondoliers, Rose Marie.* Recorded *In a Gondola* (Co-Art). Soloist First Congr. Ch., San Diego. Hobbies: theatre, dance. Studio, Thearle Music Co., 640 Broadway, San Diego, Calif. Res. Box 86, Bonita, Calif.

WIDENHAM, RUTH M.

Teacher, Calif .School of Music & Arts. b. Ill. Grad. Ill. Coll. of Music. St. piano w. Vernon Spencer, Waver Swayne, Abby Whiteside; voice w. S. Camillo Engle, William Shakespeare; harmony w. Carolyn Alchin. Taught at Girls Collegiate Sch., Hollywood Sch. for Girls, L. A. Cons. Member Dominant Club. 352 S. Westmoreland Ave., Los Angeles 5, Calif.

WIENER, FRANCES (Mrs. Lev Shorr)

Concert violinist; teacher of violin. Grad. Curtis Inst. of Music, Philadelphia. Concert tours throughout U. S. App. w. radio, chamber music organizations. Leading violinist, Music Lovers Soc. of San Francisco. Joint sonata, solo recitals w. husband, Lev Shorr. 3535 Clay St., San Francisco, Calif.

WILCOX, JOHN C.

Teacher of voice. b. Sebawaing, Mich., May 5, 1870. Att. Mehan Sch. Detroit; Mus.M. (hon.) Denver Coll. of Mus. Church, oratorio, concert soloist in U. S. Author: *The Living Voice, Voice Training for Speech and Choric Reading.* Dir. choral orgs., oratorios. Past pres. NATS, Chicago Singing Tchrs. Guild; member: Amer. Acad. of Tchrs. of Singing; MTA. Hobby, golf. Colorado College, Colorado Springs, Colo.

WILLIAMS, JEAN

Composer, teacher of piano, singing and harmony. b. Wednesbury, England. Grad. Cons. of Music, Univ. of Toronto, Licentiate Degree. St. w. Wm. Shakespeare, London; Gottfried Galston, Arthur Edward Johnstone. Comp. three *Piano Concerti;* fourteen piano solos (pub. Schroeder & Gunther) songs; choruses; two-piano music (mss.). Faculty Toronto Conservatory, St. Louis Inst. of Music. Member: Mu Phi Epsilon, Oregon MTA, Nat'l Fed. of Music Clubs. Hobbies: cooking, golf. 315 N.E. 41st Ave., Portland, Ore.

Meredith Willson

WILLIAMS, LILLIAN HINKLE

Composer, teacher of piano, harmony, ear-training. b. Yates Center, Kans., 1879. Blind at age 5. Began mus. ed. Kans. City Inst. for Blind; grad. 1896. Recovered partial sight 1897. Grad. Inst. of Musical Art (now Juilliard), 1909. St. piano w. Wesley Weyman, Arthur Hochmann, V. Coleman, Franklyn W. Robinson, Sigismund Stojowski; comp. w. Percy Goetschius, J. Cressman. Taught at Inst. for Blind, Kans. City 1899-1901; Bellville, Courtland, Kans. 1903-1906. Spec. in Normal Courses for children, incl. *Dunning System.* Founder Music Settlement School, Harlem Baptist Ch., Eastern Dist. Branch YWCA, Brooklyn. Program, choir dir. Hunts Point Presb. Ch., Van Ness Presb., Harlem Baptist Ch., N.Y.C., choir dir. Brooklyn Heights Presb. Ch., San Diego (12 yrs.). Pres. Prof. Music Guild. Member Nat'l Piano Tchrs. Guild, Amphion Club; board of dir. MTA, Mus. Merit Found. of Greater San Diego. Comp. *Children's Manual, Up the Mountain Trail, Gremlins, The Quilting Bee, The Flustered Flea, Rabboni.* Hobby, flowers. 2143 Dale St., San Diego, Calif.

WILLIAMS, VERA SALLEE

Soprano, concert singer, teacher of voice. b. Waco, Tex. St. w. Francis Stewart, New York; Spanell, Germany; Eduardo Sacerdote, George Lapier, France, various coaches in America. Mus.M. Texas Christian Univ. in theory, piano, organ. Concertized in America, Europe; joint programs with Enid Dirier, Paris. Sang w. Sacerdote Opera Group, incl. *Butterfly, Mimi, Lia.* Cond. summer master classes Cons. of Musical Arts, Amarillo, Texas. Hobbies: Book Shop and Art Gallery. Studio, Talent Workshop, 8750 Holloway Dr., West Hollywood 46, Calif.

WILLSON, MEREDITH

Composer, conductor, radio producer. b. Mason City, Iowa, May 12, 1902. Att. Damrosch Inst. of Musical Art, New York. St. theory, comp., flute w. Henry Hadley, Bernard Wagenaar, Mortimer Wilson, Julius Gold, Georges Barrere. Flute soloist w. Sousa's Band, 1922-25. First flutist, New York Philharmonic-Symphony Orch. 1925-29. Guest cond. San Francisco Sym., Highland Park Sym., others. Music dir. NBC Western Div. 1932. Major, U.S. Army in war; music dir. for Armed Forces Radio Service, incl. *Command Performances, Mail Call,* other shows. Cond. radio programs since 1926, incl. *Burns and Allen, Sparkle Time* (own show), *Family Hour,* many others. Comp. incl. *Three Symphonies* (1. *San Francisco;* 2. *Missions of California*), *The Jervis Bay* (tone poem), *Mission San Gabriel* (tone poem), numerous songs incl. *You and I, Two In Love,* various incidental pieces. Scored various films, incl. *The Great Dictator, The Little Foxes,* etc. Hobby, golf. Member AFRA, ASCAP. Mgmt. William Morris Agency, Inc., 202 N. Canon Dr., Beverly Hills, Calif.

WILSON, LILLIAN BACKSTRAND

Professor of singing, U.S.C. b. Pennsylvania. Grad. B.A. College of Mus., Univ. So. Calif. St. voice w. Wm. Shakespeare, Edmund J. Myer, Achille Alberti, Constantino, Percy Rector Stephens, Richard Hageman, Louis Graveure, Franz Proschowski. Att. Chic. Musical Coll. Concertized So. Calif.; church choirs. Univ. So. Calif. since 1914. Tchr. of Elizabeth Bolinger (Hollywood Bowl, 1944), Anne Hunter, Calvin Hendricks, Lucille Peterson, Joseph Sullivan, Annina Mueller, Catherine Cornwell. 2324 Crenshaw Blvd., Los Angeles, Calif.

WIRE, EDITH

Pianist, composer, teacher of piano; pres. Utah College of Music; pres. Wire Co., publishers. b. Salt Lake City, Utah. St. in N.Y. w. Sigismund Stojowski, George Liebling, Alberto Jonas. Concert, radio app. in U.S. Holds Papal Decoration, Order of St. John Lateran, bestowed by Pope Pius XII. First American woman to join Royal Society of Literature of United Kingdom. Piano compositions incl.: *Elfin Glade, Spanish Dance, Stairway of the Angels, Lotus Blossom.* Also author two books: *The Enchanted Island, Pageant of the Nativity.* Hon. Memb. Societe Nationale d' Encouragement au bien des Alpes Maritimes, Arts, Sciences, Lettres, Societe d' Education et d' Encouragement de Paris. National founder, honorary nat'l pres. general, Children of the American Colonists. Member: Order of the Crown of Charlemagne, Daughters of the Barons of Runnemede, past-pres., Pac. Coast Sec. Honorary State Regent (life), Daughters of the Amer. Colonists; Soc. of New England Women; D.A.R.; Daughters of Founders & Patriots of Amer.; Colonial Dames of the 17th Century; Nat'l League of Amer. Pen Women; Fed. of Music Clubs. Hobby: collecting swan ornaments. 668 Third East St., Salt Lake City, Utah.

WIRSEN, CLAUDIA EDITH

Teacher of voice; coach; composer; writer. b. Sweden. St. voice w. Grevillius, Gothenburg; also w. pvt. tchrs. in Italy, France, Germany, U.S. Head voice dept. Three Arts Sch., Chicago; faculty Univ. of West Coll. of Mus., L.A. App. in opera, concert, oratorio in Sweden under Sibelius, Stenhammar, Aulin, Andree; concertized in U.S. Sang for Illinois State Council of Defense. Pres. Am. Mus. Jr. Councillor Schubert Club. Comp. incl. songs (*Elegy,* first prize Schubert Club, 1934). Pupils inc. Erich Lawrence (S.F. Opera Co.), David Penn, Russ Whiteman, Hazel Taylor. 530 N. Orlando Ave., Hollywood 36, Calif.

WITT, MADGE de

(*See:* De WITT)

WORTH, GENE

Teacher of voice, composer, arranger, conductor. b. Portland, Ore., Oct. 19, 1912. St. voice w. father, Prof. J. A. Hollingworth, Hollingworth Sch. of Music; theory w. Will Kenton, Portland; orch., arr. w. Lowell Berry, San Francisco. Hotel, theatre app. throughout U. S.; radio, oratorio, opera, concert, road work. Comp. incl. *Blue Pastel, Modern Barcarolle, Music is Magic, Follies O Fire,* 1945 and 1946 (winner grand sweepstakes Nat'l comp. 1945). Member: AFM, AGVA, AFRA, Senior Ch. of Comm. Hobbies: psychology, psychiatry. Mgmt. Bruce Marvine, assoc. teacher. Active in musical circles. Now tenor soloist Trinity Epis. Ch., Portland. Fine Arts Bldg., 1017 S.W. Morrison, Portland 5, Ore.

WRIGHT, DOUGLAS Jr.

Teacher of piano. b. Chicago, Ill. Won gold medal as boy soloist, Choir Fest. contest, Chicago, 1903; grad. James N. Milliken Cons., Decatur, Ill. St. piano w. Charles N. Lamphere, Minor Walden Gallup; master classes w. Robert Schmidt; organ w. Wallace Sabin; theory, comp. w. Ernest Bloch. Ph. D., UC at Berkeley. Faculty Milliken Cons.; Community Mus. Sch., San Francisco 1921-32 (piano, theory, piano normal). Plays organ, bass viol. Comp. incl. *America, Land of Hope; Wise Little Owl* (Comp. Press). Pres. Neighborhood Music Sch., Los Angeles; board memb. Coleman Chamber Mus. Assn.; board memb., treas. International Inst. 2170 Chaucer Rd., San Marino, Calif.

WRIGHT, NORMAN SORENG

Composer, organist, pianist; teacher of composition, voice, piano, organ; choral director. b. Moorhead, Minn., Jan. 29, 1905. Att. Concordia Coll. (Moorhead) 1921-23; Sorbonne, Paris, 1925-26. H.D., L.A. Coll. of Osteop. Phsyc. and Surg. 1945; Mus. D. Coll. of the Pacific, 1946. Concertized in U.S., Europe. Organist Cath. Cath. Fargo, N.D. 1919-23; Trinity Ch. Moorhead, 1923-24; Eglise des Etrangers, Paris, France, 1926; solo organist Gaumont Palace, Paramount Theatres, Paris 1925-28; organist-director First Methodist Ch., Hollywood, since 1927. Excl. organ-recording artist, Pathe Freres, Paris, 1926-29. Founder-dir. annual Cesar Franck Festival, Hollywood, 1939. Dir. first U.S. perf. *Redemption* (Franck), *De Profundis* (Dupre) (w. comp. at organ); *Requiem Ebraico* (Zeisl) (w. Santa Monica Symphony); first West Coast perf. *The Bells* (Rachmaninoff) (w. Santa Monica Sym.). Concert of his sym. works perf. by L.A. Women's Sym., April 1942. Comp. incl. *David, the Boy Shepherd Who Became King* (music-drama). *A Century On Parade, Parade of the Years* (pageants), *Soldier, What Did You See? Quest, Eighth Psalm, Twenty-Third Psalm, Tired Cowboy,* numerous chorals, songs, piano pieces. Member: bd. dirs. Neighborhood Music Sch. L.A.; Rotary Intern. (hon); Authors of Hollywood (hon.). 251 N. Ridgewood Pl., Los Angeles, Calif.

Victor Young

YOST, DIXIE

Pianist, composer, teacher of piano, composition. b. Carbon, Texas. St. piano w. Pearl Cole, Roswell, N.M.; comp. w. Wright, N.M. State Teachers Coll.; Rebeil, Univ. of Arizona (piano); John Lowell (theory); Swarthout U.S.C. (piano); Toch and Kubik (comp.). B.A. Arizona State Coll. Concerts, ensembles, lecture recitals, in U.S. Comp. *Symphony in C; Desert Mood (tone poem); South Pacific (piano suite); Nocturnes, Mosquitoes,* other piano pieces, songs, etc. Pres. Arizona State Tchrs' Assn.; chairman Amer. music and Amer. comp. Arizona Fed. of Music Clubs. Member Soc. of Arizona Comp. Music Club of Phoenix; Phoenix Piano Tchrs. Assn. (past-pres., co-founder). 1338 W. Roosevelt Rd., Phoenix, Ariz.

YOUNG, VICTOR

Composer, conductor, violinist. b. Chicago, Ill., 1900. St. violin, theory in Europe; grad. Univ. of Warsaw. Concertized in U. S., Europe. Concertmaster, Chicago Theatre. Mus. dir. Brunswick Phono. Co., Decca Recording Co. Cond. Hollywood Bowl; various radio programs, incl. *Westinghouse, Texaco.* Comp., cond. for Paramount Studios. Comp. incl.: *Arizona Sketches, Hollywood Panorama, Columbia Square, Travelin' Light, Elegy to F.D.R., Leaves of Grass* (Whitman), *Perpetual Motion, For Whom the Bell Tolls* (sym. synthesis), sym. orch.; *Pearls on Velvet, Stella By Starlight* (Decca rec.) (piano and orch.); *Stephen Foster* (str. quartet); chamber music, instr. pieces, numerous songs inc. *Golden Earrings, Night Has a Thousand Eyes, Dream Girl,* etc. Film scores incl. *For Whom the Bell Tolls, Reap the Wild Wind, Frenchman's Creek, Medal for Benny, Love Letters, Two Years Before the Mast, Dr. Wassel, Calcutta, Golden Boy, The Uninvited, And Now Tomorrow, To Each His Own, Maid of Salem, Ebb Tide, California,* etc. Paramount Studios, 5451 Marathon St., Hollywood 38, Calif.

ZADOR, EUGENE

Composer; teacher of theory, composition. b. Vataszek, Hungary, Nov. 5, 1895. Att. Acad. of Music, Vienna; Leipsig Cons. Ph. D., Mus. D. Won Hungarian Nat'l Prize in comp. 1934. Prof. Vienna Cons.; hon. prof. Acad. of Music, Budapest. Comp. incl. *Diana, The Tale of Death, Asra, The Awakening of the Sleeping Beauty, Christopher Columbus* (prem. in national broadcast, Columbus Day, 1939) (operas); *The Machine Man, The Jury* (ballets); *Hungarian Caprice, Rondo, Rhapsody, Variations on a Hungarian Song, Dance Symphony, Tarantella, Biblical Triptych* (sym. orch.), numerous smaller works. Perf. by leading orchs. under Stokowski, Rodzinski, Ormandy, Krueger, Monteux, Szell, Sample, Usigli, Barbirolli, Stock, others. Recordings: *Hungarian Caprice* (RCA-Victor), *Rhapsody and Scherzo* (Decca). Member: ASCAP, Acad. of Mot. Pic. Arts & Sciences, Song Writers Prot. Assn. American citizen since 1939. Now engaged in film composing, arranging, teaching. 1433 N. Sycamore Ave., Hollywood 46, Calif.

ZAKARIAN, ARAM G. der

(See: DER ZAKARIAN)

ZAM, MAURICE

Concert pianist; lecturer; critic; writer; teacher of piano. b. New York City, 1905. St. piano w. Helen Hopekirk, Artur Schnabel, Berlin; theory w. Stuart Mason, Edward Ballantine, Harvard Univ.; voice w. von Struck, Charles Dalmores; cond. w. Hans Blechschmidt. Concertized throughout U. S., Europe; soloist w. various orchs. Radio recitals and analyses of music KECA, KFI, KHJ, KFWB, others. Program annotator, Hollywood Bowl; master classes St. Louis Inst. of Mus. and Universidad de Mexico, Mexico City; illus. mus. lec. Harvard Univ.; former dir. Los Angeles Cons. of Mus.; mus. dir. Western Inst. of Psychoanalysis. Member: Severance, Authors, Exchange (Hollywood charter) Clubs; Musicological Soc. Hobbies: swimming, table tennis. Wife: Martha Kirkbride Zam, singer. 6217 Rock Cliff Dr., Hollywood 28, Calif.

ZEIKEL, DAVID

Concert violinist, teacher. b. New York City, Feb. 8, 1904. St. violin w. Ovide Musin, Leopold Auer; comp. w. Rubin Goldmark, Percy Goetschius. Grad. Von Ende Cons., New York. Concertized in U.S. (spec. in recitals unaccompanied violin); soloist w. Boston Sym., other leading orchs. Numerous app. in radio, recordings, films. Cond. Army Air Forces, 1942-45. Advocate of concerts for unaccompanied violin, Bach and contemporaries. Comp. incl. *Introduction to Quarter-Tone Playing* (vn. alone), *The New Yorker* (Amer. Comp. Guild), *The First Nighter* (orch.) (Virtuoso Pub.), *Music for Unaccompanied Violin,* other works. Hobbies: musicology, musical research. Candell Studios of Modern Music, 518, 17th St., Oakland, Calif.

ZEISL, ERIC

Composer. b. Vienna, Austria, May 18, 1905. Att. State Academy of Music, Vienna. Awarded Austrian State prize for *Requiem,* 1934. Comp. performed by Vienna, Prague, Budapest, Warsaw, Paris, London Symphonies, NBC Symphony, CBS Orch., Wallenstein Sinfonietta, Detroit Sym. Orch., New York City Sym., Toronto Sym., Chicago Sym., Hollywood Bowl. Comp. incl. *Suite for Strings* (Universal Ed.), *Six Songs for Baritone, Seven Songs for Soprano* (Doblinger Ed.), *Childrens Songs* (Capriccio Ed.), *Requiem Ebraico* (Transcontinental Publ.), *Three Pieces for Woodwinds* (Mills Music), *Little Symphony, Four Pieces After Paintings of Roswitha Bitterlich* (orch.), *Passacaglia Fantasy* (orch.), *Overture, Dance of the Cossacks* (from opera *Job*), *Pierrot in the Flask, Uranium 235, Ballet Suites* (orch.), *Moon-picture Songs* (baritone and orch.), *Return of Ulysses,* (from stage music to Emil Ludwig's *November*), *Romantic Comedy,* (Suite from opera *Leonce*), *Lena* (chamber orch.), chorals chamber music, solo-pieces, many motion picture scores, etc. Now prof. of comp., So. Calif. School of Music. 8578 West Knoll Dr., Los Angeles, Calif .

ZIMMERMAN, DOROTHY

Piano instructor. b. Spokane, Wash., January 9, 1912. Att. Mills Coll., Calif., Hochschule fuer Music, Berlin, Germany. B.A., Mills Coll.; Abschleusszeugnia, Berlin, Germany; gen. secondary teaching credential, Mills Coll. St. piano w. Edna Barr Love, Albert Elkus, Romuald Wikarski, cembola w. Eta Harich-Schcneider; composition w. Paul Hindemith, Gmlinde; musical history w. F. Mahling, Schunemann, Seiffert, Kreichgauer. App. Hochschule fuer Musik, Germany, First Baptist Church, Modesto, Calif., Modesto Hotel, etc. Member: Lambda Alpha; Mills Coll. Music Honor Soc.; MTA. Roseburg and Nelson Aves., Modesto, Calif.

ZUNIGA, JULIA BAL de

Concert pianist, teacher of piano. b. Ghent, Belgium. St. piano w. mother, father, Herman Bal (Liszt pupil) Royal Cons., Ghent; won first prize age 9 at Brussels Cons.; st. w. Delaborde, Braud, Philipp, Paris. Debut Concerts Lamoureux (Chevillard); played Liszt Centennial (Julian Carrillo), Mexico City; soloist Mozart Festival (Enrique Arbos), San Sebastian, 1918; concertized U. S., Europe, Mexico, Central America; toured w. Argentina in *Les Noches d'Arte,* 1917-19; ensem. w. Phil. Quartet, Noack Quartet; joint recitals w. Megerlin; interp. recitals benefit L. A. Philharmonic. Taught in New York City, Mexico City, Los Angeles. Hobby, coll. laces, necklaces. 1627 N. Martel Ave., Hollywood 46, Calif.

Eric Zeisl

Julia Bal de Zuniga

Vera Sallee Williams   Edith Wire   Claudia Edith Wirsen   Gene Worth

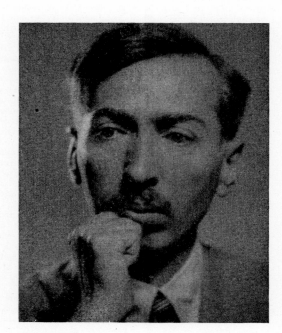

Norman Soreng Wright   Eugene Zador

Douglas Wright, Jr.   Dixie Yost   Maurice Zam   David Zeikel

281

Hollywood-Los Angeles

which brought out many rarely-heard works and commissioned many new ones; a number of both have been recorded.

The San Fernando Valley Symphony was formed in 1946 under the direction of Ilmari Ronka, with the purpose of giving several concerts a year with soloists resident in the San Fernando Valley. It is a professional group with Robert R. Frost as business manager. Also under Ronka's direction is a youth symphony of aspiring young players, residents of the Valley.

An unusual musical activity that could occur nowhere else in the world is that of several rehearsal orchestras which give no concerts and invite their own conductors and a select list of auditors. They are composed of studio and radio musicians who use their spare time, generally Sundays, to meet for the sole purpose of rehearsing masterworks and serious contemporary music for their own enjoyment.

The Los Angeles Women's Symphony has the distinction of being the oldest women's symphony in the United States. Since 1939 it has been under the efficient baton of Ruth Haroldson, leading woman conductor. It presents several concerts annually in the vicinity, many with distinguished soloists.

Highland Park, part of the northern part of the city, supports its own semi-professional symphony orchestra under the leadership of Chester A. Perry, and numerous similar semi-professional groups and youth orchestras also flourish.

Organized to provide aid and support to operatic ventures is the Opera Guild, founded by Mrs. Arthur Bergh, and currently under the leadership of William H. Richardson. The Guild gives an annual award to the individual who has done most to advance music in Los Angeles and vicinity during the preceding year.

Opera in Los Angeles is supplied by the annual visits of the San Francisco Opera Assn. each Fall. At this writing, announcement has been made of a Spring season by the Metropolitan Opera of New York. Various groups have endeavored to form permanent local opera companies, but none so far have had adequate backing to survive.

The Los Angeles Civic Light Opera Assn., under the guidance of Edwin Lester, was founded in 1938 and has grown into the most opulent organization of its kind. Its first season of four weeks now has expanded to four months and more. Its casts have featured leading grand opera artists, and its presentations have been in the form of re-creations. It added *Song of Norway* to the standard operetta repertory.

An annual summer season of light opera is presented in the Greek Theatre in Griffith Park, under the auspices of Gene Mann, its season extending from June to September.

The Bureau of Music, Department of Municipal Art, City of Los Angeles, came into being April 1, 1945, by action of the City Council and support of Mayor Fletcher Bowron, and functions under the supervision of the Municipal Art Commission. As an aid, the Citizens Advisory Committee for Music was created through appointments by the Mayor of fifteen cultural leaders. The Bureau now has functioning 26 youth choruses, 11 adult choruses and six community sings. Three bands, a symphonic band of 45, a concert band of 28 and a Mexican Tipica band of 24 provide Sunday park concerts. A Civic Center Orchestra of 50, all employees from city, state, county and federal departments. A huge chorus for the opening of the Hollywood Bowl season is now being organized. The music activities are coordinated by J. Arthur Lewis.

Concert activities include annual visits of all leading touring artists and concert groups, including Ballet Theatre, Ballet Russe de Monte Carlo, San Carlo Opera, etc. For the past sixty years, the bulk of these events have been presented by the late L. E. Behymer, as western representative for the eastern concert bureaus; they now are being continued by Mrs. Behymer.

Other managerial activities include concert series presented under the auspices of Mary Bran, Irving Parnes, and Moss & Hayman. New Venture in Music, founded by Ethel Leginska and Mary-V Holloway, presents young artists.

An important chamber music series is Evenings on the Roof, which derives its name from the *musicales intimes* originally held on the roof of the home of Pianist Frances Mullen Yates. The concerts make a point of presenting contemporary music as well as masterworks.

The growing interest in chamber music also is attested by the concerts of the Music Guild, founded and managed by Alfred Leonard, a non-profit organization begun in 1944, which has drawn packed houses to such large theaters as the Philharmonic Auditorium.

Annual events include the Cesar Franck Festival, founded in 1939 by Norman Soreng Wright, at the First Methodist Church of Hollywood, the Bach Festival, founded by John Smallman, and the Festival of Modern Music, founded by Arthur Leslie Jacobs, in the First Congregational Church, and the Mozart Festival, founded by Eunice Boyd.

Regular concerts are presented by the Ellis Club, a male choir, and the Women's Lyric Club. Opera reading clubs in Hollywood and Los Angeles dramatize several operas annually in English for their members. The Dominant Club is an organization of professional women artists. The Ebell Club, Schubert Club, MacDowell Club, Friday Morning Club and others have regular musical programs, employing both local and imported talent.

A unique organization is the Mary Carr Moore Manuscript Club which began in 1928 with students of Dr. Moore but rapidly expanded to take in other striving young composers. The aim stated in its by-laws is: "To stimulate creative musical effort; to afford composers an opportunity to hear their works performed; to receive the benefit of mutual criticism and advice; and show our appreciation of the work and inspiration of Mary Carr Moore." Programs of the club are devoted to manuscript works, but through these meetings over 200 numbers have been published by thirty publishers in the club's twenty years of existence. An annual contest, with a dozen awards in different classifications, stimulates new works. President for the current year is Mildred House.

The Armenian Allied Arts Assn. was founded in 1934 for the purpose of encouraging, aiding and sponsoring the efforts of young Armenian-American students of music, painting, sculpture, literature and drama. Auditions, exhibits and contests are held yearly, with scholarships and cash awards from a scholarship fund. Marshall G. Chashoudian is president at this time.

Famed as an outstanding organization of its kind is the Mitchell Boy Choir, founded in 1934 by Robert Bostwick Mitchell for St. Brendan's Church, where it has performed since. It has been featured in over fifty films, including *Going My Way, Love Affair, The Jolson Story, Yankee Doodle Dandy, Bishop's Wife, Paleface, The Connecticut Yankee,* has made numerous concert tours, appears regularly on the radio and has sung in many churches of various denominations.

There is a great deal of musical activity in the immediate vicinity of Los Angeles, and events in some of the contiguous cities, such as Pasadena, Burbank, Glendale and Santa Monica, are cited individually.

One of the most important is the Redlands Bowl, developed through the enterprise of Mrs. George F. Mullin. Supported by the City of Redlands, and operating through the summer months, the Bowl events present well known artists as well as local ones, ensembles and operatic performances.

The Riverside Opera Assn. has completed its 15th season under the direction of Marcella Craft, with Barton Bachmann as conductor. It has afforded opportunity to many young artists to learn or perfect themselves in opera roles, and many of its singers have graduated to major ranks.

There are a number of semi-professional symphony orchestras. Among the leaders are the Whittier Symphony, directed by Ruth Haroldson, the Palos Verdes Symphony, led by Josef Borisoff Piastro, and orchestras in Long Beach, San Pedro, and San Gabriel. Long Beach also has a Woman's Symphony, under Eva Anderson.

In the San Gabriel Valley, the Foothill Music Assn. is a non-profit organization presenting light opera under the leadership of S. Earle Blakeslee. A music series is presented at Chaffey College

Virtually all the cities and towns of Southern California

support either a Civic or a Community Concert Series and local music clubs, or music sectors of women's clubs, which offer performances with younger artists.

Music Festivals have been begun as annual events in Beverly Hills, where Franz Waxman led a symphony orchestra in several interesting programs last season, and in Ojai, near Ventura, which has hopes of becoming another Salzburg.

Los Angeles and vicinity is unique in having more music of a higher standard than can be found elsewhere in the United States, with the possible exception of New York City. A large proportion of the world's finest composers, performers and teachers either are employed by, or find it expedient to be near the film capital, which also is a rapidly expanding radio center. It now has become one of the foremost music centers of the entire world.

—Ann Wardell Saunders

San Francisco Bay Region

The San Francisco Municipal Chorus, directed by Hans Leschke, was founded in 1925 and since then has been in constant activity with a notable repertory of important choral works. The University of California Chorus also assists the Opera Chorus under Edward B. Lawton. The Orpheus Male Chorus, Mynard Jones director; the Unruh Philharmonic Chorus (annual *Messiah* and *Elijah* offerings), David P. Unruh, director, both offer several concerts each season at the Oakland Auditorium, as well as San Francisco appearances. The Loring Club is the oldest local choral group in the Bay Area. Waldemar Jacobsen and his Bach Choir also contribute concerts each summer. The Madrigal Guild, under Eileen McCall Washington, specializes in madrigals, lute songs and early English compositions. The Berkeley Chamber Singers, a new choral group directed by Iva Dee Hiatt, are offering 16th Century madrigals, motets and contemporary compositions in their program-series.

The San Francisco String Quartet, ably managed by its devoted patroness, Mrs. Edith de Lee, has given two annual subscription series. Personnel of this group is: Naoum Blinder, Frank Hauser, violins; Ferenc Molnar, viola, and Boris Blinder, 'cello. The California String Quartet has more recently come into being with concerts offered the public at Wheeler Hall, Berkeley. Felix Kuhner and David Schneider, violins; Detlev Olshausen, viola; and George Barati, 'cello, comprise this ensemble.

Mills College, Oakland, has been the center of string quartet sponsorship over a period of years and such outstanding international groups as the Pro Arte, the Parlow and the Budapest String Quartet have been in summer residence on the campus. Luther Marchant, Dean of Music at Mills College, has been honored for "eminent services to chamber music" in the award of the Coolidge Foundation Medal.

The Music Lovers' Society founded by Margaret Tilly, pianist, and specializing in first hearings of contemporary composers, offers delightful and unusual concerts each year at the Marines Memorial Theatre, San Francisco, and at Wheeler Hall, Berkeley. Resident members of this group besides Miss Tilly are Merrill Jordan, flute; Frances Weiner, violin; Lucien Mitchell, viola; and Herman Reinberg, 'cello.

A Celebrity Series, managed by Dorothy Granville, and the Opera Association Concert Series, with Paul Posz at the helm, each season bring the world's great to the War Memorial Opera House. In the East Bay, the Oakland Forum under William E. Chamberlin and the Ware-Hazelton Concert agencies present major music events at the Oakland Auditorium.

In Marin county, concerts are held at Forest Meadows, San Rafael, and at the Tamalpais Park School, Mill Valley, under the auspices of the Outdoor Art Club. At Montalvo, are occasional offerings of high calibre. A Stanford University Spring Music Festival (extending over several weeks in 1947) comprised a variety of outstanding programs with the University Choir led by Sterling Wheelwright; Richard

Purvis, organist; and the University Singers, directed by Mark Evans.

The University of California Extension Division gives the resident artist opportunity for concert appearances. In 1946-47, solo recitals and ensemble programs were heard by pianists Tanya Ury, Janet Graham, Maxim Shapiro, Estelle Caen, Corinne Lacomble, Leo Shorr and Bernard Abramowitsch; violinists Miriam Sunzer, Frances Weiner and William Kroll; 'cellist Helen Stross; singers Herta Glaz, Loraine Campbell, Mary Groom Richards, Lawrence Strauss, William Eddy, Desire Ligeti; the Morgan Trio (Virginia, harp; Frances, piano; Marguerite, violin); the Alma Trio (Adolph Baller, Roman Totenberg, and Gabor Rejto); and the University and California String Quartets.

The Composers' Forum, dedicated to the works of Bay Area residents, has been one of the most stimulating enterprises yet undertaken. Concerts in Berkeley and San Francisco have provided public hearing of ambitious compositions by students Virginia Seay, Earl Kim, Spartaco Monello, Leon Kirchner and Leonard Ralston; and master Darius Milhaud. The Museum of Art, San Francisco, is a popular locale for chamber music and small group concerts.

During the summer, thousands of listeners flock to Sigmund Stern Grove (San Francisco), Woodminster Amphitheatre (Oakland), and The Greek Theatre (Berkeley), to hear programs of wide variety: solo recitals, symphony, opera, ballet. Resident artists are featured at these events and operatic training is assured many young aspirants under the baton of Arturo Casiglia, Kurt Herbert Adler, Erich Weiler and Jan Popper. Reginald Travers and Austin Mosher are noted for their Gilbert and Sullivan productions.

Local concert managers who encourage young people entering the professional field are Curran Swint, Alice Seckels, Lulu Blumberg, Dorothy Granville, Muriel MacGurn and Marjorie Schuler.

Music clubs which offer opportunity for local talent are Pacific Musical and San Francisco Musical Clubs, San Francisco; Etude and Berkeley Piano Club, Berkeley; The East Bay Opera League, Oakland, to mention only a few. Opportunity for concert appearances and advanced study has been made available to California residents through the Gainsborough Foundation, established in 1945 with main offices in San Francisco "to assist exceptionally talented persons in the furtherance of professional careers in serious music". Auditions are annually held in San Francisco and Los Angeles.

—Helena Munn Redewill

MUNICIPAL CHORUS

The San Francisco Municipal Chorus, one of the few municipally sponsored choruses in the United States, is maintained by the City of San Francisco under the direction of the Art Commission. First organized in 1924 with Hans Leschke as conductor, it proved so great a success that the Board of Supervisors established it as a permanent institution. Men and women from all positions in life comprise its membership.

The chorus has appeared with the San Francisco Symphony Orch. in major concerts under Hertz, Monteux, Molinari, Stravinsky, Cameron, and Walter, and has given concerts in San Francisco, East Bay cities, at the University of California, Stanford University, College of Holy Names and in Hollywood Bowl. It joined with the San Francisco Symphony in recordings under the direction of Pierre Monteux.

Members of the chorus raise their standard of musicianship through participation in sight singing, vocal ensemble and conducting classes regularly given gratis by Conductor Leschke. Young singers receive encouragement and attention, and many have been recipients of the vocal scholarships which the members and friends of the chorus award annually by competitive contest.

—Edwin T. Rickman, President

COMEDY OPERA GUILD

The Comedy Opera Guild of San Francisco was founded by Erich Weiler. It has presented a regular series of operatic events throughout the Pacific Coast. Its concept was "to present the masterworks of the past, substituting good comic dialogue for the recitatives and performing entire works in English."

Its stated purposes are:
1. To give an enjoyable, entertaining show.
2. To utilize the beautiful, often wrongly neglected masterworks of great composers.
3. To give the audience an opportunity to understand every word and meaning of the opera without being compelled to read the story and synopsis.
4. To create a new repertory of comic operas.
5. To fight operatic snobbery and make opera self-supporting.

The group has developed a large repertory of operas including *The Impresario* (Mozart), *The Calif of Bagdad* (Boieldieu), *Bruschino the Grouch* (Rossini), *Maid as Mistress* (Pergolesi), *Good Night, Mr. Pantalon* (Grisar), *Women's War* (Schubert), *Secret Marriage* (Cimarosa).

Tacoma

are given opportunity to be heard, and sponsors an artist series of five concerts. This organization was founded in 1888. President is Mrs. G. Carleton Hubbey and conductor, Clyde H. Keutzer.

The Fine Arts Club is a social club with the main content of its programs music, dance and dramatics. Founded in 1916, its president is Eunice Crain.

Washington State Music Assn. Chapter in Tacoma's objective is to raise teaching standards. President is Mrs. Byron Foreman.

John Hamricks Greater Artist Series present six outstanding attractions every season, including celebrated artists.

—Lennard Anderson

Puget Sound Area

has maintained a chamber music series for three seasons, employing the best available resident artists and distinguished visitors, including Alexander Schneider, violinist, Berthe Poncy Jacobson, pianist, and presentation of William Grant Still in a lecture-recital, with the assistance of a student orchestra and soloists.

A four-day Festival of Contemporary American Works was the climax of a summer's intensive study on the part of a large corps of students under four conductors. Thor Johnson of the Cincinnati Symphony and Frederick Fennell of the Eastman School of Music jointly trained symphony and chamber orchestras, while Charles Wilson Lawrence and Eugene Linden, of the University of Washington School of Music, respectively developed a chorus and an opera company. Eugene Linden directed Menotti's *Amelia Goes to the Ball* with a local cost in which principals were Sylvia Woolfson, Don Thulean, and John Begg. The succeeding three evenings brought chamber orchestra, full orchestra, and chorus-and-orchestra performances, under the baton of Fennell. Among composers represented on the programs were Kent Kennan, David Diamond, Peter Mennin, Randall Thompson, Howard Hanson, and George Frederick McKay.

The University may be instrumental in placing resident opera on a sounder footing in the Puget Sound country. Well before Eugene Linden was brought to the School of Music on a part-time basis to conduct an opera workshop, he was identified with the Lyric or Mozart Theater. With financial support largely drawn from Olympia and Tacoma, singers from Tacoma and Seattle, and a small orchestra of Seattle Symphony members, this organization staged performances in the three cities of *The Marriage of Figaro* early in 1944, *The Barber of Seville* in December of the same year, and *The Abduction from the Seraglio* in the summer of 1946—all in lifelike English translations perfected by the conductor.

The Seattle Civic Opera Assn., after a wartime recess, came again before the public in December, 1946, with performances in English of *Die Fledermaus* and *The Bartered Bride* under the direction of the Association's new musical director, Gustave Stern.

The majority of the smaller cities on Puget Sound are supplied with artist concert series by either Civic Music or Community Concerts. Of the larger cities, Tacoma has its "Music Box Theater" series, under Impresario William Conner; while Seattle enjoys several notable series: the many and varied programs of music, dance, and drama presented at the Moore Theater by Mrs. Cecilia Schultz; the University-sponsored four-concert chamber music series at the Women's Century Club; the four winter "Music at Meany" programs on the University campus by the Associated Women Students and the four summer concerts in the same hall under the same title by the University's Summer Session; the Ladies Musical Club's five-concert series in the Metropolitan Theater; the monthly concerts in the Seattle Art Museum for its members, which feature local musicians in chamber music recitals under the direction of Francis Armstrong; the occasional public appearances of University of Washington, Seattle College, and Seattle Pacific College music faculty members and students. The Pacific Northwest Symphony presents famous guest artists, as well as accomplished resident executants, as soloists.

Varied school and college musical activities, and numerous musical clubs and societies are invaluable factors in planning and supporting musical activities in a region which, for all its 1,500,000 inhabitants, is still in the process of growing out of its pioneer, or frontier stage. The study-groups, member-concerts, scholarship funds, and artist series of the Ladies Musical Clubs of such cities as Bellingham, Mount Vernon, Everett, Wenatchee, Tacoma and Seattle; the Music and Art Foundation in Seattle; the Fine Arts Guild in Olympia; the Ladies Musical Society in Bremerton, to name only a few, share with the public schools and colleges much of the credit for what progress has been made and the responsibility for future advances.

—David B. Pennell

MUSIC AND ART FOUNDATION

The Music and Art Foundation of Seattle was organized in 1923 by the late Mrs. A. S. Kerry (Katherine A. Glen) and Mrs. Edgar Ames.

It is a foundation or fund built up by gifts, legacies and memberships which outlines and promotes a study program for its members, encourages creative expression by groups and individuals and gives financial aid to students in the fine arts.

The Foundation launched the Youth Symphony Orchestra later taken over by a group of citizens. It awards the Katherine Glen Kerry Memorial Scholarship annually at the Cornish School to an outstanding musical student and gives scholarships and awards for creative work in art, prose and poetry.

Leading Universities and Music Schools

CALIFORNIA

AMERICAN OPERATIC LABORATORY. HUGH H. EDWARDS, *General Director*; VAL ROSING, *Artistic Director*; CURTIS STEARNS, *Music Director*; ROBERT A. BRINK, *Technical Director*. 4705½ Elmwood Ave., Hollywood 4.

CALIFORNIA ACADEMY OF MUSIC. ARTHUR QUENZER, *Head of Music Dept.*; BERT PRIVAL, *Head of Dance Dept.* 5267 Bakman Ave., North Hollywood.

CANDELL STUDIOS OF MUSIC. THOMAS P. CANDELL, *Director.* 518, 17th St., Oakland 12.

Chaffey College, Ontario.

Chapman College, Los Angeles.

Chico State College, Chico.

Claremont College, Claremont.

College of the Pacific, Stockton.

Dominican College, San Rafael.

Fresno State College, Fresno.

Holy Name College, Oakland.

Humboldt State College, Arcata.

IMMACULATE HEART COLLEGE, 5662 Fernwood Ave., Los Angeles 28.

Loyola University, Los Angeles.

Mills College. Luther S. Marchant, dean of music. Oakland.

MOUNT ST. MARY'S COLLEGE, 12001 Chalon Road, West Los Angeles 24.

NATIONAL INSTITUTE OF MUSIC AND ARTS. MRS. A. W. RYAN, *President*; G. O. HUTCHINSON, *Dean*; JAMES HOWARD, *Head of Violin Dept.*; H. E. KAYSEN, *Head of Piano Dept.*; L. E. MARTIN, *Supervisor of Faculty, Northwestern Division.* 951 So. Western Ave., Los Angeles 6.

Occidental College, Los Angeles.

Palos Verdes College, Rolling Hills.

GEORGE PEPPERDINE COLLEGE. RUSSEL N. SQUIRE, PH. D., *Head of Music Dept.* 1121 W. 79th St., Los Angeles 44.

Pomona College, Claremont.

PRIVAL STUDIOS OF THE DANCE. BERT PRIVAL, *Director.* 12546 Ventura Blvd., Studio City; 5263 Bakman Ave., North Hollywood; 14418 Victory Blvd., Van Nuys.

Russo School of Music and Dance. S. Edward Russo, Director. Pittsburg.

SAMOILOFF BEL CANTO STUDIOS AND OPERA ACADEMY. ZEPHA SAMOILOFF BOGERT, *Director.* 610 So. Van Ness Ave., Los Angeles 5.

San Diego State College, San Diego.

San Francisco College, San Francisco.

SAN FRANCISCO CONSERVATORY OF MUSIC. ADA CLEMENT, *Head of Music*; RENA LAZELLE, *Head of Voice Dept.* 3455 Sacramento St., San Francisco 18.

San Francisco State College, San Francisco.

Santa Clara College, Santa Clara.

Scripps College, Claremont, Calif.

SOUTHERN CALIFORNIA SCHOOL OF MUSIC AND ARTS. HAL D. CRAIN, *Director*; LILY D. CRAIN, ERNST KRENEK, SIMON R. STEIN, ERIK ZEISL, CHARLES FOLLETT, RUTH WIDENHAM. 3173 Wilshire Blvd., Los Angeles 5.

Stanford University, Palo Alto.

University of California. Albert Elkus, Dean of Music., Berkeley.

University of California at Los Angeles, Los Angeles 24.

University of California at Santa Barbara. Van A. Christy, Head of Music. Santa Barbara.

University of Redlands. Roland Leach, Head of Music. Redlands.

University of San Francisco, San Francisco.

University of Southern California. Max van Lewyn Swarthout, dean. Los Angeles.

Whittier College. Whittier.

ARIZONA

Arizona State College. Harry Boone Harelson, head of music dept. Tempe.

University of Arizona, Tucson.

COLORADO

Colorado State College, Fort Collins.

Colorado University, Colorado Springs.

Denver University, Denver.

Lamont School of Music, Denver.

University of Colorado. Rowland W. Dunham, dean. Boulder.

IDAHO

College of Idaho, Caldwell

University of Idaho. Northern branch, Moscow; southern branch, Pocatello.

MONTANA

Montana State College, Bozeman.

University of Montana, Missoula.

NEVADA

University of Nevada, Reno.

NEW MEXICO

Eastern New Mexico College, Portales.

University of New Mexico. John Robb, dean. Albuquerque.

OREGON

Eastern Oregon College, La Grande.

Lewis and Clark College. John Stark Evans, head of music. Portland.

Linfield College, McMinnville.

Oregon State College, Corvallis.

Pacific College, Newberg.

Pacific University, Forest Grove.

PORTLAND SCHOOL OF MUSIC. ARIEL RUBSTEIN, *Head of Music.* New Fleidner Bldg., Portland.

Portland University, Portland.

Reed College, Portland.

University of Oregon. Theodore Kratt, head of music. Eugene.

VASILIEFF SCHOOL OF BALLET. NICHOLAS VASILIEFF, *Director.* Seling-Hirsch Bldg., 918 S. W. Washington St., Portland.

Willamette University. Melvin H. Geist, dean. Salem.

UTAH

Brigham Young College, Provo.

College of St. Mary's-of-the-Wasatch, Salt Lake City.

University of Utah, Salt Lake City.

WASHINGTON

College of Puget Sound. Clyde Keutzer, head of music. Tacoma.

Gonzaga University, Spokane.

Pacific Lutheran College, Parkland.

RUSSIAN-AMERICAN BALLET SCHOOL. IVAN NOVIKOFF, *Director.* 111 Spring St., Seattle.

Seattle College, Seattle.

Seattle Pacific College, Seattle.

University of Washington, Seattle.

Walla Walla College, College Place.

Washington State College, Pullman.

Whitman College, Whitman.

Whitworth College, Spokane.

WYOMING

University of Wyoming, Laramie.

FOUNDATIONS

Atwater Kent Foundation, 801 Bel Air Road, Los Angeles 24, Calif.

Gainsborough Music Foundation, 221 Sansome St., San Francisco, Calif.

MUSIC AND ART FOUNDATION. MRS. A. S. KERRY, *President.* 311 Medical Arts Bldg., Seattle 1, Wash.

ADVERTISING DIRECTORY

Mrs. Abby De Avirett

Teacher of Music

267 S. ARDEN BLVD.

LOS ANGELES   —   CALIFORNIA

CONSTANCE JEANETTE SHIRLEY
Concert Pianist—Composer

She is an artist to her finger tips. She has everything: technique, tone, poetry, fire, and musicianship—*Dr. Guy Maier.*

Brilliant young Concert Pianist-Composer has achieved distinction in both lines of her musical activities. Brilliant record not only in her public appearances but also in the serious and original character of her compositional output. As a concert artist she is pre-eminent.—*Dr. Mary Carr Moore.*

A great talent . . . charming personality . . . thorough technical facility. Her playing . . . is musicianly well conceived, and artistic in every respect. Her thorough knowledge of her score impressed me and the orchestral musicians deeply.—*Dr. John Vincent, conductor-composer.*

Virtuoso pianist . . . poised and beautiful . . . touch and tone ecstatic with youth . . . marvelous young pianist, sole product of a very gifted mother . . . climaxed one of the most brilliant orchestral debuts in our local traditions.—*Carl Bronson, L. A. Herald-Express.*

The concerto was beautifully played by Constance Shirley who showed an appealing and firmly rounded tone backed by assured technique and musicianly aplomb. She was accorded long, warm, and well deserved plaudits.—*Richard Drake Saunders, Hollywood Citizen.*

From the very beginning I recognized the great musical talent of Miss Shirley. Among the ladies who have studied composition with me she deserves recognition as one of the first rank. A former child prodigy worthy of the name.—*Arnold Schoenberg.*

Miss Shirley's composition proved of exceptional merit. It disclosed inventive genius both as to melodic line and harmonic content and more especially as to rhythmic patterns. She gave the work a capital performance.—*Vernon Steele, Pac. Coast Musician.*

AT 6:   Very, very talented.—*Harold Bauer.*

Five year old prodigy who played today on the Express Radio, has amazed many critics in her concert appearances.—*L. A. Express.*

Six year old pianist composer who was recently chosen as one of the wonder children of So. Cal. gave a most phenomenal exhibition of musical talent . . . must be the spirit of some Mozart or Chopin in her tiny soul.—*Hollywood Citizen.*

The baby "wonder" pianist scored as usual . . . remarkable young pianist composer was riotously applauded and fairly brought the audience to its feet . . . plays with great poise, technical facility, and feeling for artistic effects.—*Hollywood Citizen.*

At 7: An unparalleled success. Her technique is astonishing . . . a wonderful expression for one so young. I hope she will develop into a great artist as she has already the pianistic equipment for such a one. I never heard a more promising and so talented a child. At 16: Marvelous! Any mother who has accomplished what Mme. Shirley has with her daughter is a born musician and deserving of recognition in Who's Who in the world of music.—*Dr. Alexis Kall.*

At 9: Without a doubt the cleverest little lady I have ever seen in her line. She played for me at the Hill Street Theatre and was a sensation. In my estimation she is a genius.—*Larry Rich, (National Orpheum headliner with his band).*

JO-ANNE SHIRLEY, Mus. B.
Concert Pianist—Teacher

Pianistic mastery brilliant in style and interpretation, vigorous rhythm, and fascinating melody were displayed by Mme. Shirley.—*L. A. Times.*

She has an individual style, full of brilliancy of an airy sparkling type, and displayed great technical skill also.—*Cedar Rapids Gazette.*

A pianist of remarkable technique and powers of interpretation.—*Hollywood Citizen.*

299

The

RENNAY SHRY-OCK SCHOOL

of

MUSIC-ARTS & DRAMA

in

SAN FRANCISCO

A school dedicated,
approved and accredited
to the highest standards
in Voice, Instrumental,
Dramatic and Allied Creative Arts

———— • • ————

1353 Post Street   San Francisco, Calif.

OR-dway   —   —   5-9020

ARTURO V. CASIGLIA

General Director
Pacific Grand Opera Co.
Teacher of Voice

*

Ph.: West. 1-5443

2643 Baker St.   San Francisco 23, Calif.

ALMA BIRMINGHAM

Pianist

Teacher of Piano

*

Ph.: Fl. 8414

3299 Washington St.   San Francisco, Calif.

"Mind to Keyboard"

INSTITUTE OF MODERN MUSIC

510 - 15th St., Oakland 12, Calif.   TWinoaks 3-2573

Popular Piano	Harmony	Sight Reading
Classical Piano	Song Writing	Transposition
Arranging	Hammond Organ	Muscular Control
	Teaching Technique	

* * * *

Philip Mauro Foote (LAB) Director (Licentiate of the Associated Board, Royal College of Music, London, England)

Loretta B. Foote, Assistant

EDITH FORD KENDALL

Teacher of Singing

"Edith Kendall's success in developing young voices has been remarkably swift and sure in results." . . . Los Angeles Herald

Studio   Ph.: PR. 5-6139
990 Geary St.   San Francisco, Calif.

ROBERT   ANDERSON

Piano keyboard harmony patterns including major and minor scale pattern, diminished 7th, dominant 7th, dominant 7th and resolution pattern. $1.00 complete.

Sherman Clay & Co.
Distributors
San Francisco, Calif.

RAY MEANY'S HAWAIIAN MUSIC CENTER & GOLDEN GATE PUBLICATIONS

"Tops in Hawaiian Music for the Steel Guitar and other string instruments. Folios, Guitar Methods and Hawaiian Curios. Hawaiian Leis, Hula Skirts, Tapas, Pikaki Shells and other South Sea Island Curios.

Complimentary Folder On Request

Special discount to guitar teachers and studio operators. WRITE NOW! 5464 Foothill Blvd., Oakland 1,

EMERIE RUDLAND MURTEY

Concert Pianist

"Emerie Rudland has definite feeling for phrase, for tempo and for the nuances of expression that differentiate the uninspired instrumentalist from the artist." . . . The Argonaut, San Francisco.

Teacher
Style, Interpretation, Technique

3143 Fourth Ave.   Sacramento

The Saturday Morning Musical Club

TEMPLE OF MUSIC & ART

330 South Scott Street

Tucson, Arizona

Founded in 1907

Building Erected in 1927

Civic Groups

Temple Choral Singers
Civic Oratorio Society
Lyric String Ensemble

Annual Scholarship

Madeline Berger Scholarship
to further musical education

Junior Groups

B Sharp Club
Rhythm Club
Harmony Club
La Campanella Club
Junior Choral Group
Junior Orchestra

Concert Course
Great Artist Series

Mrs. M. L. Girton—President   * *   **Elizabeth Healy—Manager**

**HOOD RIVER MUSIC
ASSOCIATION**

Hood River, Ore.

BORIS SIRPO

Music Director

ARVO HUKARI

Music Assn. Pres.

CHAS. GUILLE

Festival Chairman

Announcing the First
HOOD RIVER MUSICAL FESTIVAL

August 5, 1948	Evening:	ALMA TRIO
August 6, "	Evening:	PORTLAND CHAMBER ORCHESTRA
August 7, "	Evening:	KING DAVID
August 8, "	Afternoon:	CHILDREN'S CONCERT
August 8, "	Evening:	SYMPHONY CONCERT. EZIO PINZA, Soloist

Paul Pierre McNeely

Nationally Known Teacher of Piano

FACULTY MEMBER of THE NATIONAL GUILD OF PIANO TEACHERS

Studio: Paramount Theatre Building
Seattle, Washington, Phone MAIN 8639

PRESS COMMENTS

DAILY CAPITOL, Topeka, Kans.—"Playing showed delicacy, ease, speed, power. Expression and tone-color reveal a fine artistic temperament."

ANACONDA STANDARD, Anaconda, Mont.—"An artist of charm and eloquence. One is enchanted by his contrast of tone, color, poetic detail of phrasing, expression and masterful technic."

TACOMA LEDGER, Tacoma, Wash.—"Proved without doubt his excellent musicianship. He has a touch which can change from the soft, soothing tones of a lullaby, to the brilliant, fiery notes of a Liszt number. His playing is clean-cut, smooth, flexible."

SEATTLE POST-INTELLIGENCER, Seattle.—"Caught the spirit of each message he gave."

MUSIC and MUSICIANS, Seattle.—"He showed himself a master pianist."

EXPONENT, Bozeman, Mont.—"He won far-reaching and very favorable comment with his finished performance. His style is very even and flowing."

COMMENTS ON TEACHING WORK

MUSIC NEWS, Chicago.—"Mr. McNeely takes the lead in Seattle as artist, pianist, and pedagogue of the highest worth, bringing to his work an unlimited fund of virtuosic knowledge, indomitable energy and power, and the keenly analytical, critical faculties of a Frenchman, also, the greatest kindliness and unceasing devotion and patience. He is deftly shaping future musical careers in a most masterly fashion." (Beldon).

TACOMA LEDGER, Tacoma, Wash.—"Difficulties of interpretation and technique were conquered with a sweep and finish which were eloquent of remarkable talent and sincere study. The success of each player reflected very great credit on the skill of the teacher."

SEATTLE POST-INTELLIGENCER, Seattle.—"Each succeeding year brings witness to the fact of the high plane of artistry manifested in the work of this well-known teacher."

TOWN CRIER, Seattle.—"PAUL PIERRE McNEELY is a rare teacher. But primarily he is a musician and an artist."

MUSICAL WEST, San Francisco.—"Great works of the greatest masters, interpreted in an authentic and artistic style, have made these recitals distinctive features of the city's musical events, and they attract capacity audiences."

MUSIC and MUSICIANS.—"The demand for pianists developed by Mr. McNEELY through his own unique system of technical mastery and tone development is increasing more and more each year."

SEATTLE STAR.—"His masterly instruction was evidenced in the playing of his skilled performers. Sensitized pedaling, delicate shadings, full-valued tone-coloring and phrasing, a fineness of interpretation—in fact, the full eloquence of the best in pianoforte, marked the production." (Talmadge)

Nationally Known Teacher of Piano

Teacher of

RANDOLPH HOKANSON, LENNARD ANDERSON, and Other Noted Artists

LETTERS OF APPRECIATION from OUTSTANDING PROFESSIONAL STUDENTS

Dear Mr. McNeely:

I take great pleasure in expressing my deep gratitude for your very superior and illuminating instruction, and also, for the excellent development in technical mastery, beauty of tone, interpretative insight and overall knowledge of the ART of PIANISM, which I gained.

New York City, N. Y.

Very sincerely, your friend and pupil,

Randolph H Hokanson

Dear Mr. McNeely:

Through the many years of study under you, I have realized that I was under a master teacher. Your fine ideals, high standards of excellence . . . genius for development of talent, unique methods . . . I have esteemed very highly.

Tacoma, Washington

Yours very sincerely,

Lennard A. Anderson

Dear Mr. McNeely:

Re-creating living music with a definite awareness . . . projection of tonal and technical proficiency . . . combined with an universal outlook, opened up new worlds of beauty, through your MASTER teaching. My years of study with you are daily a constant source of inspiration and gratitude. Gratefully,

Vancouver, B. C.

Kenneth Ross.

Dear Mr. McNeely:

With sincere enthusiasm and persistent patience, unfailing kindness you inspire your students to develop their abilities and overcome their failings through application of your ideas . . . through your inspiration and guidance, I am engaged today in the profession of music.

Seattle, Washington

Sincerely,

Gwendolyne Mines Remy

Dear Mr. McNeely:

Your great musical gifts, high standards of musicianship, remarkable interpretative powers, and unique methods . . . have been conducive to developing in me the ART of Pianoforte Playing. Sincerely your friend and pupil,

Masters School, Dobbs Ferry, N .Y.

Catherine Coleman

Dear Mr. McNeely:

With each year of piano development I am more deeply impressed with your keen perception of the individual student's needs . . . I cannot thank you enough for all you have done to help me. Most sincerely your student,

Olympia, Washington

Winifred Knox

311